# direct
# instruction
# reading

# direct instruction reading

**Douglas Carnine**

*University of Oregon*

**Jerry Silbert**

*Whiteaker School*

Charles E. Merrill Publishing Company
*A Bell & Howell Company*
Columbus   Toronto   London   Sydney

PUBLISHED BY
Charles E. Merrill Publishing Company
*A Bell & Howell Company*
Columbus, Ohio 43219

This book was set in Helvetica and Tempo.
The production editor was Cynthia Norfleet Donaldson.
The cover was prepared by Will Chenoweth.

Library of Congress Catalog Card Number: 78-71131

International Standard Book Number: 0-675-08277-3

5 6 7 8 / 85 84 83
PRINTED IN THE UNITED STATES OF AMERICA

# Preface

For the past 10 years, we've developed and implemented a curriculum used by thousands of students across the United States. In working with teachers to implement this curriculum, we've repeatedly heard complaints about the inadequacy of reading methods texts. Teachers feel that the texts often fail to relate directly to their classroom problems. While these texts discuss various approaches to teaching reading—what students should learn, and why students fail to learn — they lack specific instructional strategies. To be most useful, a methods text must address these specifics of instruction.

To give an example of their shortcomings, traditional methods books may list 10 or 15 activities to teach word recognition. However, they may leave practical questions unanswered: What types of words should be included? When should a particular activity be used? What should a teacher do when students have serious difficulty completing an exercise? What is the relationship among word recognition exercises, story reading, and comprehension?

We attempt to address these important concerns in this book, specifying in-depth procedures to teach important reading skills and providing alternatives for what to do when students fail to learn. These procedures have proven particularly effective with handicapped, bilingual, and economically disadvantaged students.

To aid the reader in using this book, it is divided into five parts: perspective, beginning reading instruction (first 6 months), primary level instruction (mid-first through third grade), intermediate level instruction (fourth through eighth grade), and developing student motivation. In each part of the book there are several sections that focus on major sets of skills taught during that grade level. Most of these sections have four parts: (1) specific skills to be taught and how to teach with precise direct instruction methods, (2) an analysis of those skills used in commercial programs and the curricular adaptations necessary for low-performing students, (3) related research findings, and (4) application exercises for the classroom.

The perspective section discusses the philosophy and techniques of direct instruction. It defines reading as consisting of understanding or *reading comprehension* and correctly identifying printed words or *decoding*. In each grade level section, a teacher or prospective teacher may first read about the selection and use of commercial programs. These sections tell how to set up a classroom program and refer readers to the pages for teaching particular skills—techniques that should prove of particular value to teachers encountering the hard-to-teach students mainstreamed into their classrooms through PL 94-142. And they should be helpful to reading specialists, resource teachers, and others concerned with reading.

This volume is not intended to be a definitive handbook. Unfortunately, a good deal of experimental evidence still is needed to support instructional procedures used in the schools. Since many commercial materials are relatively unsystematic, even using direct instruction techniques with them is far from ideal. It is our hope, however, that the systematic procedures recommended here will stimulate the development of even better techniques. Furthermore, we encourage teachers to view learning as an outcome of instruction rather than a function of the learner, and commercial publishers to provide better programs designed for low-performing students. We hope that this book will contribute to the better teaching of hard-to-teach students.

## Acknowledgments

We are grateful to many people: foremost to Zig Engelmann, whose empirical approach to instructional design has resulted in the development of numerous highly effective instructional programs. The effectiveness of these programs was documented by a national study of educational approaches (Becker, Engelmann, & Carnine, 1979). Many of the procedures in this book were derived from *DISTAR Reading, DISTAR Language,* and *Corrective Reading,* authored by Engelmann and his colleagues.

In addition to ideas gained from these programs, many ideas have been contributed by colleagues and students, including Marcy Stein, Jean Osborn, Elaine C. Bruner, Linda Carnine, Sheri Irwin, Barak Rosenshine, Jane Dougall, Sandra Schofield, Robert Dixon, Cheri Hansen, Ruth Falco, Frank Falco, Candy Stevens, Joan Thormann, Phil Dommes, Alex Granzin, Abby Adams, Joleen Johnson, Conley Overholser, and Billie Overholser. Other colleagues provided important support and encouragement: Wes Becker, Joe Jenkins, Meredith Gall, Barbara Bateman, and Ruth Waugh.

D.C.
J.S.

# Contents

# Part 3
# Primary Reading: Through Third Grade, 185

## Section 3.1
## Introduction, 187

## Section 3.2
## Phonic Analysis, 191

## Section 3.3
## Structural Analysis, 212

# Formats in Direct Instruction Reading

**To teachers,**
*whose skills and dedication make a difference*

# direct
# instruction
# reading

# PART 1

# Perspective

# *Introduction*

Reading is a complex process: complex to learn and complex to teach. Psycholinguists, information systems analysts, and cognitive psychologists each describe the reading process differently. While these descriptions are important to theoretical questions about the reading process, many of them do not address the needs of classroom teachers. Our purpose is not to survey the various theoretical positions, but to explain procedures that teachers can use to improve the reading performance of their students. We agree with Otto (1977) that many students will not become successful readers unless teachers identify the essential reading skills, find out what skills students lack, and teach students the skills they need.

Success in reading is very important to students, both for academic and vocational advancement and for the students' psychological well-being. Although some students will learn to read in almost any program, other students will not become successful readers unless they receive careful teaching. The need for careful teaching is emphasized by recent declines in scores on national measures of student comprehension and by increasing demands placed upon the schools by mainstreaming, in which handicapped students are placed in regular classrooms.

Our definition of teaching is similar to that of Bateman's (1971, p. 8): "Teaching is the teacher's intentional arranging or manipulating of the environment so that the child will learn more efficiently than if he were to learn incidentally from the world at large." If a teacher's actions do not result in more efficient learning than the actions of parents or other nonteachers, then teaching is itself called into question as a profession. A distinguishing characteristic of the teaching profession must be its ability to provide effective and efficient instructional services to students who have difficulty in school.

If teachers are to effectively and efficiently teach reading they must be knowledgeable in several areas:

1. Knowing the essential skills or objectives that make up the reading process and procedures for teaching those skills
2. Knowing procedures for evaluating, selecting, and modifying reading programs to meet the needs of all students in their classrooms

3

3. Knowing techniques for effectively presenting lessons, including techniques for pacing tasks, motivating students, and diagnosing and correcting their errors
4. Knowing how to individualize instruction by properly placing students in a program and then moving them at an optimal rate through the program
5. Knowing how to organize classrooms so that the amount of time students spend engaged in reading instruction is maximized

The remainder of this section discusses why reading is important and describes several types of answers to the question, How can educators improve reading performance?

## Why Student Success in Reading Is Important

Reading instruction is possibly the most important activity in elementary grade classrooms. Howard (1968) surveyed fourth and fifth graders from three schools located in urban, lower-socioeconomic neighborhoods. In his survey, he asked 168 questions about five areas: school, home, self, other people, and things in general. As part of the study, the students were asked to select the three most important items from the 168 items included in the survey. The three items most frequently identified were I want to learn how to read better; I want to learn how to write better; I want to learn how to spell better.

Failure in reading strongly influences children's self-images and feelings of competency. Students who fail in reading often feel inadequate and ashamed. They are anxious (Neville, Pfost, & Dobbs, 1967) and have feelings of inferiority (Athey, 1976). In many cases, the failure is so punishing that students become withdrawn, refuse to try, and attract attention through misbehavior. In discussing reading research in the affective domain, Athey (1976, pp. 363–364) states:

> The school's priorities today are such that learning to read could be considered as the *major* developmental task of the early elementary school years. . . . There can be no doubt that in American culture, learning to read is a major adjustment which the child must make to retain his own and others' respect. It is a part of the process of "growing up," a *sine qua non* of maturity, and a product of socialization processes almost as important as learning to walk and talk.

Students' experiences in reading instruction not only have important psychological effects but also important social effects. A study commissioned by the U.S. Office of Education reported that one-fifth of the population is functionally illiterate in the basic skills of writing, reading, speaking, and listening and that another third of the population is marginally literate. Only 45% are both competent and proficient (Mathews, 1975).

Stories in the public and private press continually present evidence of the social consequences of ineffective reading instruction. A report by a consortium of top Chicago business and community leaders found that the schools were ineffective in preparing an increasingly large proportion of students for careers. Fifteen out of twenty personnel managers from Chicago's largest corporation judged 60% or more of the public high school graduates to be unemployable (A secret report flunks schools, 1975, p. 1). A recent high school valedictorian was refused admission to college because he scored in the lowest 13% in verbal ability and the lowest 2% in math ability on a college entrance exam (The valedictorian, 1976, p. 52). Nor are declines in reasoning (or comprehension) scores on college entrance exams restricted to students at the lower end of the spectrum. Only 70% as many students were scoring at the *highest* level of college entrance exams in 1972 as in 1960, indicating that comprehension performance is also deteriorating for "high ability" students (Beaton, Hilton, & Schrader, 1977). Problems of this magnitude inevitably lead to a serious consideration of how to improve reading teaching and student learning.

## Improving Student Reading Performance

The question is, How can educators improve student reading performance? The answer is critical, particularly for instructionally naive students who typically have trouble learning to read. *Instructionally naive students* are those students who do not readily retain newly presented information, are easily confused, and have difficulty attending to an instructional presentation for more than a few minutes. Such students come from all socioeconomic backgrounds. When they are from a middle- or upper-middle-class background, they are typically called learning disabled; whereas, instructionally naive students from a lower-class background are frequently diagnosed as being mentally retarded.

There are three basic perspectives toward improving student reading performance. The first, the pessimist's viewpoint, states that the schools can do little unless the student's physical make-up or home and social environment are altered. The second, the generalist's viewpoint, states that the schools can improve reading performance through developing a wide range of abilities that supposedly underlie reading. The third, a direct instruction viewpoint, involves an analysis of how to teach specific reading skills. Each orientation toward reading instruction is discussed below.

## Pessimist's Viewpoint

This orientation is typified by an article from a popular news weekly. Mortimer Ad-

ler, chairman of the board of editors of the *Encyclopaedia Britannica,* was quoted as saying that there may be good reason for the rising disbelief in the ultimate educability of everyone. "Undifferentiated schooling may be doomed to defeat by differences in the children's economic, social, and ethnic backgrounds and especially differences in the homes from which they come" (New starts for America's third century, 1976, p. 29).

A major problem with the orientation that little can be done is that it minimizes the importance of teaching well.

> As long as the educational climate was such that teaching failures could be blamed on the children, there was no pressure on the teacher to learn more effective means of dealing with children. Over the years, psychologists, mental health workers, and some educators have trained teachers to ship their failures to someone else or at least to blame the child's home background, his low IQ, his poor motivation, his emotional disturbance, his lack of readiness, or his physical disability for the teaching failure. With the recent advent of the label learning disability (for children with normal IQ who fail to learn) there is no teaching failure which cannot be blamed on the child. (Becker, 1973, p. 78)

An orientation that leads to blaming students for their failure is unwarranted and harmful. *Teachers can bring about substantial improvements in students' reading performance.* Problems such as, poverty, a disruptive home life, and physiological impairments, often make teaching more difficult. We reject however, the assumption that improvement in reading achievement is not possible unless there are changes in the children's economic and social environments. Educators cannot use social and home environments as excuses for the poor performance of some students.

Research indicates that if students are directly taught fundamental reading skills, they will learn to read (King, 1978; Becker & Carnine, in press; Guthrie, 1977). Teachers, along with other members of the educational community, can provide professional services to the students who need them. Teachers do not have to turn to medical doctors, social workers, and psychotherapists for help in teaching students to read. Success can result from what teachers do in the classroom, specifically how well they design and implement a reading program. Jansky (cited in Chall 1978a) wrote, "In classes taught by adequate teachers (as rated by the principals) 23 percent of the children failed. When the teachers were characterized as poor, the failure rate rose to 49 percent." But teachers are not the only group responsible for student performance in school. School administrators, colleges of education, publishers, and other persons and institutions concerned with the education of children share this responsibility and must work together to improve educational services.

## Generalist's Viewpoint

Typical of the second orientation toward improving reading performance is the idea that reading performance can be improved by focusing on the *processes or abilities* that underlie learning. Focusing on reading skills is felt by advocates of this viewpoint to be an inappropriate emphasis. Once students "learn to learn," "become motivated," or "overcome auditory deficits" reading will be relatively easy for them. The attitudes reflected in this orientation are more constructive than those of the pessimists, in that the assumption is that students can succeed and that what the teacher does will influence the learning of the students. However, the problems with the generalist's viewpoint are these:

1. It draws attention away from the quality of reading instruction. Instead of looking at the way reading is taught, general skills such as visual perception are stressed.
2. Proposed solutions often inadvertently

result in students' receiving less actual reading instruction than they would in a normal situation.
3. Data from research reviews do not support a generalist viewpoint (Haring & Bateman, 1977; Arter & Jenkins, 1978; Hammill & Larsen, 1974).

Two important assumptions of the generalist orientation lack empirical support: "(a) that the assumed deficiencies in psychological processes can be reliably and validly assessed, and (b) that remediation of these processes will result in improved academic performance" (Haring & Bateman, 1977, p. 138). Chall (1978a) came to a similar conclusion in a separate review: "The research of the past ten years suggests, instead, that good teaching is probably the best way to help the child . . . in most instances, (good teaching is) more effective than perceptual and auditory training" (p. 40).

## Direct Instruction

The third orientation and, in our opinion, the best answer to the question of how educators can improve student reading performance is direct instruction. Direct instruction involves teaching essential reading skills in the most effective and efficient manner possible. The effectiveness of this approach has been indicated by large-scale experimental studies with instructionally naive students and by studies which investigated the characteristics of effective teachers.

A federally funded 10-year study called *Follow Through* evaluated several major approaches to educating low-income, primary grade students. Direct approaches were compared with a language-experience approach, Piaget's stages of learning, child development theory, discovery learning, and open education. Only students in a direct instruction approach consistently outperformed control students on basic, cognitive, and affective measures. Guthrie

(1977) summarized the *Follow Through* results in this way:

> Final answers about teaching are not available from this study (Follow Through)—nor will they ever be—no more than final answers about medicine, engineering, or poetry. A fully complete explanation of education is not likely, since values of the public and research methods are constantly shifting. However, the results of the Follow Through experiment endow us with evidence about the effects of teaching programs at an unprecedented level of certainty. The edge that the more successful programs have over the less successful programs is wide enough to serve as a foothold in the climb to improved, intended education. (p. 244)

A similar conclusion was reached by Rosenshine after conducting an extensive review of the research literature on teacher effectiveness (1978). In fact, Rosenshine summarized the variables that were associated with student academic success as "direct instruction."

> To give an overview of the results, direct instruction refers to high levels of student engagement within academically focused, teacher-directed classrooms using sequenced, structured materials. As developed below, direct instruction refers to teaching activities focused on academic matters where goals are clear to students; time allocated for instruction is sufficient and continuous; content coverage is extensive; student performance is monitored; questions are at a low cognitive level and produce many correct responses; and feedback to students is immediate and academically oriented. In direct instruction, the teacher *controls* instructional goals, *chooses* material appropriate for the student's ability level, and *paces* the instructional episode. Interaction is characterized as structured, but not authoritarian; rather, learning takes place in a convivial academic atmosphere. (1978, p. 17)

Although the research Rosenshine reviewed focuses on the achievement of low-income, primary grade students, other researchers (Tickunoff et al., 1975; McDonald, 1976; Stanford Program on Teaching Effectiveness, 1975) report similar results with other types of students.

## Illustrations of the Three Orientations

Three types of answers to the question of how to improve reading instruction have been discussed: pessimists look outside the school, generalists look toward abilities that underlie reading, and direct instruction advocates look to improvements in teaching methodology. The following illustrates the teacher attitudes and practices implied by these three different orientations. To clarify the orientations, three fictitious teachers, one to illustrate each orientation, are used. Assume that these teachers are sitting in a teacher's lounge discussing different students who are having difficulties reading. Although the discussion is oversimplified, it does portray common teacher attitudes. The teachers are Ms. Excuse, Mr. Indirect, and Mrs. Direct.

The first student they discuss is Arthur, who upon entering fourth grade was given the reading book for that grade. Each day an assignment is written on the chalkboard: a story to read and several written exercises to complete. Unfortunately, Arthur understands only about 60% of the words that appear in the reader and, thus, cannot figure out many of the answers to the written exercises. At the end of the reading period, he hands in his papers. They are returned at the end of the day, full of X's and sometimes a comment like, "Be more careful." After several days, Arthur begins spending more time roughhousing and talking with his neighbors. He seldom completes his assignments. Ms. Excuse complains that Arthur is educationally handicapped, comes from a broken home, and is unmotivated. Mr. Indirect suggests that Arthur receive psychological counseling, which would improve his self-concept and allow for a successful return to reading instruction at a later time. Mrs. Direct suggests *changes in the instructional program to enable Arthur to succeed.* First, she suggests placing Arthur more appropriately in the reading program, since obviously he cannot succeed in assignments that assume skills he does not have. Second, she suggests examining the tasks to determine critical component skills and devising strategies to teach these skills. If he is expected to draw inferences and know the meanings of various words for an assignment, inference skills and vocabulary words must be taught before he works the assignment. Finally, Mrs. Direct suggests instituting a system to motivate Arthur since the high degree of failure he has encountered has seemingly made reading distasteful to him.

The next student the three teachers discuss is Janice, a first grader. Janice has been taught to memorize the words *map, sat, rat, can.* When she encounters a new word, *Pam,* she misidentifies it, calling *Pam* "map." Ms. Excuse explains that Janice is not yet ready to read because she is too immature. Mr. Indirect says it's probably dyslexia and suggests a series of tasks to improve visual discrimination.[1] Mrs. Direct suggests changing the instructional program. First, she suggests testing to see if Janice knows the sound of the letter *i* and has a strategy for reading words. For deficiencies in either skill, Mrs. Direct suggests specific teaching procedures.

The last student is Dale, a sixth grader who forgets how to look up information on different topics in a textbook. The teacher explains that she has taught Dale and the rest of the class how to use a subject index in a textbook several weeks ago. Yesterday, however, when Dale was given a work-

sheet assignment that required him to list the numbers of the pages in his history book that dealt with the history of Egypt, he did not remember about the subject index or how to use it and began looking at every page in his book to find the pages that discussed Egypt. He ran out of time and was unable to finish the assignment. Ms. Excuse says that Dale did not finish his assignment because he has too many worries about his home life. She suggests contacting a social worker. Mr. Indirect suggests memory training. Mrs. Direct explains that the problem resulted because initially Dale needed *more practice* on using an index. She notes that the sixth grade text has a characteristic that causes problems for many students: it doesn't provide enough practice. She says that if Dale had received several exercises on using the subject index immediately following the teacher's initial explanation, he would be more likely to remember when and how to use a subject index. Mrs. Direct suggests reteaching the skill and providing more practice right after the reteaching.

After finishing the discussion about the students, the teachers turn to the topic of reading readiness (how to prepare students for reading instruction) which was discussed in the previous day's staff meeting. Ms. Excuse suggests delaying reading instruction until the students have had enough experiences. She says, "When the child shows a desire to read, we should start teaching." She cannot, however, answer the question of what to do when students do not show an interest in reading.

Mr. Indirect suggests a wide variety of activities which seem related to reading. He refers to Spache and Spache (1977), who classify these activities under three categories: perceptual motor, form perception, and language and thinking. Perceptual motor training includes exercises to develop hand-eye coordination, laterality, directionality, and body image. Form perception training includes some activities closely related to reading such as, match-

---

[1] *Dyslexia* is a term which implies a student has an undetectable constitutional deficit which is keeping the student from being successful in reading. See Harris & Sipay (1975, pp. 136–138) for a further discussion.

ing and reproducing letters and sounds, and some activities such as, working puzzles, drawing pictures, and identifying objects, that are not directly related to reading. Language and thinking training include receptive language exercises (understanding what is said) and expressive language exercises (communicating one's thoughts to another).

He points out that Spaches' book says that students who receive a wide range of readiness training often perform better in reading instruction than students who do not receive any readiness training. Mrs. Direct points out a problem with this approach. She says that if teachers construct and implement a program to teach all the skills, the program might take a full school year. She says the question is which of the skills are the most important and points out that this question is especially critical with instructionally naive students. Efficient instruction is essential for these students if they are to learn at a rate that will later enable them to participate in reading activities with their peers.

Mrs. Direct suggests a task analysis approach which involves teaching only important reading related skills. "Task analysis is the process of isolating, describing, and sequencing (as necessary) all the necessary subskills which when the child has mastered them, will enable him to perform the objective" (Bateman, 1971, p. 33). In this approach, just the skills which are deemed critical are taught before actual reading begins. Included are letter-sound correspondences, auditory preskills, and sounding out. She explains that the task analysis approach does not imply that other activities should be excluded since one can never be sure about the correctness of one's task analysis. Task analysis does, however, provide guidance for teachers who have limited instructional time and want to use that time most efficiently.

Note that in each situation Mrs. Direct looked for ways to improve her teaching so that her students would be more likely to succeed in learning to read. In contrast, neither Ms. Excuse nor Mr. Indirect looked at the instructional program as a factor which might be causing the problems. The discussion of these three teachers illustrates the importance of a direct instruction teacher's attitude. As teachers, we need to seek out ways to improve teaching *in the classroom.* Of course, some students are harder to teach than others, but highly skilled professionals *can* teach these students to read. Hopefully this book will contribute to improved reading instruction by providing detailed explanations of effective teaching procedures.

## RESEARCH

Research in reading is very difficult to conduct because of the many factors that affect reading performance, and, consequently, the results of any experiment on reading must be interpreted with care. Among these factors are teacher skill, pupil knowledge of preskills, and time spent in instruction. If, for example, methods A and B for teaching letter-sound correspondences are compared, the researcher must use teachers who present skills in a like manner. They must also find students whose knowledge of letter-sound correspondences are similar. Finally, instructional time must be equal. Partly because of the difficulty in conducting research, many critical issues remain unsolved. Still, there is a substantial body of research which if interpreted carefully, can provide valuable information about how to teach various reading skills.

Throughout this book, we will refer to two types of research studies, experimental studies and correlation studies. Experimental studies attempt to investigate possible cause-effect relationships by exposing one or more experimental groups to different treatment conditions and comparing the results. Often a control group that does not receive any treatment is included. An example of an experimental study would be one in which a teacher introduces six letter-sound correspondences to one group of students at one time and introduces the same six letter-sound correspondences to another group cumulatively. Differences in time required to learn the correspondences or in number of errors made during training would indicate whether one procedure was not efficient or effective. Most of the studies refered to in this book are experimental studies, since they have direct implications for how to teach specific skills.

Correlation research is not concerned with determining cause-effect relationships but merely studies the extent to which variations in one factor correspond with variations in another factor. Most correlational research in reading involves the study of characteristics possessed by students who are either doing very poorly or very well in reading. The results of correlation research are interesting but must not be confused as implying cause-effect relationships. One example of a confusion between correlation and cause and effect involves the knowledge of letter names by students entering school. Young students who read well tend to know letter names. Knowledge of letter names does not necessarily cause reading success but is correlated with reading success. Because of this correlation, some educators recommend that students should learn letter names before beginning formal reading instruction. Unfortu-

nately, teaching letter names often precludes instruction in letter-sound correspondences, which is more helpful to young students. The point is that just because a skilled person demonstrates certain behaviors in doing a task, instruction should not necessarily *begin* with those behaviors.

Research findings that have teaching implications have been included at the ends of several sections. Since more research has been conducted on decoding instruction than on comprehension instruction, most of the research involves decoding. The research summaries are not necessarily complete, nor have the studies' methodologies been critiqued. Consequently, the research material should be considered suggestive rather than definitive.

We hope that, as knowledge increases and analysis becomes more sophisticated, the quality and usefulness of reading research will increase and allow for further improvement of instructional practices. As Goodman (1976) said:

There is no simple breakthrough in reading just around the corner which will change instruction to a foolproof science. As more is understood about reading and learning to read, it becomes ever clearer how complex these processes are. No simple antitoxin can be injected into nonreaders to make them readers. But, progress will come as misconceptions disappear in favor of sound understanding. Materials and curricula based on scientific insights will replace those built on tradition, trial-and-error and expediency. And a reading curriculum will evolve tied to an effective theory of reading instruction. (p. 496)

# SECTION 1.2

## Direct Instruction

Direct instruction reading is an orientation that identifies major skills, selects and modifies commercial programs that best teach those skills, appropriately places students in the classroom program, and presents lessons each day in the most efficient manner possible. As will become apparent later in the book, no single type of commercial program, placement procedure, or presentation technique is appropriate at all times.

A commercial program is selected according to student needs. Since the average child entering school usually has adequate language and comprehension skills to understand passages from first and second grade readers, his initial instruction should focus on decoding. In contrast, decoding instruction is less important in the intermediate grades, and instruction focuses more an comprehension skills.

Likewise, no one presentation technique is suitable for all situations. Beginning readers tend to need more structure and, consequently, should work more under teacher supervision, either in small groups or at their seats. Teachers should call on them for frequent oral responses to make sure they receive the practice they need, since they are just learning how to study new material. Teachers should also use frequent praise to encourage younger students. In contrast, older students should work more independently, respond more in writing, and receive encouragement in forms other than frequent praise.

Before describing direct instruction procedures in more detail, we need to consider their application to instructionally sophisticated students. Direct instruction procedures are intended to make learning to read easier by breaking complex tasks into their component skills, teaching these components, and demonstrating to students how these components are combined. This simplification of complex tasks is particularly important for instructionally naive students but can also accelerate the learning of instructionally sophisticated students if used appropriately. A potential misuse of direct instruction with instructionally sophisticated students is unnecessarily slowing their speed of learning. When students are required to work exercises they already know how to do or are given structured teaching they do not need, valuable time is wasted. This situation can be avoided by pretesting all students. Students who do well on pretest exercises without teacher direction do not require structured teaching on the skills contained in those exercises. The teacher should proceed to exercises that students cannot do and provide instruction for those exercises. In short, instructionally sophisticated students benefit from direct instruction if they are moved through a reading program at an optimal rate and are provided no more structure than is necessary.

Many educators would disagree, arguing that direct instruction may be appropriate for instructionally naive students but not for instructionally sophisticated students. The evidence in support of this position is sparse, particularly in the area of reading instruction (Cronbach & Snow, 1977). Engelmann and Carnine (1976) found that more sophisticated students perform very well as a result of direct instruction, scoring significantly above grade level on achievement tests and demonstrating an enthusiastic attitude toward learning. Similarly, Guthrie (1977) reported that direct instruction was the only approach in the *Follow Through* study that produced benefits with both low- and middle-income students. Moreover, the incidence of middle-class reading disorders such as minimal brain dysfunction, dyslexia, and learning disabilities suggests that a substantial number of advantaged students would significantly benefit from direct instruction. Since predicting which middle-class students will succeed without careful instruction is difficult, the safest procedure is to teach essential reading skills directly to most students in the early grades, thereby reducing reading failures in later grades. Avoiding direct instruction in the first grade because the students are "too smart" can result in remedial readers in the third and particularly fourth grades. In the fourth grade, reading in the content areas begins, and vocabulary is no longer controlled. These changes result in an explosion of new and difficult words. Students who survived the first three grades through memorization but were not taught basic reading skills encounter serious difficulty in fourth grade. There are too many new words to memorize for students who have not learned generalized word attack skills. If direct instruction is used carefully, it can prevent many of these reading problems. Future research in reading instruction may well point out that many of the procedures involved in direct instruction will be of benefit to all students, not just instructionally naive ones.

The three components of direct instruction—(1) organization of instruction, (2) program design, and (3) presentation techniques—will be discussed in the following material. Adequate instructional time, well-designed materials, and effective presentation techniques are all essential ingredients of a successful reading program. An excellent reading series in the hands of a knowledgeable teacher will not produce significant gains if instructional time is too limited. Likewise, naive students will not do well in an excellent series with ample instructional time if the teacher cannot clearly present and explain the content. Finally, the potential advantages of adequate time and a teacher who presents well will not be realized if the reading series is too difficult or poorly designed.

## Organization of Instruction

### Engaged Time

Rosenshine and Berliner (1978) discuss the necessity of adequate academic-engaged time if students are to succeed in school. *Reading-engaged time* refers to the time students actually spend on reading exercises and activities. They point out that, in several studies, time spent in reading yielded higher correlations with achievement than any other teacher or student behavior studied. Note that engaged time does not refer to scheduled time, but only to the time students spend engaged in reading activities. Rosenshine (in press) reviewed studies that found only about 80% of the 85 minutes allocated to reading in second grade were academic-engaged minutes, and in fifth grade, about 75% of the 113 minutes were engaged minutes. In classrooms with little student improvement in reading over a year, only 1 to 2 minutes were spent on fundamental reading skills.

Engaged time must be put to good use. First, if students are expected to learn to read, they must be engaged in reading-related activities. Stallings (1975) found positive and usually significant correlations between achievement and engagement in reading activities. On the other hand, time spent on stories, arts and crafts, active play, or child selection of activities *always* produced a negative correlation. Second, students should be placed in a reading series at a place appropriate to their skill level. They should not be placed in material that is too easy, where they just review previously learned material. On the other hand, their placement should not be at too advanced a lesson, where they lack essential preskills and make frequent mistakes.

Similarly, independent reading exercises must be instructionally appropriate. They should provide practice for new skills and for previously introduced skills that require continued practice. The exercises should not be too easy or too hard. The match between the content of reading exercises (both teacher directed and independent exercises) and student skill is the essence of individualizing instruction. Brophy and Evertson (1976) point out the importance of appropriate independent work:

> That is, the key to successful classroom management is prevention of problems before they start, not knowing how to deal with problems after they have begun. We also strongly confirmed the additional findings of Kounin, that the best way to accomplish this is to have a variety of appropriate assignments prepared, so that students not presently involved in a lesson will have interesting and appropriate work to do at their seats. If they do, they will tend to stay involved in productive and appropriate activities. If they do not, they will tend to cause disruption. (p. 127)

A major research question yet to be answered relates to amount of engaged time. Approximately how many minutes of reading instruction is required for an instructionally naive student of a given skill level to score at grade level on an achievement test by the end of third or fifth grade? This question encompasses numerous other questions relating to various entry level skills, materials used, degree of teacher proficiency, etc. However, the basic issue is how much time should we devote to reading each day. Among other research issues that affect engaged time are types of schedules, organization of materials, training students on independent work habits, and transition from activity to activity.

## Scheduling

Since the amount of engaged time seems to be an important determinant of student success, classroom organization is critical. Teachers need to schedule ample time and implement the schedule effectively, ensuring that students do not waste substantial amounts of time during group instruction, independent work, or transitions from one activity to another. Teachers cannot spend 15 minutes getting the students settled in the morning, 5 minutes for transitions between activities, 5 minutes re-explaining assignments and rules that students should understand, and 5 minutes figuring out what to do next while students sit waiting. Teachers working with instructionally naive students must carefully schedule activities so that instructional time is well used and enough time is devoted to priority areas. In some classrooms, less important activities may need to be sacrificed so that enough time is available for reading instruction.

## Arranging Materials

In addition to adequate instructional time, organized instruction involves arranging the physical setting and the instructional materials. A teacher might save several minutes daily by indicating the page different groups are at with clips in the teacher's guide (a different colored clip for each group) so that the appropriate lesson can be easily and quickly located. Likewise, arranging student materials so the teacher can quickly hand them out when they are needed will save time. Brophy and Evertson (1976) in studying classrooms in which students made significant academic gains found "(a) each student knew what his assignment was; (b) if he needed help, he could get it from the teacher or from some designated person; (c) he was accountable for completing the assignment appropriately because he knew that his work would be checked" (p. 55). Exercises to be worked independently were placed in folders and placed in the students' desks. Additional independent work was available for students who finished the work in their folders early.

## Program Design

Teachers must also be able to evaluate reading programs so they can select programs that will best meet their students' needs. In addition, they must be able to design lessons for teaching specific skills, which often requires modifying or supplementing certain aspects of a commercial program. Six aspects of direct instruction program design are relevant when selecting a reading program, writing lesson plans, modifying reading programs, and writing IEP's (Individual Education Programs):

1. Specifying objectives
2. Devising problem-solving strategies
3. Developing teaching procedures
4. Selecting examples
5. Providing practice
6. Sequencing skills and examples

## Specifying Objectives

Objectives must be stated as specific observable behaviors. Saying that students will be decoding at first grade level by the end of first grade is not specific. The types of words the students will be expected to read must be specified, along with accuracy and rate criteria. The way in which the words will be presented must also be described, e.g., in lists or in passages. For passage reading, the complexity of sentence structure should also be specified.

Objectives of a program should be carefully evaluated according to their usefulness. Since teaching time is limited, skills should be listed in order of importance, with essential skills being taught first. If time allows, less essential skills can also be taught. A skill is essential if it is a prerequisite for a more sophisticated skill or is important in its own right.

An example of a nonessential skill is knowing where to place an accent mark in a word. Since students must be able to decode a word before they can place the accent mark, the skill is not a prerequisite for decoding. Knowledge of accent marks is necessary when students look up a word in a dictionary to figure out its pronunciation. However, that skill does not require the student to place the accent mark; its position is already indicated.

## Devising Problem-solving Strategies

Whenever possible, programs should teach students problem-solving strategies rather than require them to memorize information. A strategy is taught using a limited set of examples but can be applied to new examples. For instance, in teaching students who know the letters m, t, r, s, f, d, a, l, and o a sounding-out strategy to decode regular words, the teacher might use the words *mat, Sid, fat,* and *mom* as the initial teaching examples. Once the students master the sounding-out strategy with these words, they can use the same strategy to read words like *sit, mad, ram, it, am, Sam, rod,* and *rid.* Many students learn strategies without their being explicitly taught. For instructionally naive students, however, explicit instruction is probably necessary.

The importance of teaching strategies has been extensively analyzed and researched by Ann Brown (1976).

> Too often educators and psychologists draw conclusions about research on an educationally relevant problem without adequate analysis of the nature of the problem itself. We suspect that there are general *teachable* strategies that young children normally learn by trial and error which greatly facilitate his performance on these tasks. We therefore propose a study of these strategies with an eye toward making them an *explicit* part of reading education. . . . The main problem is one of *externalizing an internal mental event.* (pp. 1, 5)

Some researchers now suggest that strategy deficits account for many, if not most, of the educational problems of handicapped students (Ellis, 1963; Winschel & Lawrence, 1975; Martin, 1978). Research has shown that training handicapped students to apply various strategies is definitely possible. In fact, the strategy used when reading a passage may be the primary determinant of what is remembered (Zimmer, 1978). For example, Britton, Westbrook, and Holdredge (1978) reported that student performance on passage items improved after items first began to appear, suggesting that the items prompted the students to adopt a new strategy in reading the passage.

The problem with strategy teaching comes in generalization; handicapped students do not spontaneously apply a learned strategy in new situations. Because of the importance of generalization, the amount of practice and range of examples that are

provided must be carefully controlled. A student could not be expected to use a sounding-out approach with a word like *was* since the letters *a* and *s* are not representing their most common sounds, /a/ and /s/. Students must be taught different strategies to decode irregular words that do not illustrate consistent letter-sound correspondences.

## Developing Teaching Procedures

After objectives are specified and a strategy has been devised, the strategy must be translated into a *format* that specifies exactly how the teacher is to present the strategy. The format must include what to say, what words to emphasize, what to ask, how to signal, how to correct appropriately, etc. Providing detailed formats is very helpful because teaching involves very specific behaviors. Teachers do not teach students to decode words in some abstract fashion. They point to particular words, give information, ask questions, etc. Vague teaching procedures do not provide concrete suggestions for teaching a strategy in the clearest possible manner. Most design questions should be worked out *before* the teacher begins the lesson, which is the reason for having formats. Detailed formats free teachers from design questions and enable them to focus their full attention on the students' performance.

Formats often contain two stages: introduction and discrimination. In the *introduction stage* of a format, the teacher demonstrates the steps in a strategy and then provides structured practice in using the strategy. In the *discrimination stage,* the student operates with little or no teacher help and is given examples which do and do not call for use of the newly taught strategy. These two stages are very important. In the introductory stage, the teacher makes the steps in the problem-solving strategy overt so that the students can see how to approach similar examples. The importance of making problem-solving behavior overt has been stressed by various educators. "Interesting behaviors, like sequencing and translation, involve complex chains of covert activities that should be made explicit" (Frase, 1977, p. 189). In the discrimination stage, the students internalize a strategy, learning to apply it without guidance from the teacher. This stage is an essential step in developing transfer and independent work habits.

Formats must be carefully constructed so that (1) they are easy for the students to understand and (2) they contain only one new skill. For a format to be easily understood, the instructional language must be clear. Words and sentence structures that students do not understand should be avoided. This point is simple but often ignored. Formats in the teacher's guides of commercial reading programs often contain words that average and above-average students may understand, but these same words often confuse instructionally naive students. A great deal of student failure in day-to-day lessons is caused by teachers' failing to preteach critical vocabulary.

Furthermore, an acceptable format should teach only one new skill. Formats that attempt to teach more than one new skill cause two problems. First, when students have to learn two new skills at the same time, they are more likely to fail because the learning load is twice as great as when one new skill is introduced. Second, when students fail, the teacher cannot readily tell which skill caused the failure; this makes diagnosis and remediation difficult. For example, in teaching students to decode consonant-vowel-consonant-final e (CVCe) words, such as *like* or *fate,* a teacher presents this rule, When a word ends in e, say the name for the vowel. Students who were not taught vowel names *before* encountering this rule would have to learn two new skills at once: vowel names and the rule. Students who say "lik" for *like* may not know the vowel name for *i* or may not know how to apply the rule.

Consequently, a teacher would not know whether to help the students with vowel names or with applying the rule.

## Selecting Examples

Selecting appropriate examples is a critical part of format construction. Examples at the introduction stage are appropriate only if the student can use the new strategy to come up with the correct answer. For example, when teaching students to decode regular words, the examples would be limited to words that contain only the letters for which students have been taught the letter-sound correspondences. If the students know the letter-sound correspondences only for the letters *m, s, a, d, f, r, t,* and *i,* the teacher should not present the word *met* since it contains an unknown letter (e).

Selecting appropriate examples for the discrimination stage is more complex. In addition to examples of the new strategy, other examples must also be included. These other examples review previously taught strategies and are in some cases similar to the new examples. A range of examples is necessary so that students are required to differentiate when to use the new strategy and when to use previously taught strategies. If examples of the new CVCe word type are *cane* and *robe,* the teacher might include the words *can* and *rob* in the discrimination format. Including these similar words provides important discrimination practice because *a* (the letter name) represents the long sound in *cane* but not in *can.*

## Providing Practice

Learning to read requires lots of practice. Hundreds of repetitions of the same skills may be necessary if an instructionally naive student is to become a mature reader. Therefore, sufficient practice must be provided within each lesson and across lessons. When a new strategy is introduced, within-lesson practice includes a concentrated or massed presentation of examples. The practice is necessary if the student is to master the strategy. Review, which is sufficient practice across several lessons, is needed to ensure that students retain the strategies and information taught in a reading program. A pattern of massed practice in the first several lessons and systematic review later is critical for retention. Teachers must supplement reading programs that do not supply sufficient practice.

## Sequencing Skills

Sequencing involves determining an optimal order for introducing new information and strategies. Sequencing significantly affects the difficulty students have in learning some skills. Five sequencing guidelines tend to reduce student error rates:

1. Preskills of a strategy are taught before the strategy itself is presented.
2. Instances that are consistent with a strategy are introduced before exceptions.
3. High utility skills are introduced before less useful ones.
4. Easy skills are taught before more difficult ones.
5. Strategies and information that are likely to be confused are not introduced at the same time.

The most critical sequencing principle is *teaching components of a strategy before the entire strategy is introduced.* Since the components must be taught before the strategy itself, the components can be referred to as preskills. In the strategy for decoding CVCe words, knowing the names of the vowels is a preskill, which is introduced before the strategy is presented. Another illustration of preskills involves dictionary skills. To prepare older students to locate words in a dictionary, teachers should provide preskills instruction, including saying the alphabet; comparing target

words to guide words by looking at the first, second, or third letter; and knowing whether to turn toward the front or back of a dictionary after opening it to a particular page. A final example is sounding out. The preskills of the strategy are identifying the sound for each letter, blending the sounds, and then saying the blended sounds as a word.

*Introducing examples consistent with a strategy before introducing exceptions* can be illustrated with the CVCe strategy. Students are first taught a strategy to decode CVCe words in which the initial vowel represents the long vowel sounds. The words *like, cone,* and *take,* which are consistent with the strategy, are introduced first. After students become proficient with the strategy, exceptions in which the vowel is not represented by its long sound (e.g., *love, done, live*) are systematically introduced.

The procedure of *sequencing high utility skills before less useful ones* can be illustrated with irregular words. Very common irregular words, which students will encounter many times in primary readers (e.g., *was, said, have*), are introduced before less common and, therefore, less useful words (e.g., *tomb, heir, neon*). Another example involves letters: the letters *a, m, s,* and *i* are introduced earlier than the letters *v, x,* and *j* because they appear more often in words in primary readers. If students learn the more common letters, they will be able to decode more words.

The procedure of *sequencing easy skills before more difficult skills* applies to both letter-sound correspondences and word types. Easier to say sounds (e.g., *a* and *m*) should appear before more difficult to pronounce letters (e.g., *l* and *e*). Likewise, shorter regular words, which are easier to sound out than longer regular words, should be introduced first.

The procedure of *separating information and strategies likely to be confused* can be illustrated with the letters *b* and *d,* which are similar in shape and sound. If *b* and *d* are introduced within a close time span, students are more likely to develop confusion between them than if they are separated by a longer time span. If *b* is introduced during the third week of a program, *d* might be introduced in the eighth week, after eight or nine other less similar letters have been introduced. Another illustration involves the similar irregular words *when* and *where.* Since they are similar in sound and shape, they would be introduced several weeks apart.

It is important to note that the sequencing guidelines sometimes conflict with each other. Exceptions to a strategy often need to be introduced early because they are useful. For example, since students cannot decode *was* by saying the most common sound for each letter, *was* is an exception to the sounding-out strategy. However, *was* needs to be introduced early because it occurs frequently in stories for beginning readers. Similar conflicts arise when a skill is difficult, which suggests a late introduction, and yet is very useful, which suggests an earlier introduction. Obviously, compromises are necessary to resolve these conflicts. The way in which a compromise is made usually depends on the relative importance of the guidelines in conflict.

## Presentation Techniques

As mentioned earlier, different presentation techniques are appropriate for different stages of reading instruction. For example, during beginning reading, direct instruction involves small group teaching with little independent work. Later the amount of small group instruction decreases, and the amount of independent work increases. An example of how a specific technique is used differently at different times involves diagnosis. Diagnosis of student skill deficits during early decoding instruction is done by listening to students' oral reading responses. In later grades, diagnosis is often based on analysis of students' written answers to worksheet exercises. Another ex-

ample involves teacher feedback (indicating whether responses are or are not correct). For young children, feedback should be immediate; for older children, it can be delayed. In general, a primary grade teacher must be proficient in the variety of presentation techniques needed to maintain student participation in question-answer exchanges between teacher and students. On the other hand, intermediate grade teachers must be more skilled in managing students who are working independently. In both cases, however, teachers must convey warmth and active demandingness, two aspects of effective teaching identified by Kleinfeld (1975):

> The first and most important characteristic is the effective teacher's ability to create a climate of emotional warmth that dissipates students' fears in the classroom and fulfills their expectations of highly personalized relationships. The second characteristic is the teacher's ability to resolve his own ambivalent feelings about the legitimacy of his educational goals and express his concern for the . . . students, not by passive sympathy, but by demanding a high quality of academic work. (p. 318)

The remainder of this section explains some of the teaching techniques that characterize direct instruction: small group instruction, unison oral responding, signals, pacing, monitoring, diagnosis and corrections, and developing student motivation. Although most of the examples used involve situations in which younger students are being taught, teachers of older students, especially remedial students, should find much of the discussion relevant.

### Small Group Instruction

Small groups are recommended for beginning reading instruction because of their efficiency. Beginning reading instruction requires frequent oral responding, which in turn calls for teacher feedback. This feedback can be most economically provided through small group instruction. Although students would benefit from extended periods of individual attention from a teacher every day, most schools cannot afford one-to-one teaching. While some special classrooms may have enough adults to provide intensive one-to-one reading instruction, most classrooms do not have the resources. Therefore, teachers must arrange their schedules to provide for small group instruction. By working with groups of 5 to 10 students at a time for a half hour, the teacher provides students with much more teacher instruction on reading every day than would be available if the teacher worked with individuals.

A critical aspect of small group instruction is forming homogeneous groups of students with similar skills. Such groups allow for more individualization because students with advanced skills can progress quickly through a program while less advanced students receive the extra practice they need. To form homogeneous groups, the teacher divides the students into groups according to pretest performance. Although pretests indicate the skill level of a student at the beginning of a program, they cannot predict how quickly the student will learn new skills. Consequently, teachers should expect to do some regrouping throughout the year.

When forming homogeneous groups, the teacher should make the group with higher performing students the largest and the group with lower performing students the smallest. For example, in a class of 24 students, the advanced group might include 10 students; the next, 8; and the third, 6. This is done to enable the teacher to provide more individual attention to each student in the group.

During small group instruction, students are more likely to be attentive if seated close to the teacher. We recommend seating the students in chairs, without desks, in a semicircle or in two rows. The teacher sits facing the group, looking out over the classroom, so that he can monitor the entire class. Since the students in the group are facing the board and the teacher, they will not be distracted. Students should be seated about 2 feet from the teacher to make it easier for him to monitor their performance and give encouraging pats or handshakes. It is interesting to note that just the opposite pattern often occurs with less proficient students seated farthest from the teacher (Rist, 1970). Teacher monitoring of distractable and instructionally naive students is easier when they are seated in the middle of the group, rather than on the sides (see Figure 1.2.1).

## Unison Oral Responding

A critical feature of efficient small group teaching in the early primary grades is active student involvement. Unison responding, in which all the students respond at the same time, facilitates a high degree of active student involvement. The advan-

**FIGURE 1.2.1** *Suggested Seating Arrangement. An open circle (○) indicates naive or distracted students. Note that these students are not placed next to each other.*

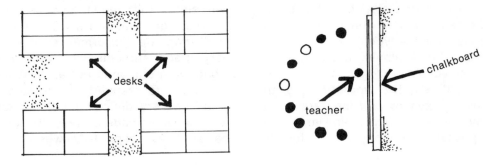

tage of frequent unison responses is that all students actively practice each skill throughout an instructional period. Unison responses also provide the teacher with frequent feedback about each student's progress. With younger students, the ratio of teacher talk to student response should be low. That is, teachers should not talk for long without calling for a response to ensure that students understand what has been said. In nondirect instructional settings, younger students often do not attend to instruction except when they are expected to answer. When a teacher calls only individuals, some students may answer only once or twice during a period. Such infrequent responding often results in limited practice on the student's part and restricted information about student performance on the teacher's part.

## Signaling

A signal is a cue given by the teacher that tells students when to make a response. The effective use of signals enables all students to participate, not just higher-performing students, who if allowed will dominate lower-performing students. For example, if a teacher points to a letter and asks the students to identify it, higher-performing students will almost always answer first, discouraging lower-performing students from responding and possibly depriving them of needed practice. A signaling procedure can avoid this problem by calling for all students to respond in unison.

The steps in a unison response signaling procedure are the directions, thinking pause, and response signal. In the directions, the teacher asks the question and tells the students the type of response they are to make. For example, in giving directions for a vocabulary task, the teacher might say, "I'll say two words. If they are synonyms, say synonym. If they are opposites, say opposite. Listen. Big, large. Are they opposites or synonyms?" After the

directions comes the thinking pause, which lasts for as many seconds as the teacher judges necessary for all students to figure out the answer. The final step is the actual signal to respond. This signal can be a hand drop, clap, or simply a change in voice inflection.

## Pacing

Appropriate pacing contributes to student attentiveness and reduces errors. Younger students are usually more attentive to varied, fast-paced representations (as in "Sesame Street") than to slow ones. However, providing a fast-paced presentation does not mean that a teacher rushes students, requiring them to answer before they have had time to determine the answer. The key to providing a fast-paced presentation is to begin the directions for the next question (or for the correction to the current task) immediately *after* the students make a response. A teacher working with younger students might work intensively for a period of 5 minutes and then take a 15 second break during which time she would acknowledge their efforts with verbal praise and physical contact in the form of handshakes, tickles, pats, etc. A 30 minute instructional session would in fact include about five smaller sessions. As students become more mature, the time they work without a break should increase.

## Monitoring

Monitoring student performance in the late primary and intermediate grades is relatively simple (although time-consuming) because assignments are written. In contrast, monitoring the performance of early primary grade students who are orally responding in unison is not easy. When several students respond at the same time, it can be very difficult for the teacher to hear mistakes made by only one or two of the students, especially when an error sounds similar to the correct response. For example, if a student says the word *sit* instead of *sick* or says the sound /m/ instead of /n/, the error will be difficult to detect. So besides listening to student responses, teachers must monitor student performance by watching their students' eyes and mouths. (They should also frequently call on individual students to respond.) By watching the students' lips and tongues, the teacher can determine if they are positioned the way necessary to produce the correct response. For example, a teacher points to the letter *m,* and a student responds with her mouth open. Since producing the *m* sound requires closed lips, the student's pronunciation is probably incorrect. In addition, students' eyes should be directed to the letter or word pointed to by the teacher. If a student is not looking at the letter, he may be mimicking other students' responses rather than initiating his own answer.

Simultaneously monitoring every student on every unison response during small group instruction is impossible. Consequently, a teacher must systematically switch from student to student, yet focus primarily on lower-performing students. For example, in a group of eight students, five seldom have difficulty while the other three often do. The teacher arranges the students' seats so that the three who have difficulty are seated in or near the center of the group. She watches them for two or three responses and then shifts her attention to the students on the left side of the group for a response or two. Then she shifts her attention back to the students in the middle for several responses before watching the students on the right side. By always returning to the students in the middle and watching them respond, the teacher monitors their responses about twice as often as responses of the higher-performing students seated on either side.

Individual tests are a very important monitoring tool because they provide a more accurate indication of mastery than a unison response. If the student makes a mistake when responding individually, the teacher provides more group practice and presents individual tests again later.

During group instruction, teachers usually should give individual tests only after all the students in the group appear to have mastered the examples presented to the group. By providing adequate group practice *before* calling on individuals, the teacher avoids needlessly embarrassing a student. Because individual tests are time-consuming, they should not be given to every child after every task. The first priority is to test instructionally naive students most often. The teacher tests them on new skills and the more critical, previously introduced skills. Higher-performing students might be tested individually just on tasks on which new skills are introduced.

In addition to individual tests during a group instructional session, a teacher might set up a system to make periodic comprehensive checks on skills introduced to date. By regularly taking data on students' errors, reading rate, and exercises completed, teachers can keep close track of students' progress, or lack of progress. Teachers need to know which students are performing well and which are performing poorly. Such information is critical in providing effective remediation and feedback to students. Often, graphs of student performance that show improvement motivate students to do better on their assignments. Data collection procedures are discussed in more detail in the section on developing student motivation (Section 5.1).

The importance of careful monitoring cannot be overemphasized. The sooner a teacher detects a problem, the easier it will be to remedy that problem. Each day a student's confusion goes undetected the student is, in essence, receiving practice doing something the wrong way. For each day a student remains confused, a teacher may have to spend several days reteaching that skill to ameliorate the confusion. Thus, careful monitoring is a prerequisite for efficient instruction.

## Diagnosis and Correction

In diagnosing the cause of a student's error during small group instruction, the teacher must first decide whether the error resulted from a lack of knowledge or from inattentiveness, since the cause of an error determines which correction procedure is appropriate. The cues a teacher uses in judging whether inattentiveness is the cause are (a) where the student was looking and (b) what the student was doing during instruction. A student who is looking at the teacher is usually attending; whereas, a student who is looking away may not be. The teacher corrects errors caused by inattentiveness by working on increasing the students' motivation to attend. The importance of using effective techniques to keep students attentive cannot be overemphasized. It is probably the most important presentation skill and, thus, will be discussed in detail in Section 5.1, "Developing Student Motivation."

When errors are judged to result from a lack of knowledge, the teacher must try to determine the specific skill deficit that caused the error. This process, called diagnosis, involves identifying deficits based on recurrent error patterns, not on random errors. The diagnosis procedure is basically the same whether the response is oral or written. If, for example, a student says "sit" for the word *set* and "mat" for *met,* the teacher would diagnose the student deficit as a confusion of the letter-sound correspondence for *e,* since the student said the wrong sound for the letter *e* in both words.

The correction procedure used in small group instruction consists of as many as six steps: praise, model, lead, test, alternate, and delayed test. For example, the teacher points to *o* and asks, "What sound?" A student responds, "/ŭ/." First the teacher *praises* another student who responded correctly.[1] Second, he *models* the correct answer saying, "ŏoooo." Third, the teacher may *lead* (respond with them). A lead provides a model as the students respond, ensuring they hear a correct response. Leading is needed only when students have difficulty making the response (saying the sound). Fourth, the teacher tests, asking the students to answer on their own. After the students respond correctly, the teacher continues the test by alternating between the missed example and other examples. He might present the missed example, a review example, the missed example, two review examples, the missed example, etc. The teacher might point to letters in this order: *o, i, o, m, e, o, u, s, i, o.* He follows an alternating pattern until the student responds correctly to the missed example two or three times in a row. This alternating pattern is very important because it requires the student to remember the response to the missed example and to discriminate the missed example from other examples. Gradually increasing the number of review examples builds student retention of the missed example while at the same time minimizing the probability of failure. Failure is minimized because the intervals that the student is required to remember the new response only gradually become longer.

The last step is a *delayed test* in which the teacher tests the student individually on the missed example at a later time in the lesson. With instructionally naive students, several delayed tests may be given during a lesson so that they receive repeated practice within a lesson if they need it. If the student makes errors on the delayed test, the teacher corrects the mistake again using the alternating pattern. A teacher should keep track of student errors

---

[1] The purpose of this praise comment is to prevent students from making errors in order to gain teacher attention and also to maintain a positive atmosphere during instruction.

so that missed skills can be emphasized on the next day's lesson.

The correction procedure is somewhat different for more advanced items. The teacher models a strategy for answering an item and tests. For example, let's say the students have read a science passage containing the rule, When objects are heated, they expand. They then work on written exercises of this form: "A metal ball was left outside. It was 40° in the morning. In the afternoon it was 95°. What do you know about the size of the metal ball in the afternoon?" A student responds, "It gets smaller." The teacher would first test to determine the specific cause of the error. Does the student understand critical vocabulary terms (*expand,* in this case), and does she know how to apply the rule? If the student does not know how to apply the rule, the teacher *models* by asking a series of questions. What's the rule that tells about temperature and size? What was the temperature of the ball in the morning? What was the temperature of the ball in the afternoon? So did the ball get hotter? So what happened to its size? Next the teacher tests the student without leading her through the steps. The teacher continues testing until the student makes three or four correct responses in a row to ensure that she is not just guessing. Later in the lesson the teacher would present a delayed test.

Not working on an exercise long enough to bring a student to an acceptable criterion of performance often leads to student failure on later tasks. For example, students who do not practice a set of sounds until they identify them all correctly will have difficulty applying the sounding-out strategy later. In contrast, when teachers correct all mistakes and repeat an exercise until the students can respond to the entire set of questions correctly (called teaching to criterion), students will have relatively little difficulty applying those skills in other situations. Teaching to criterion is a very efficient procedure in the long run. Although

40 to 50 practice examples may be required to bring a group of instructionally naive students to criterion on a new skill the first day it is introduced, only five or six practice examples may be sufficient the second day, and only one or two examples, the third day. On the other hand, when teachers do not teach to criterion, students often do not show marked improvement in learning later material.

## Motivation

Some students come to school eager to learn and eager to please the teacher. They respond well to simple praise. They work hard and have pride in their work. With such students, motivation is not a concern. Other students have little interest in learning and are not as eager to please. The teacher must accept these students regardless of their attitudes and use techniques to develop an interest in learning. A first step in motivating these students is demonstrating to them that they can succeed in reading. This is done by carefully designing and effectively presenting lesson plans. Second, the teacher shows students there is a reward in learning to read. At first, she may use extrinsic rewards like physical contact, tickles, pats, handshakes. Eventually, she works toward developing intrinsic motivation, which is discussed in Section 5.1.

## Summary

Much of the failure in schools can be attributed to deficits in the instructional system. There are numerous reasons why some students frequently fail. First, many reading programs do not carefully control the introduction of vocabulary, either in decoding or comprehension exercises. Second, preskills of complex strategies often are not taught. Students are expected to learn the component skills that make up a strategy and the strategy itself all at the same time.

Third, programs often reflect "a little of a lot" philosophy. Many different skills are presented but review and practice are minimal and are usually insufficient for many students to master new information and skills. Fourth, teachers are required to cover so many topics every day that finding the time to provide supplementary reading practice time is difficult. The result is insufficient reading-engaged time. Fifth, teachers are often not trained to place students carefully in a reading series according to skill level. Sixth, many teachers believe that students should be intrinsically motivated to learn to read and, consequently, are not prepared to manage instruction for students who are not so motivated.

Reading failure can be prevented, however, by efficiently organizing instruction, carefully selecting and modifying reading material, and effectively presenting the material. Students will not only learn the reading competencies needed for success later in life but also will feel positive about their ability to function in society.

# RESEARCH

## *Program Design*

Since the research findings concerning application of the design procedures appear at the ends of later sections, only a few studies will be illustrated here. The importance of teaching strategies can be seen in a study by Carnine (1977) that compared students who learned a sounding-out strategy to identify a set of training words with students who memorized the training words without learning how to sound out words. Both groups required a comparable amount of time to learn to identify the training words, but on a test of new words, the strategy group identified significantly more regular and irregular words. A second study (Torgensen, 1977) found that while good readers approached memorization in a more organized and active manner and performed relatively well on a recall test, poor readers exhibited different study behavior and did less well on the recall test. However, after poor readers received strategy training on how to study, their performance on the recall test approximated that of the better readers.

The importance of selecting examples is illustrated in a study by Carnine and Kameenui (1978). In learning to identify CVCe words like *hike* and *came,* one group of students received only introductory examples (all CVCe words: *cape* and *site*) while a second group received both introductory and discrimination examples (CVCe and CVC words: *cap, cape, site, sit*). On a posttest, students who received both introductory and discrimination examples identified significantly more new CVCe words.

Sufficient practice to induce overlearning, or mastery learning, seems beneficial.

> Abundant experimental research (for example, Duncan, 1959; Morrisett and Hovland, 1959) has confirmed the proposition that prior learnings are not transferable to new learning tasks until they are first overlearned. Overlearning, in turn, requires an adequate number of adequately spaced repetitions and reviews, sufficient intratask repetitiveness prior to intra- and intertask diversification, and opportunity for differential practice of the more difficult components of a task. Frequent testing and provision of feedback, especially with test items demanding fine discrimination among alternatives varying in degree of correctness, also enhance consolidation by confirming, clarifying, and correcting previous learnings. (Ausubel, p. 239, 1967)

Brophy and Evertson (1976) reported that mastery learning levels of 80% to 85% seemed to produce significant learning gains without producing negative student attitudes toward instruction.

The importance of practice is suggested by comparing student performance on two studies in which students learned letter-sound correspondences (Carnine, 1976). In one study, children received as much practice as necessary to master a correspondence before a new letter was introduced. This was the mastery learning study. In the other study, children received a total of 50 practice trials on each letter-sound correspondence. The students in the mastery learning study made 79% correct posttest identifications as compared to a mean of 28% for the students who received 50 trials on each letter.

### Presentation Techniques

*Small Group Instruction.* The research on small group instruction generally shows positive benefits. First, adult supervision apparently contributes to student engagement. Filby and Marliave (Rosenshine, in press) and Fisher, Filby, and Marliave (Rosenshine, in press) found that when students were working with a teacher or another adult, they were engaged from 79% to 88% of the time. In contrast, when students were working alone they were engaged only 68% to 73% of the time. Second, small group instruction seems to be a reasonable alternative to one-to-one instruction. Venezky and Shiloah (1972) reported that performance on language tasks was superior for students working in a small group setting than for students receiving one-to-one instruction. Working with retarded children on language skills, Biberdorf and Pear (1977) reported that group instruction was more efficient in terms of material learned per unit time than individual instruction. Fink and Carnine (1975) and Fink and Sandall (1977) reported similar results. In contrast, a single study (Jenkins, Mayhall, Peschka, & Jenkins, 1974) reported that tutorials in remedial reading were more effective than instruction in small groups. The effectiveness of small group instruction is based on the notion of students with comparable instructional needs. The student grouping in the Jenkins et al. study may not have been comparable in needs. Additional research is needed on the effectiveness of small groups for other aspects of reading instruction and for use in the intermediate grades.

*Frequent Oral Responding.* Several studies point to the importance of overt responding. Brophy & Evertson (1976) reported that low-performing students are reluctant to respond and are more likely to participate when a group of students is responding. Durling and Schick (1976) and Blank and Frank (1971) reported that overt responding (vocalizing a concept) improved performance when compared to a nonvocalizing treatment. Abramson & Kagan (1975) found that subjects who overtly responded to questions while learning unfamiliar material out-performed students who merely read the material. Frase and Schwartz (1975) reported similar results.

In terms of feedback to overt responses, Tobias and Ingber (1976) reported that feedback yielded superior achievement primarily for students with low pretest scores. Hanna (1976) found that intermediate grade students who received partial or immediate feedback during training answered significantly more pretest items than students who did not receive feedback. When and how to make a transition from overt responding and practice to covert responding are questions that await further research. Brown (1977) and other researchers have emphasized the importance of research on such transitions.

*Signals.* During small group instruction, teachers use signals to call for unison responses. Cowart, Carnine, and Becker (1976) conducted a study in which the teachers used signals for several lessons and then did not use signals for several lessons. They found that signaling resulted in more student attending and responding. When the teacher used signals, the children attended about 55% of the time and responded about 80% of the time. When the teacher did *not* use signals, the children attended about 35% of the time and responded 60% of the time. Slight improvement in test scores also accompanied the use of signals. The same study reported comparable signaling effects on attending and responding in an entire class teaching situation. For example, in one classroom the percentage of time attending averaged 53 and 54 during the two phases in which the teacher used signals and 41 and 20 during the two phases without signals. The responding percentages were 75 and 79 with signals and 67 and 47 without signals. Other research on the importance of signals has produced few effects. Consequently, we encourage the use of signals primarily as a management tool to secure student participation and to prevent higher-performing students from dominating instruction.

*Pacing.* The speed with which a teacher presents the tasks in a lesson determines how often students respond and also may affect attending behavior. Rates of presenting beginning reading tasks were compared by alternating rapid and slow pacing of lessons with the two lowest-performing first graders from three classrooms serving as subjects (Carnine, 1976b). Attending and correct answers were substantially higher during the fast-rate condition (5 seconds per task) than during the slow-rate condition (14 seconds per task). When the teacher asked approximately 12 questions per minute in the fast-rate condition, the students answered correctly about 80% of the time and were off task only about 10% of the time. When the teacher asked about 5 questions per minute in the slow-rate condition, the students answered correctly about 30% of the time and were off task about 70% of the time. Massad and Etzel (1972) found that preschoolers learned sound-symbol relationships more rapidly and with fewer errors with frequent rather than infrequent responding. They also reported that response frequency influenced performance more than various reinforcement schedules. Although we feel rapid presentations are justified because teachers present more material, research on the effects of rapid presentations beyond the first year of instruction would be useful. Also a more accurate specification of optimal rates for different tasks would provide helpful guidelines for teachers.

*Monitoring.*    Monitoring is essential both for correcting and reinforcing students' reading behavior.

> To find out unambiguously whether or not students really understand, teachers must ask questions or observe student attempts to carry out a learning task. Teachers who do this habitually will find that many students who appeared to have been attentive and to have understood a presentation are unable to apply the new material successfully by answering questions or doing exercises correctly. Thus, when we speak of "monitoring" student learning progress, we mean getting responses, not merely watching facial expressions for signs of inattention or confusion. (Brophy & Evertson, 1976, p. 68)

Not only is monitoring an indispensable ingredient for knowing when to correct and reinforce, but it also affects how students attend during reading instruction. Carnine and Fink (1974) systematically varied the amount of eye

contact directed to two students who were frequently not attending during instruction. They reported that when the teacher maintained eye contact with the first student, the student attended 91% of the time, fell to 62% when eye contact was removed, and increased to 86% when eye contact was reinstated. The second student, who started without teacher eye contact, attended 63% of the time. When eye contact increased, attending increased to 85% and then fell to 60% when eye contact was removed. Brophy and Evertson (1976) found that "More effective teachers moved around the room regularly and visually scanned the classroom regularly to keep continual track of what was going on" (p. 56).

Monitoring occurs in many forms besides teacher contact: checking worksheets, walking around the room as students work at their seats, reading graphs of student performance, etc. The effectiveness of these and other monitoring techniques deserves further research.

*Corrections.*    Although correcting student errors is usually considered an important part of the instructional process, research on error correction is limited. The importance of correcting mistakes (as opposed to ignoring them) was investigated in a study conducted by Carnine (1976a). Preschool children were taught several sets of facts: first without corrections, then with corrections, again without corrections, and finally with corrections. Accuracy on training questions averaged 55% higher during correction phases than during no-correction phases. In addition to being provided with corrective feedback, students must also attend to the feedback if it is to be effective. Fink and Carnine (1975) reported that student worksheet errors declined significantly when the students graphed their errors as compared with just being told the number of errors. Some educators (Pehrsson, 1974) suggest that errors should not be corrected, which may be reasonable when students have learned a skill and are practicing so that it will become automatic. The question of when and how to correct will be addressed several times later in the book. As with the other presentation techniques, more research questions are unanswered than answered.

Research related to the modeling aspect of a correction indicated that telling adult subjects the answer after an error resulted in quicker learning than just telling the subject whether the answer was right or wrong (Bourne & Pendleton, 1958). Furthermore, requiring the subject to say the answer following an error was more effective than just telling the subject the answer (Suppes & Ginsberg, 1962). Stromer (1975) reported that when corrections (modeling the correct answer following an error) and differential praise were introduced in tutorial situations, errors diminished. Modeling the correct answer, however, is often not sufficient to remedy many error patterns. For example, a study by Jenkins and Larson (1978) has shown that merely modeling the correct answer following a decoding error is not very effective. Only when the teacher provides a model *and extensive practice* did decoding performance improve. In providing practice, the importance of the alternating pattern, in which familiar examples are included along with difficult examples, was suggested in a study by Neef, Iwata, and Page (1977).

Although modeling and providing practice are usually appropriate for correcting mistakes on discrimination tasks (for example, a student identifies *a* as *e*), the procedure can be ineffective with errors that require the application of a multistep strategy. In these situations, the correction should prompt the student to apply the strategy (Siegel, 1977; Siegler and Liebert, 1973). A study by Carnine (1978c) investigated the importance of correcting word-reading errors by prompting students to use an originally taught sounding-out strategy. Three groups of preschoolers were taught eight letter-sound correspondences and then given practice on the sounding-out strategy until they reached a 100% correct response criterion to a set of six words. After reaching criterion on the training words, the preschoolers received daily word recognition practice, in which four new words were repeated three times. The teacher used a whole word correction procedure in which the teacher identified the word and then asked the students to identify it. The intervention, a sounding-out correction procedure, was introduced with one group at a time. The students were required to sound out and then identify the word that was missed. Consistent improvement was noted in all three groups after the sounding-out correction was introduced, both in correct training responses and correct re-

sponses to transfer words. The approximate changes in training performance on word identification were from 30% to 70% correct in group one, 20% to 35% in group two, and 15% to 25% in group three. The smaller changes with each successive intervention suggest that the longer students receive a whole word correction, the less effective is the introduction of the sounding-out correction. These results are consistent with those of Brophy and Evertson (1976), who found that phonic corrections "were particularly useful for children in general and for low SES children in particular" (p. 85).

Oftentimes errors can be anticipated and prevented. Fink (1976) investigated one such precorrection procedure with two low-performing first graders (mean IQ's were 68 and 72) who consistently misidentified vowels when sounding out CVC (consonant-vowel-consonant) and CVCC words. The students received daily practice in identifying letter sounds and in sounding out words. In addition, they were precorrected in this way: each student was instructed to identify the vowel *before* sounding out the word. Initially no precorrection was used. Then a precorrection was used for several days, and then again no precorrection was used. The mean number of correct responses (out of six possible) changed from .71 to 3.75 and back to 1.20 for the first student and from .60 to 2.56 and back to .86 for the second student. Correction is an area that requires numerous studies; whether to correct, when to correct, how often to correct, and the form of the correction are but a few of the variables that must be studied. Also, the differential application of correction procedures to students of different skill levels must be investigated. For example, for a fluent fifth grade reader, a decoding error might be ignored; however, for a second grader, the teacher might model and test the word at the end of a sentence in which the error occurred. For a beginning reader, the teacher might require the student to sound out the word immediately after the error occurred.

*Praise.* A number of studies have demonstrated that teacher attention is an effective tool in reducing children's inappropriate behavior within large group instructional settings. Thomas, Becker, and Armstrong (1968) and Madsen, Becker and Thomas (1968) showed that frequent teacher attention to appropriate behavior in the form of praise was more effective than rules or teacher reprimands in increasing appropriate behavior. Similarly, Hall, Lund, and Jackson (1968) and Cossairt, Hall, and Hopkins (1973) demonstrated that teacher attention through verbal praise and physical contact increased children's study behaviors in a large group instructional setting. In addition, Cossairt et al. reported that higher rates of teacher praise coincided with higher rates of studying behavior.

Although the effects of positive teacher attention on appropriate classroom behaviors have been well established within large group instructional settings, its effectiveness within a small group instructional setting has not received much attention. In a study by Kryzanowski (1976), four subjects displayed clear increases in on-task behavior in a small group instructional setting as a function of increased verbal praise, with the average increase being 47%.

The question remains as to whether a higher rate of on-task behavior is a necessary prerequisite to a child's learning. On-task behavior may increase a child's opportunity to respond appropriately to every task; however, it does not insure that learning will be more efficient or complete. Siegel and Rosenshine (1973) reported that praise during DISTAR Language I small group instruction was not a significant predictor of child achievement. Thus, high rates of praise may only produce better behaved children and not necessarily smarter ones. Given the contradictory data concerning this question, further research is needed to investigate the effects of praise on learning in a small group instructional setting. Research is also needed on how best to encourage older students in their academic work.

*Combined Effects.* A final study investigated the combined effects of a set of direct instruction techniques. In a *high-implementation* condition, the teacher used praise, corrections, and rapid pacing, while in a *low-implementation* condition, the teacher seldom corrected, used little praise, and presented tasks in a relatively slow manner (Carnine, 1978d). The subjects were preschoolers who were taught reading in a small group setting. For assessing the strength of the combined variables, a multi-

element design with almost daily switches in level of implementation was used.

Both on-task behavior and correct responding remained sensitive to the condition shifts throughout the experiment, with much larger changes occurring for on-task behavior than for academic behavior. The results suggest that this cluster of teacher presentation variables (praise, rapid pacing, and correcting) can strongly affect student behavior and, to a lesser extent, student performance across different educational programs. Children in this study were using the McGraw-Hill *Sullivan Reading* program, while the children in earlier cited research on isolated teacher presentation variables were using *DISTAR* materials or experimenter-designed materials.

*Other Outcomes.* A final research area of great importance is the effect of a direct approach on other outcomes as creativity or self-esteem. The studies reviewed by Rosenshine (in press) are uniformly positive. He found that the two *Follow Through* programs that produced the highest proportion of significant positive results on the Coopersmith Self-Esteem Inventory were both highly structured, direct teaching programs. In a study of middle-class students, Solomon (cited in Rosenshine, in press) found that "control and orderliness" related not only to achievement gain but also to total gain in inquiry skill, creativity, and self-esteem.

> The effective formal classrooms are not cold and critical—McDonald found criticism was relatively rare in California classrooms, being concentrated mainly in the less effective classrooms. Teachers in formal classrooms were warm, concerned, flexible, and allow much more freedom of movement. But they are also task oriented and determined that children shall learn. (p. 40)

Tikunoff, Berliner, and Rist (cited in Rosenshine, in press) also reported higher achieving classrooms were observed as being convivial, cooperative, democratic, and warm; whereas in the lower achieving classrooms there was more belittling, shaming of students, and use of sarcasm. Furthermore, competitiveness did *not* distinguish between higher achievement and lower achievement" (p. 41).

*Conclusion.* As stated earlier, these research findings suggest the effectiveness of several direct instruction presentation techniques. However, the results are not conclusive. Procedures effective with students at a certain age and skill level may not work with students who are more skilled or less skilled. Also, students who have serious behavior problems or who have major academic deficits may not respond to these techniques without concommitant changes in the instructional material and the amount of instruction they receive. The techniques are part of a larger instructional system and alone will not necessarily produce sizable effects.

Although the use of single techniques can have noticable effects in certain situations, usually teachers should think about implementing a *set* of techniques to better teach important reading skills. Another important point to remember is that as students become more skilled, different instructional procedures will be appropriate. This process is well described by Brophy:

> In particular, it should be noted that what is optimal will change to the extent that the teacher has been successful. That is, a teacher who has brought along a class (or an individual student) nicely through careful structuring eventually will get them to the point where they are ready for some independent responsibility. It is important for teachers to remain aware of this developmental trend, because what is optimal for a child who is having difficulty with initial assignments concerning tool skill mastery and who needs careful structuring and considerable encouragement is very different from what is optimal for this same child when he reaches the stage where he is mastering tool skills and has acquired the independent behavior and learning habits that make it possible for him to profit from independent and self chosen activities. (1975, p. 16)

## APPLICATION EXERCISE

1. Identifying words students will not be able to decode is an important teaching skill. Assume that students know the most common sound of all individual letters. Circle any single letter the student will not be able to decode, which means the word itself is probably not decodable. For example, the letter *g* in *gem* would be circled since it is not representing its most common sound (see the chart on most common sounds on the inside front cover).

| | | |
|---|---|---|
| mud | that | but |
| best | gem | in |
| cent | find | top |
| was | cap | some |
| of | them | sad |
| gas | tent | flat |
| clap | told | get |
| put | Tod | gin |
| cut | stand | cast |

# SECTION 1.3

# *A Model of Reading Instruction*

This section overviews a scope and sequence model for teaching reading. A *scope* of reading instruction is defined by the major reading skills that are to be taught. *Sequence* involves an order for introducing the skills. Scope and sequence are focused on here because they are directly under a teacher's control. Cognitive structures, maturational levels, etc., are of less interest because we do not yet understand how teachers bring about changes in these areas through instruction.

Reading skills usually involve decoding or comprehension (or both). *Decoding* is translating printed words into a representation similar to oral language, e.g., reading, either silently or aloud, "I am hot" for the words *I am hot.* Understanding the representation is *comprehension,* e.g., knowing who *I* in the sentence refers to and what "being hot" feels like. Although our major objective is comprehension instruction, a successful reader must be proficient in decoding in order to comprehend. For example, a 14-year-old student reads a passage about the Civil War and later answers questions about the passage. Here is one sentence: By March 15, General Grant had deployed his troops. Here is a question based on that sentence: When should General Lee have attacked General Grant, before or after March 15? Explain your answer. The question requires the student to draw an inference, which is a comprehension skill. The inference goes something like this: Grant will have had his forces deployed by March 15. Military attacks should be staged before the opponent has his troops deployed. Therefore, Lee should have attacked Grant before March 15. The student's comprehension of the sentence and his ability to answer the question would be impaired if he decoded *deployed* as *depleted.* If he decoded each word in the sentence correctly but did not know the meaning of the word *deployed,* his comprehension also would be impaired. Consequently, successful reading requires competency in both decoding and comprehension.

Although most reading educators agree about the importance of decoding and comprehension, they disagree about the nature of the reading process, whether it is a holistic, unitary process or a cluster of subskills. As will become evident throughout this book, we view learning to read as a two-step process. The acquisition of a

30

set of subskills is the first step; the assimilation of those subskills into the holistic act of reading is the second step. Teachers should be aware of the more important reading skills and how to order their presentation. The decoding model will be discussed first and then the comprehension model. Remember, the focus of the models is on instructional variables under a teacher's control. They are not intended as comprehensive representations of what occurs when a person comprehends or decodes.

## Decoding

Our conception of teaching decoding resembles a model of the decoding process outlined by Cunningham (1975–76), who synthesized the models of Venezky and Calfee (1970), Gibson (1965), and Smith (1971). According to Cunningham's synthesized model, students break words down into the largest manageable unit (Venezky & Calfee, 1970) and compare those units with familiar units. For example, when encountering *stairs,* they recognize the *air* as in *fair* and then decord the word. They then check whether their decoding of the word makes sense. ("The man fell down the stairs" would not make sense because *stairs* was read as "stars".) When they come up with a nonsensical sentence, they recheck their decoding.

A direct instruction analysis of decoding instruction includes a sequence of increasingly sophisticated decoding units and procedures for teaching students to use those units to decode words.

1. Students must be taught to identify increasingly larger units of letters and even words (letters, letter clusters, words, and phrases).
2. Students must be taught to manipulate units of various sizes through blending, segmenting, or substituting to come up

with a word; then they see if they have come up with a word that "makes sense" in the context in which it appears.
3. Students must have oral language experience with words before they are asked to decode them.

The instructional procedures explained later in the book are consistent with this model. We recommend a phonic analysis for beginning decoding instruction. Teaching begins with sounds that are represented by individual letters, since these are the smallest decoding units. As soon as the students know sufficient letters to form familiar words, they are taught a blending strategy for decoding those words. As students receive more practice in reading words, they begin to recognize words more quickly. Relatively little is understood about what occurs in the brain when students recognize words at a glance. All we can say is that, with practice, students acquire the ability to recognize words quickly.

Lessons are designed so that only words comprised of familiar letters and words in the students' speaking vocabulary are presented. When necessary, students are orally taught the meaning of a word before they encounter it in decoding exercises. For most students, the words introduced in early decoding instruction will be words in their speaking vocabulary, and, thus, extensive oral instruction will not be necessary. When students are able to decode enough words, teachers introduce phrases, sentences, and passages as well as the sound correspondences for letter combinations such as, *ea, ate, ou, al,* and *ing.*

Students must be taught other strategies in addition to phonic analysis if they are to become mature readers. These strategies include structural analysis and contextual analysis. Structural analysis involves teaching students to decode multi-syllabic words through recognition of root words, prefixes (*re, un, con*), and suffixes (*ness, ful, ion*). Contextual analysis involves syntax and semantics as aides in decoding unknown words or in checking the correctness of decoding.[1]

## Implications for Beginning Reading Instruction

The decoding model can be used to resolve many reading controversies, especially in the area of beginning reading instruction. Although extensive research has been conducted on teaching decoding, educators still disagree on many issues. For teachers of beginning readers, the disagreements result in a bewildering list of choices about what to do. Which of the following should teachers stress:

1. Letter sounds or letter names? That is, pronouncing the sound for *a* as in *cat* or the name for *a* as in *make.* Should students learn sounds before they learn the alphabet?
2. Sounding-out or whole-word reading? That is, identifying a sound for each letter in a word, blending the sounds and identifying the word, or identifying the word as a unit.
3. New words in isolation or in context? That is, presenting new words in lists or in sentences.
4. Accuracy or fluency? That is, correctly identifying words or reading sentences rapidly with expression.
5. Oral or silent reading? That is, students reading aloud or to themselves.

With the decoding model of instruction, these conflicts can be resolved by deciding *when* an objective is appropriate, not whether it is appropriate.

### Letter Sounds and Letter Names

We recommend teaching letter sounds before letter names. Although young children

are often taught the alphabet as an initial reading skill, knowledge of letter names is not as useful in beginning reading as a knowledge of letter sounds. Letter names bear little resemblance to the sounds said when a word is pronounced. For example, the word *run* is spelled using the letter names *are you en.* Knowing these letter names will not help a beginning reader decode the word. In contrast, knowing the sounds for the letters (/r/ as in *rat,* /ŭ/ as in *up,* and /n/ as in *can*) will help a beginning reader decode the word; *rrŭuunn* sounds more like *run* than *are you en* does. An important consideration with letter-sound correspondences is pronunciation variations that result from dialects or regional differences. Instruction should accommodate these variations, unless they are so extreme that students will be unable to correctly decode words. In those situations, teachers should provide practice on troublesome sounds so that word-reading performance is not impeded.

### Sounding-out and Whole-word Reading

We recommend that students learn sounding out before they read whole words as units because sounding out provides beginning readers with a relatively easy to learn strategy for attacking new words. It also prevents students from becoming confused about the relationship between letters in words and how words are said. Teaching sounding out is best done with a code-emphasis reading program in which words are selected that demonstrate consistent letter-sound correspondences. When sounding out words, students identify sounds, blend them, and identify the word. After students become proficient in sounding out, they must make a transition to whole-word reading which itself involves two stages. In the first stage, students sound out a word subvocally before pronouncing it. In the second stage, students see a word and without first sounding it out, pronounce it vocally or subvocally. As

---

[1] *Syntax* refers to the arrangement of words in a sentence and the way in which each word relates to these words. *Semantics* refers to word meaning.

mentioned earlier, we do not know what goes on in the brain that enables students to recognize words at a glance. All we can say is that recognizing words at a glance is a skill that is acquired with adequate practice. Students vary a great deal in the amount of practice they will require from sounding out to subvocal sounding out and from subvocal sounding out to recognizing words at a glance.

### Introducing New Words in Isolation and in Context

During the beginning reading stage, we recommend introducing new words in lists and then later in stories. The rationale for this sequence is that when students are acquiring decoding skills, they should be required to focus on the letters and letter combinations that make up the words and to read words using only those cues. Students are less likely to do this when the words are introduced in stories because they can use the context of the story (by saying a word that makes sense in the sentence) or pictures (by looking at objects in the picture to help them guess a word). Students who rely heavily on picture and context cues may attend only to some letters in a word and thus develop ineffective decoding strategies. In word lists, contexts and picture clues are unavailable, thereby increasing the likelihood that the student will attend to all the letters in the words.

### Accuracy and Fluency

Accuracy is defined as correctly identifying letters or words. Fluency is reading smoothly, quickly, and with expression. The relationship between accuracy and fluency might be better understood in the context of acquisition and proficiency. During the acquisition stage, a new skill is being learned. During the proficiency stage, the skill is practiced so that students can apply it quickly and will remember it. Although the two stages overlap to some extent, the

intent of each stage differs. During the acquisition stage when a skill is new, mastery of the skill (in this case, accurate decoding) is most important. After the skill has been introduced and practiced to some extent, proficiency (in this case, learning to read fluently) becomes more important. Samuels (1976a) speaks of proficiency as automaticity or "automatic habits" in decoding: "While it is true that accuracy in decoding is necessary in reading, it is not a sufficient condition. In order to have both fluent reading and good comprehension, the student must be brought beyond accuracy to automaticity in decoding" (p. 323)

The progression from accurate to fluent reading makes sense when viewed from a beginning reader's perspective. At first, the student carefully inspects and sounds out each word. The student must remember the sound for each letter, be able to blend sounds, and then transform the blended sounds into a word; e.g., the written word Sam is sounded out Ssssaaammm" and then becomes "Sam." This is the acquisition stage. If a student is encouraged to read rapidly and with expression while still in this stage, she will not have time to process the letters that make up each word. Rather, she may begin guessing, saying any word that makes sense in the sentence; perhaps she will use picture cues that accompany the words or just look at the first letter and guess. On the other hand, if the student is given time during the acquisition stage to master sounding out, she will be more likely not to develop guessing habits. It is much easier to increase reading rate with students who have appropriate decoding strategies since the teacher can concentrate solely on rate. As the rate increases, the accuracy stays high. With students who develop strong guessing behavior in early training, rate training is difficult since guessing tends to increase.

Just as stressing fluency too soon causes problems, so can stressing fluency too late. If students are required to sound out every word for months and months, they may become word-by-word readers, which in turn may cause serious comprehension problems or may result in students' not being able to complete assignments since they read too slowly.

### Oral and Silent Reading

The long-term objective of reading instruction is for students to read silently, accurately, and with comprehension. However, long-term objectives do not necessarily determine *how to begin* instruction. During early reading instruction, oral reading enables the teacher to keep students actively practicing reading and, in addition, provides information about problems the students may be having. This feedback allows the teacher to correct inappropriate strategies, thereby helping students develop the skills necessary to become successful readers. In mid- and late-primary grades, students should read silently most of the time; oral reading is used just when teaching specific skills like reading with expression or in making periodic checks of students' decoding ability. While oral reading does not interfere with improvements in reading rate and comprehension during early instruction, it could interfere at a later stage if ample silent reading practice is not provided.

In summary, with this decoding model, the controversy over the scope of decoding instruction (what skills to teach) is transformed into a question of sequencing (when to teach the skills). The alternatives described earlier as either-or questions can now be presented as compatible skills, arranged in sequence:

1. Letter sounds, then letter names
2. Sounding out, then sight reading
3. New words in isolation during the beginning reading stage; later, regular words and high-frequency irregular words introduced in context (In fact, many words must be introduced in context because of dual pronunciations, e.g., *lead* as in *lead pipe* and *lead the way*.)
4. Reading for accuracy, then reading for speed
5. Oral reading, then silent reading

Each set of objectives contains a short-term objective and a long-term objective. The initial objectives in each set are short-term goals relating to sounds, sounding out, isolated words, oral reading, and accurate reading. These short-term objectives prepare students for the long-term objectives: silently and accurately reading by words and phrases. Just because the short-term objectives are superceded by the long-term objectives does not lessen their importance.

## Comprehension

Although beginning reading instruction should stress decoding, it should not ignore comprehension. We agree with Carroll who says, "An emphasis on phonics does *not* mean that attention to meaning must inevitably decrease. Of course you can teach meaning while teaching phonics, and doing otherwise is counterproductive and absurd" (1977, p. 157). Carroll (1977) also points out that reading comprehension requires language comprehension and cognitive ability (complex reasoning skills) and that there are many more language comprehension and reasoning skills than decoding skills.

Although comprehension is more complex and more important than decoding, most reading research and analysis done in recent years have focused on decoding. Only recently have reading researchers been shifting their emphasis to studies of comprehension. Glaser (1977) explains:

The new challenge for education is to teach competencies that enable individuals to use advanced comprehension skills—to read unfamiliar text in order to gain new information, to draw inferential judgments from text rather than accept directly stated information, and to interpret complex text so that it can be related to knowledge already acquired. (p. x)

Since almost any set of thoughts or ideas can be written and given to someone to decode and comprehend, comprehension involves almost every type of "understanding" or "thinking." The close relationship between language and reading comprehension has been pointed out in a research review by Jenkins and Pany (1977). According to their review, students who do well on comprehension questions about *oral* presentations of passages also tend to do well on comprehension questions about *printed* passages. In 10 out of 12 studies reviewed by them, improvements in the comprehension of spoken messages were accompanied by improvements in the comprehension of printed messages. The implication of these studies is that the same reasoning processes are used to understand what we read as well as what we hear.

A comprehension model having implications for the classroom teacher is necessary even though comprehension instruction is more complex than decoding instruction. We believe that this orientation involves the identification of critical skills, just as is the case for decoding. Davis (1972) suggested a hierarchical skills theory in which comprehension skills are built on each other, progressing from simple to complex. In reviewing the comprehension research, he described two additional theories: an isolated skills theory and a global comprehension skill theory. In the isolated skills theory, comprehension is thought of as many unrelated skills which can be taught in any order. In the global skills theory, comprehension is made up of a single skill. According to Davis (1972),

neither of these two conceptions is consistent with the data. He suggested that a hierarchical skills theory best fits the available comprehension research data.

We agree that many comprehension skills are hierarchically related. For example, vocabulary knowledge is often a preskill for drawing inferences. Students cannot infer what two antagonists who have frequent altercations will do when they meet at a party, unless they know the meaning of *antagonist* and *altercation.* On the other hand, while comprehension can be viewed as a hierarchical relationship, requiring that some skills be taught before others, it is also a unitary process in which a student applies various skills and knowledge almost simultaneously. For example, students asked to draw an inference about the two antagonists, in a very brief interval, will have to remember relevant information from the passage, apply inference skills in determining what might happen next, and have appropriate background knowledge. In short, while skills and information can often be taught in a sequential, logical manner, they are applied in an almost instantaneous fashion, and not necessarily in the order they were originally taught.

A model similar to the one for decoding is possible for comprehension instruction because of these common elements:

1. The increasingly complex units in comprehension instruction: words, phrases, sentences, paragraphs, and passages
2. The skills for processing comprehension units: rapid decoding, identifying specific information, summarizing, drawing inferences, transforming complex syntax into a simpler form, translating difficult vocabulary into more familiar synonyms, critical reading and various study skills such as outlining and skimming
3. The knowledge base against which a reader evaluates a comprehension message (That is, does what is read make sense? The reader also may incorporate

**TABLE 1.3.1**  *A Direct Instruction Model for Comprehension*

|  | DECODING | COMPREHENSION |
|---|---|---|
| Units | letter features, letters, letter combinations, syllables, words, phrases | words, phrases, sentences, paragraphs, passages |
| Skills | sounding out, sight reading, breaking larger words into parts | literal, inference, sequencing, summarization, simplifying syntactic and semantic complexities, critical reading, and study skills |
| Knowledge Base | oral language, familiarity with words, syntax, semantic constraints | syntax, semantics, facts, logic, schema |

new information into knowledge base as he reads.)

Both the decoding and comprehension models are summarized in Table 1.3.1.[2] The hierarchical element is present in each aspect of the model: unit, skill, and knowledge base.

1. Units form a hierarchy beginning with single words and continuing to entire passages.
2. Skills begin with literal comprehension (such as finding the word *man* and circling it when an illustration of a man is given) and increase in complexity to include complex inferences and evaluations.
3. The hierarchy for knowledge base begins with simple vocabulary (such as knowing the name of common objects) and increases to include more sophisticated vocabulary such as *homo sapiens.*

The following examples illustrate how comprehension also can be viewed as a unitary or nearly simultaneous process. In a simple matching item with a picture of a man and the words *cat, man, sad,* a young student would have to know the name of the object illustrated, identify each word listed, and locate and circle the correct word. The units are words; the skills are decoding and following instructions; and the background knowledge is the name of the illustrated object and the meanings represented by the printed words. A student would deal with each of these three aspects at about the same time. A more complex example would be a reaction to this sentence: "Environmentalists claim that conservation measures will not hamper the current economy and in the long run will contribute to employment and capital formation." Critically reading this sentence involves all three aspects of the comprehension model. The unit is not only *that* sentence but also the material from which the sentence was drawn. The skills include reading critically and drawing inferences. The knowledge base includes an understanding of many uncommon words. In summary, comprehension can be viewed as at least three hierarchically ordered sets of skills that develop over time and as a unitary process that involves all three aspects whenever a reader is deriving meaning from print.

---

[2] A different, and excellent, scope and sequence for learning to read is also presented by Chall (1978).

## Three Aspects of the Comprehension Model

The following examples are intended to illustrate the components within each of the three aspects of the model: knowledge base, skills, and units.

### Knowledge Base

The knowledge base consists of several components: (1) acceptable word orderings (syntax), (2) word meanings (semantics), (3) factual information, (4) logic, and (5) frameworks for incorporating new experiences (schema). An example of each component follows.

First is syntax. A student reads, "John ran up the stepped." *Stepped* is a verb and cannot follow *ran up the.* Since the sentence violates known word order rules (syntax), the student rejects her interpretation and checks the sentence again. She notices that the word is *steps,* not *stepped.* Since "John ran up the steps" is consistent with the student's knowledge of syntax, the sentence is acceptable.

Second is an example of semantics (word meaning). A student reads, "Alice tripped and fill against the wall." The syntax is acceptable because *fill* is a verb; however, semantics is violated since *fill* does not make sense in the sentence. Again the student rechecks the sentence and comes up with an acceptable sentence, "Alice tripped and *fell* against the wall."

The third component is factual information. Larry reads, "Jackie works until 5 p.m. every morning." This rendition is rejected because 5 p.m. is in the afternoon, not in the morning. Upon rereading, Larry sees that the sentence refers to 5 a.m., not 5 p.m.

The fourth component, logic, is closely related to the factual information component. Jason reads, "It was hot and humid on a lazy April afternoon in Minnesota." April in Minnesota is usually cool, not hot and humid. When rereading the sentence, the student finds it is not April but August.

These examples of the importance of a student's knowledge base have all involved decoding errors. Decoding errors were selected to simplify the examples; however, the same process would be involved if a student misconstrued a message even if decoding were not the cause of the error, as illustrated with the next component, schema.

Schema, the fifth component of knowledge base, is a complex relationship involving information and inferences that allow students to assimilate new information (Anderson, 1977). The following illustrates how schema operates. Lisa got a letter from an old high school friend. The friend wanted to start a company to make telephones and sell them at a lower price than the telephone company did. He knew he could make them more cheaply, because he would just copy their phones. Lisa was knowledgeable about manufacturing; she had a schema including patents, royalties, and laws protecting copyrights. More specifically, she knew the telephone company had a patent on the design of their phones. Her friend could not copy them without paying a royalty or without being sued. Consequently, her friend would not be able to manufacture the phones as cheaply as he thought. Without a schema involving patents, royalties, etc., Lisa would not have realized that her friend's idea represented infringement of patent laws and would lead to unexpected expense.

It is important to note that what serves as a knowledge base for evaluating and assimilating comprehension units was at one time acquired as a skill, although not necessarily directly taught as a skill. For example, transforming complex syntactic structures into simpler ones is directly taught to some students as a skill. However, once these students comprehend a syntactic form automatically, the syntactic structure becomes part of the knowledge base for evaluating subsequent comprehension units. In short, the instructional model is portraying a dynamic system in which students learn new skills and after mastering those skills, use them as a basis for learning more sophisticated new skills and for comprehending more complex material.

### Skills

The second aspect of the direct instruction comprehension model includes the various skills that students apply to what they read. These skills include identifying specific information, rapid decoding, summarizing, simplifying syntactic and semantic information, critical reading, and various study skills including dictionary skills, outlining, and skimming.

Early instruction involves teaching students to answer literal questions (questions to which answers are directly stated in a passage). One literal skill is identifying specific information by answering who, what, when, where, and how questions based on information explicitly stated in a passage. Literal items become more difficult in later grades as the sentence structure becomes more complex. To prepare students for these exercises, the skill of simplifying syntactic complex sentences can be taught. Consider this example of transforming clauses into two simpler sentences. A student reads the sentence, "The tall man, who was seen leaving the cafe with a very old woman, lives near the cafe," and the question, "Who lives near the cafe?" The student may incorrectly respond, "The old woman," because the last part of the sentence reads "a very old woman, lives near the cafe." This type of error can be prevented by teaching students to transform longer, complex sentences into two simpler sentences: "The tall man was seen leaving the cafe with a very old woman" and "The tall man lived near the cafe." The answer to the question, "Who lives near the cafe?" is now obvious. (Note that while most stu-

dents will not need to be explicitly taught to transform syntactically complex sentences into simpler ones, teachers should be ready to provide the instruction to students who need it.)

One of the skills introduced in later grades is inference, which involves drawing conclusions beyond what is directly stated. Inferences are necessary for students to assimilate new information into their knowledge base. For example, when a twelfth grader reads about the problems of a soybean crop failure in Brazil, she infers that hardships resulting from income loss occur there just as they do in the United States. She may also use her knowledge of agricultural economics and infer that a drop in soybean production in Brazil will lead to a price increase in anchovies from Chile, since anchovies and soybeans are two major world-wide sources of protein. She infers that when supplies of one protein source become scarce, the price of the other increases.

### Units

The third aspect of the comprehension model is the increasingly larger units that a reader processes. Young readers who attend to one word at a time, forgetting what they read earlier, might have difficulty comprehending a single sentence. Initial exercises for these students would be limited to simple picture-word matching exercises. Similarly, older readers who read at a sentence level can answer questions about individual sentences but may have difficulty with comprehension items that require integrating several paragraphs. As readers become more proficient decoders, units should expand to phrases, sentences, short passages, and longer passages.

## Purposeful Reading

The comprehension model lacks one important ingredient: reader purpose. A reader does not read sentences and aimlessly apply various comprehension skills such as summarizing, simplifying, drawing inferences, etc. A reader's purpose determines the way in which she treats a passage and which comprehension skills she uses. Teachers must be sure to teach students the skills needed for reading with different purposes as well as how to read for different purposes.

Some different purposes for reading include these:

1. To be able to identify and remember specific facts or a main idea
2. To be able to follow instructions to reach a goal, e.g., assemble a bicycle
3. To enjoy
4. To be able to explain the content of a passage to someone else
5. To be able to accommodate the content into the reader's schema
6. To critique the logic or data presented in a passage
7. To edit a passage according to stylistic and organizational criteria

Several comprehension skills may be involved in fulfilling a specific purpose. For example, in pleasure reading, students must develop a story line based on main ideas derived from specific facts in a story. Reading would not be as pleasurable if we did not remember who had done what and when. So even in pleasure reading, we focus on specific details, form main ideas, sequence them, and remember them.

Going a step further, if the purpose in reading a passage is to comprehend it well enough to explain it to someone else, we will approach the material quite differently. In addition to forming main ideas and sequencing them, we will attempt to remember supporting details that justify or make sense out of our main ideas. We will also develop a rationale for selecting specific main ideas and use details from the passage to support our choice. Obviously, our self-imposed criteria for understanding or comprehending a passage are more rigor-

ous if we intend to explain it to someone, rather than just read the passage for pleasure.

The importance of purpose in determining the way in which we approach a passage suggests that purpose must be considered in any discussion of teaching comprehension. Consider reading with the intent of remembering information or main ideas from a passage for more than just a day or two. Reading for this purpose is seldom taught during the primary stage. Problems occur, however, at the beginning of the intermediate stage, when students are assumed to have had experience in reading and remembering. More specifically, third graders read narrative stories, the content of which they are not usually expected to remember over a period of days. In contrast, fourth graders read expository material with content from areas like social studies and science and are expected to remember the content. Instructionally naive students, who are not trained to "read to remember" in third grade, may have serious problems with content area materials. The implication is that instructionally naive students must be systematically taught to read to remember before fourth grade or at least during fourth grade.

## Causes of Comprehension Failure

A deficiency in any of the three aspects of the direct instruction model could interfere with comprehension. The following material will discuss some possible deficiencies.

### Inappropriate Units

Students may fail because they do not read in units appropriate to their purpose. Students who cannot process units best suited to their purpose may experience difficulties in comprehension. For example, word-by-word readers may not be able to comprehend the relationship between different parts of a sentence; whereas, students who group words into phrases will. Oakan,

Wiener, and Cromer (1971) found that poor readers, who did not organize material into phrases, did better on comprehension measures when the reading material was organized into phrases for them. The phrases were emphasized by leaving extra space between each one. (Since methodological concerns about the Oakan et al. study have been raised, their conclusions should be viewed as suggestive rather than definitive.)

### Skill Deficits

Students may have comprehension problems because they lack various skills needed to comprehend a passage: inference, summarization, simplification, etc. Students who lack these skills entirely, or possess them as oral language skills but do not apply them when reading, will have comprehension problems. A common problem among poor readers is the inability to summarize or extract main ideas from passages. For example, the owner of the Yankees made a trade for a new pitcher who was said to be the best pitcher in the league. The next day, the owner said he was looking for a new first baseman and right fielder. The paper quoted the owner as saying, "This year we will be the champs." The poor reader summarized by saying "The Yankees got a new player." She did not summarize but just picked one of the events in the story. In contrast, another student summarized by identifying the main idea as the owner tries to build a championship team. Obviously, an inability to summarize and extract main ideas has a serious effect on comprehension.

### Inadequate Knowledge Base

Students may have difficulties in comprehension because they lack an adequate knowledge base. If the syntactic or semantic load of a passage is too great, students are likely to have difficulty. Consider this sentence: Naturally, this principle is frequently violated as bureaucratic anonymity is ongoingly disrupted by eruptions of concrete humanity. This sentence would be difficult for intermediate grade students to comprehend, even if told that the principle referred to was that bureaucracy is an autonomous world of regulations. There simply are too many unfamiliar words, and the sentence structure is too complex.

### Decoding Deficits

Students with serious decoding problems will be precluded from comprehending a passage. They will misidentify too many words or read so slowly that they forget what they have just read.

In summary, comprehension failure can occur when students cannot process printed material in units appropriate for their purpose, when they lack necessary skills for interpreting printed messages, when they do not have an adequate knowledge base for evaluating their interpretation of a printed message, or when they decode so poorly that they cannot identify the words correctly or rapidly enough.

## Approaches to Improve Comprehension

Levin (1971–72) outlined two approaches to improving student comprehension performance. One approach was to carefully design the comprehension materials from which students work. The other was to teach students strategies that they then would apply to a wide range of comprehension materials. Although combining the two approaches probably has the greatest impact on students' comprehension performance, teachers are more likely to teach essential vocabulary and strategies for working comprehension items than to write a comprehension program. Teachers do not have the time or expertise to write their own comprehension program. Even so, findings that relate to designing comprehension materials will be discussed here as well as findings related to student strategies for working comprehension exercises. As mentioned earlier, research on comprehension instruction is limited, so the discussions are brief.

### Designing Comprehension Material

The following are some findings related to constructing materials:

1. Passages should be preceded by advanced organizers that summarize the upcoming content and relate it to what has come earlier in the program (Gagné & Wiegand, 1970; Richards, 1975–76).
2. Specific questions about the passage should appear frequently throughout a passage, after every 20 lines of text if possible (Frase, 1968; Frase, Patrick, & Schumer, 1970).
3. Feedback concerning performance on the specific questions should be provided as soon as possible (Frase, 1967).

These suggestions are applicable mostly for the intermedate grades and beyond. Even if teachers do not write comprehension programs, they can use these findings by writing study guides that contain advanced organizers and study questions, and they can arrange instruction so that feedback is immediate.

### Teaching Strategies

The importance of students' having comprehension strategies is illustrated in a study by Smith (1967). High IQ students were better at reading for detail than low IQ students, but neither group did well at reading for general impressions. When asked about the procedures used in reading for detail, the high IQ readers specified their strategy; whereas, low IQ readers could not explain theirs. However, neither group could explain the procedures they followed for a general impression. The re-sults suggest that superior performance of the high IQ students in finding details resulted from their having a strategy. In reading for general impressions, neither group had a strategy, and neither group did well on those items. Since students who have a strategy perform relatively well, a major goal of comprehension instruction is to teach strategies for various types of comprehension skills.

## Summary

This section has included most of the topics discussed later in the book. We have attempted here to make explicit some of the interrelationships among the topics. The topics were discussed in the context of a direct instruction model for decoding and comprehension. In both decoding and comprehension, students need to learn to process increasingly complex units, acquire skills for processing the units, and develop a knowledge base for making sense out of what they read. The units in decoding are letters, letter clusters, words, and phrases. The skills for processing the units include phonic, structural, and contextual analysis. The knowledge base is primarily familiarity with words and syntactic structures. For comprehension, the units are words, phrases, sentences, paragraphs, pages, and chapters. The skills are numerous, including summarization, drawing inferences, critical reading, and study skills. The knowledge base is extensive: logic, vocabulary, schema, etc. In addition, the comprehension model must take into account a reader's purpose since purpose determines how a passage is handled. Causes of comprehension failure and avenues for improving comprehension performance can also be accounted for by the model. The major purpose of the model is to illustrate how to organize reading instruction to meet the needs of all students.

---

# RESEARCH

## Increasingly Larger Units

Initial units are single, letter-sound correspondences (Wolf & Robinson, 1976; Santa, 1976–77); later units extend beyond single letters. These larger units have been referred to as the sound-spelling units, spelling patterns, or letter clusters. "Linguists such as Venezky, Wardhaugh, and Reed have strongly recommended that it is necessary to consider letter patterns beyond the simple sound-letter correspondence level if a more consistent relationship between oral and written language forms is to be realized" (Ruddell, 1976a, p. 24). The importance of students' learning to decode increasingly larger units is not a new finding. It was noted by Huey in 1908: "We are brought back to the conclusion of Goldscheider and Muller that we read by phrases, words, or letters as may serve our purpose best. But we see, too, that the reader's acquirement of ease and power in reading comes through increasing ability to read in larger units" (p. 116). More recently, Gibson (1965) identified three phases involved in learning to process larger units: differentiating graphic symbols, learning letter-sound correspondences, and using increasingly larger units of structure.

Various researchers have confirmed that mature readers process larger units than beginning readers. Calfee, Venezky, and Chapman (1969) reported that good readers showed an increasing mastery of multiple letter groupings through high school. Other research has indicated that mature readers identify clusters of letters rather than individual letters (Spoeky & Smith, 1973; Foss & Swinney, 1973; Savin & Bever, 1970; Glass & Burton, 1973). However, research suggests that when mature readers encounter unfamiliar words, they are able to process them by letters or letter clusters rather than as entire words (Terry, Samuels & LaBerge, 1976; Baron & Strawson, 1976, Rozin & Gleitman, in press).

## Strategies for Processing Units

Extensive research has been conducted on the importance of teaching strategies for manipu-

lating units of various size: segmenting orally presented words (a teacher says "man" and the students say "mmmaaannn"), combining sounds to form a word (a teacher says "aaaat" and a student says "at"), and blending sounds represented by printed letters (a student says "iiif" for *if*). The studies, which are discussed in Section 2.2, "Auditory Skills," indicate that strategies for manipulating various sized units are correlated with later success in reading and prepare students to correctly decode new words.

## Word Familiarity

The importance of word familiarity in facilitating decoding was suggested in several studies reviewed by Mason, Osborn, and Rosenshine (1977). Similarly, Jorm (1977) reported that familiar words were easier to decode than pseudowords (nonsense words), and pseudowords made up of familiar syllables were easier to decode than pseudowords comprised of unfamiliar syllables. Mason (1977a) found that familiar words were processed as a unit while unfamiliar words were processed at a syllable or letter level. These studies indicate that word familiarity is indeed a significant variable in how readily students can decode words. The implication is that unfamiliar vocabulary should be introduced in oral language exercises before students are expected to decode those words. Teachers will have to devote much more time to vocabulary instruction with lower-performing students. Perfetti and Hogalboam (1975) reported that skilled readers benefited greatly from a small amount of oral exposure, while less skilled readers required more exposure before their decoding rate improved.

## Letter Sounds and Letter Names

Research findings suggest that knowing letter sounds is more helpful to the beginning reader than knowing letter names. Jenkins, Bausell, and Jenkins (1972) found that while letter-sound training is more difficult than letter-name training, letter-name training did not facilitate word reading. Letter sound training did. Ohn-macht (1969) also reported that teaching letter names did not facilitate reading performance; however, teaching letter sounds did. Samuels (1971), R. J. Johnson (1970), and Elkonin (1973) reported that teaching letter names did not help students learn to read. Samuels (1972) explained that the frequent emphasis on teaching letter names may have resulted from a confusion between correlation and causation. Knowing letter names is correlated with reading achievement but does not seem to cause it. The correlation between knowing letter names and doing well in reading probably occurs because children who are taught letter names at home come from a verbally enriched background and do well in reading because of that background, not because they know letter names.

In summary, we are not recommending that students learn only letter sounds but that they learn letter sounds first and letter names later. Although knowledge of letter names is necessary for later spelling and dictionary tasks, it is not needed for sounding out simple words, a strategy we feel that students need to acquire as early as possible when learning to read.

## Sounding-out and Whole-word Reading

The limited research comparing sounding-out and whole-word reading with naive subjects supports a sounding-out approach. Bishop (1964), in a simulated learning-to-read situation with college students, and Jeffrey and Samuels (1967) and Farmer, Nixon, and White (1976), in teaching 4 to 6 year olds to read vowel-consonant words, reported that a group that was taught a sounding-out strategy read significantly more new words than a group that was taught whole words.

A study by Carnine (1977) replicated and extended Jeffrey and Samuels' findings by requiring students to learn more sounds, read more words, read longer words, and continue in training until they had reached a performance criterion. Both groups in Carnine's study received training on a set of 18 words. The students in both groups were taught to criterion (until they made 18 consecutive correct responses) and then were tested on a set of 6 new words that contained the same letters as used in the training words. The sounding-out

group in the Carnine study read 91.7% of the new regular words; whereas, the whole-word group correctly identified only 28.3% of the new words. Moreover, the sounding-out group was able to read significantly more irregular words than did the whole-word group. Although students in the sounding-out group correctly read more new words, the time required for them to reach criterion in the training program was actually less, though not significantly so, than for the whole-word group.

It is important to remember that both sounding-out and whole-word strategies are appropriate, but at different times. Sounding out appears to be more effective in initial instruction, but whole-word reading is essential for more rapid, fluent reading. When and how to make the transition are questions that must be answered in future research. In addition, the role of sounding out in decoding irregular words should be investigated.

## Introducing New Words in Isolation and in Context

Singer, Samuels, and Spiroff (1973) compared three procedures for introducing new words: words in isolation, words in sentences (context), and words with pictures. Both context and picture clues slowed acquisition. During the beginning reading stage, students often are not proficient enough in decoding to benefit from context clues (Groff, 1976; Hochberg, 1970), and, in fact, the context clues may draw their attention away from the letters that make up the word. In a review of the research on using pictures to facilitate student learning of a sight vocabulary, Samuels (1970) found that pictures hamper performance. The experiments usually compared two groups—one in which a picture appeared with each word and one without pictures. When pictures accompanied the words, students required longer to reach criterion and made more errors than when pictures were not present. More recent research tends to confirm these findings (Harzem, Lee, & Miles, 1976). Contrary findings do not test the students on word identification without the pictures (Denberg, 1976). Since the pictures were always present in Denburg's study, the students may have learned nothing more than picture reading. The reason for having illustrations is that they increase student enjoyment

(Samuels, Biesbock, & Terry, 1974). We do not recommend that pictures be done away with completely, but rather reserved until after the students complete decoding a portion of a story.

Additional research on context cues is more difficult to interpret since it was not conducted with beginning readers. Although Goodman (1965) found that students correctly identified more words when they were presented in context (rather than in isolation), other researchers did not replicate this effect (Williams & Carnine, 1978). Gibson and Levin (1975) also state that the sooner a child learns that what he says is determined by the letters that make up words, the better: "Many children start school with the notion that reading is speaking with books open in front of them. The speech is not nonsensical. Still, the earlier the realization by the child that what he says must be determined by what is printed, the better is the prognosis for early reading achievement" (p. 282).

The issue then becomes how to maximize the probability that students will learn to attend to the letters that make up words. Our suggestion is to teach words in isolation before presenting them in stories. Students cannot read words from context when they appear in isolation. Since they can decode only by attending to the letters in the words, they will more quickly learn that decoding is based on sound-symbol relationships and not on pictures or context. Questions about when to shift the instructional emphasis from reading words in lists to reading words in passages can only be answered through further research.

### Accuracy and Fluency

The importance of some minimal level of accuracy is not disputed (Golinkoff, 1975–76), and numerous studies have investigated the relationship between rate and reading achievement. Pace and Golinkoff (1976) found that proficiency in decoding words was related to comprehending word meanings. A similar relationship between decoding speed on isolated words and comprehension test performance was reported by Perfetti and Hogalboam (1975). Speer and Lamb (1976) reported a significant correlation between fluency in identifying letters and letter clusters and first grade reading achievement. In addition to these correlational

studies, two experimental studies have found that students trained to increase their reading rate also demonstrated comprehension gains (Dahl, in press; Waechter, 1972). Perfetti (1977) suggests one possible explanation for this relationship is that slow decoding interferes with recall of previously read material. He found that skilled readers recall 16% more of what they've read (six words back in a sentence) than less-skilled readers. Gough (1976) has a similar explanation: slow decoding results in pauses which disrupt memory processing of what is read.

Little research has been conducted to determine optimal accuracy and rate criteria for developing successful reading behaviors at various skill levels. Research is needed to answer several questions: How accurate should decoding be before rate is stressed? What are optimal decoding and accuracy rates for various reading stages? What are minimal rates that should be reached before new skills are introduced? What kinds of decoding errors should be corrected and when (immediately or at the end of the sentence or paragraph)? How important is oral expressive reading to comprehension? What are efficient procedures for developing reading rate?

### Oral and Silent Reading

Neville (1968) reported that reading orally before reading silently resulted in significant differences in reading fluency and number of vocalizations but not in word recognition and comprehension. Keislar and McNeil (1968) reported significantly higher word recognition and comprehension scores for kindergartners who read orally than for students who read silently. Important questions concerning how much oral reading is appropriate for different stages of acquisition and when it should occur in a lesson with respect to silent reading deserve research attention.

Research in other areas also suggests that practice is more effective with young students if they respond overtly (Durling & Schick, 1976). Similar results were reported with kindergartners in learning tasks involving pictures (Keeney, Canizzo, & Flavel, 1967) and with slow learners in learning tasks involving sentences (Taylor & Whitely, 1972), and with elementary students in recall tasks involving classification (Scribner & Cole, 1972). In all these experiments, students who responded orally during training either remembered more information or were better able to apply the information to new material than were control groups. Although these experiments did not directly relate to decoding instruction, their results suggest that overt responding is beneficial at least during certain stages of skilled acquisition.

# Classroom Reading Instruction

A teacher's role in reading instruction consists of two major phases: beginning-of-the-year planning activities and day-to-day implementation. Beginning-of-the-year activities include selecting reading material, setting up a reading program, and testing and placing students in the materials. The on-going daily activities consist of planning lessons, presenting lessons, and conducting follow-up exercises.

## Beginning-of-the-year Activities

### Selecting Materials

A major objective of this book will be to give teachers specific criteria that they can use in evaluating and selecting materials. First, the teacher should look at the skills taught in a program. It must present the major reading-related skills. Second, the teacher should note the adequacy of practice and review. Many commercial programs are not designed to meet the needs of lower-performing students. Often they do not provide adequate practice and review of important skills. Programs should provide massed practice on a skill when it

is first introduced and then intermittent review on that skill. Third, the teachers should look at the sequence and rate at which skills are introduced. A program that introduces skills very quickly or introduces skills in an order that may confuse students should not be used with instructionally naive students. Fourth, teachers should look at the strategies taught in the program. Programs should present simple, generalizable strategies.

Obtaining well-constructed materials is especially critical for teachers working with instructionally naive students, since the quality of the materials may make the difference between success and failure. Teachers working with average students should also select well-constructed programs, since poorly constructed programs may keep the students from learning at an optimal rate. High-ability students will do well in almost any program, if they spend enough time in reading-related activities.

At the core of reading instruction in most classrooms is the developmental basal reading program, which includes student and teacher materials for grades K–6. Harris and Sipay (1975) give an excellent description of the contents of basal reading programs.

Basal reader programs are not simply series of books and accompanying materials. They are preplanned, sequentially organized, detailed materials and methods used to teach and to learn the skills of developmental reading.

The pattern of a graded series starting in first grade, with a controlled vocabulary, gradually increasing difficulty, and a variety of content, has not changed greatly since the McGuffey Readers first appeared in the 1830's. For the past fifty or so years, most basal reader systems have been eclectic, trying to achieve a balanced reading program with a broad and varied set of objectives. Until the mid 1960's most of them used a look-and-say procedure for developing initial reading vocabulary, with phonics and other word-identification skills taught gradually, mainly with the second- and third-grade readers. Since then, however, there has been a decided trend toward more and earlier stress on teaching decoding skills. The following discussion deals with the eclectic basal readers that have been popular since the 1930's and the recent changes in them.

*Materials.* A representative series starts with one or more readiness books, usually in workbook form. The first actual reading materials are usually three thin paperbacks, called pre-primers. To dispel the mistaken idea that a given book should only be used in a particular year in school, however, increasingly series are numbering their books by levels. For example, a first pre-primer following two readiness books would be labeled Level 3. The pre-primers (Levels 3, 4, and 5)[3] are followed by the first hard-covered book (Primer 1[1] or Level 6), and a first reader (1[2] or Level 7) which completes the program covered by most first graders. There are usually two second reader books (2[1] and 2[2] or Levels 8 and 9), two third reader books, (3[1] and 3[2] or Levels 10 and 11) and one thick reader in each of grades 4, 5, and 6. Since the mid 1960's, there have been some departures from this traditional format, such as a choice between a conventional hard-covered reader and the same content bound in two or more paperback units. Also, a few programs now utilize a systems approach; *i.e.,* they provide a large number of components that, through skillful management,

can be used to allow for individual differences. The efficacy of such systems has yet to be adequately tested.

Each book in the series is accompanied by a consumable workbook, some of which provide self-help cues at the top of the pages, or have taped directions and answers for self-correction. Other accessory materials may include exercises printed on duplicating stencils; large cards for group practice with phonic elements, words, and phrases; introductory story cards or charts; correlated filmstrips and recordings; and supplementary paperback storybooks. The recent trend in enrichment is to provide the kinds of materials just mentioned in convenient packages as optional supplements.

Each reader is accompanied by a guide or manual which details the teaching method. Most manuals present a general plan and then give a detailed lesson plan for each selection. The manual, which is really a handbook on how to teach with the pupil book, is either a separate book or is bound together with a copy of the reader. Manuals usually provide more suggestions for skills development and enrichment than are needed for most children, while extra practice is needed for some children. The teacher must therefore judiciously select activities based on the children's needs, as well as determine the appropriate rate of presentation for different groups. (pp. 58–59)[1]

Basal reading programs are developmental in that they are designed for students learning to read for the first time. The first books in a developmental series are designed according to the interests of younger students. Later stories and assignments are geared to older students.

Developmental programs can also be used for remedial purposes in some situations. The same program that functions to teach beginning reading to a first grader can also be used as a remedial program for

[1] From *How to Increase Reading Ability: A Guide to Developmental and Remedial Methods,* 6th ed. by Albert J. Harris and Edward Sipay. Copyright © 1975 by Longman, Inc. Reprinted by permission of Longman.

a second grader, since the interest levels of first and second graders are fairly close. On the other hand, programs designed for first graders usually cannot be used for older students who have not mastered skills normally taught in first grade. These students need programs that are designed for their interest level and take into account their greater sophistication.

In addition to the basal programs are a great number and variety of other commercial materials. First are materials designed to teach or provide extra practice in decoding skills. Foremost among these materials are series of workbooks designed to provide supplementary practice on phonics. Most supplementary decoding material is designed for use in the early grades (first grade through third grade) since it is during these grades that most basic decoding skills are taught. Second are materials designed to teach or provide extra practice on comprehension and study skills. These materials are usually designed for use in the intermediate grades (fourth grade through sixth grade) since the emphasis switches from decoding to comprehension and study skills in these grades.

A third type of material is designed for the remedial reader, the student who is unable to decode and comprehend materials written for his grade level. Considering the significant number of students reading below grade level, it is surprising that there are few comprehensive programs that provide carefully integrated decoding and comprehension instruction for the remedial reader. The majority of commercially available materials for remedial readers deal only with some decoding or comprehension skills. High interest-low vocabulary books (books focusing on themes that interest older students but which use words usually taught in the primary grades) make up the bulk of material designed for remedial readers. Besides these materials are programs with activities for reteaching important decoding and/or comprehension skills. However, these programs usually are not

very comprehensive. For example, a decoding program may include just reading words in lists but not reading passages, an activity which is critical in developing fluency in using phonic, structural, and contextual cues.

Appendix E includes the names and addresses of most major and some minor publishers of commercially prepared reading programs. Since the reading materials market is very competitive, publishers constantly revise their materials. Thus, we will refrain from recommending any one program for use. Throughout the book, however, we will refer to some exercises from specific commercial programs as we discuss ways in which skills are taught and how teachers might modify the exercises to better meet the needs of low-performing students. The programs we have selected illustrations from are Scott, Foresman's *The New Open Highways,* © 1974; Houghton Mifflin's *Houghton Mifflin Reading Series,* © 1976; Ginn & Co.'s *Ginn 720,* © 1976; Lippincott's *Basic Reading,* © 1975; Harcourt Brace Jovanovich's *The Palo Alto Reading Program,* © 1973. These programs were chosen, not necessarily because they were the best programs, but because they were representative of the typical commercial programs available.

After teachers select reading instruction materials, they must decide how to use the materials. More specifically, they must schedule adequate instructional time and specify how the time will be spent.

## Setting Up a Reading Program

There are two aspects to consider in setting up a total reading program:

1. Ensuring that the program does in fact provide time for teaching all basic reading skills
2. Deciding on the type of instruction that is suitable: highly structured, teacher-guided instruction or more loosely structured, child-guided instruction.

A total reading program includes adequate provision for decoding, comprehension, study skills, recreational reading, writing, and spelling. The amount of time devoted to these activities should depend on the skill levels of the students. Teachers working with students whose home environments provide a great deal of informal instruction in basic skills need not spend as much time on these skills as teachers working with students from homes in which informal instruction is limited. Students performing below grade level should spend more time on basic skills since they must acquire more than a year's worth of skills if they are to progress at a rate that will enable them to catch up to their peers.

Furthermore, the teacher must take responsibility for providing adequate time. For example, if a teacher feels that students are unlikely to read outside of school and that their fluency indicates they need more reading practice, she must take the responsibility to provide the extra practice. In the upper grades, a teacher might do this by incorporating reading activities into all content area instruction (math, social studies, science, etc.) and by scheduling time into the day for recreational reading. These and other procedures for low-performing and remedial readers are discussed in detail later in the book.

Besides adequate instructional time, teachers must also provide a suitable type of instruction. The type of instruction students receive can vary from highly structured, small group instruction, in which the teacher presents simple skills a step at a time and calls for frequent oral responses, to unstructured student-centered learning activities, in which the students work with minimal teacher guidance. During the early primary grades (K–2), the majority of instruction should be conducted in structured, small group situations, which allow teachers to closely monitor student performance and correct errors as soon as they occur. During the intermediate grades, the type of instruction used will vary according to the students' skill levels. Students performing at or above grade level can benefit from more loosely structured, child-centered activities. Students performing below grade level may still require a more structured type of instructional setting.

In a typical intermediate level classroom, a teacher might have two programs: one for students performing at or above grade level and one for students performing below grade level. The program for the higher-performing students may include a high proportion of independent activities (e.g., research projects, independent use of audio-visual aids, etc.). Teacher-student contact would consist mostly of individual conferences and group discussions. The program for lower-performing students would include more small group instructional sessions in which activities were carefully planned to present skills in an efficient manner. Likewise, the teacher would endeavor to present skills in a manner which kept the students performing at a high success rate (90% or above) since lower-performing students are more likely to be discouraged by failure.

In some schools, reading specialists or other trained auxiliary personnel are available to assist teachers with lower-performing students. These students may be taken from a classroom for 30 minutes to 1 hour for special reading instruction. The instruction provided by the classroom teacher and the specialist must be carefully coordinated; that is, both should be teaching the student the same reading strategies. Likewise, the information being presented to the student should be carefully controlled. For example, it would be *inappropriate* for one teacher to present letter-sound correspondences in one sequence while the other teacher presented them using another sequence. Conflicting approaches overload students with too much information and confuse and frustrate them. Furthermore, teachers should not feel their responsibility for teaching reading is canceled because a student is receiving outside instruction. Lower-performing students generally need more practice than average students to master skills. Therefore, the teacher should provide practice and instruction in addition to that provided by the specialist.

## Remedial Reading Instruction

Students unable to read books at their grade level are often pre-empted from success in school since their limited reading ability handicaps their performance in nearly all other subject areas. Below grade level reading can result from a decoding deficit, a comprehension deficit, or a combination of the two. Regardless of the cause of the deficit, six guidelines are relevant to teaching remedial readers: provide extra instruction, start the extra instruction as soon as any deficit appears, use highly trained personnel, select a program that teaches essential skills and teaches them well, move remedial students through the instructional program as rapidly as possible, and motivate the students to achieve.

### Extra Instruction

*The more deficient a student is in reading, the greater the amount of instruction the student should receive.* A student should receive an extra 15 to 30 minutes of direct instruction for each year the student is below grade level. A student 2 years below grade level should receive about 1 hour of extra instruction at some other time during the day. A student decoding several years below grade level is in serious trouble. An enormous amount of practice is required to develop decoding fluency. A fifth grade student reading at a second grade level, for example, must progress *3* years in *1* year to catch up and to perform at grade level.

### Early Remediation

*The sooner remediation begins, the more likely the student can be helped.* Helping a second grader overcome a 1-year deficit is much easier than helping a fifth grader overcome a 3-year deficit. Younger students not only have less to make up but also tend to have better attitudes, because they have not failed for as long a time. Another reason for beginning remediation as soon as possible is that students identified as needing special help in early grades can continue to receive it, thus preventing failure in later grades.

Balow (1965) found that remedial instruction was effective in dealing with the problems of the disabled reader, but he also noted that severe reading disability is not corrected by short-term intensive treatment but needs continual attention.

### Careful Instruction

*The more severe the student's deficit, the more careful the instruction must be.* The instruction of remedial students must be monitored quite carefully by highly trained teachers. Until very recently, students in need of remedial help were often sent to volunteers or other untrained personnel who were asked to help the students. Many remedial readers need the help of the most highly trained professional, since they have developed serious confusions that must be carefully and consistently corrected. Volunteers and other untrained personnel are often unaware of how crucial many student errors are and do not know how to deal with them. Volunteers can perform very useful functions like listening to the students read and making simple corrections (telling the student the word and recording the error). However, they should not assume larger responsibilities unless they receive training and are monitored.

### Well-designed Program

*The greater the students' deficit, the more they will benefit from a well-designed program that teaches essential skills.* The guidelines for evaluating commercial programs for remedial readers involve the same variables as any reading program: sequence, rate, teaching procedure, and practice. However, two additional factors must be considered for remedial students. First, the program must focus on the essential skills that will prepare the students to handle decoding and comprehension exercises at their own grade level. Second, the program should be designed to interest older children. Pictures and story themes designed for first or second graders are often rejected by older students.

### Rapid Progression

*The more deficient a student is in reading skills, the more quickly she must progress through the program.* Since a remedial student is already behind, she must progress at a rate of more than 1 year for each year of instruction. If the student only progresses 1 program year for each instructional year, she will never reach grade level. To move students at the maximum rate, the teacher must know both the student's deficiencies and the order in which skills are introduced in a reading program. The teacher should spend time only on those lessons that focus on student deficits. The identification of lessons that focus on student deficits is much easier with programs that focus on essential skills.

### Motivation

*The more highly motivated a remedial reader is, the greater the student's progress and success.* Unmotivated students will not receive the full benefit of increased instructional time, careful teaching, and a well-designed program. Without motivation, covering more than 1 year of program in 1 school year is unlikely; the student will continue making the same errors and will perform poorly on new skills.

Remedial readers are often unmotivated and understandably so. Think what it would be like to be in a failure situation day after

day. No matter how hard you try, things don't get better. You can't succeed, and you can't get out of the situation. The failure has to be faced day after day, year after year. Think what that failure would do to your self-image and of how you might react. Then think of the remedial reader, who has failed day after day, year after year.

First and foremost in establishing motivation is providing a program in which the student can succeed. This occurs when the student is placed appropriately in a program that teaches only essential skills, is given extra practice, and is taught in a very careful manner. After the student is shown that he is succeeding in *reading* (and not told that success in reading is unimportant), the student's attitude and motivation will begin to change.

Second is giving the student a goal to work toward. Sometimes it will involve a point system or contract that states the student will receive a certain grade, privilege, or prize for reaching a certain performance level. The point system or contract must be carefully designed so that earning the grade or privilege is neither too hard nor too easy. The grade or privilege must be a functional reward, which means the student will work for it, and the student's daily successes must be clearly tied to his progress toward earning the grade or privilege.

## Testing

Tests given at the beginning of the school year should be designed to help teachers (1) place students of similar ability and knowledge in homogeneous groups, (2) place the groups at appropriate starting lessons in materials being used in the classrooms, and (3) identify skills and/or information the students lack which might keep them from succeeding in reading. Throughout this book, we will recommend testing procedures that teachers at various grade levels, who are faced with testing 25 to 30 students, might use at the beginning of the year. Our procedures are designed to take relatively little time per student (5 to 10 minutes) and be administered by a volunteer or teacher aide with minimal supervision.

There are two basic types of tests usually used to place students in reading instruction: norm-referenced tests and criterion-referenced tests. Norm-referenced reading tests measure the students' general knowledge and skills in reading but not the skills presented in any particular program. The results from a norm-referenced test allow for several types of comparisons. Two of the more common comparisons are percentile and grade level. Percentiles tell how the student stands in regard to other students of that age or grade level; e.g., a 35th percentile score means the student scored above 34% of similar grade or age students taking the test, but below 64% of similar grade or age students taking the test. Grade level scores indicate the average year and month in school that corresponds to a particular score. The major advantage of norm-referenced tests is that they allow for comparisons of different programs. Students from different programs can be given the same test to determine if some programs seem to result in better student performance than other programs. One problem with using a norm-referenced test to compare various programs is that the test probably covers the content of some programs more than others (even though it is not supposed to), which means that the test is biased toward some programs. An even greater disadvantage of norm-referenced tests is that they provide little information about how to instruct a student. That is, a percentile or grade equivalent score does not really indicate where to place a student in a commercial program or what a student's skill deficits are.

The second type of tests, criterion-referenced tests, focuses on specific skills, thereby providing the teacher with information about what skills the student has

and has not mastered. Criterion-referenced tests either focus on the skills from a commercial program or on important skills independent of any programs. Throughout this book, we will refer to the following types of criterion-referenced tests, which we recommend using to help place students in a program.

The first type of criterion-referenced test is an informal reading inventory (IRI), which is used to place students at their instructional level in a graded series of books.[2] The test is constructed by selecting sample passages from sequential levels of the reading series. Informal reading inventories should be used as the prime tool in placing students in basal reading programs. A more in-depth discussion of the use of informal reading inventories will appear in later sections.

A second type of criterion-referenced test focuses on various word attack skills. The diagnostic test of word attack skills can be used (1) to help the teacher group beginning readers who do not know enough words to read a selection in an informal reading inventory and (2) to help the teacher identify specific word attack deficits. Sample tests and directions for administering the tests for each reading level, appear in the appropriate testing sections for beginning, primary, and intermediate reading stages.

The third type of criterion-referenced test discussed is designed to test comprehension skills. Students should be grouped according to how they can decode and

---

[2] *Instructional level* refers to a level at which it would be appropriate to begin instruction with a student. The student should not know all the material presented at that level since if he did, no new instruction would be going on. Likewise, the level should not be too difficult since this will cause frustration for the student. A student's instructional level will vary depending on the student's personality. Some students will tolerate difficult situations better than others. In general, an instructional level in a reading book is one at which a student can decode at about a 95% accuracy level in decoding and can comprehend the major theme of the material.

comprehend. For example, a student who can decode at a sixth grade level but is unable to do comprehension exercises appropriate for that grade level may be placed, depending on the severity of the comprehension deficit, in a lower group or if placed in a higher group, may receive instruction geared toward specific deficits. Since the number of comprehension skills is much greater than the number of decoding skills, a beginning-of-the-year comprehension test can test only a small sample of the total number of skills. More thorough comprehension testing can be done during the school year.

In addition to these criterion-referenced tests, many other commercially prepared reading tests are available. Among these include the following:

1. Oral tests designed to measure various decoding skills. Some tests in this category are Botel Reading Inventory, Phonics Mastery test, Durkin-Meshover Phonics Knowledge Survey, McCullough Word Analysis test, and Rosewall-Chall Diagnostic Reading test. Some of these tests are norm referenced in that norms in grade level and percentile equivalents are provided.
2. Oral passage reading tests in which a student reads a series of increasingly difficult selections until he reaches the point at which the material is obviously too difficult. Two widely used oral reading tests are the Gilmore Oral Reading test and the Gray Oral Reading test. Although oral reading tests are valuable in judging a student's progress in a school year, they should not be used as the major tool in placing students in reading materials, since there is a great deal of variability among materials that publishers designate for a particular grade level.
3. Survey tests which provide a measure of children's general reading ability. These tests include subtests on vocabulary,

comprehension, and various study skills such as dictionary usage and chart reading. Some commonly used tests are the California Reading test, Gates-MacGinitie Reading test, Metropolitan Reading tests, and Stanford Reading tests. These tests will provide the teacher with information regarding general areas of weakness.

For a more in-depth discussion of the various uses of tests and a background in how tests are constructed, read *Teaching 3: Evaluation of Instruction* (Becker & Engelmann, 1976b).

## Day-to-day Implementation

After students are grouped and placed in a commercial or teacher-made program, a teacher presents individual reading lessons. The three components of an on-going implementation are planning, presentation, and follow-up.

## Planning

A teacher must plan daily activities for the instructional session and for independent work. The plan must be realistic. Often, teacher guides from commercial programs suggest a variety of tasks that would take many hours to present. The teacher must decide which of these tasks is necessary. Likewise, he must plan seatwork assignments appropriate for the amount of time available.

More important than planning the amount of material to present is planning for the quality of the material. Most commercial reading programs will require modifications to make them effective with instructionally naive students. The teacher must be prepared to simplify teaching explanations and provide for extra practice when appropriate. As an author of a major basal program said, "Our series was not designed for the slow learner, the non-English speaking child . . ." (Chall, 1967, p. 194). Likewise, in commenting on materials available for teaching vocabulary, Hunres (1976, p. 1) noted that they are "haphazard—in organization, sequencing, and presentation."

The extent of program modification is determined primarily by student performance. If students have no difficulty learning the skills as presented in a program, little modification will be needed. However, if students have difficulty, major modifications may be necessary. Nearly all commercial reading programs are characterized by two critical instructional design deficits in their handling of comprehension: insufficient practice and inadequate teaching procedures. First and foremost is insufficient practice. In the typical program, a new comprehension skill or vocabulary word often appears in one lesson and then disappears for several weeks only to reappear again in a single lesson. Programs seldom provide enough introductory or review examples for instructionally naive students either to master a new skill or to remember it.

The second problem is the lack of procedures for teaching students strategies for working various types of comprehension activities. Programs often provide students with one or two sample items and expect them to formulate their own strategies as they work through the remaining items. While some students can learn a strategy from a few sample items and from working practice items, many need to be directly taught strategies. They either take too much time to come up with a workable strategy, or the strategy they devise is faulty. Procedures for modifying commercial programs are included in each section of the beginning, primary, and intermediate reading parts. How skills are taught and what modifications may be necessary are discussed there.

In addition to planning and modifying instructional activities, the teacher must en-sure that the work students are to do independently is appropriate. During seatwork activity, the teacher should assign tasks containing skills the students have mastered in an instructional setting. Teachers do not want to include practice on skills the students have not mastered since such practice may be counterproductive. If, for example, teachers assign an activity which involves the student in identifying words that begin with the /n/ sound and the student is confused between the /m/ and /n/ sounds, the activity may result in the student's receiving practice in misidentifying *n,* making the confusion more difficult to remedy.

## Presenting a Lesson

A lesson consists of two major sections: (1) teacher presentation and (2) passage reading and written exercises.

The teacher presentation exercises usually involve decoding and comprehension activities (and possibly handwriting and spelling). For example, the decoding exercises during a second grade lesson might include sound identification exercises, several introductory words that illustrate a new decoding skill, and a list of discrimination words that provides practice on the new skill and on previously introduced skills recently causing students difficulty. The exercises on identifying sounds and reading words are constructed to prepare students not only for the passage and written items for that lesson but also for upcoming lessons.

Comprehension activities during teacher presentation usually include instruction on critical words, i.e., words students probably do not know and that are inadequately explained in the passage. Comprehension instruction may also be designed to introduce or provide practice on various strategies: how to draw inferences, how to paraphrase sentences with complex structures, how to summarize, etc. Finally, the teacher presentation would include going over any independent seatwork assignments that include directions the students are not likely to understand.

Passage reading and written exercises are usually done independently, unless the teacher is monitoring oral reading performance (which is often the case during the beginning and primary stages) or introducing a comprehensive strategy that applies to an entire passage. For example, if the students are learning to paraphrase sentences with clauses or passive voice constructions, the teacher might ask students to paraphrase a sentence with a clause after they read it during passage reading. When passage reading and written exercises are done independently, students should already have the decoding and comprehension skills needed to complete the assignment successfully.

## Follow-up

Follow-up exercises are intended to deal with major problems that occur during passage reading or during the written exercises. If students have decoding problems with a particular sound or word type, the teacher presents word lists or a passage that contains several examples of the troublesome skill during follow-up. If students have difficulty with a certain type of comprehension exercise, the teacher might review it with the students and then give them more practice on the same type of exercise, but with different items.

## Summary

A reading teacher's role can be seen as occurring in two phases: beginning-of-the-year activities and day-to-day implementation. Beginning-of-the-year activities include selecting materials, setting up a program, planning for use of auxiliary personnel, and testing. In selecting materials, teachers should consider the skills presented, practice and review, sequence and rate of introduction, and the use of strategies. In setting up a program, teachers should plan schedules that allow adequate instructional time and decide on the amount of structure appropriate to the students' skill levels. Teachers and auxiliary personnel, whether aides or reading specialists, must coordinate their services to individual students so that their efforts complement each other and are not in conflict. Finally, testing is important for identifying specific skill deficits, grouping students, and placing them in an instructional program.

Day-to-day implementation includes planning, presentation, and follow-up. Planning is needed to construct appropriate teacher presentations and independent work activities for the students. The planning often requires modifying program lessons for use with low-performing students. Presenting a lesson includes the teacher presentation, passage reading, and the monitoring of independent work. Follow-up is devoted to extra teaching on skill areas that are difficult for the students.

## APPLICATION EXERCISE

1. Identifying words students will not be able to decode is an important teaching skill. Assume that students know the most common sound of all individual letters. Circle any single letter the student will not be able to decode, which means the word itself is probably not decodable. For example, the letter *g* in *gin* would be circled since *g* is not representing its most common sound (see the chart on most common sounds on the inside front cover).

| | | |
|------|------|------|
| cent | tab  | put  |
| must | cut  | fat  |
| cab  | gin  | send |
| pin  | rust | son  |
| was  | ten  | con  |
| gas  | some | hat  |
| wish | fast | mind |
| tent | bent | dent |
|      | walk | cub  |

# PART 2

# Beginning Reading

The First Months of Instruction

The beginning reading stage refers to the period when students are learning to decode the first few hundred words presented in the classroom reading program. Some students may come to school able to decode many words. For these students, only several weeks of instruction may be needed before they can complete the beginning stage. Other students will enter school with little or no ability to decode words. Some of these students may require up to a full year of instruction before completing the beginning stage.

## Code-emphasis vs. Meaning-emphasis Programs

Much controversy centers around the beginning reading stage. Foremost is the controversy regarding which approach to use. There are two major approaches: code emphasis and meaning emphasis. The basic difference between them is in the manner they teach decoding. Beginning reading programs that emphasize letter-sound regularity are called code emphasis; those stressing the use of common words are called meaning emphasis. Code-em-

phasis programs initially select words made up of letters and letter combinations that represent the same sound in different words. This consistency between letters and their sound values enables students to read many different words by blending the sounds for each new word. For example, the word *sat* is sounded out as "sssaaatt" and pronounced "sat." The word *land* is sounded out as "lllaaannd" and pronounced "land." The letter *a* represents the same sound in *sat* and *land* as well as in other words that would initially appear in a code-emphasis program. In code-emphasis programs, a new word generally is not introduced until students have mastered the letter-sound correspondences that make up the word. For example, the word *mat* would not be introduced until the students knew the sounds for the letters *m, a,* and *t.* Some major basal code-emphasis programs are *Basic Reading* (J. B. Lippincott), *The Palo Alto Reading Program* (Harcourt Brace Jovanovich), *Merrill Linguistic Readers* (Charles E. Merrill), *DISTAR* and *SRA Linguistic Readers* (Science Research Associates), and *Sullivan Programmed Reading* (Webster/McGraw-Hill). Many of the instructional procedures in the beginning reading part are modeled after those found in *DISTAR.*

In contrast, meaning-emphasis programs initially select words that appear frequently in print. The assumption is that frequently appearing words are familiar and, consequently, easier for students to learn to read. Students are encouraged to use a variety of sources—pictures, context of the story, word configuration, and initial letter—as cues to use in decoding words. Meaning-emphasis programs do not control words so that the same letter represents the same sound in most initially appearing words. For example, it would not be uncommon to see the words *done, to, not,* and *book* among the first 50 words introduced in a meaning-emphasis program. Note that in each word, the letter *o* represents a different sound. Foremost among the meaning-emphasis programs are these basal reading programs: *Houghton Mifflin Reading Series* (Houghton Mifflin), *Ginn 720* (Ginn and Company), and *Basics in Reading, The New Open Highways,* and *Reading Unlimited* Scott, Foresman). These three programs are used in approximately 45% of K–8 classrooms in the United States. Some other basal meaning-emphasis programs are published by the American Book Company, The MacMillan Company, Allyn & Bacon, Harper & Row, Holt, Rinehart and Winston, and Laidlaw Brothers.

In addition to these programs are language-experience and individualized reading programs, which may also be classified as meaning-emphasis programs since the words introduced are not controlled for letter-sound regularity. In the language-experience programs, teachers write stories that students dictate and then allow the students to read their stories. The stories are intended to be motivating not only because the students dictated them but also because the vocabulary and syntax should be familiar. Students also have their own bank of words they want to learn to read. In individualized programs, students select

the books from which they will learn to read.

We recommend using a code-emphasis approach during the beginning stage over a meaning-emphasis approach because a code-emphasis approach involves the use of much simpler teaching presentations. In such programs, teachers can directly present information (letter-sound correspondences) and strategies (sounding out) using the model-lead-test procedure described previously. The advantage of the model-lead-test procedure is that it is less subject to misinterpretation, involves active student participation, and requires minimal explanations by the teacher. In contrast, meaning-emphasis programs rely more on teacher explanations of how to use a variety of strategies to decode words. Students are expected to use a fairly sophisticated combination of contextual and phonic cues in decoding unknown words. This reliance on a multifaceted strategy leads to rather complex teacher explanations. For example, the Scott Foresman teacher's guide, *Get Set* (*The New Open Highways,* 1974) recommends the following procedure in pointing out how to distinguish the word *duck* from the word *bird:* "Also draw attention to the fact that the word *duck* cannot be bird because the word begins with *d* and ends with *k.* The word does not begin with *b* and end with *d"* (p. 309). The problem with such explanations is that they are likely to confuse more naive students and are not conducive to keeping students actively involved in instruction. Moreover, instructionally naive, beginning readers have difficulty mastering strategies that begin with an emphasis on multiple sources of information: initial letter, context, pictures, configuration, etc. These students often focus on one or two sources of information (initial letter and pictures) and develop erroneous reading habits. Low-performing students are more likely to succeed in code-emphasis programs that initially stress a single strategy.

Another reason we recommend code-emphasis programs is that they allow the teacher to increase the probability that all students will be successful during the beginning stage of reading. A teacher using a code-emphasis program can readily diagnose the specific cause of student errors (e.g., when a student says "sat" for *sit,* and "ram" for *rim,* the teacher diagnoses a confusion on the letter-sound correspondence for *i* and uses presentation techniques to remedy the confusion. In contrast, teachers using meaning-emphasis programs are unable to diagnose specific skill deficits as easily. Meaning-emphasis programs teach students to use a combination of letter-sound relationships and context for identifying a word. Let's say a student is reading a sentence: The boy saw a little bird. When coming to the word *saw* the student says "said." The correction the teacher uses involves explaining that the word *saw* could not be *said* because it does not end with *d* and does not make sense in the sentence. The correction tells the student why a word couldn't be *said* but does not provide him with a strategy that enables him to figure out the word. The student might say "sees" the next time he encounters the word in the sentence.

## Overview of Skills to Teach

## Language Skills and Vocabulary

The type and quantity of comprehension instruction during the beginning reading stage depend on the entering skills of the children. Since the words introduced in most commercial reading programs are selected to be within the vocabulary of the *average* child, relatively little work needs to be done on vocabulary instruction with most students. Comprehension training for average and above-average students consists of oral training in reasoning skills and more sophisticated vocabulary.

Low-performing students, on the other hand, may require a great deal of training in basic vocabulary and expressive language. They will not know the meaning of words encountered in primary reading books. Equally important, they may not understand many terms teachers commonly use during instruction. To prepare lower-performing students for the tasks they will encounter, a teacher should provide instruction in basic language and vocabulary. Early lessons should include instruction in various attributes of objects such as, color, shape, texture, and size; labels for common classroom objects; use of comparatives and superlatives; pronoun usage; and prepositions.

In summary, oral language training during the beginning reading stage will benefit all students but is especially critical for instructionally naive students. Without extensive oral training, these students are likely to have serious problems with later comprehension activities.

## Decoding

According to the model of code-emphasis instruction, the first words students read should be regular words. In a regular word, each letter represents its most common sound. The initial strategy students are taught to decode words is sounding out. In sounding out, students start at the beginning of the word and say the sound represented by the first letter. Then they advance in left-right progression, saying the sound for each successive letter without pausing. The blending results in a word such as *Sam* being sounded out as "Sssssaaaaammm." Finally, the blended word is said at a normal rate, "Sam."

The following are preskills students need for sounding out words:

1. A knowledge of letter-sound correspondences in the word. (Note that word reading can begin as soon as the stu-

dents know enough letters to form a few words. The students need not master all letter-sound correspondences before word reading begins.)
2. The ability to telescope a series of blended sounds to form a word (e.g., the teacher says "mmmaaann" and the student says "man")
3. The ability to segment a word into its component sounds (e.g., the teacher says "man" and the student says "mmmaaannn")

Telescoping and segmenting are called auditory skills because printed letters or words are not presented. The students respond to orally presented examples.

Sounding out individual regular words is only a beginning step. As soon as students can decode a few words, phrase reading, sentence reading, and finally passage reading are introduced. Then sounding out is faded and replaced by whole-word reading in which the students do not sound out words orally before saying them. Concurrently, irregular words (words in which some letters do not represent their most common sound) are introduced. The rate at which irregular words are introduced

should be carefully controlled so that students do not become confused regarding when a sounding-out strategy will and will not work.

A scope and sequence for decoding instruction during the beginning reading stage appears in Figure 2.1.1. In the first column are five activities included in the beginning stage: letter-sound correspondences, auditory skills, regular word reading, irregular word reading, and passage reading. The numbers across the top of the chart signify lesson days. The lines next to each skill show the lessons in which the skill appears. Letter-sound correspondence tasks begin in lesson one and continue daily throughout the entire beginning stage.

An important question concerning the beginning reading stage is, When should instruction begin? This question is particularly relevant for students in lower-socio-economic areas. Formal reading instruction for these students should begin in kindergarten. Even though kindergarten students may not progress as rapidly through a reading program as first grade students would, they will receive a substantial headstart. They will enter first grade with a set of reading skills they would not otherwise

**FIGURE 2.1.1**  *Scope and Sequence, Beginning Reading Stage, Decoding Skills*

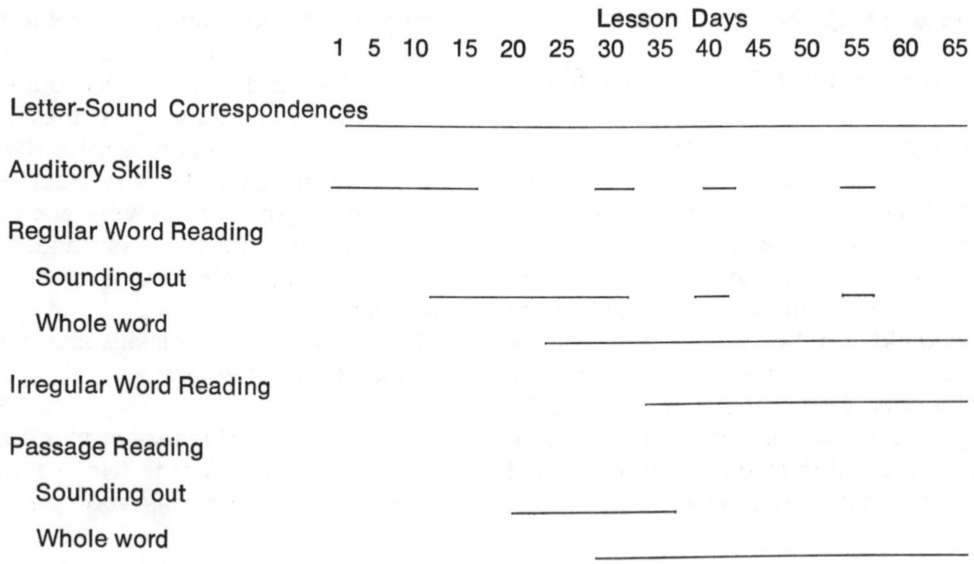

Lesson Days

| | 1 | 5 | 10 | 15 | 20 | 25 | 30 | 35 | 40 | 45 | 50 | 55 | 60 | 65 |
|---|---|---|---|---|---|---|---|---|---|---|---|---|---|---|

Letter-Sound Correspondences

Auditory Skills

Regular Word Reading
    Sounding-out
    Whole word

Irregular Word Reading

Passage Reading
    Sounding out
    Whole word

have. Our experiences and data from *Follow Through* lead us to believe that the quality of the program used is especially critical. The program must be one which teaches critical component skills, carefully controls the language used by the teacher, and provides adequate practice. If a high quality program is not used, instruction in kindergarten may not be productive. However, with a well-designed program and adequate implementation, students will definitely benefit from reading instruction in kindergarten.

## Remedial Reading Instruction

The focus of the sections in the beginning reading part will be on teaching students who are learning to read for the first time. The same principles, however, can be used with any student who has an extremely limited knowledge of reading. Nonreading second graders would progress through the same program as beginning first graders. Teachers of upper-grade students should be quite careful in using these procedures. Most upper-grade students will know most of the skills taught in the beginning stage but will have "holes" here and there. Usually the students will have trouble with vowel sounds and blends.

Teachers working with these students would *not* present the total beginning program. They would not teach sounding out of regular and irregular words but would use sight-reading procedures. Sounding out would only be taught to students who are virtually nonreaders. Specific testing and placement procedures for upper-grade remedial students will be discussed in the primary and intermediate grade parts.

## Organization of the Sections

The beginning reading stage is discussed in seven sections: "Auditory Skills," "Letter-Sound Correspondences," "Regular Words," "Irregular Words," "Passage Reading," "Vocabulary and Language Skills," and "Selecting and Using a Program." The first six sections are divided into three areas. The first one, "Direct Instruction Procedures," includes guidelines for sequencing new skills and providing practice. In addition, teaching procedures for each skill are presented. Critical teacher behaviors such as, signaling, pacing, monitoring, and diagnosing and correcting errors are discussed in detail.

The second area discusses how the skills are presented in commercial programs. Analyses of five programs are included: three meaning-emphasis programs (*Houghton Mifflin Reading Series,* © 1976, Houghton Mifflin; *Ginn 720,* © 1976, Ginn and Co.; and *The New Open Highways,* © 1974, Scott, Foresman) and two code-emphasis programs (*Basic Reading,* © 1975, J. B. Lippincott and *The Palo Alto Reading Program,* © 1973, Harcourt Brace Jovanovich. When reviewing commercial programs, keep in mind that publishers revise programs periodically. Carefully note the copyright dates listed above. Our comments reflect only what was done in the editions with those dates. Future editions no doubt will include several changes, and evaluations should be based on the revised material. The analyses of letter-sound correspondences, auditory skills, and oral language teaching in meaning-emphasis programs is based on how these skills are taught in readiness books of each series.

Code-emphasis programs do not usually include readiness programs of any significant length. Our analyses of how beginning reading skills are presented in code-emphasis programs are based on the first several books of each series. These books are not labeled as preprimers but are just labeled in order, e.g., Book A, B, C, D, etc.

After a description of how skills are taught in various programs, we provide suggestions for modifying the programs to meet the needs of students encountering difficulty. Word lists that can be used to supplement the exercises provided in commercial programs appear in Appendix A. Suggestions on how to use the lists appear in each word-reading section.

At the end of each section, is a brief presentation of research related to the teaching procedures discussed and suggestions for future research.

The final section in the beginning reading part discusses selecting and using a commercial reading program. In using a program, teachers test students, form instructional groups based on the test results, and place the groups in the program. Teachers also modify the program when needed to better meet the needs of lower-performing students. Although testing and placement is done at the beginning of the school year, this section comes last be-cause the testing procedures and suggestions for modifying programs do not make sense until after the specific teaching procedures have been read. However, teachers should not assume that all students will need to be taught sounds and auditory skills. When teachers test their students at the beginning of the year, they will often find some students who already know how to read and, consequently, do not need any of the instruction outlined in the beginning reading part. Testing procedures for these students appear in the section on selecting and using commercial programs in the primary stage. The important point is that all students are tested at the beginning of the year and receive instruction appropriate to their skill level in reading.

---

# RESEARCH

## Code-emphasis vs. Meaning-emphasis Programs

Several significant research reviews from the 1960s indicated that code-emphasis programs are more effective than meaning-emphasis programs in teaching students to decode. Chall (1967) analyzed 25 acceptable studies that were conducted between 1900 and 1960. She reported that code-emphasis programs tended to surpass meaning-emphasis programs in the areas of word recognition, oral reading, and spelling. Code programs seemed relatively more effective than meaning programs for both below- and above-average ability children. Gurren and Hughes (1965) reported similar findings after reviewing 22 comparative studies: in studies that evaluated the performance of slow learners, all significant differences favored the groups taught with code-emphasis programs. Similarly, in the six studies involving high-IQ children, five significant differences favored the code-emphasis groups.

Research reported by Dykstra (1968) on end-of-school-grade effects, and Bond and Dykstra (1967) on end-of-first-grade effects, confirmed the superiority of a code approach in teaching word recognition and spelling. Bleismer and Yarborough (1965), who compared code-emphasis and meaning-emphasis beginning reading programs during first grade, made 125 comparisons in the areas of word reading, paragraph meaning, vocabulary, spelling, and word study skills; 92 differences significantly favored the code approach. A more recent research review (Diederich, 1973) on the importance of phonics on code-emphasis instruction was consistent with earlier conclusions; "earlier and more systematic instruction is essential" (p. 7). Similarly, the work of "Hayes, Ruddell, Hahn, Tauyzer and Alpert, Mazurkiewicz and Downing has lent support to the value of greater consistency in the introduction of letter-sound correspondences" (Ruddell, 1976b, p. 454). Dykstra (1974) said:

> We can summarize the results of sixty years of research dealing with the beginning reading instruction by stating that early systematic instruction in phonics provides the child with the skills necessary to become an independent reader at an earlier age than is likely if phonics instruction is delayed and less systematic. As a consequence of his early success in "learning to read," the child can more quickly go about the job of "reading to learn."

Although some proponents of meaning-emphasis programs concede the advantage of code-emphasis programs in teaching decoding, they maintain that meaning-emphasis programs have an advantage in teaching comprehension. The research does not appear to substantiate those claims. Chall (1967) reported higher vocabulary and comprehension at the end of second-grade for students in code-emphasis programs. In analyzing 41 comprehension subtests, Gurren and Hughes (1965) reported that 22 differences in comprehension scores significantly favored the code-emphasis groups while only two favored the meaning-emphasis groups. They also reported that a code approach did not necessarily retard reading rate and that some positive effects of code-emphasis instruction were maintained through grade six. Bleismer and Yarborough (1965) reported that 20 out of 25 comparisons of comprehension performance significantly favored the code approach and none favored the meaning approach. Reports from a large scale study on beginning reading instruction (Bond & Dykstra, 1967; Dykstra, 1968) did not indicate a clear pattern of differences in the area of comprehension.

Some educators claim the research comparing code-emphasis and meaning-emphasis programs in teaching beginning reading is inconclusive. Corder (1971) maintained that the research methodology was often flawed and the findings were at times contradictory. Nevertheless, the argument for using code-emphasis over meaning-emphasis programs is strong particularly when discussing instruction for instructionally naive students. In schools in lower socioeconomic areas, the proportion of such students is quite high. In schools in mid- and upper-socioeconomic areas, the proportion of instructionally naive students is not as high. However, the significant incidence of reading failure in these more advantaged areas points out the need for careful instruction with many students.

As important as the type of program used is *how* a program is used. Harris and Sipay (1975) concluded that the quality of administrative leadership and teacher skill was more important than differences in methodology. They stressed that "efforts should concentrate on determining which program(s) work best with which children when used by certain types of teachers under given conditions and why" (p. 73). We agree with their conclusion. One cannot simply support a code-emphasis approach without insisting on its being well implemented. A code-emphasis program that is not well sequenced, provides inadequate practice, or does not teach strategies effectively will not produce optimal growth in all students.

Two auditory skills directly relate to decoding words. The first is *segmenting a word* into sounds. The teacher says a word and the student breaks it down into component sounds. The student says each sound for a second or two and switches from sound to sound without pausing between them (*am* becomes "aaammmmm"). This skill does the following:

1. Shows the student that words are composed of discrete sounds
2. Serves as a preskill for later word-reading exercises in that it provides practice in blending (students say each sound without pausing between them)
3. Serves as a preskill for simple spelling exercises in which students hear a word, break it down into sounds, and then write a letter for each sound

The second auditory skill is *telescoping sounds* to form a word. The teacher says a series of blended sounds, and the student translates the series of sounds into a word said at a normal rate ("aaammm" becomes *am*). This skill prepares the student to identify words after having sounded them out.

## Direct Instruction Procedures

## Sequence and Practice

Since auditory skills do not require knowledge of letter-sound correspondences, instruction can begin on lesson one of a program. Telescoping sounds to form a word is the easier auditory skill and, thus, should be introduced first. As soon as students can say a word after hearing the sounds, the second auditory skill (segmenting a word into sounds) can be introduced, usually several days later. Auditory tasks should be presented daily until sounding out begins. Since the auditory skills are components of sounding out, they no longer need to be presented as independent tasks after sounding out begins except for several lessons before the introduction of each new word type.

Note that instructionally naive students often will need practice on auditory skills even after decoding begins. Consequently, teachers working with these students should continue auditory skill exercises throughout the first several months of instruction. A general guideline is to use the discrimination format presented here with four to six of the more difficult regular words that appear later in the lesson in word-reading exercises.

## Telescoping Sounds

This skill involves translating a series of blended sounds into a word said at a normal rate. When sounding out a written word, students will hold each continuous sound for 1 or 2 seconds, thus producing a series of sounds, "mmmmmaaaaannnn." Then, they will have to translate this series of sounds into a word at a normal rate, *man*. Since telescoping sounds to form a word is relatively easy, an introductory format, in which the teacher models the correct response, is not needed. The skill cannot be taken for granted, however, which is the reason for including the discrimination format.

## Segmenting a Word

The teacher says a word, and the students hold each continuous sound for a second or two and switch from sound to sound without pausing (*man* becomes "mmaann"). In the introductory format, which is used just the first several lessons, the teacher models the response, then has the students imitate the response. In the discrimination format, which begins after several lessons and is used thereafter, the teacher just tests the students without first modeling the re-sponse. In both formats, the teacher presents a group of four to six words until the students master them (respond correctly to all the words).

## Critical Behaviors

### Modeling

When saying a word slowly in an auditory skills format, the teacher (a) holds each continuous sound for 2 seconds, (b) does not pause between sounds, and (c) slightly exaggerates sounds that appear at the ends of words by saying them loudly. The last consonant is emphasized because some students have a tendency to leave off the final sound, pronouncing *sad* as "sa."[1] When emphasizing the final sound, the teacher must be careful not to add a vowel sound but to say the word *sad* as "sssaaad" not "sssaaduh." Similarly, teachers must be careful not to add a vowel sound when stop sounds appear at the beginning of a word, e.g., not saying *pig* as "puhig."

### Signaling

After saying a word, teachers must be careful how they signal students to say the

---

[1] Having students pronounce regular words as they are sounded out is important in the beginning stage. In later stages when students are reading fluently, teachers need not be concerned about pronunciation as long at it is clear students understand what they read. This is particularly true when students have a dialect.

---

**Discrimination Format for Telescoping Sounds**

|  | *Teacher* | *Students* |
|---|---|---|
| 1. | Teacher gives instructions. **"Listen, we're going to play a say-the-word game. I'll say a word slowly; then you say it fast."** | |
| 2. | Teacher says the word slowly; students say it fast. **"Listen."** (pause) **"Iiiiiifffff. Say the word."** Teacher claps. | "If" |
| 3. | Teacher repeats step 2 with four more words: *sat, Sid, am, fit.* | |

## Introductory Format for Segmenting a Word

|  | *Teacher* | *Students* |

*Teacher*                                                     *Students*

1. Teacher states the instructions. **"I'll say a word. You say the sounds in the word. Each time I clap, you say a sound. Don't stop between the sounds."**

2. Teacher models segmenting. Teacher holds hands in front of chest with palms together. **"My turn. I am going to say the sounds in this word,** *sad.***"** Teacher pauses 2 seconds and then claps, leaving the palms touching after clapping. As the teacher claps, he says **"sssssss."** Two seconds later, the teacher claps again and switches to **"aaaaa"** without having paused between the /s/ and the /a/. Two seconds later, the teacher claps a third time and switches to /d/, again without pausing. The teacher does not pause between sounds or distort them. The model can be summarized in this way:

$$\underset{\text{(clap)}}{\uparrow}\ \text{s s s s s}\ \underset{\text{(clap)}}{\overset{*}{\uparrow}}\ \text{a a a a a a a}\ \underset{\text{(clap)}}{\overset{*}{\uparrow}}\ \text{d}$$

3. Teacher *leads* students by responding with the group. Teacher repeats step 2, saying **"Do it with me. We're going to say the sounds in the word** *sad.***"** Teacher signals and responds as in step 2. The teacher responds with the group until they seem able to respond correctly.

4. Teacher *tests* by having the students respond without a teacher lead. Teacher holds hands in front of chest with the palms together. **"Your turn. Say the sounds in** *sad.***"** Teacher pauses 2 seconds, then claps.

   As soon as the teacher claps the students say "sss."

   Two seconds later, the teacher claps again.

   The students switch to "aaa" without having paused.

   Two seconds later, the teacher claps a third time. **"Say the word."**

   The students say "d."
   "Sad"

5. Teacher repeats steps 2-4 with these words: *it, Sam, fit.*

6. Teacher gives *individual tests* calling on each student for one word.

\* Students do not pause when they change from one sound to the next.

sounds. This caution is particularly important for words that begin with a stop sound, such as *pan*. The teacher claps two times and simultaneously says the stop sound followed by the vowel sound ("paaaa") with no pause between them. The teacher holds the vowel sound for several seconds and then claps a third time for the third sound. Two rapid claps are needed for the stop sound and the vowel because students can say the stop sound for only an instant. The model for *pan* would be

p a a a n n n
↑ ↑     ↑
(2 claps)   (clap)

Note that the second clap comes immediately after the first one.

## Pacing

After students respond in some auditory tasks, the teacher can take a second or two to comment on their performance: "Good saying the sounds;" "Good job;" or "Good, you didn't stop between the sounds." These comments not only reinforce appropriate responding but also provide a brief rest between examples. However, the pause between the end of one response and the beginning of the teacher's direction for the next response should not be more than 2 or 3 seconds, because a longer pause may result in the students' becoming distracted.

## Correcting Mistakes

Students can make three types of mistakes in segmenting a word: pausing between sounds, not changing sounds when the teacher claps, and not saying the correct sound. Students can also make three types of mistakes when telescoping sounds to form a word: saying the word slowly (imitating the teacher), leaving out a sound (the teacher says "sssaaaat," but the child leaves off the final consonant, saying "saa"), and mispronouncing a sound (the teacher says "ssseeelll," but the student says "sil"). The correction procedure, which is the same for all types of mistakes, consists of the teacher's (a) *praising* a student who responded correctly, (b) *modeling* the correct response, (c) *leading* all the

---

**Discrimination Format for Segmenting a Word**

| Teacher | Students |
|---|---|
| 1. Teacher states the instructions. **"You are going to say the sounds in a word. Each time I clap, you say a sound. Don't stop between the sounds."** | |
| 2. Teacher tests by having the students say the sounds in each word. Teacher holds hands in front of chest with palms together. **"Your turn. Get ready to say the sounds in the word *am*."** Teacher pauses 2 seconds, then claps. | As soon as the teacher claps, the students say "aaa." |
| Two seconds later, the teacher claps again. | "The students switch to "mmmm." |
| **"Say the word."** | "Am" |
| 3. Teacher repeats step 2 with remaining words: *sat, if, sad*. | |
| 4. Teacher gives individual tests calling on several students for one or more words. | |

students by answering with them until they respond correctly, (d) *testing* them on the missed word and then alternating between the missed word and other words until they respond correctly to the missed word two times in a row, and (e) *retesting* later in the day on words missed.

When correcting mistakes, the teacher may need to provide some students with as many as 10 to 20 repetitions on the lead step before they will be able to respond correctly. Teachers must provide enough practice so that students master not just the missed word but the entire *set* of words. If an auditory skills task consists of four words and the students have trouble with two of the words, the teacher should present all four words again. Students who are required to master a set of words when the skill is first introduced will master subsequent words more quickly. A student has mastered a set of examples if she can respond to all the examples in a set without a mistake.

## Rhyming

Another auditory skill to be taught during the beginning reading stage is rhyming. Although not directly related to sounding out, it is a valuable skill since it prepares students to see the relationship between letter clusters that represent the same sound in different words such as *fan, pan, tan, man,*

In the rhyming format, the teacher first models how to form a group of rhyming words that end with the same sounds (e.g., the teacher begins with *s, r,* and *m* to form *Sam, ram, mam*). After modeling, the teacher leads the students and finally tests them. This format might be begun in the

---

**Format for Rhyming**

| *Teacher* | *Students* |
|---|---|
| 1. Teacher models. **"Listen, I am going to rhyme with** (pause) *it.* **What word?"** (signal) | "It" |
|    a. **"Rhymes with** *it* **and begins with** *ss.* **Sit."** | |
|    b. **"Rhymes with** *it* **and begins with** *ff.* **Fit."** | |
|    c. **"Rhymes with** *it* **and begins with** *mm.* **Mitt."** | |
| 2. Teacher leads. **"Let's rhyme together. We're going to rhyme with** (pause) *it.* **What word?"** (signal) | "It" |
|    a. **"Rhymes with** *it* **and begins with** *ss.* **What word?"** (clap) **"Sit"** | "Sit" |
|    b. **"Rhymes with** *it* **and begins with** *ff.* **What word?"** (clap) **"Fit"** | "Fit" |
|    c. **"Rhymes with** *it* **and begins with** *mm.* **What word?"** (clap) **"Mitt"** | "Mitt" |
| Teacher repeats steps 1 and 2 until students appear to be able to respond without leading. | |
| 3. Teacher tests group. | |
|    a. **"Your turn. By yourselves. You're going to rhyme with** (pause) *it.* **What word?"** | "It" |
|    b. Teacher repeats same signal as in step 2 except she does not respond with students. | |
| 4. Teacher tests some individual students. | |

third week of instruction. An exercise would be done daily for several weeks. Each lesson, a different word family would be used.

## Selecting Examples

Selecting the words to use in auditory tasks is relatively simple. The basic rule is to use words that will appear in early word-reading tasks. On the first day of instruction, the teacher selects four words, including some from the first word-reading task in the program.

The teacher must make sure that the words do not all contain the same letter in the same position. For example, if the same vowel appears in all words, the words form a predictable order; and the students may respond according to the pattern rather than to what the teacher says. For example, these words form a predictable order because they all contain *a: Sam, tap, nat, fat, can,* and *sat.* With this pattern, some students may develop the misrule that every word has the /a/ sound.

## Commercial Programs

The auditory skills included in most commercial programs do not include tasks similar to the telescoping and segmenting tasks discussed in Section 2.1. We recommend that these tasks be added to early lessons in all beginning reading programs using the rate, sequence, format, and example guidelines discussed here (see Appendix D for sample lessons that could be used to teach auditory skills).

Many worksheet activities in the early parts of the commercial programs include tasks that provide practice in auditory discrimination. Children are asked to signify if words have a particular sound in the initial, medial, or final position. The worksheets include a group of pictures. Students may be asked if the pictures represent words that begin with the same sound, end with the same sound, or have the same sound in the medial position.

To make these activities easier for students, in early tasks, students should compare only the initial sounds of words. One way to teach the concept of initial sound is through a model-test procedure. The teacher says a series of words and after each word identifies the initial sound. After modeling, the teacher then tests the students. Next, a strategy is taught for comparing the initial sound in various words.

1. "Listen. *Bat.* What's the initial sound in bat?"
2. "Listen. *Fell.* What's the initial sound in fell?"
3. "Do *bat* and *fell* have the same initial sound?"

Exercises in which the middle or final sounds are compared should be introduced only when students do not make any errors for several days on exercises involving initial sounds. Before introducing tasks in which students compare the middle or final sounds, the teacher should use the model-test procedure to teach the meaning of the new vocabulary word, either middle sound or final sound, and provide discrimination practice to ensure that the students can distinguish the sound in the new position from the initial sound in a word. For example:

1. "Listen. *Fat.* What's the initial sound in fat?"
2. "Now I'll say the final sound in fat. (pause) *T* What's the final sound in fat?"
3. "What's the initial sound in fat? What's the final sound in fat?"

When presenting tasks in which the students compare final sounds, the teacher would have the students say the final sounds in each word and then ask if the sounds were the same. For example, "*Fat.* What's the final sound? *Man.* What's the final sound? Do *fat* and *man* have the same final sound?"

## RESEARCH

Most of the research on auditory skills (segmenting a word into component sounds and telescoping sounds together to form a word) is correlational. Chall, Roswell, and Blumenthal (1963) reported a correlation of about .6 between performance on telescoping exercises and later reading performance. Research on segmenting is more extensive.

Helfgott (1976) and Liberman (1973) reported high correlations between performance on segmenting exercises and later reading performance. Savin (1972) noted that many children who were having reading problems could

not segment a word into its phonemes.

These findings as well as work by Venezky (1975) suggest that segmenting is an important component of a successful decoding strategy. Roberts (1975) and Helfgott (1976) found that 5 and 6 year olds learned telescoping more rapidly than segmenting, which is consistent with our recommendation of introducing telescoping exercises before segmenting exercises. Also, Roberts reported that these auditory exercises were easier for children than sounding out printed words.

## APPLICATION EXERCISES

1. This exercise introduces letter combinations (two or more letters which usually represent the same sound(s) in a significant number of words). Although letter combinations will not be discussed until later in the book (Section 3.2), we include them now so the reader may receive adequate practice to develop fluency in recognizing and pronouncing them. Assume the students know the most common sound of all single letters and these letter combinations: *th, sh, ch, ck, ar, ee, ea,* and *or.* Circle any letter or letter combination the students will not be able to decode, which means the word itself is probably not decodable. For example, the *ar* in w*ar*m would be circled because it does not represent its most common sound (see the chart on most common sounds on the inside cover).

| charm | east | gin | of |
|-------|-------|------|------|
| par | sea | cent | rob |
| warm | head | cast | mild |
| shark | porch | gun | pig |
| need | worm | put | list |
| been | corn | was | limp |
| peek | world | ten | mind |
| dead | short | post | test |
| weak | cut | lot | wet |

2. Understanding how to correct mistakes is very important. This exercise involves critiquing how errors were corrected in four different situations. Sequences a through d indicate the words a teacher presented in an auditory task. Next to each word is a plus (+) if the student responded correctly, or a minus (−) if the student responded incorrectly. For each series of responses, indicate, by checking *acceptable* or *unacceptable,* whether the teacher followed the recommended correction procedure: model, lead, test with alternating pattern, and retest if the error occurred several times. If the teacher did not follow the procedure, specify the violation and mark where it occurred. Assume the teacher is working with only one student (see page 68).

sequence a—acceptable   unacceptable   why?

sam+   fit—   (teacher corrects)   fit+   sam+   fit+   rag+   sam+   fit+
    mat+   sad+   fit+

sequence b—acceptable   unacceptable   why?

rag+   sam—   (teacher corrects)   sam+   rag+   fit+   sam—
(teacher corrects)   sam+   fit—   (teacher corrects)   fit+

sequence c—acceptable   unacceptable   why?

sam+   fit—   (teacher   corrects)   rag+   sid+

sequence d—acceptable   unacceptable   why?

sam+   fit+   rag+   sid+

3. The teacher is presenting the format for segmenting a word into sounds. In the following situations, specify what the teacher would do and the wording the teacher would use to correct the student's error when it occurs.

a. A student pauses between the *m* and *i* in *mitt*.
b. Another student says "mmmĕeet" for *mĭtt*.

# Letter-Sound Correspondences

Students should be taught letter-sound correspondences to prepare them for sounding out words. When students sound out words, they must produce the sound represented by each letter in the word, blend the sounds, and then identify the word. In this section, the specific details pertaining to teaching letter-sound correspondences are explained.

## Direct Instruction Procedures

### Preskills

The preskills needed to learn letter-sound correspondences are an ability to imitate sounds made by the teacher, understand very simple directions ("sit down" or "look at this"), and carry out simple actions by imitating the teacher. Since virtually all students entering public school in kindergarten or first grade have these preskills, we recommend teaching letter-sound correspondences beginning on the first day of instruction.

### Sequence

Here are four guidelines for determining an order for introducing letters:

1. Introduce initially only the most common sound for a new letter
2. Separate letters that are visually or auditorially similar
3. Introduce more useful letters before less useful letters
4. Introduce lower-case (small) letters before upper-case (capital) letters

### Introduce the Most Common Sound

The most common sound of a letter is the sound that is usually pronounced for the letter when it appears in a CVC word such as *man* or *sit.* (Often, groups of two or three letters are also represented by a most common sound. These groups of letters, which we call letter combinations, are discussed in Section 3.2.) The chart on the inside front cover of this book illustrates the most common sound for each of the 26 letters.

Note that the letters are grouped as continuous sounds or stop sounds. A continuous sound can be said for several seconds. All vowels and some consonants are continuous sounds. A stop sound can be pronounced for only an instant. Next to each letter in the list is a word in which the letter represents its most common sound. (Note: *Phonemes* and *graphemes* are the words used by linguists to describe sounds and the letters that represent them. *Phoneme* means sound. *Grapheme* is a letter or a series of letters that represents one sound.)

### Separate Visually or Auditorily Similar Letters

The more similar two letters are, the more likely students are to confuse them. Separating similar letters from each other in their order of introduction reduces this confusion. The greater the similarity between two sounds or letters, the greater the number of letters that should separate them. Two factors determine the probability of confusion: auditory similarity (how alike the most common sounds of two letter are) and visual similarity (how alike in appearance the two letters are). The following sounds are auditorily similar: /f/ and /v/, /t/ and /d/, /b/ and /d/, /b/ and /p/, /k/ and /g/, /m/ and /n/, and all vowels. The following letters are structurally (visually) similar: *b* and *d*, *q* and *p*, *n* and *m*, *h* and *n*, *v* and *w*, and *n* and *r*.

Our experience has shown that students have the most difficulty with sounds that are auditorily similar. Therefore, similar sounds should be separated by the introduction of three other dissimilar sounds. For example, if the sound /t/ is introduced on lesson 40, the sounds /r/, /l/, and /m/ might be introduced before /d/, which is auditorily similar. Students have the most difficulty with pairs of letters that are both visually and auditorily similar: (*b,d*) (*m,n*), (*b,p*). These letters (plus *e* and *i*) should be separated by at least six other letters. Students can also be expected to have some trouble with letters that are just visually

similar. If possible, the members of these pairs should also be separated.

### Introduce More Useful Letters First

More useful letters are those that appear most often in words. Learning such letters early enables students to decode more words than learning less useful letters. For example, knowing the sounds for the letters *s, a, t,* and *i* will allow students to decode more words than knowing the sounds for *j, q, z,* and *x*. Vowels are the most useful letters. More useful consonants are *b, c, d, f, g, h, k, l, m, n, p, r, s, t*. Less useful consonant letters are *j, q, z, y, x, v, w*.

### Introduce Lower-case Letters First

Lower-case letters should be taught before upper-case letters since the majority of words in reading material is composed of lower-case letters. A student knowing all lower-case letters would be able to decode all the words in the following sentence: "Sam had on his best hat." A student knowing only upper-case letters could read none of the words. An exception to this guideline can be made for lower-case and upper-case letters that look exactly the same, except of course for size (e.g., sS, cC). These lower- and upper-case letters may be introduced at the same time. Upper- and lower-case letters are classified according to their visual similarity in Table 2.3.1.

## A Sample Sequence

Table 2.3.2 contains one possible order for introducing letters. We are not suggesting that this is the only or even the best se-

**TABLE 2.3.1**  *Upper- and Lower-case Letters Grouped According to Visual Similarity*

| DISSIMILAR | | | | SAME | | | | | MODERATE SIMILARITY | | | |
|---|---|---|---|---|---|---|---|---|---|---|---|---|
| aA | eE | qQ | bB | cC | kK | oO | pP | sS | fF | mM | jJ | nN |
| rR | dD | gG | hH | uU | vV | wW | zZ | xX | tT | yY | lL | iI |

**TABLE 2.3.2**   *An Acceptable Sequence for Introducing Letters*

a  m  t  s  i  f  d  r  o  g  l  h  u  c  b  n  T  L  M  F  k  v  e  p  D  I  N  A  R  H  G  B  w  j  y
x  q  z  J  E  Q

quence for introducing letters. It is just one sequence that derives from the guidelines specified here.

Note the following about Table 2.3.2:

1. The letters that are visually and auditorily similar—*e,i; b,d; m,n;* and *b,p*—are separated by 17, 7, 13, and 8 letters, respectively. Other potentially confusing pairs (d,t; f,v; h,n; k,g; v,w; n,r) are also separated.
2. Upper-case letters that are not the same as their respective lower-case letters are introduced after most lower-case letters have been introduced. Upper- and lower-case letters that are identical are introduced at the same time, and, thus, these upper-case letters are not listed on the chart.
3. More useful letters are introduced before less useful letters. The lower-case letters *j, y, x, g,* and *z* are introduced toward the very end of the sequence. The first two letters, *a* and *m,* were chosen not only because they are more useful letters but also because they are relatively easy to pronounce. Starting with easy to pronounce letters makes initial sounds tasks easier for instructionally naive students.

## Rate and Practice

An optimal rate (one which introduces new letters quickly while minimizing errors) for introducing new letters to beginning readers is about one each second or third day. This rate assumes that the teacher presents daily practice on isolated sounds. Without adequate daily practice, an optimal rate is not possible. However, the rate of introduction should always be dependent on the students' performance. When the first 5 letters are being taught, a new letter should not be introduced if the students are having difficulty with any previously introduced letter. Rather than present a new lesson, the teacher would review previously taught lessons for several days, concentrating on the letters with which students had been having difficulty. (Difficulty is demonstrated by the students' more than one error on a letter in an isolated sounds task.) After the first 5 letters are introduced, a new letter can be introduced if the students are having difficulty with just one letter-sound correspondence; however, that letter should not be similar to the letter being introduced. For example, a new vowel (*e*) could be introduced even though students are having difficulty with *b* and *d*. On the other hand, the vowel *e* should not be introduced if the students are having difficulty with any previously introduced vowel since all vowel sounds are similar.

## Procedure for Teaching Letter-Sound Correspondences

The basic procedure for teaching letter-sound correspondences involves an introductory format and a discrimination format. In an introductory format, the teacher models and tests on the new letter-sound correspondence. In the discrimination format, the teacher tests the new letter-sound correspondence along with previously introduced letters. The introductory format is used the first lesson or two that a new letter appears. The discrimination format starts after the two letters have been introduced and appears in every lesson thereafter.

### Introductory Format

In the introductory format, the teacher first models by saying the sound, then leads by saying the sound with the whole group, tests by having the group say the sound

**Introductory Format for Letter-Sound Correspondences**

| *Teacher* | *Students* |
|---|---|
| 1. Teacher writes on the board: m. **"When I touch under the letter, you say the sound. Keep saying the sound as long as I touch it."** | |
| 2. Teachers *models* the sound. Teacher holds her finger 2 inches under the letter and says, **"My turn."** Teacher moves finger out and in, touching under the letter for 1 or 2 seconds if it is a continuous sound and for an instant if it is a stop sound. Teacher says the sound while touching under the letter, then quickly moves her finger away from the letter and immediately stops saying the sound. | |
| 3. Teacher *leads* by responding with the group. Teacher points under the letter and says, **"Your turn, say it with me."** Teacher touches under the letter and says the sound with the students. **"/m/"** | "/m/" |
| 4. Teacher *tests* by having the group say the sound several times. **"Your turn. Say it by yourselves."** Teacher touches under the letter. | "/m/" |
| 5. Teacher tests the students individually. Teacher points under the letter and says, **"Marie, your turn."** Teacher moves her finger out and in and touches under the letter. | |

by themselves, and finally gives individual tests to all students. The purpose of the individual test is to enable the teacher to correct mispronunciations early. A teacher should be prepared to lead lower-performing students 10 to 20 times during the first lessons a letter appears. Some students will need this amount of practice before they are able to pronounce more difficult sounds such as /l/, /n/, and /e/. In addition, teachers working with lower-performing students may want to introduce saying the sound several days before students see the letter to provide extra practice in pronouncing the sound.

### Discrimination Format

In the sounds discrimination format, students receive the practice they need to quickly and accurately identify different letters, a skill necessary for sounding out words. Students who identify sounds too slowly will have serious problems in word-reading exercises. Note that the teacher only tests the students in the discrimination format; he does not model a sound except as part of a correction or to confirm a correct response.

## Critical Behaviors

### Signaling

During the first several days of instruction, the introductory format not only teaches the students sounds associated with particular letters but also how to follow the touching signal. To follow the touching signal, students begin saying a sound as soon as the teacher touches under the letter and continue the response as long as she

## Discrimination Format for Introducing Sounds

| *Teacher* | *Students* |
|---|---|

Teacher randomly writes on board several letters that have been previously taught along with the new letter:

i

a      f      m

s    n

r

o

1. Teacher gives instructions. **"When I touch under a letter, you say the sound. Keep saying the sound as long as I touch under it."**

2. Teacher *tests* on new sound. He points to the first letter, pauses 2 seconds, moves his finger out and in, touching under the letter for about 2 seconds if it is a continuous sound and for an instant if it is a stop sound.      Students say the sound.

   Teacher immediately either corrects or points to the next letter.

3. Teacher tests on all letters. He points to a letter, pauses 2 seconds, then moves his finger out and in, touching under the letter.      Students say the sound.

   The teacher follows an alternating pattern in which he gradually increases the retention interval for the newly introduced letter by pointing to more review letters before returning to the new letter. For example, if the new letter is *f,* the teacher would point to the letters in this order:

   1st 3rd 5th     9th    11th          16th
   f a f r f m s f a i f o n i o f

   Note that at first *f* is presented as every other example, then twice as every third example, and finally once as the fifth example.

4. Teacher tests on all letters, using only 1-second pause before signaling.

5. Teacher gives *individual* tests. Every day the teacher should test several students on all vowels introduced up to that time and test all students on any sounds that have caused difficulty in the past week. By following these two guidelines, a teacher receives adequate feedback about each student's mastery of the letter-sound correspondences, which will enable him to provide appropriate practice in future lessons.

touches. This is important because during the time a teacher touches each letter, the students not only say the sound for that letter but also simultaneously look ahead to the next one. For example, while the students hold the /m/ sound in *mad,* they look ahead to figure out the sound for the letter *a.* Students who cannot hold a sound for several seconds are likely to pause when they look ahead to the next letter. Pausing between sounds often prevents students from translating blended sounds into a word.

When signaling, the teacher points under the letter (not touching the board), making sure that no student's vision is blocked by any part of the teacher's hand or body. The out and in motion is done crisply with the finger moving away from the board (about 6 inches) and then immediately back to the board (see Figure 2.3.1). When the finger touches below the letter, the students are to respond. The out and in motion should be done the same way every time it is used. Any hesitation or inconsistency makes unison responding difficult because the students cannot tell when they are supposed to respond.

A modified signaling procedure is used for the stop sounds (/b/, /c/, /d/, /g/, /h/, /j/, /k/, /p/, /q/, /t/, and /x/). Since these sounds can be pronounced for only an instant, the teacher signals by touching the board below the letter for only an instant.

During the first week or two of instruction, some students may say a sound when the teacher merely points to a letter. (Students are to say the sound only when the teacher touches under the letter after the out-in motion.) To prompt the students to say the sound only when the teacher touches under the letter, the teacher can move his finger in a small circular movement when initially pointing out the letter. This circular movement indicates to the students that they are not to respond yet.

### Modeling

Continuous consonant sounds should be said without any vowel sound added to the beginning or end. The letter *m* is said "mmmm" not "uummm" or "mmmmuuu." Saying a stop sound without adding a slight vowel sound is impossible. However, teachers should try to minimize the vowel sound. The letter *d* should not be pronounced "duh." Vowel sounds must also be pronounced accurately. Some teachers have a tendency to distort a vowel sound as they say it. They start out with a dis-

**FIGURE 2.3.1** *Point, Out-In, and Touch Signal*

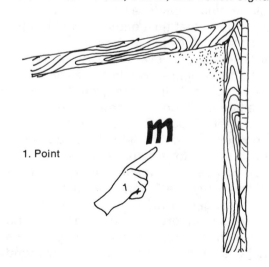

1. Point

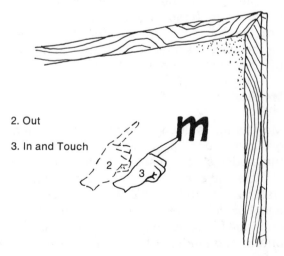

2. Out

3. In and Touch

torted sound and then change it into the correct sound (e.g., pronouncing *i* as "ŭŭĭĭĭ") or start with the correct sound and then distort it (pronouncing *i* as "ĭĭĭĕĕĕĕ"). Care should be taken to avoid distorting sounds.

### Pacing

Pacing a task is not only an important method for maintaining student attention, but it also affects their academic performance. Pacing should be fast enough to keep the students attending but not so fast that they begin to guess and make errors. *A basic pacing rule is to provide a "thinking pause" before giving the signal for the students to respond, but after they respond, quickly move to the next letter.* The thinking pause gives all students enough time to come up with a response.

The ultimate goal of the discrimination format is to provide the students with adequate practice to enable them to respond correctly with only a 1-second thinking pause. Note that in step c the thinking pause is 2 seconds; and in step d, 1 second. Step c is designed to increase the probability that students will respond correctly. Step d's purpose is to give the students the practice needed to become adept at producing the sounds. A longer thinking pause may be given on sounds that have caused the students difficulty in previous lessons. However, the teacher should provide extra practice on that letter so that by the end of the isolated sounds task, the students can respond with only a 1-second pause.

### Monitoring

Monitoring student performance during group responding is done by listening to the students' responses and watching their mouths and eyes. Since the teacher cannot watch every student on every response, she watches only a few students at a time. She continually scans the group, focusing on one or two students for one response and

then shifting attention to other students for the next response. The teacher looks at a student's eyes and mouth. If a student's eyes are not directed toward the teacher, the student is probably not paying attention. Looking at the student's mouth helps tell whether the student is responding correctly. To produce a sound, a student's lips and tongue must be in a certain position. For example, when a student makes the /l/ sound, his mouth should be open with the front edge of the tongue touching the upper palate. If the student's mouth or tongue is not in this position, he is probably not pronouncing the sound correctly. For some sounds—(c,g), (d,t), (f,v), (p,b), (s,z), and all short vowel sounds—the teacher cannot rely on looking at the student's mouth, because the lips and tongue are placed in similar positions for more than one sound. Consequently, the teacher must listen very closely to these sounds.

Even when the teacher listens and watches carefully, he cannot be sure that all students are responding correctly. Individual turns allow the teacher to catch an error before it is made so often that it becomes habitual and, thus, harder to correct. In the introductory format, teachers give individual turns to every student. Daily in the discrimination format, teachers test all lower-performing students and some higher-performing students. The individual tests should include all the vowels introduced up to that time and any troublesome consonants. Individual turns are unnecessary every day on every letter to every student, since doing so would not be good use of instructional time and would result in the students' becoming inattentive.

Teachers should test all students weekly or biweekly on all the letters introduced to date in order to determine if they are developing fluency in identifying letters. During this test, the teacher should let students respond at their own rate. This testing will tell if more practice is needed and on which letters. Teachers should note letters students are unable to respond quickly on and provide extra practice on those.

### Correcting Mistakes

There are three types of errors: a *confusion error* (saying the sound for a different letter), a *pronunciation error* (saying a sound in a distorted manner), and a *signal error* (not beginning the response when the signal is given). The basic correction for all the errors includes these five steps:

1. Directing a specific *praise* comment toward a student who responds correctly
2. *Modeling* the correct answer
3. *Leading* if necessary
4. *Testing* the group on the missed letter and then alternating between the missed letter and other letters in the format
5. Later in the lesson, *retesting* the students who made the mistake

*Confusion Errors.* In a confusion error a student might call *m* "n." The teacher would do the following:

1. Specifically *praise* a student who responded correctly. "John said mmm. Good, John."
2. *Model* the missed letter. "Listen: mmm."
3. *Lead* the students on the missed sound. "Say it with me: mmmm." (Note: Leading is necessary only if the students have difficulty pronouncing the sound.)
4. *Test* the students on the missed letter and then alternate between it and other previously identified letters, gradually increasing the number of review letters that are included. The teacher continues to alternate between the missed letter and familiar letters until the students identify the missed letter correctly two times in succession. The examples might look like this: first a test on *m,* then an alternating pattern of *a, m, s, i, m, r, t, m.*
5. *Retest* students who made an error on *m.* Later in the lesson, the teacher retests by pointing to *m* and asking, "What

sound?" If the student misses the letter, the teacher should follow the procedure in steps 1 through 4 above.

Keep in mind that the sooner confusion errors are spotted, the easier it will be to correct them. Older students who have been confused on a pair of letters for years will take much more time to remedy than younger students.

Many students encounter difficulty in discriminating between *b* and *d,* because this discrimination is the first experience they have in which the direction of a part of a letter determines what it is called. To prepare students for learning the *b-d* and also *b-p* discrimination, teachers can provide visual discrimination worksheets in which students must key on direction. Worksheet items might involve the student circling the figures that are the same as a model figure except for the position and direction of an appendage. Note in Figure 2.3.2 how the student is forced to cue on direction and location.

*Pronunciation Errors. Pronunciation errors* can be as serious as confusion errors, especially if made on vowel sounds. The more distorted the pronunciation of a sound, the greater the probability that the student will have difficulty discriminating it from other sounds that appear later in the program. For example, if a student distorts the /ĭ/ sound so that it is very familiar to the /ŭ/ sound, she will have difficulty when the /ŭ/ sound is introduced and may confuse /ĭ/ and /ŭ/ in word reading, saying "mud" for *mid.*

The correction for a mispronunciation error is similar to that for a confusion error. When a student mispronounces a sound, the teacher does the following:

1. Praises students who respond correctly
2. Models the correct response
3. Leads, checking to see whether the lips and tongue of the student who made the mistake are positioned properly. If the position is wrong, the teacher mod-

**FIGURE 2.3.2**

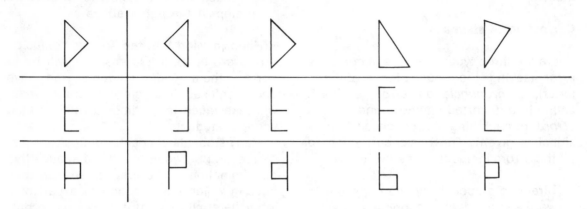

els again saying, "Watch my mouth when I say the sound." The teacher says the sound and watches the student's eyes to make sure the student is attending. Next, the teacher leads by having the student say the sound with him and watches the student's mouth. Leading is used most often when students mispronounce a sound.

4. Tests, alternating between the missed sound and other sounds
5. Finally, retests

The mispronunciation error in which a student initially says a sound correctly but then distorts it is sometimes caused by poor breath control. As the student runs out of breath, he begins to distort the sound. The modeling procedure can be used to correct this mistake. The teacher stops the student when he starts to distort the sound. He tells the student to watch, then takes an exaggerated breath, and makes the sound. The teacher tells the student, "I said the sound without changing it. Your turn. Take a big breath, and then say the sound." The prompt of taking the deep breath should be dispensed with as soon as students demonstrate appropriate breath control.

In some regions, students have unique pronunciations. Do not worry about correcting pronunciations that are natural in a region, unless the variations will interfere with sounding out. If a student has a lisp or other speech problems, do not expect him to say the sound perfectly. Work on gradual improvement.

*Signal Errors.* In a *signal error,* students do not begin and/or end their response when the teacher signals. Teachers should expect some students to need many signal corrections the first several days of isolated sounds instruction. In order to make following signals easier during the first few days of instruction, the teacher can exaggerate the signal. After pointing to the letter, the teacher exaggerates the "out" portion of the signal by moving her hand 12 inches away from the board, rather than just 6 inches. She can also emphasize when to begin responding by hitting the board to create a "thud," which tells the students to respond. To exaggerate the *end* of the signal, the teacher removes her hand with a flourish.

A second prompt teachers can use to train students to follow their signals involves varying the interval for holding a sound. The procedure works this way: the teacher points to a letter several times, each time touching the board under it for varying amounts of time. For example, the teacher might touch it for 3 seconds the first time, then 1 second, and finally for 2 seconds. The purpose is to show the students that they hold the sound as long as the teacher points to the letter and not for some fixed interval. If the students hold every sound for 2 seconds, they will soon learn to ignore the signal.

During the first few days of sounds instruction, praise or some other form of teacher attention will determine how quickly students learn to follow the signal. Even very low-performing students can learn to follow sound signals in 1 or 2 days if they are motivated.

Signal errors may occur because the students are unable to respond with just a 2-second thinking pause as in step c of the discrimination format or a 1-second thinking pause as in step d of the format. The correction procedure for this type of error is somewhat different. It involves just alternating between the missed letter and other letters until the student can respond at the specified rate. Some students will need much more practice than others to develop fluency. The students' performance tells the teacher how much practice he needs. Then the teacher must take responsibility for providing adequate practice to develop fluency.

## Selecting Examples

The introductory sounds format, used the first time a letter appears in a program, includes just the letter being introduced. The discrimination format includes six to eight letters. We recommend including no more than eight letters so that the format will not be too time-consuming and so that the teacher can concentrate on particular letters. For the first week or two, selecting examples is easy; all previously introduced sounds are included in the format. After the students know more than eight letters, the teacher must select which letters to include. The following guidelines can be used to select letters:

1. Include the newly introduced letter in every task for about 2 weeks after it is first introduced and then at least each second day for the next 2 weeks.
2. Include all vowels introduced to date in almost every lesson.

3. Include consonants that have caused the students difficulty in recent lessons.
4. Exclude letters that are highly similar (visually and/or auditorily) to the new letter until the students master the new letter (usually two lessons). Then the similar letter should appear in every task until the students can identify both similar letters (usually about a week).

During the first month of reading instruction, two isolated sounds discrimination tasks should be included in each lesson: one early in the lesson and one later in the lesson. The reason is simply to provide extra practice. Later in the program when students begin reading words, the word reading itself will be a form of practice on letter-sound correspondences and less isolated sounds drill is necessary.

## Supplementary Activities

Teachers can make up activities that can be done individually or in small groups. Regardless of the type of activity, the teachers should be careful to include only letters previously taught and mastered. One type of small group game that students like are board games. In one board game, a path of spaces is drawn with a different letter printed on each space (see Figure 2.3.3). A deck of cards with letters written on each one is also used. The students take turns selecting a card, saying the sound on the card, and then placing their cards on the right spot on the board which has that letter.

Individual seatwork activities might consist of coloring and/or cutting and pasting activities. A sample coloring sheet is shown in Figure 2.3.4. The teacher makes a key on the blackboard by using the desired color next to each letter.

### Commercial Programs

In this part of Section 2.3, how various commercial programs handle letter-sound correspondence instruction is described,

**FIGURE 2.3.3**  *Sample Board Game for Letter-Sound Correspondences*

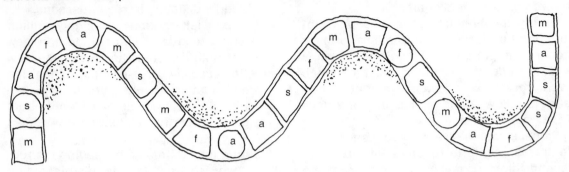

including when instruction begins, the sequence for letters, the rate for introducing new letters, teaching procedures, and example selection. We not only describe how these aspects of instruction are handled but also make suggestions for modifying the programs to make them effective with instructionally naive students.

## When Sounds Are Introduced

In most code-emphasis programs, letter-sound teaching begins very early. *Basic Reading* (Lippincott) and *The Palo Alto Reading Program* (Harcourt Brace Jovanovich) both begin letter-sound teaching on the first lesson. Most meaning-emphasis programs also begin teaching letter-sound reading very early. *New Open Highways* (Scott, Foresman), *Ginn 720* (Ginn and Co.), and the *Houghton Mifflin Reading Series* (Houghton Mifflin) all introduce letter-sound correspondences during the first weeks of instruction. We agree that letter-sound teaching should begin very early, preferably on the first or second day of instruction.

A problem noted in some programs is that a sound is taught after or at the same time the name of the letter is presented. We recommend that letter names not be taught until after students have learned the letter-

**FIGURE 2.3.4**  *Coloring Sheet for Letter Discrimination*

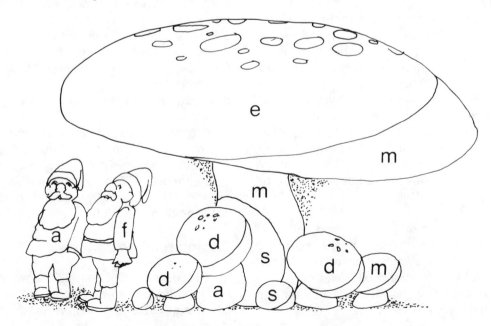

sound correspondences for all lower- and upper-case letters. Presenting a name and a sound for a letter creates too great a learning load for most instructionally naive students and for many average students as well.

## Sequence of Letter Introduction

The sequence that letters are introduced in each of the five programs is shown in Table 2.3.3.

The two code-emphasis programs (Lippincott and Palo Alto) contain some minor violations of the sequencing guidelines about separating similar letters and introducing higher-frequency letters first; e.g., *b* and *d* are introduced too close together in Palo Alto. Teachers should note potential problems in sequencing and prevent them by providing extra practice on letters that may be confused. Note also that both Palo Alto and Lippincott introduce upper- and lower-case letters at the same time, even when they are dissimilar. Learning upper- and lower-case letters that are dissimilar can be almost as difficult as learn-

ing two new letter-sound correspondences at the same time. If the students have persistent problems when dissimilar upper- and lower-case letters are introduced at the same time, delay the introduction of the dissimilar upper-case letters. These letters might not be introduced until the students know the sounds for most of the more common lower-case letters. The delaying procedure causes relatively little inconvenience. When the students encounter a word that begins with an unknown upper-case letter, the teacher prompts them by identifying the sound of the letter before asking them to sound out the word.

In all three meaning-emphasis programs, the vowels are introduced in consecutive order and only after all the consonants have been introduced. This sequence violates two guidelines: do not introduce similar letters too near each other and introduce more common letters first. We recommend altering these sequences by introducing vowels earlier in the program. *A* may be introduced after the first consonant, *i* after the fifth consonant, *o* after the ninth consonant, *u* after the thirteenth consonant,

**TABLE 2.3.3**  *Sequence of Letter Introduction*

*Palo Alto (code emphasis)*

aA mM rR tT sS nN lL fF bB oO hH gG vV dD iI zZ kK wW pP uU cC jJ eE xX qQ

*Lippincott (code emphasis)*

aA nN rR dD uU mM pP iI sS oO tT eE gG cC hH fF ar er wW aw ow lL ll bB le K cK

*Scott, Foresman (meaning emphasis)*

fF mM lL sS nN rR pP dD kK tT gG hH bB wW jJ vV zZ qQ sh ch aA eE iI oO uU

*Houghton Mifflin (meaning emphasis)*

fF dD mM gG bB sS tT wW nN pP cC kK jJ hH lL rR vV yY sh wh th ch all vowels

*Ginn (meaning emphasis)*

bB lL rR hH jJ cC fF yY nN dD gG tT vV mM sS wW pP iI pP kK

and *e* after the seventeenth consonant. A modification in which vowels were inserted into the sequence would require the teacher to provide extra practice on vowels in each lesson.

## Rate of Introduction

The rate at which new letters are introduced varies from program to program. Among the code-emphasis programs, the Palo Alto program introduces new letters at a rate of one each second or third lesson. In the Lippincott program, the rate is much faster, almost a letter each lesson. The rate at which letter-sound correspondences are introduced in the meaning-emphasis programs is difficult to determine, because the teacher's guides do not clearly state the tasks that they recommend to include in daily lessons. The rate seems to be a new letter about each second lesson.

Teachers need not be too concerned about the rate new letters are introduced during the beginning of a program, since average and above-average students will learn the first four to six letter-sound correspondences with relative ease, even if a new letter is introduced in every lesson. Consequently, unless students are making frequent errors on the first four to six letters, they will not need to go slower. After the first four to six letters are introduced, however, most students will usually need more time between the introduction of new letters, since the growing amount of information makes it harder to remember what sound goes with what letter. The rate should be slowed down if the students miss more than one sound on a letter-sounds task or need lots of repetitions before identifying letters with only a 1-second thinking pause. To slow the rate of introduction, teachers will have to construct new lessons or reteach previously presented lessons instead of doing the next lesson that introduces a new letter. (Teachers should not slow the rate of introduction if students are not having trouble.) If only

one student in a group is having difficulty, the teacher should consider either providing extra practice or transferring the student to a lower group.

## Teaching Procedures

Many programs do not teach letter-sound correspondences for isolated letters but use a series of exercises involving auditory discrimination of words in order to teach letter-sound correspondences. Among the formats typically included are the following: The teacher pronounces a series of words beginning with the same sound and asks the students what they notice is alike about each word; the teacher then asks the students for other words that begin with the same sound. A second exercise involves the teacher's asking the students to identify the word, out of a group of two or three words, that begins (or does not begin) with a particular sound. These exercises usually are followed by some type of worksheet on which the letter is written, and the students circle words that begin with the sound for that letter.

In none of the activities does the teacher say the isolated sound. The rationale given by the proponents of the whole-word method for teaching letter-sound correspondences is that knowledge of isolated sounds will not help students decode words and may even hinder them because of the distortion in the manner sounds are produced in isolation and in words. We agree with Harris and Sipay (1975) who question the wisdom of teaching sounds by a whole word method:

Although some proponents of whole-word phonics are vehemently opposed to ever mentioning the phoneme represented by a letter or phonogram as a separate entity, the wisdom of such a prohibition is decidedly questionable. If you point out to children that *baby, book, boat,* and *bunny* all sound alike at the beginning and all start with the letter *b,* the children are going to think "bee says buh" if you do not tell them that "bee says

/b/ as in baby," being careful to pronounce the consonant without an added vowel. The teacher has no control over what the child is saying to himself, and the children are better off if given a good model to imitate. Thinking the sound of a letter or phonogram is quicker and more direct than thinking of a cue word, and phonic units are easier to apply if they have been learned as separable units than when one has to refer to a cue word each time. (p. 376)[1]

## Example Selection

Most of the programs do not provide systematic review of letters in isolated sounds tasks. For several lessons, a letter appears in tasks that call for the students to produce the correct sound but then often will not appear again for many lessons. Our recommendation is to supplement the letter-sound correspondence exercises. First, we recommend that letter-sound teaching be done daily, using a model-lead-test procedure. Second, we recommend using the guidelines below to construct isolated sounds tasks:

1. Include the new letter in every task for at least a week after it is first introduced.
2. Include all vowels introduced up to that point in almost every lesson.
3. Include consonants that have caused the students difficulty.
4. Exclude letters that are highly similar (visually and/or auditorily) to the new letter until the students master the new letter (usually two lessons). Then the similar letter should appear in every task until the students can identify both letters (usually about a week).

---

## RESEARCH

For the most part, the research concerning teaching letter-sound correspondences relates to sequencing and providing practice.

### Sequencing

The following research relates to the sequencing guidelines presented in this chapter:

1. Teach the most common sound value of the individual letters before teaching other sound values for the letters.
2. Introduce higher utility letters before lower utility letters.
3. Teach letter sounds before letter names.
4. Introduce easier-to-learn examples before more difficult-to-learn examples.
5. Separate letters that are similar in appearance or sound.

*Guidelines 1 and 2.* Guidelines 1 and 2 are based more on a logical rather rather than

empirical analysis. Laumbach (1970) and Burmeister (1968, 1970a) recommend initially teaching the short sounds for the vowels because they are more frequent and more easily blended. Similarly, Johnson (1973), Bridge (1970), and Burmeister (1968) suggest initially teaching the most common sound for letters rather than minor sounds. Bridge (1970) and Laumbach (1970) recommend teaching individual letters before letter combinations. We recommend teaching lower-case letters before upper-case letters, not only because lower-case letters are more frequent but also because they are identified more quickly (Starch, 1914; Tinker, 1955).

*Guideline 3.* This guideline is to teach letter sounds before letter names. As mentioned earlier, Jenkins, Bausell, and Jenkins (1972) and Ohnmacht (1969) reported that teaching letter sounds facilitated decoding performance; teaching letter names did not. Moreover, Samuels (1971), R. E. Johnson (1970), and Elkonin (1973) found that teaching letter names did not contribute to students' decoding performance.

---

[1] From *How to Increase Reading Ability*, 6th ed. by Albert J. Harris and Edward Sipay. Copyright © 1975 by Longman, Inc. Reprinted with permission.

*Guideline 4.*    Guideline 4 is to introduce easier-to-learn correspondences before more difficult ones. Two experiments were conducted on the relative difficulty of sound-symbol correspondences of three vowels (*e, i, u*) and three consonants (*c, s, m*) (Carnine, 1978). In the first experiment, 8 preschoolers were trained to criterion on each of the letters in the context of three other previously introduced letters; i.e., six sets of letters were constructed, one for each of the six experimental letters. The mean number of trials to criterion was 92.4 for *u*, 83.0 for *e*, 76.5 for *i*, 47.9 for *c*, 23.8 for *m*, and 11.6 for *s*. The vowels required significantly more trials than *m* and *s*. In the second experiment, 18 preschoolers responded to the six experimental letters in a single set. Each letter appeared 100 times. The mean number of errors was 31.1 for *e*, 22.8 for *u*, 18.9 for *i*, 7.6 for *c*, 5.7 for *m*, and 1.7 for *s*. The vowels were significantly more difficult than the consonants, and *e* was significantly more difficult than *i*. The greater difficulty of short vowels (*e, i, u*) in comparison to consonants is consistent with Coleman's finding (1970) and Williams and Knaffe's (1977). Note that although vowels seem to be more difficult than consonants, we recommend introducing some vowels before consonants because knowledge of vowels is needed to begin word reading.

*Guideline 5.*    Research on guideline 5 (separating the introduction of similar letters) has included studies of similarity based on letter sound and on letter shape. That increased response similarity makes paired-associate learning more difficult is well documented (Brown, 1977; Feldman & Underwood, 1957; Higa, 1963; and Underwood, Runquist, & Schultz, 1959).

A study that focused on visual similarity (Carnine, 1978) was a match-to-sample visual discrimination task in which preschoolers were shown a target letter and asked to match it to one of four alternatives. Two groups of preschoolers were trained until they reached criterion on each of three consecutively presented match-to-sample tasks. One group was presented with tasks in which similar letters were separated. The other group received alternatives in which similar letters appeared together. Similarity was defined according to the number of similar alternatives that appeared in a task. The target letters were *b, d, p,* and *g*. In the similar-separated treatment, the first set of alternatives contained only one similar alternative. For example, if the target was *p*, the alternatives were *p, b, c,* and *o*. Only *b* is similar to p. In the second set, two of the alternatives were similar. In the third set all the alternatives were similar; if *p* was the target, *p, g, b,* and *d* were the alternatives. The order was reversed for the similar-together treatment: the set in which the alternatives were all similar appeared first. During training, the target letters and alternatives appeared simultaneously in the match-to-sample tasks. In the posttest, the target letter was shown but then removed before the alternatives were presented, and all the alternatives were similar. Preschoolers in the similar-separated treatment reached criterion on the posttest in significantly fewer trials than the similar-together treatment. The means were 31.0 and 69.1 trials, respectively.

The more rapid learning of the similar-separated group does not imply that visual discrimination training should not include similar alternatives. Both groups had to discriminate among similar alternatives. The difference, however, was *when* the greatest number of similar alternatives appeared, either early or late in the sequence. When the initial tasks required students to discriminate among many similar alternatives, more errors occurred and, thus, more practice was needed.

Furthermore, the results do not suggest that visual discrimination training should be done before training in sound-symbol correspondences. When similar letters are separated from each other in the order of introduction, Zoref and Carnine (1978) found that sound-symbol correspondence training alone was more effective than visual discrimination training followed by sound-symbol correspondence training. Two groups of preschoolers received 27 training sessions on nine letter-sound correspondences: *m, n, b, d, a, i, s, t*. The visual discrimination group received match-to-sample training for one day on each letter, then two days on each letter-sound correspondence. The other group began letter-sound correspondence training on the first session, receiving three training sessions on each correspondence. Each child was tested individually after the last training session for each letter. Students who received visual discrimination training made significantly more errors, indicating that the time might be better spent on letter-sound correspondence training. This finding is consistent with that of March and Desberg (1974). They suggest that training involving more response practice would be more effective than procedures, such as visual discrimination training, that do not provide practice on saying sounds.

A study that investigated the procedure of separating auditorily similar sounds (Carnine, 1978b) used a sound-symbol paired-associate task, in which the similar sounds were /e/ and /i/. The order of introduction for the similar-separated group was e, c, m, u, s, i, and the order for the similar-together group was e, i, u, s, c, m. The letters were introduced cumulatively, which meant that practice was provided on each new letter and the previously introduced letters before the next letter was introduced. In some cases, the introductions of the first and last letter was separated by several weeks. In Experiment 1, first graders in the similar-separated group made significantly more correct training responses than first graders in the similar-together group (51.7% versus 33.1%). Experiment 2 measured trials to criterion rather than number of correct responses to a fixed trial presentation. Preschoolers in the similar-separated treatment reached criterion on e and i in significantly fewer trials, a mean of 178.0 versus 293.2 trials.

Table 2.3.4 lists a sample sequence for introducing lower-case letters based on guidelines 1, 2, 3, and 4. The sequence is based on the frequency of occurrence and consistency of pronunciation of each letter (Johnson, 1973), how easy the sound is to pronounce (Coleman, 1970), and how auditorily and visually similar the letters are. Letters are labeled as follows: the 33% most frequently appearing letters are labeled H, for high frequency; the next 33%, M for moderate frequency; and the last 33%, L for low frequency. The 33% easiest to pronounce letters are labeled E for easy; the next 33%, M for moderate difficulty; and the last 33%, D for difficult. The consonants and vowels are grouped separately; however, vowels tend

to be more difficult to learn than consonants (Williams & Knafle, 1977). The rational underlying the sequence is to introduce first those letters that are useful (high frequency) and provide success (easy to learn).

### Providing Practice

Practice procedures are used after an order for introducing letters has been determined. Three questions relating to practice include these: (1) How much practice on previously introduced letters is needed before a new letter is introduced? (2) What is the best pattern for presenting practice examples? (3) How should practice be provided on a new letter (e.g., d) when it is similar to a previously introduced letter (e.g., b)?

*Procedure 1.* The first procedure for providing practice deals with how long a letter sound correspondence should be practiced before a new one is introduced. Two alternatives were compared (Carnine, 1978b): (1) a cumulative introduction, in which students reached criterion on all previously introduced letters before a new letter was introduced and (2) a simultaneous introduction, in which six letters were introduced one after another daily regardless of mastery. Preschoolers who received the cumulative introduction reached criterion on the target letters (e and i) in significantly fewer trials than students in the simultaneous treatment, a mean of 178.0 versus 260.9 trials. Also, students in the cumulative treatment made significantly more correct posttest responses, a mean of 83.5% versus 65.5%. Similarly, (Carnine, 1978b) students taught letter-sound correspondences in Experiment 1 (described previously) with cumulative introduction averaged 79% correct posttest identifications; whereas, students in Experiment 2 who received 50 presentations of each letter averaged 28%. Since these students were in two different groups, the results are only suggestive, not definitive.

The stringency of a performance criterion also affects learner retention. Carlson and

**TABLE 2.3.4**  *Sequence for Introducing Lower-case Letters*

| Letter | a | m | t | s | i | f | d | r | o | g | l | h | u | c | b | n | k | v | e | p | w | j | y | x | q | z |
|---|---|---|---|---|---|---|---|---|---|---|---|---|---|---|---|---|---|---|---|---|---|---|---|---|---|---|
| Frequency | M | H | H | H | H | M | H | M | M | M | H | M | M | H | M | H | M | H | M | M | L | M | L | L | L | L |
| Learnability | E | E | D | E | M | E | D | M | M | M | M | D | M | M | M | M | E | M | M | D | D | D | D | D | | |

Minke (1975) reported higher scores for students who had to meet a 90% criterion than an 80% criterion and higher scores with an 80% criterion than a 60% criterion. Research on mastery learning has also been conducted by Houser and Trublood (1975) and Bloom (1976).

*Procedure 2.* The second procedure for providing practice concerns the best pattern for presenting examples of a given set of letter-sound correspondences. Two common practice schedules, massed and distributed, were compared using two groups of preschoolers (Kryzanowski & Carnine, 1978). With a massed practice schedule, the same letter was presented several times in a row; with a distributed schedule, a letter was followed by a different previously introduced letter. In one group, appearances of *e* were distributed and appearances of *i* were massed; in the second group, appearances were reversed: *i* distributed and *e* massed. Consistent with the findings of other researchers who used different stimuli and subjects, preschoolers made significantly more correct posttest responses to letters presented according to the distributed schedule (a mean of 72% versus 38%), but significantly fewer correct training responses (a mean of 56% versus 73%). Although the findings suggest that for a given set of practice examples, a distributed schedule is preferable to a massed presentation, questions concerning the distribution of examples across practice sets remain. Research is needed to evaluate a procedure of massing trials when a new letter is first introduced and then distributing practice trials.

*Procedure 3.* The third procedure for providing practice concerns how to minimize the confusion that results from the introducion of a letter highly similar to a previously introduced letter. Because most preschoolers are, to some extent, familiar with letters, two geometric figures similar in appearance and name (analogous to *b* and *d*) were constructed (Carnine, 1978c). A parallelogram ( ⟋‾‾‾⟋ ) and its mirror image ( ⟍‾‾‾⟍ ) were labeled "biff" and "diff,"

respectively. Preschoolers were taught to identify examples of biff, triangle, and circle and then were randomly assigned to one of four treatments. The four treatments represented different methods for introducing diff, which was similar in appearance and name to the previously introduced biff. The terminal task for all treatments involved training to criterion on biff, diff, circle, and triangle. These were the four treatments:

1. No preteaching. Training consisted of just the terminal task. The other three methods involved preteaching.
2. Preteaching diff in the context of circle and triangle. Preschoolers labeled examples of circle, triangle, and diff, the new member. Biff, the previously introduced similar member, was excluded. In other words, preschoolers identified diff in the context of dissimilar members before discriminating diff from biff. The preteaching for the final two groups (treatments 3 and 4) included only examples of diff and biff.
3. Preteaching diff and biff. The preschoolers labeled the examples as biff or diff, which required them to make difficult discriminations based on both name and shape.
4. Preteaching biff and not biff. The preschoolers at first responded biff or not biff, allowing them to focus just on the shape discrimination because the discrimination involving similar names was postponed. The diff label was not introduced until the preschoolers reached criterion on not biff.

Preschoolers who had to make difficult name *and* shape discriminations required twice as many trials to reach criterion as preschoolers in any of the other three treatments, a mean of 30.5 versus 15.8. The findings are consistent with the guideline of separating similar sound-symbol correspondences, in that the other three treatments all involved greater separation of the similar symbols. These results are consistent with those of Williams and Ackerman (1971) using *b* and *d*.

## APPLICATION EXERCISES

1. For the letter below:
   a. Put *s* over each letter that represents a stop sound. Put *c* over each letter that represents a continuous sound (see chart on inside front cover).
   b. Circle the lower-case letters that are not identical in shape to the upper-case letters (see page 79).

   a  b  c  d  e  f  g  h  i  j  k  l  m  n  o  p  q  r  s  t  u  v  w  x  y  z

2. Assume the students know the most common sound of all single letters and the most common sound of these letter combinations: *sh, ch, ck, ar, ee, ea, th,* and *or.* Circle any single letter or letter combination the students will not be able to decode, which means the word itself is probably not decodable (see chart on inside front cover).

| | | | | | |
|---|---|---|---|---|---|
| park | bee | post | beast | was | cell |
| warm | need | do | ream | torn | rod |
| harm | been | got | shark | porch | lost |
| far | seen | gun | warn | port | of |
| chart | sheep | dead | slump | short | |
| marsh | creep | seal | cold | worm | |
| warmth | need | cheap | cheek | torn | |
| tuck | lick | peak | tot | speak | |
| shack | slop | head | gas | put | |

3. Below are lists of letters in the order they are introduced in several hypothetical reading programs. Next to each letter is the sound value taught for the letter. Write *acceptable* next to the *one* program in which the sequence is acceptable. Write *unacceptable* next to the one program that has such severe violations that it should not be used with low-performing students. Tell why the sequence is unacceptable. For the other three programs, specify the sequencing guideline below which is violated in each one and tell what step might be taken to modify it to increase the probability of student success.

   a. Separate similar letters.
   b. Introduce most lower-case letters before upper-case letters.
   c. Introduce most common sound of letters first.

   Program A
   　1. a /ă/　2. i /ĭ/　3. e /ĕ/　4. u /ŭ/　5. o /ŏ/　6. b /b/　7. f /f/　8. d /d/

   Program B
   　1. m /m/　2. a /ă/　3. f /f/　4. d /d/　5. s /s/　6. o /ŏ/　7. g /g/　8. h /h/

   Program C
   　1. m /m/　2. M /m/　3. a /ă/　4. A /ă/　5. s /s/　6. S /s/　7. d /d/　8. D /d/

   Program D
   　1. m /m/　2. a /ă/　3. d /d/　4. s /s/　5. i /ĭ/　6. b /b/　7. r /r/　8. n /n/

   Program E
   　1. m /m/　2. a /ă/　3. a /ā/　4. f /f/　5. c /k/　6. c /s/　7. t /t/　8. i /ĭ/

4. The list below shows the order in which letters are introduced in a hypothetical reading program. The number in parentheses indicates the lesson on which each letter is introduced.

m (1)   a (4)   s (7)   f (10)   d (13)   i (16)   c (19)   n (22)   t (28)   o (31)
l (34)   g (37)   h (40)   u (43)   b (46)

Below are examples for the discrimination formats that various teachers constructed for lesson 46. Two teachers constructed unacceptable tasks. Identify those teachers and indicate why their items are unacceptable. Use the guidelines below.

a. Include the newly introduced letter in every task for at least 2 weeks after it is first introduced, and then at least each second day for the next 2 weeks.
b. Include all vowels introduced to date in almost every lesson.
c. Exclude letters that are highly similar (visually and/or auditorily) to the new letter until the students master the new letter (usually two lessons).

*Teacher A*
  task 1—m   h   g   l   s   b
  task 2—c   m   f   t   k   b

*Teacher B*
  task 1—b   d   l   u   g   r   a
  task 2—d   o   b   u   h   l   i

*Teacher C*
  task 1—b   u   h   g   o   t
  task 2—a   l   i   r   b   u

5. The sequences below indicate the letters (*s, a, m, r,* and *f*) a teacher presented in a sound discrimination task. Next to each letter is a plus (+) if the student responded correctly or a minus (−) if the student responded incorrectly. For each series of responses, indicate, by checking *acceptable* or *unacceptable,* whether the teacher followed the recommended correction procedure. If not, indicate the violation and circle the first inappropriate letter that the teacher presented (see page 81).

sequence 1—acceptable   unacceptable   why?

  s+   r+   m+   a−   (teacher corrects)   a+   m+   a−   (teacher corrects)
  a−

sequence 2—acceptable   unacceptable   why?

  s+   a+   m−   (teacher corrects)   m+   s+   m+   a+   s+   f+   r+   m+

sequence 3—acceptable   unacceptable   why?

  s+   a−   (teacher corrects)   a+   m+   r+   f+   m+   s+   r+   m+

6. The teacher is presenting the sound discrimination format. The task includes these letters: *m, a, s, d, i, f, c,* and *n.* The student has identified *m, a, s,* and *d* correctly but then says /e/ for the letter *i.* Specify the steps (including the wording) the teacher should take to correct the error (see page 81).

7. The students have been taught 12 letter-sound correspondences. On Monday a student misidentifies the letter *i* several times. Assume the next lesson introduces the letter *o.* What should the teacher do? (see page 76).

Assume the next lesson introduces the letter *f.* What should the teacher do?

# SECTION 2.4

## Regular Words

A regular word is one in which each letter represents its most common sound. The teaching procedure we recommend for teaching students to decode regular words consists of two stages. In the first stage, students sound out words by saying the sound represented by each letter ("mmmm-aaaan") and then translate the blended sounds into a word said at a normal rate (*man*). In the second stage, students decode words by sight or whole-word reading. At that point, they do not sound out the word verbally but say it at a normal rate. When whole-word reading is first introduced, teachers should expect students to sound out words subvocally. Eventually, students will stop sounding out words to themselves and will begin recognizing many at a glance. This section discusses procedures for teaching students to decode words appearing in lists. (Teaching procedures for passage reading are discussed in a later section.)

### Direct Instruction Procedures

#### Preskills

A student should know the most common sounds of four to six letters and how to apply the auditory skills to simple regular words (telescoping sounds together to form a word and segmenting a word into individual sounds) before sounding out is introduced. Students who enter school not knowing any sounds may require 3 or more weeks of instruction to master these preskills.

### Sequence for Regular Words

The main guideline for introducing new regular words is that the words must contain only letters previously presented in isolated sounds tasks. For example, the word *mat* should not appear until the students have been taught the most common sound for the letters *m, a,* and *t* in isolation.

Another major factor in sequencing word types is their difficulty. A word's difficulty depends on its (1) familiarity, (2) length, (3) location of stop sounds within it, and (4) location of consonant blends.

#### Familiarity

Familiar words are easier to decode than less familiar words. Primarily, familiar words should appear in early exercises.

## Word Length

Since shorter words are usually easier for students to decode than longer words, shorter words should appear earlier.

## Location of Stop Sounds

Decoding words beginning with continuous sounds (*mit, fan, sit*) can be easier than decoding words beginning with stop sounds (*kit, tan, bid*). Two errors are more likely to occur when a word begins with a stop rather than a continuous sound. These errors are pausing between the stop sound and the sound following it ("b—pause—aaat") or distorting the sound following the stop sound. (pronouncing *bat* as "buuu-aaat"). Either error may result in word identification errors. Students may translate "b—pause—aat" into the "at" or translate "buuaat" into "but." Since words with initial continuous sounds can be easier to sound out, they should appear earlier. Note

that a stop sound at the end of a word causes no difficulty.

## Location of Consonant Blends

A consonant blend is a cluster of two or three consonants, each representing its most common sound. Students usually have less difficulty decoding words with final consonant blends than words with initial consonant blends. Consequently, words with final blends are introduced earlier. Table 2.4.1 illustrates several different initial and final consonant blends.

Table 2.4.2 shows one order for introducing regular words that follows the criteria of word difficulty and sequencing discussed earlier. In the first column (word type) the letters V and C are used to describe various word types: V stands for vowel, and C stands for consonant. Column 2 indicates the reasons for the word type's relative difficulty or ease. Column 3 illustrates each word type. The table provides general

**Table 2.4.1**  *Consonant Blends*

### Initial Consonant Blends

| TWO-LETTER BLENDS CONTINUOUS SOUNDS FIRST | | TWO-LETTER BLENDS STOP SOUND FIRST | | THREE LETTERS |
|---|---|---|---|---|
| fl (flag) | sc (scat) | bl (black) | pl (plug) | scr (scrap) |
| fr (frog) | sk (skip) | br (brat) | pr (press) | spl (split) |
| sl (slip) | sp (spin) | cl (clip) | tr (truck) | spr (spring) |
| sm (smack) | sq (square) | cr (crust) | tw (twin) | str (strap) |
| sn (snip) | st (stop) | dr (drip) | | |
| sw (swell) | | gl (glass) | | |
| | | gr (grass) | | |

### Final Consonant Blends

| TWO-LETTER BLENDS CONTINUOUS SOUND FIRST | | STOP SOUND FIRST | THREE LETTERS |
|---|---|---|---|
| ft (left) | nd (bend) | ct (fact) | words formed by |
| ld (held) | nk (bank) | pt (kept) | adding an *s* to 2- |
| lk (milk) | nt (bent) | xt (text) | letter blends, e.g., |
| lp (help) | sk (mask) | bs (cabs) | *belts, facts* |
| lt (belt) | st (west) | ds (beds) | |
| mp (lamp) | ls (fills) | gs (rags) | |
| ms (hams) | | ps (hips) | |
| ns (cans) | | ts (bets) | |

**Table 2.4.2** *Simple Regular Words—Listed According to Difficulty*

| WORD TYPE | REASON FOR RELATIVE DIFFICULTY/EASE | EXAMPLES | NOTES |
|---|---|---|---|
| VC and CVC words that begin with continuous sound | Words begin with a continuous sound. | *it, fan* | VC and CVC are grouped together because there are few VC words. |
| CVC words that begin with stop sound | Words begin with a stop sound. | *cup, tin* | |
| VCC and CVCC | Words are longer and/or end with a blend. | *lamp, dust, ask* | VCC and CVCC are grouped together because there are few VCC words. Although CVCC words that begin with a continuous sound and CVCC words that begin with a stop sound are grouped together; some students may find the words that begin with a stop sound harder. |
| CCVC | Words begin with a consonant blend. | *crib, bled snap, flat* | Words that begin with two continuous consonants are the easier of words that begin with blends. These words are grouped in with the rest of blends since there are relatively few such words. |
| CCVCC, CCCVC, and CCCVCC | Words are longer. | *clamp, spent, scrap, scrimp* | |

guides, not hard-and-fast rules. Some students may find words later in the sequence easier to decode than words earlier in the sequence. Keep in mind that *not* all possible words from an early type need to be taught before a word from the next type is introduced. Words from a new type may start appearing once the students can decode about 20 words from an earlier type.

## Rate

Specifying a standard rate for introducing new word types is not possible since some word types may cause students more difficulty than others and, thus, will take longer for the students to learn. Except for VC words, which take a few days to master, teachers can expect average students to need 1 to 4 weeks of practice on each type before developing fluency in decoding words of that type. Keep in mind that this rate assumes that students entered school with no previous reading instruction. Students with previous reading experience will require much less time. The teacher must use the students' performance as the primary factor in determining when to introduce a new word type. When students demonstrate they have mastered decoding words of the current type, they can be introduced to a new word type. Mastery is demonstrated when students decode a group of four or five new words with little difficulty (at a rate of 3 seconds a word with no errors).

## Teaching Procedure for Sounding Out

The format for teaching sounding out involves two parts. In Part I, the teacher models, leads, and tests. Part I is done only the first several days when a new word type is introduced. Continuing with a model and lead when they are no longer needed wastes time and can develop inappropriate student dependency on the teacher.

In Part II, the teacher simply tests the students and does not model. Note that in step 1 of the discrimination part (Part II), students sound out the words rather slowly as the teacher points to each letter for 1 second. After students can respond to all words at this rate, the teacher repeats the words at the faster rate specified in step 2, one letter each 1/2 second. The purpose of step 2 is to develop fluency through extra practice.

## Critical Behaviors

### Signaling

An illustrated explanation of the signaling procedure for sounding out appears in Figure 2.4.1.

### Monitoring

The teacher monitors by watching the students' eyes and mouths and by listening to their responses. To coordinate pointing to the letters with watching the students is difficult. The teacher should quickly glance at the letters to determine where to point next and then look at the students before pointing to the next letter. All these movements are done in an instant. The key is to watch the students' mouths when they say a new sound, since the position of their mouths provides feedback about the correctness of their responses and also informs the teacher whether students are responding.

### Pacing

The two important aspects of pacing are how long the teacher touches each letter and how long she pauses before signaling for the students to telescope the series of blended sounds into a word. The teacher should point to each letter long enough for the students to say its sound and look ahead to the next letter. She should not point at such a slow rate that the students get in the habit of slowly sounding out each

**Format for Sounding Out (Illustrated with the CVC Word Type)**

|  *Teacher* |  *Students* |
|---|---|

Teacher writes on board: sad, fit, man, sam.

Part I (Teacher models, leads, and tests on two words.)

1. Teacher states instructions. **"Watch. When I touch a letter, I'll say its sound. I'll keep saying the sound until I touch the next letter. I won't stop between sounds."**

2. Teacher *models* sounding out the first word. **"My turn to sound out this word."** Teacher touches under each letter that represents a continuous sound 1 to 1 1/2 seconds and under letters that represent stop sounds for only an instant. **"Sssaaad."**

3. Teacher *leads* students in sounding out the word. Teacher points to left of word. **"Get ready to sound out this word with me."** Teacher touches under letters. The teacher sounds out the word with the students until they respond correctly. Then the teacher asks, **"What word?"**    "sssaaad"

    "Sad"

4. Teacher *tests* the students on the first word. Teacher points to left of word. **"Your turn. Get ready to sound out this word by yourselves."** Teacher touches under letters.    "sssaaad"

    After students correctly sound out the word, the teacher asks, **"What word?"**    "Sad"

5. Teacher repeats steps 2, 3, and 4 with one more word.

Part II (Teacher tests students on all the words.)

1. **"Now you are going to sound out all the words by yourselves."** Teacher touches under each letter (except for stop sounds) for 1 to 1 1/2 seconds.    Students say the sounds.

    After the students correctly sound out the word, the teacher asks, **"What word?"**    Students say the word.
    (see Figure 2.4.1 for an illustrated demonstration of the signaling procedure)

2. Teacher repeats step 1 with remaining words.

3. Teacher repeats step 1 except at a faster rate (one letter each 1/2 second).

4. Teacher gives *individual turns,* pointing at a rate of one letter each 1/2 second.

**FIGURE 2.4.1**  *Signaling Procedure*

a. Instructions: Teacher points to the page about an inch to the left of the first letter in the word. "Get ready to sound out this word."

b. The signal for the first sound: Teacher looks at the students to see if they are attending, then quickly touches under the *m.* Teacher holds finger under *m* for about 1 to 1 1/2 seconds.

c. The signal for second sound: Teacher *quickly* makes a loop, moving his finger from the first letter to the second letter, *a,* and holds his finger under *a* for about 1 to 1 1/2 seconds.

d. The signal for third sound: Teacher loops quickly from *a* to *d* and instantly removes his finger from the page. When signaling for the students to say a stop sound, the teacher touches under the letter for an instant and then move his hand quickly away from the letter.

word, which makes the transition from sounding out to sight reading difficult. This is why the students first sound out the words at a slow rate and later at a faster rate.

Students should not be asked to say the word at a normal rate until they sound it out acceptably. They may have to sound out a word several times before they are ready to say it at a normal rate. The pacing of these repetitions is important. For each repetition, the teacher says, "Again," points to the left of the word, and then pauses about 2 seconds before beginning the signal. Shorter pauses before beginning signaling may not give the students time to focus on the beginning of the word. Longer pauses should be avoided because they can contribute to student inattentiveness.

Immediately after the students correctly sound out a word, they are asked, "What word?" The what word signal comes immediately after students sound out the word because a longer pause makes translating the blended sounds difficult. The longer the pause, the greater the probability that students will forget the sounds they said and make a mistake when saying the word.

### Correcting Mistakes

Three common errors are pausing between sounds, saying a wrong sound, and saying the wrong word. Pausing errors involve the student's stopping between sounds and can result in his student leaving out a sound when saying the word. For example in sounding out a CVC word, a student pauses between the first and second sounds, "ssss (pause) aaaat." When translating these blended sounds into a word, the student may leave off the sound that preceded the pause, translating "ssss" (pause) "aaaat" into "at."

Sound errors involve the student's saying a sound which is not the most common sound of a letter. In sounding out the word *fat,* a student says the sound /i/ when the teacher points to the letter *a.*

Word errors involve the student's saying the word incorrectly when the teacher asks her to say it at a normal rate. For example, a student says "fit" for *fat* when the teacher asks, "What word?" There are several possible causes for a word error. First, the student may have mispronounced a sound or stopped between the sounds when sounding out the word, and the teacher did not spot the error. A second possibility is that although the student said the sounds correctly, she did not translate the blended sounds into the right word.

The correction procedure for pausing and word errors involves the same basic steps. The teacher does the following:

1. *Praises* a student who responded correctly, "Yes Kevin, that word is *fat.*" (Pause.) "Good reading."
2. *Models* the correct response by sounding out the word and then saying it at a normal rate.
3. If the students made a pausing error, the teacher *leads* by responding with the students until they sound out the word correctly. The entire group responds.
4. *Tests* the students by having them sound out the word by themselves. The teacher continues to test by alternating between the missed word and other words in the task until the students respond correctly twice in a row to the missed word. For example, if some students missed *mad,* the teacher would correct *mad,* then alternate between *mad* and previously identified words until the students correctly identify the missed word twice in a row. The entire group responds.
5. The teacher *retests* at the end of the format on words missed. Students are tested individually.

Teachers sometimes cause pausing errors and sound errors by not pointing long enough to each letter. If the teacher moves too quickly from one letter to the next, some students will not have time to look ahead to the next letter and, consequently, will guess or pause. If students make many of these errors, the teachers should point longer to each letter. Likewise, teachers sometimes cause student errors by not signaling clearly. Teachers should make sure that their signals are not causing student errors.

The correction for sound errors is somewhat different. In correcting a sound error, the teacher uses a limited model, which involves first modeling and testing just the sound that was missed rather than the entire word. For example, if the teacher points to the letters in *sip* and the student responds "sssaaa," the teacher immediately says "iiiiii" and praises a student who said /i/. Next, the teacher points to *i* and asks, "What sound?" The teacher then tests students on the entire word. Below is a sample sounds correction for a test in which a student said /a/ for *i* in sounding out the word *sit.*

1. *Limited model.* As soon as the teacher hears the sound error, the teacher says the correct sound. "/iiiii/"
2. *Praises.* "Good saying /i/ Yvonne."
3. *Tests.* The teacher tests the whole group on the missed sound, carefully monitoring individuals who originally made the error. Teacher points to *i.* "What sound?" Teacher signals by touching *i.*
4. *Tests.* The teacher tests the whole group on sounding out the word.
5. *Retests.* The teacher retests the students individually on that word at the end of the format.

The teacher should note sounds that are frequently missed and provide extra practice on them in isolated sounds exercises.

During the first week that the students sound out a new word type, the teacher can expect some of the lower-performing students to need as many as 20 repetitions on the lead step before they are able to sound out a set of four to six words without making a mistake. As was mentioned earlier in the auditory skills section, the acceptable performance criterion is for students to correctly respond to a *set* of words without making a mistake. Bringing students to criterion on a set of four to six words will result in major daily improvement (students will master new words with less practice in each subsequent lesson); whereas, not providing adequate practice examples will result in only minimal daily improvement. Without intensive practice, students will tend to make the same mistakes day after day.

### Precorrecting

Precorrecting is a valuable technique for minimizing failure. In a sounding-out precorrection, the teacher prompts the students on a letter that has caused them difficulty in earlier lessons before having them sound out a word with that letter. For example, if the students were having difficulty with *e,* the teacher would point to *e* in the word *met* before having the students sound out the word and ask, "What sound?" The teacher would then have the students sound out the word.

A possible danger with using precorrections is in using them too much, making some students dependent on them. If precorrections are overused, the students will not try to remember difficult sounds because they expect the teacher to identify them. Teachers can avoid developing dependency by precorrecting a sound only for a few lessons. Precorrections are particularly appropriate when a new, difficult letter appears in words or when a letter that has caused students difficulty appears in a word.

## Words Beginning with Stop Sounds

Several modifications in the teaching procedure are necessary for words that begin with a stop sound. First the signaling procedure has to be modified slightly. The letter for the stop sound is touched for just an instant followed by a quick movement to the next letter, which is pointed to for the usual 1 to 1 1/2 seconds. (Note: Words beginning with the stop sound /h/ often cause students particular difficulty. When *h*-beginning words are introduced, include at least three such words in a format (*his, hat, him*) to provide massed practice.)

During the first week when stop-sound-first words appear, the teacher can use a precorrection in which she has the students say the sound of the letter that follows the stop sound before they sound out the word. For example, before the students sound out the word *cut,* the teacher points to *u* and asks, "What sound?" This precorrection is useful since the students must immediately identify the vowel following the stop sound when sounding out a stop-sound-first word, even though they have little time to look at the letter. If this precorrection is used, the teacher must have the students sound out the words later without using the precorrection so that they do not become overly dependent on it. Furthermore, the precorrection should not be used for more than a week.

## Words Beginning with Blends

Words that begin with blends often cause students difficulty. In addition to providing extra sounding-out practice, the teacher can also present several supplementary exercises. First is the auditory skills task in which students telescope a series of blended sounds into a word said at a normal rate. This exercise may be started a week or so before students begin reading words containing initial blends and can be continued for as long as students have difficulty with such words. When presenting the auditory format, the teacher would include words that the students will be asked to decode within the next few days.

A supplementary exercise for teaching words beginning with either stop sounds or consonant blends is rhyming. In this exercise, a teacher writes a group of rhyming words on the board in vertical order:

op
flop
top
crop
stop

He then has the students identify *op* and says that the rest of the words rhyme with "op." The teacher points to the first two letters in the word and says, "Rhyme with *op.* What word?" (Signal.) "flop." The same procedure is repeated with the remaining words. This format can be done daily for several weeks after words beginning with initial blends are introduced.

Precorrections can also be used when words containing blends are first introduced. The precorrection would involve the teacher's pointing to the letter with which students are likely to have problems. If the word contains a stop sound, the teacher points to the letter that follows the stop sound letter; e.g., the teacher would point to *e* in *step* and *r* in *cram.* If the word does not contain a stop sound, the teacher would point to the second consonant in the blend; e.g., the teacher would point to *l* in *flap* and the *r* in *frog.*

## Selecting Examples

The first lessons in which sounding out appears should include only 2 or 3 words since students are likely to need quite a bit of correcting before mastering the skill. Thereafter, the number of words should increase gradually until the list contains about 10 words. Students must be able to quickly identify each letter in all the words they sound out. Consequently, words included in sounding-out exercises should be made up of previously introduced letters. A letter should appear in isolated sounds tasks at least 2 days before it appears in words. The purpose of the 2-day delay is to enable the students to develop some

fluency with a letter before they identify it as part of a word. In addition, for the first few lessons after a new letter is introduced in words, several words in the list should contain the new letter.

## Sight Reading

Sounding out is taught so that students will develop a strategy of examining each letter in a word in a left-to-right progression and, thus, decode regular words accurately. However, accuracy is not the only decoding skill necessary for working comprehension items or reading for pleasure. Fluency is also necessary. One characteristic of fluent reading is instant word recognition or sight reading.[1] If students continued to sound out every word, their slow reading rate would hamper their comprehension performance. Because sight recoding is so important, teachers should introduce it as soon as students are proficient in sounding out VC and CVC words—the easiest types of words that begin with continuous sounds.

When sight reading is first introduced, most students will sound out words subvocally during the interval between a teacher's drawing attention to a word and the teacher's signal for a response. Only with considerable practice will students make the transition from sounding out to sight reading.

## Direct Instruction Procedures

### Preskills and Sequence

Sight reading of CVC words that begin with continuous sounds can be introduced when

---

[1] *Sight reading* here refers to the instructional process by which students learn to instantly recognize words. Usually sight reading refers to just the end product—instant word recognition. The end product is also our goal; we just spend more time discussing procedures that can be used to reach the goal.

students demonstrate mastery of sounding out that type of word. Since this word type is the first introduced, the criterion for mastery does not have as high a rate (a word each 3 to 4 seconds is acceptable); however, the accuracy level should be high (90%).

Students can begin sight reading a new type of word as soon as they demonstrate mastery of the previous word types. As a general rule, mastery is indicated when students read a group of words accurately (90%+) and at a rate of a word each 2 seconds. (Note: If students make several errors because of a particular confusion on just one letter, a new word type can still be introduced.)

## Sight Word Format

The format for teaching sight reading contains two basic parts. The first part, which is designed for lower-performing students, includes a model of how students should sound out words to themselves subvocally. The second part merely provides practice in sight reading words. Teachers should realize that many students will subvocally sound out words for months before they will be able to read words at a glance. The key to enabling students to make the transition is providing adequate practice. Teachers should not try to rush the transition.

## Critical Behaviors

### Pacing

The most critical signaling behavior is deciding how long to make the thinking pause in step 1 of Part II. Initially, the teacher must be extremely careful to provide the students with adequate time to sound out a word to themselves before giving the signal to respond. The teacher can estimate how long the pause should last by sounding out the word to himself. If, after several days, the teacher notes that students still have diffi-

culty sounding out words within 5 seconds, more practice on sounding out should be provided, and sight reading should be delayed. If rushed into sight reading, students may begin guessing.

In step 4, the teacher is to repeat the words until the students identify all of them correctly with a 2-second pause. Learning to identify each word with no more than a 2-second pause is critical if students are to become proficient at sight reading.

### Correcting Mistakes

Students make two types of errors in sight reading exercises: misidentification errors (a student says the wrong word or makes an incomprehensible response) and late response errors (a student responds after the rest of the group). The correction procedure for misidentification errors involves *praising* a student who responded correctly, giving a *limited model* by identifying the missed sound (e.g., if student says "fat" for *fit,* teacher points to *i* and says, "This says *i*"), *testing* the students on sounding out the word, and then alternating between the missed word and other words in the list. At the end of the lesson, the teacher *retests* students individually on any words they missed.

Below is an example of a limited model correction procedure. Alice said "fat" for *fit.*

1. Teacher praises: "This word is *fit.* Good reading, Tara."
2. Teacher gives limited model: (Teacher points to *i*.) "This says *i*. What sound?" (signal) "*i*"
3. Teacher has students sound out word: "Let's sound out the word." (Teacher points to left of first letter, pauses, then loops under each letter, "ffffiiiit What word?" (signal) "fit"
4. Teacher tests: Teacher alternates between missed words and previously identified words pointing to each word, pausing, and asking, "What word?"

**Format for Sight Reading Words**

| *Teacher* | *Students* |
|---|---|

Teacher writes on board: sat, mud, fit, sad.

**Part I**

1. Teacher models.

   a. **"You are going to tell me these words without saying the sounds out loud."**

   b. **"My turn. I'll say the sounds to myself and then say the word."** Teacher points to first word, moves lips for each sound as she points to each letter, then says, **"What word?"** signals, and says the word, **"sat."**

   c. Teacher models with one more word.

2. Teacher *tests* students on all the words.

   a. **"Your turn."** Teacher points to left of first letter. **"As I point to the letters, sound out this word to yourselves."** Teacher loops from letter to letter touching under each continuous sound letter for about a second.

   **"What word?"** (signal)

   *Students sound out words subvocally.*

   *Students say word.*

   b. Teacher repeats step a with remaining words in list. Teacher presents all words until students correctly identify them without an error.

**Part II**

1. **"Your turn. Sound out the word to yourselves. I'm not going to point to the letters. When I signal, just say the word."**

2. Teacher points to left of first word, pausing up to 5 seconds, then signals by saying, **"What word?"** and signaling.

   *Students say the word.*

3. Teacher repeats step 2 with remaining words.

4. Teacher alternates among the words until students can identify each word with only a 2-second pause.

5. Teacher individually tests several students in the group on some words.

Teacher continues alternating until students identify missed word correctly two times in a row.

5. Teacher retests: At the end of format, the teacher tests students individually on words missed during the format.

The correction for a late response depends on the cause of the error. The teacher must determine whether the student was not attending and, therefore, did not respond on time. The correction procedure for errors caused by inattentiveness (if a student is talking or not looking at the teacher) will be discussed in Section 5.1, "Developing Student Motivation."

If a student's eyes are focused on the word and the teacher can see that the student is subvocally sounding out the word, the teacher can assume the student is trying. If the student is trying but responds late, no specific correction is needed. The teacher must simply alternate between words until the student can respond at the desired rate.

## Selecting Examples

Examples must be selected so that students are successful in early sight-reading exercises. The first few lessons a new word type is introduced in word reading, the same words that appeared in that day's sounding-out format can be used. After a few lessons, previously unseen words of the new type can be introduced. For several days after a new letter is first introduced into word reading exercises, that letter should appear in several words in the word list.

The number of words in sight-reading exercises should increase gradually. For the first few days, the list might include just 4 words. Instructionally naive students may need 10 to 15 minutes of instruction to reach an acceptable criterion on just 4 words the first lesson. Lists should grow in size daily until they contain 20 to 25 words. Two-thirds of the words in a list should be of the currently introduced type; the other third should include words missed in the previous lessons.

When words with a consonant blend, either at the beginning or end of a word, are introduced, several minimally different word pairs should be included in the format. These include words that are identical except for a single letter in a certain position. The purpose of including the minimally different pairs in the list is to provide the students with discrimination practice. Unless CVC word types are reviewed when words with consonant blends are introduced, students begin overgeneralizing. For example, if a list includes all words that begin with consonant blends, some students might start overgeneralizing by adding a consonant sound to words that do not have one, e.g., pronouncing cap as "clap." Instructions for constructing minimally different word pairs appear in Table 2.4.3.

Minimally different pairs are also useful when words containing a new letter are introduced. If the letter is a consonant, we recommend that the minimal difference be in the final position in the word (e.g., sid–sit, tim–tin). The last position is used since this is the letter which is often missed. If the letter is a vowel, the minimal difference occurs in the middle of the word (e.g., hat–hit; Tim–Tom).

## Diagnosis and Remediation

Teachers must not only correct errors on specific words but must look for error patterns. Error patterns may indicate that a student needs extra practice on a previously taught component skill or that a teacher is making an error in the way he is presenting a format. A teacher error is indicated if several students in a group are making the same type of mistake. For ex-

**TABLE 2.4.3** *Preparing Minimally Different Word Pairs*

| | |
|---|---|
| *CVCC Words* | Omit the first or last consonant in the blend (*bust–bus*). <br> Vary the final consonant (*bend–bent, mask–mast, dusk–dust*). |
| *CCVC Words* | Omit the second consonant in the blend (*bled–bed, stick–sick*). <br> Vary the second consonant (*slick–stick, bled–bed*). |
| *CCVCC Words* | Omit one of the consonant letters (*cramp–camp, stand–sand*). <br> Vary one of the consonant letters (*spent–spend, cramp–clamp*). |

ample, if several students are responding late, the teacher may not be providing adequate time to figure out a word before signaling and should alter his presentation to provide students with a longer thinking pause.

The type of error patterns teachers should look for in word-reading tasks are specific letter-sound correspondence errors, word-type errors, late responding errors, and random guessing errors.

### Letter-Sound Correspondence Errors

A specific letter-sound correspondence error is indicated when students mispronounce the same letter in several words. For example, a student says "mat" for *mit* and "hum" for *him*. Probably the student does not know the most common sound for the letter *i*. The teacher should test the student individually by asking her to say the sound of *i*. If the student does not know the sound, she should be reintroduced to the letter-sound correspondence in the next lesson. The teacher would present the letter in an introductory format and then stress it in a letter-sound discrimination format for several days. During the days the letter is being reintroduced, the teacher would use a precorrection on words containing that letter. In the precorrection, the teacher tells the students the letter's sound before asking them to identify the word.

After several days, the teacher would present an introductory list of three to five words, all containing that particular letter. This list would be followed by a discrimination list in which about half the words included the letter students had missed. The discrimination list might include one or two pairs of minimally different words (e.g., *hit–hat; tin–tan*).

### Word-Type Errors

A word-type error is indicated when a student misses several words of a particular type. For example, a student says "lam" for *lamp* and "ben" for *bent*. On both words,

the student left off the second consonant of a final consonant blend in a CVCC word. To remediate a word-type error, a teacher would present daily word list reading exercises focusing on that particular word type. She would first present an introductory list of 3 to 5 words, all of which were of the particular type. (For example, if students had difficulty with CVCC words, the teacher might include the words *lamp, sink, bust, bent,* all of which are CVCC.) Next the teacher would present a discrimination list of about 10 words. About half the words would be of that particular type. The other half would be from easier types and would provide discrimination practice. Several minimally different pairs would be included. (For example, a discrimination list for CVCC words might include these words: *lie, tent, ten, bus, bust, limp, run, send, can.*)

### Late Responding Errors

A late responding pattern is indicated by a student's responding late 20% or more of the time. As mentioned before, the teacher must first determine the cause of a late responding pattern. If the student responds late because he is inattentive, the remediation involves increasing the student's motivation to attend. If the student appears to be attentive, he should be tested individually sometime during the day. During this test, the teacher notes the speed at which the student can respond. If the student is much slower than the rest of the group, he must either be provided with extra practice or placed in a lower group. The extra practice could be done both on isolated letter-sound correspondence tasks and on word-reading exercises. Sometimes late responding is caused by a student's lack of ability to say the sounds for letters at a rapid enough rate to sound out words quickly. As a check, the teacher could ask the student to produce the sounds of all letters introduced to date. The teacher would note the letters the student was unable to recognize instantly and provide practice on them. In addition to extra practice, the teacher can also use a slightly longer thinking pause on word-reading tasks so that the student does not develop a habit of copying the responses of higher-performing students.

### Random Guessing Errors

A random error pattern is indicated when a student is making errors on more than 10% of the words in exercises, and the errors do not involve a specific letter or word-type pattern. Random error patterns often result from the student's simply not examining a word carefully. The student might just look at several letters and say any word which contains those letters. Sometimes this guessing is caused by a student's not being able to respond at the rate the teacher is signaling. If so, practice should be provided and a longer thinking pause used during group reading. If the student is able to read at the rate the group is reading, the remedy lies in increasing the student's motivation to read accurately.

## Supplementary Activities

There is a wide variety of activities that can be used to provide extra word-reading practice, e.g., the worksheets from supplementary phonics programs. Figure 2.4.2 shows a typical page from one of these programs. In this activity, the students say the word above the picture and circle the word if the picture name ends in the same blend. The worksheets from such programs are usually suitable for average and above-average students. Students with limited vocabularies may have difficulty with the exercises. For example, on the worksheet in Figure 2.4.2, the student is expected to know the words *dent* (picture), *hound,* and *band.* Lower-performing students may not know those words. Consequently, teachers should not assign these worksheets as independent work to such students but should provide guidance. A peer tutor or aide could help the students by saying the word the picture represents.

Supplementary phonics programs are published by most major publishers and many minor publishers. When examining programs, teachers should look for ones that contain exercises students are likely to be able to do with a minimum of guidance. The two key factors to look at are (1) the layouts of the exercises (Do they make it clear what the student is expected to do?) and (2) the vocabulary (Are the terms used understood by the type of child with whom the teacher is working?).

## Commercial Programs

### When to Begin

All the code-emphasis programs we have examined begin word reading at reasonable times. Lippincott begins word reading exercises when the students know four letter-sound correspondences. Palo Alto begins word-reading exercises when the students know two letter-sound correspondences. Although the code-emphasis programs begin word reading at reasonable times, some instructionally naive students may need additional training on auditory skills and sounding out. Students are not ready to begin word reading until they master the auditory skills and sounding out with continuous-sound-beginning CVC words. The teacher should construct several extra practice lessons focusing on these skills. Doing so will make initial word-reading exercises easier for the students. (See Appendix D for sample lessons.)

Meaning-emphasis programs are constructed quite differently than code-emphasis programs in that they introduce very few words during the time when letter-sound correspondences are taught: only 10 to 20 words. More specific suggestions on how to use meaning-emphasis programs will be provided in Section 2.8.

### Sequence

Table 2.4.4 lists new words and when they are introduced in the code-emphasis pro-

**FIGURE 2.4.2**  *Phonics Worksheet*

Read the word above each picture.

Circle the word if the picture name ends

with the same blend. Cross out the word if the

picture name does not end with the same blend.

*Always say the names of the pictures for the pupils.*

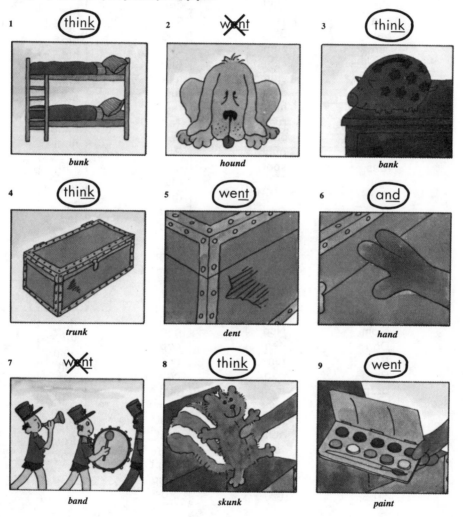

38    Letter-to-sound association: ending blends *nd, nk, nt*

grams examined. The number over each group of words indicates the lesson number. In the Palo Alto list, the letter *R* indicates that the words were introduced in a short readiness program included in the program. Asterisks appear in front of irregular words. Note that by looking at the sequence of words introduced, we can readily determine when a letter first appears. In Lippincott, for example, lesson 2 contains only the letters *a* and *n*. Lesson 3 words contain only *a, n,* and *r.* In lesson

**TABLE 2.4.4** *Sequence of Words Introduced in Two Code-Emphasis Programs*

**Lippincott**

| 2 | | | | 15 |
|---|---|---|---|---|
| an | dim | ant | pest | hat |
| Ann | rim | sat | stem | has |
| | pin | sit | step | had |
| **3** | drip | not | spent | ham |
| ran | | Tim | | hit |
| | **9** | Pat | **13** | him |
| **4** | Sid | Nat | Gus | his |
| Dan | sip | Matt | get | hid |
| Dad | sad | Tom | got | hip |
| add | Sam | Stan | dog | hot |
| and | sun | stand | dug | hop |
| | sand | stamp | tug | hum |
| **5** | us | stump | mug | hug |
| run | Russ | stop | rug | hut |
| | miss | must | rag | hand |
| **6** | pass | rust | Tag | hunt |
| mud | *is | past | peg | |
| mad | *as | punt | Peg | **16** |
| man | runs | spot | Meg | fun |
| am | spin | | pig | fat |
| ram | spin | **12** | dig | fed |
| drum | | Ed | grass | fog |
| | **10** | end | grip | fin |
| **7** | on | men | grin | fit |
| Pam | odd | met | grunt | fig |
| pan | sod | set | drug | fast |
| pad | pod | pet | | fact |
| up | pop | net | **14** | if |
| pup | mop | red | cat | off |
| map | Mom | Ned | can | sniff |
| nap | Don | den | cap | raft |
| rap | Ron | ten | cut | sift |
| pump | Ross | pep | cot | drift |
| damp | drop | mend | cup | Fran |
| ramp | pond | send | camp | Fred |
| *the | | rent | cost | *from |
| | **11** | sent | cast | frog |
| **8** | tan | tent | crop | |
| did | top | dent | crept | |
| in | tot | nest | crisp | |
| rid | tip | rest | cross | |
| mid | it | | | |
| rip | at | | | |
| dip | | | | |
| mim | | | | |
| min | | | | |

**TABLE 2.4.4** (*continued*)

**Palo Alto**

| | | | | |
|---|---|---|---|---|
| **R-3**<br>am | ran<br>nat | on<br>lot<br>Tom<br>mon | *are<br>*you<br>no | **25**<br>it<br>fit<br>sit<br>bit |
| **R-5**<br>*I | **10**<br>*look<br>*saw | **18**<br>hat<br>hal | **21**<br>van<br>val | lit<br>hit<br>did<br>hid |
| **R-6**<br>ran | **11**<br>*said | *do<br>*is<br>*yes | **22**<br>tad<br>lad | lid<br>dig<br>big |
| **R-8**<br>mat | **12**<br>Al<br>Sal<br>tan | *has<br>**19**<br>hog | sad<br>dog<br>bad | in<br>tin<br>him |
| **1**<br>*the | **13**<br>an<br>ant | log<br>fog<br>got<br>bog | *good<br>**23**<br>rod | rim<br>dim<br>Tim<br>Bim |
| **2**<br>tat | **14**<br>fat<br>fan | *this<br>in | had<br>Dad<br>don | can<br>*happy<br>*give |
| **3**<br>*see | **15**<br>Bab<br>bat<br>bam | **20**<br>tag<br>rag<br>bag | *he<br>*my<br>hand | *into<br>*she<br>*to |
| **4**<br>and | *ball | *so<br>*they<br>*me | **24**<br>Dan<br>put<br>gas<br>stop | *of |
| **5**<br>at | **16**<br>Bob<br>rob<br>not | | | |
| **6**<br>sam<br>Tam<br>sat<br>rat | | | | |
| **8**<br>man<br>Nan | | | | |

4 *d* is added, in lesson 5, *u;* in lesson 7, *p;* in lesson 8, *i;* etc.

Note that in the Palo Alto and the Lippincott programs the first word introduced begins with a continuous sound. However, words beginning with stop sounds are introduced shortly thereafter. We would suggest providing more practice on CVC and VC continuous-sound-beginning words before introducing stop-sound-beginning words. Of course, the amount of extra practice depends on student performance. After students demonstrate they can decode continuous-sound-beginning words, stop-sound-beginning words can be introduced. Providing for extra practice on continuous sound words will require teachers to construct word lists not specified in the program. This should not be too difficult. For example, assuming the students know the letters *a, i, m, r, t, d,* and *f,* the words *mad, am, it, at, if, fit, mat, fat, rat, ram, rim, mid,* and *mitt* can be included in extra drill on continuous-sound-beginning words. Possible words to use in such exercises are included in Appendix A, which provides word lists for each of the various regular word types.

As a general guideline, a new word type should be introduced only after students can read 9 of 10 words from easier types at a rate of no more than 2 seconds per word. If students do not perform at this level, we recommend that the teacher provide extra word-list and passage-reading practice on the easier word types until the students meet the performance level. Then a new word type would be introduced. Lippincott's rapid rate for introducing new word types might make it more difficult than Palo Alto for some students. Palo Alto provides much more practice on a word type before a new one is introduced than does Lippincott. Note that in Lippincott three new word types appear within a three-lesson span (see lessons 10–12 in Lippincott). Our modification suggestion is the same as that recommended when stop-sound-beginning words are introduced too early: provide more practice on the current word type if students have not mastered it by the time the next word type is introduced. Note that when referring to the introduction of a new word type, we do not mean a single instance of an advanced word type that appears in an early lesson. We mean when a group of words of a new type is introduced. Isolated examples of a new word type can either be skipped over, if students are still relatively weak on the current word type, or taught using sounding out. Extra practice lessons are necessary only when a *group* of words of a new type appears.

## Teaching Procedures

### Sounding Out

Previously, we recommended that beginning readers initially learn a sounding-out strategy for decoding regular words. Direct teaching of a sounding-out strategy can be beneficial to all students who are unable to read many words upon entering school. However, the procedure must be taught well. If it is unclear or presents a misleading model, sounding-out instruction may, in fact, hinder students. When sounding out is taught correctly, it allows teachers to teach a strategy and its component skills. Most reading programs, however, do not include sounding-out instruction.

Our suggestion is to begin regular word-reading instruction with sounding out using the procedures specified in this section. A teacher must be careful to provide adequate practice to enable students to master the skill (90% accuracy when the teacher points to each letter for 1 second). Once the students demonstrate proficiency in sounding out words, sounding out can be replaced with sight reading. The only time sounding out needs to be used thereafter is to introduce new word types or correct mistakes. The transition from sounding out should be made as soon as students are ready.

### Sight Reading

Characteristics we felt might hinder students, especially instructionally naive ones, appeared, to some extent, in most programs. These characteristics were potentially confusing demonstrations, encouragement of inattentiveness, and inappropriate correction techniques. Several of these problems are illustrated in Figure 2.4.3, which is an excerpt from the Lippincott teacher's guide.

The aspects of this format that make it potentially confusing are these:

# FIGURE 2.4.3

Decoding/Comprehension:  Vocabulary Emphasis

### Introduction

Motivate the children by telling them that now that they have learned to recognize the /m/ sound and the letter m that spells it, they will be able to read six new words.

Show the children the known word **Dan** on a Word Recognition card and ask them to read it aloud. Place the letter **m** on top of the **D** and have the children read the new word, first to themselves then aloud. Show them the two Word Recognition cards, **Dan** and **man**. Have both words read and used in a sentence, such as, **Dan is a man**. *(forming and decoding new words by letter substitution)*

Show the children the word **mad** on a Word Recognition card. Have them decode the word silently, then call on a child to pronounce it. Have another child use the word in a sentence.

Ask for a volunteer to tell you how to change **mad** to **mud**. Show the children both **mad** and **mud** on word cards. Have both words read aloud. Ask what is the same in both words. What letter and what sound is different?

Pronounce a group of words ending with /m/ such as, **him**, **Tim**, **Tom**, etc. Ask the children what sound they hear at the end of these words. (/m/) Show the children the known word **an** on a Word Recognition card. Hold the letter **m** over the **n** and ask the children to read the new word **am**. Follow the same procedure described above as you help the children decode new words. Be sure the children are not learning the words in isolation. Keep using the new words in phrases and sentences and discussing any multiple meanings the words may have. Have the children tell you how to change **am** to **ram**; **ram** to **rum**; **rum** to **dum** to **drum**. *(decoding and comprehension of new words with terminal /m/)*

The children should not "sound out" isolated or separated sounds. As the children think about each new word, move your hand under it smoothly from left-to-right. As needed, refer the children to the large cards that show the mnemonic device for each sound along with the letter that spells it. If the children cannot seem to decode a word, give a meaning clue. If they still do not read it, say the word for them.

### Using the Text

Have the children turn to page 9 in their texts. Ask if they see a word there that they can read. Call on individuals to read a word. Have the other children frame it with their fingers. Discuss the meaning of the word or have it used in a sentence.

Ask the children to read all the words in the yellow box. Tell them you are going to say two sentences. When you stop after a word, they are to point to that word in their books.

A **man** fell in the mud.

He was **mad**.

1. The use of letter names. The format assumes that students know both the names and sounds of letters. Students who do not know letter names will be at a distinct disadvantage.
2. The format assumes students understand the language concepts *same* and *end.* Students who do not understand these words will also be at a disadvantage.
3. A final potentially confusing aspect of the format is the great amount of teacher's talk. The teacher is told to use words in phrase sentences and to discuss any multiple meanings the word may have. Lengthy explanations some-

times confuse students as to the purpose of a task.

These are the aspects of the format that encourage students' inattentiveness:

1. The high proportion of teacher talk to student responding. The more teachers talk and the less students have to respond, the greater the probability that younger instructionally naive and even average students will become inattentive.
2. The use of individual turns before group responding can also cause inattentiveness. If higher-performing students are called on individually to answer a question, lower-performing students may begin to rely on just copying their responses without attending to the letters in the word or the teacher's direction.

The Lippincott correction procedure tells the teacher to help students having difficulty by giving a meaning clue and if they still do not read it, by saying the word for them. This correction procedure is inappropriate for the beginning reading stage since it may encourage a student attitude of "If you don't get the word, the teacher will tell it to you." Also, the use of meaning cues at this early stage may encourage guessing behavior in which the student looks at just the first letters of a word instead of examining the entire word closely. We would suggest using the format on pages 102–04 instead of this format.

In meaning-emphasis programs, students are taught to rely on a variety of strategies to decode words. Since the majority of words introduced are not regular, the programs teach students not to rely on the vowels but just to key on consonants. Students are encouraged to look just at the first and last letters in the word. For example, the words and pictures for two objects like *cap* and *coat* are presented. Teachers point out that they cannot distinguish the words based on initial consonants, and then encourage the students to look at the final consonants. By matching the final consonants for an illustrated object and the words, students determine which word goes with which picture. Students are never encouraged to attend to the vowels.

Meaning-emphasis programs also teach students to use the context of a sentence to figure out unknown words. In the *Houghton Mifflin Reading Series,* there are a number of exercises in which the teacher prints a word on the board and gives the students the meaning of the word or a similar cue. For the word *pencil,* the teacher might point to the word and say, "This is something you write with." The teacher then asks students the word. Next, the teacher asks students how they know the word can't be *crayon* or *paddle.* The students would respond that the word can't be *crayon* because it doesn't start with that sound. The word can't be *paddle* because it wouldn't make sense.

The problem with such formats in meaning-emphasis programs is not that they do not teach important skills, but rather that they introduce the skills too early. We agree that students should be taught strategies besides phonics to decode words. The problem in introducing a sophisticated strategy too early is that it is bound to confuse some students. Simplified decoding instruction will help many average and lower-performing students without hurting higher-performing students.

## Example Selection and Practice

Most commercial programs do not specify what exercises in the teacher's guide should constitute a daily lesson. Word list drill should be included in daily lessons. If the teacher's guide does not specify words to include, the teacher should construct a list using the guidelines on page 104 of this Section.

When using the word lists in commercial programs, the teacher should watch out for lists that are too predictable and that may inadvertently encourage guessing behavior. She should not repeat words in the same order because some students will memorize the sequence of answers and not closely examine the words. For example, if some students make mistakes on the sequence *sap, mud, fit,* and *sad,* the teacher should present the words the second time in a different order (*fit, sap, sad,* and *mud*). A different order should be used every time the words are repeated.

## RESEARCH

A growing body of data seems to point to the validity of teaching sounding out. Muller (1973), Ramsey (1972), and Richardson and Collier (1971) reported that blending is a necessary component skill for successfully applying a sounding-out strategy to unfamiliar words. Ramsey (1972) found that 40% of the errors made by nonreading second graders were due to blending difficulties. Coleman (1970) noted that blending is a strategy that students can apply to many different words, but direct instruction with many sounds is necessary before students will acquire the generalized skill. Skailand (1971) and Silberman (1964) reported that if subjects are taught sound-symbol relationships but not blending, they will not use sounding out as a decoding strategy. Bishop (1964), Jeffrey and Samuels (1967), Carnine (1977), and Vandever and Neville (1976) reported that teaching letter-sound correspondences and sounding out resulted in students' correctly identifying more unfamiliar words than when students were trained on a whole-word strategy. Haddock (1976) and Chapman and Kamm (1974) found that only when blending is directly taught will students successfully use a sounding-out strategy for attacking words.

A rhyming approach to blending was found to be effective in both the Haddock (1977) and Chapman and Kamm (1974) studies. Through direct instruction in rhyming, children tended to learn to recognize phonetically similar elements (Venezky, Shiloah, & Calfee, 1972). Venezky et al. also reported a significant positive correlation between reading achievement and rhyming performances. Recognition of phonetically similar elements through rhyming instruction should assist students to quickly identify letter combinations and syllables.

Because of individual learner differences, a specific number of examples will never be appropriate for teaching a sounding-out strategy to all students. A mastery learning approach, in which examples are presented until the student reaches a specified performance standard, probably results in higher retention scores than presenting the same number of examples to all students. Jeffrey and Samuels (1967) taught students a word-reading strategy with a fixed number of practice trials on a set of training words. Carnine (1977) taught students a similar strategy but with a mastery learning design. Subjects in the Carnine study identified about 92% of the transfer words correctly while Jeffrey and Samuels' subjects identified only about 31% of the words correctly. Since different subjects were used in the two studies, the comparison of a mastery learning and fixed practice design is at best suggestive. Research that directly addresses the question is needed.

Introducing word types according to their relative difficulty was also recommended in this section. In a study on word difficulty (Carnine & Carnine, in press), children in a synthetic phonics program (Engelmann & Bruner, 1974) were tested on three types of untaught words: CVC words with an initial stop sound, CVCC words with an initial continuous sound, and CCVC words. Students were presented with five examples of each word type (for a total of 15 words). The mean percent of correct responses was 71% for CVC words, 40% for CVCC words, and 22% for CCVC words. All differences were significant, suggesting that CVC words are easier to decode using a sounding-out strategy than either CVCC or CCVC words, and that CVCC words are easier than CCVC words.

The question of how to initially teach word recognition, is very important. As mentioned earlier Singer, Samuels, and Spiroff (1973) compared words in isolation, words in context, and words with pictures. Presenting words in isolation was the most effective procedure. Shankweiler and Liberman (1972) reported that the ability to recognize words in lists is highly correlated with accurately reading words in context. Discrimination word lists also reduce confusion errors in later reading activities. Samuels and Jeffrey (1966), McCutcheon and McDowell (1969), and Otto and Pizillo (1970–71) reported that discrimination lists (made up of similar words) resulted in fewer incorrect responses to similar transfer words than did training on lists in which the words were dissimilar. Students who learned the discrimination list usually required longer to reach criterion, but the improved word recognition skills probably warranted the additional time.

From their research on word reading, Rayner and Posnansky (1978) concluded that "since beginning readers focus so heavily on beginning letters, we suggest that a great deal of discrimination training in which the first letter is held constant will prove beneficial for children" (p. 187). Discrimination training is particularly important since primary students often mistakenly learn to identify words based on the first two letters. Venezky (1975) pointed out that 75% of the common words that appear in primary readers can be discriminated on the basis of the first two letters. Unfortunately, relying on initial letters is inappropriate since it is a useless strategy after third grade.

The ineffectiveness of picture cues has been demonstrated in several studies (Harzem, Lee, & Miles, 1976; Samuels, 1970). Similarly, research on configuration as a basis for word recognition has yielded negative results (Edelman, 1963; Smith, 1969; McClelland, 1977). Word configuration supposedly allows students to identify words on the basis of their contours, such as ⊔‾⊔ for |little| . Marchbanks and Levin (1965) tested beginning readers' preferred cues in word identification by asking them to select one word from a set of alternatives that was most similar to a standard. Children tended to use word configuration as a *least* preferred cue, after initial, final, and medial letters.

## APPLICATION EXERCISES

### SOUNDING OUT

1. Assume that a group of students knows the most common sound for all individual letters and the letter combinations: *th, sh, ch, ck, ar, ee, ea, or, oa, oo, ai, ou, ur, er.* Circle letters that will cause students difficulty. Assume students will not pronounce final *e* in words like *horse*.

| | | | | |
|---|---|---|---|---|
| roast | said | burst | steal | get |
| loan | gain | her | break | gin |
| broad | maid | fur | treat | cinch |
| moon | stain | chef | head | count |
| cool | out | chip | leak | put |
| book | four | bark | worm | stick |
| boost | ground | warn | torn | pull |
| took | pour | harm | sport | bust |
| good | stout | been | for | off |
| boot | churn | beet | of | gun |
| root | fern | need | was | cap |

2. Write each of the following words under the appropriate heading below: (See page 95)

| | | | | |
|---|---|---|---|---|
| strip | step | ant | crust | at |
| camp | fled | bets | bled | desk |
| mud | must | snap | top | skunk |
| best | cop | brat | set | slip |
| strap | ask | grab | bust | splint |

a. VC and CVC words that begin
with continuous sound:

b. CVC words that begin
with stop sound:

c. CVCC and VCC words:

d. CCVC words:

e. CCVCC, CCCVC, and
CCCVCC words:

3. (For an aid in doing this exercise, see the word lists in Appendix A.)
    a. Students have been taught to read CVC words that begin with continuous
    sounds and know the most common sounds for these letters: f, t, l, m, d, s,
    r, a, i, o. List four words that could be included in a word-reading task.
    b. Students have been taught to read CVC words that begin with continuous
    and stop sounds and know the most common sounds for these letters: f, l,
    m, d, t, s, r, h, i, o, a. Assume the letter h has been introduced 3 days earlier.
    Make a list of 10 words for a word-reading task. Four of the words should
    include the letter h. Three of the words should begin with continuous sounds.
    c. Students have been taught to read CVC and CVCC words beginning with
    continuous and stop sounds. They know the most common sounds of all
    letters except e, w, x, y, and z. Assume that CCVC words have just been
    introduced. Construct a list of 12 words, two-thirds should be of the currently
    introduced type. Include three minimally different pairs constructed by leav-
    ing out a second consonant from an initial blend.
4. The teacher is presenting a sounding-out format. In the following situations,
    specify what the teacher would do and the wording the teacher would use to
    correct the student's error when it occurs.
    a. When sounding out the word *mud*, a student pauses after saying *m*.
    b. When sounding the word *mud* a student says /i/ when the teacher points to *u*.

## Sight Reading

1. Assume that you have taught a group of students the following skills:

    The most common sound of these individual letters
        a i o b c d f g h k l m n r s t
    How to decode these word types: VC and CVC that begin with continuous
    sounds; CVC that begin with stop sounds; CVCC that end with consonant
    blends.

    a. Circle each of the following words that the student would not be able to
    decode. Next to each circled word write the abbreviation for the explanation
    below that tells why students could not decode the word. These are the
    possible explanations:

    Letter (L)—The word is regular, but a letter that the students do not know
        appears in the word.

Word Type (WT)—The word is a type that has not been taught.
Not Regular (NR)—The word is not regular. Some letter(s) does not represent its most common sound.

| | | | | | |
|---|---|---|---|---|---|
| jet | _____ | rag | _____ | said | _____ |
| slim | _____ | hot | _____ | stand | _____ |
| big | _____ | clap | _____ | tag | _____ |
| red | _____ | put | _____ | of | _____ |
| last | _____ | best | _____ | ramp | _____ |
| trap | _____ | list | _____ | stop | _____ |
| was | _____ | talk | _____ | sink | _____ |
| if | _____ | sam | _____ | fit | _____ |

b. The errors for each of two students are listed below. For each student (1) diagnose the problem, (2) specify whether an isolated letter-sounds task is called for, and (3) construct an introductory (three words) list and a discrimination list (six words) to remedy the problem. See pages 104–06.

Student A: The word was *lift;* the student said "lit."
    The word was *cast;* the student said "cat."

Diagnosis _____

Sounds Task   Yes _____   No _____

Examples for introductory word list _____

_____

Examples for discrimination word list _____

_____

Student B: The word was *bat;* the student said "bit."
    The word was *ram;* the student said "rum."
    The word was *bag;* the student said "beg."

Diagnosis _____

Sounds Task   Yes _____   No _____

Examples for introductory word list _____

_____

Examples for discrimination word list _____

_____

2. The words in a sight-reading task are *sam, rid, mad, if, at.* Below are four sequences of examples a teacher presented to different groups. A plus (+) indicates a correct response; a minus (−) indicates an error. (1) Tell whether each sequence represents an acceptable alternating pattern, and (2) explain what is wrong with the unacceptable sequences. Assume all errors were world-identification errors.

a. sam (−) (teacher corrects)  rid (−)  (teacher corrects)  mad (−) (teacher corrects   if (+)   at (+)

b. sam +   rid +   mad +   if +   at +

c. sam +   rid +   mad −   (teacher corrects)   sam +   mad −   (teacher corrects)  rid +   mad +   rid +   sam +   mad +   if +   at +   mad +

d. sam +   rid −   (teacher corrects)   sam +   rid −   (teacher corrects)   mad +   if +   at +   sam +   if +   at +

3. The teacher is presenting the sight-reading format. In the following situations, specify the wording the teacher would use to correct the student's error when it occurs.

a. A student calls *spell* "spill."

b. A student calls *bent* "ben."

4. Assume a student who knows the most common sounds of all individual letters and VC, CVC, CVCC, and CCVC word types is having difficulty with CCVC words that begin with consonant blends. Write yes next to each acceptable group of *discrimination* words. (Assume that the teacher has already presented a group of introductory words.) Write no next to each list that is not acceptable and state your reason (see page 95).

| Words | Acceptable for Discrimination Practice | |
| | Yes or No | Reason(s) |
| --- | --- | --- |
| clap, flag, plan, slap, slug | | |
| clamp, camp, cash, clash, plain, pain | | |
| cop, slip, bled, bed, clam, sip, slip | | |

# SECTION 2.5

## *Irregular Words*

This section will discuss our recommended procedures for teaching students to decode irregular words in which some letters do not represent the most common sound. We define an *irregular word* as any word which contains letter-sound correspondences the student does not know. According to this definition, a word considered irregular at an early point in a reading program may not be considered irregular at a later point in the program. For example, the words *park* and *eat* would be considered irregular words during the beginning reading stage since the letters *a* and *r* in *park* and *e* and *a* in *eat* do not represent their most common sounds. During the primary stage, however, the words *park* and *eat* would not be considered irregular because the *ar* in *park* and the *ea* in *eat* form letter combinations which the students will have been taught. Teachers must be aware of what words a student is and is not able to decode at various points in a program. With that awareness, teachers can prepare students for irregular words. If students encounter too many words for which they are not prepared, they may adopt inappropriate reading strategies.

## Direct Instruction Procedures

### When to Introduce

We recommend introducing irregular words after students are proficient (90% accuracy with only a 3-second pause) at reading regular CVC words. The reason for delaying the introduction of irregular words is that it will make the initial lessons easier. Since students will not encounter irregular words, they can successfully apply the same sounding-out strategy to all words.

### Rate

Learning to decode irregular words is a major step for beginning readers because a completely new strategy is involved. The reader cannot simply sound out a word and then translate the blended sounds into a word. For example, *was* would be sounded out as "wwwaaasss" but pronounced "wuz." Because of the complexity of decoding irregular words, students need time to master each individual word. Therefore, the first several irregular words should be separated from each other by about four lessons.

The next 10 or so irregular words can be introduced at a somewhat faster rate of about 1 new word every two to three lessons. The students' performance, of course, is the key determinant of how quickly new irregular words can be introduced. While students are learning the first 7 irregular words, a new irregular word should not be introduced if students miss any previously introduced irregular words in word list reading or in passage reading. Instead, the teacher would review missed words.

After the students have learned 7 words, a teacher can introduce a new irregular word even if a student is having difficulty with 1 or 2 previously introduced words. However, the new word should not be similar to the words the student is having difficulty with. For example, a teacher would not introduce the word *where* if students were having difficulty with *were* but could introduce *where* if students were having difficulty with *said.* If students are having difficulty with more than 1 or 2 previously introduced words, no new words should be introduced.

## Sequence

The factors governing the introduction of irregular words are frequency, similarity to other words, and knowledge of letter-sound correspondences.

### Frequency

As a general rule, words that appear more often in children's literature should be introduced before words that appear less often. The sequence of words is not particularly critical as long as the general rule is followed.

Several lists are available which order words according to their relative frequency or according to when words usually appear in reading programs. Among these lists are the following:

1. Caroll, Davies, and Richmond, *American Heritage Word Frequency Book* (Boston: Houghton Mifflin, 1971)
2. Harris and Jacobson, *Basic Elementary Reading Vocabulary* (New York: Macmillan, 1972) (available in paperback)
3. Kucera and Francis, *Analysis of Present Day American English* (Providence, R.I.: Brown University Press, 1967)
4. Thorndike and Lodge, *The Teachers Word Book of 30,000 Words* (New York: Teachers College Press, 1944)

Appendix B contains a list of words formed by combining the Dolch list of 220 words and the words in the Harris and Jacobson preprimer and first grade lists. Note that most of these words would be considered irregular during the beginning stage. These words appear often in children's literature. Students should receive adequate practice to recognize them at a glance.

### Similarity

Some isolated irregular words are very similar either to a regular word or to some other irregular word, e.g., *from–form, saw–was, of–off,* and *were–where.* The introduction of these pairs should be planned so that one of the two words is introduced long before the other (at least 15 lessons). The separation allows students to master the first word before encountering the second and, thus, decreases the probability of the students' confusing them.

### Letter-Sound Correspondence Knowledge

Whenever possible, an irregular word should be introduced after the students know the most common sound of each letter in the word. For example, the word *was* is not introduced until the students know the most common sounds for the single letters *w, a,* and *s.* Likewise, an irregular word is not introduced until students have learned to decode the word type illustrated by the irregular word. For example, the irregular word *ton* (irregular because *o* is not making its most common sound) begins with a stop sound. *Ton* should not be introduced until students can decode CVC words that begin with stop sounds.

## Teaching Procedure for Isolated Irregular Words

The initial procedure we recommend for introducing the first 10 to 15 irregular words is from *DISTAR* (Engelmann & Bruner, 1974). The procedure involves the student's sounding out the word as it is written and then translating that series of sounds into the correct pronunciation. The word *was* is sounded out as "waaasss" but is pronounced "wuz." The word *walk* is sounded as "wwwaaalllk" but is said "wauk."

Even though this procedure is somewhat cumbersome, it has several advantages. First, it increases the probability that students will continue to carefully attend to the letters making up a word. It shows students that the same basic strategy can be used to decode *all* words, even though some are pronounced differently than the blended sounds indicate. Without this demonstration, some students may develop the misrule that since sounding out does not work on some words, it will no longer work on any words. Second, it prepares students for later spelling exercises by demonstrating that students cannot rely solely on letter-sound correspondences to spell all words.

After students have learned the first 10 to 15 irregular words, the procedure of first sounding out new irregular words can be dropped and replaced by a format in which the students do not sound out the word. Remember the procedure of having students sound out irregular words is used just for 10 to 15 words during the beginning reading stage. In the primary stage, a sounding-out procedure for irregular words would not be appropriate.

## Critical Behaviors

### Demonstrating

The teacher must clearly demonstrate that the word is pronounced differently than it

---

**Introductory Format for Irregular Words**

| Teacher | Students |
|---|---|
| 1. Teacher tells students new word and sounds it out. Teacher points to *was*. **"Everybody, this is a funny word. The word is wuz. What word?"** (signal) | "Wuz" |
| **"Listen to me sound out the word."** Teacher touches each letter. **"Wwwwaaaassss. That's how we sound out the word. But here's how we say it, wuz. How do we say it?"** Teacher touches word. **"Yes, wuz."** | "Wuz" |
| 2. Teacher has students sound out the word and then say it. Teacher points to the left of *was*. **"Now you are going to sound it out. Get ready."** Teacher touches under each letter for about a second. | "Wwwaaasss" |
| **"But how do we say the word?"** (signal) | "Wuz" |
| **"Remember, how do we say the word?"** (signal) | "Wuz" |
| 3. Teacher gives individual turns on step 2. | |

is sounded out. When sounding out the word, he must say the most common sound for each letter and not just pronounce the word slowly.

### Correcting Mistakes

Students make two types of errors in step 2 of the introductory format. (1) When sounding out the word, they may say the sounds for how the word is said rather than the most common sound for each letter. For example, when sounding out the word *was,* the student says /ŭ/ instead of /ă/ for *a.* (2) After sounding out the word, they may say the word as it is sounded out rather than as it is said. For example, after sounding out the letters in *was* as "wwww-ăaaassss," the student says "wăs" instead of "wuz."

The correction procedure for both errors is to (1) model by repeating the question and saying the correct answer and then (2) return to the beginning of step 1. This procedure should be followed until the students can respond to all the steps in the format without an error.

Returning to the beginning of step 1 and repeating the entire format until the students can answer all the questions correctly is important. Students must clearly understand the difference between the way an irregular word is sounded out and the way it is said. Answering all the questions in the irregular word format indicates that the students understand that difference.

## Discrimination Format for Irregular Words

The introductory format is the only format in which the students are asked to sound out an irregular word. After the introductory format, the teacher has the students read a group of words containing the new irregular word and other previously introduced regular and irregular words. The teacher uses an alternating pattern: she presents the new irregular word, one of the previously introduced words, and then returns

to the new word. She returns to the new word several more times during the task, but each time after having presented more review words. For example, if the irregular word *said* is in a word list with *was, the, walk,* and *lamp,* the teacher would present the words in this order: *said, was, said, the, walk, said, walk, the, lamp, said,* etc. Note that more words appear between each successive presentation of *said.* The teacher keeps alternating between the new word and review words until the students are able to consistently identify the new irregular word correctly three times with only a 2-second thinking pause. No sounding out is used in the discrimination format. The teacher just points to each word and asks, "What word?"

## Critical Behaviors

### Correcting Mistakes

When the teacher asks students to identify an irregular word in a discrimination format, students may make two types of misidentification mistakes: (1) saying the word as it is sounded out (saying "wăs" instead of "wuz") or (2) saying a different word (saying "saw" instead of "wuz"). The students may also make a signal error, saying the correct answer but responding after the rest of the group.

The correction procedure for the discrimination format is quite different than for the introductory format. The teacher just tells the students the word (models), has the students say the word but *not* sound it out, and then follows the alternating pattern procedure. The students do not sound out the word at this point because sounding out may confuse them. Sounding out is used only when correcting errors in the introductory format.

If a student misses a word, the teacher returns to the beginning of the alternating pattern, presenting one review word and then presenting the missed word again. Returning to the beginning of the alternating pattern sequence is very important, since it increases the likelihood of student success and, at the same time, provides needed practice. If a student misses a word and the teacher does not return to it soon, an instructionally naive student would probably miss the word when it reappeared later.

Later in the lesson, the teacher retests by calling on the student to identify the missed word. If the student misses the word again, the teacher uses the alternating pattern. If a previously introduced irregular word is missed more than once, it should be reintroduced in the next lesson and stressed in the discrimination format. For example, if students miss the word *put* several times in Monday's lesson, the teacher would reintroduce it in introductory and discrimination formats on Tuesday. *Put* would be heavily reviewed for the next several days.

## Selecting Examples

Irregular words should appear in word list exercises for at least three lessons before appearing in stories. For the first two lessons in which a new irregular word appears in the discrimination format, the other words should be dissimilar to the new word. For example, the first time the irregular word *said* appears in a discrimination list, the other words might be *fan, jump,* and *was.* None of these words is similar to *said.* Eliminating similar words reduces confusion errors. The third day that *said* appears, a similar word like *sad* would be included. Including *sad* in a list with *said* will ensure that the students identify the critical elements of *said* (the *a* followed by *i*).

Students will need lots of practice on irregular words. Each of the first 20 irregulars should be included in sight-word discrimination tasks for about 10 consecutive lessons and then should appear daily in either a word-reading exercise and/or a story for another 2 weeks. Thereafter, the word should appear at least each second or third day in a discrimination format or story.

## Supplementary Exercises

Students should receive enough practice to enable them to recognize higher-frequency irregular words at a glance. Teachers can use a variety of board games and card games in which students read the words. Board games can have the words written in spaces. The students play the game by picking cards, saying the word, and moving to the space that has the word. Figure 2.5.1 shows an example of what the board might look like.

Card games can be played with a deck composed of 40 cards that have irregular words on them. The same word appears on 5 cards. The cards are distributed evenly to the students playing. For a turn, a student puts her card face up on the table, says the word, and collects any other card that has that word. The object of the game is to get the most cards.

## Commercial Programs

### Introduction and Rate

The rate at which new irregular words are introduced varies from program to program

**FIGURE 2.5.1**

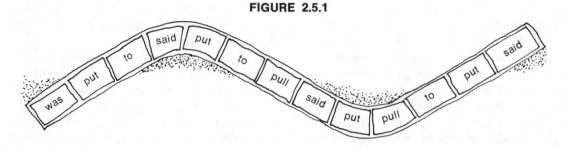

within both code- and meaning-emphasis programs. In the first 40 lessons of Scott, Foresman, we found 88 new irregular words; while in Ginn and Houghton Mifflin, there were only 29 and 24 new irregular words in the first 40 lessons. In the code-emphasis programs, Palo Alto included 13 irregular words among the first 40 lessons; while Lippincott introduced only 4 irregular words.

The rate at which irregular words are introduced has considerable significance for a teacher. The faster the rate of introduction, the higher the probability that some students will have difficulties. As mentioned earlier, when the students are learning their first seven irregular words, we recommend that a new irregular word not be introduced if students are having difficulty with any previously introduced irregular word.

Sometimes a program will introduce three to five irregular words at one time. If this is done during the beginning reading stage, the teacher should spread out the introduction of the words over several lessons, introducing the words according to their order of occurrence in passages.

## Teaching Procedure

The teaching procedures for irregular words are different in meaning-emphasis and code-emphasis programs. In meaning-emphasis programs, the procedure is the same as that described in Section 2.4 on decoding regular words. Students are encouraged to use the initial and final consonants, context, and pictures as cues.

In code-emphasis programs, students are usually not taught any specific strategy for decoding irregular words. The teacher simply points to the word, says it is a "funny word," and tells the students how it is pronounced.

The type of introductory format is not critical as long as it encourages students to look at all the letters. If students know letter names, the teacher can have the students pronounce the word and then spell it. The most important part of the teaching procedure for irregular words is providing adequate practice.

## Practice

Practice on irregular words occurs during word list reading and passage reading. Most programs do not provide for adequate word list drill on irregular words. We recommend providing increased word list reading exercises to review irregular words.

Provision for reviewing irregular words in passages is adequate in all but one program, Scott, Foresman. Scott, Foresman reviews new irregulars for several lessons, but after that time, often the words do not appear again for weeks. If a program does not provide adequate review of words in passages, the teacher should provide for extra word list practice.

Keep in mind that only common, high-frequency irregular words need be reviewed. Less common irregular words (e.g., *alligator, tiger, dinosaur*) will appear in early stories in order to make the stories more interesting to the students. Such words do not need to be reviewed unless they appear in later passages.

---

**RESEARCH**

We found no research directly related to teaching irregular words. The research questions are numerous. One is the importance of the procedure of having students sound out the first several irregular words that are introduced.

Although our experience suggests that the procedure is useful, an experimental comparison of various introductory procedures would be helpful, including sight reading and using context cues. Other questions involve amount of practice. How much word list training is necessary for accurate and rapid reading? How proficient should students be on previ- ously introduced words before new irregular words are introduced? Hopefully, research can be conducted to answer these questions.

## APPLICATION EXERCISES

1. Assume that a group of students knows the most common sound for all individual letters and the most common sound for the following letter combinations: *ai, ar, au, aw, ay, ch, ck, ea, ee, er, igh, oa, oi, oo, or, ou, oy, sh, th,* and *ur.* Underline every letter that the students will not be able to decode (see the chart on the inside front cover).

| | | | | |
|---|---|---|---|---|
| haul | stoop | greed | stork | son |
| aunt | burst | pour | horn | con |
| fault | hurt | pound | cent | mind |
| sprawl | churn | soup | can't | tin |
| spray | hood | group | rust | gun |
| play | spoon | grouch | fill | gin |
| boil | hook | park | want | rim |
| joy | said | warn | pant | test |
| boat | again | bread | an | |
| broad | gain | cheap | any | |
| cloak | need | steak | both | |
| pool | been | read | bob | |

2. The words in an irregular word discrimination task are *said, last, sick,* and *was.* Below are three sequences of examples a teacher presented to different groups. A minus (−) indicates an error. A plus (+) indicates a correct response. Tell whether each sequence is acceptable. Explain what is wrong with the unac- ceptable sequences.
   a. said +   last +   sick +   was −   (teacher corrects)
   b. said +   last +   sick +   said +
   c. said −   (teacher corrects)   last +   said +   was +
      said −   (teacher corrects)   last +   said +   sick +
      last +   said +

3. Below are the words a teacher presented in the discrimination word exercises during a 3 day period that followed the introduction of *said.* For each teacher, tell if the teacher followed the guidelines on page 122 when selecting examples appropriately. If not, specify the error made.

   *Teacher 1*
   Day 1—said, Sid, sad, do, pull
   Day 2—said, was, sad, put, Sid
   Day 3—said, to, sad, was, pull, put

   *Teacher 2*
   Day 1—said, has, was, to
   Day 2—none, do, put, pull
   Day 3—said, was, pull, push

   *Teacher 3*
   Day 1—said, was, put, push
   Day 2—said, push, put, do
   Day 3—said, was, Sid, sad, put

4. Put a check next to each of the six irregular words below that would not warrant frequent review during the first year of decoding instruction.

knob    was      scent
your    scenic   see
said    good     route
any     of       talk
pry     scarce   they

5. Assume that you have taught a group of students the following skills: Letter-sound relationships:

a, i, o, u, b, c, d, f, g, h, l, n, m, r, s, t, w

How to decode these word types: VC, CVC, and CVCC words

a. Circle each of the following words that the students would not be able to decode. Next to each of those words write the letters for the explanation below that tells why the student could not decode the word:
Letter (L)—A letter the students do not know appears in the word.
Word Type (WT)—The word type has not been taught.
Irregular (I)—The word is irregular.

_____cop        _____tin        _____spot       _____drug
_____said       _____test       _____mad        _____kept
_____last       _____bust       _____sip        _____sand
_____gram       _____was        _____can't      _____Stan
_____must       _____gin        _____don't      _____big
_____had

b. The errors for each of the two students below are listed. For each student (1) diagnose the problem, (2) specify whether an isolated letter-sounds task is called for, and (3) construct an introductory list (3 words) and a discrimination list (6 words) to remediate the problem. Be sure to include only letters the students have been taught.

*Student A*
errors: The word was *tin,* student said "tun."
        The word was *sit,* student said "sat."
diagnosis: _____

sound task:  yes _____    no _____

examples for introductory list _____

examples for discrimination list _____

*Student B*
errors: The word was *land,* student said "lad."
        The word was *fist,* student said "fit."
diagnosis: _____

sound task:  yes _____    no _____

examples for introductory list _____

examples for discrimination list _____

6. The teacher is presenting a discrimination sight-reading format which includes irregular words. A student says "sad" for *said.* Specify what the teacher would do and the wording the teacher would use to correct the student's error when it occurs and then tell what the teacher would do after making the correction.

# SECTION 2.6

## *Passage Reading*

Students are taught to read words in lists to prepare them for passage reading, which is the most critical decoding activity. Passage-reading exercises should be introduced as soon as students can decode enough words so that a teacher can present simple phrases. For the first 10 to 20 lessons in which passage reading occurs, the teacher should require students to sound out words. After that, sounding out can be faded, and students can read the stories saying each word at a normal rate without verbally sounding them out. Teachers must keep in mind that verbally sounding out words is a beginning step that must be faded. Delaying its fading too long may result in students' developing an overreliance on sounding out which, in turn, may lead to slow, laborious decoding.

Sounding-out passage reading is initially useful for many students. Teachers cannot assume that students who sound out words printed on a board will automatically transfer the skill to words in passages. Some students who perform well in sounding out word list exercises with the teacher point-ing to each letter may have difficulty transfering the skill to passage-reading exercises. In passage reading, students no longer say each sound as the teacher touches a letter but must themselves coordinate touching each letter with saying each sound. The transition from sounding out words in lists to sounding out words in passages and then from sounding out passages to sight reading passages must be made with great care.

The most important aspect of teaching passage reading is to provide the students with sufficient practice for them to read accurately and rapidly. Students differ considerably in the amount of practice they will need to become proficient readers. At first, instructionally naive students may need five times the amount of practice that average students need to read with satisfactory speed and accuracy. However, if teachers provide adequate practice, they will find that student performance will improve significantly, and gradually, the amount of practice students need will decrease.

# Sounding Out Passages

## Direct Instruction Procedures

### Preskills

Sounding-out passage reading can be introduced after the students can sound out continuous-sound-beginning CVC words in lists at the rate of a word each 3 seconds (usually 1 to 3 weeks after word list reading begins). Providing students with the practice needed to read word lists at this rate makes sounding out words in passages easier.

### Teaching Procedures

We recommend that students respond in unison, saying each sound as they move their fingers from letter to letter. Requiring students to respond in unison and to touch each letter ensures that they apply the sounding-out strategy when reading the words and serves to keep students attentive. Such a procedure is especially important with instructionally naive students, who tend to be very distractible. The touching procedure and unison responding also make monitoring easier, since they enable the teacher to more easily see and hear students respond.

The format below specifies that students should reread a passage until they are reading accurately and rapidly. The practice required to become fluent is critical. Students who can sound out words in a passage accurately and at the specified rate on the first reading need not read the passage over and over. On the other hand, students who read slowly or inaccurately should practice a passage until they can read accurately at the specified rate. The rate we recommend is reading one letter each second and beginning the next word in a sentence within 2 seconds.

## Critical Behaviors

### Signaling

Since the students are looking at their copies of the passage and not at the teacher, the signal for unison responding must be audible. Students cannot look at the passage and simultaneously watch for the teacher's signal. The audible signal we recommend has two parts—a "Get ready" and a clap. The "Get ready" tells the students to prepare, and the clap indicates that they are to begin the response. The critical teacher behavior in making the signal effective is a consistent 1-second pause between the "Get ready" and the clap. Consistency is necessary so that students will be able to use the "Get ready" as an effective cue by expecting the clap 1 second after they hear "Get ready."

During the first days of passage reading, the students may need to sound out each word several times. To ensure that the repetitions are done quickly and with little confusion, the teacher must use a clear signal for instructing the students to return to the first letter of a word. He can do this by saying, "Again, back to the first letter of the word." After giving this instruction several times, it can be abbreviated to just, "Again."

### Monitoring

The monitoring techniques used in unison story reading are somewhat similar to those a teacher uses in word list exercises. He spends about two-thirds of the time monitoring lower-performing students in the group and one-third of the time monitoring higher-performing students. Lower-performing students are seated in the middle of the group, and the higher-performing students, on the sides. This seating arrangement makes monitoring lower-performing students easier.

As in word list reading, the teacher watches the students' mouths and notes

## Format for Sounding-Out Passage Reading

| *Teacher* | *Students* |
|---|---|
| 1. Teacher tells students to touch the first word. **"Everybody, touch the first word."** | Students point below the first letter in the word. |
| Teacher checks to see if students are pointing appropriately. | |
| 2. Teacher tells students how to read the story. **"We are going to read by sounds. When I clap, say a sound. Keep on saying it until I clap again, then move your finger and say the next sound. Don't stop between sounds."** | |
| 3. Teacher signals for students to sound out and identify the first word. **"Get ready."** Teacher pauses 1 second and claps at 1-second intervals for each sound in the word. | Students say sounds, pointing to the letters as they identify them. |
| Step 3 is repeated until the students sound out the word without an error. Then the teacher says, **"Say the word."** | Students say the word at a normal rate. |
| 4. Teacher signals for students to touch the next word. **"Next word."** | Students put finger under first letter of next word. |
| Teacher pauses 1 second and claps at 1-second intervals for each sound in the word. | Students say sounds, pointing to the letters as they identify them. |
| After students sound out the word without any errors, the teacher asks, **"What word?"** | Students say the word at a normal rate. |
| Teacher repeats step 4 with the remaining words in the sentence. | |
| 5. Teacher has students reread sentence if any error was made on a word or if students could not respond at a rate of a word each 5 seconds. | |
| 6. Teacher repeats steps 3–5 with the next sentences. | |
| 7. Teacher calls on students to read individually. Each student reads a sentence or two. The teacher does not have to signal. | Other students point to the letters as the student who is reading says them. |

if lip movement is appropriate for each sound. For example, if a student's lips do not come together at the end of the word *ham,* the teacher knows that the student made an error—to say the word *ham,* the lips must be pressed together for the final sound. The teacher also watches student's fingers, noting if the student is pointing to the appropriate letter.

Individual turns are also used to monitor students' performance. As a general rule, individual turns should not be given until the group has read the passage in unison with no errors at a rate of one word each 5 seconds. Individual turns serve as a check to see if the students are actually participants in the group reading (Students often become quite good at mimicking other students rather than actually reading.) and to see if the teacher has provided the students with enough practice. During individual turns, the teacher does not have to give a signal. The students who are not reading should follow along, touching the letters as a student reads. Since the teacher can hear the responses of the student who is reading, she watches the eyes and fingers of the other students who are following along. The students who are not reading are more likely to be inattentive. Each student should read at least one or two sentences daily.

### Correcting Mistakes

Initially, some students will have difficulty following the signal for shifting from letter to letter. The teacher corrects by using a model (one of the students who is responding correctly) and, if necessary, by leading (moving the student's finger from one letter to the next). Note that students who have learned to respond to the clapping signal in the auditory preskill task, in which the teacher says a word and the students segment it into its component sounds, will probably not have much difficulty with the clapping signal. Even so, some instructionally naive students may initially require 20

to 30 repetitions before they respond to the signal by touching and saying the next letter.

If students have difficulty responding to a one-clap-each-second rate or moving from word to word, the teacher should slow the pace, clapping every 1 1/2 seconds for each sound. After reading a sentence at this slower pace, the students should then reread the sentence at the more rapid pace. They read each sentence until they read it at a pace of about a word every 5 seconds. (3 seconds to sound out the word and 2 seconds to move to the next word).

Students may *misidentify a sound or word.* The correction is similar to that specified in the word list reading section (pages 102–03). The instant the teacher hears an error, he models the correct sound or points to the letter, asks, "What sound?" and tests by having the students sound out the word again. As the final part of the correction, the teacher has the students return to the beginning of the sentence and reread the sentence or has the students finish the sentence and then reread it. The purpose of rereading the sentence is to demonstrate to the students that the teacher places a great importance on reading a passage accurately. If teachers have high expectations, students will quickly learn to read accurately. At the end of the story, the teacher retests words missed during passage reading.

# Sight Reading Passages

## Direct Instruction Procedures

### Preskills

Sight reading the words in passages can be introduced after students are able to sound out a story at a rate of about one word each 5 seconds on the first reading of the story. Some students may need only a few days of practice at sounding out passages before they are ready to sight read passages. Other students may require weeks of practice. Providing the practice needed to become proficient at sounding out is critical if students are to successfully make the transition from sounding out to sight reading.

## Teaching Procedures

In sight reading stories, students just say the word after the teacher signals. They do not sound out the word vocally. To facilitate the transition from sounding out to sight reading passages, the teacher has the students first sound out a passage and then sight read the same passage. After a week or two, sounding out a passage the first time through can be dropped. After that time, sounding out is used only in corrections.

As mentioned earlier, the critical aspect of passage reading is providing the students with adequate practice to develop fluency. However, teachers must be careful since providing unneeded practice for higher-performing students can result in their becoming bored. On the other hand,

providing too little practice for lower-performing students will result in their not developing the fluency prerequisite for success in later grades.

The sight reading procedure spelled out here is designed to help the teacher use the students' performance as the key indicator regarding the amount of practice needed on a particular passage. Note that the instructions call for the students to reread a sentence when they are unable to read it at an acceptable rate.

The acceptable rate starts out quite low and increases gradually. During the first 2 weeks of sight reading, an acceptable rate might be a word each 3 seconds (20 words per minute). After the first 2 weeks, the rate should increase to a word each 2 seconds (30 words per minute). After about 2 months of sight reading, the rate would increase to a word each 1 1/2 seconds (45 words per minute). Even though the emphasis during the beginning reading stage is on accuracy, teachers must be sure to give students the practice to gradually develop fluency.

The format we suggest involves dividing a passage into three-sentence units. The

---

**Format for Sight Reading Passages**

| *Teacher* | *Students* |
|---|---|
| 1. Students read first three sentences in unison. | |
|    a. Teacher gives instructions for unison responding. **"We are going to read this story a word at a time. Each time I clap, you say a word. Then quickly move your finger to the next word and figure it out."** | |
|    b. Teacher conducts unison reading on the first sentences. **"Touch the first word."** | Students put fingers below the first word. |
|    Teacher checks students' pointing. After a pause to enable students to figure out the word, the teacher says, **"Get ready,"** pauses a second, then claps. | Students say the word and then point to the next word. |
|    Teacher pauses to let students figure out the next word and then says, **"Get ready,"** pauses | |

**Format for Sight Reading Passages (*continued*)**

| *Teacher* | *Students* |
|---|---|

1 second, and claps. This procedure is repeated for the rest of the words in the sentence.

c. Students reread the sentence if they missed a word or if they read too slowly. Teacher repeats rereading of sentence until students read it at the appropriate rate for that lesson and make no errors. (An appropriate rate is a word each 3 seconds during the first 2 weeks of sight reading, a word each 2 seconds during the next 8 weeks, and then a word each 1 1/2 seconds thereafter for the remainder of the beginning stage.)

d. Teacher repeats steps b and c with the next two sentences.

e. If the students had to reread any sentence more than one time, the teacher has students reread all three sentences repeating the procedure in steps b and c.

2. Teacher asks comprehension questions about what was just read.

3. Teacher has students read remaining sentences in sets of three, following the procedure in steps 1 and 2.

4. Students practice reading the passage to themselves. **"Now I want you to read the story to yourselves."**

Students read the story silently.

Teacher should watch the students to make sure they are actually reading. Students who finish early should read the story again.

5. Teacher calls on students to read individually. **"No you get a turn to read by yourself. If it is not your turn, follow along and read to yourself. If the person reading makes a mistake, quietly raise your hand at the end of the sentence."** Teacher calls on individuals to read a sentence or two.

Other students follow along.

6. Students who did not read acceptably in the individual turn reread the story later. The teacher should schedule an additional 10- to 15-minute practice period for these students at a different time. During this session, the teacher would have the students reread the story following the procedure in the format.

students read each unit in unison until they are able to read it without errors at the rate appropriate for the particular lesson. Comprehension questions are asked after they read each unit acceptably. After the story is completed the students read silently. A final activity, which serves as a reward, is individual reading. The teacher uses student performance during individual reading to note who needs more practice. This practice should be provided later in the day.

## Critical Behaviors

### Finding the First Word

Since students will often have to reread a sentence several times, the teacher will want to teach students to find the first word in the sentence they have just read. This skill cannot be taken for granted. If students have difficulty returning to the first word in a sentence, much valuable instructional time will be lost. During the first weeks of sight reading, teachers should spend several minutes each day teaching students how to find the beginning of a sentence. One procedure would be to have each student keep the index finger of his left hand on the first word of the sentence while pointing to the words being read with the index finger of his right hand. The index finger of the left hand would always mark the first word in the sentence.

### Monitoring

The procedures for monitoring unison responding during sight reading are the same as used during sounding out: listen carefully to the students' response, check whether the students are pointing to each word, and watch their lips and eyes. The procedure for individual reading is slightly different.

### Pacing

When students begin sight reading passages, the teacher should allow adequate time to figure out the word. She can tell when the students have figured out a word by watching their lips as they say the word to themselves. It is important not to rush students during the early stages of sight reading, since doing so may result in guessing behavior. If students need longer than what is acceptable at that particular lesson to read any word in a sentence, the teacher has the students reread the sentence. (Teachers should allow for longer pauses for words that occur at the beginning of a new line of print, since students must move their fingers down to the next line and back to the left side of the page to locate the next word.)

### Signaling and Pacing in Individual Reading

No signals are necessary during individual reading since the students are not responding in unison. However, students who are not reading aloud should point to each word as it is read.

The teacher calls on students in an unpredictable order. If students can predict when they will be called on to read, some are likely not to attend until it is almost their turn. Others may look ahead to find "their" sentence and practice it. Sometimes inattentive students should be called on to read again after only one other student has read. This indicates to students that even though they may have just finished a sentence, they cannot become inattentive because they might be called upon again soon. Also students should read only one or two sentences in a row, since the longer one student reads, the greater the probability that some other students will become inattentive. Likewise, the more inattentive the students in a group, the fewer the number of consecutive sentences any one student should read.

Students should be instructed to stop at periods in order to read in more meaningful units. The pause also enables the teacher to call on a new student to read. *The teacher calls on the new student immediately after one student says the last word of a sentence.* This quick pace enhances student attentiveness and maintains story continuity.

### Correcting Mistakes

The two basic types of errors are the same ones students make when sight reading words in lists: misidentification errors, in which the response is wrong or unintelligible, and late responses, in which some students respond after the rest of the students. An occasional late response caused by inattentiveness may be ignored. Consistent late responding caused by inattentiveness must be corrected by increasing motivation. If a student who *is* attending responds late, the teacher assumes the student needs more practice on the word. No immediate correction is needed. The teacher simply has the group reread the sentence.

The correction for misidentification errors on regular words involves a limited model. Upon hearing the error, the teacher points to the missed letter in the word, asks the student, "What sound?" and then asks the student to figure out the word. For example, if a student said "fad" for *fat,* the teacher points to *t* and asks "What sound? . . . So what word?"

The correction procedure for misidentification errors on irregular words is different than the procedure for regular words. A simple correction of telling the student the irregular word is recommended during story reading because lengthy explanations or sounding out may disrupt the flow of the story. Words that are missed should be reintroduced the next day in word list

reading exercises and included in the word lists for several days thereafter.

### Motivation

Note that all the teaching procedures call for students to reread the sentence if a word is missed. Providing such practice is necessary for students to read a passage fluently and accurately. However, teachers must be prepared to use a combination of techniques to keep students from viewing reading as a dull, repetitive task. Teachers are challenged to provide practice in a manner that is interesting to the students and makes them like reading.

One important way teachers can do this is by treating the rereading as a challenge and rewarding the students for meeting it. If students need to reread a sentence, the teacher challenges them to read better. For example, the teacher might say, "Let's read this sentence again. You did pretty well. I bet you'll do it perfectly this time." Phrasing the challenge positively is important, since it contributes to a positive attitude toward reading. For students who require several rereadings before reading a sentence acceptably, physical rewards like handshakes, tickles, and pats should be given as well as verbal praise. When rewarding students, the teacher comments on their persistence, for example, saying "Good reading, you worked hard and didn't give up. I'm proud of you." In addition to using challenges and rewards, teachers can keep rereading from being boring by inserting short breaks after each 5–10 minutes of reading. During the break, the teacher can conduct an enjoyable game like "Simon-Says" for about 30 seconds or a minute.

## Diagnosis and Remediation

As the students read the story, the teacher should note errors on her copy of the passage. If students misidentify a word, the teacher can write the letter for the sound said above the letter in the word. For example, if a student said "but" for *bit* the teacher would write a *u* over the letter *i* in *bit*. She would also write the initial of the student who missed the word.

The words missed during passage reading should be included in the word list drill as part of the follow-up activity and as part of the presentation for the next days' lessons. In addition, the teacher should examine errors for patterns that might indicate a weakness on a particular skill. After completing a diagnosis based on passage-reading performance, the teacher should construct remediation exercises. Note that not all errors indicate a skill deficit. Students will sometimes make errors that are not caused by a particular skill deficit, but rather by inattentiveness or overreliance on context. We call these context errors. In a context error, the word the student says makes sense in the sentence but is not visually similar to the printed word. Although reliance on context is an important strategy in mature reading, it can be dangerous for a beginning reader. The beginning reader must first learn to attend to the letters and letter combinations that make up a word. Below are examples of context mistakes made by a student in reading a passage. The student's errors are written in parentheses.

The sad pup sat on a cup (cat).

The sad pup is big, but it cannot sit (stand) on a little dot.

Note that in both sentences, the missed words (*cup* and *sit*) were made up of letters the student identified correctly in previous words (*u* and *p* from *pup* and *i* and *t* from *it*). We can thus rule out letter-sound correspondences as the cause of the error. Likewise, both words are types the student decoded correctly earlier in the lesson (CVC), so we can rule out word-type difficulty as the cause. Since both mistakes involve the student's saying words that make

sense in the context of the sentences, we assume they are context errors. All students can be expected to make occasional context errors. However, if they begin to make numerous context mistakes, especially during the first year of reading instruction, the teacher should slow the rate at which students are reading and reward students for reading accurately.

The difference between mistakes that indicate a skill deficit and mistakes that do not is illustrated further in Figure 2.6.1, which shows the errors a student might make in reading a passage individually. Student's errors are noted in parentheses. Specific remediation procedures for diffent types of errors are also illustrated.

If a student frequently responds late, the teacher slows down the pace, giving students more time to figure out a word instead. After having the students read a passage at the slower rate, the teacher has the students reread the passage at the faster rate. (If only one student is having difficulty reading at the appropriate rate, teachers should consider either providing extra practice for the student or moving the student to a lower group.)

## Selecting Examples

The introduction of words into passages should be carefully coordinated with the introduction of letters and word types into the word list exercises. The guidelines for selecting words for stories are basically the same as selecting words for lists.

1. The words should contain only letters and word types that the students have been taught.
2. Systematic practice on new letters, new word types, and irregular words must be provided. For the first 2 weeks after a new word type is introduced in passage reading, the passages should contain many words of that type. For example, after words that begin with consonant blends are introduced, passages should

**FIGURE 2.6.1**    *Sample Errors in Passage Reading*

*Student A*—Letter-sound correspondence difficulty

"My hat is on the peg (pig)," said Tom. . . . "Ten (tin) hats are on it." . . . "If it is on (in) it, he will find the hat."

*Diagnosis*

The students two errors on words with *e* indicate a weakness on the *e* letter-sound correspondence. The other error, saying "in" for *on* does not indicate any specific skill deficit, since the student correctly identified other words containing the letter *o*.

*Remediation*

Present introductory and discrimination isolated letter-sound correspondence tasks, treating *e* as a new letter.

Present an introductory word list exercise with several words that contain *e*. Then present a discrimination list focusing on *e*. Some of the words should be minimally different (e.g., *beg* and *bag*). When a student encounters words with *e*, use a precorrection (Tell student the sound before asking him to identify the word.). Continue using precorrection until the student's confusion is remediated. Also include *on* in the discrimination list.

*Student B*—word-type difficulty

Ramon sat next to the tiger, which had a bed (bled) up on the deck. Ramon had fled (fed) from him without any (an) one's seeing.

*Diagnosis*

One error involves the student's adding a consonant sound (forming a blend) while the other error involves leaving out a consonant (destroying a blend). Such errors tend to indicate a weakness on words with initial blends.

The error on *any* indicates that the student may not know the irregular word *any*.

*Remediation*

Present word list exercises on words beginning with initial blends. Since errors seem to indicate confusion on the /l/ sound, the discrimination list should contain some minimally different word pairs formed by adding *l* to CVC words, e.g., *clap-cap, slip-sip, fled-fed*. Reintroduce *any* as a new irregular word. Include *any* in the discrimination word list exercise for several lessons.

contain many examples of that word type. An excerpt from a story that appears about a week after CCVCC words are introduced might be similar to this (the CCVCC words are underlined.): "A skunk went by a tramp and left a big stink. The tramp ran as swift as the wind. 'I can't stand that bad blast,' he said." Likewise, shortly after a new letter is introduced, the passages should contain quite a few words with that letter.

3. More common irregular and regular words should appear often. The more common words should be systematically reviewed, appearing several times in a story for the first week or two after they are introduced and, thereafter, at least each second or third day. The purpose of their recurrence in stories is to help students learn to recognize them at a glance.

During the first weeks of passage reading, the passages students read should contain only words that have previously appeared in word list exercises. Including previously taught words will help make the transition from word list reading to sounding-out passage reading easier. The length of passages should be controlled so that teachers can complete passage reading in 15 to 20 minutes of instruction.

Initially, the passages should be very short, containing only 2 to 4 words. As mentioned earlier, the teacher should expect to correct some students many times when passage reading is introduced. If the initial passages are too long, students may find passage reading too frustrating. The length of the passage should increase gradually, by a word or two each lesson. At the end of the first months of passage reading, passages should be approximately 25 words long. Passage length increases daily until stories are about 70 words long by the end of the second month, 110 words long at the end of the third month, and 150 words long at the end of the fourth month.

Early stories should be designed so that the students are likely to attend to the letters in the words and nothing else. Consequently, picture cues should be avoided because some students will try to use them as an aid in decoding words. A student might look at the first letter in a word and then look at the picture to find an object whose name starts with that letter. For example, a student might begin reading, "Tim had a . . . ," and then, not knowing the /o/ sound in the next word, *rock,* look at the picture for help in figuring out the word. If the picture shows a child sitting on a rock, the student is likely to use the picture as a cue for decoding the word. An effective way to avoid problems with pictures is to construct pages so that pictures appear only at the end of the passage. The students see the picture after they read the passage.

The print size in early stories should be large so that students can put their fingers under each letter. In addition, teachers should make sure that the print used in word list exercises is the same as in stor-

ies. The letters *g* and *a* have two printings each: a and a, g and g. The same printing should be used in stories and in board exercises.

## Commercial Programs

Most commercial programs examined had one or more of the following characteristics that might hinder student performance:

1. No instruction in sounding out
2. Early introduction of passage reading
3. Encouragement of picture and context cues
4. Inappropriate use of individual turns and silent reading

As mentioned earlier, we recommend that the teacher conduct the first passage-reading exercises using a sounding-out procedure. This recommendation assumes that the teacher is using a code-emphasis program.

Obviously, it would be inappropriate to use sounding out with meaning-emphasis programs, since so many of the words are irregular. In code-emphasis programs, however, we recommend using a sounding-out strategy, since it requires students to examine words in a left-to-right, letter-by-letter progression. However, the teacher must not continue sounding out too long. As soon as students become adept at it (sounding out words at a rate of one each 5 seconds), they should discontinue sounding out and begin sight reading.

Most programs introduced passage reading on the same lesson in which word list reading was introduced. For most students, the early introduction of passage reading should present few problems, since they will probably have little difficulty mastering sounding out words in lists. Teachers working with instructionally naive students, however, should not introduce passage reading until students can accurately sound out words in lists.

The teacher's guides in meaning-emphasis programs encourage students to use

## FIGURE 2.6.2

**Page 18**
**Picture Discussion**

Look at the big picture on this page.

What do you think Jan's mother might be saying?

How do you think Jan feels? Why?

**Point to the picture of Carla.** Who is this?

Who spoke first on this page?

Who spoke next?

Who spoke last?

**Silent Reading**

**Point to _nice_ in the first line of text.** Here is a word that is probably new for some of you. What letter does it begin with? . . . What other consonant do you see in this word? . . . When an _i_ or an _e_ comes right after the letter _c,_ the _c_ usually stands for a sound the letter _s_ stands for. Use those sounds to decide what word would make sense here.

**Point to _teeth_ in the third line of text.** Here's a word you may not have seen before. What consonant does it begin with? . . . You know the sound that _th_ stands for. When you come to this word, just think the sounds the letters stand for to help you decide what word would make sense in the sentence.

**Point to the commas in the first line of text.** Who can remember what this mark is called? . . . That's right. It is a comma and is used here to show who is being spoken to.

**Point to the comma in the second line of text.** Now look here. Here is another comma. This comma is used to show you that one word begins the sentence and there is a small pause between the first word and the rest of the words.

Now read this page to yourself and find out what Jan's mother said about Jan's smile.

**Oral Reading and Comprehension Checks**

Let's find out how well you read this page.

What did Jan's mother say about Jan's smile?

What did Jan's mother say Jan would have to do?

What did Jan say about her picture?

Will you read aloud what Jan and her mother said? . . .

**Have two pupils read the text aloud, with one reading Jan's lines and one reading what Jan's mother said.**

**Point to the word _nice._** What is this word?

How did you know it wasn't _fine?_   (wrong sounds)

How did you know it wasn't _nose?_   (no sense)

**Point to _teeth._** What is this word?

How did you know it wasn't _truth?_   (no sense)

How did you know it wasn't _hair?_   (wrong sounds)

Will you read what Jan and her mother said just the way you think they said these sentences? . . . Try to make Jan sound as sad as you think she sounded when she spoke. **Have two or more pairs of pupils read the page aloud. Try to get pupils to read with the proper inflection for the punctuation marks in each sentence.**

Do you think Jan will tell Carla about her problem?

You can find out. Look at page 19. **Show page 19 and point to the numeral 19.**

context and pictures as aids in decoding words. Before students read a page, the teacher usually asks a series of questions that the students answer by looking at a picture. The teacher also points out a new word and encourages students to use only one or two letters from the word to decode it. These procedures are illustrated in Figure 2.6.2 from the teacher's guide of a Houghton Mifflin first grade book. The teacher begins with a discussion of the picture. The discussion is followed by the teacher's pointing out several words. Students are encouraged to use context and one or two letters to figure out these words. Finally, the students are told to read the passage to themselves. After giving them time to read, the teacher asks comprehension questions and then calls on some students to read individually.

We feel that discussing pictures and story content before reading a passage is inappropriate for beginning readers (though the cues are appropriate with more mature readers). Since some students may begin to overrely on these cues and not rely on letter-sound correspondences as their main strategy in decoding, these cues should not be used until students are proficient at sight reading. If a teacher is using a program that has pictures containing obvious cues and if students seem to be looking for picture cues, the teacher can either rewrite stories on a Ditto or have students cover the pictures while reading the page. After the students read the passage, they are rewarded by looking at the pictures.

Maintaining a high level of student involvement in passage reading is critical. If students are not attending, they will not receive the practice required to develop proficient reading behavior. Unfortunately, the passage-reading procedures in many commercial programs do not encourage attentiveness. More often than not, just one or two students are called on to read a sentence, which is then discussed by the teacher.

We recommend not using individual turns and silent reading until students have decoded a segment of the story with unison responses. Comprehension questions should be asked only after students have demonstrated proficiency in decoding. Keep in mind that these suggestions pertain only to the beginning reading stage. In later grades, procedures for passage reading change; but in the beginning months of instruction, the emphasis is on letter-sound correspondence as the key to decoding.

In summary, passage reading can begin when students demonstrate mastery at sounding out easy word types. Students who quickly progress from sounding out words in lists to sight reading words in lists probably do not need to use sounding out when reading passages. Students who do not read words in lists as well should initially sound out words in passages. They should, however, make the transition to sight reading passages as soon as they are proficient at sounding-out passage reading. Since beginning readers should rely on the letters in words to decode them, the use of picture or context cues should be discouraged. Comprehension questions should be asked after students can accurately decode a segment of a passage. Unison reading procedures should be incorporated into early passage-reading exercises to facilitate active student involvement.

---

## RESEARCH

Research has been conducted on several aspects of passage reading: the importance of oral responding, reading rate, correction procedures, and the use of data. As discussed earlier, several researchers have reported superior performance in some aspect of reading as a result of oral reading, in contrast to silent reading (Keislar & McNeil, 1968; Neville, 1968).

### Reading Rate

Correlational evidence indicates that proficient readers read in phrases and multiple word units while less-skilled readers focus on single words or letters within words. Clay and Imlach (1971) found that the best readers read 7 words between pauses while the poorest readers read only 1.3 words between pauses. Taylor (cited in LaBerge & Samuels, 1974) reported that twelfth graders looked once or made one eye fixation for approximately every two words while first graders made about two fixations for each single word. A comprehensive comparison of three methods for instructing students

to read in units larger than single words was conducted by Dahl (in press). She compared single word recognition training, repeated readings, and hypothesis test training, in which students were trained to use context cues to predict the next word in a sentence. On various reading measures, Dahl found that the repeated readings and hypothesis test procedures produced significant gains but not isolated word drill. This finding points out the importance of providing sufficient passage-reading practice. Spache and Spache (1977) cautioned that repeated readings can be detrimental if better readers are required to follow along as less-skilled readers read. They cited eye movement studies that indicated students who followed along read with "more errors, poorer phrasing, and excessive fixations" (p. 249). To avoid this problem, we recommend that students read orally in unison and then silently before individual turns are given.

Although research suggests that rapid reading is important, research has not been conducted to determine what rates are optimal for students at various skill levels. This means that the rates suggested in this section are based on our experience and not on research findings. Research on optimal reading rates is very much needed.

### Corrections

Jenkins and Larson (1977) evaluated six correction procedures: *teacher supply* (in which the teacher said the word and the student repeated it), *no correction, sentence repeat* (the teacher said the word, the students finished the sentence, then the student reread the sentence), *end of page review* (the student read a list of missed words at the end of the page), *word meaning* (in addition to end of page review, word meanings were also provided and tested), and *drill* (same as *end of page review* except students had to identify all missed words twice in a row without any mistakes). On the next day, missed words were reread (in context and in isolation). All corrections tended to produce more accurate word reading than did *no correction*. Of the other corrections, *teacher supply* was the least effective. Only the *drill* procedure produced substantial or practically significant effects on subsequent word reading. This finding underscores the importance of follow up, in which the teacher provides practice on skill deficits. This finding was replicated for *drill* and *teacher supply* (Larson & Jenkins, 1977).

Grimes (1977) compared Jenkins and Larson's *drill* with a corrective feedback used by Hansen (1976), which consisted of six prompts; for self-correction, context cues, semantic cues, phonics cues (two different prompts), and teacher supply. *Drill* produced the greatest reduction in two types of errors, those that produced meaning change and those that did not.

### Data as a Monitoring Device

A third aspect of passage reading involves the use of data to monitor student performance.

> Research by Bohannon (1975), Jenkins, Mayhall, Peschka and Townsend (1974), and Mirkin (1977) has shown that the academic achievement of exceptional children is greater when their teachers obtain direct and daily performance measures and base their instructional decisions on these. In the best evaluation of a data-based instructional model to date, Mirkin (1977) compared children's oral reading improvement under four conditions: a) daily oral reading practice; b) daily practice plus goal setting; c) daily practice and goal setting plus daily measurement; and d) all previous components plus specific decision rules for making instructional changes. She found that under this last condition, wherein teachers systematically varied instruction in accord with the children's daily performance measurements, children showed significantly greater oral reading improvement than students in the other three conditions. (Jenkins, in press, p. 18).

## APPLICATION EXERCISES

1. Assume that a group of students knows the most common sound for all individual letters and the most common sound for the following letter combinations: *ai, al, ar, au, aw, ay, ch, ea, ee, er, igh, ing, oa, oi, oo, or, ou, oy, sh, th,* and *ur.* Underline every letter that the students will not be able to decode.

| | | | | |
|---|---|---|---|---|
| come | floor | cloak | pull | butter |
| chef | any | of | know | both |
| chest | an | stalk | Alex | painted |
| fault | went | from | wind | cheering |
| thread | soup | shed | bread | listen |
| cheap | find | color | work | brother |
| four | boot | want | for | jumping |
| strain | hood | suit | she | string |
| again | ton | cloud | folder | laugh |
| push | worm | torn | basket | was |
| weigh | steel | been | aunt | stinging |
| marsh | read | broad | hammer | hopper |

2. Assume that you have taught a group of students the following skills:
The most common sound for all single letters except *e, b, q, w, x, y,* and *z.*

How to decode these word types: VC, CVC, CVCC, and CCVC words

a. Circle each of the following words that the students would not be able to decode. Next to each of those words, write the abbreviation for the explanation below that tells why the student could not decode the word.

Letter (L)—The word is regular, but contains a letter that the students do not know.
Word Type (WT)—The word is a type that has not been taught.
Irregular (I)—The word is irregular.

| | | | | |
|---|---|---|---|---|
| fled _____ | list _____ | you _____ | nest _____ | hot _____ |
| clap _____ | stamp _____ | slam _____ | rump _____ | slug _____ |
| push _____ | bet _____ | was _____ | son _____ | stink _____ |
| led _____ | stop _____ | tint _____ | spot _____ | bent _____ |
| cut _____ | said _____ | snag _____ | free _____ | home _____ |

b. A teacher circled the errors students made when reading stories. The word above the circled word is what the student said. Your assignment is to first diagnose what skill the student needs help with and to specify what the teacher would include in the remediation exercise. Remember if a student has difficulty with a particular letter, include isolated sounds practice and a group of introductory (3 words) and discrimination words (6 words).

If the problem is with a word type, introductory (3 words) and discrimination words (6 words) are called for.

Be specific. List the examples you would include in the tasks. Be sure to include only letters students have been taught.

*Student 1*

              fat                     sap
Dan had a (flat) hat with a (snap) .

*Student 2*

              cot                                                           dad
Tim's hand had a (cut) on it. His mom did act fast. His mom is not a (dud) .

*Student 3*

         fat                   lip
Tam has a (fast) cat. It has a (limp) .

*Student 4*

Student four missed no words; however, he read quite slowly when given an individual turn. What would the teacher do?

3. In each story excerpt, the word circled was missed by a student. The error appears above the circled word. Write *c* over the circled words that were likely caused by context cuing (see page 134).

*Story 1*

                                    Hud
Hud is a big dog. Ann likes Hud. Tim likes (the dog) too.

*Story 2*

                                     him                    sot
Did it hit him on his hat? Did it hit (his) hand? I can't (spot) if it hit his hat or his hand.

*Story 3*

A bug sat in a tub. Fill it up <u>sat</u> (said) the bug.

4. Below are the words teachers presented in the discrimination word exercises during a 3-day period that followed the introduction of *where*. For each teacher, tell if the teacher followed the guidelines on page 122 when selecting examples appropriately. If not, specify the error made.

*Teacher 1*
Day 1—where   pull   do   of   were
Day 2—said   of   pull   sid   where
Day 3—where   to   said   pull

*Teacher 2*
Day 1—where   said   pull   come   none
Day 2—was   put   to   learn
Day 3—build   no   water   earth   push

*Teacher 3*
Day 1—where   said   off   put   come
Day 2—where   some   said   put   off
Day 3—where   was   were   pull   said

5. The teacher is having the students *sight* read the following passage.

  Sid was a sad bug.
  He was not big.

In the following situation, specify what the teacher would do and the wording the teacher would use to correct the student's error when it occurs.

a. During unison reading a student said "will" for *was.*
b. During unison reading a student responded late to *bug.*
c. During unison reading a student said "bug" for *big.*

# Vocabulary and Language Skills

Many beginning reading programs are written with the assumption that students have a fairly sophisticated knowledge of vocabulary and language skills. For such students, the teaching procedures in this section will not be necessary, even though comprehension instruction procedures discussed later will be. However, many students do not enter school with an adequate vocabulary and sufficient language skills. These beginning readers do not understand the meaning of many words commonly used in directions given by teachers, for example, find the letter *under* the *last* car, touch the *narrow stripe* in the first column, find the letter in the *lower right*-hand *corner.* For beginning reading students, instruction in basic vocabulary and oral language is needed if they are to succeed in reading instruction.

The vocabulary to be taught should include, at a minimum, the words that occur in teacher directions and that appear in student material in a reading program. Moreover, a language program should teach students to repeat sentences and to answer simple questions about orally presented sentences and passages.

We recommend presenting these vocabulary and language tasks *orally.* During the first year's reading instruction, students will understand and use many more words than they can decode. Limiting comprehension activities to only those words the students can decode is unnecessary and inefficient. All students, and especially instructionally naive ones, can benefit from oral instruction in basic language skills and vocabulary starting on the first day of instruction.

## Vocabulary Teaching

The procedures used to teach vocabulary are especially critical for teachers working with instructionally naive students. Teaching vocabulary to average and above-average students is relatively easy because these students have a good understanding of language and already have a sizable vocabulary. Instructionally naive kindergartners, on the other hand, often will not know many common words, will have difficulty repeating statements of more than four or five words, and often will be confused by demonstrations that are not absolutely clear.

Vocabulary can be taught orally in three ways: by the use of modeling, synonyms, and definitions. Here is an example of modeling: The teacher points to a brown crayon and says, "This crayon is brown," and to a crayon that is not brown and says, "This crayon is not brown." Modeling is used when verbal explanations of a new word would include words students do not understand. For example, when teaching the preposition *over,* the teacher cannot explain why something is over without using the term *over* or a synonym for *over* such as *above.* If the children do not know the meaning of *over,* the teacher presents examples of *over* and *not over.*

Modeling is used primarily to teach the word labels for common objects; actions; and color, shape, and size attributes. Many times, when students have learned this vocabulary before entering school, the modeling procedure has been used by their parents. When pointing to a dog, for example, a parent will say "Dog." If a child confuses a dog with a cat, the parent usually corrects by pointing to the cat and saying "No, not dog," and then pointing to a dog and saying "Dog."

The second procedure for vocabulary teaching is the use of synonyms, used when a student knows a word(s) that can be used to explain the meaning of a new, unknown word. For example, a student knows the word *over* but does not know *above.* Instead of introducing *above* through modeling positive and negative examples, the teacher just tells the student that *above* means *over,* and then tests the student on positive and negative examples to make sure he understands the synonym. Similarly, if a student knows the meaning of *wet,* the teacher can use *a little wet* to explain the meaning of *damp.* (Note: Initial synonyms do not have to be precise but must be designed to give students an approxi-

mate meaning that can be refined as they encounter the word in later reading.)

The third method for teaching new vocabulary during the beginning reading stage is by using definitions. This method is used when students have adequate language to understand a definition and when the concept is too complicated to be explained through a synonym. The teacher constructs a definition by specifying a small class to which a new word belongs and then telling how the word differs from other members of the class. For example, a simple definition of *service station* might be "a place where gasoline is sold and cars are repaired." Service station is in the class of *places.* It differs from other places in that gas is sold and cars are repaired there. After a definition is given, positive and negative examples are presented to test the students' understanding of the definition. Since definitions require knowledge of all words in the definition, this method is used only after students have developed a basic vocabulary.

## Teaching Vocabulary through Modeling

### Example Selection

The most important aspect of teaching vocabulary through modeling is selecting a set of appropriate examples. A set of examples is appropriate only if it is capable of teaching the student the meaning the teacher intends to present. When a student fails to understand a word being taught through modeling, it is more often than not because teachers use inappropriate examples. A set of examples may be inappropriate because it is too limited and does not give the student enough information to generalize to other instances of the word. For example, if the only examples for *pet* that a teacher ever presented were a dog and cat, some students would not generalize the word to other animals such as a goldfish and canary.

A set of examples may also be inappropriate because it causes students to learn an interpretation other than the one intended by the teacher; for example, a thick pen and a thick pencil presented as examples of *thick.* Since both these objects are writing tools, some naive students might interpret thick as having something to do with writing rather than with size.

Learning a vocabulary word implies applying it correctly to a set of examples. When a baby first learns the word *dog,* the baby may think that the word *dog* refers solely to the dog in his house. It is only through further experience that the child learns to expand his definition of dog to a whole set of dogs, many of which are quite different in appearance. To provide the opportunity for the same kind of learning to take place in the classroom, a teacher must provide enough positive examples of a new word to enable the student to respond to a full range of positive examples. We will illustrate with the words *pet* and *over.*

Selecting three to six examples that show the range of positive examples is the first step in constructing a set of examples for use in modeling. When teaching *pet,* the teacher could include these positive examples: dog, goldfish, canary, gerbil. Having this wide variety of positive examples rules out the student's misconstruing the concept of pet as being simply dogs or cats. When teaching the preposition *over* (as in "the pencil is over the table"), the pencil should not just be presented 12 inches above the center of the table since young children might learn that *over* has something to do with "in the middle" or a height of about 1 foot. To illustrate the full range, the teacher presents the pencil in many different positions, holding it an inch or two above the table, then several feet above, then over the left side, the right side, etc.

In addition to positive examples, an appropriate set of examples should also include negative examples. The purpose of the negative examples is to rule out incorrect generalizations. For example, if only positive examples of pet were presented (dog, cat, goldfish, canary), some students might generalize that all animals are pets. For each positive example, a negative example that is as similar as possible to the positive examples should be included in the set. The positive and negative examples will form a pair. Each pair of examples can be referred to as a minimally different pair. The purpose of using minimally different pairs is to focus student attention on the characteristics that determines whether or not an example is positive. The advantage of using minimally different pairs is illustrated in the examples below for teaching the color *orange* and the preposition *over.* A teacher might use these minimally different pairs of objects for teaching orange:

1. Two shirts exactly the same except one is orange and one is red.
2. Two pieces of paper, exactly the same except one is orange and one is blue.
3. Two plastic disks exactly the same except one is orange and one is brown.
4. Two crayons exactly the same except one is orange and one is green.

By varying just the color in each pair of objects, the teacher clearly demonstrates what characteristic is critical. Possible misinterpretations that orange has something to do with shape, texture, size, and pattern are ruled out. Likewise, students confusing orange with red is ruled out by including an example of red as a negative example.

Another example of using minimal differences is shown in Figure 2.7.1, which illustrates positive and negative examples of *over.* The circles indicate the position in which the teacher would hold an object in making the demonstration. The letters indicate the order in which the positive and negative examples are presented. Positions *A, D, E,* and *H* are positive examples of *over.* Positions *B, C, F,* and *G* are negative

**FIGURE 2.7.1**  *Positive and Negative Instances in Teaching* Over

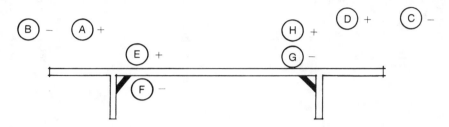

examples of *over.* The variety of positive examples is presented so that students can see the full range of positive values for *over.* The negative examples are presented so that students can see exactly when the object is no longer *over.* Minimal difference positions *A–B* and *C–D* point out that when the object is beyond the edge of the table, it is no longer over. Minimal difference positions *E–F* show that when the object is below the table top, it is not over. Minimal difference positions *G–H* show that when the object is on the table it is not over the table.

In modeling the examples of *over,* the teacher makes a dynamic presentation, which involves changing an object's position and modeling by saying, "The pencil is over" or "The pencil is not over." The use of a dynamic presentation in which just one object is used decreases the probability that students will become confused in thinking that a particular object, in this case a pencil, has something to do with *over.* Whenever possible, the same object or situation should be used initially to demonstrate positive and negative examples.

## Teaching Procedures

The basic procedure for using modeling involves three steps: (1) modeling positive and negative examples of the new word, (2) testing the students on their mastery of the examples for the new word, and (3) presenting examples of the new word along with examples of other previously taught words. As in decoding, review should be cumulative. Newly introduced words should be reviewed heavily at first, appearing daily for at least three or four lessons and then less frequently, every other day for a week or two and intermittently thereafter. Also, as is the case in introducing new decoding skills, the rate at which vocabulary words are introduced is dependent on the students' mastery of previously introduced words.

Table 2.7.1 demonstrates the similarity of formats for teaching basic vocabulary: objects, colors, adverbs, and adjectives. Each format has the three basic steps: model, test, and integrated test. Each format contains positive and negative examples and instructional wording. Note that the examples in each presentation were selected to show the range of positive examples and eliminate possible incorrect generalizations. For example, in teaching *mitten,* the positive examples vary in color and material. The purpose is to show that color and material are irrelevant to whether an object is a mitten. Also, minimally different positive and negative pairs are included, e.g., a mitten and a glove of the same size, material, and shape. Similarly, the positive examples of the color orange in Table 2.7.1 include a range of objects and minimally different positive and negative examples.

## Critical Behaviors

### *Modeling*

When modeling, examples must be presented at a rapid enough rate to keep

**TABLE 2.7.1** Formats for Teaching Vocabulary

| | OBJECT | ADJECTIVE (color) | ADVERB | ADJECTIVE (texture) |
|---|---|---|---|---|
| STEP 1 | *Teacher models positive and negative examples* Present three to six examples. | "This is a mitten" or "This is not a mitten." *Examples:* brown wool mitten brown wool glove red nylon mitten red nylon glove blue sock blue mitten | "This is orange" or "This is not orange." *Examples:* 2" red disk 2" orange disk 4x4" orange paper 4x4" brown paper | "This is writing carefully" or "This is not writing carefully." *Examples:* write on board, first neatly, then sloppily hang up coat, first carefully, then carelessly arrange books, first carelessly, then carefully | "This is rough." *Examples:* red flannel shirt red silk shirt piece of sandpaper piece of paper smooth book cover rough book cover |
| STEP 2 | *Teacher tests with yes-no question.* Present positive and negative examples until the students make six consecutive correct responses. | "Is this a mitten?" | "Is this orange?" | "Is this ____ carefully? | "Is this rough?" |
| STEP 3 | *Teacher tests by asking for names.* Present examples until students make six consecutive correct responses. | "What is this?" glove mitten sock mitten mitten glove | "What color is this?" orange brown orange red | "Show me how you ____ carefully." or "Tell me about how I'm writing?" (quickly, slowly, carefully, etc.) | "Find the ____ that is rough." or "Tell me about this shirt?" (rough, red, pretty, etc.) |

students attending. The teacher should present the examples in a lively fashion, stressing key words: "This *is* a mitten." . . . "This is *not* a mitten."

### Testing the New Word

The teacher must present the task until students are able to respond correctly to a group of at least three positive and three negative examples (six in all). It is only *after* students can make correct responses to all the positive and negative examples that a teacher can conclude that the students understand the new word.

## Teaching Vocabulary with Synonyms

Teaching new vocabulary through synonyms is similar to the procedure of modeling examples, except that the teacher first equates a new word (*huge*) with a known word(s) (*very big*) rather than modeling examples. The teacher would give the synonym ("Here's a new word, huge. Huge means very big."), rather than modeling examples ("This is huge. This is not huge."). Next, just as in the modeling format, the teacher provides a set of positive and negative examples of the new word and asks, "Is this huge?" The students answer yes or no. Third, the teacher provides practice in applying several recently taught synonyms: "Is this huge? Is this damp? Is this tiny? Find the one that is huge." The purpose of this review is to build retention. Without this drill, some students will not remember the synonyms for new words. The amount of practice the teacher provides depends on student performance. In general, a new word should appear daily for several consecutive lessons and then every other day for the next few days. Thereafter, the amount of review decreases.

## Example Selection

The selection of synonyms must be done very carefully. Students *must* understand the meaning of the familiar word since it is intended to "explain" the new word. It would be inappropriate to use the term *textile* to explain *fabric* because most students would not understand the synonym *textile.* On the other hand, using the synonym *strong* to explain *sturdy* is reasonable since most students know what *strong* means.

Teachers can find potential words to use for synonyms by referring to a dictionary or thesaurus. One or more of the words will probably be familiar to students and, thus, appropriate to use.

## Teaching Procedures

The following format illustrates synonym teaching with the word *sturdy.* The major steps include the teacher's presenting the synonym, testing positive and negative examples, and then reviewing the new word and previously introduced words. Keep in mind that the initial teaching of a word is not designed to demonstrate to the students how to use the word in everyday speech but to foster understanding of the new word during reading activities. Training in how to use the word in everyday speech should come only after students have heard the word used many times. Using a word correctly when speaking (called expressive language) is much more difficult than understanding it when someone else uses it or it appears in a printed passage (called receptive language).

## Critical Behaviors

### Correcting Mistakes

Mistakes are corrected by relating the new word to the familiar word. If a student says

## Format for Synonym Teaching

| *Teacher* | *Students* |
|---|---|

1. Teacher states the new word and the equivalent, familiar word and then tests.

   a. **"Here is a new word. Sturdy. Sturdy means strong."**

   b. **"What does sturdy mean?"** (signal) — "strong"

2. Teacher presents positive and negative examples until the students make six consecutive correct responses. Examples are not repeated in the same order.

   a. **"Tom leaned against a pole. The pole fell over. Was the pole sturdy?"** (signal) — "No"

   b. **"Tom leaned against another pole. The pole didn't move. Was the pole sturdy?"** (signal) — "Yes"

   c. **"A house didn't shake at all in a high windstorm. Was the house sturdy?"** (signal) — "Yes"

   d. **"A different house fell down when the wind started blowing. Was the house sturdy?"** (signal) — "No"

   Note: The teacher can also provide practice by asking the students to generate examples. **"Tell me about something that is sturdy."**

3. Teacher reviews new word and other words until students answer all questions correctly.

   a. **"Is it mild out today? How do you know?"**

   b. **"Is that bench sturdy? How do you know?"**

   c. **"Is my desk tidy? How do you know?"**

that the pole that fell over was sturdy, the teacher corrects by asking what *sturdy* means, by repeating the item using strong rather than sturdy, and finally by repeating the item as written.

1. "What does *sturdy* mean?" Student responds, "Strong."
2. "Tom leaned against a pole. The pole fell over. Was the pole strong." Student responds, "No."
3. "So was it sturdy?" Student responds, "No."

## Teaching Vocabulary with Definitions

The third procedure for teaching vocabulary is through definitions. Although definitions may be constructed in several ways, we will focus on a procedure that is applicable to most words. The procedure includes two steps:

1. Identifying a small class to which a word belongs

2. Stating how the word differs from other members of that class

In constructing definitions, teachers must be concerned with making them understandable to students rather than technically correct. For example, a liquid might be defined as something that you can pour. Although scientists might disapprove of this definition, it is adequate to teach the meaning of *liquid* to young children. Definitions are also kept understandable by using only words students know.

Some sample definitions appear below. Note the effort to keep them as understandable as possible.

1. Container—an object you can put things in.
2. Vehicle—an object that can take you places.
3. Seam—a place where two pieces of material are sewn together.
4. Glare—to look at someone as if you are angry.

Examples used to teach vocabulary by definitions must be carefully controlled. Just as in modeling, both positive and negative examples should be used, including minimally different instances. When selecting examples, teachers should not try to teach multiple meanings of a word but should first concentrate on the most common meaning. If a teacher tries to teach multiple meanings of a word when it is first introduced, young students may become

quite confused. The teacher would first concentrate on the main stage. Other usages of the word can be taught later.

## Teaching Procedures

The teaching procedure involves first telling the students the definition and having them repeat it. Next, the teacher tests the students on positive and negative examples. It is essential that they understand the definition and are not just memorizing a series of words that have no meaning for them. Understanding is indicated by the correct identification of positive and negative examples. Finally, review of previously taught words is included. The format below illustrates definition teaching with the word *exit*.

## Written Vocabulary Exercises

During the beginning reading stage, written vocabulary exercises usually involve students' selecting a word or phrase that defines a picture. A student may either (1) look at a picture and select a word, (2) read a word and select a picture, or (3) answer a question based on an attribute of the object illustrated in the picture. Each type of exercise is illustrated in Figure 2.7.2.

The simplest type of picture-related vocabulary item is multiple choice with one obviously correct alternative. Items increase in difficulty as more alternatives seem reasonable, even though only one

**FIGURE 2.7.2**

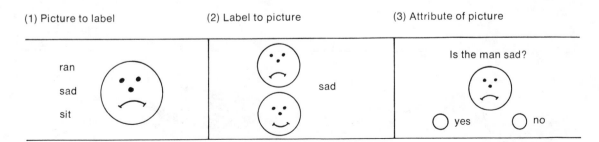

(1) Picture to label            (2) Label to picture            (3) Attribute of picture

## Format for Teacher Vocabulary with Definitions

| Teacher | Students |
|---|---|
| 1. Teacher states the new word and its definition and has students say definition. | |
|    a. **"An exit is a door that leads out of a building."** | |
|    b. **"What is an exit?"** (signal) | "A door that leads out of a building." |
| 2. Teacher presents positive and negative examples. | |
|    a. Teacher holds up a picture or points to a closet door. **"Is this an exit?"** | "No" |
|      **"How do you know?"** | "It doesn't lead out of the building." |
|    b. Teacher holds up a picture of a movie theater, points to door, **"Is this an exit?"** | "Yes" |
|      **"How do you know?"** | "It leads out of the building." |
|    c. Teacher continues presenting examples until the students answer five consecutive questions correctly. | |
| 3. Teacher reviews words recently introduced. | |
|    a. Teacher holds up picture of barracks. **"What is this?"** | "A barracks" |
|      **"How do you know?"** | "It's a building full of bunk beds." |
|    b. Teacher holds up picture of an exit. **"Is this an exit? How do you know?"** etc. | |

answer is correct. For example, a picture shows a young boy. The answers are: *boy, kitten, man.* A student may think that *man* is correct. However, the correct answer is *boy* because the person in the illustration is young. Vocabulary items are also more difficult when they ask about object attributes rather than object names. In Figure 2.7.3, item a, which involves naming an object, is easier than item b, in which the

**FIGURE 2.7.3**

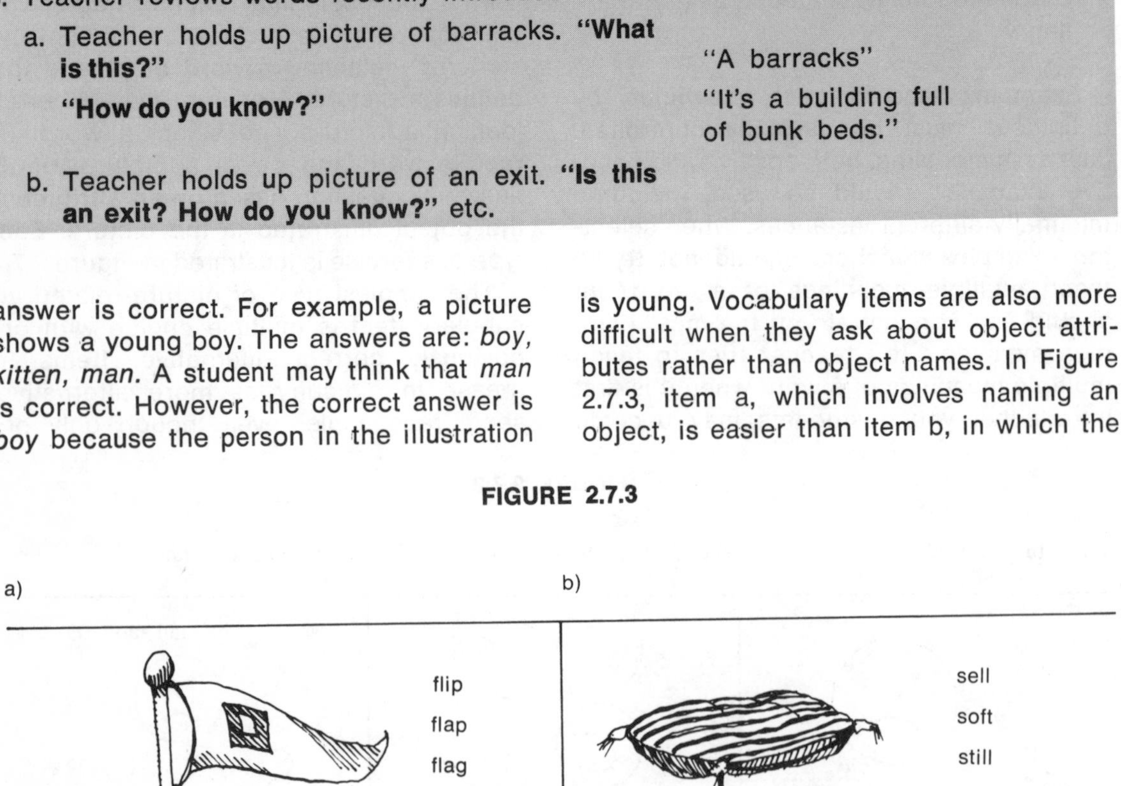

a)

flip
flap
flag

b)

sell
soft
still

students must identify an attribute of an object. In item b, the student must make the association between pillow and soft.

## Teaching Procedure for Object Labels

Many students will be able to work this simple type of picture-related item without any teacher guidance. Obviously, these students do not need the teaching procedure. However, instructionally naive students will benefit from being led through the steps outlined below. Students should be led through about five structured examples daily for several days. The items should include only words that are labels for objects. The teacher (1) asks the students what they see in the picture, (2) tells them to touch and read each word, and (3) asks if the picture shows that word. Students should be taught to examine all the choices in a multiple-choice exercise before selecting the correct answer. Doing so prepares them for more difficult items which contain more than one plausible answer.

The item for the format below includes a picture of a hat and the words *sad, sun, hut*, and *hat*.

## Teaching Procedures for Characteristics

A significant proportion of students will need direct teaching on items that involve object characteristics. For example, an item includes a picture of a pillow and the words *set, soft,* and *still.* The teacher first has the students say the name of the object in the picture and decode each word, asking if that word names the object. Next the teacher tells the students that since no word names the object, one of the words must tell about the object. The teacher has the students decode each word and asks, "Is a pillow _____?" Note that students must already know the vocabulary words used in the task. If necessary, vocabulary words should be taught before the written task is presented.

# Language Skills

Beginning language skills include statement repetition, sentence comprehension, and comparisons. Sentence comprehension involves teaching students to answer

---

**Format for Teaching Object Labels**

| *Teacher* | *Students* |
|---|---|
| 1. Teacher asks students about the picture. | |
|    a. **"Touch the first picture."** | Students touch picture of a hat. |
|    b. **"What do you see?"** | "A hat" |
| 2. Teacher asks students to touch and read the first word, then asks if the picture illustrates the word. | |
|    a. **"Touch the first word under the picture."** | |
|    b. **"What word?"** | "Sad" |
|    c. **"Does the picture show sad?"** | "No" |
|    d. **"So are you going to circle the word sad?"** | "No" |
| 3. Teacher repeats steps 2a–2d for the words *sun* and *hut*. | |
| 4. Teacher instructs students to circle correct word. | |

simple questions involving who, what, when, where, and why. Comparisons include expanding the notion of the concepts *same* and *different*. Although average and above-average students come to school with many of these oral language skills, instructionally naive students do not. They need oral language teaching during the early months of decoding instruction before comprehension exercises on written passages appear. Consequently, oral language training should begin very early in the school year.

## Statement Repetition

Statement repetition is an often-overlooked preskill for learning definitions and answering questions about statements. If students have difficulty saying a statement to themselves, they are likely to have difficulty understanding the intent of the sentence and answering questions about it. For example, if in the statement, The little girl is not running in the park with her big brother, the child leaves out the word *not,* the entire meaning of the sentence is changed. We are not claiming that students must remember a sentence verbatim to understand it. However, if a student cannot repeat a statement after two or three corrected repetitions, the student may have trouble answering comprehension questions based on short passages and even single sentences. Fortunately, relatively few students will have difficulty repeating statements. However, teachers need to be prepared to help students who do have difficulties.

Teachers should test statement repetition ability during the first school week by having students repeat several 6- to 10-word sentences. Daily practice on saying statements should be provided for students who have difficulty. Such practice should consist of short drills (3 to 5 minutes) in which students practice saying statements. Practice should start on sentences of a length slightly longer than those a student can say without error.

## Teaching Procedures

Providing sufficient practice is the key to improving statement repetition performance. When providing practice, the teacher first models by saying the statement and then tests by asking the students to repeat it. If the students are unable to say the statement, the teacher says it again, stressing deleted or mispronounced words. After three or four such corrections, the teacher notes how close the students are to saying the statement correctly. If they appear to need only a few more trials, the teacher continues modeling and testing. On the other hand, if the student needs many more trials, the teacher uses a *backward chaining* technique in which the teacher first models, leads, and tests on just the last part of the statement, then the middle plus the last part, and finally the entire statement. The final step in the format is modeling the statement in a normal speaking manner and testing the students on saying the statement in a normal fashion. Without this final step students may develop a stilted, singsong way of saying statements.

### Critical Behaviors

#### *Modeling and Pacing*

Each word in the sentence should be said at a normal pace. Teachers have a tendency to speak slowly in statement repetition tasks. We've found that, if anything, a slow model makes repeating the statement more difficult for the students.

The teacher leads the students until they appear to be able to say the sentence without assistance. After each leading trial, the teacher should pause about 2 seconds, say "Again," and then say the statement with the students. Too short a pause be-

**Format for Statement Repetition**

| Teacher | Students |
|---|---|
| 1. Teacher models and tests entire statement. **"Listen. The little cat is under the old table. Say that."** (signal) | "The little cat is under the old table." |
| If students cannot say the statement after several attempts, the teacher goes on to steps 2, 3, 4, and 5. | |
| 2. Teacher models, leads, and, tests on the last part of the statement and has students repeat it. **"Listen. The old table. Say it with me."** (signal) **"The old table."** | "The old table." |
| **"Say it by yourselves."** (signal) | "The old table." |
| 3. Teacher models, leads, and tests on middle and last part of the statement. **"Listen. Is under the old table. Say it with me."** (signal) **"Is under the old table."** | "Is under the old table." |
| **"Say it by yourselves."** (signal) | "Is under the old table." |
| 4. Teacher models, leads, and tests saying the entire statement. **"Listen. The little cat is under the old table. Say it with me."** (signal) **"The little cat is under the old table."** | "The little cat is under the old table." |
| **"Say it by yourselves."** (signal) | "The little cat is under the old table." |
| 5. Teacher models and tests saying the statement at a normal pace. **"Listen. The litte cat is under the old table. Say it by yourselves."** (signal) | "The little cat is under the old table." |

tween each trial may confuse the students, while too long a pause may result in the students' becoming inattentive.

## Critical Behaviors

### Correcting Mistakes

When the teacher models the entire statement, some students may leave out a word. For example, the teacher says, "This ball is not big," but the student says, "This ball not big." The correction procedure is to model the statement again, stressing the word left out, "This ball *is* not big."

A second type of error involves mispronunciation. If the word is one or two syllables, the teacher corrects by stressing the missed sound. If the student said "ba" instead of "bat," the teacher says "ba*t*," stressing the final /t/ sound. If the student said "mid" instead of "mud," the teacher says "m*u*d," stressing the /u/ sound. If the word is more than two syllables, the teacher can use a backward chaining procedure: model, lead, and test on the last one or two syllables, then add one new syllable at a time. For example, in saying *skyscraper,* the teacher would say "er," then "scraper," then "skyscraper."

## Sentence Comprehension

### Introducing Question Words

Sentence comprehension begins with exercises to teach students to identify what happened in a sentence, who was involved, when the event happened, where the event occurred, and why the event occurred.

Students should be able to repeat five-to-seven-word statements (e.g., *The boy ran in the park. The girl hit the ball.*) before questions about sentences are introduced. If students cannot retain the information in a sentence long enough to repeat that sentence, they are unlikely to remember the information from the sentence needed to answer simple who or what did questions.

The rate for introducing new question words is determined by student performance. A new question word is not introduced until the students have mastered questions involving previously introduced question words.

### Sequence

Who and what did questions should be presented first because they are easiest. "John went to the store. Who went to the store?" "John." "What did John do?" "Went to the store." Where and when can be introduced next. How and why are introduced later because they are more difficult.

### Teaching Procedures

To introduce who and what did questions, first say a sentence, ask the questions, then model the answers.

---

**Format for Introducing Who and What**

| Teacher | Students |
|---|---|
| 1. Teacher models. **"John ran in the park. Who ran in the park? John. What did John do? Ran in the park."** | |
| 2. Teacher provides practice and tests. | |
| a. **"Listen. Tom fell off his bed. Say that."** (signal) | "Tom fell off his bed." |
| b. **"Who fell off the bed?"** (signal) | "Tom" |
| c. **"What did Tom do?"** (signal) | "Fell off the bed." |
| 3. Teacher repeats steps a–c with these sentences and questions: | |
| a. **Ann hit the ball.** | |
|     **Who hit the ball?** | "Ann" |
|     **What did Ann do?** | "hit the ball" |
| b. **The cat ate the food.** | |
|     **Who ate the food?** | "the cat" |
|     **What did the cat do?** | "ate the food" |
| c. **The dog jumped up and down.** | |
|     **Who jumped up and down?** | "the dog" |
|     **What did the dog do?** | "jumped up and down" |

**Format for Introducing When and Where**

| Teacher | Students |
|---|---|
| 1. Teacher models. | |
| a. **"I'll say phrases that tell *when*. Yesterday morning tells when. Last night tells when. Before it got dark tells when. After dinner tells when."** | |
| b. **"Now I'll say phrases that tell *where*. In the park tells where. At the beach tells where. On my chair tells where. Under the couch tells where."** | |
| 2. Teacher tests. **"I'll say a phrase. You say if it tells when or where."** | |
| a. **"In the park."** (pause and signal) | "Where" |
| b. **"After dinner."** (pause and signal) | "When" |
| c. **"Yesterday morning."** (pause and signal) | "When" |
| d. **"On my chair."** (pause and signal) | "Where" |
| e. **"At the beach."** (pause and signal) | "Where" |
| f. **"Last night."** (pause and signal) | "When" |

As soon as students answer who and what questions without difficulty, where and when can be introduced. Most student will have little difficulty with this task and may need only a few minutes of practice.

After students can discriminate when from where phrases, they can be introduced to where and when questions. The teacher uses all four question words to do this. (Note: If students had difficulty learning who and what, introduce when but delay where until students can correctly answer who, what, and when questions.)

The next step is to introduce *how*. The procedure for doing this is to model the answer for one or two how questions and then test the students on a series of sentences.

The last step is to introduce *why*. The procedure for teaching *why* is similar to that for earlier question words in that the teacher gives several practice examples with why and then provides discrimination

**Format Using Four Question Words**

| Teacher | Students |
|---|---|
| 1. Teacher says, **"John played in the park yesterday morning. Say the sentence."** (signal) | "John played in the park yesterday morning." |
| a. ***"Who* played in the park?"** (signal) | "John" |
| b. ***"What* did John do in the park?"** (signal) | "Played" |
| c. ***"Where* did John play?"** (signal) | "In the park" |
| d. ***"When* did John play?"** (signal) | "Yesterday morning" |

## Format for Introducing How

| Teacher | Students |
|---|---|
| 1. Teacher models. **"She ran like a deer. How did she run? Like a deer."** | |
| 2. Teacher tests. | |
| a. **"He worked quickly. How did he work?"** (signal) | "Quickly" |
| b. **"He wrote carefully. How did he write?"** (signal) | "Carefully" |
| c. **"They worked like dogs. How did they work?"** (signal) | "Like dogs" |

practice. A teacher should not always include the word *because* in passages that call for a response to a why question, since students may learn that *because* is the only word that tells why. To prevent students from learning this misrule, teachers include examples containing *to* (He went home to get his coat.), *since* (He ran home since it was late.), and finally *and* (He fell down and cried.).

After several days of practice on why questions, they can be incorporated into exercises that include other question word items.

## Similarity Comparisons

Similarity comparisons involve examining several objects or actions to determine ways in which they may or may not be similar. Student success on similarity comparison items is particularly dependent on the knowledge of common dimensions along which objects and events can be compared. Some major dimensions are listed below:

1. Classification, e.g., a knife and a saw are the same because they are both tools.

## Format for Introducing Why

| Teacher | Students |
|---|---|
| 1. Teacher models. **"He cried because he was hungry. Why did he cry? He was hungry."** | |
| 2. Teacher provides practice and tests. | |
| a. **"Since she was late to school, she ran. Why did she run?"** (signal) | "She was late." |
| b. **"He went home to get his coat. Why did he go home?"** (signal) | "To get his coat." |
| c. **"She tried her best and won the race. Why did she win the race?"** (signal) | "She tried her best." |
| d. **"They lost because they made mistakes. Why did they lose?"** (signal) | "They made mistakes." |

2. Use, e.g., a knife and a saw are the same because they both cut.
3. Materials, e.g., a knife and a hairbrush are the same because their handles are often made of wood.
4. Parts, e.g., a knife and a saw are the same because they both have handles.
5. Location, e.g., a toothbrush and a hairbrush are the same because they are both found in a bathroom.
6. Attributes, e.g., shape, color, texture, etc.

Obviously, if students are not knowledgeable about the dimensions relevant to comparison items, they will not understand the item. For example, if students do not know the class of tools or that a knife and a brush both have handles, they will fail an item that asks how a knife and a hairbrush are the same. Thus, vocabulary knowledge is critical for teaching comparison tasks.

The first step in teaching similarity comparisons involves expanding the students' understanding of *same* by showing them that things are the same when they possess similar attributes. Many students understand the concept *same* in only a limited sense, i.e., whether two objects look alike. Below is a sample format designed to expand the students' understanding of *same.*

Students have more trouble with items in which they are asked to tell how two objects are different than they do with items that ask how objects are the same. This difficulty is sometimes caused by the students' not knowing what *different* means and sometimes by a lack of vocabulary. The format illustrated is one that might be used to teach the concept of different. Note how similar it is to the format for teaching how objects are the same. However, this concept should not be introduced until stu-

---

**Format for Teaching the Concept of Same**

| *Teacher* | *Students* |
|---|---|
| 1. Teacher says, **"Let's see some ways a chair and a table are the same."** | |
| a. **"Does a chair have legs?"** (signal) | "Yes" |
| **"Does a table have legs?"** (signal) | "Yes" |
| **"So a chair and a table are the same because they both have legs. A chair and a table are the same because they both"** (signal) | "have legs." |
| b. **"Can a chair be made of wood?"** (signal) | "Yes" |
| **"Can a table be made of wood?"** (signal) | "Yes" |
| **"So a table and a chair are the same because they both can"** (signal) | "be made of wood." |
| c. **"Is a chair in the class of furniture?"** (signal) | "Yes" |
| **"Is a table in the class of furniture?"** (signal) | "Yes" |
| **"So a table and a chair are the same because they are both"** (signal) | "in the class of furniture." |
| d. **"Name three ways a chair and a table are the same."** Teacher calls on individuals; accepts appropriate answers; has whole group repeat each answer. | |

## Format for Teaching the Concept of Different

| *Teacher* | *Students* |
|---|---|
| 1. Teacher says, **"Let's see how a chair and a table are different."** | |
| a. **"Does a chair have a back?"** (signal) | "Yes" |
| **"Does a table have a back?"** (signal) | "No" |
| **"So a table and a chair are different because a chair has a back but a table doesn't."** | |
| b. **"Do you usually sit on a chair?"** (signal) | "Yes" |
| **"Do you usually sit on a table?"** (signal) | "No" |
| **"So a table and a chair are different because"** (signal) | "you sit on a chair but you don't sit on a table" |
| c. **"Does a table have a top?"** (signal) | "Yes" |
| **"Does a chair have a top?"** (signal) | "No" |
| **"So a chair and a table are different because"** (signal) | "a table has a top but a chair doesn't" |
| d. **"Tell me three ways a chair and a table are different."** Teacher calls on individuals. | |
| e. **"Now tell me some ways a chair and a table are the same."** Teacher calls on individuals; accepts appropriate answers. | |

dents have little difficulty with comparisons involving same.

## Commercial Programs

Although nearly all reading programs include exercises designed to teach vocabulary in their readiness books, few of these programs provide the systematic teaching necessary for instructionally naive students to learn at an optimal rate. Most programs are characterized by inappropriate teaching demonstrations and insufficient practice.

Scott, Foresman teaches vocabulary by introducing an object each day. The teacher tells the students the name of the object and then leads a discussion about the characteristics of the object. In teaching the word *vest,* for example, the teacher's guide suggests that the teacher develop the following concepts:

1. A vest may be a sleeveless, close-fitting short garment.
2. A vest may be of different color and materials.
3. A vest may be worn by a person.
4. A vest may be worn under a jacket or over a shirt or blouse.

An exercise such as this assumes that the students know basic characteristics such as colors, prepositions, and materials. Although the exercises in Scott, Foresman may serve as interesting items for students who have a basic vocabulary, they are not likely to be effective in teaching instructionally naive students.

## Suggested Modifications

Most reading programs contain activities appropriate for average students but inappropriate for instructionally naive students. The major type of modification needed for teachers working with average and above-average students might be to redesign activities to provide for more student involvement and extra practice on tasks causing students difficulty. The situation is not so simple for teachers working with instructionally naive students. Major modifications are necessary to make most commercial reading programs suitable for teaching these students vocabulary and oral language skills.

Unfortunately, modifying the vocabulary and oral language component of a program is much more difficult than modifying the decoding component of a program, since constructing demonstrations to teach the meaning of a new word can require many illustrations or objects. Likewise, providing for adequate review and practice can be difficult since the lessons in the programs do not serve as a guide in determining what skills to include or review. Our suggestion is not to try modifying the vocabulary teaching component of reading programs, but rather to obtain a program specifically designed to teach vocabulary and language skills to instructionally naive students. When selecting a program, teachers should spend most of their time examining *how* the programs teaches skills, rather than determining what skills are taught, since most programs cover basically the same content. Teachers should look at individual lessons, noting the formats and examples used. The wording in the formats should be simple and direct. The examples, as mentioned earlier, are critical. Example selection is the key to effectively teaching vocabulary. Note if positive and negative examples are provided. If the program does not provide adequate examples, it will prob-

ably not be effective with instructionally naive students.

After looking at the way in which several tasks are constructed, teachers should look at 5 to 10 consecutive lessons noting how many times each new skill or word is reviewed. The purpose is to determine the adequacy of initial practice and review. If a new skill or word is not reviewed, many students will not learn it. Programs with inadequate review are difficult to modify.

In summary, examine a beginning language program by looking at *how* it teaches language skills and vocabulary rather than by looking at what it claims to teach. Look at (1) the language used in the formats, (2) the adequacy of example selection, and (3) the provision for review. These three areas will tell the teacher how effective a tool a program will be.

An example of an effectively constructed program designed to teach basic vocabulary and language skills is the *DISTAR Language Series*. This program is designed to be taught independently of decoding; thus, it may be used in conjunction with any commercial reading program. The program begins by teaching simple vocabulary (e.g., words like *big, red, in, on*) and expressive-language tasks (e.g., teaching students to say statements like *"The ball is not big"*) and proceeds gradually, eventually teaching complex reasoning and inference skills. The program consists of two modules. Both include 160 daily lessons. Module I would be used with instructionally naive students since it stresses basic vocabulary teaching and expressive language. Module II would be used with average and above-average students during beginning reading. It stresses reasoning skills rather than basic vocabulary. Module II would be used with instructionally naive students after they complete Module I.

*DISTAR Language I* is unique in that it provides for cumulative introduction and practice of skills (when new skills are introduced, previously introduced skills are reviewed) and introduces new material at a realistic rate. For example, prepositions are introduced at the rate of about one each 10 lessons; *on* appears in lesson 28, *over* in lesson 31, *in front of* in lesson 36, *in* in lesson 47, *in back of* in lesson 57, *under* in lesson 67, *next to* in lesson 76, and *between* in lesson 86. When a new preposition is introduced, previously taught ones are reviewed.

The *DISTAR Language I* program is also unique in its emphasis on expressive language. Tasks range from early ones designed to teach simple identify statements (e.g., "This is a dog." or "This is not a dog.") to more complex statements ("This rabbit will eat the big apple that has leaves."). Simple reasoning skills are also introduced in Module I. Module II reviews the vocabulary from Module I and presents more complex reasoning tasks like absurdities, descriptions, definitions, multiple classifications, and analogies.

## Setting Up a Program

If a teacher is unable to obtain a program that adequately teaches vocabulary and language skills, he will have to do the best he can. The teacher should test students informally on particular areas of knowledge. For sentence comprehension, he could present a sentence and ask simple questions. Students having difficulty should be asked questions about several sentences every day. Teaching vocabulary will be much more difficult because of the need to test and teach many different words. Appendix F lists some of the vocabulary words students need to know and suggestions for testing each class of vocabulary word. The teacher should test and teach more basic words first and then teach the rest later. Teachers should present daily exercises, using modeling and, in some cases, synonyms to teach unfamiliar words. Review should be systematic.

---

## RESEARCH

"According to Goodman, readers 'construct the meaning' on the basis of their past experience of language. School beginners, he asserts, 'are already possessed of a language competence and an ability to learn language which are powerful resources'" (Downing, 1977, pp. 1–2). Our emphasis is on instructional procedures that will utilize students' ability to learn language. This emphasis seems appropriate since students who do well on oral language tasks tend to do well on written comprehension tasks (Jenkins & Pany, 1977; Perfetti, 1977; Berger, 1975). Early written tasks are limited by the student's decoding ability to relatively simple items.

The importance of statement repetition has not been documented in experimental research; however, there is correlational evidence to suggest its importance. After comparing the performance of good and poor readers on their ability to remember what they just read, Perfetti said, "The point at which it seems adaptive to forget the words recently heard appears

to be the end of a sentence (Jarvella, 1971). Up to that point, it is helpful to remember the sequence of words or phrases verbatim so that the unheard portion of the sentence (e.g., the verb) can be related to the first part of the sentence" (1977, p. 33). Perfetti's work underscores the importance of students' being able to remember words in a sentence. If a reader cannot say a sentence verbatim, she probably has difficulty remembering sentences that are read.

Although research suggests that vocabulary can be developed and expanded through classroom experiences and visual aides such as films or field trips (Davis, 1968; McCullough, 1969; Lieberman, 1967) and context clues (Eicholz & Barbe, 1961; Wittrock, Marks, & Doctorow, 1975; Gipe, 1978), vocabulary can also be more directly taught (Jenkins & Pany, 1976; Petty, Herold, & Stoll, 1968; Otterman, 1955). Many of our specific guidelines for teaching basic vocabulary have been validated in experimental research. One of the

**FIGURE 2.7.4**

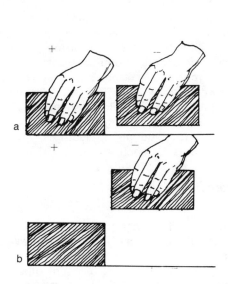

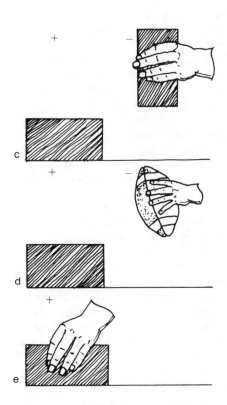

first points made in Section 2.7 is that a *presentation should be consistent with only one interpretation.* If a presentation is consistent with several interpretations, students may learn an interpretation other than that intended by the teacher. An application of this principle is illustrated in Figure 2.7.4, which contains positive and negative examples of the discrimination *on.* The pair of examples from teaching set <u>a</u> illustrates the minimum difference between positive and negative examples of *on.* In set <u>a</u>, the number of possible interpretations for *on* is minimized because of the small difference between the positive and negative examples. In contrast, the subsequent sets of examples (sets <u>b</u> through <u>e</u>) differ in terms of several features, which suggest additional interpretations. A student presented with set <u>e</u>

examples might learn that *on* means a block, something not held in a hand, horizontally positioned objects, etc. None of these interpretations are possible from set <u>a</u>. When Carnine (1978c) presented examples similar to those in Figure 2.7.4 to different groups of preschoolers, he found a significant linear trend between the number of possible interpretations and errors on a transfer test. Preschoolers presented with set a examples responded correctly to 10.2 transfer items; whereas, preschoolers presented with set <u>e</u> responded correctly to only 5.0 transfer items. In other words, the greater the number of possible interpretations that are consistent with a teaching demonstration, the greater the likelihood that some students will learn an interpretation other than the one intended by the teacher. Designing a presentation as in set a that is consistent with only one interpretation increases the likelihood of students' not becoming confused regarding what is relevant.

Ensuring that a presentation is consistent with only one interpretation requires selecting not only minimally different positive and negative examples (whenever possible) but also *a range of examples.* For example, Flanders (1978) worked with a student who did not understand the difference between singular and plural nouns; e.g., the experimenter would present two sets of examples (one dog and two dogs), touch the one dog and ask, "Am I touching dogs?" The student would be likely to answer, "Yes." Flanders followed a commonly used procedure to teach the student to correctly answer questions involving singular and plural nouns. The problem was that the procedure implied a misrepresentation. All examples were presented in pairs: a single object for singular and two identical objects for plural. Testing revealed that the student had learned the misinterpretation that plural meant two. The teacher presented a set of two objects and a set of four objects, pointed to the four objects, and asked "Am I touching dogs?" the student answered, "No" and pointed to the two dogs saying, "dogs."

Other research suggests that misinterpretations can result from a limited sample of negative examples (Carnine, 1976d). Students were presented with a narrow range of negative examples keyed on the features of the negatives but not the positives. The same positive examples (figures with saw-toothed edges) were presented to three groups of students. One group of students was presented with straight-sided negatives (or narrow range of negative examples) while two other groups were presented negatives with many different characteristics (a full range of negatives). The group with the narrow range of negatives did poorly on a transfer test because they identified figures with straight sides as negatives and everything else as positives, regardless of whether the figure had saw-toothed edges. The preceding two studies suggest that a full range of positive *and* negative examples is needed to ensure appropriate "generalization."

Another study (Carnine, 1976d) suggested the importance of presenting intended irrelevant characteristics in both positive and negative ex-

amples. Any feature that appears only in positive examples may be treated as relevant, whether the teacher "intends" for a feature to be relevant or not (Reynolds, 1961). Carnine (1976d) presented a concept to one group that had both a dotted pattern and three points. The students in the group treated the dots as critical. The concept for another group had the dotted pattern in both positive and negative examples and only the three points in positive examples. These students treated the three points as critical. For a third group, the dots appeared only in positive examples. These students treated dots as critical. The point is that students learn what is easiest (Samuels, 1976b). Consequently, teachers must be sure that what is easiest for students to learn is what the teacher wants to teach.

### Sequencing Examples

Several procedures are relevant for sequencing examples. *First, minimally different positive and negative examples of a discrimination* should be sequenced adjacent to each other and simultaneously rather than successively. Sequencing minimally different examples in this way increases the obviousness of the discriminations' relevant features (Granzin & Carnine, 1977). Students taught conjunctive and exclusive disjunctive concepts with simultaneously presented minimally different positive and negative examples reached criterion in about half as many trials as students presented the same examples but successively and with multiple differences between adjacent examples. Similar results have been reported by Stolurow (1975); Tennyson, Steve, and Boutwell (1975); and Tennyson (1973).

A second sequencing procedure is that, whenever possible, positive and negative examples should be generated by changing a single stimulus (a dynamic presentation) rather than presenting a set of discrete stimuli, either simultaneously or successively (a static presentation). Carnine (1978j) reported faster acquisition and higher transfer scores for preschoolers who were taught to discriminate between *diagonal* and *convex* with a dynamic rather than static presentation. In the dynamic treatment, examples of diagonal were generated by rotating a single line segment. In the static treatment, examples consisted of pairs of line segments drawn on cards. The differences in trials to criterion for the two treatments was 46.4 versus 10.6 for diagonal and 5.8 versus .05 for convex.

Carnine (1978h) also compared all three sequencing procedures discussed above. Preschoolers were taught a discrimination defined by an angle using material developed by Tra-

basso (1963) in his study on various types of prompts. Preschoolers who received the dynamic presentation with minimum differences reached criterion in an average of 7.6 trials; preschoolers who received a static presentation with minimum differences took 12.8 trials; finally, preschoolers who received a static presentation with multiple differences required an average of 26.0 trials.

## APPLICATION EXERCISES

1.  For each of the following sets of examples, specify at least one misinterpretation a student might learn.

    a. *rough*
       negative examples: desk top and mirror
       positive examples: wool shirt and burlap bag

    b. *narrow*
       positive examples:  a picture of a narrow European street and a narrow alley next to the school, with buildings on each side
       negative examples: none

    c. *vehicle*
       positive examples: Pinto   Gremlin   Mustang   Cadillac
       negative examples: none

2.  Assume you are working with young children (5–6 years old). Tell which method —examples only, synonyms, or definitions—you would use to teach the following words. (A synonym can be a word or a phrase.) Also, for each word specify two positive and two negative examples.

    a. avoid
    b. damp
    c. striped
    d. nurse

3.  Write a format to teach students two ways milk and orange juice are the same.

4.  Construct four sentences that answer the question, 'Why did Tom win the race?' Use *because* in one sentence, *since* in the second, *and* in the third, and *in order to* in the last. Why must teachers be aware of different phrases that indicate an answer to a *why* question?

5.  On the following picture-comprehension item, the student makes this wrong response:

    How would you determine what caused the error?

6.  Specify the correction procedure for the following error:

    a. The teacher asks students to repeat this statement: The old man is walking the little dog. A student says, "The old man has a dog" (see page 153).

7. Assume that a group of students knows the most common sound for all individual letters and the most common sound for the following letter combinations: *ai, al, ar, au, aw, ay, ch, ea, ee, er, igh, ing, oa, oi, oo, or, ou, oy, sh, th,* and *ur.* Underline every letter that the students will not be able to decode:

| | | | | |
|---|---|---|---|---|
| spout | some | peach | boost | spurt |
| hood | broad | burst | hook | mind |
| boat | caught | gain | pour | hound |
| walk | tough | chord | starch | stoop |
| again | round | steak | put | church |
| much | stain | gray | park | storm |
| bread | strewn | beach | groan | none |
| four | straw | steel | torn | |

8. The teacher is having students sight read the following passage:
   "Jim will get it if he is wet," his mom said. "I told him not to swim today."

   In the following situations, first specify what the teacher would do and the wording the teacher would use to correct the student's error when it occurs (see page 133).

   a. During unison reading, a student says "sad" for *said.*
   b. During unison reading, a student says "got" for *get.*
   c. On individual turns, a student reads very slowly.

# Selecting and Using a Program

This section includes three parts. The first one deals with selecting a basal program to use during the beginning reading stage. The second deals with tests the teachers can use to group students and place the groups in a classroom reading program. The third part covers using a program, setting up daily lessons incorporating direct instruction techniques.

## Selecting a Program

The following material is designed to help the classroom teacher select a program that (1) requires relatively little modification and (2) can serve as an effective tool for teaching reading to all students. Decoding instruction is the major reading activity during the first 2 years of reading instruction. Consequently, programs for the early primary grades should be selected according to how well they teach decoding. We recommend using a code-emphasis program for the first 2 years of reading instruction. The rationale for this recommendation was spelled out in detail in Section 2.1, the introduction to beginning reading.

Teachers can determine whether a reading program is meaning-emphasis or code-

emphasis by looking at the number of regular words that appear among the first 50 words introduced in the program. In meaning-emphasis programs, the number is usually around 20, while in code-emphasis programs the number is usually closer to 40. Table 2.8.1 lists the first 50 words introduced in several code- and meaning-emphasis programs. The number in parentheses indicates how many of the first 50 words are regular. Note the marked difference between code- and meaning-emphasis programs. The number of regular words included in the first 50 words is 17 for Houghton Mifflin, 22 for Ginn, 18 for Scott, Foresman, but 47 for Lippincott, and 36 for Palo Alto. The reason for the difference is that meaning-emphasis programs do not select words according to the letter-sound correspondences. In contrast, code-emphasis programs take great care in limiting words to ones that are made up of letter-sound correspondences that have been taught.

## Selecting a Code-emphasis Program

The major design factor to consider in selecting a code-emphasis program is the

**TABLE 2.8.1** *First 50 Words Listed in Several Reading Programs*

| MEANING EMPHASIS | | | CODE EMPHASIS | |
| --- | --- | --- | --- | --- |
| HOUGHTON MIFFLIN | GINN | SCOTT, FORESMAN | LIPPINCOTT | PALO ALTO |
| (17) | (22) | (18) | (47) | (36) |
| is | *Bill | girl | *an | *am |
| *in | *Lad | *man | *Ann | I |
| the | *runs | *dog | *ran | *ran |
| *will | hides | horse | *Dan | *mat |
| go | *Jill | the | *dad | the |
| I | *and | *is | *add | that |
| to | go | *on | *and | see |
| *on | I | *not | *run | *and |
| *and | *am | boy | *mud | *at |
| *it | rides | puppy | *mad | *Sam |
| *not | *run | *and | *man | *tam |
| you | hide | find | *am | *sat |
| *get | *can | likes | *ram | *rat |
| *Jill | this | baby | *drum | look |
| Andy | *yes | sandwich | *Pam | saw |
| *help | no | thumb | *pan | said |
| *cat | *is | *man | *pad | *Al |
| *truck | here | cake | *up | *Sal |
| *can | *not | pie | *pup | *tan |
| see | *duck | cherries | *map | *an |
| come | *get | *bed | *nap | *ant |
| *stop | *Ben | eating | *rap | *fat |
| here | *Ted | shells | *pump | *fan |
| where | *Nan | people | *ramp | *Bob |
| *its | look | look | the | *bat |
| rocket | *at | car | *did | *bam |
| are | said | *cat | *in | *rob |
| *bus | park | *sun | *rid | *not |
| tiger | the | rainbow | *mid | *on |
| have | *will | *red | *rip | *lot |
| this | like | apples | *dip | *Tom |
| me | to | horse | *dim | *man |
| with | we | *duck | *rim | *hat |
| tigers | *help | *pig | *pin | *hal |
| zoo | are | saw | *drip | do |
| want | *stop | *ran | *Sid | is |
| *can't | heres | house | *sip | *yes |
| real | *it | children | *sad | has |
| going | eat | woman | *Sam | *hog |
| *am | you | orange | *sun | *log |
| I'm | *can't | tree | *sand | *fog |
| wants | helps | *lots | *us | *bog |
| fish | me | of | *Russ | this |
| school | with | *got | *miss | *in |
| sick | we'll | ate | *pass | *Tag |
| fishing | I'll | *big | is | *rag |
| day | what | little | as | *bag |
| today | come | potato | *runs | so |
| play | turtle | *fox | spins | they |

Asterisk Indicates a Regular Word

rate at which letters and letter combinations are introduced. If letters and letter combinations are introduced at too rapid a rate, teachers may be forced to construct lessons that provide extra practice to slow the rate of introduction of new letters. The rate factor is especially important for teachers working with students who come to school with little knowledge of letter-sound correspondences. Unfortunately, determining the rate at which letters are introduced in a program is often difficult since many commercial programs do not specify what tasks make up a lesson. Most teacher's guides merely list a series of tasks. The teacher is supposed to decide what tasks to include in a lesson. To figure out the rate at which a new letter and letter combinations are introduced, teachers must decide what tasks would make up a daily lesson. The teacher should keep in mind that a lesson includes letter-sound correspondence tasks, word list reading, story reading, comprehension exercises, and independent activities. The tasks should be grouped into lessons and the lessons numbered.

After dividing the teacher's guide into lessons, the teacher notes the lesson on which each letter or letter combination is introduced. In nearly all programs, the lesson in which a new letter or letter combination is introduced will be very obvious. A page in the student reader will contain a list of words, all of which include the new letter. For example, in the Palo Alto program, the words: *it, fit, sit, bit, lit, hit, did, hid, lid, dig, big, in, tin, him, rim, dim, Tim,* and *bim* all appear on the page on which the letter *i* is introduced. Table 2.8.2 lists the sequence and rate at which new letters and letter combinations are introduced in several code-emphasis programs. Since we had to decide which tasks would be included in a lesson, our lesson numbers are only approximate.

Note that Lippincott introduces a new letter or letter combination almost every other day, while Palo Alto introduces one new letter every several lessons. In Lippin-

cott, 71 letter-sound correspondences are introduced in the first 150 lessons, while the Palo Alto program teaches only 27 letters in the first 150 lessons. We would not recommend Lippincott for teachers working with students who come to school with little knowledge of letter-sound correspondence since most likely the students could not learn the letter-sound correspondences at the rate they're introduced. Teachers would have to construct many extra practice lessons.

If two programs introduce letters and letter combinations at about the same rate, the teacher should look at a combination of other factors in deciding which program to use. These factors are (1) example selection (Does the program provide guidance in specifying which letters and words to include in drill exercises and are exercises constructed so that adequate practice is provided?) (2) sequence (Are there any violations of the sequencing principles that may cause extensive time-consuming modifications? Fortunately the sequences in most major programs are reasonable, if not ideal, according to our standards.) (3) adequacy of supplementary activities (Are written worksheet exercises relevant? Are the directions clear? Can students be expected to do them independently?).

Some other programs which teach beginning reading skills using a code-emphasis approach include these:

1. *DISTAR Reading* (Science Research Associates)
2. *Merrill Linguistic Readers* (Charles E. Merrill)
3. *Miami Linguistic Readers* (D. C. Heath)
4. *Programmed Reading* (Webster/McGraw-Hill)
5. *SRA Basic Reading Series* (Science Research Associates)

## Selecting a Meaning-emphasis Program

Students are more likely to progress at an optimal rate if placed in a code-emphasis

**Table 2.8.2** *Sequence and Lesson Number for Introducing Letters and Letter Combinations in Two Code-emphasis Programs*

| LIPPINCOTT | | PALO ALTO | | |
|---|---|---|---|---|
| 1. aA | 52. oa | *P. aA | 219. wh | 431. wr |
| 2. nN | 54. j | P. mM | 226. ch | 436. ph |
| 3. rR | 56. v | P. rR | 252. ck | |
| 4. dD | 58. sh | P. tT | 254. es | |
| 5. uU | 60. ch | 7. sS | 263. ing | |
| 6. mM | 61. th | 10. nN | 277. ar | |
| 7. pP | 63. wh | 14. lL | 284. or | |
| 8. il | 64. qu | 17. fF | 300. ea | |
| 9. sS | 64. x | 19. bB | 305. ay | |
| 10. oO | 65. y | 20. oO | 313. ai | |
| 11. tT | 65. z | 23. hH | 316. oy | |
| 12. eE | 70. ing | 29. gG | 316. oi | |
| 13. gG | 78. ar | 34. vV | 320. er | |
| 14. cC | 84. y | 36. dD | 334. est | |
| 15. hH | 84. ay | 43. il | 336. al | |
| 16. fF | 84. ey | 54. zZ | 341. c/s/ | |
| 17. ar | 89. c/s/ | 56. kK | 345. ar | |
| 19. er | 95. g/j/ | 60. wW | 345. ture | |
| 20. ed | 99. tion | 62. pP | 349. y | |
| 21. w | 101. o | 68. uU | 357. oe | |
| 25. aw | 101. oo minor | 77. cC | 358. ow | |
| 27. ow | 106. ow | 83. yY | 361. oa | |
| 28. IL | 106. ow minor | 84. sS | 364. g/j/ | |
| 30. b | 108. ou | 87. eE | 370. igh | |
| 31. le | 115. oi | 92. xX | 376. ou | |
| 33. k | 119. ew | 93. gG | 379. ow/ō/ | |
| 34. Vce | 121. aw | 148. ee | 386. ew | |
| 37. ee | 121. au | 157. a_e** | 390. aw | |
| 40. ea | 122. ph | 180. i_e** | 391. au | |
| 42. ai | 122. ch/k/ | 192. o_e** | 405. tion | |
| 45. i_e** | 122. ch/sh/ | 198. sh | 409. ea/ĕ/ | |
| 46. ir | 124. wr | 205. ol | 416. le | |
| 48. o_e** | 132. igh | 208. th | 417. al | |
| 49. or | | 210. oo | 451. kn | |
| | | 212. oo minor | | |

\* Preprogram
\*\* Indicates the vowel in a VCE pattern word. See Section 3.2.

program. Unfortunately, some teachers may not be able to use a code-emphasis program. The following discussion is directed to the teacher who must select a meaning-emphasis program.

The key factors to examine in selecting a meaning-emphasis program are (1) the rate at which irregular words are introduced and (2) the amount of practice provided on those words. The rate at which ir-

regular words are introduced is important since too fast a rate may result in the teacher's constructing numerous additional practice exercises to delay the introduction of new words.

Table 2.8.3 lists the irregular words introduced in what we estimated to be the first 50 lessons of three popular meaning-emphasis programs. Note the significant difference between Scott, Foresman and the other two programs, Houghton Mifflin and Ginn. Scott, Foresman introduces about three times as many irregular words in the first 50 lessons. (Numbers in parentheses indicate the total number of irregular words introduced in the first 50 lessons.) An examination of the review provided on each word also showed a significant difference between Scott, Foresman and the other two programs. Both Ginn and Houghton Mifflin provided more review than did Scott, Foresman. In both Houghton Mifflin and Ginn, the more common irregular words were reviewed daily or every other day in stories. In Scott, Foresman, although words were reviewed heavily when first introduced, later review was much less frequent than in Ginn or Houghton Mifflin. For example, the word *has* appeared daily for 3 lessons in Scott, Foresman but then did not appear again for 15 lessons.

Since the rate and practice are more controlled in Houghton Mifflin and Ginn than in Scott, Foresman, we feel that one of those first two programs would be easier to use, both from the viewpoint of modifications necessary and of relative difficulty for students.

Some other publishers of programs which teach beginning reading using a meaning-emphasis approach are Allyn & Bacon; American Book Company; Harcourt Brace Jovanovich; Harper & Row; Holt, Rinehart and Winston; Laidlaw; MacMillan; and Rand McNally.

## Tests for Placement and Grouping

The following material discusses tests that can be used to initially group and place students who have had no previous reading instruction, in kindergarten or first grade. The two tests we recommend are a diagnostic test of word attack skills and a language screening test. Both tests should be given during the first few days of school.

When reading this section, keep in mind that the procedures are designed for use by a classroom teacher with 20 to 30 students in her class. Consequently, the testing procedure is as brief as possible. Also realize that any beginning-of-the-year testing and grouping procedure will not be 100% accurate. A student's performance on one test may not indicate what the student knows. Likewise, a test of what a student knows at a particular point in time will not indicate how quickly he will be able to learn new skills.

Grouping students is a difficult task, since it involves compromising what is ideal for each individual student with what is practical for the entire class. Classroom teachers do not have the luxury of making decisions based solely on what is best for each student. Since the time available for instruction is very limited, teachers must balance the needs of each student with the needs of other students. How to group the students initially and how quickly to move a group through a program are complex questions.

## Diagnostic Test of Word Attack Skills

The beginning level of the diagnostic test of word attack skills (Figure 2.8.1) tests students' specific letter-sound correspondence knowledge and simple word attack strategy skills. The test will tell a teacher if a student has the skills to be placed at a lesson within a program or if he should be placed at the beginning of a program.

### Materials

The teacher needs a copy of the test form (Figure 2.8.1) and a class record form (Figure 2.8.2). When preparing the test form for reproduction, use a primary typewriter or print with large letters.

### Seating Arrangement

The student should be seated at a desk

**TABLE 2.8.3**   *Irregular Words Introduced in the First 50 Lessons of Three Meaning-emphasis Programs.*

| HOUGHTON MIFFLIN (38) | GINN (39) | SCOTT, FORESMAN (125) | | |
|---|---|---|---|---|
| 1. David | 1. hides | 5. find | 31. eat | 39. Susan |
| Andy | 4. go | the | play | Maria |
| go | I | horse | Simon | goes |
| Becky | 7. rides | girl | says | 41. bike |
| 3. you | this | 8. boy | all | too |
| 5. I | 10. no | puppy | clapped | sometimes |
| 12. come | here | 11. sandwich | hopped | 41. they |
| see | 13. look | thumb | ate | animals |
| here | said | 14. pie | 33. boots | them |
| 16. where | 16. the | cherries | shoes | lion |
| are | park | eating | feet | father |
| TV | like | 18. look | warm | what's |
| 18. have | to | people | dry | 42. that |
| me | 19. we | shells | keep | won't |
| tiger | are | now | safe | have |
| 22. want | 27. circle | 21. car | these | marble |
| real | eat | rainbow | dance | 43. peanuts |
| zoo | you | apples | 34. snow | line |
| 39. fish | 29. me | 22. house | blue | thank |
| school | with | saw | make | 44. seals |
| 40. day | 33. what | 23. woman | angels | giraffe |
| today | core | oranges | ride | 45. lived |
| play | turtle | tree | 36. coat | farm |
| park | 35. guess | ate | Karen | chicks |
| 41. take | little | 24. little | hair | other |
| no | 37. do | potato | paper | wheat |
| 42. there | 39. don't | 27. one | paint | grain |
| funny | 40. read | two | paper | 46. soon |
| 44. smile | books | three | 37. he | take |
| picture | 42. you're | four | sign | 47. bread |
| look | mother | five | who | oh |
| nice | 45. zoo | fish | put | work |
| 45. teeth | who | shop | yard | 49. Vicky |
| for | parrot | 29. building | waited | tired |
| my | hello | streets | then | wanted |
| 46. Mrs. | say | cars | with | story |
| be | 48. seal | city | she | 50. school |
| 47. your | play | there | said | story |
| | ball | this | name | library |
| | | 31. house | 38. why | Melvin |
| | | foot | because | mouse |
| | | | | home |

facing away from the rest of the class. The teacher should be seated to the side of the student so that the student cannot see the teacher recording errors.

## Administering and Scoring

*Step 1*—Test Letter-Sound Correspondences (Lower-case letters). Point to the

**FIGURE 2.8.1**  *Diagnostic Test of Word Attack Skills Beginning Readers Section*

| a | m | t | s | i | f |
|---|---|---|---|---|---|
| d | r | o | g | l | h |
| u | c | b | n | k | e |
| v | p | y | j | x | w | q |

D    A    R    H    G    B    E    Q

| 1 | 2 | 3 | 4 | 5 |
|---|---|---|---|---|
| it | cat | must | flag | stamp |
| am | him | hats | step | strap |
| if | hot | hand | drop | split |
| sam | tag | last | skin | skunk |
| mad | | | | |

**FIGURE 2.8.2**  *Record Form for Diagnostic Test of Word Attack Skills—Beginning Level*

first letter (a) and ask the student, "What *sound* does this make?" Continue in row 1, then row 2, 3, and 4. On the class record form, write a (+) for each sound correctly produced; write a (0) for each letter not identified correctly. If a student tells you the letter name, say to the student, "Yes, that's the letter name but can you also tell me the *sound* it makes?" If the student cannot tell you the sound but does know the letter, write L.N. next to the letter. If a student doesn't respond in 5 seconds and seems unable to answer, tell her the sound, mark the letter with a (0), and move to the next letter. Continue testing letters until the student makes three incorrect responses in a row.

*Step 2—Test Letter-Sound Correspondences (Upper-case Letters).* The procedure is the same as for step 1.

*Step 3—Test Regular Words.* Point to the first word in column 1 and ask the child, "What word is this?" Repeat this question with each word in column 1, then columns 2, 3, 4, and 5. On the class record form, write a + next to words correctly read. Write a 0 next to each word not read correctly. If the student misidentifies a word but then immediately corrects himself, count it as correct. If a student does not respond in 5 seconds and does not seem to be able to decode the word correctly, give the answer and move to the next word. Continue testing until the student misses three words in a row.

## Oral Language Screening Test

The oral language screening test is designed primarily to alert teachers to students who may have vocabulary and/or language deficits. It should be administered to all students during the first days of school. The test results can also be used to help in forming groups.

### Materials

The teacher needs a test form (Figure 2.8.3) and a class record form (Figure 2.8.4).

### Teacher Directions

Start at Item 1 and test all items.

### Recording

Use the class record form (Figure 2.8.4). For a correct answer, write a plus (+) under the appropriate heading. For an incorrect answer, write a zero (0).

## Informal Reading Inventory

An informal reading inventory is a test in which students read selected passages from a reading textbook. The purpose of the test is to determine the appropriate lesson at which to place students in the textbook. Students who read 12 or more words on the beginning level diagnostic test of word attack skills should be given an informal reading inventory. Directions for constructing and administering an informal reading inventory are included in Section 3.6 of Part 3.

## Recording Test Results

The results of the tests should be listed on a class summary form (Figure 2.8.5). The students should be listed according to the total number of letter-sound correspondences correctly identified on the diagnostic test of word attack skills. Students who made the fewest correct responses should be listed first. Across from the student's name, the number of correctly identified letters (total of lower- and upper-case) and words should be written along with the number of items the student answered correctly on the language test. If the students read a passage from the in-

**FIGURE 2.8.3**  *Oral Language Screening Test*

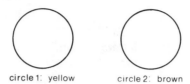

circle 1: yellow        circle 2: brown

Directions—Color circle one yellow. Color circle two brown.
1. (Point to circle one and ask) "What color is this?"
2. (Point to circle two and ask) "What color is this?"
3. "I'll say sentences. Say them just the way I say them."
   "Listen." (pause) "A big boy and a little girl are sitting on a dirty bench."
   (Repeat the sentence once if the student did not say it verbatim. If the student says it correctly verbatim on the first or second trial, score the item correct.)
4. "Listen." (pause) "Mary was baby-sitting for her little sister last night. Say that."
   (Repeat the sentence once if the student did not say it verbatim. If the student says it correctly verbatim on the first or second trial, score the item correct.)
5. "I'm going to say a sentence, then ask you some questions. Listen carefully.
   A little cat slept in the park yesterday. Listen again, a little cat slept in the park yesterday."
   "Where did the cat sleep?" (In the park)
6. "When did the cat sleep in the park?" (Yesterday)
7. "How are a mouse and a cow different?" (Accept reasonable answers.)
8. "Listen. Monday, Tuesday, Wednesday, Thursday, Friday. Say that."
   (Repeat the days once if the student did not say them correctly. If the student says them correctly on the first or second trial, score the item correct.)
9. "What is a person who fixes your teeth called?"
10. "What is a pencil usually made of?"

**FIGURE 2.8.4**  *Record Form for Oral Language Screening Test*

| Student's Name | 1 yellow | 2 brown | 3 statement (1) | 4 statement (2) | 5 where | 6 when | 7 different | 8 days | 9 pencil | 10 wood |
|---|---|---|---|---|---|---|---|---|---|---|
|  |  |  |  |  |  |  |  |  |  |  |
|  |  |  |  |  |  |  |  |  |  |  |
|  |  |  |  |  |  |  |  |  |  |  |
|  |  |  |  |  |  |  |  |  |  |  |
|  |  |  |  |  |  |  |  |  |  |  |

**FIGURE 2.8.5**  *Class Summary Form for Beginning-of-the-year Testing*

| | PHONICS TEST | | LANGUAGE TEST | IRI |
|---|---|---|---|---|
| | *letters correct* | *words correct* | *items correct* | *lesson rate* |
| Ann | 0 | 0 | 6 | |
| Samuel | 0 | 0 | 8 | |
| Jason | 2 | 0 | 4 | |
| Cheryl | 2 | 0 | 5 | |
| Heidi | 2 | 0 | 9 | |
| Eric | 3 | 0 | 6 | |
| James | 4 | 0 | 8 | |
| Mary | 5 | 1 | 8 | |
| Mendy | 5 | 0 | 5 | |
| David R. | 5 | 1 | 8 | |
| Lois | 6 | 2 | 6 | |
| Alex | 6 | 0 | 9 | |
| Phillipe | 8 | 2 | 7 | |
| Gerald | 10 | 2 | 8 | |
| Dianne | 10 | 1 | 8 | |
| David P. | 10 | 3 | 9 | |
| Sean | 11 | 2 | 9 | |
| Toni | 12 | 4 | 10 | |
| Dina | 14 | 3 | 8 | |
| Jerome | 17 | 5 | 10 | |
| Sandy | 19 | 7 | 10 | |
| Alfred | 21 | 14 | 10 | 30 |

formal reading inventory successfully, the passage number and the student's reading rate on the passage should also be listed on the class summary form. The class summary form is the basis for grouping students.

## Grouping Beginning Readers

While reading specialists, tutors, and resource room teachers may be able to work with individual students, most classroom teachers cannot. With 20 to 30 students in their classrooms, they must group students. In making groups, teachers should first look at the number of letter-sound correspondences students know. Students who know the most letter-sound correspondences would form a high group. The students who know the lowest number of letter-sound correspondences would form

the lowest group. When many students know about the same number of letters, the teacher uses the number of words identified and scores from the language screening test in deciding which students belong in a high, middle, or low group. In setting up groups, the teacher will want to have the lowest-performing students in the smallest group.

Teachers must keep in mind that initial groupings are tentative. No matter how much time is devoted to pretesting, some regrouping will be necessary. Regrouping should be done after the first week or two of instruction. The student's performance should serve as a basis for changing group assignments. A student who makes few errors and is facile (does not hesitate) in responding during instruction might be moved to a higher group while a student who makes more errors than other members of the group might be moved to a lower group. Indications that a student might be ready to be moved to a higher group include mastering new skills with less than half the practice required by the other students in the group and being ready to answer before the other students. Students possibly belong in a lower group when the opposite occurs: the student always needs many more practice examples to master a new skill than the other members of the group or the student is often not ready to answer when the others are. Early regrouping is very important. If regrouping is delayed too long, students who could progress at a faster rate might be separated from the next higher group by several skills, making regrouping difficult.

## Using the Program

## Using a Code-emphasis Program

Three areas dealing with using a code-emphasis basal program are discussed here. First, how to place a group at a particular lesson in a program and progress through the initial lessons at an optimal rate are discussed. Since many students come to school with some knowledge of letter-sound correspondences, teachers often can progress through early lessons quite quickly. Second, the tasks that would be included in daily lessons are outlined. Third, guidelines for modifying the following various parts of a decoding program are reviewed: isolated letter-sound correspondences, auditory skills, regular word reading, irregular word reading, and passage reading.

### Placement

Some students will read well enough on the diagnostic test of word attack skills to warrant being given the informal reading inventory (IRI). Procedures for placing students who do well on an IRI are given in

Section 3.6, "Selecting and Using a Program," in the primary reading part. Here, we deal exclusively with procedures for placing students who cannot decode enough words to read the passages in early lessons.

Teachers working with instructionally naive students may find it difficult to use code-emphasis programs that begin word-reading exercises on the first lesson of the program. We recommend that teachers in such a situation teach the tasks from the 20-lesson beginning decoding program in Appendix D before placing the students in the commercial program. The program in Appendix D outlines the examples that might be used in teaching auditory skills, early letter-sound correspondences, and sounding out. The formats for the tasks outlined can be found on the following pages: letter introduction, page 77; letter discrimination, page 78; telescoping, page 67; segmenting, page 68; sounding-out word list reading, page 97; sight word list reading, page 103; irregular words, page 120; and sounding-out passage reading, page 128. Teachers working with very low-performing students might expect to teach just one lesson a day. Higher-performing students may be able to complete several lessons a day.

After completing the 20 lessons outlined in Appendix D, the teacher would proceed to the first lesson in the commercial program on which there was a letter-sound correspondence which a student did not know and present the lessons.

### Sample Lessons

During the first week of instruction, a teacher working with students who do not know any letter-sound correspondences would include just letter-sound correspondences and auditory skills in the decoding section of lessons (see Lesson 5 in Appendix D). Word list reading would not be introduced until students know four or five letter-sound correspondences (see Lesson

7 in Appendix D). The remaining instructional time during the first weeks should be spent on oral language training, vocabulary training, and teaching students how to work exercises independently at their seats. Later, lessons in the beginning reading stage would include word list reading and passage reading (see Lesson 20 in Appendix D).

A sample decoding lesson taken from a later part of the beginning reading stage might include the following tasks:

1. Letter-sound correspondence tasks (2–3 minutes). Teacher writes eight letters on the board, points to each asking, "What sound?"
2. Introductory format for irregular words (2 minutes). Teacher introduces new irregular word and reintroduces previously taught words that had been missed in passage-reading exercises.
3. Sight reading words in isolation (8 minutes). Student reads 20 word list, including irregular and regular words.
4. Passage reading by sight (15 minutes). Student read passage of 90 words.
5. Instruction in activities to be done independently as seatwork activity (5 minutes).

A period for comprehension instruction should also be included. For students who enter school with vocabulary and language deficits, a 20–30 minute period for instruction should be incorporated into the schedule in addition to the period scheduled for decoding instruction.

The type of comprehension activities that a teacher presents depends primarily on the skills students bring to school. Instructionally naive students will need instruction in basic vocabulary and expressive language. An early lesson for these students might include these activities:

1. Colors (3–5 minutes)
2. Object characteristics such as, large, shiny, rough (5–10 minutes)

3. Prepositions (3–5 minutes)
4. Names of objects and of object parts (3–5 minutes)
5. Pronoun and tense usage (5 minutes)

We strongly recommend that teachers obtain a supplementary oral language program for use with students who get less than seven items correct on the oral language screening test. These students will likely have significant difficulty in later grades if they do not receive intensive language and vocabulary work early. When selecting an oral language program, the teacher should be quite careful to select a program that uses very carefully designed presentations. Revising a poorly constructed language program is very time-consuming since so many pictures and objects are needed.

If teachers cannot obtain a well-prepared commercial oral language program, they will have to do the best with the program they have. They should test students individually to detect deficits in basic vocabulary and systematically teach this vocabulary. The language and comprehension tasks should be modified to increase student involvement and provide clear demonstrations. Revising these tasks is much more difficult than revising decoding tasks because so many pictures and objects are needed as examples.

Oral training would also benefit higher-performing students but is not critical for them as it is for instructionally naive students. Oral comprehension activities for instructionally sophisticated students should focus on reasoning skills such as inference and summarization (See Section 3.5.) as well as vocabulary teaching for less common colors, characteristics, and object names.

### Guidelines for Modifying Code-emphasis Programs

*The Letter-Sound Correspondences.* Most code-emphasis programs do not adequately teach isolated letter-sound correspondences. The formats in the commercial programs are often potentially confusing, and the practice opportunities are usually inadequate. They also present letter names before or at the same time as sounds. We recommend replacing the letter-sound correspondence tasks in the commercial programs with the formats specified on pages 145–147. Also we recommend that no reference be made to letter names until students know the most common sound for most letters.

In selecting examples for isolated sounds tasks, teachers should follow these guidelines:

1. A new letter should appear in every task for a week or two after it is introduced.
2. All vowels introduced to date should be reviewed each lesson.
3. Previously introduced consonants that are missed in an isolated sounds tasks or in word-reading tasks should be reintroduced and appear daily for a week.
4. When a new letter that is highly similar to a previously introduced letter is introduced, the similar previously introduced letter should not appear in that or the next day's sounds' task but should appear daily thereafter for about a week. The purpose, at first, is to avoid presenting two confusing correspondences and then after two lessons, to provide discrimination practice on those correspondences.

*Auditory Skills.* Most commercial code-emphasis programs do not include formats similar to the format for segmenting words into sounds and telescoping sounds into words. We recommend adding both formats, starting with lesson one. Four to six words should be included in each task. The words should be drawn from word-reading tasks students will do in the upcoming week. The auditory skills tasks should be done for about 2 weeks and after that, for

four or five lessons prior to the introduction of each new word type.

*Regular Words.* Sounding out should be continued no longer than it takes students to develop fluency. Fluency is demonstrated by the students' correctly sounding out a group of words at a rate of about a word each 4 seconds. For students with no prior reading instruction, acquiring fluency in sounding out will usually take from 1 to 4 weeks. Sight-word reading should be introduced after students are fluently sounding out new words.

The words to be included in word list exercises should be drawn from the story that will be read by the students two or three lessons hence. All new words that have not previously appeared in a passage should be presented in word lists. Preteaching all words that will appear in a passage is just done during the first several weeks of word reading. After that time, only words that contain a new letter or illustrate a new word type need appear in word lists. When words containing blends are introduced, some words without blends should also appear in the list to provide students with discrimination practice. In addition, any words missed by students in previous lessons should appear in the word list.

In most programs, the sequence for introducing new word types is acceptable. However, in some programs, more difficult word types are introduced quite early. If students are still having difficulty decoding words of an easier type, the teacher should consider delaying the introduction of the more difficult type of words, by either reteaching earlier lessons or constructing practice lessons. If just one or two words from a difficult type appear early in the program, teachers can just provide extra practice on these words but do not need to construct extra lessons.

*Irregular Words.* When students are learning their first 7 irregular words, they should not be introduced to a new irregular word if they are having difficulty with previously introduced words. The teacher delays the teaching of the new irregular word simply by identifying the word when it appears in a passage. If possible, teachers should try to avoid delaying new irregular words by providing extra practice on previously introduced irregulars. After the first 7 irregular words are introduced, a new irregular word can be introduced, even if students are having difficulty with a few previously introduced irregulars. The new irregular should not be similar to a word with which a student is having difficulty. If it is, the teacher skips that word and introduces the next irregular. The similar word is delayed until the student has mastered the previously introduced words.

Irregular words are included in word list exercises if they appear in upcoming passages or were missed in a passage-reading exercise. The teacher inspects passages and worksheet pages 3 days prior to presenting them to determine what words are irregular. These words are presented in word list exercises for three lessons before students encounter them in a story. More common irregular words should be reviewed frequently. Teachers should include common irregulars in word list exercises daily for about 2 weeks after they are introduced. Less frequent irregular words (e.g., *Lisa, alligator, soup*) do not need to be reviewed unless they appear in later passages.

*Passage Reading.*   Passage reading is introduced on lesson one in many code-emphasis programs. However, it should be delayed if students cannot sound out words in lists. We recommend that initial passage-reading exercises be conducted using the sounding-out format specified on pages 127–29. Just as with word list reading, sounding out should be replaced with sight reading once students have demonstrated a mastery of sounding out. (Students demonstrate mastery by sounding out words at

a rate of a word each 5 seconds, 90% accuracy.) Becoming proficient in sounding-out passage reading usually takes 1 to 3 weeks, although higher performers may need only a day or two of practice.

Teachers should delay passage-reading exercises until students are able to sound out words in lists. Sounding out words in passages is more difficult than sounding out words in lists since students must coordinate touching the letters and saying the sounds. If sounding-out passage reading is introduced too early, lower performers may encounter a great deal of frustration.

The procedures in commercial programs for conducting whole word passage-reading exercises often do not encourage student attentiveness. We recommend teachers use the format on pages 129–34. It involves the use of unison reading, silent reading, and individual oral reading in a manner which will keep students attentive.

The most critical aspect of passage reading is providing the students with enough practice to develop fluency in sight reading. Students will require varying degrees of practice. Higher-performing students may need only one reading of a story while instructionally naive students may require four, five, or more readings of a story before they can read it at an acceptable rate. Remember, the teacher starts the passage-reading exercises at a rate at which the students can read accurately and gradually increases the rate for each subsequent reading.

## Using a Meaning-emphasis Program

In the introduction to the beginning reading stage, we recommended that all beginning readers be placed in a code-emphasis program. We pointed out that using a code-emphasis program is of particular importance for instructionally naive students. Here we deal with what to do if a teacher is required, for one reason or another, to use a meaning-emphasis program.

Our first suggestion involves not using the readiness books which accompany meaning-emphasis programs. Most of the commercial readiness programs provide little practice on the actual decoding of words; only 10–15 words are introduced in the average readiness program. The programs usually teach (1) letter names and sound recognition and introduce upper- and lower-case letters, (2) use of contextual cues to figure out unknown words, (3) auditory exercises involving word likenesses and differences, (4) visual training exercises in which students match or select similar letters, and (5) left-right awareness. In addition, some programs include language development exercises.

One problem with these programs is that some exercises encourage strategies that are inappropriate for instructionally naive beginning readers (e.g., contextual clues) or are unnecessarily difficult (the simultaneous introduction of upper- and lower-case letters as well as letter sounds and names). Another problem with these readiness programs is that they introduce so much that relatively little time is spent on the more critical skills (e.g., letter-sound correspondences). Since so much is included in the programs, the review provided on the more essential skill is usually inadequate for lower-performing students and many average students. Instead of using a readiness program, we recommend placing students in a code-emphasis program which will act as the readiness program. A student could be transitioned from the code-emphasis program once she (1) can decode all types of regular words, (2) knows the most common sound of all single letters, several more common letter combinations (*th, sh, wh, ch, ar, ea*) and several affixes (*er, ing, ed, est, y, le*), and (3) can read words with these letter combinations and affixes.

When making the transition from the code-emphasis to meaning-emphasis program, the teacher would administer an in-formal reading inventory to determine a proper placement.

Our second suggestion deals with the daily use of a meaning-emphasis program. We recommend that daily lessons include the following tasks. (Note that this recommendation assumes that students have mastered the skills described in the previous paragraph.)

1. Letter-sound correspondence teaching. The rest of the lower-case consonant letters, then upper-case letters, should be introduced. When students know just about all single letter-sound correspondences, the teacher would introduce more letter combinations and affixes (see Sections 3.2 and 3.3).
2. Word list reading. Practice on reading regular words containing blends, both in the initial and final position, should continue. After students master regular words, words containing letter combinations, VCe patterns, and affixes can be introduced (see Sections 3.2 and 3.3). Remember that sounding out is *not* used.
3. Irregular word introduction and practice. A new irregular word introduction procedure, which is described in the primary part irregular word section, should be used. In this procedure, students no longer sound out a word. Instead, the teacher encourages the use of a combination of phonic and context cues to figure out unknown words. The critical part of irregular word teaching is providing adequate practice on the word. New words should be reviewed daily for several weeks.
4. Passage reading. We recommend using the procedures on pages 130–31. As students progress, more individual reading can be incorporated into lessons.
5. Preparation for independent activities. Teachers should check the worksheets to see if they contain any words students will not be able to decode. Such words should be pretaught. Directions should be explained when necessary.

## Progressing at an Optimal Rate

A critical teaching skill for both code- and meaning-emphasis programs is knowing how to move a group at an optimal rate. A rate is optimal when a teacher spends no more time on a task than is necessary for students to master it. The students' performance dictates the rate to progress. If students require a substantial number of corrections before successfully completing a lesson, the teacher will not be able to present more than a lesson a day. Since the students are obviously learning new skills, this is an optimal rate. On the other hand, if students are able to complete the tasks in a lesson with few corrections or repetitions, the teacher can proceed at a faster rate than a lesson each day.

There are two ways in which a teacher can present more than a lesson a day. One is simply to present the tasks from several lessons in the time set aside for one lesson. The other way is to skip lessons. Teachers can skip lessons if they see that students have little difficulty with the tasks in a current lesson, and no new skills are introduced in the following lesson. The teacher would skip to the next lesson in which a new skill is introduced. She can continue skipping until the students' performance on a new skill indicates that they need the continued practice on that skill rather than introduction of a new skill.

Teachers should be careful to take both rate and accuracy into consideration before deciding to skip lessons. Skipping a student who performs accurately but is slow in responding would be inappropriate.

## Monitoring, Diagnosis, and Remediation

Monitoring is a critical teacher skill for ensuring that all students are in fact mastering the skills the teacher is presenting.

During group instruction, a teacher monitors by looking at and listening to students and by giving individual turns. In addition to the monitoring done during group instruction, teachers should set up a supplementary individual testing system in which weekly or biweekly in-depth tests of student performance are made. The tests should include all the letters and irregular words introduced to date as well as five regular words of the most recently introduced word type.

Administering comprehensive individual tests is time-consuming. The average classroom teacher does not have time to give more than one or two tests daily and, thus, can only test students about once a month. If possible, teachers should use a volunteer, parent, or an older student to administer the tests.

The teacher makes the test by writing the letters and words on a sheet of paper and then writing the same words and letters on a group answer form similar to that in Figure 2.8.6.

When administering the tests, the tester writes a plus (+) across from each letter or word said correctly and a minus (−) across from each letter or word the student misses. For each error, the tester writes in what the student says. If the student does not answer, the tester writes N.R. If the student responds correctly but takes longer than a second to produce a sound, the tester marks an L (Late) in the space across from that letter. If a student takes longer than 3 seconds to identify a word the tester marks an L even if the student eventually identifies the word correctly.

The teacher should use the results of the comprehensive individual tests in evaluating his teaching, regrouping students, and in planning remediation lessons. A teacher can use the results to evaluate his teaching by noting how well the group as a whole performs. If several students perform below a 85% accuracy criterion, the teacher must

**FIGURE 2.8.6**  *Within-year Testing Form*

LETTERS & WORDS                                    STUDENTS

| Letters | date tested_____<br>Jim | date tested_____<br>Sarah | date tested_____<br>Tammy |
|---------|---------|---------|---------|
| m | + | + | + |
| a | + | + | + |
| s | + | + | + L |
| d | + | + | + L |
| f | + | + | + |
| i | + | + | + L |
| r | + | + | + |
| t | + | + | + |
| c | − N.R. | + | + L |
| o | + | + | + |
| n | + | + | + |
| g | + | + | + |
| b | + | + | + |
| u | + | + | − ŏ |
| k | + | + | + |
| **Irregulars** | | | |
| was | + | + | + L |
| put | + L | + | + L |
| pull | + | + | + L |
| walk | + | + | + L |
| said | + L | + | − sad |
| **Regulars** | | | |
| last | + | + | + L |
| cent | + | + | + L |
| ask | + | + | + L |
| lift | + | + | + L |
| sand | + | + | + L |

improve daily monitoring procedures to ensure that tasks are repeated until students have mastered them. Similarly, if several students in the group respond late to more than just one or two letters or words, the teacher is probably not providing enough rate training practice.

The results of the individual tests may also help to regroup students. If one or two students perform significantly poorer than the other students in the group, the teacher should consider either placing these students in a lower-performing group or providing them with extra practice to improve their performance. On the other hand, students who are noticeably more fluent in reading words than the other students in their group may be considered for placement in a higher-performing group.

The third way teachers can use the results of the tests is in planning lessons to remedy specific skill deficits. If several members of a group miss more than two or three letters or words, the teacher should consider not progressing in the program but rather repeating several lessons and concentrating on deficits. If the students accuracy is high but they answer slowly, the teacher should concentrate on providing the practice needed to increase fluency.

## APPLICATION EXERCISES

1. Below are the first 20 words in two hypothetical reading programs.

   *Program A*

   | sat | ram | fat | mam | am | it | cat | ram | was | sit | fit |
   |-----|-----|-----|-----|-----|-----|-----|-----|-----|-----|-----|
   | ham | go | tan | Sid | mad | dad | had | sad | dim | | |

   *Program B*

   | Robin | Larry | house | go | into | the | was | happy | new |
   |-------|-------|-------|-----|------|-----|-----|-------|-----|
   | soon | at | if | when | there | what | did | them | you | find |

   Which program is probably a code-emphasis program? Which program is probably a meaning-emphasis program? Explain your answers.

2. Below are the words introduced in the first 20 lessons of three hypothetical code-emphasis programs.

   | Lesson | Program A | Program B | Program C |
   |--------|-----------|-----------|-----------|
   | 1 | Sam, am | at, tam | a    During the |
   | 2 | at, sat | tim, mit | m    first 15 |
   | 3 | mad, tam | rat, rim | lessons, the |
   | 4 | tad, mat | sit, sat, Sam | s    program |
   | 5 | it, sit | mad, rid, did | teaches |
   | 6 | Tim, mit, miss | if, fat | t    auditory |
   | 7 | rim, ram, rat | gas, dig, tag | skills but |
   | 8 | rid, mam | ham, him, his | not word |
   | 9 | fit, fat | hot, hit, rot | r    reading. |
   | 10 | if, dim | lit, hill, till | |
   | 11 | rag, tag | tan, man, Don | |
   | 12 | gas, go | pan, pot, Pam | i |
   | 13 | fill, till | hut, mud, hum | |
   | 14 | lad, lid, to | tub, but, sub | f |
   | 15 | had, ham, has | kiss, kit, kid | |
   | 16 | hig, him | cat, sick, lock | if, sat |
   | 17 | cat, sick | net, ten, bet | am, Sam |
   | 18 | tack, sack | wet, wing, was | rat, at |
   | 19 | hot, sock, lock | tax, tex, box | sad, sit |
   | 20 | mom, lot, tom | yes, yet | Sid, ram |

   a. For each program, fill in the chart below with the letters introduced on each lesson.

   | | 1 | 2 | 3 | 4 | 5 | 6 | 7 | 8 | 9 | 10 | 11 | 12 | 13 | 14 | 15 | 16 | 17 | 18 | 19 | 20 |
   |---|---|---|---|---|---|---|---|---|---|----|----|----|----|----|----|----|----|----|----|----|
   | A | | | | | | | | | | | | | | | | | | | | |
   | B | | | | | | | | | | | | | | | | | | | | |
   | C | | | | | | | | | | | | | | | | | | | | |

   b. Tell which program would be the easiest to use with low-performing students. Explain why.

   c. Tell which program would be the next easiest to use with low-performing children. Explain why.

   d. Tell which program would be the most difficult to use with low-performing students. Explain why.

3. Below is a summary table which shows the performance of Mr. Andrews' first graders on the diagnostic phonics test. (None of these students was able to read acceptably on the IRI). Make two groups. Tell which students would be in each group.

|        | m | a | s | d | f | i | c | n | t | o | r | l | h | g | u | b | T | L | M | F | k | th | e | v | p |
|--------|---|---|---|---|---|---|---|---|---|---|---|---|---|---|---|---|---|---|---|---|---|----|---|---|---|
| John   | O | O | O |
| Ann    | + | + | + | + | + | O | + | + | O | + | + | + | + | O | + | + | + | + | + | + | + | O | O | O |
| Sue    | + | + | + | + | + | + | + | + | O | + | + | + | O | O | O |
| Ramon  | + | + | + | + | + | + | + | + | + | + | + | + | O | + | + | + | + | O | + | + | + | + | O | + | + |
| Dina   | + | + | + | O | + | O | + | + | + | + | O | O | O |
| Rachel | + | + | + | O | + | O | + | + | + | + | O | + | + | O | O | O |
| Sandy  | O | O | O |
| Tomas  | + | + | + | + | + | O | + | + | O | O | O |
| Jill   | O | + | O | O | O |
| Jason  | O | O | O |

4. Below is a scope and sequence chart of the skills taught in a hypothetical reading program.

| Lesson | Letter-Sound Correspondences | When the Word Types First Appear | Irregular Words |
|--------|------------------------------|----------------------------------|-----------------|
| 1  | m |                  |         |
| 4  | s |                  |         |
| 6  | a |                  |         |
| 9  | t |                  |         |
| 11 | r |                  |         |
| 14 | g |                  |         |
| 16 | i |                  |         |
| 19 | f | CVC (continuous) |         |
| 22 | n |                  |         |
| 25 | d |                  |         |
| 28 | o |                  |         |
| 31 | h |                  |         |
| 34 | l | CVC (stop sounds)| was     |
| 37 | b |                  | said    |
| 40 | u |                  | have    |
| 46 | c | CVCC             | give    |
| 50 | k |                  | no, go  |
| 55 | p |                  | the     |
| 60 | v | CCVC             | were    |
| 63 | e |                  | of      |
| 68 | j |                  | most    |

a. Specify the tasks you would include in Lesson 31 on this program. For each task, write the page in this book on which the format appears. Also write the examples you would use in each task. Use the lessons in Appendix D as a guide.

b. Specify the tasks you would include in Lesson 68 of this program. For each task, write the page in this book on which the format appears. Also write the examples you would use in each task. See page 176 for an outline of tasks to include.

# PART 3

# Primary Reading
## Through Third Grade

# SECTION 3.1

## *Introduction*

As was the case for the beginning reading stage, each primary stage section has three major components: (1) recommendations for instruction, (2) how instruction is handled in commercial programs and how the recommendations can be applied to commercial programs, and (3) research applicable to this stage. While applying the procedures recommended to commercial programs is not necessary for many students, it is critical for students who have difficulty in learning to read.

The primary stage begins when students are able to decode all types of regular words and lasts until the students have learned nearly all the basic components of word attack skills. High-performing students may begin the primary stage soon after entering school and complete it midway through their second year of instruction. Low-performing students, on the other hand, may not begin primary stage activities until their second year in school and may take until their fourth year to complete it. Although the major emphasis of instruction during the early part of the primary stage is on decoding, the emphasis gradually shifts to comprehension.

## Direct Instruction Decoding

During the primary stage, students learn strategies and skills that will enable them to decode an increasingly large number of words. The strategies include using phonic, structural, and contextual cues. A scope and sequence chart outlining when specific skills might be introduced can be found on page 276 of Section 3.5.

## Phonic Analysis

In phonic analysis during the beginning stage, we recommend teaching the most common sound for individual letters. During the primary stage, students are taught sound correspondences for groups of letters, referred to as *letter combinations.* An example of a letter combination is *ar,* which usually represents the /är/ sound as in the word *far.* Learning the sound for this letter combination enables students to decode a set of previously unknown words (e.g., *bark, barn, farm, cart, hard, start, card, star, dark,* and *harm*).

After students are taught the most common sound of several letter combinations, they are introduced to the concept of *minor sounds*. We define a minor sound as a sound made by a particular letter or letter combination in less than 50 but more than 20% of the words in which it appears. Letters and letter combinations which have minor sounds are *c, g, a, e, i, o, u, ea, oo, ow,* and *th.* Students are taught a general strategy of first pronouncing a word saying the most common sound of the letter or letter combination and determining if the word as pronounced represents an actual word. If the pronounced word does not make sense, students are taught to pronounce the word saying the minor sound of the letter or letter combination.

Students are also taught a rule for decoding words with a VCe pattern such as, *like, made,* and *hope.* In VCe words, a single vowel is followed by a consonant and a final *e.* Since the initial vowel represents its long sound in approximately two-thirds of such words, we recommend teaching a generalized strategy for decoding them. The strategy involves teaching the students the rule, "An *e* at the end of a word tells us to say the name of the vowel." The teaching of the rule is followed by careful guidance in applying the rule.

## Structural Analysis

Structural analysis involves teaching students to decode words formed by adding prefixes, suffixes, or another word to a base word. Initially, we recommend teaching the relatively simple strategy of identifying a word a part at a time. The word *repainting* would be presented as *re + paint + ing.* A complication appears when VCe derivatives (words formed by adding a suffix to VCe pattern words, e.g., *hope +ing*) are introduced. Students are taught a strategy to discriminate words derived from VCe patterns from words derived from VC patterns,

e.g., *hopping–hoping.* Also included in structural analysis are procedures to teach students to decode *y* derivative words (e.g., *funniest, happier, babies*) and contractions (*I'd, you've, he's*).

Teaching students phonic and structural analysis skills will allow them to decode a great number of words. However, there will still be words the students are not able to decode. We call these words *irregulars.* Teachers must be aware of what words a student cannot rely on his knowledge of letter-sound relationships to decode. These words need to be introduced systematically and practiced quite often.

## Contextual Analysis

Contextual analysis is useful in decoding irregular words. It involves teaching students to rely on the syntax (word order) and semantics (word meaning) of the sentence in which a word appears as an aid to decoding the word. The first type of context cue, word order or syntax, limits the number of possible words that can come next in a sentence. Thus, syntax cues allow students to make inferences regarding the possible pronunciation of a word. For example, the next word in the sentence *John ran to the _____* might be any of several nouns (e.g., *store, shore, station*) but could not be a verb (e.g., *stay, shave*), adverb (e.g., *slowly*), or pronoun (e.g., *she*), etc. The second type of context cue, meaning or semantics, further limits the number of possible words that can come next in a sentence. For example, although the next word in the sentence *Alice threw away the _____* must be a noun, only certain nouns make sense (e.g., *cup, old clothes, broken TV,* etc.). Other nouns would not make sense and would not come next in the sentence (e.g., *Jerry, woman, railroad,* etc.). Since context cues (semantic and syntactic) restrict the words that can come next in a sentence, students are more likely to be able to figure out the pronunciation of an unknown word in context than when it appears in a list of words.

Students also use context cues to check their decoding of words in passages. If a student reads the sentence, *The rabbit went hopping down the street* as "The rabbit went hoping down the street," he can infer that he made a decoding error since the sentence does not make sense. The student would reanalyze *hoping* so that the sentence makes sense.

Context cues also allow students to determine the meaning of an unknown word. By considering the sentence the word is in and the sentences which precede and follow that sentence, students use context to figure out the meaning of the word. This topic will be discussed in Part 4, "Intermediate Reading."

The final aspect of decoding instruction is passage reading, which is the vehicle through which students develop fluency. Passage reading accounts for an increasingly larger proportion of decoding activities as students progress through the primary stage. Recommended procedures for conducting passage reading change during the primary stage. Unison reading is faded out and replaced by individual and silent reading. Comprehension is stressed more. Teachers use a modeling procedure for demonstrating reading with expression. Finally, the criterion for reading rate is gradually increased.

## Direct Instruction Comprehension

During the primary stage, the scope of written activities expands. Literal comprehension becomes more complex as passage length increases, pronoun usage is introduced, and instructions become more complicated. New types of written exercises are introduced: summarization, which includes selecting the main idea or best

title that describes a passage; inference in which the students must use the information in a passage to come up with an answer not stated in the text; sequencing, which involves ordering a series of events; and vocabulary application including synonyms, antonyms, and classification. The scope of comprehension activities will depend on the skill of the students. Since the vocabulary introduced in primary grade literature is generally controlled to be in the receptive vocabulary of the average child, relatively little vocabulary teaching is necessary for average and above-average students. Low-performing students, on the other hand, may require a great deal of vocabulary instruction.

## Selecting and Using a Program

A code-emphasis program should be used for students entering the primary stage since decoding remains the main objective of reading instruction. Code-emphasis programs allow for easier teaching of generalizable decoding skills while meaning-emphasis programs, because of the greater number of irregular words, make teaching generalizable decoding skills more difficult. Our rationale for recommending code-emphasis programs is developed more fully in the overview of Part 2, "Beginning Reading."

Code-emphasis and meaning-emphasis programs become increasingly similar in the latter part of the primary stage since by this time, most decoding skills have been taught. Thus, a third grade teacher with students who know most decoding skills need not look at how decoding is taught but rather at how different programs teach comprehension.

The rate at which new skills are introduced is the main criteria for selecting commercial programs. Teachers selecting among code-emphasis programs should look at the rate at which decoding elements are introduced while teachers evaluating meaning-emphasis programs should look at the rate at which irregular words are introduced. Programs with an unrealistic rate for introducing new skills are difficult for a teacher to use, since a great deal of time must be spent in constructing supplementary exercises to meet the needs of lower-performing students. Both code-and meaning-emphasis programs handle written comprehension activities in a similar manner. Most do not provide enough practice on critical skills, nor do they provide for systematic vocabulary instruction. Teachers must be prepared to supplement the comprehension activities provided in most programs.

# *Phonic Analysis*

During the primary stage, students should be taught to see words as units of letters rather than just single letters. Primary stage phonics instruction includes teaching students (1) the most common sound(s) represented by several consecutive letters, referred to as letter combinations, (2) a strategy to decode words which contain a VCe pattern in which the initial vowel represents its long sound and the final *e* is silent as in *make, hope, use,* and (3) minor sounds of letters and letter combinations and a strategy for trying these sounds if a word pronounced with the most common sound of a particular letter does not make sense. Teachers should also test and review, as necessary, phonic skills taught during the beginning stage: knowledge of single letter-sound correspondences and decoding of various types of regular words. Special emphasis should be given to words beginning with consonant blends since they are often troublesome (see page 100 for directions on teaching words with blends).

## Words with Letter Combinations

A letter combination is a group of consecutive letters that is quite predictable regarding the sounds it represents. Knowing the most common sounds of letter combinations greatly expands students' ability to decode new words. For example, a student who can decode all types of regular words and has just learned the *ee* letter combination will be able to decode these new words: *bee, bleed, beet, breed, peel, see, teen, weed, creek, deer, flee, fleet, green, greet, jeep, keep, weep, canteen, indeed, upkeep,* and *fifteen.*

Table 3.2.1 lists the letter combinations that we suggest presenting. We recommend presenting a letter combination if it represents one sound in over half the words in which it appears and if it appears in 10 or more common words. The letter combinations are listed alphabetically in the left column of the table. The second column contains words that illustrate the most common sound of each letter combination. The third column shows the phonetic representation of the most common sound. The fourth column lists the percentage of total words in which the letter combination represents its most common sound. The fifth column tells the number of words in which the particular letter combination represented its most common sound in a computer analysis of the most common 17,310 English words (Hanna et al., 1966). (Note

**TABLE 3.2.1** *Letter Combinations*

| LETTER COMBINATION | SAMPLE WORD | PERCENTAGE | FREQUENCY | TYPE |
|---|---|---|---|---|
| ai[a] | ma*i*d | 90% | 254 | vowel digraph |
| ar | c*a*r | 75% | 518 | r-controlled |
| au | h*au*l | 94% | 146 | vowel digraph |
| aw | l*aw*n | 100% | 75 | vowel digraph |
| ay | st*ay* | 97% | 131 | vowel digraph |
| ch | *ch*ip | 63% | 313 | consonant digraph |
| ea[a] | b*ea*t | 60% | 294 | vowel digraph |
| ee[a] | n*ee*d | 98% | 285 | vowel digraph |
| er | f*er*n | 97% | 313 | r-controlled |
| eu | f*eu*d | 73% | 28 | vowel digraph |
| ew | shr*ew*d | 95% | 38 | vowel digraph |
| ey | hon*ey* | 67% | 46 | vowel digraph |
| igh | h*igh* | 100% | 88 | vowel digraph |
| ir | f*ir*st | 100% | 104 | r-controlled |
| kn | *kn*ow | 100% | 41 | consonant digraph |
| ng | si*ng* | 100% | 362 | consonant digraph |
| oa | l*oa*d | 94% | 126 | vowel digraph |
| oi | b*oi*l | 98% | 92 | vowel digraph |
| ol | h*ol*d | n.a. | n.a. | l-controlled |
| oo | b*oo*t | 59% | 173 | vowel digraph |
| or | sh*or*t | 55% | 312 | r-controlled |
| ou | cl*ou*d | 84% | 285 | vowel diphthong |
| ow | *ow*n | 50% | 124 | vowel digraph |
| oy | t*oy* | 98% | 48 | vowel diphthong |
| ph | *ph*one | 100% | 242 | consonant digraph |
| qu | *qu*ick | 100% | 191 | none |
| sh | *sh*op | 100% | 398 | consonant digraph |
| th[b] | *th*ank | 74% | 411 | consonant digraph |
| ue | c*ue* | 67% | 27 | vowel diphthong |
| ur | b*ur*n | 100% | 203 | r-controlled |
| wh | *wh*ale | 85% | 89 | consonant digraph |
| wr | *wr*ap | 100% | 48 | consonant digraph |

*Note.* Double consonants are usually *not* letter combinations in that they represent their most common sound. For example:

bb: ebb
dd: add
ff: stuff
gg: egg
ll: fill
nn: inn
ss: boss
tt: mitt
zz: buzz

We did not list these as letter combinations since no special teaching procedure is needed. Students can decode words in which double consonants appear using the sounding-out and sight-reading procedures discussed earlier. The same holds true with the consonant digraph *ck*. Since both the *c* and *k* represent the /k/ sound, students have little difficulty decoding words that contain *ck*.

[a] When computing percentages from the Hanna et al. study (1966), we combined some combinations that were followed by *r* (*air, eer*) with the respective combination without *r* (*ee, ai*). We found that even though there is a sound difference when *r* follows the combinations, students can decode words by pronouncing the most common sound of the letter combination and then saying the /r/ sound.

[b] Although /th/ represents the unvoiced sound in most words (e.g., *think*), in many high frequency words (*this that, them, than, then, the, those, these*) the *th* is voiced. We recommend introducing this less common, or minor sound of *th* first, because students use it in sounding out many high frequency words.

that these percentages vary from study to study, depending on the sample of words used.) In the sixth column, the letter combinations are classified as vowel digraph, consonant digraph, r-controlled vowel, or diphthong. A digraph consists of two consecutive letters that represent one sound. An r-controlled vowel is a vowel followed by the letter r. A diphthong consists of two consecutive vowels each of which contributes to the sound heard.[1]

The consonant and vowel digraphs and dipthongs in Table 3.2.2 were not included in the letter combination list because they appeared in less than 10 common words and/or they did not represent a particular sound in more than half the words in which they appeared. The source for these figures is Burmeister (1975) who also utilized Hanna and Hanna's (1966) computer analysis of letter-sound correspondences. The vowel digraph ie is not taught as a letter combination but receives special attention in the structural analysis section. The ie combination is often formed when an ie suffix, er, ed, or est, is added to a y-ending word (e.g., happy + er = happier).

## Direct Instruction Procedures

### Preskills

The first letter combinations can be introduced after students know the most common sounds of about 15 to 20 single letters and can decode passages made up of regular words at a speed of about 30 words per minute. This speed indicates that students are no longer laboriously sounding out but are perceiving words as units, which makes decoding words that contain letter combinations much easier.

---

[1] The distinction between which letter combinations are digraphs, diphthongs, or r-controlled vowels is more important to speech teachers than reading teachers. Nonetheless, reading teachers should be aware of the terms since they often appear in teacher's guides and professional literature.

## Sequence

Two factors determine the order in which letter combinations are introduced in a reading program. The first is the number of words in which the letter combination appears. When planning a sequence for introducing letter combinations, the number of words containing the letter combination should be considered not only in terms of total occurrence but also in terms of how many of the words are common or high frequency. For example, although the digraph ph appears in a large number of words, many of these words are fairly uncommon words (words which would not appear in primary grade books). Consequently, ph would not be introduced as early as indicated by its frequency of occurrence. On the other hand, the letter combination ol appears in relatively few words, but the words are very common (hold, told, cold). Thus, ol would be introduced relatively early.

The second sequencing consideration is the similarity of letter combinations. If letter combinations make similar but not identical sounds, they should be separated by at least two other combinations. Letter combinations to be separated include these:

1. sh and ch: These consonant digraphs are made by forming the lips in a very similar manner. This factor, along with their similar sound and appearance (both contain the letter h) can cause confusion.
2. oa, oi, oo, and ou: In addition to the fact that these letter combinations sound somewhat similar, they are part of a bigger group of letter combinations that begin with o (oa, oi, ol, oo, ou, ow, and oy). The large number of combinations beginning with the same letter and sounding similar can confuse students.
3. r-controlled vowels: The three sounds produced by r-controlled vowels (/ä/ as in arm, /û/ as in fur, bird, her, and /ô/

## TABLE 3.2.2

| LETTER COMBINATION | SAMPLE WORD | PERCENTAGE OF WORDS WITH MOST COMMON SOUND |
|---|---|---|
| ae | algae | 83 |
|  | aesthetic | 17 |
| bt | debt | 100 |
| ei | reign | 40 |
|  | deceit | 26 |
|  | foreign | 13 |
|  | seismic | 11 |
| eo | pigeon | 67 |
|  | leopard | 20 |
|  | people | 13 |
| lf | often | 100 |
| ie | chief | 64 |
|  | tie | 36 |
| gh | rough | 45 |
|  | ghost | 48 |
| gm | phlegm | 100 |
| gn | gnat | 100 |
| kh | khaki | 100 |
| ld | could | 100 |
| lf | calf | 100 |
| mb | tomb | 100 |
| mn | autumn | 100 |
| oe | foe | 59 |
|  | shoe | 22 |
| ps | psychic | 100 |
| rh | rhetoric | 100 |
| sc | scene | 100 |
| sl | island | 100 |
| st | listen | 50 |
| tw | two | 100 |
| ue | clue | 75 |
| ui | build | 47 |
|  | fruit | 29 |
| uo | buoyant | 100 |
| uy | buy | 100 |

as in *sport*) all sound similar. Thus, the letter combinations which represent these sounds should be separated.

Letter combinations representing the same sound (*ee* and *ea, ai* and *ay, oi* and *oy, au* and *aw*) need not be separated. Only letter combinations which represent *similar* sounds should be separated.

In Table 3.2.3 we have constructed a sample order for introducing letter combinations. Keep in mind that the order suggested is *not* meant to represent the only order for introducing letter combinations.

**TABLE 3.2.3**  *Sample Order for Introducing Letter Combinations\**

| th | ai | ou |
|----|-----|-----|
| er | ch | aw |
| ing | or | ir |
| sh | ay | kn |
| wh | igh | oi |
| qu | ow | ph |
| ol | ur | ey |
| ar | oa | wr |
| ea | au | ue |
| oo |  | oy |
| ee |  | ew |

\* Read vertically.

It should serve as an example of how the sequencing guidelines can be applied.

Here is our rationale for determining the placement of specific letters:

1. *Th, wh* and *ol* are introduced early because they appear in very common high frequency words (e.g., *this, that, when, where,* and *sold*).
2. *Er* and *ing* are introduced early because, in addition to serving as letter combinations, they also function as affixes (e.g., *cutter, cutting*).
3. *Sh* and *ch* are separated by eight other combinations since if introduced too near each other, they might be confused by some students.

## Rate of Introduction

Learning to decode words containing a new letter combination is more difficult than simply learning the sound of a letter combination in isolation. When reading a word that contains a letter combination, the student can no longer decode by looking at it letter by letter but must see the word as being composed of one or more combinations of letters. This transition from decoding letter by letter to decoding words as units requires extensive practice. The stu-

dents' performance in decoding words containing previously taught letter combinations should determine when to introduce a new letter combination, rather than their ability to identify a letter combination in isolated sounds tasks.

As a general rule, students should be able to read a list of words containing letter combinations introduced to that date at a rate no slower than a word every 2 seconds with 95% accuracy before a new letter combination is introduced. (Toward the middle of second grade, the rate should increase to a word each 1 1/2 seconds.) In a developmental program being taught to average ability students, nearly all letter combinations can be introduced by the end of the second year. This translates into a new letter combination being taught about every 2 weeks. A new letter combination should not be introduced if a student is having difficulty with a previously introduced letter combination that is similar to the new combination. For example, if a student is having difficulty with the combination *oo* and the next combination is *ou,* the teacher would not introduce *ou.* Instead, the teacher would skip to the next letter combination that is not similar. If, however, a student is having difficulty with more than one previously introduced combination, the teacher should generally work on firming up the student's knowledge of these combinations before introducing a new one.

## Teaching Procedures

Two basic formats are used in teaching words that contain letter combinations: an isolated sounds format in which students learn to identify letter combinations in isolation and a sight format in which the students identify part of a word before reading the entire word. The isolated sounds format is nearly identical to the formats used to teach the most common sounds of individual letters. It combines the steps from the introductory and discrimination formats into one format. In the sight-reading format, for the first half of the words in a list, the students first identify the sound of the letter combination and then the whole word. Then, the students reread those words and the remaining words without first identifying the sound of the combination.

## Critical Behaviors for Teaching Isolated Sounds

### Correcting Mistakes

The corrections are the same as those specified on page 81 of Section 2.3. If a student misidentifies a letter combination or responds late, the teacher tells the student the correct sound, has the student say the sound, and then alternates between the missed letter combination and other letter combinations that the student knows. If a student continues to make errors on a previously introduced letter combination, extra practice should be provided on that combination.

## Example Selection for Isolated Sounds

The format should include five to eight letter combinations. The following are guidelines for selecting examples:

---

**Isolated Sounds Format for Letter Combinations**

| Teacher | Students |
|---|---|
| Teacher writes on the board: *ea, or, ee, th, sh,* and *ing.* | |
| 1. Teacher models by saying the sound of the new letter combination and tests by having the students pronounce it. Teacher points to *ea.* **"These letters usually say /ē/. What do these letters usually say?"** (signal) | "ē" |
| 2. Teacher alternates between the new combination and other combinations. Teacher points to *ea,* pauses 2 seconds, and signals with out-in motion. | Say most common sounds. |
| Teacher presents the remaining letter combinations using an alternating pattern similar to this: *ea, or, ea, ee, th, ea, sh, ing, or, ea.* (See letter-sound correspondence format on page 77 for direction on signaling.) | |
| 3. Teacher presents the letter combinations again but this time with a 1-second thinking pause. | Say most common sounds. |

1. Review the most recently introduced letter combination daily until the students consistently identify words in passages that contain the combination. This usually takes a week or two.
2. Exclude previously taught, similar letter combinations the first 2 days a new letter combination appears. On the third day after the new combination appears, include any previously introduced letter combinations that are similar to the newly introduced combination. For example, on the third day after *ch* is introduced, the combination *sh* should be included because it sounds similar. Likewise, on the third day after the letter combination *or* is introduced, the letter combination *ar* should be included. Do not, however, include a similar letter combination unless it has been taught earlier.

## Correction Procedure

If a student misidentifies a word, the teacher points to the letter or letter combination pronounced incorrectly and asks students to produce its sound. For example, if a student says "boot" for *bout,* the teacher points to *ou* and asks, "What sound do these letters usually make?" After the student produces the correct sound for the letter, the teacher asks, "What word?"

## Example Selection for Sight Format Words

A new combination appears in one-syllable words 3 days after it appears in isolation. The first 2 or 3 words in a list should contain the new letter combination. The word list can contain a total of 10 to 15 words. About one-half of the words should contain the new letter combination. The rest of the list should include words containing previously introduced letter combinations. Include two minimally different pairs of words focusing on newly introduced letter combinations. In such pairs, words would be identical except for the letter combination (e.g., *bout–boot, hail–haul*).

## Multi-syllabic Words Containing Letter Combinations

Two-syllable words containing a letter combination should be introduced about a week after the first one-syllable words with that letter combination are introduced. A format for introducing multi-syllabic words is discussed in Section 3.3.

---

### Sight-reading Format for Single Syllable Words

| *Teacher* | *Students* |
|---|---|
| Teacher writes on the board: *bout, round, loud, boot, beam, trout, proud, stain, moon, pound.* | |
| 1. Students identify the sound of the letter combination, then read the word. Teacher underlines *ou* in *bout* with fingers and asks, **"What do these letters usually say?"** (signal) | "ou" |
| Teacher points to word. **"What word?"** (signal) | "Bout" |
| Teacher repeats step 1 with five words. | |
| 2. Students reread list *without* first identifying the sound of the letter combination. Teacher points to *bout,* pauses 1 second, and signals. **"What word?"** (signal) | "Bout" |

# Words with a VCe Pattern

In a VCe pattern word, a single vowel is followed by a consonant, which in turn is followed by a final e. Note the VCe patterns in the following words:

|  VCe  |  VCe  |  VCe  |
| lake, | stripe, | smile |

In approximately two-thirds of one-syllable words that contain VCe patterns, the initial vowel represents the long sound (the letter name).[2] In the other one-third of the words in which there is a VCe pattern, the vowel sound is sometimes the most common sound of the initial vowel (give) and sometimes a sound that is neither the most common sound nor the long sound (done).

Since the initial vowel represents its long sound in most one-syllable, VCe pattern words, we recommend teaching the rule that when a word ends in e, the initial vowel says its name. The other one-syllable, VCe pattern words in which the initial vowel makes a sound other than its long sound should be treated as irregular words: the teacher identifies each word and then tests the students. Although a few irregular VCe pattern words (e.g., have, give, come) will need to be introduced early because of their high frequency, most irregular VCe words should not be introduced until after students learn to decode "regular" VCe words in which the vowel represents the long sound.

## Direct Instruction Procedures

### Preskills

The strategy to decode VCe pattern words should be introduced after students have been taught to identify several letter combinations and can decode words containing those combinations. Reading words with letter combinations gives students practice in looking at units of letters. This skill will prepare students for VCe words, in which the initial vowel sound is determined by a letter at the end of a word (the final e). In addition, students must be taught letter names for the vowels. Letter names can be introduced once students know the most common sounds for all the vowels. They are taught by having the students say the sound for a vowel, telling them the name of the letter, and then testing them on saying both the sound and the name of the vowel. A new vowel name can be introduced every three to five lessons. Review should be cumulative; i.e., on a given lesson all previously introduced vowels should be included in each letter name exercise. Note that many students will know the names for the vowels and will not require instruction. However, instructionally naive students may need several weeks of instruction to master all the vowel names. These students should not be introduced to VCe words until they master the letter name and sound for each vowel.

## Sequence

In order to make initial exercises on VCe pattern words easier, teachers can introduce them in groups made up of words containing the same initial vowel. The groups should be introduced according to the relative frequency of the initial vowel in VCe pattern words. Since the letter a appears most frequently in VCe pattern words, VCe words with a should be introduced first. The second most frequently appearing vowel is i, the third o, the fourth u, and the fifth e. In this way, students do not have to figure out initially which of the five vowel names (or sounds) to say when discriminating VCe pattern words from CVC pattern words. Rather, they can concentrate on determining whether the vowel represents its long sound or its short sound.

---

[2] Various researchers report different percentages for the number of words in which the initial vowel in a VCe pattern represents its long sound. Clymer (1963) found the percentage to be 63%; Burmeister (1968), 61%. The differences result from the different words included in the studies.

## Rate

A group of VCe pattern words that begins with a new initial vowel might appear about every five lessons, depending on student performance. As always, the criterion for introducing a new skill is student mastery of previously introduced skills. However, if the second group of VCe words (those containing *i*) is delayed much more than a week, instructionally naive students may develop the habit of always saying /a/ whenever they see an *e* at the end of a word. To avoid teaching this misrule, a second initial vowel should be introduced no more than a week after the first one.

## Teaching Procedures

The teacher presents the rule: "When a word ends in *e*, we say the name (points to initial vowel) of this letter." The wording of this rule is designed to be free of language concepts that might confuse the students. The format includes three steps: telling the students the rule, prompting them to apply the rule, and practicing nonprompted sight reading.

## Critical Behaviors

### Fading

Steps 1 and 2 of the format are used only the first few days when a new vowel is introduced. After that, only step 3 for the discrimination words is used.

### Correcting Mistakes

Most mistakes will involve the students' saying a wrong vowel sound. If students make this mistake, the teacher corrects by asking, "Is there an *e* at the end of the word? So do we say the name of this letter? What do we say for this letter? What's the word?" The teacher then alternates between the missed words and previously identified words. If the students require

many trials to identify the word correctly in the alternating pattern exercise, the teacher can use a precorrection for the next several VCe words in the list. In the precorrection, the teacher points to the end of the word and says, "Does this word end in *e*?" The teacher then points to the initial vowel and says, "Think about what you say for this letter." If this precorrection prompt is used, the teacher should retest the students on all the words later, without the prompt.

## Example Selection

The first several words should end with *e* and contain the newly introduced vowel. The rest of the list should include some CVC and some VCe words. Two of the words should form a minimally different pair (e.g., *same–Sam*). The list should include some CVC and VCe pattern words with initial vowels that were introduced in earlier lessons. Below is an example of a group of words that might be included in a VCe exercise for primary stage readers. Assume that VCe words with *a* and *i* have been taught and words with *o* as the initial vowel are being introduced.

> *home   hope   note   Sam   same   not*
> *bone   rode   ham   like   robe*

Note that the list is constructed in an unpredictable order. A VCe word is not always followed by a CVC word. Also, the same vowel does not appear in several consecutive words except for the three introductory words. Ordering the words unpredictably discourages guesses based on word order.

During the first several weeks of instruction, most VCe words should begin with a single consonant rather than a consonant blend. Since words that begin with single consonants are easier to decode, the students will be better able to concentrate on correctly identifying the vowel. Also, higher-frequency words like *name, same, home, like, take,* etc., should be included

**Format for VCe Words**

|                                                    Teacher | Students |
|---|---|

Teacher writes on the board: *game, hate, lake, Sam, same, made, fan, land, sad, late*

1. Teacher states the rule, **"An e at the end tells us to say the name of this** (pointing to *a*) **letter."**

2. Teacher demonstrates how to apply the rule with the first three words, which are all VCe words.

   a. Teacher points to *game*. **"Is there an e at the end of this word?"** (signal)                    "Yes."

   b. Teacher points to *a*. **"So do we say the name of this letter?"** (signal)                    "Yes."

   c. **"What's the name of this letter?"** (signal)    "a"

   d. **"Get ready to tell me the word."** Teacher pauses 1 or 2 seconds, then signals.    "game"

   e. Teacher repeats steps 1–4 with the next two words.

3. Teacher tells students that the next words will sometimes end in *e*. **"Be careful, some of these words end in e and some do not."** Teacher points to first word, pauses several seconds, then signals, asking, **"What word?"** The same procedure is repeated with the remaining words until the students make six to eight consecutive correct responses. Only when students respond correctly to a set of examples can the teacher assume they can apply the rule.

in lists, rather than less common words such as, *hive, cope,* etc.

## Words with Minor Sounds

The following material deals with teaching students a strategy for decoding words containing letter(s) representing a minor sound. A minor sound for a letter or letter combination occurs less often than the most common sound but frequently enough to justify teaching the minor sound in isolation. We define a minor sound as a sound that represents a letter in less than 50% of the words in which it appears but in more than 20% of the words.

The letters and letter combinations that have minor sounds are listed in Table 3.2.4. In the first column are the letters. The second column contains words that illustrate the most common sound. The number next to the word indicates that percentage of words in which the letter represents the most common sound. The third column contains words that illustrate the minor

**TABLE 3.2.4**    *Minor Sounds of Single Consonants and Letter Combinations*

| LETTER(S)[a] | MOST COMMON SOUND | | MINOR SOUND | |
|---|---|---|---|---|
| c | call | 74% | cent | 25% |
| g | gun | 65% | gin | 35% |
| ea | treat | 60% | bread | 26% |
| oo | moon | 59% | book | 36% |
| ow | blow | 52% | now | 48% |
| th | thank | 74% | this | 26% |
| ch | chip | 63% | chord | 29% |

Note. Percentages based on study by Hanna et al., 1966.

a Single vowel letters were not included in this list since a strategy for figuring out minor sounds of vowels is discussed in Section 3.3 "Structural Analysis."

sound and the percentage of occurrence. The percentages do not total 100 because some letters represent sounds besides the two listed.

## Direct Instruction Procedures

### Minor Sounds of Consonants

Two consonants have minor sounds: *c* and *g*. The letter *c* is quite predictable in that whenever it appears in front of the vowels *a, o* or *u*, it represents its most common sound, /k/. Whenever it appears in front of the vowels *i, e,* or *y*, it represents its minor sound, /s/. The minor sound for the letter *g* is not as consistent. It represents its most common sound in front of the vowels *a, o,* or *u*. However, when it appears in front of the vowels *i* and *e,* it does not always represent its minor sound /j/, as in *gin* and *gym;* it sometimes represents its most common sound, /g/ as in *give, gill,* and *get.*

#### When to Introduce

More common words with the minor sounds of *c* and *g* should be treated as irregular words during the first and early part of the second year of decoding instruction. Toward the middle of the second year, however, the teacher can present a format for teaching students to decode new words in which *c* and *g* represent their minor sounds. Words with *c* should be taught first since *c* appears in more words than *g*.

## Minor Sounds of Letter Combinations

Unlike *c* and *g*, the sounds of letter combinations are not usually determined by the letters that come next in a word; thus, the teaching procedure is different. For letter combinations, teachers present a strategy in which the students first try the most common sound and see if they come up with a "real" word. If they do not come up with a familiar word, they pronounce the word using the minor sound of the letter combination.

Students should not be taught a minor sound strategy until about a month after the most common sounds for several combinations have been introduced. The purpose of this delay is to enable the students to become proficient in decoding words which contain the most common sound of various letter combinations.

Some words in which a letter combination represents its minor sound will produce a familiar word if the student says the most common sound for that word. For example if *ea* in *dead* is pronounced with the /ē/ sound, the word is "dēd." When encountering such words, the teacher

**Format for Teaching Minor Sound of *C* or *G***

| Teacher | Students |
|---|---|
| Teacher writes on the board: *cent, city, call, center, cod, cut.* | |
| 1. Teacher presents rule about most common sound and minor sound. | |
|    a. Teacher points to *c.* **"What does this letter usually say?"** (signal) | "k" |
|    b. **"When the next letter is *e* or *i*, it says *s*. What does it say when the next letter is *e* or *i?"** (signal) | "s" |
|    c. **"And what does it usually say?"** (signal) | "k" |
| 2. Teacher prompts students on words. | |
|    a. Teacher points to *c* in *cell.* **"What letter comes next?"** (signal) | "e" |
|    b. **"So do you say /k/ or /s/ for this letter?"** (signal) | "s" |
|      To correct, teacher used step 1b. | |
|    c. **"What word?"** (signal) | "Cell" |
|      Teacher repeats steps a, b, and c with the rest of the words. | |
| 3. Teacher points to each word. **"What word?"** (pauses, then signals) | Students read entire list of words with no prompts. |

Note: When doing the format for *g,* change the wording in step 1b to **"When it comes before *e* or *i*, you sometimes say /j/."**

should say a sentence in which the word is left out. For example, "The _____ man was buried." The teacher would point to the word *dead* when coming to the blank in the sentence. The students must come up with a word that makes sense in that context.

## Example Selection

Examples used in teaching students to decode words with minor sounds must be selected with care. The proportion of words containing common and minor sounds should be similar to the percentages in Table 3.2.1. For example, since 60% of *ea* words say /ē/, about two-thirds of the words would have long *e*. Words should be familiar and made up of familiar letters and letter combinations. If students are not familiar with a word, they will not know which of two possible pronunciations is correct—the one with the most common sound or the one with the minor sound. If, for example, the word *bleak* appears in a list and a student has never heard the word, she will have no way of knowing whether the pronunciation is blēk or blĕk.

**Format for Minor Sounds of Letter Combinations**

| *Teacher* | *Students* |
|---|---|

Teacher writes on board: *thread, treat, cream, spread, least, meant.*

1. Teacher presents rule about most common and minor sound.

   a. Teacher points to *ea.* **"What do these letters usually say?"** (signal)      "ē"

   b. **"In some words they say /ĕ/. What do they say in some words?"** (signal)      "ĕ"

   c. **"What do these letters usually say?"** (signal)      "ē"

   d. **"But in some words they say . . ."** (signal)      "ĕ"

2. Teacher prompts students on first four words.

   a. Teacher points to *ea* in *thread.* **"What do these letters usually say?"** (signal)      "ē"

   b. **"Say the word."** (pause, signal)      "Thrēd"

   c. **"Is that a word?"** (signal)      "No"

   Do steps d–f only if answer to step c is no.

   d. **"What else can you say for these letters?"** (signal)      "ĕ"

   e. **"Say the word."** (pause, signal)      "Thread"

   f. **"Is that a word?"** (signal)      "Yes"

   g. **"What word is this?"** (signal)      "Thread"

3. Students sight read entire list without any prompts. Teacher points to each word, pauses several seconds, and signals. To correct, use step 2.

4. Students reread list with only 1-second pause before signal.

More common words that contain a minor sound should appear frequently enough in word lists and stories so that the students will be able to identify them as sight words and not have to go through a laborious procedure to decode them. These more common words should appear daily for at least a week and then intermittently.

## Supplementary Activities

A great variety of activities can be used to help students develop fluency in phonic analysis. The activities encourage students to see words as being composed of units of letters. Some worksheet exercises that may be done independently appear in Figure 3.2.1.

When assigning supplementary materials, teachers must carefully coordinate the words selected for the activities with the words being taught in the program. All the words in the activity should be words the student can decode. Teachers must be especially careful to use familiar words in fill-in exercises.

**Figure 3.2.1**

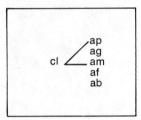

_ich

st sl sn

_ip

ch wh sh

_ain

dr gr tr

Make a line between the letters in column one and column two which form real words.

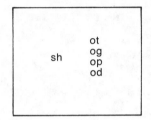

cl

ap
ag
am
af
ab

sh

ot
og
op
od

fl

ame
am
ag
ate

Fill Ins

I will _____ (meet, met) you at two o'clock.

She will _____ (shop, chop) down the tree.

She has two _____ (cans, canes) of pop.

## Commercial Programs

Keep in mind that since the 1960s the teaching of phonic analysis skills has improved dramatically. It is rare now to find a new program which presents false generalizations like "when two vowels go walking, the first one does the talking." Even with the improvements, however, modifications are needed to ease the learning of low-performing students. Specifically, teachers will need to construct word and review lists to explicitly teach many of the phonic analysis skills discussed here. The formats in Section 3.2 provide suggestions for teaching procedures and the word lists in the appendix provide examples to include in the formats.

## Letter Combinations

### Sequence

Several of the programs we examined had violations of the sequencing guideline re-

garding separating similar letter combinations. In Lippincott and Houghton Mifflin, for example, *sh* and *ch* are introduced consecutively. Also in Lippincott, several similar letter combinations appear quite near each other (*oo, ow, ou,* and *oi*).

Teachers have several options in dealing with sequencing problems. The first is to simply teach the program as it is written, carefully monitoring student performance and providing extra practice if necessary. A second option is to delay the introduction of a similar letter combination by not presenting it when it appears in the program. The teacher would present other tasks in upcoming lessons but not include examples containing the new letter combination. Only after several other letter combinations were introduced would the delayed letter combination be presented. This procedure is difficult to implement and should be used only with very low-performing students.

Another sequencing problem in commercial programs involves the introduction of the minor sound of a letter combination.

It often appears on the same lesson or shortly after the lesson on which the most common sound is introduced. We recommend separating the introduction of most common and minor sounds by at least 20 lessons since introducing both sounds at the same time confuses some low-performing students.

### Practice

Providing adequate practice on letter combinations in isolation and in words is necessary for students to develop fluency. Unfortunately, most programs had only a lesson or two in which the sound of a letter combination was presented in isolation and/or in word lists. While that amount of practice may be adequate for most average and above-average students, some students will need more practice and review. Teachers should construct supplementary isolated sound and word list exercises to provide the necessary extra practice. This suggestion is reasonable since it would require only a few minutes of extra work each day on the teacher's part. Constructing word lists to provide extra practice is especially critical for teachers using meaning-emphasis programs, since in these programs, what is taught in the phonics portion of a lesson is not coordinated with the words that appear in passages.

### Rate

The rate at which new letter combinations are introduced varies considerably from program to program. The students' performance should dictate whether the teacher modifies the program. If students have no trouble, no modifications are needed. If students are having difficulty with more than one previously introduced combination, the introduction of new combinations should be delayed while the teacher firms up knowledge of the previously taught combinations. If a student is having difficulty with just one previously taught letter combination, the teacher introduces the next letter combination which is not similar to the one the student is having difficulty with. The teacher works on the letter combination causing problems. When the student knows this combination, the teacher introduces the skipped one.

### Teaching Procedures

The teaching procedure for words containing letter combinations are often constructed in a potentially confusing manner in commercial programs. Most programs do not provide isolated sounds tasks in which the teacher pronounces the letter combination's most common sound in isolation. Instead, the teacher says a group of words containing the most common sound of the letter combination. For example, in introducing the *or* letter combination, a teacher's guide might recommend the teacher write the words *or, for,* and *nor* on the board. The teacher has the students say the words and then asks, "Do these words rhyme? Do all three words end in the same letters? What are these letters? The letters *o* and *r* stand for the ending sound in *or, for, nor."* Such a demonstration may be adequate for most students; however, for lower-performing students, it has the potential of being confusing. We recommend that teachers use the format presented earlier in the section.

## Minor Sounds

### Minor Sounds of C and G

Two characteristics of commercial programs that might cause students difficulty are (1) excessive or ambiguous teacher explanations and (2) lack of practice.

The explanations in some programs involve the words *hard c* and *soft c.* The students are told that when *c* is followed by *i, e,* or *y,* it represents its soft sound; whereas, when followed by *a, o,* or *u,* it represents its hard sound. We recommend not using the terms *hard* and *soft* when first introducing the minor sound for *c,* since the inclusion of the extra terms will cause difficulties for some students. Instead of using those terms, we suggest that the teacher point to *c* and say, "This letter usually says /k/, but when the next letter is *e, i,* or *y,* it says /s/." Additional terms such as, following, preceding, and in front of, are also included in commercial programs. Some students can be expected to have difficulty applying rules containing these words, especially when programs do not provide enough demonstrations of how the rule is applied and how these words function. Teachers should not assume that students can apply a rule just because they can say it. Teachers must ensure that students know the meaning of all terms used.

A second problem is lack of sufficient practice. Several weeks of practice may be needed before students can be expected to apply the minor sound rule when reading independently. Typically, programs provide only one or two lessons for teaching the rule. Consequently, teachers should construct their own daily supplementary exercises until students are facile in applying the rule independently.

### Minor Sounds of Letter Combinations

We noted two characteristics present in some commercial programs that might cause students difficulty: (1) introducing the minor sound too soon after the most common sound and (2) including words in which a letter combination represents neither the most common nor the minor sound on the same lesson the minor sound was introduced.

Some programs introduce the most common sound and minor sound when the letter combination is first introduced. The introduction of two sounds at one time for a single letter combination may confuse some students. Therefore, we recommend delaying introduction of the minor sound either by providing several practice lessons on the most common sound before introducing the minor sound or by simply skip-

ping the instruction on the minor sound, teaching the next lessons and presenting the minor sound later.

The second problem concerns introducing words in which the sound represented by a letter combination is neither the most common nor the minor sound, on the same lesson the minor sound is presented. For example, in the Lippincott program, the words *steak, learn, pearl, heard, search, earn, heart,* and *hearts* are introduced on the same page as the minor sound of *ea.* The introduction of these other words should be delayed until students have learned to use the most common and minor sound strategy. The delay procedure involves deleting the words from list-reading exercises and identifying them for students when they appear in passages.

## VCe Pattern Words

The commercial programs we examined have one or more of the following characteristics that might cause difficulties for some students: (1) inadequate teaching of the discriminations between letter sounds and letter names, which is a critical preskill, (2) use of verbal explanations that were potentially confusing, (3) inappropriate example selection, and (4) inadequate practice.

### Letter Names and Letter Sounds

An essential preskill for learning VCe words is the ability to discriminate the name from the most common sound of a vowel letter. In most commercial programs, students are taught the letter names and sounds quite early in the beginning stage. The discrimination between letter sounds and letter names often is just briefly reviewed the week before VCe words are introduced. We recommend supplementing the teaching of this critical discrimination several weeks before VCe pattern words are introduced. The teacher should present a format in which the teacher writes the vowels on the board, models saying the *sound* of the letter and the *name* of the letter, and then tests the students. "What's the name?" "What's the sound?" Each several days, a new vowel would be introduced while the others are reviewed.

### Confusing Explanations

We noted two wording problems that might cause problems for some students. The first problem occurred in programs where students were introduced to the terms *long sound* and *short sound* in the same lesson in which VCe words were introduced. Adding the words *long* and *short* makes the task of teaching VCe words somewhat more difficult since the students must remember what *long* and *short* mean. We recommend just using the term *name* and *sound.* If the terms *long* and *short sounds* are to be used, they should be introduced *before* students are required to use them in reading VCe words. A second problem involved the use of lengthy explanations that did not teach a specific rule. Keep in mind that the more lengthy and complex explanations are, the more likely they are to confuse instructionally naive students.

### Example Selection

Inappropriate example selection is a problem in some programs because of the lack of adequate discrimination examples. It is quite important that students receive practice in determining when a rule does and does not apply. If the program does not provide discrimination practice, we recommend including a discrimination list composed of some VCe words and some CVC and CVCC words. Students read the words in the discrimination list after they read the introduction list provided in the original program.

### Practice

The final problem concerns inadequate practice. Again, the problem is more severe in meaning-emphasis programs because they do not provide massed practice on new word types in passages as do code-emphasis programs. Teachers using meaning-emphasis programs should be prepared to include several weeks of supplementary word list reading exercises focusing on VCe words.

Teachers using code-emphasis programs should also be prepared to make some modifications. First, VCe words should be introduced in lists about a week before they appear in passages. Second, more than a day or two of VCe word list reading is needed. We've found that some students need a week or more of practice, being lead through applications of the VCe rule, before they will be able to apply it independently.

---

## RESEARCH

Teaching students letter combinations greatly reduces the irregularity of common words by allowing students to treat them as a special type of regular word (Mason, 1977). Other studies indicate that good readers attend to letter combinations. Glass and Burton (1973) and Spoeky and Smith (1973) studied successful readers to determine how they decode. In the Glass and Burton study, the possibilities included generalizations, syllabication rules, single letter analysis, affixes, and letter clusters. According to self-reports from the readers and experimenter observations, over 80% of the successful identifications were accounted for by a letter cluster analysis. Our assumption is that if students learn the most common (and in some cases, minor) sound for letters and letter combinations, the students will automatically learn to combine letters and combinations into larger chunks (letter clusters) so that they can sight read. Decoding individual letters and combinations is too slow a process for fluent sight reading.

For example, Spache (1939) identified several high-frequency letter clusters that exhibit a consistent sound-symbol relationship:

| | | | | |
|------|------|------|------|------|
| ail  | con  | ick  | ter  | it   |
| ain  | eep  | ight | tion | ite  |
| all  | ell  | ill  | ake  | le   |
| and  | en   | in   | ide  | re   |
| ate  | ent  | ing  | ile  | ble  |
| ay   | er   | ock  | ine  |      |
|      | est  |      |      |      |

It is interesting to note that all these clusters are composed of letters and letter combinations discussed earlier in the text; e.g., *ail* is composed of *ai* and *l; ain* is composed of *ai* and *n.* Research is needed to determine whether teaching letters and combinations results in students' automatically mastering letter clusters, or whether letter clusters need to be directly taught after single letters and letter combinations have been taught.

A great deal of research has been conducted concerning the utility of phonic generalizations taught to students. Clymer (1963) identified 121 generalizations that appeared in four basal reading programs. By combining overly specific generalizations and deleting overly general ones, Clymer ended up with 45 generalizations. He then prepared a composite list of all the words introduced in the four basic series from which the words were drawn plus the words for the *Gates Reading Vocabulary for the Primary Grades.* Once this list was prepared, each phonic generalization was checked against the words in the list to determine which words were pronounced as the generalization stated and which were not. A percent of utility was computed for each generalization by dividing the number of words pronounced as the generalization claimed by the total number of words the generalization applied to.

Of the 45 generalizations, 6 were found to be extremely nonfunctional as they had only a 35% utility figure. Another 6 of the generalizations had a utility rate between 36 and 50%. An additional 16 had a utility rate between 51 and 75%, and 17 had a utility rate of above 75%. Further studies by Emans (1967), Baily (1967), and Burmeister (1968) showed similar but not exact findings due to the variations in the words studied. The results of these studies point out the need for teachers to have a specific knowledge of phonic generalizations so they may delete or modify ill-founded generalizations that appear in commercial programs.

Unfortunately, little research has been conducted on teaching words that contain letter combinations or VCe patterns. Two studies by Carnine and Stein (1979a) dealt with issues relevant to teaching procedures. They compared the efficacy of two common procedures for teaching students to decode words with letter combinations. In one procedure, words containing *oi* were introduced in a passage, which the students read twice. If the students missed the word, the teacher told it to them. In the other procedure, the letter combination *oi* was introduced in isolation followed by *oi* words in introductory and discrimination word lists. Then students read the training passage containing *oi* words *one* time. Both groups were tested on a transfer passage containing *oi* words the students had never before seen. The results showed that the group introduced to the letter combination in isolation and in word lists identified significantly more *oi* words on the transfer passage than the passage-reading group.

Another important question regarding letter combinations is sequencing. Should one sound value be introduced when a new letter or letter combination is introduced, or should several sound values be introduced when the new letter or letter combination is introduced? We recommend a constant introduction in which just one sound is presented for a letter or letter combination when it is first introduced. In contrast, Gibson and Levin (1975) recommend a variable introduction, in which multiple sound values are presented for a letter when the letter first appears; i.e., a vowel is introduced in isolation and as a member of letter combinations to demonstrate that it represents various sounds. Stein and Carnine (1978) compared constant and variable introductions by constructing two sequences made up of three vowels and six letter combinations; each vowel appeared alone and as part of two letter combinations. In the constant treatment, the sound represented by each single letter was taught before the sounds of any letter combinations; the order of introduction was *a, o, u, aw, or, ur, ow, oa,* and *ou.* In the variable treatment, different sound values represented by a single letter were taught before a second vowel; the order of introduction was *a, aw, oa, o, or, ow, ou, u,* and *ur.* Nonreading preschoolers were pretrained on consonant sounds, on the vowel *a,* and on the sounding-out strategy. After pretraining, the preschoolers were presented a set of introductory words, all of which contained the most recently introduced single vowel or vowel-letter combination. After the introductory words, the preschoolers were presented a set of discrimination words, including those which contained the recently introduced letter or combination, and others containing previously introduced letters and combinations. Introductory and discrimination word lists were presented for each letter and letter combination. The results were mixed: preschoolers receiving the constant introduction made more correct responses to words that contained three of the nine letters and combinations (*o, oa, ow*), while preschoolers in the variable treatment made more correct responses to one-letter combination (*ou*). Transfer scores for the two treatments were comparable.

The mixed findings may have resulted from the limited practice received in the fixed trials design and from the brevity of the constant introduction. In the constant introduction, only three vowels were presented before letter combinations with different values for the vowels were introduced. The limitations that result from a fixed trials design are illustrated by two experiments on separating similar sounds (Carnine, 1976d), where the post-test scores were over three times higher for students involved in the trials to criterion experiment than for students who received a fixed number of trials. Further research comparisons of constant and variable introductions with more letters and using a trials to criterion design are needed.

Carnine and Stein (1979b) also conducted a study concerning varying teaching procedures with VCe pattern words. Three procedures for teaching VCe words to lower-performing children were compared to a control group: rule stated, rule applied to introductory and discrimination list, and rule applied to introductory list. The VCe rule was "When there's an *e* at the end of the word, this letter (tester points to the vowel) says its name." The students in the

rule stated group were told the rule and then presented with three introductory words (all VCe words) until they correctly identified all three consecutively or until the list had been presented three times. After the introductory list, the students were asked to identify nine words in a discrimination list (VCe and CVC words) until they correctly identified six consecutive words or until the last had been presented three times. All errors were corrected by the teacher's saying the word and asking the students to repeat it.

The students in the rule applied to introductory list group were also presented the VCe rule. When they were presented the introductory word list, however, the tester prompted each word by asking, "Is there an *e* at the end of the word? So, what does this letter say? What is the word?" Following the introductory list, the tester presented the discrimination list. To correct errors on the discrimination list, the tester used the same VCe rule prompt that was used with the introductory words.

The third group differed from the second group in that the discrimination words were replaced by five additional VCe words; i.e., the students were presented an introductory list only. In all other ways, the groups were alike.

Following training, all three groups were tested on an 11-word transfer discrimination list and a paragraph containing 5 new VCe words. Mistakes were not corrected. The students in the control group were given the transfer test without having had any previous training on VCe words. Students in the two rule application groups made significantly more correct transfer list responses than students in the rule stated or in the control group. This result suggests that students should be prompted to apply the VCe rule and not just told it. Also, all students who were presented word lists made significantly more transfer responses than the control group, indicating that practice on word lists improves decoding performance on new words in lists. The absence of significant differences in paragraph reading indicates that the relatively brief intervention (3.19 minutes on the average) did not substantially affect reading performance in context. Mean correct identification of VCe words in passages was about 35%. Longer interventions that include some passages with transfer words are needed to replicate the earlier finding (Carnine & Stein, 1979a) that word and passage training contribute to superior transfer passage performance.

Another study on procedures for teaching VCe words (Carnine & Kameenui, 1979) evaluated the importance of discrimination lists. The results indicated that teaching with discrimination lists results in superior transfer performance in both lists and passages compared to training with all VCe words and to passage reading with a high density of VCe words. A second finding was that transfer performance for the group with list training on all VCe words was also superior to the transfer performance for the group that received paragraph reading training.

Although research has found that students have difficulty learning minor sounds (Calfee, Venezky, & Chapman, 1969), we could find no research relating to teaching procedures for words with minor sounds. The strategy of trying the most common sound for a letter or combination and then trying the minor sound needs to be compared with a sight or context procedure for teaching words that contain minor sounds. Additional research is also needed to determine what kind and how much phonic instruction is beneficial for various skill levels. We assume that in the beginning stage, much of the instruction involves word lists, but in the primary stage, more instruction occurs in passage reading. Research on how best to make this transition would be helpful.

## APPLICATION EXERCISES

1. Assume that you have taught the students the following skills:
   a. Most common sound of all individual letters
   b. How to decode all regular word types
   c. All irregular words in Appendix B
   d. Strategy to decode VCe words with long vowel sound
   e. The most common sound of the following letter combinations: *ar, ea, ee, oa, th, sh, wh, ck*

   Circle each of the following words the student would not be able to decode. Next to each of the circled words, write the abbreviation for the explanation below that tells why the student could not decode the word.

   Letter (L)—The word contains letter combination that the student does not know.
   Irregular (I)—Some letter or letter combination is not representing its most common sound.

   | | | |
   |---|---|---|
   | _____ground | _____those | _____warn |
   | _____boat | _____which | _____farm |
   | _____speak | _____spoil | _____break |
   | _____wish | _____cheer | _____sack |
   | _____stew | _____stick | _____cheer |
   | _____done | _____went | _____groan |
   | _____build | _____broad | _____spout |

2. Circle the three letter combinations below that the authors do *not* recommend teaching. Explain why.
   *ai    ea    ei    oa    ou    oe    oy    ui*

3. Circle the three pairs of letter combinations below that students are most likely to confuse.
   *(ch–sh)   (ph–wr)   (ai–ea)   (ea–ou)   (ou–oo)   (ar–ir)*

4. The following letter combinations have been introduced in this order: *th, wh, sh, ar, ea, ou, igh, ai, ee, ol,* and *ch.* Below are the letter combinations three teachers included in isolated letter-sounds tasks when the lesson *ch* was introduced and in the two following lessons. One teacher constructed his examples

acceptably. Two teachers did not. For each teacher, tell if the examples are acceptable. If not, tell why.

Teacher A: Lesson 1—*ch, sh, wh, ar, ol*
　　　　　　　Lesson 2—*ch, sh, ou, ol, ee, ea*
　　　　　　　Lesson 3—*ch, sh, ar, ai, igh, ee*

Teacher B: Lesson 1—*ch, ar, ea, ol, wh*
　　　　　　　Lesson 2—*sh, wh, th, ar, ea, ow*
　　　　　　　Lesson 3—*ch, sh, ar, ol, ee, ai*

Teacher C: Lesson 1—*ch, ol, ee, igh, ea*
　　　　　　　Lesson 2—*ch, th, wh, ar, ea, ol*
　　　　　　　Lesson 3—*ch, sh, ai, igh, ol, ee, ea*

5. Describe the difference in the manner in which teachers would present words such as, *like, made,* and *hope,* and words such as, *have, none,* and *live.*

6. Below are the words three teachers included in a VCe format. One teacher's examples are acceptable. Identify that teacher's examples. Tell why the other examples are unacceptable. This is a list presented when VCe words are first introduced.

Teacher A: *lake, cape, tame, bake, same, made, late, name*
Teacher B: *lake, same, cape, cap, sat, fame, name, tap*
Teacher C: *flame, shape, grade, clap, grape, crab, stale*

7. The following letter combinations have been taught so far in a program: *th, sh, wh, er, ai, oo, ar,* and *ea.* On an individual test, a student identifies all the letter combinations correctly except *oo* (see rate of introduction for letter combinations). Assume the program introduces the letter combination *ch* on the next lesson. Should the teacher delay *ch*? If so, why?
What if the program introduced the letter combination *ou* on the next lesson? Should the teacher delay *ou*? If so, why?

8. In the following situations, specify what the teacher would do and the wording the teacher would use to correct the error. Then describe what the teacher would do next after the students responded correctly to the missed item.
   a. During an isolated sounds format, the student says "o" for *ou.*
   b. During the sight format for one-syllable words containing a letter combination, a student says "bat" for *bait.*
   c. During the VCe format, a student says "hop" for *hope.*

9. Construct a list of 10 words for each lesson described below. Also specify the page number of the format you would use (see example selection sections for respective types of words). Refer to Appendix A for words to include.
   *Lesson 198*
   Assume the students know all single letters and the letter combinations *sh, th, wh, ar,* and *ea.* The lesson should focus on the letter combinations *ch,* which was introduced five lessons ago.
   *Lesson 206*
   Assume the students know VCe pattern words with the vowel *a.* The lesson should focus on VCe pattern words with the vowel *i.*
   *Lesson 248*
   Assume the students know these letter combinations: *th, sh, ch, ee, ea,* and *oa.* The lesson should focus on the letter combination *ou,* which was introduced three lessons earlier.

10. (Review item)
    a. Tell which method (examples only, synonyms, or definitions) you would use to teach the meaning of the following words:
       red    thin    poster    vehicle    plastic
    b. Describe six examples, three positive and three negative, that could be used in teaching *plastic.*

# *Structural Analysis*

Structural analysis* involves teaching students strategies to decode words formed by adding a prefix, suffix, or another word to a base word. The initial strategy we recommend is quite simple. The students simply read a long word a part at a time. For example, the word *repainting* is read as *re + paint + ing*. The strategy becomes somewhat more complex as students encounter VCe derivative words (words formed by adding suffixes to words that end in a VCe pattern) since students must be able to distinguish these words from CVC derivatives, e.g., *hopping* and *hoping*. This section also discusses *y* derivative words (e.g., *funnier, happiest*) and contractions (e.g., *he's, I'm, you're*), both of which require special treatment. Following our recommendations is an overview of how structural analysis skills are taught in commercial programs.

## Direct Instruction Procedures

### Introducing Affixes (Prefixes, Suffixes, and Inflectional Endings)

Two factors should be taken into consideration: (1) the number of primary level words in which each prefix or suffix appears and

(2) the relative similarity of the prefixes or suffixes. Those that are similar should not be introduced too close to each other. For example, the suffix *le* would not be introduced soon after the suffix *ly* because they both contain the letter *l* but represent significantly different sounds.

Table 3.3.1 lists prefixes and suffixes in one possible order of introduction. It is not the only acceptable sequence but serves as a concrete example of how our recommendations are applied. In column one is a word which represents the most common pronunciation of the particular suffix or prefix. Many suffixes have several pronunciations. The suffix *ate* for example is pronounced differently in the words *private* and *regulate*. Column two tells whether the word is a prefix, suffix, or inflected ending.[1] The affixes are listed in alphabetical order on the inside of the front cover.

## Sequence for Introducing Word Types

Compound words (words formed by combining two words, like *outside, into,* over-

---

[1] The discrimination between what is a suffix and what is an inflected ending is not critical for teaching decoding. We list them simply because the terms appear in reading literature.

---

* Structural analysis is sometimes referred to as morphemic analysis. Morphemes are the smallest meaningful units of language. All words include one or more morphemes. An in-depth discussion of morphemes appears in the sections on decoding and vocabulary instruction in Part 4.

**TABLE 3.3.1**  *Sample Sequence for Introducing Prefixes and Suffixes*

| SAMPLE WORD | | TYPE |
|---|---|---|
| s | hits | inflected ending |
| er | batter | inflected ending |
| ing | jumping | inflected ending |
| le | handle | suffix |
| ed | jumped[a] | inflected ending |
| y | funny[b] | suffix |
| un | unhappy | prefix |
| est | smallest | inflected ending |
| re | refill | prefix |
| a | about | prefix |
| de | defeat | prefix |
| es | misses[c] | inflected ending |
| ness | kindness | suffix |
| a | formula | suffix |
| ly | sadly | suffix |
| al | formal | suffix |
| be | become | prefix |
| in | inside | prefix |
| con | confuse | prefix |
| ment | payment | suffix |
| teen | sixteen | suffix |
| ful | handful | suffix |
| en | happen | suffix |
| dis | distant | prefix |
| able | enjoyable | suffix |
| less | useless | suffix |
| pro | protect | prefix |
| tion | invention[d] | suffix |
| ad | address | prefix |
| age | package | suffix |
| ence | sentence | suffix |
| ish | selfish | suffix |
| pre | preschool | prefix |
| ex | expect | prefix |
| over | overtime | prefix |
| ion | million | suffix |
| ship | friendship | suffix |
| com | compare | prefix |
| ist | artist | suffix |
| ive | detective | suffix |
| ac | accuse | prefix |
| ous | joyous | suffix |
| ward | forward | suffix |
| ic | heroic | suffix |
| ize | realize | suffix |

a *Ed* sometimes represents the /d/ sound, the /t/ sound or /ed/ sounds.

b *Y* is sometimes a suffix in itself and is sometimes a letter in other suffixes (e.g., *ty*, *dy*).

c The inflected ending *es* usually forms an additional syllable (e.g., *boxes, misses, churches*). However, when added to words that end in *f*, a special case results. The *f* is changed to *v* and the *es* does not add a new syllable (e.g., *half–halves, wolf–wolves*).

d The suffix *tion* is often formed by adding *ion* to a word ending in *t*, (*interruption*). We list *tion* as a high-frequency suffix for convenience.

time) may be introduced as soon as students can identify each of the words that make up the compound word. Words formed by adding a suffix, prefix, or inflected ending can be introduced when students are able to sight read single syllable regular words at a rate of about a word each 2 seconds. At first, very few words exceeding two syllables are introduced. Words formed by adding a prefix and suffix to a base (e.g., *re + paint + ing*) should be introduced only after students have been reading words formed by adding only one prefix or suffix to a base for several weeks.

VCe derivatives (words formed by adding a suffix to words ending in a VCe pattern) should not be introduced until students have developed fluency in decoding words formed by adding suffixes to regular words. This will usually be 6–10 weeks after suffixes are first introduced. *Y* derivative words (words formed by adding a suffix to

words that end in *y*) are difficult because the *y* is often changed to *i* as in *happy–happier–happiest. Y* derivative words may be introduced after students know about 10–15 words ending in *y*.

As a general rule, teachers should introduce a prefix or suffix in isolation several days before students read words that contain it. The teacher would use the same procedure as for teaching letter combinations (see page 196).

In the word-reading format, the teacher would first have the students read some words by saying each part in the word (the prefix, root, and suffix) and then saying the entire word. The students would then reread these words, as well as the rest of the list, without the prompt. As in all board exercises, the teacher would first go through the list with a pause longer than 1 second if the students need the extra time to figure out the word. The teacher would,

---

**Format for Introducing Prefixes and Suffixes**

| *Teacher* | *Students* |
|---|---|
| Teacher writes on board:<br>slimmer    topping    sweeping<br>hopping    slimmest    hopped<br>smallest    hardest    tallest<br>cleaned    runner    handed | |
| 1. Students read words by first identifying each part of the word and then saying the word. | |
|    a. Teacher covers *er* and points to *slimm.* **"What is this part?"** (signal) | "Slimm" |
|    b. Teacher points to *er.* **"What do these letters say?"** (signal) | "er" |
|    c. Teacher points to *slimmer.* **"What's the word?"** (signal)<br>   Teacher repeats steps a–c with about a third of the list. | "Slimmer" |
| 2. Students read all the words from the beginning without first identifying each part. | |
|    a. Teacher points to each word, pauses 2 seconds, then signals. | Students say the word. |
| 3. Students reread the list from beginning with the teacher only allowing a 1-second pause between pointing to the word and signaling. | Students say the word. |

however, repeat the list until students can respond with just a 1-second pause.

## Example Selection

The format should contain 10 to 15 words. About half the words should contain the most recently introduced prefix or suffix. The root words should all be ones the students can decode with relative ease. This means that the word should contain only letters or letter combinations that were introduced earlier.

## Introducing Words Formed by Adding *ed*

The suffix *ed* may represent one of three pronunciations. When *ed* is added to a word that ends in *d* or *t,* the *ed* is pronounced as a separate syllable (e.g., hand*ed* batt*ed*). When *ed* is added to other words, the *ed* sometimes represents the /t/ sound (e.g., *jumped, tricked*), and sometimes, the /d/ sound (e.g., *hummed* and *begged*). The teaching procedure for words that contain the *ed* suffix consists of two steps. The first step is a verbal exercise in which the teacher writes *ed* on the board, says a word, then says the word with the *ed* ending. The teacher does this with six words, two each representing the /d/ sound, the /t/ sound, and the /ed/ sound. A sample

list would include *hand, jump, fill, land, hop,* and *hum.* The advantage of using this verbal format is that it clearly demonstrates how the base word determines the sound *ed* will make.

Since the students do not have to read the base word, they can concentrate on saying the ending appropriately. This format should be presented daily for about a week before the students read words with the *ed* suffix. Note that familiar words are selected so that students will be familiar with the pronunciation of the past tense forms of the verbs.

The second step in teaching students to decode words with the affix *ed* involves reading words. In the format, the teacher covers up the *ed* and has the students sight read the root word. Since the *ed* represents several sounds, the students do not identify the /ed/ sound in isolation. The teacher then uncovers the *ed* and has the students identify the entire word.

## Introducing Words Formed by Adding *s* or *es*

Some students may have difficulty with the plural endings *s* or *es* since *s* may represent the /s/ sound as in *hops* and *hits* or the /z/ sound as in *hums* and *runs.* The *es* usually forms an extra syllable as in *boxes* and *misses,* but sometimes not, as in *lives*

---

**Format for Verbally Presented *ed* Words**

|  | *Teacher* | *Students* |
|---|---|---|
| 1. | Teacher writes *ed* on the board. Teacher then models and tests saying different words with the *ed* suffix. | |
| | a. **"Say *hop*."** (signal) <br> **"I'll say *hop* with this ending."** <br> Teacher points to *ed*. **"Hopped."** | "Hop" |
| | b. Teacher points to *ed*. **"Say *hop* with this ending."** (signal) | "Hopped" |
| | c. Teacher repeats steps a and b with *hum, jump, lift.* | |

**Format for Presenting Written *ed* Words**

| *Teacher* | *Students* |
|---|---|
| Teacher writes on board: | |
| hummed   begged | |
| jumped   tripped | |
| lifted   handed | |

1. Students read each word by first identifying the root word and then saying the whole word.

   a. Teacher covers *ed* in *hummed* and points to *hum*. **"What do these letters say?"** (signal) — "Hum"

   b. Teachers uncovers *ed*. **"Get ready to say the word with this ending."** (signal) — "Hummed"

   To correct, if students say "humm-ed," the teacher says, ***"Hum* with this ending says hummed."**

   c. Teacher repeats steps a and b with remaining words.

2. Teacher tests students on reading words.

   a. Teacher points to *hummed*. **"What word?"** (signal) — "Hummed"

   b. Teacher repeats step a with remaining words.

and *haves.* If students have trouble with words with these endings, teachers should use a verbal format in which they say the word without the plural ending, then say it with the plural ending. The wording would be the same as for the verbal format for *ed* words (see page 215).

## Introducing Words Formed by Adding a Suffix to VCe Pattern Words

When an affix that begins with a vowel is added to a word that ends with VCe, the final *e* is dropped; e.g., fine + al = final; hope + ing = hoping;   tame + ed = tamed; time + er = timer. We call these words VCe derivatives because they are formed by adding an affix to a word that has a VCe pattern. To decode a VCe derivative, students must realize that the word is derived, in fact, from a VCe pattern word and is not simply a CVC word plus an affix. Naive

readers are quite apt to call *hoping* "hopping," since they see *hoping* as *hop* + *ing.* To discriminate words like *hopping* and *hoping, diner* and *dinner,* and *cuter* and *cutter,* students must cue on the number of consonants in the middle of the word. One consonant in the middle indicates that the word was derived from a VCe pattern and that the initial vowel will probably represent its long sound. Two consonants in the middle indicate that the word was not derived from a VCe word and that the initial vowel usually will not represent its long sound. Very few VCe derivatives should be introduced during the first 2 months when common affixes are being introduced, since forcing students to cope with this discrimination too early can cause needless confusion. Exceptions can be made for very high-frequency words (e.g., *taking, liked, used*). The format we recommend teaches students to cue on the number of consonants in the middle of the word, and then to use the context of a sentence to determine if the decoding of the word was proper.

In the first part of the format, the teacher tells the rule for which sound to try first for the vowel. The teacher says, "If there are two *m's* in the middle, we say the *sound* of this letter." Teacher points to initial vowel. "But if there is one *m* in the middle, we usually say the *name* of this letter."

Next, the teacher tests by pointing to each word and asking the following set of questions: "Do we say /ā/ or /ă/ for this letter? How do you know?" The "how do you know" question serves to provide practice on referring to the rule.

Third, the teacher leads the students through the steps in actually applying the rule to reading words. After applying the rule, the students check their decoding by seeing if the word makes sense in a sentence. Finally, the students read the words without teacher assistance.

When a word in which there is one consonant in the middle yet the initial vowel is short is introduced, several new steps need to be added to the format. These steps would only be used with words like *having, giving,* or *lived* in which the initial vowel is short. When the answer to step d of part 3 is "no," the teacher would add steps e, f, and g.

Note that this format does not use the words *consonant* or *vowel* but just has the teacher refer to the name of the consonant letter(s) in the middle and point to the vowel. Teachers working with above-average students may wish to teach the students to identify letters as vowels or consonants before introducing this format. If students can identify letters as consonants or vowels, the teacher can change the rule: "If there are two consonants in the middle, we usually say the sound of this (point to initial vowel) vowel. If there is one consonant in the middle, we say the name of this vowel first." The advantage of using this wording is that it allows the teacher to use words with two different consonants in the middle, (e.g., *jumping, standing*). However,

we recommend that teachers working with lower-performing students use the format as written. The advantage of including words with two different consonants is outweighed by the added complexity resulting from using the term *consonant*. Lower performers may need weeks to develop fluency in identifying letters as vowels or consonants.

## Example Selection

This format should be done daily with 6–10 words for about a month. About half the words in the format should have two consonants in the middle. The other half should have one consonant. The words with two consonants in the middle should all have a short initial vowel sound, since the initial single vowel usually represents its short sound in words with two consonants in the middle. The words with one consonant should all have long vowel sounds for the first 2 weeks. After that some words in which the initial vowel represents its short sound should be included.

The words used in the format must be in the students' speaking vocabulary so they can determine which pronunciation is correct. If the teacher has any doubts about the student's familiarity with certain words, he should present the words in a vocabulary exercise for several lessons before presenting them in the decoding exercise.

## Introducing VCe Derivatives with *s* Endings

VCe derivatives with *s* endings form a special subgroup since the students cannot key on the number of consonants to discriminate them from CVC derivatives but must key on the presence or absence of the letter *e* (e.g., *cans–canes, hops–hopes*). Students should be taught VCe derivatives with *s* endings shortly after words with VCe patterns are mastered. When presenting the words, the teacher would construct a set of words composed of some VCe pat-

## Format for Keying on Consonants

|  *Teacher* | *Students* |
|---|---|

Teacher writes on the board: *later, batting, naming, hoping, hitter, timing, tapping, roping.*

1. Teacher states the rule.

   a. Teacher points to *t* in *later.* **"Listen. If there's one t in the middle, we say the name** (points to *a*) **of this letter first."**

   b. Points to *tt* in *batting.* **"If there are two t's in the middle, we say the sound** (points to *a*) **of this letter first."**

2. Teacher prompts students on keying on the number of consonants.

   a. Teacher points to *later.* **"How many t's in this word?"** (signal)     "One"

   b. Teacher points to *a* in *later.* **"So what do we say for this letter, ă or ā?"** (pauses 2 seconds, then signals)     "ā"

   Teacher repeats steps a and b with three or four more words.

3. Teacher guides students in applying the rules.

   a. Teacher points to initial vowel. **"What do we say for this letter?"**     "ā"

   b. **"Say the word."** (signal)     "Later"

   c. **"I'll say a sentence with that word. I will go home later. Does *later* make sense in the sentence?"** (signal)     "Yes"

   Teacher repeats steps a to c with each word.

   Additional Steps for One-consonant Words with Short Initial Vowels:

   d. **"He is hāving fun. Does hāving make sense in the sentence?"**     "No"

   e. **"So let's try the sound."** Teacher points to ă. **"What's the sound?"** (signal)     "ă"

   f. **"Get ready to pronounce the word saying the sound of the letter."** (pause, signal)     "Having"

   g. **"I'll say the sentence with that word. He is having fun. Does having make sense?"**     "Yes"

4. Students reread list without teacher guidance.
   a. **"Let's read the list again."**

   b. Teacher points to each word, pauses, and signals.

5. Teacher calls on some students to read several words.

tern words plus *s* and some CVC words plus *s* (e.g., *cans, canes, names, cats, hates, hats*). The teacher would first present the list by covering the *s* in each word and having the students identify the root word, then the teacher would uncover the *s* and have the students say the whole word. The teacher repeats this prompting procedure with each word. After the prompted reading, the teacher would have the students reread the list without any prompts.

## Introducing Words Formed by Adding a Suffix to Words Ending with *y*

When a suffix is added to a word that ends in *y*, the *y* is often changed to an *i* (e.g., *funny + er = funnier; baby + es = babies; fry + ed = fried*). Decoding such words will be easier if the student is aware that the word has been derived from a word ending in *y*. A format for presenting these words is shown below. Note that the teacher first has students identify the root word, then the entire word.

## Example Selection

The letter *y* at the end of a word usually represents the /ē/ sound, e.g., *happy, funny, silly.* However, in some words it represents the /ī/ sound, e.g., *try, fly, apply.* Thus, most words in the *y*-derivative format should be formed from words in which *y* represents the /ē/ sound. About one of each four words should be derived from words in which *y* represents the /ī/ sound.

## Introducing Contractions

Contractions are unique in that two words are joined and some letter(s) are omitted and replaced by an apostrophe. For ex-

---

**Format for Adding Suffixes to Words Ending in *y***

| *Teacher* | *Students* |
|---|---|
| Teacher writes on board:<br>baby + es = babies<br>funny + er = funnier<br>silly + est = silliest<br>cry + ed = cried<br>play + ed = played | |

1. Teacher tells rule, **"When we add an ending to a word that ends in *y*, we sometimes change the *y* to an *i*."**

2. Teacher has students identify root word, then whole word.

   | | |
   |---|---|
   | a. Teacher points to *baby*. **"What word?"** | "Baby" |
   | b. Teacher points to *babies*. **"What word?"** | "Babies" |

   Teacher repeats steps a and b with remaining words.

3. Teacher erases first two columns and has students just read the new words.

   | | |
   |---|---|
   | a. Teacher points to *babies*. **"What word?"** (pauses 1 second, signals) | "Babies" |
   | b. Teacher repeats step a with remaining words. | |

**TABLE 3.3.2**    *Contractions to Introduce in the Primary Stage*

| | | | | |
|---|---|---|---|---|
| 1. they—they'd | they're | they've | they'll | |
| 2. she —she'd | she's | | she'll | |
| 3. he —he'd | he's | | he'll | |
| 4. we —we'd | we're | we've | we'll | |
| 5. I —I'd | I'm | I've | I'll | |
| 6. you —you'd | you're | you've | you'll | |
| 7. not —hasn't | wasn't | isn't | doesn't | couldn't |
| shouldn't | wouldn't | won't | don't | aren't |
| mustn't | | | | |

ample, in the contraction *aren't*, the *o* is left out of *not* when combining *are* and *not*. In the contraction *he'll*, the letters *wi* are dropped from *will*. Contractions can be grouped according to base word or last word. In Table 3.3.2 is a list of some of the more important contractions introduced in the primary stage.

A group of contractions can be introduced a few weeks after students learn the base word for that group. The teaching procedure for contractions involves the teacher's modeling how the word with a contraction is pronounced, then testing the students on the word.

Exercises in which the students translate a contraction into its two constituent words (*they'll = they + will*) can be done at the same time the contraction is introduced. More naive students, however, may be confused by these exercises. We recommend just concentrating on decoding the contraction for these students and delaying translation exercises until several weeks later.

## Structural Analysis Correction Procedure

The basic correction procedure when students make a misidentification error during reading a list of words involves use of the

---

**Format for Contractions**

| Teacher | Students |
|---|---|
| Teacher writes on board: *they'll, they've, they're, they'd.* | |
| 1. Teacher models. | |
|    a. Teacher covers *'ll*, points to *they*. **"What word?"** | "They" |
|    b. Teacher uncovers *'ll*. **"Now the word is they'll. What word?"** | "They'll" |
|    c. Teacher repeats steps a and b with rest of words. | |
| 2. Teacher tests. | |
|    a. Teacher points to first word, pauses, and asks, **"What word?"** (signal) | "They'll" |
|      To correct, teacher models. | |
|    b. Teacher tests students on the rest of the words, repeating the entire list until students respond correctly to all words. | |

cues in the respective format for that type of word. If a student makes an error involving a prefix or suffix, e.g., saying "tallest" for *taller,* the teacher has the student identify both parts of the word—*tall* and *est*—and then say the entire word. If a student makes an error on a VCe derivative, e.g., saying "tapping" for *taping,* the teacher asks, "How many *p's?* So what do we say for this letter?" Teacher point to *a.* "What word?" If a student makes repeated errors on a previously taught prefix, suffix, or word type, the teacher should provide extra practice on that skill.

## Supplementary Activities

Supplementary worksheet exercises can be extremely useful in teaching structural analysis. In Figure 3.3.1 are some examples of appropriate exercises.

## Commercial Programs

In general, the main problem we noted with commercial programs was a lack of adequate practice on structural analysis teaching. Programs would include exercises for just several lessons here and there rather than sustained daily practice. For higher-performing students, the lack of practice may not be a problem. If students have no difficulty using structural analysis skills in decoding, teachers need not construct extra practice exercises. Teachers working with lower-performing students will probably have to construct word list exercises

**FIGURE 3.3.1**

1. Word Building

   a. Put the parts in the right order to make up a big word.

   | | | | | | |
   |---|---|---|---|---|---|
   | ed vent pre | = _____ | ness use less | = _____ |
   | teach ing re | = _____ | care ly less | = _____ |
   | out side in | = _____ | ful care ly | = _____ |
   | point dis ap | = _____ | less ly care | = _____ |

2. Fill-Ins

   a. Write the right word in the blank.
   I am _____ (hopping, hoping) it does not rain.
   I ate two _____ (cans, canes) of soup.
   We ate _____ (dinner, diner) at 10 o'clock.
   He _____ (hats, hates) to be late.

3. Root Word Selection

   a. Write the word under its root word.

   happiest    reusing    cares

   caring    happier    happiness

   happening    cars    happened

| happy | care | happen | car |
|---|---|---|---|
| | | | |

and worksheet exercises to supplement those in the program. Guidelines for constructing word list exercises were discussed earlier in the section.

Two specific problems pertaining to structural analysis were (1) inappropriate introduction and teaching of VCe derivatives and (2) a confusion about the function of syllabication as an aid in decoding words. VCe derivatives must be handled carefully so that students learn to discriminate VCe derivatives from VC derivatives (e.g., *hopping, hoping*). We recommended not introducing VCe derivatives until students had learned to decode CVC derivatives formed by adding some common endings like *ed, ing,* and *er* (e.g., *running, hitter*). In Lippincott, only one lesson separated the introduction of CVC and CVCe derivatives. We recommend delaying the introduction of VCe derivative words for several weeks until after students are proficient at decoding CVC derivative words. If any VCe derivatives appeared in stories, the teacher would treat them as irregular words. Even though some higher-performing students may not have difficulty discriminating the two word types when introduced, delaying introduction will make learning easier for all students, especially lower performers.

The second problem area involved syllabication. We agree with Johnson and Pearson (1978) that "syllabication is probably the most misclassified and misused of the word identification skills" (p. 6). The confusion surrounding syllabication comes because the term is applied to two essentially different skills. Students are taught one for figuring out the pronunciation of unknown multi-syllabic words and one for breaking words into written syllables. The former is a decoding skill; the latter is a writing skill. The overlapping definitions have led to creation of exercises in commercial programs which are unnecessarily complicated. Most syllabication exercises require students to put a line between the letters in a word at which one syllable ends and the next begins.

Teachers should realize that teaching students to divide words into syllables is in itself nonfunctional as a decoding aid. The only time students need to syllabicate a word is when they do not have room at the end of a line to finish writing a multi-syllabic word. Since the set of rules that governs syllabicating words is so complicated, we recommend not teaching syllabication rules until the intermediate grades. Even then, only one or two of the simple rules need be taught. Teachers need not bother teaching all the exceptions but should teach students how to use the dictionary as a reference source.

The decoding skill of trying different sounds to figure out pronunciations of syllables should be taught. Since vowel sounds cause the greatest difficulty in multi-syllabic words, students should be taught the strategy of pronouncing the word with one vowel sound and then if the pronounced word does not make sense, trying the other vowel sound. Worksheet exercises should be kept simple so that students can clearly see the purpose of the tasks. Instead of having students draw lines between letters to indicate where a word is syllabicated, the teacher would have the students indicate how the word is pronounced. The student would simply make a diacritical mark over the vowel to indicate how it is pronounced in the word ( ⁻ if it's the long sound of the vowel and ˘ if it's the short sound of the vowel).

An independent assignment might look like this:

Look at the word in each box. Figure out the sound the underlined vowel makes. Put a mark over the vowel to show how it is pronounced.

1. They slept in a ⬚motel⬚ .

2. She is going to build a ⬚mo̲del⬚ plane.

3. She plays the  bugle .

4. Look at that  robin  in the sky.

A prerequisite for student success in all these exercises is that students are familiar with the words. If students are not familiar with the words, they will have no idea which pronunciation is correct since neither represents a real word for them. For example, if a student has never heard of the word *model,* he will have no way of knowing which pronunciation is correct, *mōdel* or *mŏdel.*

A similar confusion over the role of accent marks results in too many exercises in which students write accent marks. Accent marks, which designate a stressed syllable, help students pronounce words. Consequently, teaching students how to interpret accent marks in dictionaries is functional. However, teaching students where to put accent marks in words is not functional. Much time is wasted in teaching this skill. If students can pronounce a word, little is gained by requiring them to decide which syllable is stressed more and to draw in an accent mark at the beginning or end of that syllable.

## RESEARCH

The research concerning structural analysis deals with syllabication generalizations and correlations of student performance rather than experimental studies to determine more effective ways of teaching structural analysis skills.

Waugh and Howell (1975) discussed various problems associated with syllabication rules. They pointed out that syllables are often treated as a group of letters rather than a unit of speech. When syllables are viewed as conventions for where to divide a word, they are not functional decoding units. The syllables for *abrupt* are *ab-rupt,* but people don't say "ab rupt"; they say "a brupt." Thus the most widely accepted syllabication rule—a word is divided between adjacent consonants and before a consonant—is of questionable utility.

Spache and Badgett (1965), McFeely (1974), Aaron (1960), Burmeister (1968), and Canney (1976) suggested that most syllabication rules are not worth teaching. Rather than emphasizing generalizations and rules, various researchers suggest teaching students to identify root words, suffixes, and prefixes (Venezky, 1967, 1970; Chomskey, 1970; and McFeely, 1974). Also, several affixes can be taught as letter combinations: *ing, est, iest, pre, re, de, pro, con, tion, tain, ly,* and *ness* (McFeely, 1974; Venezky, 1970). We agree that teaching syllabi-

cation rules is not a good use of time. We'd rather see teachers concentrate on demonstrating how to find prefixes, roots, and suffixes in longer words and how to use a strategy of trying various sounds when encountering a syllable one does not know how to pronounce.

Although the correlational research and analyses of syllabication are important, they are no substitute for experimental research. Experimental research is needed to answer several questions. Many of these questions are the same ones raised with regard to teaching letter combinations: Should affixes be introduced in isolation? What is the optimal mix of word list training and passage reading? How proficient should students be with a set of affixes before a new affix is introduced? When should identification errors be corrected by prompting the missed structural element rather than through a context or whole-word correction, or no correction at all? Other research questions relate more specifically to structural analysis. How should spelling, morphemic analysis (for deriving meaning), and structural analysis (for purposes of decoding) be integrated? Can syllabic analysis exercises be designed that help students decode new words? When should *y* derivative and VCe derivative words be introduced? What formats should be used? As can be seen from this extensive list of questions, many of the suggestions we make in this section have not been experimentally investigated. Although our recommendations are consistent with research in phonic analysis and our own experience, research studies could provide information that would improve the recommendations.

## APPLICATION EXERCISES

1. Assume that the teacher has taught the following skills:
   a. Decoding all types of one- and two-syllable regular words and words containing letter combinations
   b. The most common sounds of all single letters
   c. The most common sound of these letter combinations and affixes (introduced in the order indicated): *ai, ar, ea, ee, ck, ou, th, sh, wh, ch, er, ing, ed, y, igh, al,* and *oa*
   d. VCe words with long sound for initial vowel
   e. All irregular words in Appendix B

   Circle each of the following words the student would not be able to decode. Next to each of the circled words, write the abbreviation for the explanation below that tells why the student could not decode the word.

   Letter (L)—The word contains a letter combination that the students do not know
   Irregular (I)—Some letter or letter combination is not representing its most common sound

   | | | |
   |---|---|---|
   | _____spoil | _____blind | _____which |
   | _____ground | _____blame | _____smell |
   | _____blew | _____goes | _____tone |
   | _____none | _____wreck | _____done |
   | _____trait | _____cheer | _____roam |
   | _____groan | _____bleach | _____grew |
   | _____straw | _____sigh | _____shame |
   | _____stem | _____reach | _____string |

2. Assume the students know the letter combinations *sh, th, ol,* and *wh,* all single letters, and the suffixes, *ing* and *er.* Below are word lists that various teachers prepared 6 days after the suffix *est* was introduced. Tell which teacher constructed an acceptable list. Specify the problem with the other two lists.

   *Teacher 1*
   biggest  hottest  hotter  fattest  coldest  colder  hitting
   *Teacher 2*
   hottest  biggest  fattest  coldest  maddest  wettest
   *Teacher 3*
   cheapest  cheaper  shortest  trainer  smallest  falling

3. Assume the students know the most common sounds of all single letters and can decode all types of regular words. Circle the prefixes and suffixes below which the students would *not* be able to decode.
   ment  ist  un  pro  re  ion

4. Specify what the teacher would say and do to correct the following error made when reading a list of words:
   a. A student says "hop-ped" for the word *hopped.*
   b. A student says "hopping" for the word *hoping.*
   c. A student says "topic" for the word *topic* (see steps 3d-3g on page 218).

5. Below are descriptions of pages that appeared in a reading workbook. Three of the pages contain activities that would be difficult for lower-performing students and would not warrant the time required to teach the skill. Identify these three pages.

*Page A*

The student is asked to classify a group of words according to their initial vowel sound.

*Page B*

The student is asked to designate which of two minimally different words belongs in a blank space in a sentence; e.g., The boy is _____ it will not rain. (hopping, hoping)

*Page C*

The student is asked to indicate where a word would be divided into syllables

*Page D*

The student is asked to select the word that corresponds to a picture

time
tin
tame

*Page E*

The student is asked to place the accent mark over the proper syllable.

6. Construct a 10-word list for each lesson described below. Include two minimally different pairs. Also specify the pages for the formats you would use.

*Lesson*

The students know all single letters, and the letter combinations and suffixes *ar, ee, ea, er,* and *ing.* The teacher is introducing words that end in *le.*

*Lesson*

The students know all single letters and the letter combinations *ar, ee, ea, er,* and *ing.* The teacher is introducing VCe derivative words.

Contextual analysis involves a student's using the meaning of the sentence in which a word appears as a decoding cue. Contextual analysis is used in conjunction with phonic and structural analysis to decode words. This section discusses two aspects of contextual analysis: decoding irregular words (words that contain letter-sound correspondences the student is unable to figure out) and passage reading.

## Irregular Words

In the beginning reading section on irregular words, we defined an irregular word as any word that contains a letter-sound correspondence students do not know. Some words like p*ou*nd, tr*ea*t, and st*ai*n should be considered irregular until the students learn the most common sound of the letter combination in each word. Other words will always be irregular because some of the letters or letter combinations do not represent their most common sound (e.g., *was* and *said*) or because they contain vowel digraphs that we do not recommend teaching (e.g., *build, ceiling,* and *duel*).[1]

---

[1] We do not recommend teaching the most common sound of digraphs and dipthongs that appear in few common words and represent no particular sound/s/ in over half the words in which they appear (see page 194 for a list).

As a general rule, we recommend not introducing a word as an irregular word if it contains letters and letter combinations which the student eventually will be taught. For example, we would not recommend that the word *treat* be introduced until the students learn the most common sound for the letter combination *ea.* Exceptions to this rule would have to be made for some very common words like *boy, house, soon,* and *may.* These common words often appear in stories students read before the letter combinations in them have been taught.

The procedure for introducing irregular words during the primary stage is significantly different from the procedure for the beginning stage. It involves the teacher's encouraging students to use the context of a sentence and the letter sound relationships in the word to figure out the word. In addition to this context procedure, we recommend enough word list drill on the words in isolation to allow the students to recognize the word at a glance (as sight words).

### Direct Instruction Procedures

#### Sequence

The sequencing guidelines for introducing irregular words remain the same as during the beginning reading stage. More common words should be introduced before lower-frequency words. Also, previously introduced words that are very similar to a new word should not appear in the discrimination list until 2 days after the new irregular word is introduced. For example, if students already know the irregular word *tough,* it should not appear in the discrimination list during the first two lessons on which the new irregular word *though* appears. On the third, fourth, and fifth lessons, *tough* can appear in the discrimination list to give students practice discriminating the two similar words.

A new sequencing guideline is to introduce groups of irregular words that contain letters representing the same sound so that students can see the relationship among them. Below are some of the more common related irregular words:

he, she, me
my, by, cry, try, fly, spy, sky
do, to
go, no, so
walk, talk chalk, stalk
pull, full
could, would, should
any, many
other, brother, mother, another
half, calf
door, floor
mind, kind, find

## Rate

During the beginning reading stage, we recommend introducing irregular words at a relatively slow rate. Initially, one word is introduced every fourth lesson, then one each second or third lesson. During the primary stage, the rate can increase until several new words are introduced each day.

## Example Selection

The amount of review that needs to be provided for new irregular words will decrease as students become more sophisticated

readers. Even so, more difficult irregular words will have to be reviewed quite extensively. Several factors determine the difficulty of an irregular word. First is the difference between how the word is sounded out and how the word is pronounced. The greater the discrepancy between the sounds and the actual pronunciation, the more difficult the word is. The word *though,* for example, is more difficult to decode than the word *put* because several letters in *though* do not represent their most common sound (ough), while in *put* only one letter does not represent its most common sound (*u*). Another factor that determines the relative difficulty of an irregular word is familiarity. The more familiar a word is to students, the easier it will be for them to decode. A word like *pull* will be easier for students to decode than a word like *agile,* since *pull* is more likely to be in the students' speaking vocabulary.

More difficult words should be reviewed daily for 1 week and each second day for 2 weeks thereafter. Easier words need not be reviewed as often; for several days when they are introduced and then each second day for a week.

## Teaching Procedures

For the introductory format, the teacher encourages the students to use context as an aid in figuring out an unknown word. The first step in the format involves the teacher's writing the word on the board and pointing out that it is a "funny word." (You can't rely on letter-sound correspondences.) The teacher would then say a sentence with the word left out. When the teacher comes to the irregular word in the sentence, she points to the word on the board but does not say it. For example, the teacher would write the irregular word *soup* and say a sentence like "He needed a big spoon to eat his vegetable _____." She would point to *soup,* signaling the group to respond or calling on a volunteer to supply the word. At first, teachers should construct sentences with the unknown word coming at the end since this form is usually easiest for students.

Even though context cues are used, the teacher still encourages the students to look at all the letters in the word. After the students identify a word, the teacher might ask how the students know the word is not another similar word that would make sense in the context (e.g., pointing to *soup,* "How do you know this word is not *stew?*")

The critical aspect of the teaching procedure remains the discrimination format in which the teacher has students sight read irregular words. After presenting several words with the introductory format, the teacher presents the discrimination format in which the students sight read a list of about 10 irregular words. The teacher has the students read the list of words until they can identify any word with only a 1-second pause. If the student has difficulty with a word, the teacher alternates between that word and other words, giving the student more practice on the difficult word.

A special procedure is useful to students in decoding multi-syllabic words in which a vowel is followed by a single consonant. In the structural analysis section, we recommended that students be taught to decode VCe derivatives by first trying the long sound for the initial vowel and then if that pronunciation did not produce a word that made sense, trying the short sound of the initial vowel. The same strategy can be used when students encounter multi-syllabic words that have a vowel followed by a single consonant but are not VCe derivatives (e.g., *camel, rapid, bacon, motel, copy,* and *baby*).

The format below is an example of the wording the teacher would use in presenting the strategy with the word *camel.*

## Abbreviations

Table 3.4.1 includes a list of abbreviations students should know at the end of the primary stage. Teaching abbreviations is simple. The teacher simply models by telling students what the abbreviation stands for, tests, and reviews. The rate for introducing abbreviations depends on how fa-

---

**Format for Multi-syllabic Words with a Vowel Followed by a Consonant**

| Teacher | Students |
|---|---|
| 1. Teacher points to *camel.* **"How many *m*'s in this word?"** (signal) | "One" |
| 2. Teacher points to *a* in *camel.* **"So what do we say for this letter?"** (signal) | "ā" |
| 3. **"Say the word."** (signal) | "Cāmel" |
| 4. **"I'll say a sentence with that word, A cāmel has humps on its back. Does cāmel make sense in that sentence?"** (signal) | "No" |
| Note: If the answer to step 4 is yes, do not do steps 5, 6, and 7. | |
| 5. **"So let's try the sound. What's the sound?"** (signal) | "ă" |
| 6. **"Get ready to pronounce the word saying the sound of the letter."** (pause, signal) | "Camel" |
| 7. **"Does that word make sense in the sentence?"** (signal) | "Yes" |

**TABLE 3.4.1**  *Abbreviations*

*Days*
Sun.  Mon.  Tues.  Wed.  Thurs.  Fri.  Sat.

*Months*
Jan.  Feb.  Mar.  Apr.  Jun.  Jul.  Aug.  Sept.  Oct.  Nov.  Dec.

*Persons*
Mr.  Ms.  Mrs.  Dr.  Rev.  Hon.  Pres.  Gov.  Gen.  Jr. (junior)  Sr. (senior)

*Time*
sec.  min.  hr.  wk.  mo.  yr.

*Language usage*
e.g.,—for example
etc.—and so forth
p.—page
pp.—pages
chap.—chapter

*Locations*

| | |
|---|---|
| N—North | Rd.—Road |
| S—South | St.—Street |
| E—East | Ave.—Avenue |
| W—West | Blvd.—Boulevard |

*Measurement*
*American*

| | |
|---|---|
| oz.—ounce | mi.—mile |
| lb.—pound | pt.—pint |
| in.—inch | qt.—quart |
| ft.—foot | gal.—gallon |
| yd.—yard | |

*Metric*

| | |
|---|---|
| mm—millimeter | km—kilometer |
| cm—centimeter | gm—gram |
| m—meter | |

miliar the word is. Familiar words such as *feet* can be introduced at a faster rate than less familiar words such as *liter.* The sequencing guidelines are the same as for all irregular words: (1) introduce more useful ones first and (2) separate abbreviations that may be confusing from each other. Systematic review should be provided through independent worksheet items in which students match the abbreviation to its name or write the name or abbreviation when the other is given; e.g., Write abbreviations for these words: pound, cen-timeter, . . . or Write the words these abbreviations stand for: lb., in., . . . .

## The Schwa Sound

In many multi-syllabic words, one of the syllables is pronounced with less stress. This syllable is referred to as the *unstressed syllable.* The vowel sound in unstressed syllables rarely represents the most common sound but rather a unique vowel sound somewhat similar to the /ŭ/ sound. This is called the schwa sound and is represented by the symbol / ə /. Note in the following words how similar the sound of the underlined vowels are: bottom, nickel, victim, momma. Words containing schwa sounds can be introduced several weeks after students have been reading two-syllable words formed by adding a common suffix to a regular word.

The teacher should treat the first 15 two-syllable schwa sound words as irregulars. The teacher would introduce 2 or 3 words every day for several days, writing the words on the board, modeling by telling the students each word, and then testing on pronouncing each syllable and saying the entire word. After introducing 15 words listed as irregulars, teachers can drop the use of the irregular format and simply include new schwa words in word list exercises. Students will probably not have much difficulty with new words that have a schwa sound unless the word is difficult for another reason. Table 3.4.2 contains some common words that include schwa sounds.

## Commercial Programs

The major problems regarding irregular words in commercial programs concern adequacy of practice and rate of introduction. Few programs include systematic word list practice on irregular words. We recommend supplementing these programs with word list exercises including irregular words. A new irregular word should appear in a supplementary word list exercise several days before appearing in a story and should appear daily for a week after that and then each second day for about 2 more weeks. The amount of review provided in lists is contingent in part on the amount of review provided in stories. Programs differ considerably in the amount of review provided on irregular words in stories. Teachers can determine the adequacy of the review by looking at the 10 stories that follow the introduction of a new irregular word and counting how many times that word appears. The less often the word appears, the greater the need to supplement lessons with word list exercises containing the irregular word.

The rate at which irregular words are introduced also varies from program to program. Teachers should use the students' performance as the guide in determining if a program is introducing words at too fast a rate. If students are missing irregular words, provide extra practice. Several short review periods of 2 to 3 minutes scattered throughout the school day can be quite helpful. Another alternative if students are having serious difficulty with irregular words is to slow down the rate at which they are introduced by not presenting words when they are introduced in the program. Delay introducing the words until students master other previously taught words. The delay method is less preferable because it complicates the teacher's job. The teacher must tell students the irregular word when it appears in stories and must keep track of the delayed words so they can be introduced at a later time.

**TABLE 3.4.2**  *Common Words with Schwa Sounds*

| | | |
|---|---|---|
| bottom | wagon | carton |
| nickel | basket | victim |
| button | forest | season |
| husband | happen | apron |
| gallon | sudden | pocket |
| cotton | color | gallop |
| extra | doctor | |
| momma | dragon | |
| kitten | hidden | |

Finally, the procedures for introducing irregular words vary from program to program. In some programs, the teacher simply tells the students the word; while in other programs, the word is written in a sentence, and students are urged to use the context to figure it out. Either procedure is acceptable. Remember, what is critical in the teaching procedure is providing enough practice.

## Passage Reading

The goal of decoding instruction is to prepare students to read for meaning. Passage reading instruction is the key step in making the transition from decoding to comprehension. As students progress through the primary stage, an increasingly greater proportion of group instruction and independent seatwork activities are devoted to passage reading. During the primary stage, teachers work on developing both accuracy and fluency.[2]

Accuracy in passage reading is facilitated by adequate preteaching of words that will appear in passages and through the application of motivational techniques. Preteaching ensures that the students have the knowledge needed to decode every word in the passage; motivational techniques include pay-offs for accurate reading, like praise, activities (e.g., extra recess, free time, etc.), and acknowledgement (e.g., name on bulletin board, membership in a "good readers" club, etc.). For example, if a group made no errors on a several hundred word passage, they might receive 10 minutes extra recess; for one to two errors, 8 minutes; for three to six errors, 5 minutes. Note that a motivational system will be effective only if students earn the pay-offs. Consequently, the teacher should structure lessons so the pay-off is readily available to all students. She does this by placing the students at a proper lesson in the reading program and by adequately preteaching the skills needed to decode the words in passages. The motivational system may be ineffective or even if effective, involve too much negativism if the teacher does not do an adequate job of preteaching.

Fluency in passage reading is facilitated primarily by providing the students with adequate practice. A major point in this book is that the teacher takes the responsibility for providing adequate practice to facilitate mastery of skills. The amount of practice students will require varies considerably. Teachers should try to facilitate reading outside the classroom by encouraging students to read at home, contacting parents, setting up a reading club, etc. In the classroom, the teacher should schedule enough practice time to enable students to reach specified rates (rates are usually expressed in words per minute). In this book, we specify minimal rates for students at various skill levels. These rates are based on our experiences and on a search of the research literature regarding rates. Unfortunately, little experimental research deals with the question of optimal reading rates for various skill levels. Authorities in the field of reading specify widely differing rates. The rates we chose (see Table 3.4.3, page 237) may seem to some to be high. However, we chose them because we feel that the more fluently students read, the more likely they are to engage in reading as a leisure time activity. A second reason for recommending somewhat high rates is that the ability to read fluently makes written comprehension exercises easier. Students who read slowly may be handicapped in doing exercises in which they have to answer questions regarding the content of long passages. They are more likely to have difficulty integrating the sentences from a passage to form a meaningful theme. Al-

---

[2] Students read accurately when they make few errors, none of which change the meaning of a sentence; students read fluently when their rate approximates their speaking rate and also when they group words into phrases with appropriate inflection.

though primary grade students may be able to answer items correctly, in spite of their slow rate, the handicap of a slow rate will become apparent in the intermediate grades. The amount of reading required in assignments increases dramatically in the intermediate grades, especially in the content areas (science, health, social studies, etc.). Students who cannot decode fluently may have difficulty completing their assignments in the allotted time.

## Direct Instruction Procedures

## Teaching Procedures

Before students begin passage reading in the primary stage, they should learn to find the beginning (and end) of paragraphs. The time spent in teaching this skill will result in more efficient use of instructional time since the students will be able to follow teacher instructions. To teach students to identify paragraphs, the teacher holds up a page from a passage, points to the first paragraph indention and says, "Writing that starts over here shows the beginning of a paragraph." The teacher points to the next paragraph. "Here's where the paragraph begins. Now it's your turn. Point to where the first paragraph begins." The teacher checks students' pointing. "Show me where the next paragraph begins." The teacher checks. Each day, the teacher has the students identify the paragraphs on two or three pages until they make no mistakes on two pages. After reaching that criterion, students no longer need to do the exercise.

The basic teaching procedure for passage reading involves the students' reading a passage one section at a time. A section may consist of one longer paragraph or several shorter paragraphs. The students read a section silently once or twice and then orally with individual turns. After students orally read a section, the teacher asks comprehension questions about what occurred and sets a purpose for reading the next section. The students then read the next section silently, after which the

### FIGURE 3.4.1

STORY 141

#### The Lion and the Mouse

There once was a lion who lived in the jungle. The lion was the king of all the animals in the jungle. He was big, and he was mean. If he said, "Get out of my way," the other animals got out of his way. If he said, "Come here," the other animals came to the lion.

One day a little mouse came up to the lion. The mouse said, "I want to be your friend. I am just a little mouse, but I will be a good friend."

The lion laughed. "Ha, ha," he said. "What do I need with a little friend like you? What can you do for me? I am the strongest animal in the jungle. I am the best hunter. I am king of all the animals."

The little mouse said, "But I will be a good friend."

The lion laughed so hard that the mouse fell down. Then the lion said, "Go

From *Distar® Reading II, 2nd Edition* by Siegfried Engelmann and Elaine C. Bruner. © 1975, 1969 Science Research Associates, Inc. Reprinted by permission of the publisher.

teacher again conducts individual oral reading and asks comprehension questions. After the students complete the story, the teacher has them reread it, first concentrating on reading with expression and then on developing fluency.

An example of the passage reading procedure appears in the format below. Assume the students are reading the first page of the passage, "The Lion and the Mouse," (Figure 3.4.1) from *Distar Reading II* (Engelmann & Bruner, 1975, Book 4, p. 60).

## Reading with Expression

Training in reading with expression is necessary to demonstrate to students that written passages express meaning in the same way as spoken language. Oral reading behaviors that characterize reading with expression include pausing at periods and punctuation marks, emphasizing the appropriate words in questions, and when reading quotations, using inflections that reflect the mood of the character speaking. Expression training can begin when students

---

**Format for Passage Reading**

| *Teacher* | *Students* |
|---|---|
| A. Procedure applied to first section of passage. | |
| 1. Teacher sets purpose. **"The title says the lion and the mouse. Let's see what the story tells about the lion and the mouse."** | |
| 2. Teacher has students read silently, then orally. | |
| a. **"Point to the end of the second paragraph."** Teacher checks students' pointing. | Students point to end of second paragraph. |
| **"Read the first two paragraphs to yourselves."** Teacher watches students' eyes to monitor their silent reading. | Students read silently. |
| b. After all students finish reading two paragraphs silently, the teacher says, **"Put your fingers on the first word. I'll call on people to read."** Teacher calls on individuals to read one or two sentences until both paragraphs have been read. | Individual students read orally. |
| 3. Teacher asks comprehension questions. | |
| a. **"Was the lion nice?"** | |
| b. **"What happened if the lion said, Come here?"** | |
| c. **"Whom did the lion meet?"** | |
| d. **"What did the mouse say?"** | |
| B. Procedure from step A is applied to second section of passage. | |
| 1. Teacher sets the purpose for the next section. **"I wonder what the lion will do. Read the rest of the page to yourselves and find out."** | |
| 2. Teacher has students read silently, then orally. | |

**Format for Passage Reading (continued)**

| Teacher | Students |
|---|---|

3. Teacher asks comprehension questions.

C. Procedure from step A is repeated with remaining sections.

D. Reading with expression training.

1. Teacher models reading first one or two sentences with expression then calls on a student to reread those sentences.

2. Teacher repeats step 1 with several more sentences.

Note: Step D would be done daily until students begin reading with proper expression on the first reading of a story. Thereafter, expression training can be faded.

E. Students read in pairs.

1. Students read to each other, switching after each sentence. This step is optional. It need only be done with students who are reading below the desired rate for their instructional level (see Table 3.4.3). A more extensive procedure for developing fluency is described under diagnosis and remediation.

are able to read at a rate of 45 words per minute. A 5–10 minute training session should be incorporated into the lesson following the reading of the passage.

We recommend a modeling procedure for teaching students to read with expression. The teacher says, "We're going to practice reading this story as if we were telling it to someone. I'll read a sentence. Then you read it the same way I do." The teacher then reads the first sentence or two, using slightly exaggerated expression. Students should be instructed to keep their fingers on the first word in the sentence and just follow along with their eyes as the teacher reads. (Pointing to the first word enables the students to find the beginning of the sentence when it is their turn to read.) After the teacher reads, an individual is called upon to read with expression. If the student reads with expression, the

teacher praises her. If the student does not read with expression, the teacher repeats the model. Exercises for teaching reading with expression should be done until students read new material with expression without first receiving a teacher model.

## Encouraging Attentiveness

The success of the passage reading procedures outlined above is contingent on students' actively practicing reading even when they are not reading orally. Initially, all students should point to the words as another student reads. Not pointing to each word as another student reads should be considered a privilege that students earn by demonstrating that they can keep their place. Teachers should encourage attentiveness through a positive motivational system. During group reading, teachers can offer a bonus pay-off if nobody loses his place while reading the story.

The teacher should rely mainly on positive attention, praising students who are pointing or watching the page as another student reads. He should not nag students who are not reading. If a teacher notes a student not reading during this time, the teacher might use a natural consequence of having the student read after the group is dismissed or during recess time.

Another procedure that can be used to encourage attentiveness during individual oral reading is calling on a student to correct an error made by another student. The teacher calls on a student at the end of the sentence in which the error occurred. The student would be expected to correctly identify the missed word. The teacher does not ask for a volunteer but simply calls on a student at random. For this procedure to be effective, the teacher must not allow any students to make negative comments about other students. When an error is made, the students are not to say or do anything. They wait till the end of the sentence, at which time the teacher calls on a student to identify the missed word.

## Correction Procedure

Since all reading is done individually, the only type of errors teachers have to worry about are misidentification errors. As a general rule, we recommend that teachers make corrections at the end of a sentence. The reason for waiting is to give the student the opportunity to recognize that a word does not make sense and then self-correct. If a student says a word that does not make sense in the context of the passage and does not correct himself, the teacher points out that the sentence does not make sense and tells the student to try again. For example, a student reads, "The boy was going to the beat," saying *beat* instead of *beach.* The teacher might say, "Beat doesn't make

sense. Boys don't go to a beat. Look at that word again and figure it out." If the student still does not identify the word, the teacher either tells the student the word or gives him some type of phonic or structural cue. The cue depends on the type of word missed. If a student misidentifies a word with a letter combination, the teacher points out the letter or letter combination missed, tells the student the sound, and then asks the students "What word?" For example, if a student says *beat* for *beach,* the teacher would say "*Ch* says /ch/. So what's the word?" If the word has a VCe pattern, the teacher would remind students of the VCe rule. If the student misidentifies an irregular word, the teacher simply tells the student the word, since a phonic or structural cue will not help in figuring out an irregular word. For all errors involving a meaning change, the student should go back to the beginning of the sentence and reread it. The purpose of rereading the sentence is to make sure the student gains the proper meaning.

When making corrections, the teacher should be careful not to use words or tone of voice that may inadvertently embarrass the student. As a general rule, the less said by the teacher when making corrections during passage reading, the smoother the lesson probably will progress.

## Diagnosis and Remediation

Student performance during passage reading indicates whether a student has mastered previously taught skills, and, if not, what skill deficits need to be remedied. During passage reading itself, teachers do a minimum of remediation, since too many interruptions may result in students' losing interest or not understanding the passage.

The teacher quickly corrects errors and notes the word missed and the response the student made. This record is necessary to diagnose a student's skill deficits. We suggest using abbreviations. For example, if a student named Linda said *turn* for the word *torn,* the teacher would write the letter *u* over the *o* in *torn* to indicate the mistake, then a capital *L* for Linda. Writing lower-case letters to signify what a student said and upper-case letters for the student's name will minimize confusion. This record of errors serves three purposes. First, it provides an accurate list of words missed during passage reading that should appear in the next lesson's word list exercises. Second, it serves as a guide for the teacher in indicating any deficit on previously taught skills. Third, the record serves as a guide in rewarding students for improvements in reading performance.

In diagnosing errors, teachers may identify several types of deficits: (1) phonics or structural analysis errors, (2) lack of knowledge of irregular words, (3) phrasing and expression errors, (4) inappropriate context usage which indicates either an over- or underreliance on context cues, and (5) rate deficits.

Phonics errors are indicated when students misidentify a particular letter or letter combination in several words. For example, if a student misses several words containing the letter combination *ea,* she probably needs remediation on *ea.* The remediation would involve the teacher's presenting *ea* in an isolated sounds tasks and then *ea* words in a word list exercise. (Remediation exercises are included as both part of the follow-up portion of the same lesson in which the deficit is identified and as part of the next lesson's teacher presentation.)

An irregular word deficit is indicated when a student is consistently unable to identify an irregular word. The remediation procedure involves treating the missed irregular as a new irregular during the next several lessons. The teacher would include the word in word list exercises and during the exercises, would have the students identify that word several times.

Phrasing and expression deficits are indicated when a student ignores various punctuation marks and/or reads without grouping words into thought units. Such deficits should be remedied through the modeling procedure specified earlier in this section for 5 to 10 minutes each day. These exercises would continue until students incorporate reading with proper phrasing and expression into all oral reading exercises.

Context errors may involve either an over- or underreliance on context cues. An overreliance on context cues is indicated by the student misidentifying many words (more than three per hundred) which the student is able to identify correctly in isolation and/or inserting or leaving out words whose omission or insertion results in a change in the meaning of the sentence (e.g., reading The boy was not happy as "The boy was happy.").

The remediation procedure for a pattern that indicates an overreliance on context involves instituting a motivation system to encourage accurate reading. A teacher might have a student read several excerpts from passages orally each day. A reward would be established for accurate reading. For example, five points might be awarded for 100% accuracy; three points, for 99% accuracy, and so on. A minimally acceptable level of 97% should be established. If a student reads below this level, the student is to reread the passage. The standards for this exercise should be quite stringent. The student should be told that a word will be counted as wrong even if she self-corrects. The student should be encouraged to take her time. Some students who overrely on context will also have a reading rate deficit. The teacher should not work on remediating both types of deficits at first. He should first work on developing accuracy. Only after the student has begun reading accurately on a consistent basis should the teacher work on increasing rate.

An underreliance on context would be indicated by students' saying words that do not make sense in the context of a passage. For example, when reading, *The man went to the shop,* a student reads, "The man went to the she." If students make many meaning-changing mistakes, the teacher should institute oral language training exercises to teach students to identify context errors. In one type of exercise, the teacher says sentences, and students indicate whether the sentence makes sense. Once students learn to identify context errors in spoken sentences, they are more likely to identify context errors when they read. In presenting the exercise, a teacher might say, "I'll say some sentences. You tell me whether they make sense."

1. "The ran ate the corn. Does that make sense?"
2. "The rat ate corn. Does that make sense?"
3. "The boy played on the pouch? Does that make sense?"
4. "The girls ran to the sore? Does that make sense?"
5. "The boy played on the porch. Does that make sense?"

In addition to exercises such as this one, the teacher should establish a motivation system to encourage more careful reading.

Deficits in reading rate are indicated when students read new material at a rate more than 10% slower than the indicated desired rate for the instructional level at which they are reading (see Table 3.4.3). Note that a student's instructional level may be different than her grade level. If a student is reading in a book designated for late second grade, the student's instructional level is at late second grade regardless if the child is a first, second, or third grader.

At the beginning of the school year, the teacher should administer informal reading inventories to each student (see Section 3.6 on testing and placing students during the primary grades). These tests will tell the teacher the reading rate of each student. We recommend rereading exercises for students whose reading rate is 10% below the desired level. Rereading exercises involve students' reading passages they have previously read until they can read them at a specified rate.

To prepare for rereading exercises, the teacher first determines an acceptable rereading rate. The rereading rate should be 40% higher than the student's current reading rate. The purpose of setting the rereading criterion significantly higher than the first reading criterion is to ensure that students receive the massed practice on familiar material that is needed to improve their rate on new material. We found that having lower performers reread a story one time results in minimal improvements in rate. On the other hand, if students reread a passage until they read it at a rate significantly higher than their rate on the first reading, their rate on new material gradually improves.

If a student were currently reading at a rate of 60 words a minute, the teacher would have the student reread a passage until the student could read it at 84 words a minute [60 + (40% of 60 = 24) = 84]. If

**TABLE 3.4.3**  *Desired Reading Rates for Various Instructional Levels*

| INSTRUCTIONAL LEVEL | WORDS PER MINUTE ON FIRST READING |
|---|---|
| First half of year 1 | 45 |
| Second half of year 1 | 60 |
| First third of year 2 | 75 |
| Second third of year 2 | 90 |
| Last third of year 2 | 110 |
| First half of year 3 | 120 |
| Second half of year 3 | 135 |

a student were reading at a rate of 90 words a minute, the student would reread the passage until he read it at the rate of 126 words a minute [90 + (40% of 90 = 36) = 126]. Next, the teacher uses Table 3.4.4 to translate the acceptable rereading rate into seconds needed to read a 100 word passage. In order to read a 100 word passage at 84 words a minute, the student would have to read a passage in about 1:11 seconds. Then the teacher prepares the reading material by marking off several 100 word excerpts in a previously read story. A teacher might put a star at the beginning and a bracket at the end of each 100 word excerpt.

**TABLE 3.4.4**   *Translation of Seconds Required to Read 100 Words into Reading Rate*

| SECONDS | WORDS PER MINUTE | SECONDS | WORDS PER MINUTE |
|---|---|---|---|
| :30 | 200 | 1:46 | 57 |
| :32 | 187 | 1:48 | 56 |
| :34 | 176 | 1:50 | 55 |
| :36 | 167 | 1:52 | 54 |
| :38 | 158 | 1:54 | 53 |
| :40 | 150 | 1:56 | 52 |
| :42 | 143 | 1:58 | 51 |
| :44 | 136 | 2:00 | 50 |
| :46 | 130 | 2:02 | 49 |
| :48 | 125 | 2:04 | 48 |
| :50 | 120 | 2:06 | 48 |
| :52 | 115 | 2:08 | 47 |
| :54 | 111 | 2:10 | 46 |
| :56 | 107 | 2:12 | 45 |
| :58 | 103 | 2:14 | 45 |
| 1:00 | 100 | 2:16 | 44 |
| 1:02 | 97 | 2:18 | 43 |
| 1:04 | 94 | 2:20 | 43 |
| 1:06 | 91 | 2:22 | 42 |
| 1:08 | 88 | 2:24 | 41 |
| 1:10 | 86 | 2:26 | 41 |
| 1:12 | 83 | 2:28 | 40 |
| 1:14 | 81 | 2:30 | 40 |
| 1:16 | 79 | 2:32 | 39 |
| 1:18 | 77 | 2:34 | 39 |
| 1:20 | 75 | 2:36 | 38 |
| 1:22 | 73 | 2:38 | 38 |
| 1:24 | 71 | 2:40 | 37 |
| 1:26 | 70 | 2:42 | 37 |
| 1:28 | 63 | 2:44 | 37 |
| 1:30 | 67 | 2:46 | 36 |
| 1:32 | 65 | 2:48 | 36 |
| 1:34 | 64 | 2:50 | 35 |
| 1:36 | 62 | 2:52 | 35 |
| 1:38 | 61 | 2:54 | 34 |
| 1:40 | 60 | 2:56 | 34 |
| 1:42 | 59 | 2:58 | 34 |
| 1:44 | 58 | 3:00 | 33 |

The teacher begins the exercise by pointing out the excerpt a student is to read and telling the students how long he has to complete it. The teacher would let the student time himself reading the story. The student practices reading the excerpt to himself until he is able to read it within the specified time. When the student feels he is able to read at the specified time, he raises his hand for the teacher to check him out. The teacher times the student as he reads the excerpt orally. The student's reading of the excerpt would be deemed acceptable if he read the passage in the specified time with two errors or less. If the student read acceptably, he would begin practicing another excerpt. During one 15-minute session, the student might work on three to five 100 word excerpts. If a teacher is working with a group of students, the teacher should structure the session so that while one student is being tested, the other students are practicing reading to themselves.

A motivational system should be incorporated into rate-building exercises. Each excerpt read acceptably might earn a point, with each 20 points leading to some type of reward.

Every 2 weeks, the teacher would have a student read a passage the student has never read before. The student's performance tells the teacher if the rate training exercises are, in fact, working. If the student's rate has improved, the teacher increases the acceptable rate on rereading exercises to the student's new rate plus 40%. For example, if a student had been reading at a rate of 60 words a minute at the beginning of the year and is now reading at 75 words a minute, the acceptable rate for rereading exercises would increase from 84 words a minute (60 + 24) to 105 words per minute (75 + 30). If the student's rate had not improved, the teacher should consider providing more practice time.

The exercise described above may be conducted in a small group setting with one adult and three or four students. Parent volunteers or paraprofessionals could be used to conduct the training sessions. The length and number of training exercises each day would depend on the students' relative deficit. Students reading at a very slow rate might participate in two 15–20 minute sessions daily.

Teachers can and should also use other exercises to increase fluency. Teachers working with older students can make a line graph (see Figure 3.4.2). These graphs on which a student's rate is recorded periodically are popular with many students.

Another way to develop rate is through phrase drill. The teacher prints phrases like "the tall man," "in the house," "went home" on separate cards and presents the phrases until the students identify them by sight. Students can also work in pairs

**FIGURE 3.4.2**

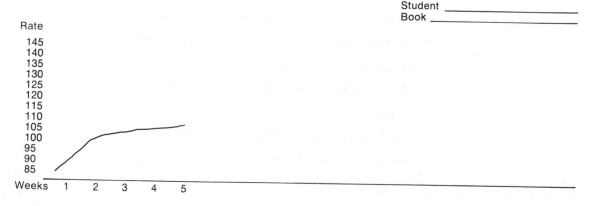

and present the cards to each other. The goal is for the students to read a phrase by sight, as soon as it is shown. Teachers can also use tachistoscopes, which present words at a controlled rate.

## Commercial Programs

Some programs use individual turns inappropriately and include too much discussion about what is going to happen before students read a passage. The problem with too much discussion is that it uses up too much of the time allocated for reading. Inappropriate use of individual turns is caused by some programs recommending that the teacher call mostly on higher-performing students. While calling on higher-performing students is advantageous in that these students will usually provide a clear model of reading with expression, this procedure may cause lower-performing students to become inattentive. Individual turns and discussion play a valuable part in the teaching procedure; however, they should not be misused.

**FIGURE 3.4.3**

STORY **137**

### The Frog and the Turtle
### and the Snake Get Along

Flame the snake was sliding into the weeds. He was going after the frog.

"Save me, save me," the frog yelled. "Please save me from this snake."

Suddenly, the turtle took a big bite out of the snake's tail. "Ow, ow," the snake yelled. "Why did you do that?" Flame asked. "I must do what snakes do."

The turtle said, "I have to do what turtles do."

Then Flame called, "Frog, oh frog. Come out here." The frog hopped out of the weeds. He looked scared. Flame looked at him and began to slide after him.

"Stop," the turtle called. "Stop, or I will bite your tail again."

So Flame stopped. Then the turtle said, "You can be a sneak when you are not

From *Distar® Reading II, 2nd Edition* by Siegfried Engelmann and Elaine C. Bruner. © 1975, 1969 Science Research Associates, Inc. Reprinted by permission of the publisher.

Ideally, passages that are to be read as part of the lesson should be constructed to provide practice on newly introduced phonic skills and irregular words. Words containing letter combinations, VCe words, affixes, etc., should appear frequently in passages soon after they are introduced in word list exercises. For example, after words with VCe patterns appear for several days in word list reading, the next three to six passages should be designed so that quite a few VCe words appear. The story in Figure 3.4.3 is an example of a story that stresses VCe words (Englemann and Bruner, 1975).

Passages provide important practice and review not only on new letter combinations and word types but also on new irregular words. High-frequency irregular words should appear several times after they are first introduced so that students receive enough practice to remember them. Because passages are used to provide practice on a great number of skills, they should not contain too many new irregular words. Too many new words in a passage will disrupt some students' decoding strategies, causing numerous errors. Teachers can avoid the introduction of too many *new* words in a passage by looking ahead for stories that contain too many new irregular words and introducing some of the words in word list exercises before the lesson that contains the story.

## RESEARCH

Correlational evidence indicates that proficient readers read in phrases and multiple word units while less skilled readers focus on individual words or letters within words. Clay and Imlach (1971) found that the best readers read 7 words between pauses while the poorest readers read only 1.3 words between pauses. Taylor reported that twelfth graders made one fixation (eye movement) for approximately every 2 words while first grade readers made about two fixations for each single word. A comprehensive comparison of three methods for instructing students to read in units larger than single words was conducted by Dahl (in press). She compared single word recognition training, repeated readings, and hypothesis test training, in which students were trained to use context cues to predict the next word in a sentence. On various reading measures, Dahl found that the repeated readings and hypothesis test procedures produced significant gains but isolated word drill did not. This study points out the need for specific training in passage reading. Teachers cannot assume that training in word list reading will result in students' acquiring passage-reading skills. Specific teaching is needed to develop the various passage-reading skills.

Another variable involved in passage reading is student interest. In reviewing the literature on the importance of student interest, Collins, Brown, Morgan and Brewer (1977) reported that interest significantly affects the performance of boys up through third grade but has no affect after third grade. This finding would suggest that using high interest material is important for boys in the first three grades. However, more recent research included in the review suggested that students may be more interested in areas in which they are knowledgeable, in which case an appropriate knowledge base would be the critical variable in student performance and not interest. The data are insufficient to resolve this question.

**TABLE 3.4.5**  *Average Reading Rates of Students Scoring 70% or Better in Comprehension*

| Grade | 1 | 2 | 3 | 4 | 5 | 6 | 7 | 8 | 9 | 12 |
|---|---|---|---|---|---|---|---|---|---|---|
| Words per Minute | 80 | 115 | 138 | 158 | 173 | 185 | 195 | 204 | 214 | 250 |

*Note. From Grade Level Norms for the Components of the Fundamental Reading Skill, Bulletin #3 by S. E. Taylor et al. New York: Huntington, Educational Development Laboratories, 1960.*

Taylor, Frackenpohl and Pettee (1960) studied students who scored 70% or better in comprehension when reading material of average difficulty for the grade. The average heading rates are shown in Table 3.4.5.

Unfortunately, experimental studies have not been conducted to establish optimal accuracy and rate criteria for various skill levels. Nor have studies compared differing passage reading procedures. Studies of this type might determine an optimal mix and sequence for oral and silent reading activities. Questions about how to correct errors during passage reading also need to be researched. The contribution researchers could make in the area of instructional practices for passage reading is substantial.

## APPLICATION EXERCISES

1. The errors in each item below reflect a deficit in a particular passage-reading skill. State the skill and describe the procedure for remedying the deficit.
   a. When reading the sentence, *The girl tripped when running down the stairs,* a third grade student says "stars." Next the student says "later" for *landed* in the sentence, *She landed on her head.*
   b. When reading the sentence, *Ann built a large house,* a student says "bought" for built. The student has missed *built* several times.
   c. When reading two sentences, the student ignores the period. The student has done this several times.
   d. A student reading late second grade material reads at a rate of one word each 2 seconds.
   e. A student reads "bet" for *beat* and "set" for *seat.*
2. Specify the desired reading rates for the following students (see Table 3.4.3).
   A third grade student reading at a mid-second grade level.
   A first grade student reading at a early-first grade level.
   A fifth grade student reading at a late first grade level.
   A second grade student reading at a beginning third grade level.
3. For each student described below, tell if they should receive training to improve their reading rate. If they need such training, specify what the acceptable criterion would be on rereading exercises.
   William—A third grader whose instructional level is at early second level. He is reading at a rate of 75 words per minute.
   Jackie —A third grader whose instructional level is at mid-third grade. She is reading at a rate of 75 words per minute.
   Andra —A second grader whose instructional level is at a early second grade level. He is reading at a rate of 40 words a minute.
4. Listed below are the errors made by two students when reading the following passage. The word the student said is in quotes next to the missed word from the passage.

   The farmer had a gleam in his eye. He was hoping that all his wheat would be cut by that night. Later he would load it on his truck and take it to the coast.

   For each student, tell if the student's errors indicate a specific skill deficit. If so, state the deficit. Remember skill deficits are indicated by patterns of errors rather than a single incorrect response.
   Bill—gleam, "glow"; load, "lay"
   Wilma—hoping, "hopping"; load, "loud"
5. You have several parents who have volunteered their time in the classroom. One of the parents will be conducting a rereading exercise with Jason who is reading at mid-second grade level and who is reading at a rate of 50 words a minute. Write an instruction sheet for the parents. Specify exactly what they are to do during the session with the student.

# SECTION 3.5

## *Comprehension*

Written comprehension begins with simple questions that are directly answered in a passage. These early literal comprehension exercises, which focus on specific details from a passage, introduce the concept that answers to questions often appear in print. Before written comprehension exercises are introduced, many young children will never have used a printed passage as an information source. Rather, they will have learned by watching and listening to others. Early items must be kept simple, in part because of students' limited decoding ability. This limitation can be overcome by presenting more advanced comprehension exercises verbally during the early primary stage. As the students' decoding ability increases, the difficulty of passage-related exercises gradually increases as questions become less literal, passages become longer, pronoun usage is introduced, and instructions become more complex. The written comprehension activities also become more sophisticated, including inference, summarization, and sequencing exercises. The content of comprehension instruction also depends on students' vocabulary and language skills. Instructionally naive students will need continued vocabulary and language training if they are to successfully work more complex items. Teachers should keep in mind, though, that many students will not require direct instruction in answering literal question word items and even summarization and sequencing exercises.

These exercises focus student attention on the overall structure of a passage, rather than just on specific details. Summarization exercises involve selecting the best title, main idea, or summary for a passage. Sequencing requires students to order several events from a passage according to when they occurred in the passage. Inference items require using the information in a passage to respond to questions that are based on the passage but not directly answered in the passage. In addition to passage-related comprehension activities, several vocabulary-related activities are introduced during the primary grades; opposites (or antonyms), synonyms, and classification.

Written comprehension exercises provide students practice in decoding as well as in gaining information from print. By the end of the third grade, written comprehension exercises will probably account for more than half of the decoding students will be doing during a school day. Therefore, coordination between the decoding skills being taught and the words that appear in written exercises is essential. Students will be seriously hampered if they are given materials that contain words they are unable to decode or do not understand.

The amount of direction students receive before working passage-related exercises independently depends on their ability to understand and retain what they read. Many students will be able to read a passage and remember enough information from the passage to answer a variety of summarization, sequencing, and inference questions. For these students, minimal guidance is needed. The teacher just models items that contain unfamiliar instructions.

On the other hand, instructionally naive students may require substantial guidance in doing passage-related items. These students often will not remember what they have read and even may not know how to refer to a passage to locate information (scanning). They will need teacher direction in working passage-related exercises until they can work the items independently.

One way to prepare students for passage-related items is to ask questions while students read a passage. The teacher asks questions after each group of several sentences. Asking comprehension questions ensures that students realize that the purpose for reading is to gain meaning. Below is a passage and the questions a teacher might ask after the students read each paragraph in the passage that follows. Questions 1, 3, and 4 are literal. Questions 2 and 5 are inference questions, because they are not directly answered in the story; the answers are based on information in the story. Teaching procedures for inference items appear later.

Tanya was fourteen years old. She liked school a lot. Every day she worked very hard in school. She wrote neatly. She practiced her arithmetic, and she read lots of books.

1. Did Tanya like school?
2. Do you think Tanya was in first grade? How do you know?
3. What did Tanya do in school?

The first thing on Monday morning, the teacher talked to Tanya's mother. That night Tanya's mom called her into the kitchen. Tanya's mom was smiling.

4. What happened first on Monday?
5. Do you think Tanya's mom was happy? Why?

## Direct Instructional Procedures

### Preskills

We recommend not asking comprehension questions until after students can decode a passage with relative fluency. Laborious decoding will often cause students to miss comprehension questions. Students may forget words that appeared in earlier sentences if they decode too slowly, or they may give a wrong answer because they are attending almost exclusively to decoding. For average and above-average students who are having no dfficulty with decoding, the comprehension questions can be incorporated into the first reading of a passage. In contrast, instructionally naive students may need to reread a passage several times before comprehension questions should be asked.

### Literal Comprehension

Literal comprehension, which is the simplest written comprehension exercise, is the first type of written exercise introduced in most reading programs. In a literal comprehension exercise, the answer is directly stated in a passage. The difference between literal and nonliteral comprehension is illustrated in the passage and items in Figure

**FIGURE 3.5.1**

Passage:

A cat was sleeping in the sun. Then a dog walked by. The cat jumped up and hid in a can.

Items: Write the right word in the blank.

literal 1. The cat hid in a _____.  can  house  box

nonliteral 2. The cat was _____.  happy  afraid  big

3.5.1. Item 1 is literal because the answer is directly stated in the passage. In contrast, item 2 is not literal since the answer (afraid) does not appear in the passage. In item 2, students must infer that since the cat ran from the dog and hid, the cat was afraid.

## Teaching Procedure for Literal, Passage-related Items

The following procedure is designed to introduce literal comprehension items. The procedure would be used only if students were unable to work literal items on their own. Even with students who initially require the structured teaching procedure, the procedure should be faded as soon as students can accurately work literal items independently.

In presenting passage-related items, the teacher (1) has the students decode the passage until they can do so fluently, (2) explains and tests the students' understanding of the instructions, (3) has the students read the first item, asks if they remember the answer, and, if not, directs them to reread the passage until they come to the sentence that contains the answer (a rudimentary form of scanning; more complex forms will be discussed in later sections).

## Developing Student Retention

After a few days of teacher-directed instruction, the students should do several passage-related items independently. The teacher watches students carefully while they read the passage and answer the items. She notes the strategy students use: do students refer to the passage for every item or just for unknown items?

If students refer to the passage to answer most of the items, they should be encouraged to remember what they have read. One way of doing this is to present a passage and items on separate pages or require the students to cover the passage before they begin answering the items. The teacher says, "Today you're going to have to remember what you read. When you remember what you read, you can write your answers without looking back at the story. Let's try it. Read the story over until you remember what happens. Then cover the story like this (demonstrates) and write the answers." The teacher monitors the students to make sure that they cover the passage before they begin to work the items. When students make an error or cannot remember an answer, they are allowed to refer to the passage. The teacher calls attention to students who correctly answer all the items without looking at the passage. For example, "Students who didn't have to look at the story are in the good remembering club." The teacher reads the names of students who are members of the club for that day. This procedure for building retention can be used on almost all comprehension exercises. In order to ensure a successful experience for instructionally naive students, initial exercises should include relatively short passages. Passage length should be increased gradually.

## Difficulty of Literal Comprehension Items

Several variables affect the difficulty of passage-related items: (1) the degree to which the items are literal, (2) the length of the passage, (3) the order in which questions are asked, (4) the complexity of the instructions, and (5) the use of pronouns.

### Literal Items

The easiest type of passage-related item is one that can be answered by matching words in the item with those in the sentence. The following item, written in a nonsense language, illustrates a strictly literal item.

Sentence: yjr, sm gr;; gpp jod jptdr
Item:     yjr, sm gr;; gpp jod _____.

Adults cannot decode the nonsense item; yet, they can answer it correctly by matching the words in the item with those in the sentence and writing *jptdr* in the blank. Likewise, a child can answer a completion item by using a matching strategy rather than decoding each word.

Items become less literal when they are not identical to a corresponding sentence in a passage. Changes include alterations in words or word order. For example:

**Format for Literal Comprehension**

Passage:

A little cat lived in a mud house. It rained. A bug ran in the house. The mud house got wet and fell apart. The cat and the bug sat in the rain and got wet.

Items: Fill in the blanks.

1. What got wet and fell apart? _____
2. A cat lived in a mud _____.  house  bug  hut
3. The _____ and the bug sat in the rain.  bug  dog  cat

| Teacher | Students |
|---|---|
| 1. The teacher focuses on decoding fluency. **"Touch the first word."** Teacher checks pointing. | Students touch the first word. |
| The teacher alternates between unison and individual responses until the students read the passage fluently. Students may need to reread the story several times. | Students read the passage. |
| 2. Teacher tests students' understanding of the instructions. Often the instructions for early comprehension activities are not written because the students do not have the decoding skills necessary to read the words that appear in instructions. Whether the teacher gives the instructions or the students read them, the teacher then asks, **"How are you going to answer the question? Tell me what you're going to do. Show me where you put the answer."** | |

**Format for Literal Comprehension (*continued*)**

| *Teacher* | *Students* |
|---|---|
| 3. Students read the first item and then mark the answer. If necessary, they find the appropriate sentence in the story that answers the item. | |
| a. **"Touch the first question."** Teacher checks pointing. **"Get ready to read."** Teacher claps for each word. | Students touch the first question. Students read the question. |
| b. **"Raise your hand if you know the answer to that question."** If the question has only one correct possible answer, the teacher calls on the group to respond. If the question has several possible correct answers, she calls on individuals to respond. **"What's the answer?"** | Students answer. |
| c. If any students do not remember the answer, the teacher says, **"Let's find the answer in the story. Find the words *got wet and fell apart.*"** If students cannot find the words, have them read each sentence. | Students find the sentence. |
| After students find the sentence, the teacher repeats the item. **"What got wet and fell apart?"** **"Right, the mud house. Write the answer."** | "the mud house" Students write the answer. |
| d. The procedure in step 3 is repeated until the students have completed all the items. | |

Sentence: The cat lived in a mud house.
Literal item: The cat lived in a mud _____.
Altered word order: In a mud _____, lived a cat.
Word change: The _____ lived in a mud home.

Question word items are also less literal, e.g., *Where did the cat live?* because the word order is altered, and the student must understand particular question words, e.g., *where* calls for a location answer.

### Passage Length

Finding the sentence that contains the answer to a completion item is more difficult in longer passages. For example, extracting the answer to the question, "Who sat on a mat?" is easier in the sentence, "A mad cat sat on a mat." than in this passage: "A fat rat sat on a bat. A mad cat sat on a mat. A sad man sat on a bed."

### Question Order

Items ordered so that they parallel the sequence of events in a passage are easier than items that do not. When items follow the sequence of a passage, students can start at the beginning of the passage and work through the items in order. Otherwise, they must skip around in the passage to locate the answers. Below are two sets of items, one that follows the sequence of events in the passage (set a) and one that does not (set b).

Passage:

Sam ran in a hut. He sat in a cup. He said, "I am hot." He fell off the cup. He got wet. "I am not hot," he said.

Items: Fill in the correct answer.

    a. Items follow the order of events in the passage:
        Did Sam run in a hut? _____
        Where did Sam sit? _____
        He said, "I am not _____."

    b. Items do not follow the order of events in the passage:
        He said, "I am not _____."
        Did Sam run in a hut? _____
        Where did Sam sit? _____

### Instruction Complexity

Instructions indicating how students are to respond range from simple ones, in which students circle the word that goes in a blank or fill in a missing word, to more complex ones in which students make several different responses, e.g., "Circle the word that tells what the boy did. Underline the word that tells what the girl did."

### Pronouns

Pronouns increase the difficulty of items because students must identify a pronoun antecedent before they can answer the item. Note the differences between passage a and passage b.

    Passage a: Tom got a car. It was dirty.
    Passage b: Tom got a car. The car was dirty.
    Item: Was Tom dirty?

A naive student would be more likely to incorrectly answer yes after reading passage a because of the pronoun *it*. Passage b is easier in that it directly states that the car was dirty. If students do not understand pronouns, they will have some difficulties with comprehension. To prevent these difficulties, teachers should present oral language exercises to teach pronouns. Students can then apply their understanding of pronouns when reading. Although most students will *not* require instruction in pronouns, teachers should be prepared to work with students who need the instruction.

## Teaching Procedure for Pronouns

The first step in teaching proper pronoun usage involves oral exercises to ensure that students know the meaning of key pronouns: *he, she, we, they, it, you, them, her, him.* Pronouns that cause particular difficulty are *it, they,* and *them* because they can refer to inanimate objects. The format below, which assumes students know *he, she,* and *it,* demonstrates how the pronoun *they* might be taught. Note that students are taught that the pronoun *they* refers to objects as well as people. This is an example of including a full range of positive examples.

The second step in teaching pronoun usage involves leading the students through a series of passages containing pronouns. A sample passage appears below.

Passage:
    Tom and Lisa got in trouble with their parents. They had to stay in all weekend. He cried. She got mad.

Item:
    a. Did Lisa stay in all weekend?
    b. Did Tom get mad?
    c. Who cried?

The teacher or students read the passage. The teacher asks questions after each sentence:

1. **"Tom and Lisa got in trouble. Who got in trouble?"**
2. **"They had to stay in all weekend. Did Tom have to stay in?"** "yes"
    **"Did Lisa have to stay in?"** "yes"
3. **"He cried. Did Tom cry?"** "yes" **"Did Lisa cry?"** "no"
4. **"She got mad. Did Tom get mad?"** "no"
    **"Did Lisa get mad?"** "yes"

If students make errors, the teacher refers to the pronoun; e.g., **"She got mad. *She* tells about a girl. Is Tom a girl?"**

## Format for Teaching Pronouns

| *Teacher* | *Students* |
|---|---|
| 1. Teacher demonstrates. **"Here's a new pronoun. They. They tells about more than one."** | |
| 2. Teacher provides practice on saying the definition. **"What does the pronoun *they* tell about?"** | "More than one." |
| 3. Teacher provides practice on applying the definition. **"Listen: John and Mary. Do we say *they* when we talk about John and Mary?"** | "Yes" |
| **"How do you know?"** | "John and Mary are more than one." |
| 4. **"Listen: John. Do we say *they* when we talk about John?"** | "No" |
| **"How do you know?"** | "John is only one." |
| **"What pronoun could tell about John?"** | "He" |
| 5. **"Listen: fork. Do we say *they* when we talk about fork?"** | "No" |
| **"Why not?"** | "Fork is only one." |
| **"What pronoun could tell about fork?"** | "It" |
| 6. **"Listen: fork and spoon. Do we say *they* when we talk about a fork and spoon?"** | "Yes" |
| **"How do you know?"** | "Fork and spoon are more than one." |
| 7. **"Listen: boys. Do we say *they* when we talk about boys?"** | "Yes" |
| **"How do you know?"** | "Boys are more than one." |
| 8. **"Listen: Mary. Do we say *they* when we talk about Mary?"** | "No" |
| **"Why not?"** | "Mary is only one." |
| **"What pronoun could tell about Mary?"** | "She" |

The final step is to teach students that a pronoun antecedent comes just before the pronoun in a passage.[1] The key to making this procedure work is selecting items in which the antecedent comes just before the pronoun. If the antecedent is separated from the pronoun by too many nouns, the students will have difficulty finding it.

## Sequence

The major sequencing guideline for the variables relating to item difficulty is to present easier items first. After students are proficient at easy items, they can be introduced to more difficult items. More

---

[1] The antecedent of a pronoun is the word the pronoun represents. In the sentences *John went to bed early. He was very tired*, the antecedent of *he* is *John*.

**Format for Pointing Out Pronoun Antecedents**

Passage

Jane and Mary wanted to go away for the weekend. Jane went to the beach. Mary had to work all weekend. Mary cried, but she still worked. On Saturday night, she went to a ball game. Who went to a ball game?

| *Teacher* | *Students* |
|---|---|
| 1. Teacher has the students read the passage. | Students read. |
| 2. Teacher has the students locate the antecedent. **"The story says, 'she went to a ball game.'"** | |
| **"Find the girl just before the word *she* in the story."** (pause) | Students find the antecedent. |
| 3. **"What is the name of the girl?"** | "Mary" |
| **"So who went to a ball game?"** | "Mary" |

specifically, initial passage-related items should be quite literal, with later items involving word and syntax (word order) changes and question word items. Initial exercises would be based on a single sentence, with later items refering to longer passages. Items for longer passages at first should parallel the order in which events occur in a passage; later, the item can appear in a different order. One-step instructions should be used at first, with multi-step instructions appearing later. When pronouns first appear, the antecedent should be very obvious; e.g., only one female should be presented by *she,* and the female's name should appear immediately before the pronoun. Later passages could include several possible antecedents with a greater separation between the pronoun and its antecedent.

## Motivation

The teacher should set up a system to motivate the students. Her goal should be for the students to answer all questions correctly. Since literal comprehension is one of the first written exercises students will do, it is quite important to instill the habit of doing tasks correctly the first time. If a student is unable to perform acceptably, the

teacher should try increasing the motivation (see section entitled "Developing Student Motivation"). If increasing motivation does not lead to an acceptable improvement in student performance, the teacher has probably placed the student in material that is too difficult and should provide easier assignments.

## Summarization

Summarization not only allows the students to identify the key ideas from a passage but also reduces the information in a passage to key ideas that students can remember. Since students cannot remember everything they hear or read, acquiring summarization skills ensures that they will remember major events rather than random details. A summary condenses a passage into a few sentences. A one-sentence summary can be considered a main idea. A title is the shortest summary because it contains only a word or phrase.

During the early part of the primary stage, the bulk of written summarization items are multiple choice. Students are asked to pick out a title or phrase describing an entire passage from among a series of possible answers. The incorrect titles often describe just one aspect of the passage. For example, in the exercise in the first format below, answers 1, 2, and 3 tell just one thing Linda did while answer 4 describes the entire paragraph.

In the teaching procedure for selecting the best title or main idea, the teacher has the students read a passage, presents different titles or main ideas, and asks which is the best and why. Students must select the title or main idea that encompasses all the major events and not just one event. A verbal explanation of why one title is better than the others is the most important part of the teaching procedure.

Selecting the best main idea or title is not the only critical summarization skill that students must learn. They must also learn to summarize longer passages by coming up with several main ideas. Summarizing longer passages assumes mastery of the skill of selecting the best title or main idea for a brief passage and, consequently, should not be introduced until students are proficient at selecting the best title for a short passage.

---

### Format for Summarization (Early Primary)

Passage:

Every day Linda got up early and played catch with her mom. She wanted to get stronger so she could throw a baseball harder. In the afternoons she would spend two hours pitching. At night she would read books about baseball.

Items: Put a check in front of the best title.

1. _____ Linda gets up early.
2. _____ Linda reads about baseball.
3. _____ Linda throws a baseball.
4. _____ Linda wants to get better at baseball.

| *Teacher* | *Students* |
|---|---|
| 1. **"We're going to learn about titles. A title tells what the whole story is about."** This step is used only when the teacher first introduces select the best title exercises. | |
| 2. Teacher has the students read the passage. | Students read. |
| 3. Teacher asks about the first title. | |
|   a. **"Read the first title."** | "Linda gets up early." |
|   b. **"Does that title tell about the whole story or just one event in the story?"** | "Just one event" |
|   c. **"So is Linda gets up early a good title for this story?"** | "No" |
|   d. **"Why not?"** call on individuals. | "It just tells about one event" or "It does not tell about the whole story." |
| 4. Teacher repeats steps a–d with remaining possible titles. | |

**Format for Summarization of Longer Passages**

| Teacher | Students |
|---|---|
| 1. Teacher has the students read until they finish the first major event in the passage. | Students read. |
| 2. After the students read about the first major event, the teacher asks, **"What has happened so far?"** | Students describe the event. |
| 3. The students continue reading. After they read about the next major event, the teacher asks, **"What just happened? Now tell me what we've read about so far."** | Students describe the first and second events. |
| 4. Teacher continues the procedure of asking about each major event and then having the students summarize the passage up to that point. | |

## Critical Behavior

### Correcting Mistakes

Some students will answer the question, "What just happened?" by citing a trivial detail. Correct by agreeing that the student told about what happened but not about the most important thing that happened. The teacher might say, "More than that just happened." If another student cannot answer correctly, the teacher should model the correct answer. Sometimes students forget an event when asked, "Now tell me what we've read about so far." When this happens, the teacher rereads key sentences and asks what happened. He then repeats the original instruction, "Tell me everything we've read about so far." If the students still cannot summarize the passage, the teacher models by summarizing the passage and then tests by asking the students to summarize the passage.

### Sequencing

Sequencing requires ordering several events according to when they occur in a passage. For example, a student reads a passage and then writes numbers in front of several phrases that describe events, writing 1 in front of the event that occurred first, 2 in front of the event that occurred next, etc. The difficulty of sequencing items depends on the length of the passage, the order in which the events to be sequenced appear in the passage, and the number of items to be sequenced. Obviously, the longer a passage is and the more items to be sequenced, the more difficult the exercise will be. Likewise, items based on passages in which the events are not listed in their order of occurrence are difficult. In sentence 1 below, the events are listed in the order in which they occurred, while in sentence 2, the second event appears first.

1. John played with Mary, then he played with Tom.
2. John played with Tom after he played with Mary.

In sentence 2, "John played with Tom" appears first but the event itself did not occur first; John played with Mary first.

To do such items, students must know the meaning of key words that dictate sequence: *before, after, today, yesterday,* etc. In sentence 2, the key word dictating sequence is *after.* If *after* were replaced by *before,* the meaning of the sentence would change.

A teacher should not assume that young students know the meaning of *before* and *after*. Students with suspected language deficits should be tested on both words. Knowing *before* and *after* is critical also because these words are used to teach the meaning of other sequencing words. For example, *tomorrow* comes *after* today, or *yesterday* comes *before* today.

Many students will need little or no train-

**Format for Sequencing**

Passage:

Alice went home after school. Later she went to the park. At the park she saw her friend Bob. Alice and Bob played catch all day. Then they got an ice cream cone.

Items:
Write a 1 in front of what happened first, a 2 in front of what happened next, and a 3 in front of what happened third.

_____ Alice went home
_____ Alice got an ice cream cone
_____ Alice and Bob played catch

| Teacher | Students |
|---|---|
| 1. Teacher has students read the story and directions. | |
| a. "Read the story." | Students read the story. |
| b. "Read the directions." | Students read directions. |
| 2. "Find where it says *Alice went home* under the directions." | Students find event below directions. |
| 3. "Now find that event in the story and underline it." | Students locate and underline the sentence. |
| 4. Teacher repeats steps 2 and 3 for the remaining two events. | |
| 5. "Look at the story, find the first sentence in the story that is underlined and place a 1 next to it, then place a 2 next to the second sentence and a 3 next to the third underlined sentence." | Students locate the first event and write a 1 next to it. Students locate the item and write a 2 next to it, etc. |
| 6. a. "Look at the events listed under the directions and find *Alice went home*." | |
| b. "Now find where it says *Alice went home* in the story." | Students point to sentence. |
| c. "What number is written next to the sentence that says Alice went home?" | "One" |
| d. "Write that number in front of Alice went home." | Students write one. |
| Teacher repeats steps a–d with remaining items. | |

ing on written sequencing items. If students cannot do sequencing items correctly, we recommend they be taught to use a strategy of underlining the sentence in the passage that contains each event. After underlining each event in the passage, the students number the events and then write the appropriate numbers next to the items that appear below the passage. Underlining should be used only with students who cannot work the items on their own.

The key to teaching this strategy is adequate practice. The teacher uses this sequencing teaching procedure with two or three passages each day. When the students seem able to perform the task with relative ease, they are asked to do the task independently. If students do not stop underlining items on their own, the teacher should say, "See if you can write the answers without underlining the sentences."

After students perform acceptably on sequencing items based on longer passages in which events appear in their order of occurrence, passages in which events are not listed in their order of occurrence can be introduced. To prepare students for these passages, the teacher focuses on key sequence words such as *before, later,* and *after.* She should provide concentrated practice on single sentences which contain these sequence words and in which events are not listed in their order of occurrence. Possible sentences include:

1. Before John sat down at the table, he finished his homework.
2. The newspaper is delivered after the mail.
3. Alice got home later than Jane.

The students read each sentence, and then the teacher asks two sequencing questions. The questions for the first sentence are **"What did John do *before* he sat down?"** "He finished his homework." **"So what happened first?"** "He finished his homework." The questions for the second sentence are **"What was delivered last?"** "newspaper"

**"So what was delivered first?"** "the mail" The questions for the third sentence are **"Who got home later?"** "Alice" **So who got home first?"** "Jane." After asking two questions about several sentences, the teacher should repeat the sentences, asking only the second question and using the first question when correcting mistakes; e.g., a teacher asks, **"What did John do first?"** A student says, "sat down." The teacher corrects by asking, **"What did John do *before* he sat down?"** "Finished his homework." **"So what did he do first?"** "Finished his homework." When students can do these items verbally, written exercises can be introduced.

## Inferences

There are many types of inference items. In the primary stage, two types of exercises make up the bulk of inference items students encounter. These are (1) naming an event, object, or attribute when a description is given and (2) predicting what will happen next in a story based on preceding events. Several more advanced types of inferences are discussed in Part 4, "Intermediate Reading." A key prerequisite for drawing inferences is knowing the vocabulary that appears in a passage and items. The importance of vocabulary can be seen in the following items. The key vocabulary word is *considerate.* (In item 1 students are to name an attribute; in item 2 students are to predict what will happen next.)

1. Students name an attribute of John:

   Passage:

   John was hurrying to the movies. He wanted to see the cartoons. When running down the stairs, he saw a big puddle of oil. He thought someone might slip, so he wiped it up. He was in a hurry, but he was still careful to get it all.

   Item: John was _____.
      selfish   considerate   athletic

2. Students predict what will happen next in a story:

Passage:

John had always been very considerate of other people. One day he was hurrying to the movies when he noticed a puddle of oil on the stairs in his apartment. He almost slipped on the oil.

*Item:* What do you think John did next?

_____ Ran to the movies so he wouldn't be late.

_____ Told himself to remember to clean up the oil after the movie.

_____ Wiped up the oil right away.

To work either item, students would have to understand the word *considerate.* In item 1, the student would have to recognize *wiping up the oil* as an example of being considerate. In item 2, the student would have to identify which of the three possible answers illustrates being considerate.

In short, before students can work inference items, they must understand the critical vocabulary words. Although the vocabulary words that appear in primary grade programs will be familiar to most students, the meanings of many words will need to be taught to instructionally naive students. The teaching procedures for new vocabulary are the same as explained in Section 2.7 on oral language: examples, synonyms, and definitions. For example, before giving students the preceding items, a teacher would teach the meaning of *considerate.* He might use a definition and then test the students on examples, as illustrated in the format below.

Note that the teacher not only asks the students whether the situation illustrates considerate behavior but also asks them

---

**Format for New Vocabulary**

| Teacher | Students |
|---|---|
| 1. Teacher says definition. **"Being considerate is doing things that show you care about other people. What does being considerate mean?"** | Students give definition. |
| 2. Teacher tests students on examples of considerate. | |
| a. **"Tom was driving to a movie. A woman had run out of gas. Tom did not stop to get gas for the woman. He went to the movie. Was that considerate?"** | "No" |
| **"Why?"** | "He went to the movie. He didn't show that he cared about the woman." |
| b. **"Alice was driving to help her friends move furniture. The people were waiting for her. She drove by a movie she wanted to see, but she did not stop to see the movie. She drove to her friend's house. Was that considerate?"** | "Yes" |
| **"Why?"** | "She went to help her friends." |
| 3. The teacher continues presenting examples until the students make several correct responses in a row. | |

to justify their answers. Student answers to the *why* question should refer to the action described in the item; e.g., "He didn't help the woman get gas." and "She went to help her friends. She didn't stop and go to a movie."

In addition to teaching key vocabulary, we recommend teaching students a strategy in which they underline the key words that are the basis for the inference.

The underlining strategy will only be practical when one word, phrase, or sentence holds the key information. If several bits of information from a passage must be synthesized to determine an answer, the teacher probably should not require students to use the underlining strategy.

## Following Directions

Direction following is an integral part of all written comprehension exercises. Students may be asked to circle, cross out, underline, draw a line to, make a check in front of, or put a line over a correct response. Teachers must make sure that students understand the meaning of words used in the instructions. For example, if a teacher tells students to circle all pictures that have

---

**Format for Underlining Key Details**

Passage:

John had always been very considerate of other people. One day he was hurrying to the movies when he kicked over a can of oil on the stairs in his apartment.

Items:  What do you think John did next?

Ran to the movies so he wouldn't be late.
Told himself to remember to clean up the oil after the movie.
Wiped up the oil right away.

| *Teacher* | *Students* |
|---|---|
| 1. Teacher has students read the passage, then the question. | "What do you think John did next?" |
| 2. **"Let's look in the story and see what kind of person John is. If we know what kind of person he is we can say what he might do next. Raise your hand when you find a word that tells what kind of person John is."** Teacher calls on individuals. | "Considerate" |
| **"Underline that word."** | Students underline *considerate*. |
| 3. Teacher asks about each possible answer. | |
| a. **"Would a considerate person run to the movies after he spilled some oil?"** | "No" |
| **"How do you know?"** | Student justifies response. |
| b. **"Would a considerate person tell himself to clean up the spilled oil after the movie?"** | "No" |
| **"How do you know?"** | Student justifies response. |
| c. **"Would a considerate person wipe up the oil?"** | "Yes" |
| **"How do you know?"** | Student justifies response. |

**FIGURE 3.5.2**

Do the following with the words in the box.
1. Make a circle around the third letter in the word quiet.
2. Put a line under the word that means the same as little.
3. Cross out the word quiet or old.
4. Put a circle around all the words that have the letter o in them.

| quiet | small | old | top |
|-------|-------|-----|-----|

the same *initial* sound as the word *egg,* he must make sure that the students understand the word *initial.* If they do not, failure on the task is likely.

Special direction-following exercises can be incorporated into reading exercises. These exercises are useful since they encourage students to read instructions carefully. One type of activity involves the students' following a set of written instructions (see Figure 3.5.2).

The activity in Figure 3.5.2 can be made more difficult simply by writing the directions out in paragraph form rather than in list form (see Figure 3.5.3). The meaning of words like *circle, box, all, some, or, same as* would have to be taught to lower-performing students before appearing in this type of activity.

The strategy we recommend teaching students involves their first reading a set of directions and then rereading the directions a sentence at a time. After rereading each sentence, the students do the action speci-

fied in the sentence and place a check at the end of the sentence before doing the next action. The purpose of the check is to help the students locate where they left off. This strategy obviously will not work for all types of activities. If practiced enough, though, it will develop the habit of carefully examining directions.

Toward the latter part of the primary stage, the teacher can introduce new types of directions in which some of the sentences do not tell what to do but merely explain something about the task. Figure 3.5.4 is an example of such a set. A new step would be added to the strategy for following instructions exercises of this type. It would involve the students' underlining each sentence in the directions that actually told them to do something. For lower-performing students, teachers would have to teach the distinction between sentences that specified actions and sentences that didn't. This would be done by having the students read the directions a sentence at

**FIGURE 3.5.3**

Make a circle around the third letter in the word *quiet.* Next, put a line under the word that means the same as old. Third, cross out the word *quiet* or *old.* Finally, put a circle around the words that have the letter o in them.

| quiet | small | old | top |
|-------|-------|-----|-----|

**FIGURE 3.5.4**

Some words in the sentence tell you where the action happened. Circle the words that tell where the action happened. Other words tell why, who, how and when. It is important to be able to find words that tell when something happened. Underline the words in each sentence that tell you when something happened.

1. The girls played baseball in the park yesterday morning.
2. After each lunch I went to the swimming pool.
3. Jack and Jill were running in the park this afternoon.

a time and asking after each sentence if the sentence told them to do something. The teacher would repeat the set of directions until the student could correctly identify all sentences that specified actions. Several of these exercises should be done each day. Only three or four items should be included after each set of directions so that the tasks do not become too time-consuming.

## Vocabulary

Vocabulary instruction in the primary stage involves the same methods as in the beginning reading stage: examples, synonyms, and definitions. As pointed out earlier, the teacher is responsible for teaching any critical vocabulary occurring in reading exercises. In addition to the general attention to new, critical vocabulary, teachers must also be prepared to introduce unique vocabulary applications: synonyms, opposites (antonyms), and classification.

In addition to initially teaching critical vocabulary, teachers must also consistently review it. A major difficulty in reviewing vocabulary words is deciding what specific words from comprehension exercises and stories to include in review exercises. Students encounter literally hundreds of different vocabulary words. Since time is too limited to review them all, the teacher must decide which words to review. These decisions are important because many students will forget the meaning of vocabulary words that are not reviewed. Teachers should follow two criteria in selecting vocabulary words to review. First, they must be careful to review vocabulary words that students will frequently encounter and will be expected to know in later grades, i.e., useful words should be reviewed. Second, high-frequency words that were initially confusing and difficult for students to learn should be reviewed more frequently than easier words. Although word utility and difficulty are not the only criteria for se-

lecting words to review, they provide a basis for sorting through the hundreds of words that appear in elementary grade texts.

As a rule, vocabulary words selected for review should be presented daily for several lessons and periodically thereafter. Words not selected for review because they appear infrequently should be defined or illustrated on the day the students work the exercises that contain them, but not reviewed after that time.

## Synonyms

Synonyms are relatively easy to teach. The key step is explaining clearly what synonyms are. We recommend this explanation. "A synonym is a word that means the same as another word." After saying this definition, the teacher asks for a synonym for a word, "Tell me a synonym for *big*." If a student does not give a synonym, the teacher corrects by referring to the definition of a synonym. For example, if a student says that little is a synonym for *big,* the teacher corrects by saying, "A synonym is a word that means the same as another word. *Big* and *little* don't mean the same thing. Tell me another word that means the same as *big*."

## Opposites (Antonyms)

Opposites usually cause students little difficulty since the words included in exercises during the primary stage are usually simple (e.g., *big–little, cold–hot, wet–dry*). If students do not understand the meaning of *opposite,* the teacher models by verbally presenting a series of examples. "Listen: The opposite of *big* is *little*. The opposite of *old* is *young*. The opposite of *cold* is *hot*. The opposite of *happy* is *sad*." Next the teacher tests the students: "What is the opposite of *big*? What is the opposite of *old*? What is the opposite of *cold*? What is the opposite of *happy*?"

Obviously, to succeed, students must know the meaning of the words included in the tasks. Vocabulary knowledge becomes an even more important factor when less common pairs such as, *smooth–rough* or *straight–crooked,* are introduced.

Once the students know the term *opposite,* they can be taught that *antonym* is a word that means *opposite.* "*Antonym* is another word for opposite. Antonym means opposite." Table 3.5.1 lists some of the opposites and synonyms that students might encounter during the primary grades. This list does not include all pairs but is merely a sample.

## Classification

In classification exercises, students select objects or events that are in some way similar. Items may specify a key word (e.g., *vehicle*) and call for students to find examples of that word. Or items may consist of a list of examples and call for students to find the ones that do not belong with the rest (e.g., *truck, plane, car, plate*). The format below is an example of a classification vocabulary item and a teaching procedure.

If the students make a mistake in independent exercises (e.g., circling the word *dinner* in the item above), the teacher corrects by asking if the remaining words are all in the same class. "Are lunch, coat, and breakfast all in the same class?" The teacher would then present the classification format.

## Diagnosis and Remediation

Teachers should mark students' independent work daily and keep track of errors. If students are not functioning at about a 90% accuracy level, teachers should determine what is causing students difficulty. There are five main reasons why students may miss items:

1. Lack of effort
2. Decoding deficits
3. Lack of knowledge of critical vocabulary
4. Inability to understand directions
5. Lack of appropriate strategy

The first step in the diagnosis process involves setting aside a time when the students redo any items they missed on daily

---

**Format for Classification**

Item: Cross out the word in each group that does not belong.

1. lunch   dinner   coat   breakfast

| *Teacher* | *Students* |
|---|---|
| 1. **"Read the instructions."** | Children read. |
| 2. **"Read the words in Item 1."** | "Lunch, dinner, coat, breakfast" |
| 3. **"Tell me how the first two words are the same."** | "Lunch and dinner are meals." |
| 4. **"Let's try another word. Does *coat* fit in the class of meals?"** | "No" |
| 5. **"What word does not belong with the other words?"** | "Coat" |
| **"So what do you do?"** | "Cross out coat" |

**TABLE 3.5.1**  *Opposites and Synonyms*

### OPPOSITES

| | | |
|---|---|---|
| big–little | to push–to pull | raw–cooked |
| awake–asleep | strong–weak | healthy–ill, sick |
| hungry–full | laugh–cry or weep | coming–going |
| sad–happy, glad | smile–frown | to begin–to end |
| bad–good | long–short | on–off |
| same–different | old–new | fast–slow |
| deep–shallow | wet–dry | difficult–easy, simple |
| shine–dull | outside–inside | far–near |
| win–lose | brave–cowardly | tall–short |
| easy–hard | quiet–loud, noisy | hot–cold |
| careful–careless | wild–tame | straight–crooked |
| open–shut, closed | alive–dead | heavy–light |
| ugly–pretty, beautiful | to remember–to forget | old–young |
| hello–goodbye | to whisper–to yell, to shout | full–empty |
| thin–fat, thick | wide–narrow | loud–soft |
| cool–warm | up–down | fat–skinny |
| full–empty | clean–dirty | smooth–rough |
| dumb–intelligent | bumpy–smooth | soft–hard |
| safe–dangerous | stop–begin, start, go | light–dark |

### SYNONYMS

| | | |
|---|---|---|
| to shout–to yell | healthy–well | near–close |
| above–over | big–large | to cry–to weep |
| pretty–beautiful | sad–unhappy | bright–shiny |
| to shut–to close | a pain–an ache | alike–same |
| sick–ill | thin–skinny | smart–intelligent |
| to start–to begin | small–little | to end–to finish |
| loud–noisy | glad–happy | to pick up–to lift |
| to shove–to push | quick–fast | quiet–silent |
| easy–simple | hard–difficult | |
| under–below | dumb–stupid | |

worksheet assignments. The students' performance on redoing the items may tell if the errors were caused by lack of effort; e.g., a student who usually is able to answer all missed items correctly when redoing a worksheet is likely to have a motivation problem. A special procedure to increase the student's motivation should be instituted (see Section 5.1, "Developing Student Motivation"). Teachers should be quite cautious in diagnosing errors as being caused by lack of effort. Sometimes students seem not to be trying when in fact they do not know what to do.

A second step in the diagnosis procedure involves individual testing of students who are functioning below the 90% level and who do not respond to increased motivation. Teachers would have students reread missed passages and items aloud to determine whether errors were caused by decoding deficits. If the students can decode the words with minimal errors and at a rate which would not interfere with comprehension, the teacher will have to continue the diagnostic process. The remaining three steps can be done in any order. The teacher should start with the step that deals with the probable cause of the student's errors. One step would be to determine if a vocabulary deficit caused the problem. The teacher does this by testing the students on key words. If the problem is not vocabulary, the teacher has the students redo the item, watching them carefully to see the strategy they use and noting whether they follow the directions. Once the cause is determined, whether it involves motivation, decoding, vocabulary, directions, or strategy, remediation on the particular skill deficit should be provided.

Again, let us point out the importance of developing good independent work habits during the primary stage. Teachers must ensure that they have taught all the prerequisite skills before assigning students work to do independently. Only when this is done will students be able to have the successful experiences so important to fostering a positive attitude toward school. If students are constantly given exercises containing prerequisite skills the students have not been taught, they will quickly develop guessing behaviors and a negative, "what's the use" attitude. "Even if I work hard I don't succeed, so why work hard."

## Commercial Programs

The majority of basal commercial reading programs have three characteristics that may cause instructionally naive students difficulty on comprehension activities:

1. Lack of massed practice on new skills
2. Lack of vocabulary teaching and review
3. Unnecessarily complicated directions

Providing massed practice when a skill is introduced is critical if students are to master it. In most commercial reading programs, a new skill appears in a workbook one day and then does not appear again for several weeks. For example, in the Houghton Mifflin program the initial exercise on choosing the best title appears on page 59 of the student's first workbook. Only one more exercise on selecting the best title is included in the rest of the 140

page workbook. That exercise is on page 127. This pattern of limited practice, scattered throughout a program, characterizes most commercial programs. They seldom provide adequate massed practice when new skills are introduced.

The problems and remedies for insufficient practice on a certain type of item are similar to those for insufficient practice on vocabulary. However, problems resulting from inadequate practice and review on a certain type of item are more difficult to remedy than lack of practice on one vocabulary word. One possible solution is to assign all written tasks of one type from a workbook at the same time. For example, if a program has sequencing tasks on workbook pages 18, 47, and 73, the teacher might make copies of the activities on pages 47 and 73 and present them on the same day as the task on page 18, or wait until lesson 73 and present them all. The problem with introducing worksheets from later lessons earlier is that they may contain words the students will not know. The teacher either must identify these words as the students encounter them or preteach the words as irregular words before students are assigned the worksheets.

An alternative to presenting all the items of one type at the same time is for the teacher to prepare written exercises or use exercises from supplementary comprehension programs. Since written comprehension tasks are not too complex in the primary grades, preparing supplementary worksheets is not too time-consuming. In all cases, care must be taken so that an exercise is made up of words the students can decode.

In addition to providing massed practice when a skill is introduced, teachers also need to provide review after a skill is introduced. For example, when main idea is introduced, the teacher might present three main idea items every day for about 2 weeks. Thereafter, the teacher should include at least one main idea item in each lesson. Likewise, when any new skill appears, it should be reviewed heavily at first and then systematically reviewed. Primary grade teacher should try to include daily written exercises that review the major written comprehension skills: sequencing, inference, summarization, literal comprehension, and vocabulary.

Most programs also assume that students have average vocabularies. Words like *pounce, mounds,* and *limb* will appear in the programs without earlier vocabulary teaching. Instructionally naive students will not know how many of these less common words. Teachers should supplement a program by examining written tasks several days before they are assigned. Any vocabulary words that must be understood in order to work items should be taught before students are expected to work the items.

Some basal programs contain worksheets that are quite difficult in that it is not obvious what the students are supposed to do. In an effort to make workbook exercises more interesting, publishers rarely have the same layout on more than several pages in a workbook. Unfortunately, the lack of uniformity in worksheet exercises requires teachers to spend considerable amounts of time explaining how students are to go about working the exercises on each new page. For higher-performing students, the task of figuring out the directions may be challenging and worthwhile. For lower-performing students, though, the amount of teacher time and effort needed to explain an exercise should be weighed against the value of that exercise. If teachers spend too much time explaining exercises, they waste valuable time which the student might otherwise spend reading.

However, teachers should go over the directions of worksheet exercises that will be used. Let's say a workbook has quite a few exercises like Figure 3.5.5 in which the students have to fill in the blanks using the words in the line above the sentences. The teacher would present a strategy to use in working such pages. For this exercise, the strategy might be having the student read

**FIGURE 3.5.5**

deer    feet    met    feel

His _____ are dirty.

Do you _____ good?

I _____ him this morning.

Did you see that _____?

a sentence and then search the line at the top for the word that makes sense in the blank. The first days when a new type of item appears, the teacher might lead students through the exercise, telling them to read a sentence and then find the answer. After several days, the teacher should just preview it during a group lesson asking:

1. "What do we do on this worksheet?"
2. "Show me where you find the words that can go in the blank."

After the students have done several worksheets of this type, the preview would be dropped. Teachers must be careful not to develop too much student dependency on the teacher. Consequently, teacher guidance should be faded as soon as possible. As the year progresses, teachers should provide explanations of instructions only for unique assignments.

## Supplementary Comprehension Programs

In order to satisfy a demand brought on by dissatisfaction of some teachers with basal workbooks, many publishers have prepared supplementary comprehension material. There are two basic types of supplementary comprehension programs: general skill programs and specific skill programs. General skill programs usually consist of sets of workbooks or kits with individual cards, each workbook or kit being written at a slightly higher difficulty level than the preceding workbook or kit. The exercises usually consist of short passages followed by a set of questions including a variety of question types (literal, inferential, sequential, and/or summarization).

Specific skill series programs are different in that a workbook or series of cards in a kit focus on just one type of comprehension skill. One series of exercises might involve selecting the best title; another, set sequencing items. A program might include about 50 workbooks. For example, the *Specific Skills Series* published by Barnell Loft includes separate series of booklets entitled *Working with Sounds, Following Directions, Using the Context, Locating the Answer, Getting the Facts, Getting the Main Idea, Drawing Conclusions*, and *Detecting the Sequence.* Each skill is developed through a series of 12 booklets which gradually increase in difficulty from late first grade through high school levels.

## RESEARCH

Although some research suggests correlations among various skills (e.g., Smith-Burke, Reid, & Nicholich, 1978, found that correctly identifying the main idea of a passage correlated with students' classification performance), we found little research on teaching procedures (other than the use of reinforcement) for primary stage comprehension skills. Our own research has focused on literal comprehension, summarization, and sequencing. The research on summarization has been of a pilot nature. In one study, three groups of instructionally naive first graders were taught to select the best title for a brief passage according to the procedure outlined earlier in this section. The results indicated that student performance on selecting the best title improved dramatically after training was instituted. Students were asked to select the best title rather than construct one because, as mentioned earlier, constructing a title is more difficult (Otto, 1977). In a second study, two students who could not consistently answer literal, sequencing, and main idea questions served as subjects. Both subjects received the same practice exercises each day; however, initial summarization training accompanied the exercises for only one student. Later, the second student received the training. The results indicated that after a student was trained to summarize the major events from a brief passage, performance on literal, sequencing, and main idea items based on a transfer passage improved.

Two studies by Carnine, Prill, and Armstrong (1978) investigated the underlining procedure for answering sequencing items and the skimming procedure for answering literal passage items. In the first study, three educable mentally retarded students received the same sequencing practice exercises each day; however, training on the underlining procedure was introduced to one student at a time. The results indicated that performance on the sequencing items improved dramatically after the introduction of training. Further research is needed to investigate the transition from the underlining procedure to less structured summarization procedures. In the second study, a group of economically disadvantaged fifth and sixth graders who made frequent errors on literal passage items and sequencing items received training in the skimming and underlining procedures. As in the first study, performance improved after training was introduced. Performance did not improve on other types of items for which a strategy was not taught. Since both studies were conducted with older students in a remedial setting, the applicability of the procedures to younger students' learning the skills for the first time needs to be investigated.

Various researchers have noted the importance of summarization, in part, because students seem to remember a summary of a passage rather than series of discrete events (Brown, 1976). The content of the summary depends on perceived importance (R. E. Johnson, 1970). When a theme is vague or difficult to discover, summarization is difficult and the content of the text is hard to understand and remember (Dooling & Mullet, 1973; Bransford & Johnson, 1972).

### Decoding Fluency and Comprehension

LaBerge and Samuels (1974) suggest that for high-level comprehension to occur, students must be able to decode and identify word meanings automatically so that attention will be free to organize the meanings represented in sentences. Research suggesting the importance of decoding in comprehension has been reviewed by Golinkoff (1975–76), who reported that poor comprehenders make more decoding errors and often make correct responses more slowly than skilled comprehenders. Similar findings were also reported by Perfetti (1977) and by Guthrie and Tyler (in press). Poor comprehenders are also more likely to make errors that change the meaning of a sentence and are less likely to correct their errors than are skilled comprehenders (Golinkoff, 1975–76). When good comprehenders read silently, they make fewer and briefer fixation pauses, suggesting that they are using context to read more rapidly. Poor comprehenders, on the other hand, tend to read in the same way whether reading silently or orally. Their eye movements indicate that they attend to single words or parts of words rather than covering multiple word units. Isakson and Miller (1976) studied the decoding errors good and poor comprehenders made when reading sentences. The good and poor comprehenders were selected so that they were comparable in identifying isolated words. Poor comprehenders made more errors on words in sentences than good comprehenders. Similarly, Pearson (1975) reported that late primary readers' identification of high frequency words benefited from minimal context cues, which was not the case for beginning readers. The various findings suggest that good comprehenders decode accurately, rapidly, and use context cues. The implication is that training should foster accurate, rapid, and context-related decoding.

## APPLICATION EXERCISES

1. Specify whether each question below is a literal question or an inference question:
   The rocket landed on the soft sand. Minutes later Zorn walked out of the rocket. He had never seen such a place. The sky was black. He could see nothing but sand.
   a. Did Zorn land at noon time?
   b. What landed on the soft sand?
   c. What color was the sky?
   d. Did Zorn land in New York City?
2. Assume some teachers are presenting sets of examples to teach the range of the word *it*. Tell which of the three teachers below has constructed the best set of examples. Explain why.
   *Teacher A*—a pen, a fork, a cup, a hat
   *Teacher B*—a bed, a chair, a table, a dresser, a stool, a closet
   *Teacher C*—a lion, a dresser, the moon, a pen, a spider
3. Specify the teacher wording in correcting the following errors made by a student on a worksheet assignment. (Assume the student can decode all the words.) Note that the correction procedures are not usually specified in the section. In most cases, the correction procedure follows the steps in the initial teaching procedure.
   a. Passage: Tom hit the ball to Jim. He dropped it.
      Item: Who dropped it?    Tom
   b. Read each group of words and put a circle around the one that does not belong.
      talk   whisper   (shout)   jump

c. Passage: The beach was crowded. It was Sunday, and it was hot. Babies played in the sand. Children jumped in the waves. Parents sat and talked. Everyone was having a good time.

Item: Circle the best title.

(Children play in the waves)    Babies make sand piles    A day at the beach

d. Passage: Bill and Sally walked to the park this morning. Sally played baseball and Bill ran around the track. Before they went home, they got a drink of water.

Item: Write 1, 2, 3 in front of the events in the order they happened.

   3   They got a drink of water.

   2   They went home.

   1   Bill and Sally went to the park.

e. What is a synonym for big?    little

f. Passage: Bill was a very stout lad. He had been stout since he was a baby. He liked being stout. Which team do you think he will join?

Item: Circle your answer.

(a—cross country team)    b—football team

4. A teacher tested a group of students and found the students did not know the following words that will be appearing in a written comprehension task within the next few days: daring, contented, rudder, and parallelograms.

For each word (1) describe the procedure you would use to teach the word (examples, synonyms, or definitions) and if applicable, write the synonym or definition and (2) write a set of four examples that could be used in teaching *daring* (specify two positive and two negative examples)

# Selecting and Using a Program

This section discusses three areas. The first one concerns variables to consider when selecting programs. The second one deals with testing, placing, and grouping procedures for primary stage students. The construction and use of an informal reading inventory and a written comprehension test in the placing and grouping process are explained. The third area suggests how to incorporate direct instruction into a classroom reading program. Much of the material applies to either a code-emphasis or a meaning-emphasis program. However, special considerations for each type of program are discussed. This area also includes a diagnostic test of word attack skills and a scope and sequence chart for the primary stage. These are tools to be utilized in incorporating the instructional procedures described in the previous sections with a selected commercial program.

## Selecting a Program

This material is divided into two parts: materials for students reading at a second grade level and materials for students reading at or above a third grade level.

## Second Grade Level

We recommend that students reading at a second grade level receive instruction in a code-emphasis program. (The distinction between meaning-emphasis and code-emphasis programs is discussed on pages 59–61 of Section 2.1.) Code-emphasis programs provide students with much more practice on phonic and structural analysis. In a code-emphasis program, the introduction of a new phonic or structural analysis skill is followed by stories that include a number of words in which students apply that skill. For example, after students are taught the letter combination *ee,* the stories for several days will contain quite a few words with *ee.* Also in code-emphasis programs, almost no words requiring a phonic skill are introduced before the phonic skill is taught. Thus, in the lessons before the letter combination *ee* is introduced, few or no *ee* words would appear. In contrast, meaning-emphasis programs do not coordinate phonics and structural analysis instruction with the words that are introduced in stories. For example, words with *ee* appear in stories before students are taught this combination. Also, words with *ee* would not be stressed in stories immediately following the introduction of a strategy for decoding those words.

Since code-emphasis programs provide concentrated practice on new phonics skills after they are introduced, while carefully controlling the rate of introduction of irregular words, students have the opportunity to become facile with skills they can generalize to new words. By emphasizing generalizable skills, teachers better prepare students to become independent readers.

The major factor teachers selecting a code-emphasis program should consider is the rate at which new letter-sound correspondences are introduced. The rate should average somewhere around one new letter-sound correspondence each three to five lessons. Programs that introduce letter-sound correspondences at a faster rate will probably need time-consuming modifications to provide extra practice for lower-performing students. Programs that introduce letter-sound correspondences at a slower rate present only a minor problem, since teachers can either skip lessons or present two lessons in one period with higher-performing students.

Teachers will find that many code-emphasis programs are fairly equal in regard to the rate at which new decoding skills are introduced. Other factors to be considered are: sequence control of irregular words, story content, and workbook construction.

Compare the sequence in which decoding skills are introduced. Note if programs introduce skills in an order likely to confuse students.

Note the rate of introduction and adequacy of practice. A new irregular word should appear in several consecutive lessons after it is first introduced and at least each second or third lesson thereafter.

Note story content. Stories should be written to promote an appreciation for the multi-cultural composition of our society. Likewise, stories should be free of racial or sexual stereotyping. Stories should be interesting and enjoyable.

Check the student workbook. The teacher should consider several factors. First is the adequacy of practice on more critical comprehension skills such as, summarizing, drawing inferences, and sequencing. The program should contain enough exercises to let a student develop mastery. Second, the workbook should not be unduly complicated. Students should be able to work exercises independently with a minimal amount of teacher direction. Third, the vocabulary control should be realistic. Exercises should not contain many words students will not understand.

Although we suggest a code-emphasis program for students reading at a second grade level or below, we recognize that for various reasons, teachers may use a meaning-emphasis program. The factors to consider in selecting a meaning-emphasis program during the early primary stage are basically the same as during the beginning stage (see Section 2.8). The rate of introduction of irregular words and the amount of practice on irregular words are the critical aspects. If programs are equal in this respect, teachers should evaluate the workbook and story content.

## Third Grade Level

When examining materials for students decoding at or above a third grade level, teachers should consider comprehension instruction and story content as the major factors in selecting a program. By third grade, most of the basic phonic and structural elements will have been introduced. Code-emphasis and meaning-emphasis programs at this level are essentially the same in their treatment of decoding skills. Neither stress them. Thus, just because a particular code-emphasis program was used during first and second grades does not mean that the program needs to be used in third grade.

During third grade, we suggest that teachers consider the possibility of using a supplementary comprehension program in addition to the basal workbook. Most basal workbooks do not provide the massed practice to enable most lower performers and many average performers to develop mastery of the more critical comprehension skills. A discussion of these supplementary programs can be found in Section 3.5.

## Testing, Grouping, and Placing

Here we describe a testing procedure a classroom teacher can use to group students homogeneously and place the groups at an appropriate level for instruction. Keep in mind that the procedure described is designed to provide maximum information in a relatively short period of time. (In a day or two a teacher with one parent volunteer could administer tests that would provide a basis for initial grouping and placing.) A teacher with 20 to 30 students simply does not have time for time-consuming testing. After a week or two of instruction, the teacher should assess the performance of students to see which students might function better in another group and if groups are placed at appropriate instructional levels. At the end of the section, we will discuss a more in-depth testing procedure that might be used with nonclassroom teachers who have more time for initial testing. We recommend two testing instruments for initial placing and grouping: an informal reading inventory and a written comprehension test.

## Informal Reading Inventory

An informal reading inventory (IRI) is the major tool for placing students during the primary stage. An IRI is a criterion-referenced test constructed by selecting representative passages from the reading series being used in the classroom. The purpose of administering an IRI is to determine the appropriate lesson at which to place students. This lesson is usually referred to as the student's *instructional level.*

### Constructing the IRI

The test is constructed by selecting 100-word passages from various lessons in the books designated for first, second, and third grade students. If the teacher is using a traditionally constructed basal text, he will find there are five books designated for first grade (three preprimers, a primer, and a first level book), two second grade books, and two third grade books. The teacher would select a passage from near the beginning of each book except the first preprimer.

If the teacher is using a series which includes more or less books than the traditional basal, the teacher would pick passages from about each fiftieth lesson during first and second grade and each seventy-fifth lesson during third grade.

When selecting the specific passage for students to read, the teacher should, if possible, find a page containing 100 words. If the teacher is using a code-emphasis program, he should try to avoid passages that stress any one particular phonic or structural element but should find pages that review phonic and structural skills presented to date. Likewise, the teacher should avoid pages which are significantly more difficult or easy than surrounding pages.

After identifying the selections to test, the teacher goes about preparing the test. On each page, he finds the beginning of the first paragraph and counts off 100 words, placing a line or star at the end of the hundredth word. The teacher can attach a clip to each page on which a selection to be read appears. If possible, the teacher should photocopy the pages and make a testing booklet. Photocopying the pages will make administering the test easier since the teacher will not have to deal with several different books.

### Administering the Informal Reading Inventory

The student should be seated at a desk facing away from the rest of the class. The teacher should be seated to the side of the student so that the student cannot see the teacher recording errors.

*Where to Begin.*  For beginning readers (kindergarten or first grade), the teacher begins testing with the earliest first grade selection. For second grade, the teacher begins testing with the earliest second grade selection. For third grade students, the teacher begins with the earliest third grade selection. A note of caution: several code-emphasis programs include a series of relatively short books. There might be four to six books used in each grade level. Teachers should consult the teacher's guides to determine the grade level designation for the various books.

*Instructions.*
1. The teacher explains the purpose of the test. "I want to find out where to start you in reading. I am going to ask you to read from different stories. Start here." (The teacher points to where students begin.) "If you make a mistake, I want you to look at the word again and say it the right way."
2. The teacher should use a stopwatch to time the student on each 100 word selection. She starts the watch when the student begins to read and stops it when the student finishes reading the 100th word.
3. If a student hesitates more than 5 seconds on a word, the teacher should tell the student the word.
4. If a student misses a word, the teacher says nothing (no correction) unless the student tries to figure out the missed word and hesitates for 5 seconds. After 5 seconds, the teacher says the word.
5. If a student is reading a passage very laboriously and is making many errors,

the student does not have to read the entire passage. The teacher can stop the student and present an earlier passage.

## Recording

We have prepared a simple recording form that teachers can use when testing students (see Figure 3.6.1). Spaces are provided for recording scores on the eight passages that will be used in testing students (four first grade, two second grade, two third grade). Before administering the test, the teacher fills in the book and page of each selection and the student's name in the left-hand column. The teacher records the student's performance on the first passage under the column for that passage.

The teacher records errors by making vertical lines in the error box. The teacher makes a line if the student does the following:

1. Mispronounces a word (Do not make marks for proper nouns: names of persons or locations.)
2. Is unable to figure out a word in 5 seconds (Do not make marks for proper nouns.)
3. Omits or adds a word (Do not make marks for the words *a* and *the.*)

If the student self-corrects (self-correcting involves the student's making a word identification error and then saying a word correctly without any prompting from the teacher), the teacher circles the mark. For example, if the student says "was" for the word *will,* the teacher makes a line in the error box. If the student self-corrects, the teacher makes a circle around the line (e.g., 11 ①). After the student completes the passage, the teacher records in the time column the time the student took to read it.

### What Passages to Test

After the student completes the first passage, the teacher counts the number of lines in the box that are not circled. If there are six uncircled lines or more, the teacher has the student read the next lower passage. The teacher continues testing lower passages until the student reads a passage with five errors or less. If a student read very laboriously and made many errors on a passage, the teacher might skip down several passages. Students unable to read acceptably on the earliest passage from a first grade book should be given the beginning level diagnostic test of word attack skills, which can be found on pages 167–72.

If there are five or less uncircled lines, what the teacher does next is determined by the time it took the student to read the passage. The schedule in Table 3.6.1 tells the teacher what to do next. The teacher continues testing higher passages until the student either makes five or more errors that are not self-corrected or reads a passage in a time which dictates stopping testing.

If a third grade student reads a passage from late in the third grade book in less than the specified time, the teacher need not at this time test the student in fourth grade material. The student would be tested on fourth grade material only if the student's performance on the written comprehension test was above 90%. Procedures for placing students at a fourth grade level are discussed in Section 4.7 of the intermediate grade part.

When deciding to continue or stop testing, the teacher should use judgment in borderline instances (e.g., a student reads a story in slightly more than the designated time or makes six or seven errors instead of five). If a student were reading fluently but made six or seven errors because of an overreliance on context, she might be retested on a passage from a lesson near the one from which the particular passage was taken. If the student read acceptably on this passage, she would be tested on a higher passage.

## Written Comprehension Test

The second test we recommend giving is a written comprehension test. To prepare this test, the teacher would select several pages from the student workbook corresponding to the student's instructional level in the textbook as determined by the student's performance on the IRI. Students whose instructional level was in the 3–1 textbook would be given several pages from early in the 3–1 workbook. Students whose decoding level is in the 2–1 textbook would be given pages from the 2–1 workbook. The purpose of the test is to give the teacher additional information in deciding how to group a borderline student. The test will also indicate any students who have severe comprehension deficits.

The workbook pages selected should be ones that require little explanation from the teacher. What the students are expected to do should be obvious, and the items should be passage related. The students read a passage and answer questions about it. If possible, the teacher should try to select some items that test main idea, in-

**TABLE 3.6.1**

TIME

| | | |
|---|---|---|
| First grade student with five less errors | below 2:00 | test next higher passage |
| | more than 2:00 | stop testing |
| Second grade student | below 1:30 | test next higher passage |
| | more than 1:30 | stop testing |
| Third grade student | below 1:00 | test next higher passage |
| | more than 1:00 | stop testing |

**FIGURE 3.6.1** *Informal Reading Inventory, Class Record Form*

| Student Name | Bk. ___ Pg. ___ | | Bk. ___ Pg. ___ | | Bk. ___ Pg. ___ | | Bk. ___ Pg. ___ | | Bk. ___ Pg. ___ | | Bk. ___ Pg. ___ | | Bk. ___ Pg. ___ | | Bk. ___ Pg. ___ | |
| | Errors | Time | Errors | Time | Errors | Time | Errors | Time | Errors | Time | Errors | Time | Errors | Time | Errors | Time |
| --- | --- | --- | --- | --- | --- | --- | --- | --- | --- | --- | --- | --- | --- | --- | --- | --- |
| Becky | | | | | | | | | | | | | | | | |
| Bill | | | | | | | | | | | | | | | | |
| Rich | | | | | | | | | | | | | | | | |
| Susan | | | | | | | | | | | | | | | | |
| Betsy | | | | | | | | | | | | | | | | |
| Jake | | | | | | | | | | | | | | | | |
| Ramona | | | | | | | | | | | | | | | | |
| Elton | | | | | | | | | | | | | | | | |
| Tonia | | | | | | | | | | | | | | | | |
| Kirsten | | | | | | | | | | | | | | | | |

ference, and sequencing, as well as literal comprehension. A test might include three or four workbook pages.

## Beginning-of-the-year Testing and Grouping

The informal reading inventory should be given to all students during the first day or two of school. If possible, an aide or volunteer should be trained to assist the teacher in administering the test. The written comprehension test should be administered after the teacher has administered the IRI to all students.

The results of the informal reading inventory are recorded on a summary sheet similar to the sample in Table 3.6.2. Students are listed according to their performance on the IRI. Students at the lowest instructional lesson are listed first. (The instructional lesson is the lesson corresponding to the most advanced IRI passage in which the student reads with no more than five errors and within the designated time period.) The instructional lesson and the time it takes students to read the passage are listed across from each student's name.

The teacher works from this summary sheet in forming instructional groups. Student performance on the IRI is the major determinant of group composition. The performance on the written comprehension test is referred to when a teacher has doubts about the placement of a student. When making groups during the primary stage, teachers should try to place students so that there is not a significant spread between the highest- and lowest-performing student in the group.

In a normal primary level classroom, a teacher may find that instructional levels vary from nonreader to several years above grade level. To illustrate how students in a classroom might perform on an IRI, we have listed in Table 3.6.2 the testing results for one second grade class. Note that one student (student 22) is performing sig-

nificantly above grade level and one (student 1) is performing significantly below grade level. Appropriately placing these students in instructional groups in the classroom is almost impossible, since no other student is functioning near their levels. The teacher is faced with some very difficult choices. The student below grade level needs more instruction in order to catch up. Unfortunately, the teacher may not have time to spend with that one student since the other students also have needs, including the student who is above grade level.

As mentioned earlier, the best way to minimize the problems involved with grouping is intergrouping among classrooms. If several teachers from adjacent grade levels (1–2, 3–4 or 5–6) or from the same grade level join together in grouping students who are either very low or very high, the problem involved in setting up groups will be greatly reduced. The basic rule concerning grouping is that the larger the number of students and teachers involved in setting up groups, the easier it will be to form groups that meet the instructional needs of each individual student. If it is not possible to intergroup, however, the teacher may set up a semi-individualized program for those students who cannot be grouped appropriately.

The teacher starts forming groups with the lowest performers, keeping the group size small (4–6 students). On the summary score form in Table 3.6.2, student 1 has almost no reading skills and must be handled as a special case. Similarly, student 22 must be handled as a special case. Students 2, 3, and 4 scored at the same lesson. Student 5 tested out higher but had a slow reading rate. We would, thus, look at his performance on the written test. If he did poorly, we would place him with students 2, 3, and 4 resulting in a low group of 4 students. Next, we note that 11 other students scored at book 2, page 10. When deciding how to group them, we would look at the students' reading rates and compre-

**Table 3.6.2**   *Mrs. Muntz's Second Grade Class*

| | STUDENT'S INITIALS | INSTRUCTIONAL LEVEL GRADE | PAGE | TIME |
|---|---|---|---|---|
| 1. | F.G. | | | |
| 2. | M.T. | 1 | 150 | 2:38 |
| 3. | T.L. | 1 | 150 | 2:18 |
| 4. | B.N. | 1 | 150 | 2:40 |
| 5. | T.R. | 1 | 200 | 3:10 |
| 6. | T.M. | 2 | 10 | 2:05 |
| 7. | R.J. | 2 | 10 | 2:00 |
| 8. | D.H. | 2 | 10 | 1:55 |
| 9. | J.B. | 2 | 10 | 1:40 |
| 10. | L.T. | 2 | 10 | 1:23 |
| 11. | M.B. | 2 | 10 | 2:05 |
| 12. | R.A. | 2 | 10 | 1:48 |
| 13. | D.C. | 2 | 10 | 1:56 |
| 14. | L.S. | 2 | 10 | 2:23 |
| 15. | R.L. | 2 | 10 | 2:14 |
| 16. | A.M. | 2 | 10 | 1:08 |
| 17. | S.J. | 2 | 110 | 1:45 |
| 18. | E.K. | 2 | 110 | 1:17 |
| 19. | A.L. | 2 | 110 | :59 |
| 20. | B.A. | 2 | 220 | 1:35 |
| 21. | G.B. | 2 | 220 | 1:14 |
| 22. | L.G. | 3 | 250 | :48 |

hension performances. Note that student 16 decodes at a much faster rate than the other students who scored at this level. We would consider placing her with the next highest group if her comprehension score indicates that her comprehension is also high. The mid-group might, thus, contain 10 students (6 through 15). The high group would include the remaining students. Ideally, the high group should contain the most students. However, as in this class, such grouping is not always possible.

Teachers should expect some regrouping to be necessary after the first week or two of instruction. Students who have consistently made more errors on comprehension items and/or passage reading should be considered for a lower group. By placing the student in a smaller group, teachers can provide more individual help. Regrouping might also be necessary if a student shows marked improvement and demonstrates an ability to learn information at a rate more commensurate with a higher-placed group. Student personality characteristics also need to be taken into consideration when regrouping. Some students will function better when slightly pressured to keep up with other students; other students may perform much better as the high member of a lower group.

## Specifying a Starting Lesson

Teachers are better able to gear their instruction to the needs of individual students with small group instruction than with entire class instruction. However, small group instruction does not allow for perfect individualization, since not all students in a group will be at the same instructional level. A teacher will have to make some deviations from the ideal placement when dealing with groups. There are several alternatives. A teacher may start at the instructional level of the lowest-performing student in the group. The advantage of starting at this lesson will be that all students will be successful in initial instruction. A disadvantage of this starting point is that the instruction may not initially challenge the higher students. A second, and usually more practical, alternative is starting at a lesson midway between the instructional lesson of the highest and lowest students in the group. A problem with this starting point is that the initial lessons might be somewhat difficult for the lower performers in the group. The teacher must usually do what is most efficient for the majority of students. For example, if five students in a group were performing at a level 50 lessons higher than the lower two students in a seven student group, the teacher might start at a lesson nearer that of the higher students. During the early weeks of instruction, the teacher would provide supplemental instruction for the lower-performing students on deficient skills. The teacher would also have to work on keeping the two lower-performing students from becoming discouraged or feeling incompetent.

## Rationale for Testing, Grouping, and Placement Procedure

The method we suggest for administering the informal reading inventory differs from the method suggested in most textbooks in three ways: (1) we include rate criteria; (2) we include a written comprehension test rather than asking oral comprehension questions for each selection the student reads; and (3) we do not call for extensive recording of errors.

Our rate criteria function this way. We recommend not placing students in books higher than their respective grade level unless their reading rate is at or above the desired rate for their grade level. For example, we specify that a third grade student who takes longer than 1 minute to read a passage should not be placed over

a third grade instructional level. Reading a 100-word passage in 1 minute translates into a rate of 100 words per minute. This is near the desired reading rate for students reading at a beginning third grade level. Only students who read faster than 100 words a minute would be tested in the 3–2 book. We recommend not placing students above grade level if their rate is below the desired level because they need ample practice with relatively easy material to develop fluency before they begin intermediate grade materials. Fourth grade textbooks are usually significantly more difficult than third grade books. Vocabulary becomes less controlled, and sentence length and complexity increase. Likewise, the volume of assigned reading increases in fourth grade as content area books (science, social studies, health education) become an integral part of the curriculum.

On the other hand, students should be placed in their grade level textbook as long as they can read with acceptable accuracy (95%) and with reasonable accuracy on comprehension exercises (70%). Placing students in below grade level materials solely because of a slow reading rate would be inappropriate.

A second feature of our procedure is the inclusion of a written comprehension test rather than having teachers ask oral comprehension questions after each passage. One reason for not asking oral questions after each passage is to save time. Another reason for recommending a written test is that it will give a teacher an indication of how a student functions independently.

The third way our procedure varies from traditional ones is the inclusion of group record forms. We recommend group record forms because they do not require extensive scoring or preparation of materials. The disadvantage of the forms is that they do not allow a full analysis of student performance. During the first days of school, however, the teacher's main objective in testing is to allow him to quickly group students, place the groups, and begin instruction. More extensive diagnosis can be done once instruction begins. See the primary level diagnostic test of word attack skills at the end of this section.

## A More In-depth Testing Procedure

The testing procedure outlined is not meant to serve as a comprehensive diagnostic assessment of a student's reading behavior but as a practical method for quickly testing, grouping, and placing a large number of students. The procedure will not be 100% accurate. Teachers will have to watch student performance during the first week of instruction and make adjustments.

Reading specialists and other personnel who have more time to test should conduct more thorough initial testing. Lovitt and Hansen (1976), suggest a procedure in which students read several passages from various books over a period of several days before being placed at an instructional level. Obviously, the more thorough testing will yield a highly accurate placement. Likewise, the more reading a student does, the better the teacher will be able to diagnose specific phonic and structural deficits. Specialists should record all errors and look for patterns that indicate a skill deficit.

## Using a Program

As students progress through the primary stage, the length of a lesson becomes increasingly dependent on student ability to learn new information. Higher-performing groups may not require teacher guidance when reading a passage and may need relatively little direction for doing comprehension exercises. On the other hand, groups with lower-performing students may require extra instructional time for work on basic vocabulary and language skills and to develop adequate fluency in decoding.

## Using a Code-emphasis Program

Teachers will most likely have to construct word list and letter-sound exercises to supplement those in the teachers guide of the particular program being used. Instructions on how to select words for word list exercises and letter combinations and affixes for isolated sounds drill are contained under the heading Example Selection in Sections 3.2 and 3.3.

A sample lesson during the primary stage might include the following tasks:

1. Phonics instruction (5 minutes)
   a. Isolated letter combination practice
   b. Word list reading 10–15 words
2. Structural analysis instruction (5 minutes)
   a. Isolated prefix and suffix identification
   b. Word list reading 10–15 words
3. Irregular word practice (5 minutes)
   a. Introduction of new words
   b. Practice on previously introduced words
4. Passage reading (15 minutes)
5. Preparation for written comprehension exercises (5–15 minutes)
   a. Vocabulary instruction
   b. Instruction explanation
   c. Strategy introduction or review

## Using a Meaning-emphasis Program

A sample lesson for teachers using a meaning-emphasis program would be the same as for a teacher using a code-emphasis program. The difference in using the programs is that much more teacher effort will be required to make a meaning-emphasis program into an efficient instructional program.

Most meaning-emphasis programs have varying degrees of instruction in phonic and structural analysis skills. However, re-

**FIGURE 3.6.2** *A Sample Scope and Sequence for the Primary Reading Stage*

| SKILL AREA | END OF BEGINNING READING STAGE *Late First Grade* | *Early Second* | *Mid Second* |
|---|---|---|---|
| 1. Phonic Analysis | | | |
| Letter combinations | th sh wh qu ol ar ea oo | ee ai ch or ay igh ow | ur oa au |
| Words with letter combinations | | | |
| VCe pattern words | <u>VCe</u> | | <u>c-ea-g</u> |
| Minor sounds words | | | |
| 2. Structural Analysis | | | |
| Prefixes and suffixes | s er ing le ed y un | est re a de es ness ly | al be in |
| Multi-syllabic words | | | |
| VCe derivatives | | <u>y deriv.</u> | <u>VCe deriv.</u> |
| Y derivatives | | | |
| Contractions | | | <u>Contractions</u> |
| 3. Irregular Words | | | |
| 4. Passage Reading (rate in words per minute) | 60 wpm | 75 wpm | 90 wpm |
| 5. Comprehension | | | |

| SKILL AREA | Late Second | Early Third | Mid Third | Late Third |
|---|---|---|---|---|
| **1. Phonic Analysis** | | | | |
| Letter combinations | kn | | | |
| Words with letter combinations | ou aw ir | oi ph ey | wr ue oy ew | |
| VCe pattern words | | | | |
| Minor sounds words | | oo—minor | ow—minor | |
| **2. Structural Analysis** | | | | |
| Prefixes and suffixes | con ment teen ful en dis able less | pro tion ad age ence ish | pre ex ion ship com | ist ive ac ous ward sion ic ize ure ation |
| Multi-syllabic words | | | | |
| VCe derivatives | | | | |
| Y derivatives | | contractions | | |
| Contractions | | | | |
| **3. Irregular Words** | | | | |
| **4. Passage Reading (rate in words per minute)** | 110 wpm | | 120 wpm | 135 wpm |
| **5. Comprehension** | | | | |

277

view is usually inadequate, and the formats are often potentially confusing. Thus, we recommend setting up an independent supplementary program to systematically teach the critical phonic and structural analysis skills.

Figure 3.6.2 includes a suggested scope and sequence chart for introducing phonic and structural skills during the primary stage. Teachers can use this scope and sequence chart as a guide in establishing an independent supplementary program.

In order to determine where on the chart to begin instruction, teachers administer the primary level of the diagnostic test of word attack skills (Figure 3.6.3) to each student individually during the first 2 weeks of school. (Note that the order of skills is roughly parallel in the test and the sequence chart.) The teacher begins the supplementary program with the first skill on the chart that any student in a group missed on the primary level test of word attack skills. The formats for presenting these skills appear in the phonic and structural analysis sections (Sections 3.2 and 3.3). The teacher presents the isolated sound formats on letter combinations and affixes and daily word list reading exercises focusing on these new elements.

The teacher should move across the chart in all areas simultaneously. For example, at the point in the program where the teacher is introducing the *wh* combination, the students should have met criterion on the *th* and *sh* sounds, they should also have met criterion on the suffixes *s*, *er,* and *ing* and be building toward a passage reading rate of 60 words per minute.

Appendix A includes a list of words that the teacher can refer to in selecting words to use in teaching the various elements. When preparing word list exercises, the teacher should include adequate discrimination practice. Guidelines for constructing word lists can be found under the heading "Example Selection" in Sections 3.2 and 3.3.

In addition to presenting phonic and structural analysis skills, the teacher presents new irregular words that appear in upcoming stories. Teachers should expect lower-performing students to have some difficulty learning irregular words during the early part of the primary stage. Therefore, they should provide extra practice on irregular words through drill and gamelike activities. The procedures for teaching irregular words, conducting passage reading, and dealing with comprehension exercises are the same as for code-emphasis programs.

## Progressing at an Optimal Rate

After a teacher forms reading groups and places them in the program, he must move the students through the program at an optimal rate. A rate is optimal when students spend the minimum amount of time mastering new skills. Higher-performing students will often be able to progress through the primary stage in less than 2 years while lower-performing students may require 3 or 4 years to finish this stage. The teacher uses the students' performances as the key indicator of how quickly to progress through a program. Three main factors should be taken into consideration: accuracy in passage reading, rate in passage reading, and comprehension accuracy. If students read with a high accuracy level (97%), read at the rate specified for their level in the program, and perform with 90% accuracy in comprehension, the teacher should structure lessons so that more material can be covered. The teacher would do this in two ways: remedy skill deficits during the first few weeks of instruction and, thereafter, increase the amount of passage reading assigned each day and have most passage reading done independently. The primary level diagnostic test of word attack skills appears at the end of this section (Figure 3.6.3).

We recommend administering this test to all primary level students during the first weeks of school. The results of this test, along with a student's performance on oral reading tasks, will enable a teacher to pinpoint specific phonic and structural deficits. Teachers should note the phonic and structural skills (letter combinations, VCe, prefix, suffix, etc.) introduced in lessons that follow the IRI placement and then look at the student's results from the diagnostic test to determine which ones a student knows. By remediating phonic and structural elements introduced in coming lessons, teachers may be able to teach lower-performing students skills that prevented them from reading at a higher level on the informal reading inventory.

Assigning more pages to be read each day would mean that new phonic and structural elements would be introduced more rapidly. The amount of material assigned each day would depend on the skills introduced in upcoming lessons. If few new words or skills were to be introduced, the teacher would assign more pages to be read than if a large amount of new material were being presented in each lesson. If students continue to read accurately and rapidly, and score at or above a 90% level on comprehension exercises, even after the teacher increases daily reading assignments, they can either be readministered the IRI, or the teacher can introduce a skipping schedule. The purpose of readministering the IRI would be to determine whether a more advanced placement is appropriate. Sometimes students will do poorly on tests given soon after school begins but within a few weeks, their performance will improve dramatically. In other cases, students might be doing very well, learning new material at a rapid rate but not be able to perform 60 or 90 lessons ahead in the program. The teacher need not readminister an IRI to these students but rather introduce a skipping schedule. Skipping can be approached in various ways: skipping every second (third, fourth) lesson or skipping lessons that do not introduce new skills. In either case, skipping should be stopped or slowed when decoding rate or accuracy or comprehension accuracy falls below the prescribed levels.

An optimal rate with high-performing students requires going quickly enough. An optimal rate with lower-performing students requires going slowly enough. A major theme of this book is that teachers should supply instruction on strategies and additional practice so that students will succeed. The extra teaching may result in students from low-performing groups spending 2 days on a lesson. By following the suggestions for student performance levels specified in the formats, teachers can determine how long to spend on various instructional activities. A note of caution is needed, however: do not move low-performing students through a program too slowly. When they reach the performance criterion specified for an activity, present the next activity. Do not continue to spend time on mastered tasks.

## The Remedial Reader

Second and third grade teachers can expect to have some students reading below grade level. We have two basic recommendations for such students. The first concerns the amount of time allocated for reading instruction. As a general guide, we recommend at least 15 minutes extra instruction for each half-year the student is below grade level. The second recommendation involves the program used. A well-constructed code-emphasis program should be used. Students functioning below grade level need a program that teaches skills as efficiently as possible and enables the teacher to provide the students with a high degree of success.

Teachers should be quite careful to distinguish nonreaders from poor readers. A nonreader is a student who is unable to read a passage from an early first grade book at anywhere near an acceptable level (95%) and who is unable to identify more than 10 words on the primary level test of word attack skills. Such students should be given the beginning level test of word attack skills (Figure 2.8.1). If the student scores poorly on this test, he will need to be placed at a stage in the program where basic beginning skills are taught (see Section 2.8 for guidance in establishing a program to teach beginning reading skills).

Students who are able to read some passages on the IRI acceptably do not require an extensive program to teach beginning skills, although they will probably need remediation on some individual letter-sound correspondences. There are no unique techniques that need to be used with these students; the key is to provide these students with the extra practice that will enable them to catch up to their peers.

The quality of instruction provided to students performing below grade level must be excellent. Teachers should take the prime responsibility for teaching these students. If aides or volunteers are used, they should be carefully trained and their duties should be clearly designated. Initially, the teacher should observe the person quite carefully. The person should be allowed to work independently with the student only after she has demonstrated competence in the specified duties.

## The Diagnostic Test of Word Attack Skills— Primary Level

This test is an individually administered oral test in which the student reads words

**FIGURE 3.6.3**  *Diagnostic Test of Word Attack Skills*

| | Phonic Analysis | | | Structural Analysis | | |
|---|---|---|---|---|---|---|
| **1** | **2** | | | **3** | **4** | **5** |
| short vowels | a i o u e | initial blends | spot trap club | that her sing shop when quick fold | ed ending  y deriv. | handed licked hopped  happier funniest | handle sunny biggest refill poppa depend misses |
| | | initial final blends | splint stamp brand | cart team toot peep raid chop torn clay sight grow turn loan Paul knock loud yawn firm coin phone key wrap clue joy stew | VCe deriv. | taping hoped | sadly mental beside handful golden display adjustable protect action package sentence prevent million active joyous forward mission classic realize summary mixture vacation |
| | | VCe words | fine hope cute | words with letter comb. | | | |

in lists. The purpose of the test is to give the teacher an indication of specific phonic and structural skill deficits. Note that we use the word *indication* because no one test is a definitive indicator of skill deficits. An error on a word presented in isolation

**FIGURE 3.6.4**   *Phonic Analysis, Group Record Form*

| Phonic Element / Students | | | | | | | | | | | | | | | | | | | | | |
|---|---|---|---|---|---|---|---|---|---|---|---|---|---|---|---|---|---|---|---|---|---|
| **vowels** | | | | | | | | | | | | | | | | | | | | | |
| a | | | | | | | | | | | | | | | | | | | | | |
| i | | | | | | | | | | | | | | | | | | | | | |
| o | | | | | | | | | | | | | | | | | | | | | |
| u | | | | | | | | | | | | | | | | | | | | | |
| e | | | | | | | | | | | | | | | | | | | | | |
| **blends** | | | | | | | | | | | | | | | | | | | | | |
| 2 letters | | | | | | | | | | | | | | | | | | | | | |
| 3 letters | | | | | | | | | | | | | | | | | | | | | |
| vce | | | | | | | | | | | | | | | | | | | | | |
| th | | | | | | | | | | | | | | | | | | | | | |
| er | | | | | | | | | | | | | | | | | | | | | |
| ing | | | | | | | | | | | | | | | | | | | | | |
| sh | | | | | | | | | | | | | | | | | | | | | |
| wh | | | | | | | | | | | | | | | | | | | | | |
| qu | | | | | | | | | | | | | | | | | | | | | |
| ol | | | | | | | | | | | | | | | | | | | | | |
| ar | | | | | | | | | | | | | | | | | | | | | |
| ea | | | | | | | | | | | | | | | | | | | | | |
| oo | | | | | | | | | | | | | | | | | | | | | |
| ee | | | | | | | | | | | | | | | | | | | | | |
| ai | | | | | | | | | | | | | | | | | | | | | |
| ch | | | | | | | | | | | | | | | | | | | | | |
| or | | | | | | | | | | | | | | | | | | | | | |
| ay | | | | | | | | | | | | | | | | | | | | | |
| igh | | | | | | | | | | | | | | | | | | | | | |
| ow | | | | | | | | | | | | | | | | | | | | | |
| ur | | | | | | | | | | | | | | | | | | | | | |
| oa | | | | | | | | | | | | | | | | | | | | | |
| au | | | | | | | | | | | | | | | | | | | | | |
| kn | | | | | | | | | | | | | | | | | | | | | |
| ou | | | | | | | | | | | | | | | | | | | | | |
| aw | | | | | | | | | | | | | | | | | | | | | |
| ir | | | | | | | | | | | | | | | | | | | | | |
| oi | | | | | | | | | | | | | | | | | | | | | |
| ph | | | | | | | | | | | | | | | | | | | | | |
| ey | | | | | | | | | | | | | | | | | | | | | |
| wr | | | | | | | | | | | | | | | | | | | | | |
| ue | | | | | | | | | | | | | | | | | | | | | |
| ew | | | | | | | | | | | | | | | | | | | | | |
| oy | | | | | | | | | | | | | | | | | | | | | |

does not definitely pinpoint a specific deficit. A teacher can only be sure of a specific skill decit when a student makes several errors on a particular skill.

**FIGURE 3.6.5**  *Structural Analysis, Group Record Form*

| Structural Element | Students |
|---|---|
| ed | |
| y drv | |
| vce drv | |
| le | |
| y | |
| est | |
| re | |
| a | |
| de | |
| es | |
| ly | |
| al | |
| be | |
| ful | |
| en | |
| **dis** | |
| able | |
| pro | |
| tion | |
| age | |
| ence | |
| pre | |
| ion | |
| ive | |
| **ous** | |
| ward | |
| ic | |
| ize | |
| ary | |
| ture | |
| ation | |

### Materials

The teacher needs one copy of the test (Figure 3.6.3) and two group record forms (Figures 3.6.4 and 3.6.5), one labeled *phonic analysis* and one labeled *structural analysis*.

### Administering Part 1—Phonic Analysis

*Column 1—Short Vowel Sounds.* Point to the letter *a* in the first column and ask, "What sound does this letter make?" If the student says the name of the letter, say "Yes, that is the name of the letter, but what sound does it make?" Repeat the same procedure with the letters *i, o, u,* and *e.* On the record form, write a + across from each letter identified correctly and a circle (O) for each letter not identified correctly. Go to column 2.

*Column 2—Blends and VCe Words.* Point to the words across from the *initial blends.* Ask the student to tell you each word. Write a plus on the record form across from initial letter blends if the student identifies all three words in the box correctly. Write a O if the student misses any word. Repeat the procedure with words across from initial-final blends and the VCe words. Go to column 3.

*Column 3—Words with Letter Combinations.* Point to the word *that.* Ask the student, "What word?" If the student correctly identifies the word, write a + across from *th* on the record form. If the student misidentifies the word, write a O across from *th.* Continue asking the student to identify each word and make a + or O across from the respective letter combination on the record form. Go to column 4 after four consecutive errors.

### Administering Part II—Structural Analysis

*Column 4—Ed Endings, Y Derivatives, and VCe Derivatives.* Point to the words across from *ed endings* and ask students to read all the words. If the student reads all the words in the box, write a + on the record form across from ed endings. If a student misses any word, write a O on the record form across from ed endings. Repeat the same procedure with words across from *y* derivatives and VCe derivatives. Go to column 5.

*Column 5—Words Containing Prefixes and Suffixes.* Point to the word *handle* and ask the student, "What word?" Ask the student to identify each word. Mark a + or O across from the respective prefix or suffix. Stop testing after four consecutive errors.

---

## RESEARCH

The issue of how students can be placed accurately at their instructional level has been discussed widely, but not researched extensively. Harris and Sipay (1975) discuss the problems in using students' grade level scores on standardized test scores as a guide in placing students in basal programs. They point out that students who scored at a particular grade level on a standardized test may not have mastered many of the skills taught in the books that are designated for students of that grade level. Educators tend to agree that an IRI is preferable to standardized tests for placing students.

One problem with IRI's and other testing procedures is making a placement based on a student's performance on a single day. Jenkins and Fleisher (1977) tested students over a 3-day period. They found that for 50% of the children in their study three consecutive days of IRI measures resulted in different placements than did a single IRI measure. We have tried to minimize the variability that results from a single IRI measure by suggesting that students be regrouped early in the year. Reading specialists and teachers who have the time may wish to do more extensive testing. Our procedures though were designed for classrooms, teachers with limited time, and 20 to 30 students to test.

The research on moving students at an optimal rate is also limited. Lovitt and Hansen (1976) evaluated a skip and drill procedure. Students were given a criterion of performance in terms of reading rate and correct comprehension responses. Students skipped ahead to the next book as soon as they reached the criterion. Students who did not reach criterion within 7 days received drill in deficient areas. Greater oral reading improvements occurred when the skip and drill procedure was in use.

Although research on procedures for testing, grouping, and placing students is time-consuming, more research is definitely needed. For example, teachers would benefit greatly from knowing how rapidly students should read and how accurately they should read and answer comprehension items before introducing new skills.

Another question relates to the comparative effectiveness of a code-emphasis program and a modified meaning-emphasis program; i.e., how beneficial are the modifications we suggest? The list of important questions is too long for us to adequately discuss. Hopefully, educational researchers will address these questions in the near future.

## APPLICATION EXERCISES

1. For each student below, state which of the following steps should be taken in the initial IRI testing procedure: (1) test the next higher passage, (2) skip down a passage or two, (3) administer beginning level diagnostic test of word attack skills, or (4) place the student at the level tested.
   a. When Joe, a second grader, reads the first 100-word passage, he makes 12 errors and completes the passage in 1 minute, 29 seconds.
   b. When Susan, a second grader, reads the first 100-word passage, she makes 3 errors and completes the passage in 1 minute, 15 seconds.
   c. When Ann, a first grader, reads the first 100-word passage, she makes 12 errors and completes the passage in 2 minutes, 30 seconds.
   d. When Tom, a second grader, reads a 100-word passage, he makes 6 errors and completes the passage in 1 minute, 10 seconds.
   e. When Allan, a third grader, reads the highest 100-word passage, he makes 3 errors and completes the passage in 1 minute, 45 seconds.
   f. Tom, a first grader, makes 10 errors on the first 30 words of the earliest selection from a first grade book.
   g. Bill, a third grader, reads the first 100-word passage making 15 errors and completing the passage in 4 minutes, 12 seconds.
2. Mr. Harris is using a meaning-emphasis program to instruct a group of students who are placed at early second grade level. He is using the scope and sequence in Figure 3.6.2 to introduce phonic and structural elements. Assume that he introduced the letter combination ee and the suffix un several days earlier. Today he wants to introduce the next letter combination and the next suffix listed on the chart. Construct a sample lesson in phonic and structural analysis for Mr. Harris' group. Specify the page(s) in this book on which appropriate presentation formats can be found.
3. Ms. Adamson, a second grade teacher, has administered IRI's to her class. Figure 3.6.6 is a partial summary of the testing. List the students in order of their performance on the test. Specify each student's instructional level.

**FIGURE 3.6.6** Informal Reading Inventory—Class Record Form

| Student Name | Bk. B Pg.___ Errors | Time | Bk. C Pg.___ Errors | Time | Bk. D Pg.___ Errors | Time | Bk. E Pg.___ Errors | Time | Bk. F Pg.___ Errors | Time | Bk. G Pg.___ Errors | Time | Bk.___ Pg.___ Errors | Time | Bk.___ Pg.___ Errors | Time |
|---|---|---|---|---|---|---|---|---|---|---|---|---|---|---|---|---|
| Becky | | | | | ///// | 2:10 | ||Ø||Ø||| | 2:40 | | | | | | | | |
| Bill | | | | | | | |Ø||| | 1:10 | //////// | 1:30 | | | | | | |
| Rich | | | | | | | || | 1:10 | ||| | 1:08 | ||| | 1:45 | | | | |
| Susan | | | | | | | |||Ø | 1:30 | | | | | | | | |
| Betsy | /// | 2:10 | //////// | 2:30 | ////////| 2:40 | /////// | 3:00 | | | | | | | | |
| Jake | | | | | | | ØØ//// | 1:4 | | | | | | | | |
| Ramona | | | | | ///ØØØ | 1:48 | //////// | 1:35 | | | | | | | | |
| Elton | | | | | | | //// | 1:20 | Ø||ØØ||| | 1:58 | | | | | | |
| Tonia | | | | | | | || | 1:45 | | | | | | | | |
| Kirsten | | | | | | | ||| | 1:03 | ||Ø | :58 | ////ØØØØ | 1:40 | | | | |

4. Below are the results of the IRI administered by Ms. Adamson to her second
   grade class. Book A, B, C, D, and E are first grade books; F and G, second grade
   books; and H and I, third grade books.
   a. Would you place student 3 in a group with students 1 and 2 or students 4, 5,
      and 6? Why?
   b. Would you place student 7 in a group with the students who scored at level C
      or level E? Why?
   c. Students 1 and 2 could not successfully read any passage on the IRI. What
      would you do next to determine their relative skill levels?
   d. Assuming that interclass grouping is not feasible, set up four instructional
      groups.

|  | INSTRUCTIONAL LEVEL | |
| STUDENT | BOOK | TIME |
| --- | --- | --- |
| 1 | NF | — |
| 2 | NF | — |
| 3 | B | 2:20 |
| 4 | C | 2:30 |
| 5 | C | 2:40 |
| 6 | C | 2:30 |
| 7 | D | 2:40 |
| 8 | E | 1:50 |
| 9 | E | 1:45 |
| 10 | E | 1:58 |
| 11 | E | 2:04 |
| 12 | E | 1:42 |
| 13 | F | 1:51 |
| 14 | F | 1:38 |
| 15 | F | 1:50 |
| 16 | F | 1:56 |
| 17 | F | 1:48 |
| 18 | F | 1:52 |
| 19 | F | 1:32 |
| 20 | F | 1:30 |
| 21 | F | 1:24 |
| 22 | F | 1:14 |
| 23 | F | 1:38 |
| 24 | F | 1:42 |
| 25 | G | :51 |

NF = did not finish passage

# PART 4

# Intermediate Reading

## Through Eighth Grade

# SECTION 4.1

## *Introduction*

The scope of reading instruction expands greatly during the intermediate grades. While in the primary grades the reading program usually centers around the various components of the basal reading program, in the intermediate grades the basal reading program should comprise a much smaller part of the total reading program.

Reading instruction in the intermediate grades expands to include (1) instruction in the various content areas (science, social studies, health, etc.), (2) independent reading of various types of literature, and (3) study skills which will prepare students for using reading as a vehicle to learn new information.

The increased scope of reading instruction in the intermediate grades might result in students' reading literature from a basal or library book, learning how to deal with content area texts from a science text, developing study skills while using a social studies book, and receiving practice on specific comprehension skills from a supplementary comprehension program. Because of the range of materials students might be working from, we have organized this part by skill area, so that the teacher can work on a skill with a variety of materials. For example, a teacher should be prepared to preteach important, difficult-to-decode words, whether they appear in a basal, a short story, or a science text.

The skill areas discussed in the intermediate sections are decoding, vocabulary, comprehension, content area skills, and study skills. As in the beginning and primary parts, each section begins with a discussion of direct instruction procedures for major skills and continues with an overview of commercially available materials.

The first section focuses on decoding instruction. Teachers have several responsibilities relating to decoding. The first responsibility is to test and, if necessary, remedy any phonic, structural, or contextual analysis skill deficits. A second responsibility is to introduce words from upcoming selections that students may have difficulty decoding. The teacher selects shorter words with unusual letter-sound correspondence (e.g., *aisle, psychic, gnat*) and multi-syllabic words (e.g., *preventive, isolation, occupation*). As students become more proficient in decoding multi-syllabic words, only words which contain unusual letter-sound correspondences need to be taught before students read selections.

The third, and probably most important, teacher responsibility relating to decoding is to establish a literature program which demonstrates to students that reading is an enjoyable and useful activity. In establishing such a program, the teacher must first select a variety of materials that represent a careful balance between making reading enjoyable and exposing students to various types of good literature. Teachers must also ensure that students have adequate time to read. Through conversations and meetings with parents, teachers should encourage reading outside of school. If, for one reason or another, students do not read much outside of school, extra time should be provided for reading during the school day. If necessary, teachers should set up a motivation system to encourage reading and to develop positive student attitudes toward reading.

The second section deals with vocabulary instruction. The careful control of vocabulary exercised in primary grade material is not present in intermediate grade material. While nearly all words in primary grade books are in the speaking vocabulary of most students, many words in intermediate grade books are not in the speaking vocabulary of lower-performing students. Unfortunately, few programs make adequate provision for teaching the meanings of these words. Consequently, teachers must be prepared to supplement instruction with vocabulary exercises.

The vocabulary section reviews methods for presenting vocabulary that were discussed in earlier sections and shows how the same techniques can be used to teach more complex concepts. In addition, procedures are outlined for teaching students to use the dictionary to determine the meanings of unknown words. Since using the dictionary interrupts the flow of the material being read, students should learn to figure out the meaning of an unknown word from the context of the selection. Using context to figure out the meanings of un-

known words is a very important skill, since authors often use context to explain new terms. If students know how to use context to infer meanings, they will find reading more enjoyable and expand their vocabularies through recreational and school-related reading. A final topic discussed in the vocabulary section is morphemic analysis. Morphemes are the smallest meaningful units of a word. Teaching students meanings of more common morphemes will help them to figure out the meanings of some words. The utility of morphemic analysis in figuring out the meanings of words is limited though because many morphemes have several meanings, and for most words, a literal translation of the morphemes in a word does not translate into a functional meaning for the entire word.

The third section is entitled "Written Comprehension." Two types of advanced reasoning tasks are discussed: (1) inferential tasks in which the students apply a stated or implied relationship to answer questions, the answers to which are not directly stated in the passage and (2) critical reading tasks in which students have to identify an author's conclusion and whether the evidence and logic support that conclusion. Quite detailed teaching procedures are suggested for both types of tasks. In addition, the section discusses syntax variables that make intermediate grade passages more difficult to comprehend than primary grade passages. Teaching procedures for two major syntactic variations, passive voice and clause constructions, are discussed to illustrate how to comprehend sentences that are syntactically complex.

The fourth section focuses on incorporating reading instruction into the teaching of the various content areas (science, social studies, health, math, etc.). Reading demands and expectations drastically shift when students begin reading content area materials: Vocabulary is more difficult to decode, writing style is rather terse, and information is organized into units, indicated by various organizational styles (headings, subheadings, etc.).

Content area textbooks should be selected quite carefully since the readability level of many is several years above that designated by the publisher. A textbook should not be selected if it is at a readability level higher than the grade level for which it is designated. This point is very important. Time limitations dictate that much content area instruction will be conducted with relatively large groups of students. Programs with too high a readability level will frustrate low performers.

The fifth section is entitled "Study Skills." It includes teaching procedures on how to use various types of reference material such as, dictionaries, encyclopedias, almanacs, and telephone books; how to use various graphic aids such as maps, tables, and charts; and how to go about studying and taking notes when reading expository material.

The final section in the intermediate part is concerned with setting up a total reading program. Intermediate grade teachers should be prepared to establish one or more of three types of reading programs, each of which is designed to accommodate students at different skill levels: (1) a remedial program to meet the needs of students reading significantly below grade level, (2) a highly structured program to meet the needs of students reading at about grade level but who, without significant teacher preparation, would not be able to succeed in material designated for their grade level, and (3) a low structure program for students who possess the skills to succeed with minimal guidance from a teacher. The text specifies testing procedures to help teachers group students and determine suitable programs.

# Decoding Instruction

Decoding instruction during the intermediate grades should begin with a remediation of any deficits in skills taught during the primary grades. Teachers can determine skill deficits by administering the primary level of the diagnostic test of word attack skills (see page 280 of Section 3.6). Procedures for remedying specific skill deficits can be found in Section 3.2, "Phonic Analysis," and Section 3.3, "Structural Analysis."

This section is divided into two areas. The first one deals with introducing new, difficult to decode words that students will encounter in passages. The objective of the formats is not only to teach students the particular words in question but also to teach them strategies that can be used in decoding unknown words. Particular stress is given to multi-syllabic words.

The second area deals with establishing a total literature program: how to select and use various types of books. Research is not discussed in this section because of a lack of research on teaching advanced decoding skills.

## Decoding Preparation for Passage Reading

During the intermediate grades, students will read selections from a wide variety of sources: basal textbooks and workbooks, supplementary comprehension materials, content area books (science, math, English, social studies), and recreational fiction and nonfiction books. Since teachers cannot preteach words from a book that only one student will read, decoding instruction focuses on words from selections that an entire group of students will be reading. To prepare students for a selection, teachers should identify and preteach words that students will be unable to decode.

Three factors determine the difficulty that students are likely to have decoding a word: (1) the regularity of letter-sound correspondences, (2) the relative frequency of the word, and (3) the length of the word. Irregularities in common, shorter words usually present few difficulties. A short word *steak,* for example, contains an unusual letter-sound correspondence: the *ea* represents the long *a* sound. However, at an intermediate grade level, students who do not know the word would be likely to figure it out from the context of the sentence in which it appeared, since *steak* is a familiar word. On the other hand, the short word *czar* is not a word often used by intermediate grade students and is not likely to be figured out by many students since it contains unusual letter-sound correspondences. Less common, shorter words that contain irregularities and are unlikely to be identified through context should be pretaught. When introducing shorter words, the teacher simply tells the student the word and discusses its meaning.

Multi-syllabic words can be divided into two types: first are words in which the pronunciation of each syllable is relatively easy to decode. For example, in the words *pre-ven-tion, re-gard-less, ad-just-ment,* and *care-less-ly,* each syllable is decodable by students who have mastered primary level decoding skills. After several months of practice on decoding longer words of this type, students can be expected to have relatively little difficulty with them. The second type of multi-syllabic word includes one or more syllables in which there is a letter-sound correspondence that is difficult to decode. Note the underlined letters in the following words: *interference, stimulate, hazardous, radiation.* Each is not representing its most common sound. Many multi-syllabic words contain some type of irregularity. Students can be expected to have more difficulty with these words, especially less common ones.

When introducing multi-syllabic words, the teacher uses the following steps:

1. Students identify decodable prefixes, bases, and suffixes in the word.
2. The teacher says a sentence with the new word deleted. Then calls on a student to identify the word.

3. The students pronounce the word part by part.

## Example Selection

A daily exercise might contain 15–20 words of which about half are new. The remaining words would be previously introduced words that were difficult for the student or that appear frequently in intermediate material.

When introducing words that contain an unusual letter-sound correspondence, or a low frequency morpheme, the teacher can introduce several related words at the same time. For example, let's say that the word *physics* is introduced in a story. The teacher might also introduce the words *physical* and *physician.* Likewise, when the word *diaphragm* is introduced, the words *dialect, diagnosis,* and *diatribe* can be introduced. Presently, one aid is available to teachers in finding related words, a study by P. R. Hanna et al. published by the U.S. Government Printing Office © 1966, entitled *Phoneme-Grapheme Correspondence as Cues to Spelling Improvement.* This book is the result of a computer analysis of words. For each of the phonemes (sounds) in our language, the book lists all the letters and letter combinations which represent it. A comprehensive list of words appears for each letter(s)-sound correspondence.

A format that can be used to introduce related multi-syllabic words is the build-up format, which teaches students to look for familiar morphemes in a word. The teacher first writes a root word on the board and has the students identify it. Then the teacher adds one or more affixes to the word and has the students identify the new word. The teacher continues adding or deleting affixes, each time having the students identify the word. This exercise is particularly useful in introducing *y* derivative words (e.g., *rely, reliable, unreliable; vary, variation*). Y derivative words

**Format for Introducing Multi-syllabic Words**

| *Teacher* | *Students* |
|---|---|
| A. Teacher writes on board: isolation, undetectable, recognize, demonstrate, relationship, graduation. | |
| B. Teacher introduces word. | |
|   1. Teacher has students say familiar parts in word. | |
|     a. Teacher points to *isolation*. **"Let's say the parts in this word."** | |
|     b. Teacher points to *ol*. **"What do these letters usually say?"** (signal) | "ol" |
|     c. Teacher points to *ation*. **"What do these letters usually say?"** (signal) | "ation" |
|   2. Teacher gives context hint. **"Listen, I'll say a sentence. The doctors put him in an** (points to *isolation*) **ward because they didn't want anyone to catch his disease. Raise your hand when you know the word."** Teacher calls on an individual. After the student says the word, teacher asks the group to say it. **"What's the word?"** (signal) | "Isolation" |
|   3. Students pronounce word part by part. | |
|     a. **"Let's say the word part by part."** | |
|     b. Teacher points to *is*. (signal) | "is" |
|     c. Teacher points to *ol*. (signal) | "ol" |
|     d. Teacher points to *ation*. (signal) | "ation" |
|     e. **"What word?"** (signal) | "Isolation" |
|   Teacher repeats steps 2 and 3 with remaining new words. | |
| C. Students practice reading. | |
|   1. After introducing all the words, the teacher repeats the entire list until students can identify the words with only a second pause. If a word is particularly troublesome, the teacher would alternate between that word and the other words. | |

are particularly difficult since the *y* is often changed to an *i* when a suffix is added. For example, the *y* in the word *marry* changes to an *i* when the suffix *es* is added, *marries*. If a student sees *marries* as a derivative of *marry,* the student is more likely to be able to decode the word correctly.

To provide systematic review and to ensure that students are in fact mastering new words being presented, teachers can

## Build-up Format for Multi-syllabic Words

| Teacher | Students |
|---|---|
| Teacher writes on board: response. | |
| 1. Teacher points to *response*. **"What word?"** (pause and signal) | "Response" |
| 2. Teacher erases *e*, adds *ible* to form *responsible*. **"What word now?"** (pause and signal) | "Responsible" |
| 3. Teacher erases *ible*, adds *ity* to form *responsibility*. **"What word now?"** (pause and signal) | "Responsibility" |
| 4. Teacher adds *ir* to form *irresponsibility*. **"What word now?"** (pause and signal) | "Irresponsibility" |

write new words on dittos, making a list of 30–50 words. Every several days, the teacher runs off copies of a ditto and gives copies to the students. Students should practice reading the list several minutes each day. This practice might be done in pairs or individually. Students should practice a list until they can read the words at a rate of two words a second. (This fast rate will ensure that students receive the practice necessary to recognize the words at a glance.)

To facilitate record keeping, each student might be given a form like the one in Figure 4.2.1. After several practice periods with a word list, the teacher would have a testing period. The testers would be higher-performing students or adults (volunteers or aides). When testing the student, the tester records the date of the test, the number of errors made on the test, and the seconds it takes the student to read the list.

Directions to the tester should be simple (i.e., tell the student the word if he makes an error or asks for help). The teacher examines each student's record form periodically (once a week) and evaluates the student's performance. If the student was unable to read the list quickly enough, the teacher schedules extra practice sessions. In addition, she has students keep old word lists and review them. For example, after

the students have been given three worksheets, they might be directed to review worksheets one and two.

## Establishing a Literature Program

During the beginning and primary stage, we recommended that passage reading be integrally coordinated with the introduction of phonic and structural elements. Ideally, passage reading during these stages would provide practice on utilizing the various word attack skills (phonic, structural, and contextual) being taught. In the intermediate grades, passage reading becomes an end in itself since the basic phonic, structural, and contextual analysis skills have been taught.

Here we explain how to establish the literature component of an intermediate grade reading program. From our perspective, the main goal of a literature program is to develop a positive attitude toward reading, which in turn results in students' spending a significant amount of time engaged in reading activities. The importance of students' engaging in a significant amount of daily reading cannot be overemphasized. Independent reading, in itself, is one of the main factors that contributes

**FIGURE 4.2.1**

| Practice Sheet | Test 1 | | | Test 2 | | | Test 3 | | | Test 4 | | |
|---|---|---|---|---|---|---|---|---|---|---|---|---|
| | Date | Err. | Sec. | Date | Err. | Sec. | Date | Err. | Sec. | Date | Err. | Sec. |
| 1 | | | | | | | | | | | | |
| 2 | | | | | | | | | | | | |
| 3 | | | | | | | | | | | | |
| 4 | | | | | | | | | | | | |
| 5 | | | | | | | | | | | | |
| 6 | | | | | | | | | | | | |
| 7 | | | | | | | | | | | | |
| 8 | | | | | | | | | | | | |
| 9 | | | | | | | | | | | | |
| 10 | | | | | | | | | | | | |
| 11 | | | | | | | | | | | | |
| 12 | | | | | | | | | | | | |
| 13 | | | | | | | | | | | | |
| 14 | | | | | | | | | | | | |
| 15 | | | | | | | | | | | | |
| 16 | | | | | | | | | | | | |
| 17 | | | | | | | | | | | | |
| 18 | | | | | | | | | | | | |
| 19 | | | | | | | | | | | | |
| 20 | | | | | | | | | | | | |

to vocabulary development, fluency, and interest in further reading. Teachers should judge all proposed activities by how the activity relates to the goal of developing a positive attitude toward reading.

Establishing a literature program involves several tasks: selecting material for students to read, presenting stories, and facilitating independent reading.

## Selecting Material

Materials are usually basal reading textbooks and hard- or paperback books. Intermediate grade level basal readers include a wide variety of literature, ranging from short poems to chapters from books and short stories. The main advantage of basal textbooks is that they allow the teacher to present the same selection to a group of students. Consequently, the teacher can preteach critical words and use the selection as a basis for group discussion.

Two problems teachers must attend to in selecting a basal textbook are interest level and readability. A disproportionate number of selections from basal programs represents "good literature" that students should be reading but that often is not interesting to students. While having students read good literature is an important goal, it must be approached carefully. If students are required to read too much good literature that does not interest them, they may not develop a habit of reading for pleasure.

*Readability* is a term used to describe the relative ease or difficulty of a passage. The level of difficulty is usually expressed in terms of grade equivalent. A book with a rating of 2.5 would be deemed readable by a student in the fifth month of second grade. Numerous formulas have been developed to determine readability. While each formula is somewhat unique, some or all of the following factors are taken into consideration in most of them:

1. The average length of words. Passages with longer words are considered more difficult than passages with shorter words.
2. The relative frequency of the words. Passages with more common words are easier than passages with less common words.
3. The length of sentences. The longer the length of the average sentence, the more difficult the passage.
4. The relative complexity of the sentences. The more clauses and the greater the use of passive voice, the more difficult the passage.

Figure 4.2.2 is a graph of the readability levels of different stories from a fifth grade basal textbook (Britton & Lumpkin, 1977). Note the variability in readability levels.

As can be seen in Figure 4.2.2, intermediate basal textbooks often include a high proportion of selections written at a readability level significantly higher than the grade level for which the textbook is designated. Stories written at a grade level several years above the level at which students are reading should be skipped. Also, some selections found near the end of a book or in the book for the next grade level will be easier than some found at the beginning of a book. A teacher should not feel constrained to introduce stories in the order they appear in the textbooks but can introduce stories in an order suited to meet the students' skill level.

For information regarding readability levels of stories within basal textbooks, we recommend writing to:

Britton & Associates, Inc.
Instructional Materials Analysis Service
1054 N.W. Filmore
Corvallis, OR 97330

They have made computer readability analysis of the textbooks in several major basal reading programs.

Teachers can also use a formula to estimate readability of different selections. Among the more popularly known formulas are ones developed by Spache, 1953, 1974;

**FIGURE 4.2.2**   *Readability Level of Stories in a 5th Grade Basal Textbook (Fry Formula)*

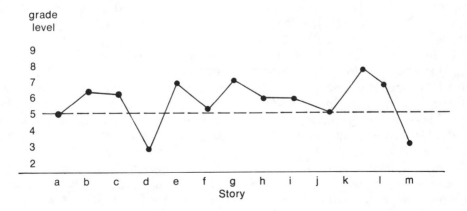

Dale and Chall, 1948; and Fry, 1968, 1972, 1975. The formula we recommend for use by classroom teachers is the Fry Formula (1975) since it is the least time-consuming. Readability level is computed in the Fry formula by determining the average number of sentences and syllables per 100 words. For a copy of the Fry Readability Scale, write:

Jamestown Publishers
P.O. Box 6743
Providence, RI 02940

Readability formula calculations only offer an estimate of difficulty. A more specific check on the suitability of a selection is having a student from a group read several 50–100-word passages from the selection.

If the teacher is going to preteach difficult words before students read passages, the book should be at the student's instructional level. A selection is at a student's instructional level if the student can decode it at about 95% accuracy without any preteaching of difficult words. The supposition is that the teacher will present difficult-to-decode words in preparatory exercises. On the other hand, selections for which the teacher will not preteach difficult-to-decode words should contain no more than 1 word per 100 that the student is unable to decode. This is referred to as the student's independent level.

A second source of literature material is the numerous soft- and hard-covered books. An excellent guide for selecting books likely to be relevant and enjoyable to students is *The New Hooked on Books* by Daniel Fader et al. Also, a list of books appropriate for lower-performing students is provided in a book by George Spache entitled, *Good Reading for Poor Readers.* Spache includes lists of books in various areas: sports, biographies, adventures, etc. Appendix C includes a list of books that are commonly requested by intermediate grade students. Furthermore, students should be taught various resources for ob-

taining books and a strategy for previewing books so that they select those they find enjoyable and interesting.

The most commonly used resource is usually the school library. The study skills section discusses teaching procedures for several skills relating to locating books in a library. Less common methods for obtaining books involve purchasing or sharing. Teachers should inform students that while they can buy books at a bookstore, they can save money by shopping at used bookstores and garage sales. Sharing books is not only another way of obtaining books but also a method for getting students to talk to one another about books. Teachers can encourage sharing of books by establishing a sharing club. Each time a student shares a book with another student, the student might get a star or point on a chart. A specified number of points can lead to special recognition or rewards.

Even after students know where to obtain books, they still must learn how to select books. Naive students often select books according to the title or the picture on the cover. Since the content often turns out to be difficult or uninteresting, the students do not read the books they check out. To prevent students from selecting books they will not read, teachers should teach students how to preview books.

The first step in a previewing strategy is to locate a summary of the book. Students should check the back cover or inside cover or look for an introduction. Next, they should read one or two pages from various sections of the book and ask themselves if they are interested in what they read and if they understood it. As a general rule, students should read books in which they can decode 99% of the words and comprehend at a 90% level. However, teachers should be careful not to always discourage students from reading books that are too difficult for them. If a student is very interested in a topic, he should be allowed to read the book. The teacher should monitor the students carefully. If after several days a teacher sees that a student seems frustrated with a book, the teacher might recommend another book on that topic written closer to the student's independent reading level.

Another alternative is for the teacher to set up a mini-library in the classroom in which books are classified according to their difficulty level. This is especially useful with lower-performing students.

## Presenting Stories

The teaching procedure that would be used in introducing stories from basal texts begins with the introduction of difficult-to-decode words and critical vocabulary. After this, the teacher attempts to generate interest in the story. This is called setting a purpose for reading. The teacher might give background information or ask questions that are answered in the passage. The teacher's guides that accompany basal texts often give useful suggestions for setting a purpose for reading.

After setting the purpose, the teacher usually has the students read the passage silently. Oral reading would be done only with material of a complicated nature in which teacher questioning would facilitate comprehension or with material of a unique nature (e.g., plays, poems, or passages which contain sentences with several clauses).

Activities following passage reading should extend student interest to related reading. For example, after discussing a selection by a particular author, the teacher can point out other books written by the author; or after discussing a selection about a particular topic, the teacher can tell the students about other books written on that topic.

These and other teacher-directed activities should be carefully planned to ensure that they don't defeat the goal of developing a positive attitude toward reading. Teachers should not quiz students on details from the passage. Comprehension

questions should be of an interpretive level. "What would you have done? What do you think might have made her do that? What do you think will happen?" Teachers should use other material to systematically build comprehension skills (see the sections on comprehension, study skills, and content area reading).

## Facilitating Independent Reading

Teachers should not expect students to read books just because they are exposed to them. Teachers must set up an environment that will provide students the time for reading the books. If necessary, the teacher may have to set up a motivation system to encourage independent reading, possibly at home and at school. While teachers can schedule recreational reading during the school day, they must work with parents in setting up a time for students to read at home. Some suggestions teachers can make to parents include these:

1. Setting a time that will not interfere with the child's doing some other activity (e.g., trying to set up a reading period at the same time as the child's favorite TV show will not work). A good period is bedtime because staying up and reading can be treated as a privilege.
2. Being interested in what the child reads but not badgering him to tell about what he has read.
3. Providing a model. Read when the child is present. Point out interesting or funny selections when they occur.

If necessary, teachers can set up a motivational system in which time spent reading at home is recorded and leads to special recognition in the classroom. The parents might send in a weekly report of the time spent reading at home each day. The teacher would record the time on graphs and charts similar to the ones in Figure 4.2.3. The teacher should reward students who read a certain amount out-

**FIGURE 4.2.3** *Graph and Chart for Recording Student Reading*

Graph

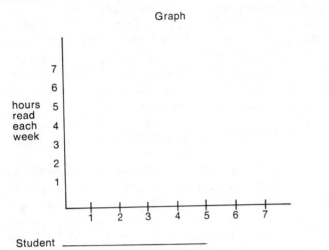

Chart

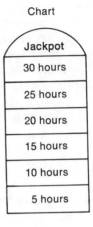

Student _____

Student _____

side class with praise or extra activities, such as a weekly party or certificates for membership in a class reading club.

If a student's home environment does not provide adequate time for recreational reading, the teacher should provide this time during the school day. Teachers might provide a 30-minute period in the morning or afternoon during which all students in the class would be reading. To ensure that students actually spend this time reading, the teacher might initially monitor students, carefully noting if students' eyes are directed toward the book, rather than staring off into space. The teacher might also grant special privileges to students who read continuously throughout the period.

Motivating students to read in their spare time is a difficult goal to reach but very important. Nagging and moralizing are usually ineffective. Motivational techniques must be somewhat subtle and convey the message that reading is fun. Reading excerpts from books is an excellent way to develop student interest in books. A teacher might set aside a 5–10-minute daily period for reading excerpts from different books to students. Another example was described by Krumboltz and Krumboltz

(1972). As students entered the room after recess, the teacher would be reading silently to himself, occasionally laughing loudly. When the students would ask what was so funny, the teacher would say "Oh, nothing" and put the book down. After several days, the students became more insistent on knowing what was so funny. Reluctantly the teacher would point out what he had read, laughing as he told the students. Eventually, the students asked him to read the funny parts to them. He did. The next step involved the students' asking where they could get books like that and if they could read with him during recess. This teacher may have been a unique individual; still what he did was very important. He showed that reading could be fun.

## Developing Reading Rate

During the first weeks of the school year, the teacher should have each student orally read several 100-word excerpts from the various materials that constitute the reading program basal text, comprehension worksheets, content area texts). These tests can be administered by a parent volunteer. The tester would record the number of errors made by the students and the time the student takes to read the passage (to avoid the rate's being distorted because of difficulty with just one or two words, the tester should tell the student any word he cannot figure out within 5 seconds).

The purpose of these oral reading tests is to ensure students have been placed at their proper instructional level and to determine if the student might benefit from exercises designed to improve reading rate. We recommend that intermediate grade students be able to read orally at a rate of 150 words a minute. A student who reads a 100-word passage in 40 seconds is reading at 150 words a minute. An oral rate of 150 words a minute will be equivalent to a higher silent rate since students read silently at a more rapid rate. We recommend an oral rate test because it is more reliable than a silent rate test. During a silent test, a teacher does not know if the student is actually reading and cannot judge if the student's accuracy level is acceptable.

As mentioned earlier in the book, research does not suggest ideal rates for specific grade levels and materials. The rate criteria we specified during the primary grades were based on our observations, a review of rates specified on standardized tests, and a study in which the rates of students who did relatively well on comprehension tasks were recorded (see Section 3.6). Our recommendation for reading rate for intermediate grade students has a similar basis.

If students are not able to read orally at about 150 words per minute, we recommend instituting rate-building procedures. The amount of time devoted to rate-building exercises would be dependent on the severity of the student's deficit. For students reading over 100 words a minute, a 15-minute daily session might be sufficient. For students reading below 100 words a minute, more time should be scheduled (see Section 3.4 on passage reading for procedures for conducting rate-building exercises).

## Commercial Programs

Many commercial programs do not provide for preteaching of difficult-to-decode words that appear in passages. Teachers should always preview material before assigning it to students, noting which words students may not be able to decode. These words should be presented before students are required to read passages independently.

Several publishers produce sets of workbooks designed to provide supplementary practice on decoding skills. Although these programs are usually very useful for providing practice for beginning and primary grade students who are learning decoding skills, the intermediate-grade books are often less useful since they include numerous exercises of questionable value. For example, most include numerous exercises involving syllabication. The problem with the exercises is that instead of presenting a strategy for figuring out difficult letter-sound correspondences, they introduce complicated rules regarding how a word is divided when written. Also, the programs often include busy work activities that involve practicing skills students will have already mastered in order to be reading at an intermediate level. For example, a typical exercise might require a student to classify the words *head, dream, lead, steak, lain, weight,* and *spain* according to whether the vowel sound in the word is short *e*, long *e* or long *a*. Obviously, to do this task students will have to already know how to decode the words. Teachers should avoid exercises which may take a great deal of time to explain but provide little practice on new skills. The time spent explaining such exercises to students and having them complete the exercises might be better spent on other activities, such as independent reading.

## APPLICATION EXERCISES

1. Below is a passage students will be reading. Pick five words from the passage that fourth grade students are likely to have difficulty decoding. Specify what the teacher would do and say in presenting each word.

   Alice Thomas had an older friend. It was Ann Lewis, a sophomore, who was the school's star soccer player. Ann gave Alice a great deal of encouragement. Some day Alice would be the team's leader. One day the two young women were having a conversation. Alice said "I want to be an entertainer. I want to tour the country."

2. During the first several days of the school year, Ms. Atkinson administered the primary level diagnostic test of word attack skills to the students in her fourth grade class. Below is a list of skills missed by a student in her group.

   Bill: letter combinations: ar, au, oi

   affixes: tion, ous

   a. Construct a word list (12 words) to teach the letter combination *ar*. Specify the pages in Section 3.2 for the formats you would use to present this skill. Half the words in the list should include *ar*. Include two minimally different pairs.

   b. Do the same as in step a for the affix *tion* (see Section 3.3, "Structural Analysis").

   c. During passage-reading exercises, a student often says words that do not make sense in the context of the sentence. Describe the remediation procedure (see Section 3.4 on passage reading in the primary stage).

   d. During a testing of a student's oral reading rate, the student read at a rate of 80 words a minute. Describe in detail a plan to improve his reading rate (see Section 3.4 on passage reading in the primary stage).

3. It is possible for a teacher to predict the relative difficulty students will have decoding new words. Put a check in front of the six words below which students are likely to have the most difficulty decoding. Assume students have mastered all phonic and structural analysis skills taught during the primary stage (see Sections 3.2 and 3.3).

   | | | |
   |---|---|---|
   | _____ predictable | _____ inactive | _____ peril |
   | _____ hilarious | _____ ratio | _____ invention |
   | _____ detective | _____ souvenir | _____ basketball |
   | _____ hopelessly | _____ returning | _____ buttercup |
   | _____ sodium | _____ inspection | _____ malaria |

4. In the build-up format, a teacher generates derivatives from a single word to show how a base word remains when various structural changes occur; e.g., from *prosecute* come *prosecution, prosecutor*. List two derivatives for each of the following words:

   a. apply

   b. rely

   c. inspect

5. Specify if the book tested in each of the following situations would be appropriate for the situation:

   a. A student makes no errors in a 100-word selection from a book which she desires to take out of the library to read at home.

   b. A student makes two errors in a 100-word selection from a book that will be used in a reading group.

   c. A student makes 4 errors in a 100-word selection from a book that he will be taking home to read.

# Vocabulary Instruction

Vocabulary used in primary grade reading books is usually controlled in that words are limited to those in the average student's speaking vocabulary. In the intermediate grades, vocabulary is not as carefully controlled and, consequently, it becomes a source of difficulty for many students. Many passages are written at almost adult reading levels, particularly books in the content areas: social studies, English, science, and math. Teachers must be prepared to spend additional time teaching vocabulary. They must work on increasing students' general vocabulary and their knowledge of specific words that will appear in upcoming passages.

The procedures we discuss in teaching vocabulary during the intermediate grades include those discussed earlier (modeling, synonyms, and definitions) and several new strategies: morphemic analysis, contextual analysis, and dictionary usage.

## Morphemic Analysis

All words are composed of morphemes, which are the smallest linguistic units that have meaning. Morphemes may be free (whole words) or bound (found only as parts of words such as prefixes and suffixes and nonword bases). Morphemic analysis as a vocabulary aid involves dividing a word into its component morphemes and using the meanings of the individual morphemes to figure out the meaning of the entire word. Morphemic analysis as a vocabulary aid can be illustrated with the word *unworkable*, which includes three morphemes: *un* meaning not, *work,* and *able* meaning able to. Through morphemic analysis, *unworkable* can be translated as *not able to work.* Teaching students the meaning of morphemes will give them a strategy for analyzing some unknown vocabulary words. However, teachers must realize that this strategy works with only a limited set of words. Three factors limit the usefulness of morphemic analysis. First is the difficulty of translating individual morphemes into a functional definition. For example, the word *accurate* is composed of three morphemes: *ac,* which means toward; *cure,* which means care; and *ate,* which means that which is. The morphemic definition of *accurate* is thus *that which is toward care.* For a sophisticated reader who was able to use the context of a passage, this definition might be helpful; however, for the less sophisticated students, such a definition would not be helpful.

A second reason why morphemes are of limited value in figuring out word meanings is that many morphemes have dual meanings. For example, the morpheme *dia* sometimes means through as in diameter and sometimes day as in *diary*.

A third reason for their limited value is that students often will not be able to determine the morphemes that have been combined to make up the word. For ex-

ample, the word *recognition* is composed of the morphemes *re* + *cogno* + *ite* + *ion*.

Table 4.3.1 includes some morphemes that lend themselves to relatively easy translation. Next to each morpheme is (1) a word that illustrates use of that morpheme, and (2) the morpheme's common meaning. Note that the meaning we use is designed to be functional rather than technically correct. We tried to construct definitions that will make morphemic analysis easier for students. When a morpheme has a second meaning that occurs in a significant number of words, that meaning is listed under the first meaning.

## TABLE 4.3.1

| MORPHEME | SAMPLE WORD | APPROXIMATE MEANING |
|---|---|---|
| able | portable | able to be |
| al | rental | related to |
| bi | bicycle | two |
| cent | century | 100 |
| dis | dishonest | not |
|  | disappear | opposite of |
| er | bigger | more |
|  | worker | one who |
| est | biggest | the most |
| ex | exhale | out |
| ful | hopeful | full of |
| il | illegal | not |
| inter | interstate | between |
| intra | intrastate | inside |
| ion | invention | an act of; state or quality |
| ist | artist | one who |
| ity | normality | state or quality |
| ive | inventive | one who; having the power of |
| less | fearless | without |
| ly | sadly | how something is |
| ment | agreement | something that is |
| ness | kindness | something that is |
| ology | biology | study of |
| pre | preschool | before |
| psych | psychology | the mind |
| re | repay | again |
| sub | submarine | below |
| tri | tricycle | three |
| un | unable | not |
|  | untie | opposite of |
| ward | backward | toward |

For a more thorough listing of morpheme meanings, see *Dictionary of English Word-Roots* (R. Smith, 1966).

## Direct Instruction Procedures

### Sequence

The meaning of morphemes should be taught after or at the same time students are taught to decode the morphemes. At first, intermediate grade teachers should concentrate on teaching students the meaning of morphemes the students were taught to decode during the primary stage. After students have learned the meaning of these morphemes, the meaning of the less common morphemes can be taught at the same time a morpheme is introduced in a decoding lesson.

### Teaching Procedures

Our teaching procedure includes two teacher-directed formats, an introductory format for presenting the meaning of new morphemes and a build-up format used to demonstrate the relationship between words with the same base morpheme. Also included in the teaching procedure are several types of independent exercises: ones in which students match morphemes and meanings, ones in which students match words and meanings, and ones in which students fill in missing words in sentences.

The introductory format includes several steps. In the first step, the teacher tells students the meaning of a new morpheme and tests students on how the addition of the morpheme affects the meaning of several words. In the second step, the teacher provides discrimination exercises in which the students review previously taught morphemes. In the third step, students use their knowledge of those morphemes to determine word meanings.

In the build up format, several new words are formed by adding different affixes to the same base word. For example, when the word *investigate* is introduced, the teacher can also introduce *investigation* and *investigator*. When *politics* is introduced, the words *political, politicians,* and *politically* can also be introduced. Introducing words in groups is an efficient and relatively easy way of teaching several new words at once. An example of a format for introducing words as a group is illustrated below. First the teacher has the students decode the new word and related words. Second, the teacher models and tests the students on the meaning of each word. Third, the teacher says a sentence with a word missing. The students fill in the missing word. A group of new words should be reviewed for several days and intermittently thereafter to develop student retention. The exercises can include words containing morphemes that have not been introduced in isclation. The teacher just tells the students the meaning of the words.

### Seatwork Exercises

A good deal of practice on morphemic analysis can be provided through independent worksheet activities like those in Figure 4.3.1. In exercise 1 on the worksheet, students select the correct meaning for each morpheme. In exercise 2, students select words for sentence completion items. The teaching procedure involves leading the students through the directions the first few times the worksheet appears. In each item, the teacher has the students read the directions and asks questions to make sure that the students know what to do. For example, after the students read the directions for exercise 1, the teacher says, "Point to the morphemes. Now point to the meanings. Write the correct meaning for *un*." After students read the directions for exercise 2, the teacher says, "Show me the blanks you're going to fill in. Now show me the words you'll write. Fill in the first

**Format for Introducing Morphemes**

| *Teacher* | *Students* |
|---|---|
| 1. Teacher introduces a new morpheme. | |
|    a. **"Listen. *Less* usually means without."** | |
|    b. **"What does *less* usually mean?"** (signal) | "Without" |
|       **"So what does the word *careless* mean?"** (signal) | "Without care" |
|    c. **"What does *less* usually mean?"** (signal) | "Without" |
|       **"So what does the word *winless* mean?"** (signal) | "Without a win" |
|    d. **"What does *less* usually mean?"** (signal) | "Without" |
|       **"So what does the word *homeless* mean?"** (signal) | "Without a home" |
| 2. Teacher reviews morphemes. | |
|    a. **"What does *pre* mean?"** (signal) | "Before" |
|    b. **"What does *un* mean?"** (signal) | "Not" |
|    c. **"What does *tri* mean?"** (signal) | "Three" |
|    d. **"What does *less* mean?"** (signal) | "Without" |
|    e. **"What does *able* mean?"** (signal) | "Able to be" |
| 3. Teacher applies morphemes to figuring out meaning. | |
|    a. **"Listen. *Careful.* Tell me the morphemes in *careful*."** (pause, then the teacher claps two times pausing a second between each clap) | "Care . . . ful" |
|    b. **"What does *ful* mean?"** (signal) | "Full of" |
|    c. **"Now think and get ready to tell me what *careful* means."** (pause several seconds, signal) | "Full of care" |
|    d. Teacher repeats steps a–d with these words: *preschooler* (one who is before school), *triangle* (three angles), *winless* (without a win). | |

blank." If students make a mistake (e.g., saying that *hopeful* is acceptable for the first sentence), the teacher says the sentence (e.g., Tom did not want to hopeful any words on the test.) and asks if the word *hopeful* makes sense in the sentence. The teacher then tells them to find the correct word. If students cannot find the correct word, the teacher explains the answer (e.g., "The answer is *misspell*. Tom did not want to *misspell* any words on the test. *Misspell* means spell wrong, so we could say that Tom did not want to spell any words wrong on the test."). The teacher tests the student on that item later in the lesson.

Similar exercises can be done with related words formed by adding affixes to the same root word. For example, when *predict* is introduced the words *predictable, predicted, unpredictable* and *prediction* can be used in a written exercise similar to the one in Figure 4.3.2.

**Format for Teaching Related Words**

|                     *Teacher*                      |     *Students*     |
| :-- | :-- |

Teacher writes on board: predict
                                predicted
                                prediction
                                predictable
                                unpredictable

1. Students read each word.

   a. Teacher points to *predict*. **"What word?"** (signal) — "Predict"

   b. Teacher points to *predicted*. **"What word?"** (signal) — "Predicted"

   c. Teacher points to *prediction*. **"What word?"** (signal) — "Prediction"

   d. Teacher points to *predictable*. **"What word?"** (signal) — "Predictable"

   e. Teacher points to *unpredictable*. **"What word?"** (signal) — "Unpredictable"

2. Teacher models and tests meanings.

   a. Teacher points to *predict*. **"What word?"** (signal) — "Predict"

   b. **"When you say something is going to happen, you predict."**

   c. **"What do you do when you predict?"** (signal) — "Say something is going to happen"

   d. Teacher points to *prediction*. **"What word?"** (signal) — "Prediction"

   e. Teacher points to *ion*. **"We added this morpheme to make *predict* into *prediction*."**

   f. **"What does *ion* mean?"** (signal) — "An act of"

   g. **"So a prediction is the act of predicting. It is what you make when you say something is going to happen. What is a prediction?** — "What you make when you say something is going to happen."
   **"I'll use it in a sentence. We made a prediction about the weather. Say that sentence."** (signal) — "We made a prediction about the weather."

   h. Teacher repeats steps d–g with the rest of the words.

3. Teacher gives completion items.

   a. **"I'll say a sentence with a missing word. You say the missing word."** (The teacher says "blank" for the missing word.)

   b. **"Television shows are boring if they are too _____."**

| Teacher | Students |
|---|---|
| c. **"What word is missing?"** (pause several seconds, signal) | "Predictable" |
| d. **"Say the sentence with that word."** (signal) | "Television shows are boring if they are too predictable." |
| e. Teacher repeats steps b–d with these sentences: Yesterday Tom _____ we would lose the game. (predicted) <br> Tom's _____ did not come true. (prediction) <br> The weather here changes quickly. It is very _____. (unpredictable) | |

**FIGURE 4.3.1** *Worksheet for Morphemic Analysis*

1. Write the correct meaning next to each morpheme.

   un _____     less _____     re _____     mis _____

   ful _____     able _____     est _____     er _____

   most, not, without, able to be, full of, again, wrong, more than

2. Fill in the blanks using these words:
   hopeful     hopeless     misspell     preschool

   Tom did not want to _____ any words on the test.

   My brother is too young for this school; he goes to a _____.

   We are _____ our team will win.

   After trying for two months to get his dog to sit down, Tom thought it was _____ to continue.

**FIGURE 4.3.2**

Fill in the blanks using these words:

predict     prediction     predicted     predictable     unpredictable

Yesterday Tom _____ we would lose the game.

Tom's _____ did not come true.

Did the weatherman _____ rain?

Take a jacket because the weather here is _____.

## Example Selection

Daily practice should be provided on morphemic analysis in verbal and/or written exercises. New morphemes should appear for three to five lessons after being introduced and then be reviewed each second (then each second or third) lesson for the next several weeks. Since morphemes do not always have the same meaning in different words, teachers must be careful to include only words in which the meaning of the morpheme is the same as that taught to students.

# Contextual Analysis

In contextual analysis, a reader uses the words that surround an unknown word to figure out the unknown word's meaning. Contextual analysis is an essential skill for students in the intermediate grades, since it allows them to determine the meaning of many of the unknown words they will encounter. Writers often define words that they feel the reader is unlikely to know. Many times the definition is given through the use of an appositive construction in which a synonym or definition immediately follows the unknown words in the passage.

1. The *drouge,* a small parachute for slowing down an object, shot out of the rear of the space capsule at 10,000 feet.
2. The *surplus,* that is the amount left over, was so great that the storage bins were full and grain was lying on the ground.

A definition or synonym can also be stated as a negation, which is more difficult for students:

1. The older brother was quite *affable,* not argumentative, like his younger sibling.
2. Janice was a *versatile* athlete while Ann, who was not so versatile, was able to play only one sport.

Contextual analysis is made more difficult not only when negative examples are used but also when a synonym or definition is separated from the unknown word in a passage. In example 1 below, the definition immediately follows the new word. In example 2, the definition is separated from the new word, which makes example 2 more difficult.

1. The food is *preserved,* kept from spoiling, by special refrigeration cars.
2. The food is *preserved* by special refrigeration cars. These specially made cars keep the food from spoiling.

Contextual analysis is also more difficult when the meaning of a word is implied by a description rather than directly stated as a synonym. Often a paragraph or a series of sentences provide example(s), either positive or negative, that students must use as the basis for inferring the meaning of a new word:

1. Byron's muscles strained as he pulled at the door. He leaned back and pushed as hard as he could. He *exerted* all the force he could.
2. In the sea, bones and shells are not eaten away and harmed by the air. Objects are covered with protective layers of sand so years from now they will be undamaged. Life from the sea is being *preserved* for the future.

## Direct Instruction Procedures

### Teaching Procedures

The teaching procedure involves leading students through a series of passages in which context is used to define an unknown word. For each passage, the teacher: (1) points out the unknown word, (2) has the students find the words that tell what the unknown word means, and (3) has the students restate the sentence substituting a synonym or description for the unknown word. The definition or synonym would be derived through contextual analysis.

The most critical aspects of teaching contextual analysis are sequencing of examples from easy to difficult and providing adequate practice. Students will learn the skill if they are given enough practice and review on the various types of context constructions: synonym or definition (which can be close to or separated from the new

**Format for Teaching Vocabulary through Context**

| *Teacher* | *Students* |
|---|---|
| An advanced exercise might include four to six passages such as this one: | |

> When the first men came to our country, they saw a dark, living cloud of birds. The cloud was so huge that it almost <u>eclipsed</u> the sun. When this happened, men could hardly see what was happening.

| | |
|---|---|
| 1. Students read first passage and identify unknown word. | |
|   a. **"Read the passage."** | |
|   b. **"A new word is underlined, what word is that?"** (signal) | "Eclipsed" |
| 2. Teacher calls on a student to find synonym or definition. | |
|   a. **"Who can find the words that tell what happened when the birds eclipsed the sun?"** (signal) | "The men could hardly see." |
|   b. **"Because of the eclipse of the sun, the men could hardly see. What do you think an eclipse does to the sun?"** (signal) | "Covers it up." |
| 3. Students say the sentence substituting the meaning of the new word. | |
|   a. **"Read the sentence with *eclipse* in it."** (signal) | "The cloud was so huge that it almost eclipsed the sun." |
|   b. **"Now tell me what that sentence means. Don't use the word *eclipse*."** (signal) | "The cloud was so big that it covered up the sun." |
| 4. Teacher repeats steps 1–3 with remaining passages. | |

word), negation, and inference. Providing sufficient and appropriate examples is more important than the teaching procedure itself. Many students can learn contextual analysis through practice alone.

# Dictionary Usage

## Direct Instruction Procedures

Using the dictionary to determine the meaning of a word is often difficult. First, a definition may include words that a student does not understand. For example, a dictionary may define *habituate* as to accustom; unfortunately, many students will not know what *accustom* means. Teachers should try to select dictionaries written at an appropriate level for the students. The dictionary should use clear definitions made up of words with which intermediate grade students are familiar.

Second, many words have more than one meaning listed for them. Teachers cannot take for granted that students will know how to find the appropriate meaning. Exercises should be presented to teach students how to determine which of several meanings listed for a word is appropriate for a given sentence. To teach the skill of finding the appropriate meaning, we recommend an exercise in which the teacher writes on the board a sentence that contains a word having several meanings. The students look up the word, examine each meaning listed for the word, indicate which meaning seems most appropriate for the sentence, and explain why. The first exercises should be limited to words in which the differences between the meanings are fairly obvious. For example, two possible meanings for the word *cold* are chilly and emotionless. In the sentence *The doctor's eyes were cold as he performed the operation,* the meaning of cold is somewhat obvious. To correct mistakes, the teacher would have the student read the sentence substituting the dictionary definition and then ask the student if the sentence makes sense.

As students become more proficient in finding words in the dictionary (see study skills section for exercises designed to teach this skill), teachers can use dictionary exercises as a means for introducing new vocabulary words that will be ap-pearing in future passages. Since the meanings written in dictionaries are often difficult for students to understand and since more than one meaning is listed for each word, we recommend that teachers prepare written worksheets similar to the one in Figure 4.3.3. The need to rewrite definitions will be determined by the students' vocabulary skills and the clarity of the dictionary's definitions. Note that in the first part of the exercise the students are to match a word with its meaning. The purpose of writing the definitions this way is to help students understand potentially difficult dictionary definitions. For example, in a dictionary the word *inflate* might be defined as "to swell up with air or gas." Some students are likely not to know what *swell up* means. Our definition, to fill with air, is not technically correct but functional for a student with limited vocabulary.

## Using a Dictionary during Independent Reading

Although teachers should encourage students to look up new words they encounter during independent reading, teachers should not require students to look up so many words that reading be-

**FIGURE 4.3.3**

1. Look up the meaning of the words in column one in your dictionary. Write each word in column one in front of its definition in column two.

Column One                    Column Two
inflate        _____ — able to be bent or changed
picturesque    _____ — about to happen
flexible       _____ — leave out
imminent       _____ — very colorful or attractive
omit           _____ — to fill up with air

2. Fill in the blanks in the sentences below with a word from column one.

This postcard shows a _____ fall day in Oregon.

Don't _____ any words when you copy the sentence.

Rubber is a _____ material.

We asked the mechanic to _____ our front tires.

With only two seconds left, and our team ahead by eight points, I think victory is _____.

comes tedious. Looking up every unknown word makes reading too laborious while never looking up words can result in students' reading without understanding what they read. The decision of whether a word is important is dependent on the student's purpose for reading the passage. When reading to learn new information, students would look up most unknown words. On the other hand, students do not need to look up many adjectives or adverbs during pleasure reading. Knowing when to figure out the meaning of a new word is an important skill that is usually not taught.

The basic strategy that students learn is that when they encounter an unknown word, they continue reading the paragraph in which the word appears to see if the context gives the word meaning. If the context does not give the meaning, the students decide if knowing the meaning of the word is important to the understanding of the passage. If so, the students look up the word. To demonstrate when looking up a word is necessary, a teacher should conduct exercises in which he leads students through several passages, helping them to see if the context tells the meaning of an unknown word. If the context does not tell the meaning, he asks if knowing the meaning of that particular word is essential to understanding the passage. For example, adjectives describing scenery are often not critical to understanding a passage. Teachers must be careful to strike a delicate balance between encouraging students to use the dictionary for critical words and requiring the students to look up every new word regardless of its importance.

A note on sentence writing has to do with the expressive use of a word versus the receptive use of a word. *Expressive usage* refers to how a person uses words to communicate with other people while *receptive usage* refers to a person's understanding of the words another person has said. Teachers should keep in mind that expressive language (using a word properly) is much more difficult than receptive language (understanding the word). Thus, exercises in which students are asked to generate sentences using a new word should not be done until at least several days after the word has been introduced. During the introductory period, the teacher should model how the word is used in sentences. The more the teacher can use the word throughout the school day, the better. Using the word in sentences during the school day provides excellent models of how to apply the word.

# Examples, Synonyms, and Definitions

We discussed three methods for teaching vocabulary in Section 2.7 on oral language training: (1) teaching through modeling examples, which is used when students do not understand words that could be used to explain the meaning of the new word, (2) teaching through a synonym, which is used when the student knows a word that has a meaning similar to a new word; for example, the word *deceive* can be taught by using the synonym *trick,* and (3) teaching through definition, which is used when a longer explanation is needed to define a word and the students understand the words that make up the explanation.

Example teaching is used primarily to teach young children vocabulary words. For example, parents respond to their children by saying, "Yes, cat" or "No, that's not a cat. It's a dog." Example teaching alone is rarely used in later grades.

Synonym teaching begins to supplement example teaching as the child's vocabulary grows. For example, a parent explains that *below* means the same as *under* or *glad* means the same as *happy.* Synonym teaching can be continued throughout all grade levels. Some examples of less common words that can be taught through synonyms are these:

merge–join
exterior–outside
amity–friendship
assault–attack
secure–safe
brief–short
vary–change
mentor–teacher

An excellent resource for the teacher in thinking up synonyms is a thesaurus.

Definitions are used more often as students progress through the grades and the meanings of words become increasingly complex. A major way of defining words involves putting the new word in a class and then specifying the unique characteristics of that word that distinguish it from other words in the class:

> *decathlon*—an athletic contest that includes ten track and field events
>
> *pediatrician*—a doctor who works with children
>
> *slander*—a false report that says bad things about someone
>
> *cutlery*—tools used for eating
>
> *nonentity*—a thing that is of no importance

When presenting a new word, teachers should not try to teach all the meanings of the word at one time. If the word is a familiar one, the teacher might present just one or two of its less common meanings. If the students are probably not familiar with a word at all, the teacher should present just one meaning for it when it is introduced and not present other meanings until the students have mastered the first meaning. For example, the word *beat* can refer to (1) winning a game, (2) striking repeatedly, (3) being exhausted, (4) rhythmic stress in music, and (5) a regularly traveled course. When it is introduced, since students might be familiar with several of its meanings, the teacher might present two less common meanings: being exhausted and rhythmic stress in music.

When a less familiar word like *faculty* is introduced, the teacher might present just one meaning for the word (teachers in a school or college). Other meanings of a word may be taught once students demonstrate an understanding of the more common meanings.

## Direct Instruction Procedures

The teaching procedure for new vocabulary involves three steps. First, the teacher models the meaning of the word, either through modeling examples, synonyms, or a definition. Second, the teacher tests the students on various positive and negative examples. This step ensures that students really understand the meaning of the word and are not just memorizing a rote definition. Third, the teacher incorporates the new word into review exercises. The teaching procedure is illustrated in format form with the words *perpendicular* and *respite*.

Perpendicular is a good example of why including positive and negative examples is important, even when definitions are used. Students would probably not understand degrees so the teacher cannot use an explanation involving degrees or right angle. The teacher's definition of perpendicular (*when an object comes straight out from another object*) is not very clear, in that it could be easily misinterpreted. The strength of the teaching procedure comes from the examples presented. The teacher initially uses a single object, such as a pencil, which would be placed in various positions. By changing the position of the pencil, the teacher illustrates a full range of positive examples and several minimum difference examples (see Section 2.7 for a full discussion of the range of positive examples and minimal differences).

Note that for teaching new vocabulary, the teacher asks, "How do you know?" after each answer. The purpose of this question is to require the students to use the definition in explaining their answers.

**Format for New Vocabulary (*Perpendicular*)**

| *Teacher* | *Students* |
|---|---|

1. Teacher models the pronunciation and definition of *perpendicular*.

   a. **"Listen, perpendicular. Say that."** (signal)    "Perpendicular"

   b. **"Perpendicular is a position in which an object comes straight out from another object."**

2. Teacher tests definition.

   a. Teacher holds pencil perpendicular to a table ⊥ . **"Is this perpendicular? How do you know?"**    Students respond to all questions and justify their answers.

   b. Teacher slants the pencil to the left on the table ⊥ . **"Is this perpendicular? How do you know?"**    "No"    "The pencil is not straight."

   c. Teacher slants the pencil to the right on the table ⊥ . **"Is this perpendicular? How do you know?"**    "No"    "The pencil is not straight."

   d. Teacher holds pencil perpendicular to the table ⊥ . **"Is this perpendicular? How do you know?"**    "Yes"    "The pencil is straight."

   e. Teacher holds pencil perpendicular to the wall ⊢ . **"Is this perpendicular? How do you know?"**    "Yes"    "The pencil is straight."

   f. Teacher holds pencil slanted against the wall ∠ . **"Is this perpendicular? How do you know?"**    "No"    "The pencil is not straight."

3. Teacher reviews recently introduced words.

Requiring students to use definitions in this way is a powerful review procedure.

## Sequence and Examples

The words that are taught and the sequence in which they are introduced will be dictated by what the students are expected to read. All important words that students probably do not know should be taught for a day or two before students encounter them in their independent reading. The question of which words to teach, though, is not as difficult as the question of which words to review. Students will en-

## Format for New Vocabulary (*Respite*)

| *Teacher* | *Students* |
|---|---|
| 1. Teacher models the pronunciation and definition of *respite*. | |
|    a. **"Listen, respite. Say that."** (signal) | "Respite" |
|    b. **"A respite is a short rest. What is a respite?"** (signal) | "A short rest" |
| 2. Teacher tests definition. | |
|    a. **"John worked hard all day. Then he went home and slept for ten hours. Did he take a respite? How do you know?"** | Students answer all questions and justify answers. |
|    b. **"Ann worked hard all morning. At twelve she stopped and ate a quick lunch and then went back to work. Did she take a respite? How do you know?"** | |
|    c. **"Sue did fifty push ups. Then she splashed cold water on her face and lay down for five minutes. Then she did twenty-five more push ups. Did she take a respite? How do you know?"** | |
|    d. **"Bill did fifty push ups this morning and then twenty-five this afternoon. Did he take a respite? How do you know?"** | |
| 3. Teacher reviews recently introduced words. | |

counter hundreds of new words during a year. There is not enough time to adequately review all the words. Teachers must select which words to review.

In selecting words to review, teachers should consider student ability as well as the likelihood of the students' encountering the word in future assignments. Teachers working with higher-performing students will be able to focus on less common words while teachers working with instructionally naive students will have to review more common words. Only by allocating extra time to instructionally naive students will teachers be able to review less common words with them. Extra practice should not, however, all be in the form of directed instruction or worksheets. Teachers should make up game-like activities. For example, a "Bingo" game might in-

volve each student's getting little cards with words written on them and big "Bingo" cards with several words written on them. The teacher would say a definition or synonym, and the students would find the card with the correct word and put it on their board.

The second criterion for selecting review words is usefulness. The more likely students are to encounter a word, the more frequently it should be reviewed. In deciding which words to review, teachers must not restrict themselves to words that appear in reading books but must include words from all the content areas: math, social studies, science, music, and health. As a guide in determining the relative usefulness of a word, teachers can consult a word list that tells the relative frequency of words. Below are several such lists:

1. Albert Harris & Milton Jacobson, *Basic Elementary Reading Vocabularies* (New York: The Macmillan Company, 1972).

   The list is based on 14 series of textbooks used in grades one through six. A word is listed when it appears in three or more basal readers. The study is available in paperback at a relatively low cost. Words are listed according to the grade in which they first appear.
2. John Carroll, Peter Davies, & Barry Richmond, *The American Heritage Word Frequency Book* (Boston: Houghton Mifflin, 1971).

   This list is based on textbooks used in grades three through nine. Words are listed in order of their relative frequency.
3. Henry Kucera & W. Nelson Francis, *Computational Analysis of Present Day American English* (Providence, R.I.: Brown University Press, 1967).

   This list is based on samples from adult printed material rather than material designed for younger students.

Teachers should record in a notebook words they intend to review. A new word should be reviewed daily for several days and then every other day for the next week or two. After that, it can be written out on a ditto or on the board along with other review words, and students can be assigned to match or write a definition or synonym and then write a sentence containing the word.

## Teaching Figurative Speech

Intermediate grade textbooks contain hundreds of figurative or idiomatic expressions such as, *down and out, bottom of the heap, in hot water,* and *to be out of line.* Students should be taught the meaning of figurative expressions just as they are taught the meaning of any unknown vocabulary word. Teachers should preview upcoming passages that students will read and select figurative or idiomatic expressions that students may not understand and are not explained through the context of the passage. These expressions should be taught and reviewed before the passage is presented. As extra practice, the teacher can prepare worksheets in which the students have to match figurative expressions with their meanings and then have the students fill in expressions in the appropriate blanks in sentences (see Figure 4.3.4).

## Independent Review of Words

Teachers should set aside several minutes each day for students to review the meanings of new words. In one review method,

**FIGURE 4.3.4**

Draw a line from each numeral to the correct letter.

|   A   |   B   |
|-------|-------|
| 1. down and out | a. in trouble |
| 2. in hot water | b. very happy |
| 3. high as a kite | c. without hope |
| 4. heavy heart | d. sad |

Fill in the blanks with the phrases in Column A.

1. That kid was _____ after she spilled the ink on her Dad's shirt.
2. With a _____ the coach told the team that he was leaving.
3. We were _____ after winning a big game.
4. The old tramp was _____.

**FIGURE 4.3.5**

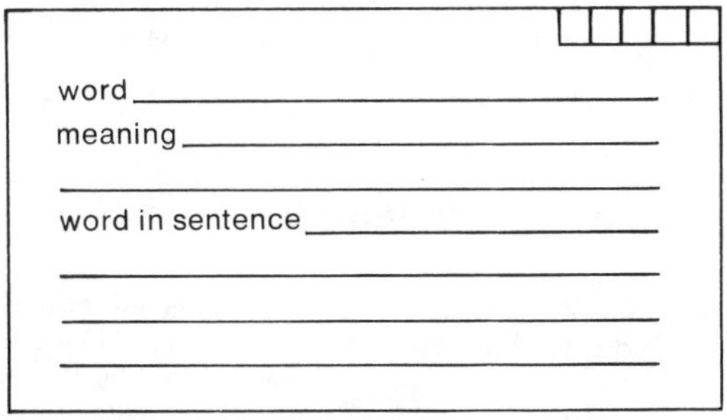

the students write each new word on a card similar to the one in Figure 4.3.5.

Students can work in pairs testing each other on words. Each day that students define a word correctly the first time they try, they make a check in one of the boxes in the upper right-hand corner of the card. After defining a word correctly on 5 different days (and having made the five checks), students can put the card at the back of their deck. Students do not have to review cards with five checks that appear at the back of the deck. However, teachers should collect cards with five check marks and informally test students on those words soon after the student makes the fifth check. If students miss a word when the teacher presents it, the five checks are erased and the card for that word returns to the front of the deck.

## Commercial Programs

Teacher's guides for basal reading programs, supplementary comprehension programs, and content area programs usually specify words that should be introduced before students read selections. Unfortunately, many difficult words, which naive students may not understand, are not included in these lists. Teachers should preview selections that students are to read to determine words with which students will have difficulty. Fortunately, teachers do not have to preteach every difficult word that is likely to be unfamiliar. Rather, teach-

ers should concentrate on words that (1) are critical to the meaning of the story or necessary to answer a question and (2) are not defined in the context of the story. When teaching new words, teachers should alter any unclear definitions that appear in a program and use positive and negative instances to illustrate each word's meaning. Of the words whose meanings are taught, only those words that students are likely to encounter often should be reviewed. Much of the review can be done through an individualized vocabulary-building program and worksheet exercises in which the students match a word with its meaning and fill in missing words in sentences. Once students know how to use the dictionary, the teacher can assign students the task of looking up difficult words prior to reading a passage.

Several publishers market separate programs for teaching vocabulary. The demand for these programs comes in part from teachers' dissatisfaction with the lack of adequate emphasis on vocabulary instruction in intermediate grade basal programs for lower-performing students. Unfortunately, these supplementary programs generally do not meet the needs of students having difficulty in that they do not provide adequate practice. Words will appear in just one or two exercises.

A strength of these supplementary vocabulary programs is that they often provide a great deal of practice in using context to figure out meanings of words. A teacher might wish to use the exercises from supplementary vocabulary programs to teach context usage. Teachers, however, should not rely on these programs to actually increase student vocabulary unless the teachers provide a great deal of extra review.

---

# RESEARCH

The hypothesis that vocabulary concept knowledge plays a major role in reading comprehension is supported by many findings. In a research review, Carroll (1971) concludes:

> much of the failure of individuals to understand speech or writing beyond an elementary level is due to deficiency in vocabulary knowledge. It is not merely the knowledge of single words and their meanings that is important, but also the knowledge of the multiple meanings of words and their grammatical functions. (p. 175)

Chall (1958) stated, "of the diverse stylistic elements that have been reliably measured and found significantly related to difficulty, only four types can be distinguished: vocabulary load, sentence structure, idea density, and human interest" (p. 157). She said that vocabulary was the most significantly related to the difficulty criteria used.

Although vocabulary knowledge is an essential ingredient of comprehension, systematic instruction is not usually provided in school. Collins, Brown, Morgan, and Brewer (1977), making observations in an urban classroom, said:

> the following kinds of problems arose when children were working exercises designed to teach vocabulary skills: 1) items were inappropriate to the level of skill or the background of the child, 2) tasks were of doubtful value to teaching vocabulary skills, 3) the children did not understand what to do, 4) the teachers did not know what kinds of problems children were having. (p. 27)

Becker (1977), in discussing research data from the *Follow Through Program,* made a case for the problems caused by lack of adequate vocabulary teaching:

> Other analyses of our Follow Through data tend to support the view that vocabulary-concept knowledge is not systematically taught by schools. Analysis of the MAT Reading tests indicates a progressive loss on percentiles from end of grade one to end of grade three, which is paralleled by a progressive change in the tests toward an adult vocabulary by the end of third grade. On MAT Total Reading, low-income children in our program are far above the median at the end of first grade (70th percentile), but they drop progressively by the end of second grade (56th percentile) and at the end of third grade (40th percentile). This drop is found for all reading subtests—Word Knowledge, Word Analysis, and Reading (Becker & Engelmann). Such losses are not found in decoding, math measures, or spelling, in all of which substantial percentile gains occur during kindergarten and first grade and are then maintained. (p. 35)

Even when systematic vocabulary instruction is provided, it may need to go beyond drill on new words and their meanings. For example, Paney and Jenkins (1977) found that having learning disabled students recite word meanings before reading a passage containing the words enhanced vocabulary test scores; however, the recitation did not improve students' performance in literal comprehension. They suggest:

> Perhaps teaching word meanings is only one step in teaching comprehension; disabled readers may also require training to integrate individual word meanings within sentences and then to relate meanings within sentences and then to related meanings of several sentences contained in a passage (Otto; Chapman, 1973). Unless a training sequence includes all of those skills, a student's understanding of a passage may not be appreciably improved. A second possible factor is passage redundancy. If a passage is sufficiently redundant, students' comprehension may not be impaired even if they do not know the meaning of several key words. (p. 18).

In a redundant passage, the same theme is portrayed in different ways by different sentences. Students can comprehend such a passage even if it contains some words they do not know. The redundancy interpretation does not mean that the meaning of vocabulary words need not be taught but it does alert teachers to the fact that students do not have to know the meaning of every word in a passage. Teachers should be selective, picking words that are critical to understanding the passage and which are not defined by the context. When previewing a passage, teachers must keep in mind the relative sophistication of the students and the obviousness of the context cues.

To evaluate the effects of integration training and passage redundancy on comprehension, Kameenui and Carnine (1979a) conducted a study that compared student performance on inference items based on sentences containing either difficult synonyms or familiar words. Passages were designed to compare five treatments: familiar words, difficult synonyms, difficult synonyms with sentences added to increase passage redundancy, difficult synonyms with training on their relationship to the familiar words, and difficult synonyms with integration training (using familiar words to restate sentences initially presented with a difficult synonym). Students from all treatments did comparably well on literal items on sentences made up of familiar vocabulary. On inference items, performance differed according to the treatment. A preliminary inspection of the data indicates that increased redundancy leads to more correct inference responses. However, performance of students in the increased redundancy treatment was still well below that of students given vocabulary training on the difficult synonyms. Integration training resulted in

performance only slightly better than just vocabulary training. The results suggest that the importance of vocabulary knowledge depends to an extent on the redundancy of a passage and whether students are taught to integrate synonyms for difficult words in sentences. However, the most powerful effect was from directly teaching students familiar words for difficult synonyms.

The need to teach students how to use context to derive word meanings was illustrated in another study by Kameenui and Carnine (1979b). They tested students on the meaning of an unknown word after the students had read passages in which the new word was defined by the context. Student error rate ranged from 34% on relatively simple structures in which a synonym was used to define a word to 54% when context cues were involved. Research is needed to determine how best to teach students to deal with the variables that affect learning vocabulary from context. Research is also needed to evaluate various strategies for teaching students to remember the meanings of vocabulary words after they are learned through direct instruction, context, or from a dictionary. Unfortunately, few of the teaching procedures used in the intermediate grades have been subjected to experimental investigation.

## APPLICATION EXERCISES

1. Circle the five words in which the use of morphemes will enable intermediate grade students to figure out the meaning of a word. Assume the students know the meaning of the root word.

   | | |
   |---|---|
   | unusable | emphasis |
   | decisive | discord |
   | misspell | dejected |
   | carelessly | rewashable |
   | absent | usefully |

2. Rank the three passages according to the difficulty students would have in determining the meaning of each underlined word through contextual analysis. Write 1 for the easiest, 2 for moderate, and 3 for most difficulty. Explain why 2 is harder than 1 and why 3 is harder than 2.

   Our center fielder, Bill, is ambidextrous. He bats third in the lineup. He can use his right hand and his left hand.

   I wish I was ambidextrous. Then I would be able to use my left hand as well as my right.

   Our center fielder, Bill, is not ambidextrous. He bats third in the lineup. He can use his right hand but not his left hand.

3. Which three of the following dictionary definitions would be most difficult for fifth graders to understand? Why?

malpractice — dereliction of professional duty
mammoth — a very great size
burnish — to polish using something hard
fossil — trace or impression of the remains of a plant or animal preserved in the earth's crust from past ages
infirm — deficient in vitality
fortunate — coming by good luck

Rewrite the more difficult definitions to make them more understandable.

4. Tell which method (examples only, synonym, definition) you would use to teach the meaning of the following words. If you would use a synonym or a definition, specify the wording you would use.
   1. residence
   2. retrospect
   3. diabolic
   4. invalid
   5. sanctuary

5. Specify a set of examples, two positive and two negative, you would use in the teaching of *residence.*

6. Which five of the following vocabulary words should a fourth grade teacher review in later lessons when working with more naive students?

congress    region
impend      myriad
defend      professional
enscond     suspend
wrest       trough

7. The following words are to appear in passages the students will be reading several days from now. Write V in front of each word that should be included in a vocabulary exercise. Write D in front of each word that should be included in a decoding exercise. (Some words need not be included in either type of exercise.)

| | | | |
|---|---|---|---|
| _____ pauper | _____ exported | _____ extinction | _____ cleft |
| _____ surround | _____ finch | _____ gymnasium | _____ footstep |
| _____ essay | _____ architect | _____ void | _____ dynamite |
| _____ noun | _____ swear | _____ neutral | _____ brittle |

8. (Review—primary stage decoding)

Assume you have just administered the primary level test of word attack skills to your class. Below are some of the skill deficits exhibited by Tom, a fourth grade student:

Tom: letter combination ou
     VCe derivatives

a. Construct a word list (12 words) to remediate the letter combination deficit. Specify the pages in the phonics analysis section (3.2) for the formats you would use to present this skill.

b. Do the same for the VCe derivative skill deficit (see Section 3.3, "Structural Analysis").

c. During passage-reading exercises, Tom often inserts or omits words. Describe the remediation procedure (see diagnosis and remediation in Section 3.4).

d. During a testing of Tom's oral reading rate, he read at a rate of 90 words a minute. Describe in detail a plan to improve his reading rate (see diagnosis and remediation in Section 3.4).

# SECTION 4.4

## *Comprehension*

The bulk of comprehension exercises in intermediate grade workbooks involves basically the same type of exercises which appear during the primary level (i.e., literal, vocabulary, inference, sequence, summarizing). The main differences between the exercises appearing in the primary and intermediate levels are the increased length and complexity of passages and the appearance of less common vocabulary in the intermediate level. Since teaching procedures for these skills have already been discussed (Section 3.5), they will not be covered again here.

In this section, we deal with three new types of comprehension skills: making inferences based on relationships, comprehending sentences with complicated syntactic structures, and critically reading passages—identifying an author's conclusion and evaluating the adequacy of the evidence and the legitimacy of the arguments. Although these topics do not appear frequently in most commercial material, they are very important. Making inferences based on relationships is a fundamental thinking skill. Similarly, critical reading is necessary if students are to intelligently evaluate material they read.

## Inference

Inferential questions require knowledge of relationships between two objects or events. The statement, When people run faster their hearts beat faster, implies a relationship between changes in running rate and changes in heart beat. Sometimes the relationship is directly stated in a passage (see example A in Table 4.4.1). More often, the relationship is not specified; students are expected to know a particular relationship (see example B in Table 4.4.1) or are expected to infer the relationship using the information stated in a passage (see example C in Table 4.4.1). In passage A the relationship, When people run faster, their hearts beat faster, is directly stated. Since the relationship is stated, students are more likely to answer the item about Rachel correctly. In passage B, the relationship is not stated, and examples are not provided that would allow the reader to figure out or induce the relationship. Obviously, students who do not know the relationship between exertion and heart rate have no basis for answering the item. Although the relationship is not directly stated in passage C either, several exam-

## TABLE 4.4.1

| RELATIONSHIP STATED | RELATIONSHIP NOT STATED |
| --- | --- |
| *Knowledge of Relationship Is Assumed* | *Examples for Figuring Out the Relationship Are Provided* |
| A. When people run faster, their hearts beat faster. On Monday, Rachel ran a mile in 5 minutes. On Tuesday, she took 7 minutes. On Wednesday, she took 4 minutes. | B. On Monday Rachel ran a mile in 5 minutes. On Tuesday, she took 7 minutes. On Wednesday, she took 4 minutes. | C. On Friday, Rachel ran a mile in 8 minutes. Her heart was beating 78 times a minute. On Saturday, Rachel ran a mile in 6 minutes. Her heart was beating 93 times. On Sunday she ran a mile in 9 minutes. Her heart was beating 68 times. On Monday, Rachel ran a mile in 5 minutes. On Tuesday, she took 6 minutes. On Wednesday, she took 4 minutes. |

On which day did Rachel's heart beat fastest?
Monday
Tuesday
Wednesday

On which day did Rachel's heart beat fastest?
Monday
Tuesday
Wednesday

On which day did Rachel's heart beat fastest?
Monday
Tuesday
Wednesday

ples illustrate the relationship between running rate and heart beat. When Rachel ran a mile in 8 minutes her rate was 78 beats per minute. When she ran faster (a mile in 6 minutes), her rate was faster (93 beats per minute). Students are given information that enables them to induce the relationship and then figure out the answer. (Using specific information to derive a general relationship, as in example C, is called induction. Applying a stated relationship to come up with a specific answer is called deduction.)

We first discuss procedures for teaching students to make inferences based on stated relationships. Second, we discuss procedures for teaching students to complete items when a relationship is not stated. This type of item accounts for the majority of inference items in commercial programs. Third, we discuss procedures for teaching students to induce relationships when examples are provided that illustrate the relationship.

When introducing inference items, the teacher can refer to them as "detective" problems. The students must use the information in the passage to figure out the answer to the question.

## Direct Instruction Procedures

### Relationship Stated

Much of the material that students read in the intermediate grades is expository. It is designed to convey information. A common characteristic of expository material is the inclusion of key sentences which specify a relationship. Table 4.4.2 includes examples of sentences which specify relationships with items that can be used to teach students to draw inferences. Several of these examples could be presented as a pretest. Students scoring below 80% should receive instruction as described below.

First the teacher presents oral exercises in which she states the relationship then asks a set of predictive (what will happen if) and causal (why did this happen) questions. The purpose of these oral exercises is to teach the students how to work from a statement that directly specifies a relationship. Note that in these items the students must work from the stated relationship. They should be discouraged from attempting to use explanations besides the stated relationship.

### Written Items

When students are able to use a stated relationship as the basis for making predictions and determining causes, they can be introduced to written items similar to those in Table 4.4.2. After students can perform at an 80% accuracy level on this type of item, written passages can be introduced. When introducing these passages the teacher tells the students that the answer is not explicitly stated in the passage. To determine the answer, students must find the sentence(s) that states the relationship. This can be done by having the students read the question and then go back to the passage and locate the relationship sentence. If necessary, students should read sentence by sentence until they find the sentence that states the relationship. An example of an easier written item and the teacher directions to the students appears below.

> John runs at the track every day. When he finishes, he counts his breath to see how hard he ran. When he breathes harder, it means that he ran faster. On Monday he took 100 breaths in 1 minute. On Tuesday, he took 90 breaths in 1 minute. On Wednesday, he took 110 breaths in 1 minute. When do you think John ran the hardest? Why?

Unfortunately, few commercial programs include systematic instruction in how to search for and utilize specified relationships. One program which does is *Distar*

**TABLE 4.4.2**  *Simple Relationships and Items for Teaching Inference*

| RELATIONSHIP | ITEMS |
|---|---|
| 1. Students who study hardest make the best grades. | 1. Jim got a lower mark on the test than Bill. Who studied harder? |
| 2. The steeper a stream, the faster the water flows. | 2. Bill is fishing in a stream on some land that is flat. Sarah is fishing in a stream on a hill. Which stream is moving faster? |
| 3. The higher you go up, the less oxygen in the air. | 3. There is less oxygen where Ann is walking than where Margie is walking. Who is walk- at a higher place? |
| 4. The greater the rainfall, the greener the grass. | 4. There were 5 inches of rain in Oregon last month, 2 inches in New York, and 1 inch of rain in Arizona. Where is the grass greener? |
| 5. When you buy a lot of the same thing, the price is cheaper. | 5. Ann, Tom, and Jill bought some cans of chicken soup. Ann paid 14 cents for each can. Tom paid 13 cents for each can. Jill paid 11 cents for each can. Who bought more cans of soup? |
| 6. The more weight you lift, the bigger your muscles get. | 6. Bob's and Susan's muscles were the same size in November. Now Bob's muscles are smaller than Susan's muscles. Who lifted more weight? |
| 7. The faster you run, the more energy you use. | 7. On Monday Agnes ran 3 miles in 15 minutes. On Tuesday she ran 3 miles in 13 minutes. On which day did she use more energy? |
| 8. The less a car weighs, the further it goes on a gallon of gas. | 8. Tim's car went 23 miles on a gallon of gas. Bill's car went 17 miles on a gallon of gas. Who's car is heavier? |
| 9. The less you eat, the thinner you get. | 9. Bill lost 4 pounds in January, 3 pounds in February, and 5 pounds in March. In which month did he eat the least? |

*Reading III* (Engelmann & Stearns, 1973). Content area books, especially science and social studies books, are also good sources for finding passages which contain stated relationships.

## Relationship Not Stated

In many inference items, the student is assumed to have the prerequisite information and knowledge of a less common relationship needed to answer the question. For example, a social studies book might ask, "Is the border between the U.S.A. and Mexico or the border between Oregon and Washington more heavily watched by po-

lice?" To answer the question, the students must know that since U.S.A. and Mexico are separate nations, that border is more closely watched than the border between Oregon and Washington, which are states. Knowledge of the relationship between type of boundary and how heavily it is guarded is assumed. Teachers, especially those working with lower-performing students, should preview inference items in all types of material; content area, literature, and workbooks. When previewing the material, the teacher notes what information the student needs to know to comprehend the material and answer questions. The information may be a simple fact (e.g.,

**Format for Answering Question Based on a Stated Relationship**

| *Teacher* | *Students* |
|---|---|
| 1. Teacher says the relationship, then students repeat it. | |
| a. **"Listen. The less a car weighs, the better the gas mileage. Tell me about weight and gas mileage."** | "The less a car weighs, the better the gas mileage." |
| 2. Teacher asks predictive questions. | |
| a. **"Car A weighs 6000 pounds. Car B weighs 4000 pounds. Which will get better mileage?"** **"How do you know?"** | "Car B" Student states relationship. |
| b. **"My truck weighs 2 tons. My car weighs 3 tons. Which will get better mileage?"** **"How do you know?"** | "Your car" Student states relationship. |
| c. To correct, teacher says, **"Tell me about weight and gas mileage. Which weighs most, the 3 ton car or the 2 ton truck? So which will get better mileage? How do you know?"** | |
| 3. Teacher asks causal questions. | |
| a. **"My new Datsun gets better mileage than my new Ford. Why is that? What is one possible reason?"** | The Datsun is lighter than the Ford. |

Oregon is a state) or an unstated relationship (e.g., international boundaries are watched more closely than state boundaries). Teachers should preteach prerequisite information or relationships students are not likely to know and which are not stated in the passage. The distinction between items which do and do not require preteaching can be seen in the following sets of passages and items. Note that the first set will not require preteaching because it assumes knowledge of a relationship which most students will in fact know (when you play in the rain you may get a cold). The second set assumes knowledge of a less well-known relationship (if a cactus is watered every day it will die). This relationship should be taught before students are assigned the item.

Exercise 1—obvious relationship, no preteaching needed

*Passage:*

Thomas was big for his age and tired quickly, but today he kept on playing handball even after the rain started. He was so concerned about improving his serve, he didn't care about being tired or notice the cold rain beating down on his head and arms.

*Item:* Circle the best answer.

Thomas _____

1. is probably a ninth grader.
2. plays handball every day.
3. may get a cold.

Exercise 2—less common relationship, preteaching required

*Passage:*

Tom brought his mother two plants, a cactus and a fern, for her birthday. He watered the plants every day for three weeks. He wanted the plants to look nice when he gave them to his mother.

*Item:* Circle the best answer.

Tom _____.

1. probably will be very happy when he gives his mother the plants.
2. will be disappointed because one of the plants will be dead.
3. probably took a course in how to care for plants.

## Relationship Must Be Induced

Relationship-based inference items, in which students must induce a relationship (i.e., the relationship is not stated), are much more difficult than items in which a relationship is directly stated in a passage. Items of this type can be introduced after students have learned to answer questions based on stated and assumed relationships.

An exercise that involves inducing relationships is forming analogies. Analogies require specifying the relationship of how a series of events or objects are similar or different. For example, the relationship between a broom and a closet is that of an object to where the object is found. Because analogy exercises are a relatively simple form of induction exercise, they should be presented before other types of induction items. In the illustrated verbal format, students apply analogy relationships.

After a week or two, the teacher can introduce exercises in which students must induce the analogy relationship. In this exercise, the teacher makes a worksheet with several items, similar to the one in Figure 4.4.1.

Once students have mastered the analogy concept, teachers can present passages in which relationships are not specified but must be induced from information in the passage.

A procedure for teaching students to induce a relationship based on information in a passage is described in the format. The format can be presented verbally or in written form. In either case, the teacher asks questions so that students induce the

---

**Format for Applying Analogies**

| Teacher | Students |
|---|---|
| 1. **"An analogy is a statement that tells the same thing about some objects. Let's make up analogies that tell where you find objects. What is the analogy going to tell?"** (signal) | "Where you find objects." |
| 2. Teacher writes on board: a *broom* is to a _____<br>as a *sink* is to _____<br>as a *bird* is to _____ | |
| 3. **"The first object is a broom. Raise your hand if you can tell me where you find a broom."** Teacher calls on an individual; accepts reasonable answer. | |
| 4. **"Let's use closet. Say the first part of the analogy."** (signal)<br>Teacher points to words on board as students say the analogy. | "A broom is to a closet" |
| 5. Teacher repeats steps 3 and 4 with the remaining objects. | |

**FIGURE 4.4.1**

a word is to _____          a word is to _____

    happy is to glad                    happy is to sad
    big is to large                    big is to little

an object is to _____          an object is to _____

    a robin is to birds                a robin is to a wing
    a trout is to fish                 a trout is to a fin

**Format for Inducing Analogies**

Complete the analogy and fill in the missing example:

A _____ is to a whole object

  a. a fin is to a fish
  b. a leg is to a table

| *Teacher* | *Students* |
|---|---|
| 1. Teacher leads the students through the worksheet. **"Read the instructions."** | "Complete the analogy and fill in the missing examples." |
| 2. **"Read a."** | "A fin is to a fish." |
| 3. **"How is a fin related to a fish?"** Teacher calls on an individual student. | "A fin is part of a fish." |
| To correct, teacher tells the answer; points out why student's answer is wrong. | |
| 4. **"An analogy has to fit all the examples. Let's see if we can say the same thing about b."** | |
| 5. **"Read b."** | "A leg is to a table." |
| **"Can we say that a leg is part of a table?"** | "Yes" |
| 6. **"So the analogy is A part is to a whole object. What's the analogy?"** | "A part is to a whole object" |
| **"Fill in the blank to finish the analogy."** | |

Example Selection

Each lesson should include several analogy relationships. Among the various relationships that could be used are:

    A word is to its opposite: big is to little; happy is to sad

    A word is to its synonym: big is to large; happy is to glad

    A word is to its color: grass is to green; snow is to white

    An object is to its function: a knife is to cutting; a pen is to writing

## Format for Inducing Relationships

Passage:

A beggar asked Alice Jones for some food. Alice said, "No." Another beggar came by and asked to sit on the porch and rest. Alice said, "Yes." The next day a different beggar came to the house. He asked to stand by the fire and warm up. Alice said, "Yes." A week later, a beggar asked for some gas for his car. Alice said, "No."

Items:

1. A beggar asked to lay in Alice's yard and sleep. What do you think Alice said?
2. Another beggar asked for some clothes. What do you think Alice said?

| *Teacher* | *Students* |
|---|---|
| 1. **"You're going to read about Alice and some beggars. We're going to figure out why Alice treats them the way she does. Start reading the story."** | Students begin reading the passage. "A beggar asked Alice Jones for some food. Alice said, 'No.' Another beggar came by and asked to sit on the porch and rest. Alice said, 'Yes.' " |
| 2. **"One time Alice said yes; one time she said no. What happened before she said yes?"** | "The beggar asked to sit and rest." |
| **"What happened before she said no?"** | "The beggar asked for food." |
| **"Why do you think Alice said no to food and yes to sitting and resting? How is letting someone have food different from letting someone sit down and rest?"** If students do not indicate that food costs money but letting someone sit and rest doesn't, the teacher should point out this relationship. **"Let's read on and see if Alice says no when beggars ask for things that cost money."** | "The next day a different beggar came to the house. He asked to stand by the fire and warm up." |
| 3. **"Would it cost money to let the beggar stand by the fire?"** | "No." |
| **"So what do you think Alice will do?"** | "Let him stand by the fire." |
| **"Read on and see if she does."** | "Alice said, 'Yes.' A week later, a beggar asked for some gas for his car." |
| 4. **"Would it cost money to let the beggar have some gas?"** | "Yes." |
| **"So what do you think Alice will do?"** | "Not give him any gas." |
| **"Read on and see what happens."** | "Alice said, 'No.' " |
| 5. **"You were right. Giving the man gas would cost money; so Alice said no. Read and work the items on your own."** | |

**FIGURE 4.4.2**  *Stone Soup* by Aesop

A poor man came to a large house during a storm to beg for food. He was sent away with angry words, but he went back and asked, "May I at least dry my clothes by the fire, because I am wet from the rain?" The maid thought this would not cost anything, so she let him come in.

Inside he told the cook that if she would give him a pan, and let him fill it with water, he would make some stone soup. This was a new dish to the cook, so she agreed to let him make it.

The man then got a stone from the road and put it in the pan. The cook gave him some salt, peas, mint, and all the scraps of meat that she could spare to throw in.

Thus the poor man made a delicious stone soup and the cook said, "Well done! You have made a wonderful soup out of practically nothing."

Item:

Why did the man ask to dry himself by the fire?

relationship that when a beggar asks for something costing money, Alice says no.

The critical aspect of the format is teaching the students to recognize what is the same when one event occurs (Alice said, "No" when requests involved money) and what is different between two recurring events (when Alice said, "No" and when Alice said, "Yes"). Learning to induce relationships is difficult and will require extensive practice. Passages that contain implied relationships are scattered throughout reading programs, making them difficult to locate and present during several consecutive lessons. Whenever implied relationships occur in passages, the teacher should ask inference questions.

The passage and item in Figure 4.4.2 illustrate an exercise that involves induction (Collins et al., 1977). Note that this exercise is more difficult since there are only two instances where the beggar approaches the house.

The answer to the question in Figure 4.4.2 is that the man wanted something to eat. Asking to warm himself by the fire was a tactic to enable him to get something to eat. The need to teach students to induce relationships was illustrated in a pilot study conducted by the authors in which only 30% of a sixth grade class answered the item correctly. Note that exercises of this type are often referred to as determining a character's motive; i.e., "What was the poor man's motive in asking to dry himself by the fire?"

## Difficulty Variables

Three factors contribute to the difficulty of inference items:

1. The degree to which the problem statement is separated from the relevant information
2. The ease with which relevant information can be used in drawing an inference
3. The number of distractors that appear in the passage (A distractor is irrelevant information that calls attention to a plausible, but incorrect answer.)

These three difficulty variables are illustrated in the two passages in Figure 4.4.3. Most students find passage A easier because relevant information is directly stated; the sentences containing the problem statement and the relevant information appear together, and passage A contains no distractors.

1. In passage A, the information about the speed of the planes immediately follows John's statement about wanting to fly

## FIGURE 4.4.3

*Passage A*

John was planning a short vacation. He walked into a travel agency and said, "I like to visit big cities. The city I enjoy visiting the most is San Francisco."

"Are you sure you want to go to San Francisco?" asked the agent. "It's raining there and you won't be able to enjoy the parks and beaches."

"Yes, I'm sure," John replied. "It's a beautiful city with many interesting people and lots of fun things to do. I can see friends, go to museums, see new plays and enjoy good food. The last time I was in San Francisco the weather was stormy. It was a holiday and there was a special show at a theater. I went and saw folk dancers, listened to music and watched a magic show. There is always something new and exciting to do there."

"Let me tell you about the flights to San Francisco then," said the agent. "There are two planes that travel non-stop to San Francisco."

"Well," said John, "when I travel all I care about is flying on fast planes."

The agent said, "The Air Worst plane takes one hour. The Untied plane takes one and a half hours."

Which plane do you think John will take?

*Passage B*

John was planning a short vacation. He walked into a travel agency and said, "I want to fly to San Francisco. When I travel, all I care about is flying on fast planes."

The agent said, "Are you sure you want to go to San Francisco? It's raining there and you won't be able to enjoy the parks and beaches."

"That's all right," said John, "I don't mind rain. I'm sure I want to go to San Francisco. It's my favorite city. There is always something new and exciting going on there. I can visit friends, go to concerts, see new plays and enjoy good food. I always have a good time in San Francisco. The rain won't matter."

"Let me tell you about the flights to San Francisco," said the agent. "There are two planes that fly non-stop. The Air Worst plane is a small jet which leaves at 10:30 and arrives at 11:30. The Untied plane is a huge jet. It has one of the fastest engines built. It carries 300 passengers, serves a great meal and shows a movie. If you don't want to see the movie you can listen to music with headphones. Or, you can just rest comfortably. The Untied plane leaves at 9:30 and arrives at 11:00. I think you would enjoy flying on the Untied plane, but it's up to you."

Which plane do you think John will take?

on fast planes. In passage B, John's statement about wanting to fly on fast planes is separated from the relevant information about the speed of the planes. Students reading passage B must remember the problem statement that John's major concern is flying in a fast plane.

2. In passage A, relevant information can be easily processed since the flying time for each plane is stated: 1 hour and 1½ hours. On the other hand, stu-

dents reading passage B must know to translate departure and arrival times into total flying time. "The Air Worst plane is a small jet which leaves at 10:30 and arrives at 11:30."

3. Finally, passage A contains few distractors. Little is said about the Untied plane which flies slower. In passage B, many advantages of the Untied plane are listed; that it is big, serves a good meal, and shows movies. Students who read passage B must be careful to ap-

ply John's criterion for selecting a plane and not be misled by all the benefits listed for the Untied plane.

While no single format can prepare students to handle all inference items, a teaching procedure can be helpful. The first step is to teach students to find the problem statement and the information needed to draw an inference based on the problem statement. Naive students must be shown that they sometimes have to skim a passage to find both the problem statement and the information they need to draw an inference based on the problem statement. (See Section 4.6 on study skills.) For example, if students had just read the item asking about which plane John will take, the teacher would say, "In what kind of plane does John like to fly?" "Fast planes." "Find the part of the story that tells about how long it takes the planes to get to San Francisco." Note that this passage assumes student knowledge of the unstated relationship: vehicles that get to a place the quickest travel the fastest. This relationship may have to be taught to some naive students before presenting the passage.

Next, students must learn to translate any relevant information into a form that directly fits the problem statement. In the example about John, who likes to fly on fast planes, the student must be able to subtract time notations and determine that 10:30 until 11:30 is 1 hour while 9:30 to 11:00 is 1½ hours. When students do not have the skills needed to translate information into a direct form, they will have trouble with comprehension items. Consequently, teachers must preview comprehension exercises and identify assumed preskills. The teacher must then either teach preskills that students do not have or delete items requiring those preskills.

Finally, students must learn to deal with distractors in a passage. The distractors in the item about John consist of the positive aspects of the Untied plane, which is the slower plane. The Untied plane is bigger, serves a meal, and has music and a movie. Students who do not carefully attend to the statement that John wants to fly in the fastest plane might think that John would take the Untied plane. When introducing items with distractors, teachers must emphasize the statement that determines the answer to the item. For example, after students read, "Which plane do you think John will take?" the teacher says, "In what kind of plane does John want to fly?" "The fastest plane." "Did John say he wanted a plane with a meal or with a movie?" "No." "So what kind of plane are you going to look for when you answer the item?" "The fastest plane." "Figure out what plane John picked." Whenever students make a mistake because of a distractor, the teacher should require the students to locate the part of the passage that specifies the problem statement. The teacher then points out that the distractor has nothing to do with the problem statement and does not lead to the correct answer.

Although teachers can and should use formats for teaching students to handle the various difficulty variables, the most critical aspect of teaching involves providing a carefully designed sequence of items in which difficulty variables are introduced one at a time.[1] They should sequence items

---

[1] Education has long been enamored with higher order or inference questions. While educators are correct in calling for numerous inferential items, they must realize that large doses of inferential items will not necessarily improve students' inference skills, especially for instructionally naive students. The problem occurs when the inference items assume knowledge and skills the students do not have, and yet teacher guidance is not provided. For example, consider this inference item: "As the location of a subatomic particle becomes more precise, what would you infer about its momentum?" Or consider this example: "When John walked out onto the street, he nictitated rapidly. Where do you think John had been?" These are inference items but working many items similar to these would not improve an average adult's skill in drawing inferences. Similarly, exposing students, especially low-performing ones, to inference items is not sufficient. The examples must be carefully

from simple to complex and provide sufficient practice on easier types before introducing more difficult types. When sequencing items, teachers should begin with relatively simple items which call for commonly known relationships; complexity of passages should be gradually increased, and new difficulty variables should be introduced one at a time. More specifically, teachers should pretest and, if necessary, teach students to make inferences based on stated relationships. Next, items based on assumed relationships can be introduced. Less common relationships should be pretaught. Items for both stated and unstated relationships should be drawn from the students' reading assignments. Next, the difficulty variables can be introduced, one at a time: separation, ease of using relevant information, and distractors. Finally, induction items should be presented. Again, the items should be taken from literature and content area assignments.

## Sentence Structure

During the intermediate grades, sentence syntax becomes increasingly complicated. A great variety of sentence constructions are introduced including these:

1. Participles (underlined words):
   The man taking the money looked to his side.
   The mountain towering above the plain was 12,000 feet high.
   Thinking about the upcoming test, Jack decided not to go out last night.
   Wearing her new sneakers to the meet, Ann was confident she would be the next state champion.

2. Clauses: Trig, who comes from the planet Floss, was over 80 feet tall.
   Eugene, which is in west central Oregon, has a population of 100,000.

3. Sentences containing these connectives:
   consequently, although, therefore, provided that, unless, so that, as, whether, while, yet, whether or not, while, during, some, all, none, either, or, neither, nor.
   Note the difference in the meanings in these sentence pairs.
   a. Neither Jim nor John will win.
      Either Jim or John will win.
   b. They played while it rained.
      They played until it rained.
   c. He gave pencils to some of the students.
      He gave pencils to all of the students.

4. Passive constructions:
   John was carried down the mountain by Liz.
   The man was led into the arena by a black stallion.

5. Numerical and class inclusive notations:
   The lion and the gladiator walked into the arena, the former snarling and vicious, the latter tense and alert. (*Former* and *latter* are numerical terms.)
   His dog barked a lot during the night. The animal seemed to be on edge. (Dog is included in the class of animals.)

6. Pronouns referring to an action or series of actions:
   The baseball game went into extra innings. This caused Tom to worry if he would be late getting home.
   The rocket took off. Faster and faster it went until it had climbed 386 feet. It was the beginning of the space age.

---

selected and sequenced, and careful instruction must be provided. Students must know relevant vocabulary, assumed relationships, and how to draw inferences if practice exercises are to be helpful.

The teaching procedure for each type of construction is somewhat different. Since we cannot discuss the procedures for each type of syntactic construction, we will illustrate direct instruction procedures that can be used to show students how clauses and passive voice construction function. Similar procedures can be used for other constructions. (Note: Directly teaching all types of syntactic structures is not necessary since many may not cause difficulty for students. However, syntactic structures that cause students difficulty in comprehension could be taught using the steps similar to those outlined below for clauses and passive constructions. Difficulty can be assessed by having students answer written items similar to those on pages 336 and 337. Additional items could be constructed to sample students' comprehension of other syntactic structures. Instruction would be provided only on structures which were in items failed by a student.)

## Direct Instruction Procedures

## Clauses

A sentence with a clause, such as, *John, who was helped home by Jack, fell off his bike,* will be more difficult for students to comprehend than two separate sentences: *John fell off his bike. Jack helped John go home.* The difference in difficulty in the two versions becomes apparent when students are asked, "Who fell off his bike?" Some students reading the sentence *John, who was helped home by Jack, fell off his bike* will answer that Jack fell off his bike.

The teaching procedure for clauses involves teaching students to transform a longer sentence that contains a clause into two shorter sentences that students can readily comprehend. For example, from the sentence *Tom, who had a date with Mary, was very happy,* two simple sentences can be constructed: *Tom had a date with Mary. Tom was very happy.* An important prerequisite skill for introducing clauses is reading with expression, pausing at commas, and grouping words into units. Stu-

dents will have less difficulty comprehending sentences with complex structures if they read with proper expression.

The first exercises, in which students transform sentences with clauses into simpler sentences, can be verbal ones. When students master these, written exercises can be provided. Note that these exercises are relatively simple and might be introduced in late third or early fourth grade.

### Critical Behaviors

*Correcting Mistakes.* If students are unable to generate the two sentences, the teacher models by asking the question and saying the correct answer. The teacher should repeat the three questions pertaining to a sentence until the students answer them correctly:

1. What word comes in front of *who/ which?*
2. Say the first sentence.
3. Say the second sentence.

Students must be able to answer all three questions consecutively if they are to develop a generalized understanding of the structure. More naive students may need up to 10 corrected repetitions on each sentence when the skill is first introduced. Taking the extra time to teach the task to criterion will pay off in future lessons.

### Written Format for Clauses

After the students can verbally generate two short sentences for a sentence that contains a clause, the teacher presents written worksheet exercises based on sentences with clauses. Below are sample items that would appear on the worksheet.

1. Tom, who practiced with Bill, won the race. Who won the race?
2. Tom practiced with Bill, who won the race. Who won the race?
3. The lake, which is near the mountain, is pretty. What is pretty?

**Oral Format for Clauses**

| *Teacher* | *Students* |
|---|---|
| 1. Teacher tells the rule about transforming sentences with clauses. | |
|    a. **"When you hear the words *who* or *which* in a long sentence, you can usually say it as two shorter sentences. Say the person or object that comes in front of *who* or *which* as part of both sentences."** | |
| 2. Teacher models and tests. | |
|    a. **"Listen. Tom, who works with Alice, is a friend of Jim's."** | |
|    b. **"What word comes in front of *who*?"** | "Tom" |
|      **"So we say *Tom* in both sentences."** | |
|    c. **"I'll say the two sentences. Tom works with Alice. (pause) Tom is a friend of Jim's."** | |
|    d. **"Tom, who works with Alice, is a friend of Jim's. Say the first sentence."** (pause, signal) | "Tom works with Alice." |
|    e. **"Tom, who works with Alice, is a friend of Jim's. Say the second sentence."** (pause, signal) | "Tom is a friend of Jim's." |
| 3. Teacher tests. | |
|    a. **"Listen. The book which is on the table is dirty."** | |
|    b. **"What word comes in front of *which*?"** (signal) | "Book" |
|      **"So we say *book* in both sentences."** | |
|    c. **"The book which is on the table is dirty. Say the first sentence."** (pause, signal) | "The book is on the table." |
|    d. **"The book which is on the table is dirty. Say the second sentence."** (pause, signal) | "The book is dirty." |
|    e. **"Listen. Jim likes Mary, who is Scott's sister."** | |
|    f. **"What word comes in front of *who*?"** (signal) | "Mary" |
|      **"So we say *Mary* in both sentences."** | |
|    g. **"Jim likes Mary, who is Scott's sister. Say the first sentence."** (pause, signal) | "Jim likes Mary." |
|    h. **"Jim likes Mary, who is Scott's sister. Say the second sentence."** (pause, signal) | "Mary is Scott's sister." |

4. The lake is near the mountain which is pretty. What is pretty?

5. The book is on the table, which is dirty. What is dirty?

6. The book, which is on the table, is dirty. What is dirty?

7. Jack, who won the race, ran for a long time. Who ran?

8. The book, which is on the bottom shelf, is red. What is red?

Note that several pairs of sentences are nearly identical; the only difference is the position of the word *who* or *which*. The worksheet should include three to five pairs of similar sentences, some with *who* and some with *which*. The items should be sequenced unpredictably.

After students can do tasks in which the subject or object is a single word, noun phrases can be introduced as the subject or object. For example, "John's vacation house, which sits at the base of a mountain, is a fun place to stay in the winter." The item asks, "Where is a fun place to stay in the winter?" The answer is, "John's vacation house." Noun phrases cause some students difficulty because students tend to look for a single word antecedent rather than a phrase.

## Passive Voice

The procedure for teaching students to understand passive voice is somewhat different than that for sentences with clauses. The teacher asks questions about an active and passive version of the same sentence. The format involves the teacher's presenting an active voice sentence and asking (1) who was acted upon and (2) who did the acting. After each active voice sentence, the teacher presents a passive voice sentence and asks the same questions. By answering these questions, students will learn to comprehend both active and passive constructions. For example:

1. "I'll say sentences and then ask a question."
   "John hit Mary." (Active)
   "Who got hit?" ("Mary")
   "Who did the hitting?" ("John")
2. "Listen to a different sentence."
   "John was hit by Mary." (Passive)
   "Who got hit?" ("John")
   "Who did the hitting?" ("Mary")

In the active construction (John hit Mary), Mary got hit. In the passive construction (John was hit by Mary), the subject, John, got hit. Since the question, "Who got hit?" is identical for both the active and passive constructions, the students must attend carefully to the words *was* and *by*. These words signal a passive construction, in which the subject is the recipient of the action. (John *was* hit *by* Mary. Who got hit? John.) Only by carefully watching for the words that signal a passive construction will students learn to distinguish passive from active constructions and thereby be able to answer questions such as, Who got hit?

The situation is almost identical for the Who did the hitting? question. This question is asked about both the active and passive constructions. Again, only by watching for the words that signal a passive construction (*was* and *by* in this example) will the students learn to distinguish active from passive voice and thereby be able to answer the question. More specifically, "John hit Mary" is active so the subject (John) did the hitting. "John was hit by Mary" is passive so the subject (John) didn't do the hitting; Mary did. The verbal exercises should include three to five pairs of sentences. Corrections should involve modeling and testing.

After several days, a worksheet exercise can be presented in which pairs of similar sentences, one in the active voice and one in the passive voice, are followed by literal comprehension questions. Note that in both sentences in each item in Figure 4.4.4, the names appear in the same order; e.g., in item 1 the order is rabbit–chicken. Maintaining a consistent order prevents students from learning a misinterpretation that the actor in a sentence always comes first.

The items included in these tasks should be low probability items. That means the answer should not be one that would be expected based on common knowledge. An example of a bad item would be The

**FIGURE 4.4.4**   *Worksheet Practice on Passive Voice Constructions*

Item 1.  a. The rabbit helped the chicken.
Who got helped? _____
Who did the helping? _____
b. The rabbit was helped by the chicken.
Who got helped? _____
Who did the helping? _____

Item 2.  a. John was found by Mary.
Who got found? _____
Who did the finding? _____
b. John found Mary.
Who got found? _____
Who did the finding? _____

Item 3.  a. The dog sold the cat.
Who got sold? _____
Who did the selling? _____
b. The dog was sold by the cat.
Who got sold?_____
Who did the selling? _____

child was bitten by the dog. Since the answer is highly predictable from common knowledge (dogs bite children), the item is of high probability. It can be answered through common sense, without the students carefully attending to the words that signal a passive voice construction.

In contrast, the items on our sample worksheet are low probability items. Common sense does not indicate whether a rabbit or chicken is more likely to be helpful, whether a dog would sell a cat, or whether John would find Mary rather than Mary find John. Since the answers for items 1, 2, and 3 are not based on common knowledge, students must learn sentence structure to determine who is the actor and who is the recipient of the action.

## Application to Passages

The preteaching of clauses and passive voice will help most students succeed in passages with complex constructions. For some students, more guidance may be needed. The students may perform acceptably when skills are taught in isolation but not when the students must apply the skills when reading a passage. These students will need structured guidance in transforming complex sentences into simpler forms. In Figure 4.4.5 is a sample worksheet exercise that might be used to provide practice on using the previously taught skills.

If a student makes errors, the teacher leads the student through reading the passage. As the student finishes reading a sentence that contains a clause, the teacher asks him to generate two shorter sentences. For passive voice constructions, for example, the teacher would ask who did the action and who was the recipient of the action.

The procedures we described dealt with relatively easy sentence forms. Teachers will find that naive students will benefit from a daily 15–20 minute oral reading session during which they read passages containing complex sentence structures. The students read each page twice. During the first reading the teacher paraphrases sentences that were difficult. During the second reading the teacher calls on students to paraphrase difficult sentences or asks questions to see if the students comprehend the sentence.

A written exercise aimed at fostering an understanding of complex sentences involves students having to tell which of

**FIGURE 4.4.5**

Jan and Ann had played on the same soccer team for two years. Jan, who was tall and quicker than Ann, played forward. In one game Ann was helped by Jan in scoring three goals.

Who played forward?
Who scored three goals?

several sentences has the same meaning as a model sentence. In Figure 4.4.6 is a set of sentences that could be used. Note that the correct answer is both 2 and 4.

# Critical Reading

Critically evaluating assertions, arguments, and proposals, whether presented orally or in print, is possibly the most important comprehension skill related to preparing students for their various roles in life. Many personal, professional, and social decisions are based on what we are told by other people. Because faulty arguments and propaganda are so common, critical thinking has a role in almost every important decision we make. To simplify instruction in critical reading, we will outline a standard procedure that students can apply to increasingly sophisticated arguments. As in the material on inferences, sequencing exercises from simple to complex and providing sufficient practice for students to master one level of complexity before introducing the next are indispensable if students are to learn a strategy for critical reading. The steps in teaching critical reading involve teaching students to do the following:

1. Identify the author's conclusion; i.e., what does the author want the reader to believe?
2. Determine what evidence is presented; i.e., what does the author present to convince the reader? Evidence or opinion?
3. Determine the trustworthiness of the author; i.e., can the reader trust what the author says?
   a. Does the evidence come from a qualified person?
   b. Does the person have biases?
4. Identify faulty arguments; i.e., does the conclusion derive from the evidence?
   a. Tradition, either old or new (sometimes called a bandwagon effect)
   b. Improper generalization
   c. Confusing correlation with causation (or coincidence)

A rather advanced example of the propaganda devices that students will encounter and how students should analyze them are illustrated in the following passage and discussion:

Thomas Edison, the inventor of the light bulb, was seriously concerned about the increasing use of alternating current as a form of electricity. Edison believed that because alternating current involved so much more current than direct current, alternating cur-

**FIGURE 4.4.6**

*Model Sentence:* Before our ship was sunk by an iceberg, it tossed in waves 20 feet high.
1. Our ship was sunk by an iceberg then tossed in 20 foot high waves.
2. Our ship, which was sunk by an iceberg, had been tossed around by 20 foot high waves.
3. A 20 foot high iceberg sunk our ship after it had been tossed around by waves.
4. After it was tossed in waves 20 feet high, our ship was sunk by an iceberg.

rent was a threat to the nation. Many fires were caused by alternating currents. In fact, alternating current was used in Sing Sing to electrocute criminals. Direct current was used with light bulbs for many years. Edison felt direct current was still the best form of electricity.

First, the students must use details from a passage (seriously concerned, a threat to the nation, direct current is still the best) to form a main idea (or an author's conclusion). Identifying an author's conclusion is a continuation of summarization skills (main idea, best title) discussed earlier.

The second step is for the student to decide whether the author's conclusion is based on opinion or evidence. If a conclusion is based on opinion, students should know that the author's conclusion is really nothing more than a suggestion by the author about what people should think. A conclusion based on opinion does not imply that the student should believe or act on it. In the alternating current example, both opinion and evidence are used to support the author's conclusion. The statement that alternating current is a threat to the nation is an opinion. The other details are evidence used to justify the author's interpretation, i.e., the occurrence of fires, electrocution of criminals, and the initial use of direct current as an energy source.

The third step consists of several questions, all relating to the reliability or trustworthiness of the person presenting the argument. Question a is whether the evidence comes from a qualified person. Since Edison was definitely an expert on electricity in the late 1800s, he was qualified. Question b concerns biases that the expert might have. In Edison's case, two major biases existed. One was his deep personal and financial involvement in a company that provided direct current. He stood to lose money if alternating current replaced direct current. Also his reputation was at stake. He became famous, in

part, because of his discovery of the light bulb and a distribution system for electricity, which was based on the use of direct current. If alternating current replaced direct current, his reputation might be diminished. Since Edison's biases would contribute to the passage's conclusion, the evidence may not be trustworthy.

Since there is doubt about the trustworthiness of the author, students must seek information from different experts. The statement that direct current is the best form of electricity is disputed by many experts. Alternating current can be transmitted great distances, but direct current cannot. If remote areas are to receive electricity at a reasonable rate, alternating current is a necessity. Since the expert is biased and alternative interpretations of the evidence are compelling, the evidence is probably not trustworthy.

The final step in the critical reading process is deciding whether a conclusion legitimately derives from the evidence. In many arguments, valid evidence will be presented, but then a conclusion will be drawn that does not derive from the evidence. In the alternating current example, one possible interpretation is that since direct current has been used with light bulbs for many years, it should continue to be the best form of electricity. This improper argument illustrates the use of tradition; what has been the best must continue to be the best. Conclusions based on tradition are not necessarily true. What has worked well may continue to be the best procedure, or a better procedure may be developed. Students can disregard conclusions based on tradition. (Note that the same attitude can be taken toward newly developing traditions; i.e., Everybody is starting to use alternating current; therefore, you should too. A conclusion that a product or procedure is better because it is popular is not reasonable.)

Since the passage about alternating current does not illustrate the other two types of improper arguments (improper generalization and confusing correlation with causation), the following additional passages provide better illustrations of these invalid forms of conclusions. The first additional passage illustrates improper generalization. One valid example is presented, but then a conclusion is drawn that applies to all examples.

> Another example of the dangers of alternating current has just occurred. A house wired with alternating current caught fire and burned to the ground. The fire started when an electrical wire became so hot that a wall caught fire. Alternating current will eventually cause a fire whenever it is used. Direct current should be used for lighting rather than alternating current.

One fire caused by alternating current does not mean that alternating current will cause a fire every place it is used. Improper generalization occurs often: "I saw a rich person who was rude. What makes rich people so rude?" "We sat next to a long-haired man in the movies. He smelled. I'll bet he hadn't bathed in weeks. Long hairs should take better care of their bodies."

The next passage involves a confusion of causation and correlation. An event that is associated with success or some other positive outcome through coincidence is erroneously concluded to be the cause of the positive outcome.

> The Daily Post used direct current to light its press room for over a year. Reporters are much happier now. They say that the light from bulbs does not hurt their eyes as much as the gas lights the paper used before. Also the rooms are much cooler in the summer because the light from direct current does not give off heat like gas lights do.

Direct current lighting is associated with less eye strain and more comfortable temperatures; however, direct current did not necessarily cause reporters to be happier. The electric lighting that produced the positive outcomes could have been achieved with direct or alternating current.

Conclusions suggesting causation that are, in fact, based on correlation can be disregarded. Confusion of correlation and causation is often made: "Joe Blow uses Squirt-Squirt deodorant, and girls always chase him." "Silly Sally took You-Bet-Your-Life vitamins every day. She lived to be 106!"

## Direct Instruction Procedures

### Sequence

Before the complete critical reading strategy can be introduced, the component skills must be taught separately and then combined to form the strategy. The four steps in the critical reading process can be treated as the major component skills: (1) identifying the author's conclusion, (2) distinguishing opinion from evidence, (3) determining the trustworthiness of evidence (qualifications of evidence source, biases, alternative interpretations of evidence), and (4) identifying faulty arguments (tradition, improper generalization, and a confusion of correlation and causation.)

Students can be taught relatively early to identify an author's conclusion and details that support the conclusion. Next, procedures for discriminating evidence from opinion can be introduced. After that, instruction in determining the reliability of evidence and then the validity of arguments can occur. Finally, the component skills can be combined to form the complete strategy.

### Teaching Procedures

We will discuss teaching procedures for the four component skills of the critical reading strategy separately.

#### Identifying an Author's Conclusion

This skill is closely related to selecting a main idea. A major difference is that students must generate a conclusion rather than select the best alternative in a multiple choice format. Since every passage is unique, specifying a detailed format to teach students to generate an author's conclusion is difficult. This skill, however, can be taught through modeling and extensive practice. A teacher would model by presenting a passage, identifying the author's conclusion, and listing supporting details from the passage that led to the conclusion. Then the teacher would test by presenting a series of passages and asking students to identify the author's conclusion and justify their conclusion by citing supporting details. The teacher and the students should discuss unacceptable answers, pointing out why they are unacceptable. At first, items should be quite simple (see Section 4.6 for more detailed teaching procedures). Below are examples of items which might be done initially.

1. I hope Tom comes back to our team. Ever since he left, we have lost every game. (Conclusion: We are losing because Tom isn't on the team.)
2. Those ABC tires are great. I've been getting super gas mileage on my new car with ABC tires. (Conclusion: I'm getting better gas mileage because I'm using ABC tires.)
3. Mary has looked so sad since our team lost the game. She doesn't go out at night. I never see her in the store after school. (Conclusion: Mary doesn't go out any more because she's sad about our team losing the game.)

Verbal exercises would be done for several days and then replaced with written exercises. The length of the passages should be increased gradually.

### Discriminating Evidence from Opinion

This skill can be taught after students learn to identify an author's conclusion or at the same time. Teaching students to discriminate fact from opinion is done in two stages. In the first stage, all opinion statements include phrases that indicate that an opinion is being given (I think, I believe, I feel, in my opinion, in my judgment). The examples would include about 10 statements, half of which are opinions and half of which are facts. Below is a set of statements that might be included in such a format.

1. I believe Tom won the race.
2. Tom won the race yesterday.
3. I believe he is faster than his brother.
4. He beat his brother in a race.
5. I think it will rain.
6. It is raining.
7. I think chocolate is the best flavor.
8. More people eat chocolate than any other flavored ice cream.
9. In my opinion she is the best player on the team.
10. She is the oldest girl on our team.

The teacher might introduce the items by explaining the difference between fact and opinion saying, "When somebody tells you something that actually happened they are telling you a *fact*. When somebody tells you how they feel about something they are telling you an *opinion*. Sometimes the way a person tells you something lets you know if it's an opinion. If a person says: I think, I believe, or I feel, they are giving an opinion." The teacher would then present the statements asking the students to tell if the statement is one of fact or opinion.

The second stage of the procedure introduces more sophisticated items which do not include phrases such as I think or I believe. Teaching students to distinguish fact from opinion with this type statement has to do with consensus. If a person says something with which almost everybody who is knowledgeable would agree, the statement is one of fact. If, on the other hand, it is a statement with which people who are knowledgeable disagree, the statement is one of opinion. Consider the following statements:

1. *Traveling by train is not as exciting as traveling by car.* This is a statement of opinion. No special knowledge base is needed. In the general population, there are many people who would not agree with the statement.
2. *Traveling across the country by plane is faster than by car.* This is a statement of fact. Most people knowledgeable about travel agree.
3. *It rains too much in Oregon.* This is a statement of opinion. It reflects how some people feel but not how all people feel.
4. *Oregon has more rain than New Jersey.* This is a fact.

Distinguishing opinion from fact is not easy. It will require lots of practice with a great variety of statements. For example, when an author uses opinion rather than evidence to sway the reader, he will use emotional words as a tactic. (See the format for teaching students how to identify emotionally charged words when evaluating conclusions. Since this format is independent of the other formats, it can be introduced at a teacher's convenience.)

### Determining the Trustworthiness of an Author

An important aspect of determining author trustworthiness is examining the qualifications of the person stating the argument. Much advertising is based on nonexpert endorsements. Sometimes a popular figure will endorse products about which he or she has no knowledge.

The first step in determining the trustworthiness of the author is determining his expertise regarding what he is talking about. A second step involves examining the motives of an author to determine if he has anything to gain by convincing the reader of his position. For example, if a

student knows that a person invented an object and stands to make a good deal of money if the object is sold, there is good reason to be suspicious of the person's claims. Passages like the one below could be presented to develop the concept of author motive.

Edwin Water, an inventor of the Sunglass Water Camera and owner of Water Camera Company of America, made the following remarks at a photographer's convention. "I was a professional photographer for several years. During that time I felt that a PHXTVW-23 Sunglass Water Camera gave me the greatest resolution, both with close work and when using a telephoto lense. Its light weight and small size make it very convenient. I don't need to tell you the importance of quality and convenience when it comes to cameras."

After students have been taught to evaluate author's trustworthiness, they should work exercises that incorporate the critical reading skills discussed thus far. A sample exercise appears below. (Assume that the students have previously learned to identify an author's conclusion and to distinguish evidence from opinion.)

Thomas Edison invented the electric light bulb and a system for distributing direct current to people to light their homes and businesses. He owned part of a company that made light bulbs and one that sold direct current. After direct current had been in use for a few years, alternating current was invented. Many people bought alternating current because it was cheaper and could be distributed long distances. Edison opposed the use of alternating current, though. He felt it was a threat to the nation. Edison argued that people should continue to use direct current.

1. What was the author's conclusion?
2. Was evidence or opinion used to support the conclusion?
3. Was Edison a qualified expert on electricity? Explain your answer.
4. Was Edison biased? Did Edison have

**Format for Identifying Emotional Words**

| *Teacher* | *Students* |
|---|---|

1. Teacher explains emotionally charged words.

   a. **"Most peope like some words and don't like other words. Here are some words that most people like:** *love, freedom, beauty, democracy, kindness, confidence, creativity.* **Here are some words that most people do not like:** *murder, hate, ugliness, loneliness, cruelty, selfishness.* **Sometimes words people like are used to convince people to accept a conclusion."**

2. Teacher models.

   a. **"Listen to this conclusion. The F.U.N. Reading Program is colorful, fun packed, and enlightening. All teachers should use the F.U.N. Reading Program."**

   b. **"When you read or hear an argument, ignore words that people like or dislike. When we get rid of the words people like or dislike, we see that there is no evidence for using the F.U.N. Reading Program. It's just someone's opinion."**

3. Teacher tests.

   a. **"I'll make a claim. You tell me the words people like or dislike. Then you tell me if any evidence is left to support the conclusion."**

   b. **"Everybody should use smiley toothpaste. It makes them pleasant all day and free to do all the things they really want to do."**

   c. **"What are the words people like or dislike?"** Teacher calls on individuals.                    "Pleasant, free"

   d. **"Is there any evidence left to support the conclusion?"**                    "No"

4. The teacher presents several more items. After students can correctly respond to verbally presented items, they should be assigned written items. The students would cross out emotionally charged words and then indicate what evidence remains to support the conclusion.

any personal reason for opposing alternating current? Explain your answer.

5. Would you be suspicious of Edison's conclusion? Why?

Items 1 and 2 assume that students have been taught to identify an author's conclusion and to distinguish evidence from opinion. To answer items 3 and 4, students use the information in the passage about Edison. If students have doubts about the trustworthiness of an author, they must seek additional information about the subject. Item 5 requires the student to synthesize the information from items 1–4.

### Identifying Faulty Arguments

Earlier we mentioned three types of fallacious arguments: those based on tradition (It's been done this way in the past, so it should be done this way in the future), improper generalization (X is no good, X is a Y, so Y is no good), and

coincidence or a confusion of causation and correlation (S and Y happened at the same time, so S must cause Y). We picked these three fallacies since they occur relatively often. For a discussion of other fallacies, we recommend a book by Alex C. Michalos (1970) entitled, *Improving Your Reasoning.*

The formats are similar for each of the three types of invalid arguments (tradition, improper generalization, and a confusion of causation and correlation). The teacher

---

**Format for Identifying Invalid Conclusions Based on Tradition**

| *Teacher* | *Students* |
|---|---|
| 1. **"Sometimes an author makes a conclusion that is based on a faulty argument."** | |
| 2. **"One type of faulty argument is called tradition. A conclusion based on tradition says that something should be a certain way because it has always been that way. What does a conclusion based on tradition say?"** (signal) | "That something should be a certain way because it has always been that way" |
| 3. **"Here is an example. Mr. Rotter said our family has always bought Brand X shoes and should keep on buying Brand X shoes. The conclusion that we should continue doing something just because we have done it in the past is based on the faulty argument of tradition."** | |
| 4. **"Listen to this argument: Mr. Jones said the Yankees are a sure bet to win this year since they won last year. Do you agree with Mr. Jones' conclusion?** (signal) | "No" |
| **"Why not?"** Teacher calls on individual students; accepts reasonable answers. **"Right, his conclusion was based on tradition. Just because something has been done a certain way in the past doesn't mean that is the way it should be done."** | |
| 5. **"Listen to this argument. Mrs. Spencer told her daughter, 'When I was a young girl, my mother had me come home at 9 P.M. from a date. So when you go out, you should be home at 9 P.M.' Do you agree with Mrs. Spencer's conclusion?"** (signal) | "No" |
| **"Why not?"** Teacher calls on individual students; accepts reasonable answers. **"Right, the conclusion was based on tradition."** | |

**Format for Identifying Invalid Conclusions Based on Improper Generalization**

|                                    *Teacher*                                    |                                    *Students*                                    |
|---|---|

1. **"Sometimes authors make a conclusion that is based on improper generalization. An improper generalization says that because a part has a certain characteristic, the whole thing must have that characteristic. What does an improper generalization say?"** (signal)

   "That because a part has a certain characteristic the whole thing must have that characteristic"

2. **"Here are some examples. When a store sells a gallon of spoiled milk, that doesn't mean that all the milk they sell is spoiled. The conclusion that the store always sells spoiled milk because it sold some spoiled milk once is based on the faulty argument of improper generalization. When a student does well in sports, that doesn't mean that all the student's brothers and sisters are athletic. The conclusion that everyone in the family is athletic because one person is athletic is based on improper generalization."**

3. **"Listen to this argument. The cobra car has super tires. You should buy the cobra car. Do you agree with the conclusion?"** (signal)

   "No"

   **"Why not?"** Teacher calls on individual students; accepts reasonable answers. **"Right, that argument is faulty because it is based on improper generalization. Just because one part of something is good doesn't mean the whole thing is good."**

states a rule about an invalid form and presents a series of examples, asking whether the argument in each example is valid. After students have learned the first two forms of invalid conclusions, they receive discrimination practice in determining which form accounts for an invalid conclusion. In this discrimination exercise the teacher presents a series of examples and asks, "Is the argument faulty?" If students answer yes, the teacher asks, "Why?" The students then have to indicate what invalid argument was used to draw the conclusion. This discrimination exercise also appears again after the third form of invalid argument is introduced; students identify which of three forms accounts for an invalid conclusion. Below we present formats for teaching students

to identify conclusions based on tradition, improper generalization and confusions between correlation and causation. Then we discuss an exercise that requires students to apply the entire critical reading strategy discussed in this section.

The format for improper generalization is identical to the format for tradition. Only the rule for explaining why the argument is invalid is different. The rule for improper generalization is that a conclusion is invalid if it tells about a whole group of people or things based on evidence for just one person or thing.

After arguments based on improper generalizations are introduced, a discrimination exercise in which students must discriminate between tradition and improper generalization should be introduced. In this format, the teacher reviews the definitions of tradition and improper generalization and then presents a series of items.

The final type of faulty argument is a confusion of correlation with causation. When two things happen at the same time, one does not necessarily cause the other.

After students correctly work verbally presented items, they should be given written items in which they must discriminate among the causes of faulty arguments: tradition, improper generalization, or coincidence.

## An Overall Critical Reading Strategy

Exercises in which students must apply several of the critical reading component skills in analyzing the validity of an author's conclusion should be presented after students have been taught the component skills (identifying conclusion, distinguishing evidence from opinion, determining reliability of evidence, and spotting faulty arguments). Exercises should include a mixture of supportable and unsupportable conclusions so that students do not develop a habit of automatically disagreeing with an author's conclusion. There should be variety among the passages that have unsupportable conclusions. In some passages, the cause of the conclusion's being invalid should be lack of evidence; in others, faulty arguments; and in others, lack of reliable evidence.

When written items are first introduced, the teacher follows each passage with a

**Discrimination Format**

| Teacher | Students |
|---|---|
| 1. "An argument may be faulty because it is based on tradition or because it is based on an improper generalization." | |
| 2. "What does an argument based on tradition say?" (signal) | "Something should be a certain way because it has always been that way." |
| 3. "What does an argument based on improper generalization say?" (signal) | "That because a part has a certain characteristic the whole thing must have that characteristic." |
| 4. "I'll say some arguments that are faulty. You tell me why the argument is faulty, because of tradition or because of improper generalization." | |
| a. "Tomas can spell very well. I bet he is the smartest student in the class. Why is that argument faulty?" | "It is based on improper generalization." |
| b. "New York had the first good subway system. Its subway system must be the best. Why is that argument faulty?" | "It is based on tradition." |
| c. "Mr. Ricardo has lived on this street since 1970. He'll never move. Why is that argument faulty?" | "It is based on tradition." |
| d. "That restaurant serves delicious pies. It is the best restaurant in town. Why is that argument faulty?" | "It is based on improper generalization." |

**Format for Identifying Faulty Arguments Based on Coincidence**

| *Teacher* | *Students* |
|---|---|
| 1. "An argument is faulty if it is based on coincidence. An argument is based on coincidence when we say that one event caused another event just because they both happened at the same time. When is an argument based on coincidence?" (signal) | "When we say that one event caused another event just because they both happened at the same time." |
| 2. "Here are some examples. Joe is shown eating muscle man hotdogs. Joe is handsome and strong. Eating muscle man hot dogs and looking handsome and strong happen at the same time. A conclusion that muscle man hot dogs caused Joe to be handsome would be faulty. Just because two things happen at the same time, you cannot make a conclusion that one caused the other to happen. That argument is based on the faulty argument of coincidence." | |
| 3. "Listen to this argument. Sam fights a lot, and he has lots of friends. Sam has lots of friends because he fights a lot. Do you agree with the conclusion?" (signal) | "No" |
| "Why not?" Teacher calls on individual students; accepts reasonable answers. "Right, a conclusion that fighting causes people to have friends would not be reasonable; it is based on coincidence. Just because two things happen to the same person, you cannot make a conclusion that one caused the other." | |

series of questions and instructions designed to lead students to decide if the conclusion is supportable or unsupportable. Below is a sample worksheet exercise.

Mrs. Asper was talking to her neighbor, Mr. Trump. Mrs. Asper told him she thought it would be terrible if he sold his house to the Parkinson family. Mrs. Asper said that the Parkinsons were from that terrible country Lispania. Her husband had been in the war against Lispania. She had worked with a person from Lispania who always came late to work and did not dress neatly. She said that if the Parkinsons moved into the neighborhood, it would never be the same.

1. What is Mrs. Asper's conclusion?
2. Did Mrs. Asper use evidence? If so, list the evidence used.
3. Would you be suspicious of Mrs. Asper's evidence? If so, explain why.
4. Are faulty arguments used? If so, tell which type.
5. Do you agree with Mrs. Asper's conclusion? Explain your answer.

When initially presenting exercises of this type, the teacher instructs the students to answer the questions one at a time, occasionally inserting additional instructions. More specifically, before students identify the author's argument, the teacher instructs the students to cross out all emotionally charged words. In the example above, the students would cross out the phrase *terrible country.* The teacher would also make sure the students explain why Mrs. Asper's opinions are unreliable. The teacher would check the students' answers to each item before instructing them to answer the next item.

After carefully monitoring student performance on several exercises, teachers should allow students to work independently. After students can successfully work items independently, they can omit the first four items, and just answer the question, "Do you agree with the author's conclusion? Explain your answer." In explaining their answers, students should discuss the reliability of the author's opinions, the evidence, and any faulty arguments. Working exercises of this final form is difficult and will require extensive practice. However, the practice should be provided because the skills are very important and should be taught until students master them.

## Implementing a Comprehension Program

Four basic steps in implementing a comprehension program are (1) placing the students appropriately, (2) setting up a motivation system, (3) preteaching critical vocabulary and strategies, and (4) establishing a follow-up system.

The first step is to place students at an appropriate point in a program. Teachers can do this by constructing placement tests for the specific program they are using (some commercial programs include testing procedures). The test can consist of several sample exercises from each of the various levels. Placement should be at a level where the student can do about 70–80% of the items correctly without any assistance from the teacher. This 70–80% level is based on the assumption that stu-

dents will be taught critical vocabulary and preskills before doing worksheet exercises; i.e., the teacher will present information students need to get the other 20–30% of the items correct. If the teacher does not plan on preteaching critical skills but just on having the students do the exercises with minimal teacher guidance, the percentage correct on the pretest should be closer to 85–90%. No program can guarantee 100% student success; students will occasionally make several errors on a set of items. However, students should average 85–90% correct. A high level of success is particularly important for students who are not intrinsically motivated. It will be more difficult to "turn on a kid" to school if the student encounters a great deal of failure.

The second step involves establishing a motivation system. With higher-performing, intrinsically motivated students, the system can be a limited one in which students simply record their performance each day and work toward meeting a certain quota. With less motivated students, a back-up reinforcer such as extra recess may be needed. See the section on developing student motivation for further details, including suggestions for recording the number of errors students make each day and rewarding improvements in performance.

The third step involves preteaching critical vocabulary and strategies needed to work the exercises. Teachers must be careful to teach in a manner that encourages students to use the skills taught and not constantly rely on the teacher for guidance. Strategies should be demonstrated on several sets of problems; then students should be expected to do problems independently.

The fourth step involves establishing a follow-up system in which the teacher ensures that students understand all items they missed on worksheet exercises. To be effective, a follow-up system should have the following characteristics:

1. Papers should be marked daily.
2. Students should have to redo any items missed. Note: If students are unable to figure out an answer, they circle the item or write a question mark.
3. The teacher should inspect the items the student redid to see if they are correct.
4. The teacher should work with students to diagnose the cause of failure on items which the student is unable to rework correctly; i.e., the teacher looks for a pattern of errors. First, the teacher determines if a decoding or vocabulary error caused the problem by having the student identify key words and tell their meaning. If the student identifies words and knows their meanings, the teacher might next ask questions to determine the strategy the student used when answering the item.
5. If the errors are caused by vocabulary or strategy deficits, the teacher must increase the amount of preteaching done on those skills and the amount of practice provided.
6. If the student misses many literal type questions or exhibits behavior of not examining questions carefully (i.e., answering a question like "Why did the captain turn the ship around?" with a yes or no answer), the remediation procedure should begin with a change in the motivation system. We have found that for most students increasing motivation leads to significant improvement in the quality and quantity of work.
7. If, after several weeks, a student's performance is significantly below other members of the group and there is no sign of gradual improvement, the teacher should consider placing the student in lower level material.

## Commercial Programs

As mentioned in the comprehension section for the primary grades (Section 3.5),

there are two basic commercial sources of comprehension exercises: the workbook component of basal reading series and supplementary comprehension programs. For low-performing students, we recommend the use of supplementary programs. Basal program workbooks usually have one or more of the following characteristics:

1. A lack of systematic development of skills from easy to more complex
2. A lack of adequate practice on component skills
3. Excessive use of terms and concepts with which some students will be unfamiliar
4. Unnecessarily complex directions which make it difficult for students to function independently.

Since the workbook components of most basal series do *not* contain questions related to the stories in the textbook, using a supplementary program will cause no problem.

Supplementary commercial comprehension programs come in two forms: general skill format and specific skill form. A general skill supplementary comprehension program includes exercises in which a passage is followed by various types of questions: inference, summarization, literal, and sequencing. Specific skill programs include exercises in which a passage will be followed by just one type of question. A specific skills series might include a series of workbooks or kits, each focusing on different skills. Unfortunately, teachers will not find supplementary programs to be panaceas. They too are not constructed in what we would consider an ideal manner. Few include definitive directions to the teacher on how to teach problem-solving strategies nor do they provide specific guidance in working corrections. Also, presently there are few programs that systematically teach the more complex inferential and critical reading skills discussed earlier in this section.

Some factors to look at when examining programs, either basal or supplementary, include these:

1. Significance of exercises. Does the program include summarization, inference, and critical reading? Few programs include critical reading. We believe in the future more programs will focus on this important skill.
2. A progression from simple to more complex skills.
3. Readability. The readability level of the selections in each unit should be at the level designated by the publisher. This point is critical. If a great number of selections differ significantly from the designated grade level, the program will not be suitable for independent use by the students without extensive preteaching of difficult words and concepts.
4. Clarity of directions. When a new skill is being taught, the students should be able to concentrate on that new skill. The directions should be brief and clear and the layout of the page simple. Simplicity of directions will allow a teacher to concentrate on the more significant skills rather than on explaining where to put answers.
5. Consistency in assignment length. When planning seatwork activities, it is useful if a teacher can predict how long an assignment will take students.
6. Practice. Sufficient practice when a skill is introduced and later review is important.

A program which is rather unique in its approach to comprehension is the comprehension component of the *SRA Corrective Reading Program* by S. Engelmann et al. (1978). Even though this program was constructed primarily to serve as a remedial program at the junior and senior high levels, it has been used quite successfully in the intermediate grades.

---

## RESEARCH

Extensive research has been conducted to determine what types of inferences students at different grade levels are able to make. A summary of intermediate grade studies reviewed by Roberge (1972) indicates that about 50% of the fourth, fifth, and sixth grade students studied could correctly make inferences in answering items of this form: "If metal is heated, it will expand. This metal glass was heated. Did it expand?"

Our own research in the areas of inferences has focused on procedures for teaching students to draw inferences based on abstract rules, which often occur in content area reading (Carnine, Kameenui, & Ludlow, 1978). The rule was, "The lower you eat on the food ladder, the more protein goes directly to you." Transfer questions were of the form, "Which food gives more protein directly to you, peanuts or fried chicken?" After a student answered, the teacher asked, "How do you know?" and the learner answered, "Peanuts are lower on the food ladder." The last question tested whether the learner applied the rule in arriving at an answer. We used primary grade students in comparing three rule teaching treatments:

1. Saying the rule and the key concept from the rule (the concept being "A food ladder has plants on the low step, little animals on the next step, and big animals on the high step")
2. Working application items relating to the key concept in addition to rule and concept saying
3. working rule application items in addition to concept application items and rule and concept saying.

Only students in the third treatment responded correctly to transfer items at a level significantly higher than chance. The results suggest that merely saying a rule and even learning the key concept from a rule are not sufficient to ensure that students can apply a rule. Direct application exercises seem necessary to ensure successful applications. Further research is needed to determine how and when various inference principles are best taught.

Student performance on drawing inferences depends on more than the difficulty of the relationship on which the inference is based. As discussed earlier in this section, the question of whether a relationship is explicitly stated, the ease with which relevant information can be applied, the dispersal of relevant information in a passage, and presence of distractors all potentially affect students' performance on drawing inferences. A study to evaluate the impact of these four variables was conducted by Golick, Kameenui, and Carnine (1978). Although not all combinations of the four variables were presented in passages, results indicated that when a relationship is stated and direct information is provided, distractors and separating relevant information detract from inference performance. Also, stories without a stated relationship and with indirect information were more difficult than those with a stated relationship and direct information.

Research on the role of syntax is sometimes interpreted as indicating a hierarchy of difficulty, beginning with simple, affirmative sentences such as, "The girls went to the store" followed by negative sentences, passive sentences, and passive negative sentences (Athey, 1977). Various approaches to identifying difficulty hierarchies have been taken. One is to count the frequency of children's speech patterns, either spoken or from children's literature. Four of the five studies illustrating this approach that were reviewed by Collins, et al. (1977) suggest that more frequent structures are easier for students to comprehend. However, they also found that in certain contexts, frequency of a structure is not a reliable predictor of difficulty; i.e., when negative or passive constructions are expected, they tend to be easier, which is usually not the case. Finally, they noted that certain types of examples of a structure are more difficult; i.e., reversible passives such as "The boy was kissed by the girl" are more difficult than nonreversible passives such as "The car was kissed by the girl." While a girl can be kissed by a boy, a girl is never kissed by a car. The instructional impli-

cations of these findings is that since syntactic structures do differ in difficulty, teachers should be aware of the syntactic complexity of materials used in the classroom and of student competency with various syntactic forms.

A second area of research addresses the relative importance of syntax and semantics in comprehension. Siler (1973–74) suggested that syntax is the single most important dimension available to students when they read. Syntactic violations of prose resulted in more oral reading errors than semantic prose violations for second and fourth graders. Siler interpreted several other studies as supporting the relative importance of syntax over semantics. In contrast, a review by Jenkins & Pany (1977) focused on comprehension rather than oral reading errors as a dependent measure. Reviewing studies which used comprehension as a dependent measure, Jenkins and Pany found that syntactic variations had a relatively slight impact on comprehension. We could possibly reconcile these disparate findings by saying that syntactic violations greatly affect oral reading but not comprehension. From our perspective, such an interpretation is unnecessary. We assume that students must be able to decode and understand sentences reflecting differing semantic and syntactic content. Consequently, we would interpret these findings as supporting the importance of both aspects of reading.

A final area of research on syntax has to do with educational interventions; teaching procedures can improve student comprehension or decoding of various syntactic forms. Carnine & Kameenui (1978) evaluated the procedures outlined in this section for teaching students to transform sentences with passive voice or clause constructions into simpler forms. Three third graders who did not consistently respond to comprehension questions based on sentences with passive constructions or clauses served as subjects. The training was introduced to subjects one at a time. As a control for practice effects, subjects not receiving training worked the same training items as subjects receiving training. Performance on transfer items did not improve merely from practice and feedback but did improve for each subject after training was initiated. Since the research was conducted with brief paragraphs, the generalizability of the procedures to students' reading longer passages requires further research. Other intervention studies have involved alterations of the material the students read. For example, Mason and Kendall (1978) found that low ability readers benefited from shortened and segmented sentences. This finding is consistent with those reported at the beginning of this section; simpler syntactic forms result in fewer decoding errors. Interventions based on simplifying the sentences in a passage must be approached carefully, however. As Pearson (1976) stated:

> What happens can be explained as a trade-off relationship between explicitness on one hand and simplicity on the other. The causal relationship in (36) is explicit. If one rewrites (36) as (37), he has reduced grammatical complexity and average sentence length, but he has placed a new inferential burden on the reader.
>
> (36) Because the chain broke, the machine stopped.
> (37) The chain broke. The machine stopped.
>
> What was previously complex but explicit becomes simple but implicit. (p. 100)

In summary, research findings suggest that syntactic structures do vary in difficulty, that both syntactic and semantic aspects of sentences are important in teaching reading, and that teaching students to deal with increasingly complex syntactic structures is not only possible but preferable to always simplifying the syntactic structure of sentences in passages.

## APPLICATION EXERCISES

1. Label each passage with an *RS* (relationship stated), *PKA* (prior knowledge assumed), and *IIP* (information for induction provided).

    _____ Fresher vegetables contain more vitamins. The two pounds of carrots in the blue bag were picked today. The two pounds of carrots in the red bag were picked three days ago. Which carrots have more vitamin A?

    _____ The two pounds of carrots on the ground have four hundred units of vitamin A. They were picked today. The two pounds of carrots on the table have two hundred units of vitamin A. They were picked a week ago. The two pounds of carrots in the can were picked yesterday. Which carrots have the most vitamin A?

    _____ These carrots are all from the same garden. The two pounds in the sack were picked today. The two pounds in the box were picked a week ago. Which carrots have more vitamins?

2. Specify what the teacher would say to correct a student who answered the question below incorrectly.

    "Fresher vegetables contain more vitamins," Mrs. Ampston told her boy, Robbie. "When you go to the store always try to buy the freshest vegetables." Saturday morning Robbie went shopping for his mother. When he got to the vegetable counter he asked the man about carrots. The man told him they had two types of carrots, Mighty-Fine carrots and Blue Label carrots. Mighty-Fine carrots were delivered to the store Tuesday. They were from the biggest farm in the state. They were also on sale today, one pound for 36¢. Blue Label carrots had been delivered just after the store opened this morning. They were packed in plain wrappers and cost 38¢ a pound. They had been grown on a small farm outside the city.

    Which carrots should Robbie buy? (The student answers Mighty-Fine carrots.)

3. For each of the following selections:
    a. Identify the author's conclusion
    b. List the evidence
    c. Determine the author's trustworthiness by indicating whether she is qualified or has biases

    d. Identify any faulty arguments

- Mr. Ragster had been a top race car driver and mechanic when he was young. Now he was a salesman for the Snazy Truck Company. Mr. Ragster had heard that Kevin McNeer wanted to buy a new truck. Wednesday morning Mr. Ragster called Kevin. He said "Kevin, you should buy a Snazy truck. Your Dad always drove a Snazy truck. I bet I sold him 10 different Snazy trucks. *Automotive News,* a magazine that has reports on trucks, says that the new Snazy truck gets better mileage than any truck that is comparably priced. You'd be making a mistake if you didn't buy a Snazy truck."

- Tom Jackson was a star baseball player. He worked for the Ace Toothpaste Company during the winter. He said, "I think Ace toothpaste is the best toothpaste there is. I have white shiny teeth and I use Ace toothpaste. If you want bright shiny teeth, you too should use Ace toothpaste."

4. For each of the following inference items, state the problem statement and the information students must know to answer the item correctly.

    a. Tim lived in San Francisco. Bill lived in New York. When waking up each morning, one of the boys would look out his window and watch the sun rise over the ocean. Tell which boy. Tell why you chose that boy.

    b. Janice was a star athlete. She hoped to make the Olympic team; however, first she wanted to complete medical school. It is now 1978. Janice has 3 years of medical school left. Do you think Janice will try out for the next Olympics? Why?

    c. Bill and Susan were carpenters who were building a house. They had completed everything except putting the floor in. Jack, their good friend, told them that he had lots of cedar wood left over and would sell it to them for a cheap price. Do you think they will buy the cedar? Why?

5. Which two of the following four sentences would not be good items for a passive voice exercise?

    a. The dog was put in the house by Tom. Who was put in the house?

    b. Bill was put in the house by Bob. Who was put in the house?

    c. Ann is getting a scolding from Jill. Who is scolding?

    d. Ann is getting a scolding from her mother. Who is scolding?

6. (Review. See sequencing and summarization in Section 3.5.) Briefly describe the strategy you would teach students who were having difficulty with the following types of problems:

    a. sequencing items that called for students to place sequential numbers in front of a group of sentences describing events from a passage

    b. summarization items like the one below:

    *Passage:*

    Bill was an unusually persistent boy. He wasn't a super student but he worked very hard. He studied one hour each morning before going to school. At school he always paid attention. At night he would only watch television after he completed his work.

    *Item*

    What sentence best describes this passage:

    Bill doesn't like TV.

    Bill gets up early.

    Bill is a good student.

    Bill goes to school.

7. (Review)

The following words are to appear in passages the students will be reading several days from now. Write *V* in front of each word that should be included in a vocabulary exercise. Write _D_ in front of each word that should be included in a decoding exercise.

| | | |
|---|---|---|
| _____ anvil | _____ bragging | _____ reins |
| _____ enjoyment | _____ uranium | _____ alley |
| _____ breech | _____ efficient | _____ coil |
| _____ harmlessly | _____ plague | _____ deerskin |
| _____ suffix | _____ pollster | _____ choir |

# SECTION 4.5

## Reading Instruction in the Content Area Textbook

by Anita Archer

The major emphasis in the intermediate grades should move from learning to read to reading to learn. Intermediate children begin extensive reading in expository materials such as content area textbooks and reference books designed to convey factual information or to explain what is difficult to understand. These materials differ substantially from the narrative or story material generally found in code-emphasis and meaning-emphasis basals. New organizational structures are used, the vocabulary is often more difficult to decode and understand, unique typographic features as well as graphics are introduced, and the density of concepts is higher. Not only are the characteristics of expository materials more difficult for the naive reader to cope with, the demands placed on the reader also increase. The reader is expected to extract, integrate, and retain significant main ideas and details presented in the material and to learn many specialized vocabulary terms; expectations seldom demanded in narrative reading. Because of the unique characteristics of expository materials and the demands placed on the reader, explicit instruction in reading and

understanding expository materials must be provided the intermediate student, beginning with the classroom content area textbooks.

This section focuses on content area lessons beginning with an analysis of the differences between expository and narrative materials. Following that discussion is an overview of how written assignments should be constructed for passages in content area textbooks. Next is a discussion of the steps a teacher takes in preparing students to read expository selections and to do written assignments. After the section on preparing students, directions for actually giving the written assignment and conducting follow-up exercises are discussed.

## Characteristics of Expository Materials

Before discussing teaching procedures for content area textbooks, it is helpful to examine the unique characteristics of expository materials and some of the problems that these characteristics might pose to the naive reader. To illustrate these characteristics, examine Figure 4.5.1, a selection from a fifth grade science book.

## Vocabulary

One of the major differences between narrative and expository materials is the vocabulary used. The vocabulary of content area material is often more difficult to decode and pronounce than that found in narrative material. For example, in the selection in Figure 4.5.1, the child must decode the words *igneous, sedimentary, metamorphic, average, diagram, kilometers, regions, magma,* and *photograph.* The density of multi-syllabic words and words containing unfamiliar morphemes increases the decoding difficulty of expository materials.

Pronunciation is made more difficult by lack of familiarity with the words and their absence from the child's listening or speaking vocabulary. Though the child may use appropriate decoding strategies, he may make slight errors in pronunciation because of his inability to correct the pronunciation against his known vocabulary.

The challenges posed by expository vocabulary go beyond decoding. Expository materials are more likely to include vocabulary terms that are hard to understand or unfamiliar to the child. It is unlikely that the child has had an opportunity to use such terms as *igneous, sedimentary,* or *metamorphic* in his own speech or has had much prior exposure to their meanings. Expository materials not only present a large number of new vocabulary terms but also include technical terms (e.g., *kilometers*), words used in unusual ways (e.g., "*pockets* of hot liquid rock"), symbols and abbreviations to convey concepts or to replace vocabulary terms (e.g., 1290°F, 700°C), and figures of speech.

Not only is the vocabulary difficult to decode and unfamiliar to the reader, but the terms are often presented in rapid succession. For example, in one paragraph the terms *molten rock, magma,* and *igne-*

*ous* are presented using definitions or contextual cues but with little elaboration. Children, particularly children new to the content area or naive readers in expository materials, will need careful preparation in order to handle the vocabulary load found in content area selections.

## Content

In addition to the vocabulary terms, the general content of expository materials is often beyond the child's experiences. While narrative stories generally focus on situations, events, or concepts that the child has dealt with or been exposed to, expository materials include content that is new and unique to the child. Within the illustrated passage, the reader is introduced to various rock formations, the process of erosion, the various layers of the earth's rock, and the formation of igneous rocks. The content includes many unfamiliar concepts as well as a much higher density of ideas than found in narrative materials.

## Style and Organization

Expository material is usually written in a terse, straightforward style with explanation minimized, a pattern seldom found in narrative materials. The organization of ideas presented in narrative and expository materials often differs. In narrative or story selections, there is generally a gradual building of sequential events or related ideas, climaxing near the end of the selection and tapering to the selection's conclusion. The reader is literally carried by the author from event to event, from situation to situation, from idea to idea. Unlike narrative materials that provide a continuous, uninterrupted stream of information, expository materials usually segment the selection into a number of topics delineated by headings and subheadings. Like a huge puzzle, each paragraph provides an explicit or inferred main idea with suppor-

**FIGURE 4.5.1**

We live on a planet that is always changing. Sometimes we can see the changes taking place. But more often they take place too slowly for us to notice. Maybe you have been lucky enough to have seen an erupting volcano spilling red hot rock out over the land. If you have, you watched one of the most dramatic changes that takes place on our planet.

Discuss the question, "Is Earth's surface changing?" See TM.

What happens to the hot liquid rock that wells up through cracks in the top layer of Earth, called the crust, and spills out over the land? It cools and hardens, yes. But what happens to it a year later, a century later, or a million years later?

Rain, wind, and frost slowly wear this rock away by breaking it down into tiny pieces. The pieces are blown overland by the wind, or they are washed away by streams and rivers and carried to the sea. There they are spread out over the sea floor. Century after century, one layer settles on top of another and still another layer on that one, and so the layering continues.

**178**

The older and deeper layers are packed tighter and tighter. They are pressed and squeezed together by the great weight of the materials on top. During this pressing and squeezing the packed material is slowly cemented together and becomes new rock. Often this new rock is later churned up, folded, and twisted. Then, over a period of several million years, the rock may be pushed upward, to form new mountains.

After the children have read the text, take a walk and observe natural changes that are taking place on Earth. See TM for discussion.

See TM for Additional Activities and Correlating Suggestions.

Over many, many more years, the rocks of a new mountain also are worn and broken down by wind and weather. The rocks beneath our feet are changing, too. To find out more about the way these rocks are changed, let's take a close look at the three main kinds of rocks. They are igneous (ig'nē əs), sedimentary (sed ə men'tə rē), and metamorphic (met'ə môr'fik) rock.

Lesson 2—See TM for Teaching Strategy.

## IGNEOUS ROCK

First Day

The solid rock forming Earth's crust, or top layer, is very thin. If Earth were an apple, the top layer of rock would be nearly as thin as the skin of the apple. Actually, the average thickness of the crust under the continents is 20 miles (35 kilometers). Under the oceans, the crust is much thinner.

As the diagram shows on page 180, <u>most of Earth is made up of the mantle rock</u>. The mantle is nearly 1800 miles (3000 kilometers) deep. The rock making up both the mantle and the deep regions of the crust is very hot. It may be up to about 1290°F (700°C) in the crust and much hotter than that in the mantle.

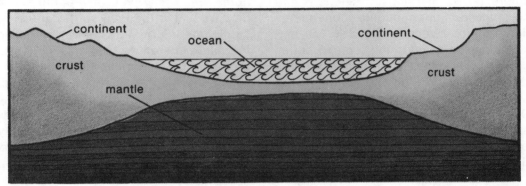

**179**

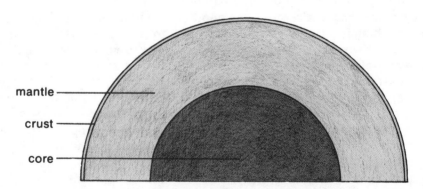

It is not surprising then, to find here and there in the crust, pockets of hot, liquid rock that can be squeezed and pushed around this way or that. More of this molten rock, called <u>magma</u> (mag′mə), may also be in the mantle. Our first main kind of rock, igneous rock, is <u>made of magma that has cooled and hardened</u>. The word "igneous" comes from the Latin word *igneus,* which means fiery.

From Teacher's Edition of *Intermediate Level* A of the GINN SCIENCE PROGRAM by J. Myron Atkin and others,
Copyright © 1975.

tive details which, when combined with other paragraphs, define a single topic. These topical segments in turn are combined with other segments to form an overall body of knowledge. For example, the selection in Figure 4.5.1 begins with introductory paragraphs that present the chapter's theme and content outline. Each of the subsequent major headings introduces a different type of rock formation. Within each of these major sections, subheadings indicate topics directly related to the major heading. To develop the topic, a series of paragraphs, each containing a main idea and supportive details, follows each subheading.

Other characteristics of organizational design also contribute to the complexity of expository materials. For example, cause and effect relationships and comparisons are prevalent in expository materials, particularly in science and social studies textbooks. These relationships occur less often in narrative materials. Inverted time sequences are also found in expository materials but seldom in story material. Within narrative materials, the discourse is smooth and seldom disturbed until the selection's conclusion. However, expository reading is interrupted by subheadings and headings; referrals to glossaries and pronunciation keys; and references to graphic aids. These complex organizational patterns and disruptions in the discourse can pose problems for the naive reader who has not been systematically introduced to this type of organizational design.

## Special Features

Narrative stories have few special features outside of the title and occasional illustrations. The student, however, must cope with and attend to many special features in content area material. Graphics and illustrations that accompany narrative stories are included to enhance enjoyment and interest and to enrich the story. Graphics and illustrations found in expository materials, on the other hand, contribute directly to the information presented either by supplementing or expanding on concepts found in the discourse. In narrative materials, the student need not examine illustrations with any intensity. However, in expository materials, she must scrutinize graphics and illustrations with special attention given to the title and explanatory notes. Each new type of graphic aid must be carefully introduced so that the student can locate information, make comparisons, formulate inferences, and draw conclusions based on the information presented. In the selection on igneous rocks, two diagrams are presented illustrating the various layers of rock found in the earth. Though the written discourse discusses the various layers of rock (e.g., the crust, mantle and core), their interrelationships are not clear until the student has examined the labeled graphics.

## Content Area Lessons

Content area lessons should be designed to promote *mastery of the salient information* presented in the selection and *acquisition of critical reading study skills* that can be applied to other expository materials and at the same time, *foster independence in the learners.* This is a difficult but important balance to reach. Often teachers give total responsibility to students for reading the selection and completing written assignments. Though independence is maximized in this case, the lack of preparation for reading and guidance given may result in lowered comprehension and inadequate use of reading study skills. On the other hand, teachers may provide extensive preparatory exercises and direction to all students, across all selections throughout the year. Though this might provide for mastery of the information and for an excellent introduction to critical reading study skills, it would not foster student responsibility for learning or independent use of previously taught reading study skills. For the majority of elementary students and the majority of selections found in content area textbooks, a compromise between these extremes should be reached. Preparation and guidance should be limited to critical passage variables, should be gradually faded as the students become more sophisticated in their reading, and should be matched to individual learner needs. To accommodate learner differences, it will not be possible to provide the same instruction to all students. Preparation, written assignments, amounts of the textbook to be read, and time allotted for reading may need to be varied for groups of learners at various skill levels. On a specific selection, one group may be able to read the selection independently and complete the written assignment; another group may need extensive preparation and guidance; and still another group may be able to complete the reading and written assignment after minimal preparation.

Content area lessons generally include the following steps: preparation for passage reading, silent reading of the selection, completion of written assignments, and follow-up on passage reading and assignments. During the preparation step prior to reading, instruction is presented on significant variables within the material (e.g., new vocabulary, difficult to decode vocabulary, unique graphics, or a unique organizational pattern) that can contribute to passage comprehension. Preparatory exercises may also include a survey of the passage's content. Usually these activities are followed by silent reading of the passage and independent completion of written assignments. Assistance in selection of appropriate silent reading rates and strategies for completing assignments may also be provided as preparatory activities. When written assignments are complete, assignments may be corrected and discussed, and information in the selection is reviewed and/or extended using additional resources. The selection may also be used

to teach additional reading study skills such as scanning, skimming, summary writing, outlining, interpretation of graphics, and critical comprehension (see Section 4.6).

To determine the critical aspects of the selection to be stressed in each of these steps, the teacher must first decide what information students will be expected to learn. Many selections are too long and complex for students to be held accountable for everything contained in the selection. Likewise, the teacher cannot preteach all aspects of every selection. By deciding what students should learn, the teacher provides a focus not only for reading a selection but also for preparing antecedent activities to facilitate student success within the selection. Since decisions about what students are expected to learn are best made by specifying responses to be made following reading (e.g., answering questions, completing a chart, filling in an outline), the first step in planning a content area lesson is to construct a written assignment. After the teacher has identified questions or other written responses that students will be required to make, the specific vocabulary, graphics, and organizational patterns can be scrutinized for difficult aspects that should be included in the preparation activities. Similarly, an analysis of the critical aspects of the selection helps in identifying strategies that students may need to apply as they read the selection.

## Constructing Written Assignments

Written assignments may include answering unit or end-of-chapter questions, summarizing information in the passage, outlining the chapter's content or utilizing the information to independently complete a visual representation of the information. Written assignments not only firm up the information by summarizing salient points but also provide children with practice in written expression. Within the primary grades, mastery of knowledge is usually ascertained through verbal responses or minimal written responses (e.g., circling answers, filling in the blank, or selecting the correct answer from a number of choices). As children approach secondary

**FIGURE 4.5.2** *Written Assignment—Outline*

Chapter 7, Sections 1 and 2

Ginn Science Program, Intermediate Level A

*Directions:* Read this content guide *before* you read the chapter. What information should you learn about rocks? What information is important to think about? After reading the content guide, put it away and read the chapter. When you finish reading, try to fill out as much of the outline as possible without the book then look for answers in your book.

I. The earth's layers.

    A. _____

    B. _____

    C. _____

II. Igneous Rocks

    A. Igneous rock is made of _____ .

        1. To become igneous rock, magma must _____ .

        2. Magma that has welled up and spread over the land or sea is called

        _____ .

        3. A mountain formed from magma is called a _____ .

    B. Types of igneous rock

        1. Rock that cools on the surface has _____ grains.

        2. _____ and _____ are examples of igneous rock that has cooled on the surface.

        3. Rock that cools underground has _____ grains.

        4. _____ and _____ are examples of igneous rock that cools underground.

III. Sedimentary rocks.

    A. Sedimentary rocks are made from _____ .

        1. Sediment includes pieces of _____ and _____ , and

        _____ .

        2. Sediment is carried to the oceans by _____ .

        3. Sediment collects on the bottom of _____ and _____ .

        4. Sedimentary rock is formed when _____ .

    B. Types of sedimentary rock.

        1. Shale

            a. Shale is made from _____ .

            b. Clay turns into solid rock when _____ .

        2. Sandstone

            a. Sandstone is made from _____ .

            b. Sandstone is formed when _____ .

        3. Limestone

            a. Limestone is made from _____ .

            b. Limestone is formed when _____ .

**FIGURE 4.5.3**   *Written Assignment—Map Outline*

Chapter 7, Sections 1, 2, 3, and 4

*Directions:* This chapter discusses the nervous system. Look at this outline. Read the chapter carefully. When you are done try to fill in the boxes of this outline. Use the words under the outline to fill in the boxes.

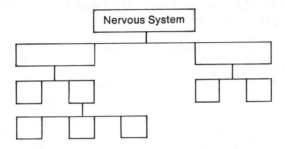

cerebrum, brain, motor nerves, cerebellum, central nervous system, sense nerves, medulla, peripheral nervous system, spine

school levels, written responses (e.g., sentences, paragraphs, reports, and summaries) almost totally supplant verbal responses. Children can be handicapped in secondary schools by a lack of writing skills promoted by little practice in elementary school. For this reason, written responses are appropriate and necessary additions to the content area lesson.

When writing or selecting questions for written assignments, the teacher should use the following criteria. The questions should (1) stress *major* concepts presented in the material, not insignificant facts, (2) include both literal and inferential comprehension responses, (3) go beyond yes and no responses, and (4) be well worded to promote ease of interpretation. Since one

**FIGURE 4.5.4**   *Written Assignment—Chart*

Chapter 7, Sections 1, 2, and 3

Ginn Science Program, Intermediate Level A

*Directions:* This chapter will tell you about *three types of rocks.* Look carefully at this chart. What should you learn about each type of rock? Read the chapter carefully. When you finish reading, try to fill out some of the chart. How much did you remember? Use your book to fill out the rest of the chart.

| TYPE OF ROCK | What is this type of rock made from? | How is this type of rock formed? | What are some examples of this type of rock? (name appearance) |
|---|---|---|---|
| Igneous Rock | | | |
| Metamorphic Rock | | | |
| Sedimentary Rock | | | |

**FIGURE 4.5.5**   *Written Assignment—Diagram*

Concepts in Science
pages 278 to 280

*Directions:* These pages talk about the digestive system. Read this content guide before you read the chapter. What information should you look for? What is important? Read the chapter. Try to answer the questions and label the diagram without your book. Check your answers with the book.

Digestive System

Label the parts of the
digestive system:
  mouth
  salivary glands
  stomach
  small intestine
  large intestine

Draw an arrow beginning
at the mouth to show
where the food goes.

Questions on the digestive system.

1. Where does food enter the body?
2. What helps you break up the food?
3. What mixes with the food to help you swallow?
4. Where does the food go from your mouth?
5. What happens to the food in your stomach?
6. What happens to the food in your small intestine?
7. Where does the dissolved food go when it passes through the wall of the small intestine?

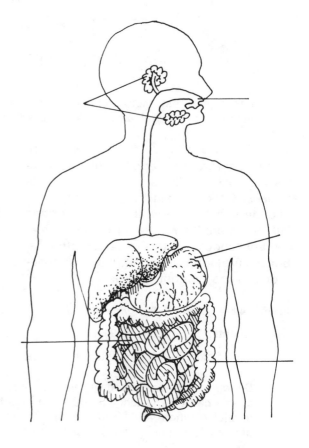

of the purposes of the questions is to ascertain passage understanding, the majority of questions should be "passage dependent," that is, the answers should be based on passage information rather than solely on experiential background. The answers should also involve significant concepts and relationships. Often teachers and authors write questions that focus on insignificant facts rather than main ideas. As a result, students become detail seekers who cannot separate the important from the unimportant. Teachers can change this pattern through the prudent selection of questions. Ask yourself, "What do I *really* want the children to remember from this selection?"

In addition to sets of written questions, written assignments can take many other forms: outlines, flow charts, time lines,

**FIGURE 4.5.6**  *Written Assignment—Flow Chart*

Concepts in Science
pages 278–280

*Directions:* Today you will be reading about the digestive system. After you read
the section on the digestive system, you will be completing this flow chart to tell
what happens at each point in the digestive system. Read carefully so that you
can fill in your flow chart.

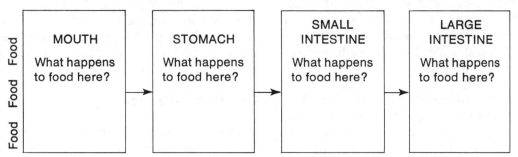

diagrams, maps, bar graphs, pictographs, and vocabulary summaries (see Figures 4.5.2–4.5.6). Potential advantages of these items include : visual representation of the information to facilitate recall ; illustration of relationships among concepts, main ideas, and supportive details; increased student interest; and reinforcement of other study skills (e.g., writing outlines, reading charts, and interpreting graphs). Partially completed outlines are particularly useful written assignments. Outlines not only demonstrate the organization of information within the selection and relationships among ideas, but they also can serve as the initial introduction to independent note-taking and outlining.

The form of the written assignment, though partially determined by the sophistication of the students, depends primarily on the content organization. If the material has a chronological pattern, a flow chart or time line might be used. If the discourse stresses spatial relationships, a diagram or sketch might be used to summarize the relevant information. If the content stresses comparisons or contrasts, graphic representation might be appropriate. However, in most expository discourse the unifying factor is not time or space, but the ideas

or facts. Outlines can be used to summarize this information.

### Accommodating Individual Differences

Because student reading and written expression skills differ, assignments given to children should reflect these differences. Assignments should be difficult enough to challenge the learner but not so difficult that they defeat the learner. The following variables within the written assignment can be altered to match individual differences: the number of responses demanded, the sophistication of the responses (e.g., completing simple questions rather than filling in a comparative time line), the amount of writing demanded to complete the responses (e.g., sentences versus paragraphs), the difficulty of the responses (e.g., literal versus inferential or critical comprehension), and the amount of prompting provided to assist the learner in completing the responses (e.g., direct instruction on a response strategy, page number cues for locating the answer, key words highlighted in the question). For example, more naive readers might be required to complete 10 questions on the material. A question answering strategy would be taught before the written assignment was given. Underlined key words and page number references would be provided to assist the learners in locating and verifying their answers. A more sophisticated group of readers might be given this same set of questions without the highlighted key words, page references, and instruction on question answering. In addition, some extra questions might be added to the assignment. While the more naive readers might be required to write word or phrase answers, the higher group might be required to write full sentence answers and paragraph summaries. A group of very sophisticated readers might be required to complete the set of questions without any prompts and to write a written summary of the most salient information presented. Though the assignments might be differentiated across groups throughout the school year, the difficulty of items should gradually be increased for all learners as their reading and writing skills improve.

# Preparation for Selection Reading

When critical information that students will be held accountable for has been determined and translated into written assignments, the other steps in the content area lesson can be initiated. The first step, preparing students for selection reading, is designed to preteach or alert students to significant variables within the material (e.g., new vocabulary, difficult to decode vocabulary, organizational patterns, new graphics) that will facilitate comprehension and extraction of the desired information.

The amount of preparation needed for a given selection depends on the complexity of the material, the experience of the children with the given textbook, the reading level of the children, and their familiarity with the topic. Certainly, the fourth grade student reading the first selection in her new social studies book will need substantially more preparation than the more advanced student. Just as the written assignments must be matched to learner needs, so must the amount and type of preparation. Though most students will require some teacher direction to successfully read a selection and complete an accompanying assignment, these interventions should only be used when necessary and should be gradually faded as the learners become more competent readers in expository materials.

## Decoding Assistance

When selecting words for decoding instruction, the teacher should focus on words that are difficult "stopper" words, central to the understanding of the passage, and whose pronunciations are not cued within the discourse. When presenting the words, the teacher should not restrict the presentation to whole word methodology. Instead, she should capitalize on the decoding skills that have been introduced to the children: phonic, structural, and contextual analysis.

In designing prior instruction on decoding of vocabulary, the teacher should begin by carefully selecting the words. Words can be listed on the board and introduced individually, leading the children to use the desired decoding strategy. To assist children in using structural analysis, the root might be listed first followed by the derivative. The teacher identifies words that are quite irregular and probably unfamiliar to the students. The following lesson based on a fifth grade science lesson will illustrate these procedures (see Figure 4.5.7).

To ensure that students receive adequate practice to become fluent at reading words from the content areas, the teacher might prepare dittoed lists of new words introduced each week, distribute the lists to the students, provide practice time, and set up a check out system in which each student is tested on reading the words either by the teacher or a peer.

A potentially important aspect of decoding instruction in content areas involves directly teaching children to use the phonetic spelling often found in parentheses following foreign words or difficult to pronounce words in elementary content materials. The teacher should not assume that children will be able to use these prompts without direct instruction, substantial practice, and occasional review of the process. Begin by examining the textbook and determining the pronunciation key used for respelling in the text. The following were extracted from two science texts.

*Ginn Science*
(Ginn and Company, 1975)

| | |
|---|---|
| igneous | ig' nē es |
| sedimentary | sed ə men' tə re |
| metamorphic | met' ə môr' fik |

*Modern Elementary Science*
(Holt, Rinehart and Winston, 1971)

| | |
|---|---|
| vegetarians | veh-juh-TAIR-ee-unz |
| algae | AL-jee |
| aphids | AY-fids |
| forsythia | for-SITH-ee-uh |

As noted in these examples, some authors use pronunciation keys similar to those

---

**FIGURE 4.5.7** *Lesson Example—Prior Instruction on Decoding of Difficult Words*

Step 1. Examination of text and selection of words.

Difficult words to decode that are crucial to passage understanding: countdown, spacecraft, gravitation, gravitational force, unbalanced, investigate, apprentice, inference, astronaut, and Isaac Newton.

Step 2. Select a decoding strategy you plan to stress with each word.

*Structural analysis:* countdown, spacecraft, gravitation, gravitational force, unbalanced, inference, apprentice, astronaut, Newton

*Phonic and contextual analysis:* none

*Whole word approach:* Isaac.

Step 3. Write on the board to stress desired strategy.

New Words

| | |
|---|---|
| spacecraft | infer |
| gravity | inference |
| gravitation | invest |
| gravitational | investigate |
| balance | countdown |
| unbalance | apprentice |
| unbalanced | astronaut |
| | Isaac Newton |

Step 4. Present the words to the children stressing the desired decoding skill.

(See detailed step 4)

Step 5. Drill the children on the words until they are firm using group and individual responses.

*Figure 4.5.7 cont'd.*

## Step 4.    Presentation to Children

| Teacher | Word Written on Board | Child Response |
|---|---|---|
| a. "Listen. These words are from your chapter, 'Man and Earth—Their Journeys in Space.' You may know some of the words, but wait for the signal before saying the word." | | |
| b. "The first two words are compound words. A compound word has two real words. Say the first small word in this compound word. Say the second small word." "What's the whole word?" Repeat step b with *spacecraft*. | Countdown | "Count" "Down" "Countdown" |
| | Spacecraft | "Space, Craft" "Spacecraft" |
| c. "Read this root word." (signal) "Each of these words is made from the root word, *gravity*. What is their root word?" (signal) | Gravity | "Gravity" |
| | *Gravit*ation *Gravit*ational Gravitation | "Gravity" |
| "This word ends with t-i-o-n. What do we say?" (signal) "Ready to read this word." (Pause) "What word?" | | "Shun" "Gravitation" |
| (Point to *al*) "What do we say for these letters?" "Ready to read this word." (Pause) "What word?" Continue same format for *un(balance)d*, *(infer)ence, and (invest)igate*. Remember to use a fast pace to maintain interest. | Gravitational | "ul" "Gravitational" |
| d. "Let's review these words quickly. When I touch the word, you say it." | List of words presented thus far | Children say each word on signal. |
| "This time I am going to mix up the list. When I touch the word, you say it." | | Children say each word on signal. |
| e. "Let's say each part of this word." Point to ap          prent          ice "What word?" | Ap prent ice | "Ap" "Prent" "Ice" "Apprentice" |
| f. "Let's say each part of this word. We say ō for this letter." (point to o) Point to astro          naut "What word?" | Astro naut | "Astro" "Naut" "Astronaut" |

*Figure 4.5.7 cont'd.*

| Teacher | Word Written on Board | Child Response |
|---|---|---|
| g. "The next word is the name of the scientist in the chapter. His first name is Isaac. What is his first name?" | Isaac Newton | "Isaac" |
| "Ready to read his last name." (pause) "What word?" (signal) | | "Newton" |
| h. Present all words until the students identify them correctly. | | |
| i. Individual turns may be given if felt desirable. | | |

found in glossaries and dictionaries, while others use phonetic respellings. After discovering the system used by the author, the teacher should present lessons that teach the children to use this decoding strategy. The teacher should present the pronunciation system, demonstrate decoding of words using the system, lead children through decoding of unknown words written in the author's style, and finally test the children on their use of this strategy. If the pronunciation system is very complex and difficult to interpret or will directly interfere with use of the dictionary pronunciation system used in the classroom, you may elect not to introduce the pronunciation key and instead present the words using direct instruction.

## Vocabulary Assistance

Since vocabulary understanding is critical for passage comprehension, the teacher should include vocabulary instruction in his preparatory activities. The teacher must begin by examining the chapter or selection and carefully selecting words for instruction. Words for vocabulary instruction should be limited to a small number of words that are crucial for passage understanding and beyond the children's experiential background. Children should not be overwhelmed with a large number of difficult to understand words in a single pre-

sentation. Critical words should be carefully introduced, practiced, and reviewed in subsequent lessons.

In this book, we have discussed a number of strategies for vocabulary instruction that apply equally well to content area instruction: (1) teaching through examples, (2) teaching through a synonym, (3) teaching through definitions, (4) locating the meaning in the dictionary, (5) determining the meaning using morphemic analysis, and (6) teaching the use of context clues. Though all of these strategies can be used in content materials, emphasis should be placed on developing contextual analysis. Since authors of elementary textbooks realize that many of the words will not be in the children's experiential background, explicit and inferred context clues are generally given. Contextual analysis is a student's major tool for vocabulary expansion. Because contextual analysis can be used by the reader when no instructor is present, proficiency in its use leads to independent vocabulary growth. Many children (and adults) have developed the habit of reading right past unfamiliar words. Direct instruction on contextual analysis will alert children to the use of these clues and encourage them to hunt for the word's meaning within the discourse.

Following selection of words for vocabulary instruction, the teacher can use the following guidelines to determine the best teaching strategy:

1. *Contextual analysis:* Does the author include a definition, explanation, or synonym for the word? Can a definition or synonym be inferred from the discourse? If you answered *yes* to either of these questions, the words should be presented to the children using the context presented in the text. If contextual analysis cannot be used, consider one of the remaining strategies.

2. *Morphemic analysis:* Does the derivative include meaningful free and bound morphemes? Do the combined meanings of the free and bound morphemes lead to an appropriate definition of the unknown word? If these questions cannot be answered in the affirmative and contextual analysis is not appropriate, another strategy should be selected.

3. *Examples, synonyms, definitions, or dictionary use:* As discussed earlier, teaching through examples should only be done when the children do not understand words that would be used to explain the meaning of the unknown word; a situation that is less likely to occur in the intermediate grades. Synonym instruction can be used when the child knows a word with a similar meaning to the new vocabulary term. Definitions are used when a single word or phrase synonym will not suffice and more explanation is needed. If you are also teaching dictionary or glossary skills, dictionary determination of the meaning would be appropriate. In order to give children practice in determining the appropriate meaning for the word, the vocabulary term used should be presented in its context.

In summary, the following steps should be followed in designing a vocabulary lesson to accompany a content area selection:

1. Examine the text and select vocabulary words that are crucial to passage understanding and unlikely to be in the children's experiential background

2. Select a teaching strategy for each word using contextual analysis when possible
3. List the focus words on the board
4. Present the words to the children using the designated strategy
5. Test the children on their vocabulary knowledge.

If you have selected to use contextual analysis when teaching a vocabulary term, the context may be copied on the board or overhead, or the children may be referred to the relevant content in the textbook. When possible, the order of vocabulary presentation should stress the interrelationships among the terms or the order of presentation in the material. By teaching in this manner, you allow the children to preview the material and to understand the relationships of ideas to be found in the material. The following lesson will illustrate application of these principles to a fifth grade science text (see Figure 4.5.8).

As children become more familiar with the use of context clues, direct instruction on vocabulary meanings that are explicitly stated in the material or can be reliably inferred should be faded. However, prior to passage reading, the teacher may wish to delineate the important vocabulary to alert the children to the use of context clues:

"In your chapter today on rocks, these are the most important words: *sedimentary, sediments, sandstone, conglomerates,* and *limestone.* (Words written on the board) As you read, watch for these words. Read the sentences around these words carefully to determine their meanings. Write down the meanings so we can discuss them after your reading."

After the children have completed silent reading of the selection, elicit their definitions. If their definitions are inadequate or too limited, go back to the context and lead them to the correct definition. The majority of elementary content area textbooks indi-

**FIGURE 4.5.8** *Example Lesson for Vocabulary Instruction*

Based on pages 34 to 40, Ginn Science Program, Intermediate Level A

Selection of words and teaching strategy.

| *Word* | *Teaching strategy* |
|---|---|
| seedling | *definition* paired with picture |
| record (unusual usage) | *definition* paired with context |
| minerals | *contextual analysis (inference)* |
| cell | *glossary* paired with context |

| *Stimulus* | *Teacher Response* | *Student Response* |
|---|---|---|
| Book and Words on board | "Today we are going to read a chapter in your science book about plants. First, we need to learn some of the new words in the book. Open your book to page 34." | Opens book |
|  | "The first part of the chapter tells us how plants grow. Look at the first word on the board. Ready." (pause) "What word?" (signal) | "Seedling" |
| Seedling | "A seedling is a young plant that grows from a seed. What is a seedling?" | "A young plant that grows from a seed." |
| Pictures in text | "Is this a seedling?" (points to full-grown tree) | "No" |
|  | "How do you know?" | "It isn't a young plant." |
|  | "Is this a seedling?" (points to a seedling) | "Yes" |
|  | "How do you know?" | "It is a young plant that grows from a seed." |
|  | "To decide if a plant were a seedling, what would you need to know?" (individual turns) | "If it is young. If it grew from a seed." |
| Record | "Read the next word on the board." (pause) "What word?" | "Record" |
|  | "Turn to page 35. Find *record* on the yellow chart and put your finger on it. A record is a piece of paper where we write down what has happened. What is a record?" | "A piece of paper where we write down what has happened." |
|  | "Read the title of this record. What is this a record of?" | "Seed growth" |
|  | "What will we write on this record?" (individual turn) | "How many inches the stem grows." |
| Mineral | "Turn to page 37. This section of the chapter tells us how plants |  |

*Figure 4.5.8 cont'd.*

| Stimulus | Teacher Response | Student Response |
|---|---|---|
| | grow. Look at the word on the board. What word?" | "Mineral" |
| | "Read the first paragraph on page 37. Watch for the word *mineral*." | |
| | "What does the plant need besides water and sugar?" | "Minerals" |
| | "Yes, minerals are food for plants. Where do the minerals come from to the plant?" | "From the ground" |
| | "What size are the minerals?" | "Very small" |
| | "How do you know?" | "They come in through the roots." |
| | "Tell me what we know about minerals." (individual turns) | "They are small substances." "They come from the ground." "They come from the ground through the plants' roots." "The plant needs minerals to live." |
| Cells | "Find the word *cell* in your glossary." | Children look up word cell. |
| | "Read the definition for the word cell. Ready." | "A small unit of living matter of which plants and animals are made" |
| | "Good. A cell is a small unit of living matter. Read the first sentence on page 40. Look for the word *cells*." | Children read sentence. |
| | "Listen to me read the sentence with the definition instead of the word cell. In your body, small units of living matter that do the work of making you grow taller are along your bones, muscles, and other parts of you. What do we call small units of living matter?" | "Cells" |

Review and firm up new concepts.

cate important words to the reader through boldface type, alternate type style, underlining, color highlighting, or italics. If this occurs in the textbook, the teacher may simply remind children to attend carefully to the highlighted, key words.

Though we have limited these examples to words having difficult meanings that are crucial to understanding the passage, the teacher should also be alert for other spe-cial vocabulary terms that may need direct instruction prior to passage reading: abbreviations, symbols, figures of speech, and words used in unusual ways.

### Assistance with Graphics

In addition to assistance with vocabulary meanings and decoding, children will often need preparation to adequately read and interpret visual, representational aids. Since content area materials generally provide children with their first exposure to charts, tables, graphs, diagrams, maps, and interpretive illustrations and photographs, direct instruction must be provided. The goals of this preparation are to increase the student's ability to read and interpret the information presented as well as increase awareness of the importance of these features to expository writing.

At the beginning of the school year, the teacher should examine the various visual aids appearing in the text and determine the necessary prerequisite skills for using these visual aids. For example, upon examination of maps in a social studies text, the teacher might conclude that the following skills are necessary to map reading: read title and determine subject of the map, speculate as to the type of information presented in the map, determine directions, locate various places, understand symbolic language presented in the map, read the legend of the map, identify geographic characteristics presented in the map, and read the map's scale. These preskills should be systematically taught during the early weeks of instruction (see Section 4.6, "Study Skills"). With systematic preteaching early in the year, the teacher can later focus on teaching students to apply the skills in interpreting information, forming conclusions, making comparisons, and/or using the information for problem solving. Often the teacher will need to demonstrate interpretive strategies before child

responses are demanded. For example, the teacher might show children how to compare the various points on a line graph and how to interpret the graph's trend (slope). Following demonstration of the processes, the teacher should again present structured questions that allow interpretation, problem solving, or inference formation. Teaching procedures for graphics are discussed in Section 4.6.

In addition to instruction on reading and interpreting graphic aids, students must be taught *when* to refer to graphic material and how to move from discourse to the graphic aid and back. Authors use different techniques to direct the reader's attention to graphic material: explicit directions to refer to graphic material (e.g., "see diagram," "the scale shown in the margin"), general discussion of the graphic material within the discourse, and symbols that appear in the text to indicate to what graphic material a statement refers. In Figure 4.5.9, the ☐ and the △ refer the student to specific illustrations.

Naive readers could be taught to read the discourse until the author refers to a graphic aid, place their finger at that place in the discourse, refer to the graphic material, examine the material carefully reading all captions, and then resume reading. The critical concept to convey to students is that in content area material, you don't skip over diagrams, charts, pictures, and other illustrations. You examine them carefully. The behavior of examining graphic elements can be encouraged by including

**FIGURE 4.5.9**

You can approximate the time of day by noting the length of your shadow.
■ shows what a person's shadow would look like at midday. ▲ shows what a person's shadow would look like late in the day.

questions referring to the graphic aids in written assignments.

### Previewing the Selection

Another preparatory step for expository reading involves previewing information-laden sections of the chapter, such as the chapter title, introduction, critical illustrations, headings, subheadings, and summaries. Through this preview, the reader gains an idea of the content material covered and the organization of that information, and develops a framework for reading the selection. Previewing the chapter can be teacher guided when the content or organizational structure is complex, the textbook is new to the reader, or the readers are less skilled in expository reading. As children become more familiar with the text organization and general content of the book, the teacher may simply review the sections to be previewed to gain a global understanding of the content. The teacher may set a limited time for previewing followed by questions to verify the accuracy of the children's preview techniques. As proficiency in independent previewing develops, the teacher can fade discussion of the sections to be previewed and simply give a period of time for preview followed by questions.

When guiding children in preview activities, begin by having the children read the chapter title and introductory paragraphs. From this information, the children can speculate as to the topic of the chapter and its general scope and begin to formulate questions that might be answered in the discourse.

In order to facilitate this process, the teacher can lead the children in discussion using structured questions. For example, after the students have read the following introduction (Figure 4.5.10), the teacher could inquire the following:

1. Are the roots and stem all a plant needs to keep alive?

2. What other parts of the plant are necessary?
3. What is the whole chapter going to talk about?
4. Right, the whole plant. What parts of the plant might the chapter discuss?
5. What will the first unit be about?
6. What would you like to know about stems? (These questions could be recorded on the board or overhead.)

Next, have the children examine key illustrations, photographs, and graphics in the text to verify their early speculations as to the chapter content. Again, the teacher can guide this process to maximize the children's attention to relevant variables.

1. Look at the illustration on page 35. What does it show us?
2. Yes, a growing plant. What do you think the book will tell us about young plants?
3. Look on page 37. What kinds of plants are here? Read the question under the picture of the violet. What part of the plant are they talking about?
4. Look on the top of the next page. What type of plant is this? Read the caption under the picture. What part of the plant do they want us to look at?
5. Look at the picture on page 40. What part of the plant is it showing?

One of the unique features of expository writing is the use of headings and subheadings to delineate the hierarchical ordering of information. Though there is variance among different textbooks and reference books, chapter organization and accompanying typographical features are similar throughout a given text. When reading the initial chapters of a textbook, the distinctive typographic features (type style, use of color, indentations) need to be introduced so that children can understand the organization of content. Initially, these features can be identified by locating the headings and subheadings within the material or examining reproductions of the

**FIGURE 4.5.10**

## IS ANY ONE PART OF A PLANT MOST IMPORTANT?

Lesson 1—See TM for
Teaching Strategy.

Although a plant might
technically stay alive
without flowers, buds,
and fruits, it would not
be able to reproduce it-
self. Without these re-
productive parts, the
species of plants would
become extinct. A plant
cannot normally survive
without its leaves,
since it is here that
photosynthesis, or food
production, occurs.

Have you ever seen a tree growing out of the bank of a river or a stream? Sometimes a lot of the soil has been washed away and you can see a great tangle of thick <u>roots</u>. If you crawled around in this root cave and looked up under the tree, you would see that the thick roots all come together and form the lower part of the tree's <u>stem</u>. The tall part of a tree from the roots up is all stem, even the branches and twigs.

Could the roots and stem keep the plant alive all by themselves? The plant's <u>leaves</u> and <u>buds</u>, <u>flowers</u> and <u>fruits</u>, and all its other parts are important, too. Each part does certain jobs that make the plant grow and keep it healthy. Take away any one of these parts and the plant will die.

So, to understand what a plant is, we must keep the whole plant in mind. Yet, to understand how a plant lives and grows, we must look at it part by part, just as we would look at the parts of an alarm clock to find out how it works.

In this unit we are going to take a close look at stems. As we do, you may notice many ways that the stem and the other parts of a plant work together.

**34**

From Teacher's Edition of *Intermediate Level* A of the GINN SCIENCE PROGRAM by J. Myron Atkin and others, Copyright © 1975.

text on an overhead or opaque projector. The relationships of the major topics and subtopics (headings and subheadings) can then be illustrated in outline form.

While many elementary texts use question headings or subheadings (e.g., How does a stem grow taller? Why do plants have stems? How do plants grow taller?), students can also be taught to transform statement headings into questions and to generate additional questions based on the headings. To do this, have the students examine the headings and subheadings and record them on the board or overhead projector. Point out the distinction between headings and subheadings. Careful examination of the headings and subheadings not only provides information on the content and organizational structure, but also raises new questions about the content. In Figure 4.5.11, the teacher recorded the headings and subheadings after the children had located them. Question trans-

formations and child-generated questions were also recorded. These questions will help the reader establish a purpose for reading and can serve as the focal point of follow-up discussion.

Though few elementary textbooks provide summaries, if available they can be used in the last step of the preview procedure. The summary, like the examination of the headings, should confirm the children's speculations concerning the selection content. Because the summary usually includes broad statements of the chapter's main ideas, reading of the summary will also alert the reader to the salient information within the selection.

### Selection of Appropriate Reading Rate

Intermediate students often lack strategies for adjusting reading rates in expository materials. Many read content materials with the "once over lightly" approach more

**FIGURE 4.5.11** *Headings and Subheadings*

EXPLORING THE WORLD OF ROCKS

| | Children's Questions |
|---|---|
| Igneous Rock | What is igneous rock? How is it made? What does it look like? |
| Where magma comes from | What is magma? Where does magma come from? |
| Kinds of igneous rock | How many kinds of igneous rock? What are their names? |
| Changes at Earth's Surface | How does the surface change? |
| Mechanical weathering | What is mechanical weathering? Does this include rain, wind and snow? What happens? |
| Contract-expand | What does *contract* mean? What does *expand* mean? Do the rocks contract and expand? Why? |
| Chemical weathering | What is chemical weathering? What chemicals? What happens? |
| What plants can do to rocks | Do plants change rocks? What do the plants do to rocks? |
| How to identify limestone | What does limestone look like? |
| Oxygen can change rock also | What does the oxygen do to the rocks? Does oxygen affect *all* rocks? |

Headings were extracted from GINN SCIENCE PROGRAM *Intermediate Level A*, by J. Myron Atkin and others, Copyright © 1975, 1973, by Ginn and Co. (Xerox Corp.)

suitable to narrative selections and recreational reading; while others plod through all the information as if it were crucial to the central theme or reading purpose. Not only do naive readers often select the wrong reading rate, they are often not aware of the differential importance of various parts of the passage and, thus, the necessity of employing a flexible reading speed. Whether the child is a "one pace plodder" or a "one pace cruiser," he would benefit from a brief discussion prior to reading as to the appropriate reading approach. The teacher should point out segments in which rapid reading for background information would be adequate and other segments needing close, careful reading in order to handle the density and complexity of ideas.

# Preparation for Written Assignments

Written assignments can be presented either after the selection has been read or before silent reading. When presented before passage reading, the written assignment becomes a *study guide* that extends the preview of the selection by alerting students to the salient information in the passage and establishing specific purposes for reading. Children can be taught a number of strategies for completing the study guide. One procedure would involve answering written questions or items on the study guide when the answer was located during silent reading. Thus, the written assignment would be completed during, not after, silent reading. A similar procedure would be simply to write down the page number on which the answer was found in the discourse, completing the written answers after the entire selection was read. The advantage of this procedure is that the flow of information in the selection is not interrupted by stopping to complete written responses. Still another strategy involves reading the entire selection, then answering the questions.

Students, particularly lower-performing students, may also need specific instruction on how to complete their written assignments or study guides. For example, low-performing students may not have a strategy for locating an answer to a question in the discourse using key words from the question and scanning techniques. As a result, the teacher should introduce procedures for completing written assignments with this instruction quickly faded as the children become more proficient.

### Integration of Preparatory Activities

The teacher can present each of these activities in isolation or in tandem. For example, difficult to decode words often have meanings that are also unfamiliar. Both aspects of the word could be simultaneously introduced rather than presenting decoding instruction for all words and then returning to review meanings. In the same way, vocabulary instruction can be integrated with the survey of the material, especially if context clues are being used. As children preview a section, critical vocabulary can be highlighted and guidance in meaning determination given. Likewise, introduction to graphic material can be injected into the chapter survey. Within a specific section of the material, attention can be given to graphic information and its relationship to section headings or subheadings.

If the content is complex, the readers less skilled, or the discourse demanding in reading study skills, preparation can begin 1 or 2 days in advance of passage reading. Pronunciation of words, word meanings, and new graphics introduced in prior lessons should be reviewed before passage reading. The survey of the chapter should not be separated from the actual reading of the passage since many of the benefits of the survey (e.g., speculating as to the content, formulating questions, establishing a reading purpose, and understanding the organizational structure) would be diminished, if not lost.

### Accommodating Individual Differences

Since children's decoding skills and comprehension abilities in expository materials vary, preparatory activities should be tailored to individual needs. The *amount of preparation,* the *type of preparation,* and the *amount of teacher direction* given can be varied to meet individual needs. Below are two outlines of a teachers' content area lesson for three groups of children. One outline (Figure 4.5.12) illustrates how a lesson presented early in the school year might be structured. The second outline (Figure 4.5.13) illustrates how a lesson presented later in the year might be structured. Notice that the amount of preparation across all groups is reduced as the skills of the learners increase and as familiarity with the textbook and expository reading expand.

In this example, the teacher divided the students into three groups for differential preparation for content area reading. At the beginning of the year, all groups needed instruction on reading and interpreting graphic aids as well as preview techniques. These preparatory activities were done with the whole class, followed by further preparatory activities for the low and middle groups. These two groups received instruction on critical vocabulary meanings and use of contextual analysis for determining definitions of words. In

**FIGURE 4.5.12**  *Social Studies Lesson, Beginning of the Year*

| Low Group | Middle Group | High Group |
|---|---|---|
| Whole class, teacher-directed preview of the selection Whole class instruction on new graphic aid | | |
| Teacher-directed instruction on 10 new vocabulary terms and use of contextual analysis | | Presented a list of important words to learn while reading the passage |
| Teacher-directed instruction on 15 difficult to decode words with individual tests | | |
| Guided reading and completion of written assignments | Silent reading and completion of written assignments appropriate to skills of the group | |

←——————— Follow up ———————→

contrast, the high group received no direct instruction on critical vocabulary meanings but received a list of words to focus on during reading. The low group also received direct instruction on decoding of important vocabulary words and guided reading instruction with the selection.

As the year progressed, the amount of preparation given to all groups declined. In the lesson at the end of the book, the high group no longer was involved in teacher-directed previewing of the chapter but independently previewed the chapter before silent reading. The middle group and low group were given some guidance in previewing the chapter; however, this consisted of reminding the students to review specific aspects of the selection rather than

**Figure 4.5.13**  *Social Studies Lesson, End of the Year*

| Low Group | Middle Group | High Group |
|---|---|---|
| Teacher assistance with previewing the chapter (e.g., reviewing sections to preview, asking questions after the preview) | | Independent previewing of the selection |
| Review use of graphic aid stressing interpretation and reaching conclusions based on the information | | |
| Testing on difficult vocabulary (decoding and meaning) followed by direct instruction if students having difficulty | | |
| Silent reading and completion of written assignments appropriate to skills of group | | |

←——————— Follow up ———————→

total teacher guidance through the preview. Instruction on graphic material was given to the low and middle group though the focus had moved from reading the graphic aid to interpretation of the material. Only the low group received assistance on decoding and vocabulary meanings at the end of the year. The teacher tested the students on decoding of the words and determination of word meanings using contextual analysis and only provided instruction as student performance warranted. Though this example cannot be applied to all content area textbooks or groups of children, it illustrates important concepts in preparing children for selections. The amount and type of preparation must be matched to the students and the content area selection with the major goal being to reduce the amount of preparation so that all students can become more independent in their reading.

## Silent Reading of the Selection

After preparatory activities are finished, silent reading should be initiated. Though oral reading is often used in beginning reading instruction, we would not recommend oral reading of expository material. When reading orally, the student must concentrate on intonation, pronunciation, phrasing, inflection, and stress; variables that channel attention away from the concepts being presented. Silent reading rates also surpass oral rates in the majority of intermediate readers. Oral reading of specific sections should be reserved for follow-up exercises in which the students read material that explains an incorrect answer or in rate-training exercises in which the students reread selections until they develop a minimal fluency.

### *Accommodating Individual Differences*

Special accommodations for passage reading may be necessary for the low-performing student including teacher guidance through the material, reduced amounts of assigned reading, and, in extreme cases, alternate inputs. The selection may be broken down into smaller segments using a *guided reading procedure.* When using guided reading, the teacher divides the selection into meaningful segments of appropriate length for the students. The students read a portion of the selection for a specific purpose (e.g., "Read to find out two causes of the Civil War."), discuss the selection with the teacher, and respond to questions on the content. When the children appear firm on the material, another reading purpose is established, and the children read the next segment of discourse silently. This process is continued throughout the selection.

Another alternative for low-performing readers is to assign only portions of the chapter or selection for silent reading. This alternative is especially appropriate for children with very low reading rates. For example, the teacher might assign the introductory and summary paragraphs and key paragraphs found in the discourse. Page numbers or headings of sections to be read can be indicated as a part of the study guide. Also, items from written exercises that these students are expected to answer can be marked.

With the increased prevalence of mainstreaming in the elementary school, the problem of the low reader or the nonreader poses a special challenge to the regular classroom teacher. Though these children should certainly be receiving special reading instruction, access to content area information should not be denied due to their reading skill deficits or handicapping conditions. If the textbook cannot be read even when preparation, guided reading, or minimal reading assignments are provided, other alternatives must be explored. The textbook material can be taped for use by the low-performing child. These supplementary tapes can be prepared by a competent student in the class, a parent, or a volunteer. The taped material need not cover all of the textbook selection but only key segments. Since one of the purposes of content area instruction is expansion of reading skills, other options involving reading are preferable. One option is to rewrite the material or to locate parallel material that covers the same topic presented in the textbook. Trade books, magazine articles, chapters in content area textbooks prepared for lower grades, high-interest low-vocabulary books, and narrative material can be used for this purpose. School librarians can assist the teacher in locating parallel materials.

When using these alternatives, special care must be given not to single out the special child. When possible, alternative assignments should be presented to the individual child or group of children without whole class attention given to the alternative materials. Also, children must be held accountable for specific information even when alternate materials or assignments are used. Though the input might be altered, expectations should still exist for their performance.

## Completion of Written Assignments

Though the written assignment may be introduced before or after silent reading of the passage, it is generally completed after silent reading. In either case, clear expectations for completion of assignments and for correct and complete answers must be communicated to the students. Time should be allotted for completion of the assignment within the classroom schedule. The allotted time should be carefully regulated by the difficulty and complexity of the written responses.

## Follow-up

Feedback on written assignments can be provided through answer keys, whole class or small group corrections, or through teacher feedback, either written (e.g., comments on written assignments or circled answers to be redone) or verbal. Following feedback on written assignments, students should be required to complete incorrect or incomplete responses using their textbook. To assist low-powered readers, page or heading referents can be included in answer keys to aid in corrections.

Performance on written exercises should be recorded on some type of chart, which would be the basis for a motivational system. All students should be performing at about a 90% accuracy level. If students are not performing at this level, teachers should either increase the amount of preparatory activities or decrease the difficulty of the written assignments (the former is usually preferable). Let us once again stress the importance of having students function at a high accuracy rate. Typically, lower-performing students function at a low accuracy level because the assignments presented are too difficult and/or the students do not receive adequate preparation. When students constantly encounter failure, they are likely to develop faulty study habits (random answering just to finish an assignment) and negative attitudes.

Whole class or small group discussion designed to firm up difficult concepts can follow individual corrections. The teacher may pose additional literal and inferential questions on the content, elicit verbal answers, and engage the children in discussion. Questions recorded during the chapter preview can be used. To clarify concepts, the teacher may visually summarize information using a table, chart, graph, time line, or flow chart. Visual representation of information is particularly helpful when explaining relationships across conceptual, spatial, or temporal dimensions. If a chapter outline of headings and subheadings was established prior to reading, this outline can be supplemented with additional chapter detail.

Further exploration of the topic can be encouraged through many creative activities: viewing a filmstrip or movie, reading narrative trade books on a related topic, locating maps in the atlas on the country studied, reading further information in the encyclopedia, locating a magazine article on the topic, gaining a current perspective on the topic through newspaper articles, or reading a biography on one of the people mentioned in the selection.

### Review of Major Concepts

In addition to firming up difficult concepts immediately after completion of passage reading and written assignments, critical concepts and relationships should be reviewed in subsequent lessons through teacher-posed verbal questions or written items on later written assignments. Students must learn that the information presented in the content area textbook is important and should be retained beyond completion of written assignments. End-of-chapter or unit tests can also be used to insure review of critical concepts.

## Selecting and Using a Content Area Textbook

Two major factors to consider when examining content area textbooks are readability level and adequacy of new vocabulary introduction. Many content area textbooks are written at a readability level several years above the grade level for which the book is designated. The teacher or selection committee should use a standard readability formula for comparing textbooks in content areas. We recommend using the Fry readability scale since it is the easiest to compute.

The second major factor to consider is the vocabulary load. Note if the book carefully defines terms that students are not likely to understand. Also note the rate at which difficult terms are introduced. No more than two or three new words should be introduced on a page. If a book does not provide for adequate definition of words and/or introduces words too quickly, lower-performing students will be at a distinct disadvantage. If a program is not written at a consistent readability level or has grossly inadequate vocabulary control, we recommend not selecting it.

The next factors to look at are the adequacy of the teacher's guide and written assignments provided in the program. Both of these factors are important since deficiencies in either area will require extra work by the teacher or some other school personnel, either in the form of previewing lessons or preparing supplementary worksheet exercises.

The teacher's guide should point out specific words that should be included in vocabulary and/or decoding exercises. Furthermore, the definitions for words should be clear. Critical concepts the students are expected to master should be pointed out. In science programs, suggested experiments and demonstrations should be reasonable, not requiring unrealistic amounts of preparation.

Written assignments should (1) stress major points rather than insignificant detail, (2) include both literal and inferential comprehension questions, and (3) be cleanly worded to promote ease of interpretation. The majority of questions should be passage dependent: i.e., answers should be found in or implied by the text rather than being dependent on the students' experiential knowledge. This last point is of particular importance to teachers working with students from limited experiential backgrounds. An answer key that is easy to use and may be used by students in marking their own assignment should also be included.

The spacing of written assignments is also important. The program should be structured so that written assignments appear after segments of about three to six pages. This structuring allows for daily student practice on the material. Student learning is greatly enhanced through frequent exercises.

Another major factor to consider is the organization of information. The book should be written so that critical points are made obvious. Paragraphs and units should be written so that one clearly sees the points being made. In addition, terms which are critical for the reader to understand should be pointed out.

A final factor to consider is the interest level of the text. Information should be presented in a manner that fosters student attentiveness.

## Summary

Reading in content area textbooks presents new challenges to intermediate students due to the divergence of expository material from more familiar narrative or story material. Students need explicit instruction on the use of content area textbooks that not only promotes mastery of information presented in the text but also assists students in the acquisition of critical reading study skills that can be used independently. Preparation for content area lessons begins with the teacher's determining the information in the selection that should be mastered by the students. This information is translated into written assignments that will be completed during or after reading of the selection. These assignments may consist of written questions or a visual representation of the information, such as, a chart, graph, time line, or outline.

When the critical information has been determined and the written assignment either designed by the teacher or selected from the materials accompanying the content area textbook, the teacher can prepare students for reading of the selection. Preparatory activities may include preteaching of vocabulary (decoding and meanings), introduction of critical graphics, previewing the selection, and instruction on the appropriate reading rate to be used. The amount and type of preparation for passage reading should be adjusted to accommodate the individual differences among students with more preparation given to low-performing students. As the students become more competent content area readers, the amount of preparation should be gradually faded leading to independent reading of the selections.

Following preparation for passage reading, students should read the selection silently and complete written exercises on the material. When the written assignments are complete, corrections, either group or individual, should be given followed by students correcting any incorrect or inadequate answers. Additional follow-up activities to extend or review critical concepts may also be initiated.

## APPLICATION EXERCISES

The following pages (Figure 4.5.14) are taken from a recently published social studies program, *Understanding the United States* by George Vuicich et al. (McGraw-Hill, 1979).

1. The program reflects a movement toward improving the quality of content area programs. Tell three positive features of the program.

2. Which two of the following words are not defined in the context of the passage? How would you teach them to students who do not know them?

    ancestor          regions
    native American  seacoast
    continent        international boundary
    landform        elevation

3. Because of the importance of using contextual analysis to determine word meanings, you would like to use these initial pages in the textbook to introduce contextual analysis. Describe the strategy you would model for your students, using the vocabulary terms *continent, landform,* and *regions.*

4. You are teaching a low-performing group of children who have mastered sounding of one and two syllable words with common consonants, consonant combinations, single vowels, and vowel pairs. However, they are less proficient at decoding three and four syllable words, words with suffixes, and longer words containing irregular graphemes. Which four of the following words would you select for decoding instruction prior to silent reading? How would you present each of the words?

    landforms     international
    spacious      continent
    regions       elevation
    seacoast     tabletop

5. How might you assist children in decoding the word *Appalachian?*

6. What is the critical information in this selection that should be mastered by the students? Would the questions at the end of the selection adequately measure attainment of that information? Why? Why not?

7. Look at question 2 of the selection. State all the information a student needs to know to answer this question.

8. Write four questions, two to determine if students understand the elevation key and two to determine if students understand how to determine regions.

9. Evaluate each of the following questions designed to measure selection understanding, using the criteria presented in the chapter.

    a. When might your ancestors have arrived in North America?
    b. Is North America a continent?
    c. What are the three large nations on the continent of North America?
    d. What is a region?
    e. When do we sing the song, "America, the Beautiful?"
    f. What do international boundaries separate?

**FIGURE 4.5.14**

# The Continent of
# North America

You are one of the people living in North America. Your ancestors may have come here sometime in the last 400 years. During that time, many people from all parts of the world came to North America. Native Americans lived here even before that time. If you are a Native American, your people have lived in North America for thousands of years.

Have you heard the song that begins "Oh beautiful, for spacious skies"? Do you remember the rest of the words? This song is called "America, the Beautiful." It tells about the beauty of North America. It tells how big the land is, how wide the skies are, how rich the crops are.

North America is a *continent*, or large land mass, on Earth. There are three large nations on the continent of North America. They are Canada, the United States, and Mexico.

Because North America is so large, it has many different *landforms*, or kinds of land. In some places, the land is as flat as a tabletop. In others, it is as jagged as the edge of a saw. Some land in North America is covered with thick forests. Some land is covered with drifting sand. How do we study a land with so many differences?

We can begin by dividing the continent into seven *regions*. These regions are large areas where the landforms are similar. The seven regions are:
    the Atlantic and Gulf coastal plain
    the Appalachian (ap′ ə lā′chən) Mountains
    the Central Lowlands and the Great Plains
    the Rocky Mountains
    the Great Basin
    the Pacific Coastal Ranges and Lowlands
    the Canadian Shield
Find each of these regions of North America on the map on the following page.

The *elevation* key on the map tells how high some of these regions are. The color green stands for the lowlands. This land is usually found along seacoasts. The highest land is colored in purple. Look at the key. How many meters high is this land? Now look at your map and find the areas in purple. What regions of North America have the highest land?

The other key on your map gives the *symbols*, or small drawings, that stand for national capitals, largest cities, and *international boundaries*. Find the symbol for national capitals. Then, find the national capital of the United States.

International boundaries are the lines on a map which divide one nation from another. They show where one nation ends and another begins. Find the symbol for international boundaries on your key. Now look at the map. With your finger, trace the international boundary between Canada and the United States. Then find and trace the international boundary between the United States and Mexico.

Notice that the land regions of North America do not stop at international boundaries. Landforms do not change suddenly as you go from one country into another. For example, the Great Plains extend from Canada through the United States and into Mexico. The coastal plains lie along the seacoasts of both the United States and Mexico.

In the next few lessons, you will learn about the land and resources of the seven main regions of North America.

---

Choose the best answer:
1. North America is (a) a landform, (b) a nation, (c) a continent, (d) a region of the United States.

*Figure 4.5.14 cont'd.*

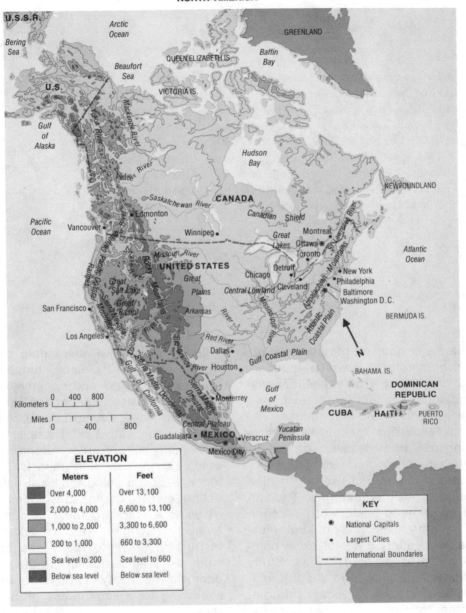

NORTH AMERICA

2. An international boundary separates (a) one land region
   from another, (b) Mexico from the United States, (c) the
   Great Plains from the Rocky Mountains.
3. An elevation key is useful because it tells you (a) how high
   land regions are on a map, (b) where nations are located,
   (c) how far one place is from another.

4. Look at the map on page 12. Try to find the general area
   where you live. What large city is nearest to the place
   where you live?
5. In which region of North America do you live?

ON YOUR OWN

# Study Skills

by Anita Archer

One of the major goals of the intermediate reading program is to develop independent and efficient use of expository materials including content area textbooks, reference materials, and tradebooks. The tremendous explosion of knowledge now confronting children as well as adults makes it imperative that we effectively teach students to find and use information contained in expository materials. The student not only needs basic word recognition and comprehension skills but must also be able to apply a set of skills commonly referred to as study skills. Study skills include the ability *to locate* information in parts of a book; *to locate* information in other printed references such as the dictionary or encyclopedia; *to locate* information using the card catalog and other library aids; *to read and interpret* graphic material; *to select* appropriate references and relevant information within those materials to answer a question or solve a problem; *to organize* information for later retrieval using such skills as notetaking, outlining and summarizing; and *to use* appropriate reading rates.

Study skills, like all reading skills, will not be obtained by many students unless they receive direct and systematic instruction on their use, independent practice in using the skills, and structured review and maintenance activities. There is evidence that many upper-grade elementary students cannot use such important skills as locating books using the card catalog, locating entries in an encyclopedia index, or using a standard table of contents effectively (Gengler, 1965). Lack of direct instruction leads to faulty and inefficient study skills as evidenced by the older student who randomly thumbs through a book searching for a small piece of information rather than referring to the index, by the student who proceeds through the library pulling books from the stacks rather than consulting the card catalog, by the elementary student who reads page after page in a dictionary in search of one word, or by the high school student who reports, "I take notes in class but I sure can't understand them." These and many other problems can be avoided through systematic instruction on study skills in the elementary grades. Study skill instruction must not be delayed until the student enters secondary school where the skills must be applied daily and where the necessary training and practice may not be available.

Study skills involve a large number of rather discrete skills, which necessitates the different organizational pattern used in this section. Following an introduction to general teaching procedures for study skills, each of the major sets of study skills will be discussed with the suggested sequences, teaching procedures, and child responses summarized in tables.

## Direct Instruction Procedures

### Selecting Study Skills for Instruction

Because of the vast number of study skills, the teacher must carefully select and prioritize them for instruction. Study skills that are frequently used and, thus, have higher utility should be introduced before less frequently used skills (e.g., tables of contents, index, and glossary *before* footnotes, prefaces, and appendixes; dictionaries, encyclopedias, and telephone books *before* atlases and alamanacs). When possible, less complex study skills should be introduced before more complex study skills (e.g., glossaries *before* dictionaries; simple informal outlining *before* formal outlining; table of contents *before* index). Also, skills that serve as the basic or foundation of higher level skills should be taught first (e.g., locating words in an alphabetized list *before* using the index; rapidly locating given pages in a text *before* locating pages using the table of contents).

Study skills should be introduced when they are demanded by expository materials or by a particular assignment. When students begin using a new textbook, the content of the title page, the copyright page, and the table of contents can be introduced. Before students begin library re-

search on a science or social studies topic, the card catalog, general organization of the library, and use of the encyclopedia should be taught. Instruction followed by immediate use of the study skill to solve a problem or to function in a content area textbook insures immediate practice of the study skill. If a skill is taught in isolation and students do not see its usefulness or have an opportunity to apply the skill, transfer to self-initiated use of the study skill is unlikely. If students are taught to use an index but are never called upon to use it in answering questions or locating information, they probably will not master the skill or use it independently.

In summary, study skills should be ordered from more frequently used to less frequently used, from least complex to most complex, from basic foundation skills to higher level skills and should be introduced when they have immediate usefulness to the students in solving a problem or functioning in a textbook.

### Determining Component Skills

The majority of study skills are quite complex and must be broken down into smaller steps for instruction. For example, location of information using the index involves the following component skills: locating the index at the back of the book, reading the entries, locating entries and corresponding pages when given a main topic, locating entries when given a main topic and subtopic, using cross references, locating names listed last name first, determining a key word in a question and locating the corresponding entry, and determining alternate main topics when the key word is not located in the index. Each of these component skills needs to be taught separately, though some might be introduced in the same lesson, before the overall strategy for using an index is applied. Component skills for the major study skills are listed later in this section.

## Introducing Component Skills

As with other areas of reading instruction, the teacher must provide explicit and direct input on how to perform study skills. Depending on the particular study skill, the teacher can explain how to perform the behavior or strategy and/or demonstrate actual skill performance. For example, the teacher can demonstrate how to locate a page in a book, how to write a simple outline for a paragraph, how to locate a topic in the encyclopedia, or how to use the card catalog. She can explain how to use guide words in the dictionary followed by a demonstration.

During introduction of the component skills, the teacher must elicit responses from the students not only to maintain their attention but also to verify understanding of the strategies being introduced. These responses might involve answering questions on information provided by the teacher or actually performing the desired skill (e.g., writing supporting details in an outline, locating chapter or unit titles in the table of contents, selecting the correct encyclopedia volume for a specific topic). During this supervised practice when unison or individual responses are elicited, the teacher should provide feedback on correct use of the strategy ("Great. You wrote an important detail right under the main idea.") and corrections when errors occur ("Watch me. First I write down the main idea for the paragraph. Then I indent and write down an *important* detail in my own words"). Suggested teaching procedures and child responses are outlined for each of the component skills in the tables later in this section.

## Providing Independent Exercises

In order to insure mastery of the strategy, teachers must provide ample practice. Written exercises can be designed to provide practice on the information and strategies introduced during direct instruction (see Figure 4.6.1). These exercises not only allow for more practice and an opportunity to firm up the skill but also provide feedback to the teacher on the need for additional input.

## Providing Opportunities for Continued Practice

Self-initiated use of a study skill seldom occurs after a single lesson or even a series of lessons and written exercises. The teacher must provide situations and problems that demand use of the skill, provide review lessons on the more difficult skills, and remind children when to use the skills. For example, after the table of contents has been introduced and location skills practiced using it, the teacher should continually demand use of the table of contents (e.g., "Today we are beginning Chapter 5 in Unit 3. Where can I find the page number of Chapter 5? Good, in the Table of Contents. Find Unit 3, Chapter 5 in the Table of Contents. What is the title of the chapter? What page does it begin on? What page does it end on? Turn to Chapter 5 in your book."). It is particularly important that students get actual practice, not simulations, in applying the more complex strategies (e.g., outlining sections of a book, researching a topic for a report, locating information using the index of the encyclopedia).

## Materials for Study Skill Instruction

The reading difficulty of any material used for study skill instruction should be minimized. Attention on a particular study skill should not be diverted by difficult to decode material, a heavy concept load, or complex sentences. As a result, readability level should be a major concern when selecting appropriate content textbooks, classroom dictionaries, or reference, materials such as encyclopedias or atlases.

**FIGURE 4.6.1**  *Independent Practice Exercise on Use of the Table of Contents*

Exploring Science                 Name _____
Table of Contents

1. When you want to find out about units, chapters, and page numbers in your science book, you use the _____  _____  _____ .

2. Name the six units in the science book.

   _____

   _____

   _____

   _____

   _____

   _____

3. Unit 1 begins on page _____ .
   Unit 2 begins on page _____ .
   Unit 5 begins on page _____ .

4. Chapter 1 of Unit 1 begins on page _____ and goes up to page _____ .
   The title of Chapter 1 is _____ .

   Chapter 3 of Unit 1 begins on page _____ and goes up to page _____ .
   The title of this chapter is _____ .

   Chapter 4 of Unit 5 begins on page _____ and goes up to page _____ .
   The title of this chapter is _____ .

   Chapter 3 of Unit 6 begins on page _____ and goes up to page _____ .
   The title of this chapter is _____ .

5. If you wanted to find out about animals, what unit would you look in?
   _____  What pages? _____

6. If you wanted to find out how animals protect themselves, what chapter would you look in? _____  What pages? _____

7. If you wanted to find out about plant beginnings, what unit would you look in?
   _____  What chapter? _____  What pages? _____

8. If you wanted to find out about simple machines, what unit would you look in?
   _____  What chapter? _____  What pages? _____

Classroom textbooks in such areas as science, social studies, and health are particularly useful in study skill instruction for a number of reasons: all students in the classroom have a copy, the materials are generally written at a level the students can read with some preparation, skills taught using classroom textbooks have immediate usefulness, and the consistency of the textbook allows for later application of study skills. Study skill lessons can be interspersed with content lessons. For example, the title page, copyright page, and table of contents could be introduced before the first chapter is read. Following the first chapter, use of the glossary could be introduced to complement vocabulary study. In the same manner, lessons on reading and interpreting graphics, use of the index, outlining and note-taking could be taught along with chapter content. Often it is helpful to use a chapter or unit within a textbook for study skill instruction *after* the students have read the chapter so that sole attention can be given to use of the study skill. Teachers should teach the majority of study skills using the initial chapters in the textbook with continual review and practice given in remaining chapters.

After study skills have been introduced

in the content area textbook, they can be extended to outside reference materials. For example, when students can locate information using the index in their science or social studies textbook, they can apply the same skill to encyclopedias, atlases, and commercial catalogs (e.g., Wards, Sears). When they can outline passages in their textbooks, they can apply this strategy to articles found in magazines, journals, or encyclopedias. Outside materials should also be used to supplement textbooks when the number of available examples are limited. Many social studies textbooks contain a limited number of maps, diagrams, and graphs, not an adequate sample to practice reading and interpreting these graphics.

Though the classroom textbook is the most appropriate stimulus for study skill instruction, additional instructional materials including multi-skill workbooks, single skill workbooks, exercises in basal readers, and support materials accompanying children's reference materials (e.g., dictionaries, atlases, encyclopedias) are available to assist the classroom teacher. These materials can be used to determine a hierarchy of study skills, as a stimulus for initial instruction and for limited practice of the study skills. Though these materials focus on important skills and present useful information to the student, they have a number of deficits. The most critical deficits are the lack of direct teacher instruction provided (usually independent practice material) and the lack of applied practice with actual textbooks and reference materials. If these materials were to be used, the teacher would need to model or explain the use of the study skill prior to completion of the prescribed activities and provide exercises using actual materials.

The rest of this section illustrates application of direct instruction procedures to various study skills: locating information within a book, in graphic aids, in reference material, and in a library; recording information through outlining and note-taking; and gathering information through skimming and scanning. Many of these teaching procedures are quite complex. To assist you in understanding the formats, we suggest going through the procedures using the appropriate reference material.

## Locating Information Within a Book

Fundamental to all other study skills is the ability to locate information within books. The most basic skill is the ability to locate a given page within a text. Though most intermediate students have developed a strategy for rapidly locating a page, the intermediate teacher should verify this skill through assessment. Working with 10 to 15 children, dictate a page number in a book and have them locate the page. During this activity, carefully observe performance of the children. Children who cannot quickly find the page, who proceed page by page, or who have difficulty deciding whether to go forward or backward in the book will need instruction on this skill. To make practice more interesting, the students could time their successive attempts at locating pages and record their progress on this skill.

Because of earlier exposure to the tables of contents in basal readers, intermediate students often are able to locate a page when given a specific chapter or story title. However, the table of contents in expository materials is used for additional purposes: to determine the scope of the book's content and to locate pages in the book when given a general topic rather than a specific title. After assessing location of a specific page given a title in the table of contents, students should be introduced to these specialized uses of the table of contents beginning with classroom textbooks and expanding to expository trade books.

While the table of contents can be used to find sections of the book discussing general topics, the index enables students to locate information on very specific topics needed to answer questions, write reports, or complete projects. Use of the index is a very complex skill not only because of the requisite alphabetizing skill but also the need to select *key words* that might be index entries and to generate alternate entries when a key word is not listed. Use of the index should be taught in a number of structured lessons followed by written exercises and continuous review. Timed exercises can be used to increase motivation during practice. Careful instruction on using the indexes in classroom textbooks should occur before this skill is transferred to indexes found in reference materials (e.g., encyclopedias, newspapers, trade books, atlases).

Use of the glossary in content area textbooks is another important location skill. Though primary basal readers often contain glossaries, their use is more critical in expository materials that include difficult terminology. Glossary instruction, particularly on locating meanings, substituting meanings in context, and determining the word's pronunciation, provides the basis for more complex use of the dictionary. In the following tables, a simple strategy for locating words in the glossary, relying primarily on the first letter and scanning for the word, is suggested.

Other location skills within the textbook can also be introduced. Younger students can be introduced to the title and copyright pages; older children, to the preface, introduction, list of illustrations, and appendixes. The following tables outline the component skills for locating information within a text and corresponding teaching procedures.

## Locating and Interpreting Information in Graphic Material

Pictorial graphics including illustrations, diagrams, charts, and photographs are the most common graphic material found in elementary textbooks. When teaching children to use graphic material in their content area textbooks, our goal is not only to increase their ability to accurately extract and interpret information but also to increase their awareness of the importance of graphics to an understanding of the material. Since early reading experiences occur in fictional materials, students may not realize that photographs and drawings are included not only for aesthetics but also to convey information. Students must realize that graphics are included for a purpose: to explain, summarize, or expand information presented in the discourse. Teachers can help students develop the habit of referring to graphic material by emphasizing the importance of graphics, by teaching them to efficiently read the graphics so that the task is less formidable, and by asking them both literal and inferential questions concerning graphic material.

Content area textbooks include relatively few graphic aids. Nevertheless, the unique organization of information, use of symbols, and the density of information in graphic material can be frustrating to the naive learner. The teacher must present each type of graphic aid introduced in the content area textbook and when the samples are limited, extend practice to supplementary study skill and reference materials.

Though actual information presented for each type of graphic aid differs, consistent instructional procedures can be used. The student must first be taught how to determine the topic of the graphic material using the title, caption, or author's description. Next, the unique organization style and symbols found in the graphic aid must be taught. Armed with this knowledge, the student can be taught to locate information in the graphic aid. When he can read the graphic aid with understanding, comprehension exercises can extend to making inferences (comparisons, contrasts, conclusions) based on the information presented. Finally, the student must synthesize the information presented in the graphic

(Continued on p. 396)

**TABLE 4.6.1** *Locating Information within a Book*

| SKILLS | TEACHER RESPONSE (Additional examples and questions should be provided.) | CHILD RESPONSE |
|---|---|---|
| A. *Can rapidly locate a page in a book.*<br>Preskill:<br>Can determine if a number is smaller or larger than a given numeral.<br>Component Skills:<br>1. Given a page number, can determine whether to move forward or backward to locate the page. | T. models with book. ("We are on page 23. We are looking for page 45. If the page number we are looking for is larger, we go toward the back of the book. We are on page 45 and are looking for page 98, so we go toward the back. If the page number we are looking for is smaller, we go toward the front of the book. We are on page 90 and we are looking for page 64, so we go toward the front of the book." T. tests with questions of this form: "We're looking for page 21 and we're on page 50. Do we turn toward the front or back of the book?") | C. tells if you must go toward the front or back of the book to find page. |
| 2. Given a page number, can open to an approximate location in the book. | T. models. ("This book has 200 pages, page 178 would be close to the end. I am opening the book close to the end.") T. tests with questions of this form: "This book has _____ pages, where would page 56 be?" | C. tells if page number would be at the beginning, end, or middle of the book. |
| 3. Given a page number, can locate an approximate location and proceeds forward or backward rapidly locating the page. | T. tells how to locate a page. ("If we want to find a page we open to the beginning, middle, or end of the book and then go toward the front or back of the book to find the page. Find page _____.") | C. locates page in book. (Timing page locations may be interesting to children.) |
| B. *Can locate information in the book using the table of contents.*<br><br>Component Skills:<br>1. Can locate the table of contents at the beginning of the book. | T. tells location of table of contents and shows in book. | C. locates in book. |
| 2. Can survey the table of contents to determine the general topic and scope of the book. | T. explains how to survey the table of contents to determine the general topic. ("To find out what the book is about, you can read the title and major headings in the table of contents. Let's read the title and major headings. What will this book be about?" | C. reads title and headings.<br>C. tells what the book is about. |
| 3. Can read the entries within the table of contents (e.g., Unit 1, Chapter 1 "Plant Beginnings" beginning on page 8 and going to page 22.) | T. models reading entries and explains how to determine the first page of the section and where the section ends. | C. reads entries and tells where section begins and ends. |

| | T. (Teacher) | C. (Child) |
|---|---|---|
| 4. Can determine the organizational pattern of the book from the table of contents (e.g., organized into units and chapters).<br><br>*Sample:*<br>UNIT 1 PLANT GROWTH<br>  1. Plants with seeds<br>  2. Plants without seeds<br>  3. What plants need to grow<br>UNIT 2 THE ANIMAL WORLD<br>  1. Animals with backbones<br>  2. Animals without backbones<br>  3. Animal reproduction | T. shows how a book is divided into segments and the relationship among the segments. ("This book is divided into units. A unit is a long section that tells about one big topic." T. points to two different unit headings. "This is a unit, etc. How many units in this book? What is the big topic for Unit 1? Each unit is divided into chapters. What are the units divided into? Each chapter tells us more about the big topic. How many chapters in Unit 1? What does Chapter 1 tell us about plant growth (unit heading)? What does Chapter 2 tell us about plant growth? etc.) | C. tells number of segments (units, chapters, subtopics).<br>C. identifies the topic of each unit and chapter. |
| 5. Given a chapter, unit, or section title (e.g., "Plant with seeds") or designation (e.g., Chapter 5, Unit A) can locate the entry in the table of contents and corresponding pages within the text. | T. models locating an entry using the title or section designation. ("Let's find pages in our book using the table of contents. I want to find the first page for Chapter 6 in Unit 5. I find Unit 5 and read down to Chapter 6, look for the first page for Chapter 6, and then turn to it in my book. Your turn. Find Chapter 8 in Unit 2.") | C. locates pages in the book when given the unit, chapter, or section title or number designation. |
| 6. Given a general topic (the index should be used to locate specific topics), can locate related entries and corresponding pages. *Note: This skill may be taught in conjunction with component skill 9 for using an index, since both skills are basically the same.* | T. models locating an entry using a general topic. ("Let's find pages in our book when we know the general topic but not the exact unit or chapter title. I want to find pages on weather. I start with the title for the first unit. Will this unit talk about weather? No. So I go to the next unit heading until I find a unit that might talk about weather. Then I look at the chapter titles to see if they talk about weather. Your turn. Find the pages in your book that talk about planets.") | C. locates pages in the book when given a general topic. |
| C. *Can locate information within the glossary.*<br><br>Preskill:<br>  Can say the alphabet.<br>Component Skills:<br>  1. Can locate the glossary within a textbook and explain its purpose. | T. shows the location of the glossary in a textbook and explains what information is included there. ("A glossary is a list of important words from the textbook listed in alphabetical order. How are the words listed? After each word is its meaning and how to say the word. What is given after each word?") | C. locates glossary in book.<br>C. tells how words are ordered in the glossary and the type of information included. |
|   2. Can rapidly locate a word in the glossary.<br>  *Note: Glossaries are generally quite short with a limited number of words beginning with each letter. Because of their length, no* | T. explains how to locate a word and demonstrates with glossary. ("Let's find some words in the glossary. I want to find the word *plantation.* I open my book to the first page in the glossary. What is the first letter in *plantation?* Right, plantation begins with *p.* I turn the pages in the glossary quickly until I find the list of words that begin with the letter *p.* What words | C. determines first letter in word, opens to the first page in the glossary, turns pages until he finds the list of words beginning with the first letter, and scans the list for the word. |

Table 4.6.1 cont'd.

| SKILLS | TEACHER RESPONSE | CHILD RESPONSE |
|---|---|---|
| guide words are provided. This simple strategy has been selected because it can be introduced to young children and is efficient for locating words in the glossary. | am I looking for? When I find the list of words beginning with p, I put my finger on the first word, quickly moving my finger down the list reading the p words until I find plantation. Where did I first put my finger? When did I stop? Your turn. Find the word factory in your glossary.") | |
| 3. Can locate and read the meaning of a target word in the glossary. Note: Unlike dictionaries, glossaries usually only give one meaning for a word, the meaning used within the textbook. For this reason, exercises involving selecting the correct definition to fit a given context should be introduced with the dictionary not the glossary. | T. explains how to locate the meaning of a word in the glossary and models. ("If we want to know the meaning of an important word in our textbook, we can look it up in the glossary. Where can we find the meaning? . . . Quickly locate the word matter in the glossary. After the word matter is its definition. What is the definition?") Provide additional practice. | C. locates word in glossary and reads definition. |
| 4. Can use the glossary definition to understand a statement in the textbook. | T. explains how to substitute the glossary definition into the textbook discourse to aid understanding. ("Today we are going to learn how the glossary can help us understand what we are reading. Let's say I read this sentence, The growth of an embryo begins as soon as there is water. I don't understand this sentence because I don't know the meaning of embryo. I look up the word in the glossary. Find the word embryo in the glossary. What is its meaning? Yes, it means a tiny plant inside a seed. To help me understand the sentence, I am going to reread it with the definition instead of the word. The growth of a tiny plant inside a seed begins as soon as there is water. To help me understand the sentence, I looked up the unknown word, found its meaning, and put the definition in the sentence. Now its your turn." Provide additional examples and practice exercises. Further explanation of this strategy is found in the intermediate vocabulary section.) | C. locates word in glossary. C. reads the definition. C. substitutes definition for word in the sentence. |
| 5. Can determine the pronunciation of a word using the glossary. | T. should present sounds for the various symbols beginning with the more common symbols (e.g., short and long vowels). When the sounds for the isolated symbols are mastered, practice in reading words written on the board or overhead can be given followed by practice using glossary entries. Note: When the pronunciation symbols differ substantially from the dictionary used in the classroom (and thus might interfere with dictionary use) or the respellings are exceptionally difficult to decipher, this skill should not be introduced with the glossary. | C. says isolated sound when given glossary symbols. C. pronounces words using the glossary. |

D. *Can locate information within the text using the index.*

Preskill:
Can locate an entry within an alphabetized list.

Component Skills:

| | T. (Teacher) | C. (Child) |
|---|---|---|
| 1. Can locate the index at the end of the book. | T. tells the location of the index and shows in the book. T. tells use of index. ("The index lists specific topics in alphabetical order. We can look up specific topics in the index and find the pages that talk about that topic.") | C. locates index.<br>C. tells purpose of index. |
| 2. Can read entries in the index including page designations and abbreviations (35–89; 296, 309), (ill., m.).<br>Sample:<br>Roads, 45, 85–92, 103<br>Slaves and slavery, 56, 132, 345–356, *ill*.357. | T. models reading entries and explains special features of entries. ("Look at these entries. First they give the topic. The topic here is roads. What do entries give first? After the topic the pages where we can find information on the topic are listed. What is listed after the topic?<br>The different pages that talk about roads are separated by commas, e.g., pages 85, 86, 87, 88, 89, 90, 91, and 92. When there is a dash between page numbers, all of the pages beginning with the first number up to and including the second number talk about the topic, e.g., 85–92 means that pages 85 up to and including page 92 talk about roads. Read this entry. Say the topic and page numbers where we can find information." Extend similar instruction to abbreviations used in the index. Abbreviations and symbols used in the index are generally explained at the top of the first page in the index.) | C. answers structured questions on parts of entry.<br><br>C. reads entry. |
| 3. Given a main entry, can locate entry in index and corresponding pages. | T. uses the procedure for finding a word in a glossary. | C. locates entries in the index. |
| 4. Given a main entry and subentry, can locate entry and corresponding pages in the index.<br>Sample organized in two ways:<br>ships, 59–65<br>  American Indian Boats, 68–71<br>    ill. 71.<br>  British, 155, 158–160<br>ships, 59–65; American Indian Boats, 68–71, ill. 71; British, 155, 158–160 | T. explains subentries and relationship to main entries. ("Find the main entry, ships, in the index. Under ships are subentries. Subentries are more precise, specific entries about the main entry. What is a subentry? What subentries are listed under ships?" Repeat with additional examples. If the subentries are listed horizontally rather than vertically, introduce the semicolon as a marker between subentries.) | C. finds main entry.<br>C. defines a subentry.<br><br>C. reads entries under main entry. |
| 5. Given a main entry, can locate entry and cross references<br>(See ———; See also ———.)<br>*Sample:*<br>Social groups, 67, 156–178, 245, | T. explains cross references and models use. ("Find the main entry, factories. After factories it says 'See manufacturing.' No page numbers are listed, so we look up manufacturing to find the pages. Find manufacturing in the index." Repeat with additional examples.) | C. locates main entry.<br>C. reads cross reference and locates in the index. |

Table 4.6.1 cont'd.

| SKILLS | TEACHER RESPONSE | CHILD RESPONSE |
|---|---|---|
| *See also* Families and Tribes Factories, See Manufacturing | ("When the index says See _____ or See also _____ we look under a new entry for page numbers. These are called cross references. What are they called?") | |
| 6. Given name of a person, can locate entry in the index (first name and surname reversed). | T. explains how names are listed last name first in the index. | C. locates names of persons in the index. |
| 7. Given a question or problem statement with a *single* key word from the index, can select the key word, locate the entry in the index, locate the corresponding pages in the book, and verify the relevancy of the information to the problem or question. | T. explains how to select a key word from a question to look up in the index. ("When you use the index to find information that will help you answer a question, you must first decide what word from the question to look for among the main entries. What must we do before we look in the index? This word is called a *key word*. This is my question, How are volcanos formed? The key word is *volcano*. I will look up *volcano* in the index. Try to choose a *key word* that names what the question asks about. What should the *key word do?*" Provide numerous questions with only one possible key word. When children are proficient at determining the key word, have them locate key word, locate corresponding pages, and read to find the answer to their question.) | C. selects key words from question or problem statement. <br><br> C. determines key word, locates entry in index, locates corresponding pages and reads to verify relevancy of information. |
| 8. Given a question or problem statement with *more than one* key word from the index, can select the key words, locate the entry in the index, locate the corresponding pages in the book, and verify the relevancy of the information to the problem or question. | T. explains how to look up entries when more than one key word is contained in the question. ("In some questions there may be more than one key word. Look at this question, What resources come from the ocean? We should look up *resources* and *ocean*. If we only looked up one of the words, we might only find part of the information needed to answer our question. Why should we look up both words?" Provide additional question examples, some having one key word and others having two key words. When children can determine key words, have them locate the entries, locate corresponding pages, and read to find the answer to the question.) | C. selects key words from question or problem statement. <br><br> C. determines key words, locates entries in index, locates corresponding pages and reads to verify relevancy of information. |
| 9. Given a question or problem statement *using vocabulary not explicitly stated in the index*, can locate entries within the index and corresponding page to verify if the information is relevant to the question or problem. | T. explains how to determine alternate key words when the original is not found in the index and models the process. ("Read this question, Why does weather change? What is the key word? Look for *weather* in your index. We can't find the word *weather* in the index, and there aren't any cross references. We have to think of other words that mean the same thing or almost the same thing as weather that might be main entries in the index. Another word for weather might be *climate*. Look for *climate* in your index. Now it's your turn. Determine the key word in this question. If it is not listed in the index, think of other words that mean the same thing or almost the same thing that might be main entries.") | C. gives other possible words that might be main entries in the index when the word is not listed. |

394

Students should be taught several strategies for determining alternate entries: to generate synonyms or near synonyms (e.g., villages—towns; nations—countries), a broader term (e.g., pine tree—forest or trees; manure—fertilizer) or a related word (e.g., shuttle—weaving; wigwam—Indian; harbor—ports, ships—shipping); or if the key word is very broad, more specific related words should be located in the index (e.g., weather—rain, snow).

Much practice should be given on determining alternate entries. The topic in question must be familiar to the students so that they can make the necessary associations. The teacher should supplement the list of possible main entries. When children are proficient at determining alternate entries, practice should be given on locating entries, finding corresponding pages, and reading to determine if the information answers the given question.

C. determines alternate main entries, locates entry words and corresponding pages, and reads to find the answer to the given question.

---

E. *Can locate information using other aids in the book.*

Component Skills:

1. Can locate and state significance of information found on the title page (e.g., title, author(s), publisher, location of publisher, editor's name, name of series, edition).

T. explains each aspect of the title page and shows in book. ("Turn to the 1st page in your book. This page is called the title page. What is it called? It tells us the title and the authors. The authors are the people who wrote the book. Who are the authors? The names across the top are the authors. How many authors wrote this book? Look at the authors' names as I read them.")
With older children, this lesson can be expanded to include the publisher, editor's name, name of series, and edition.

C. locates the title page.
C. locates the title and authors on the title page.
C. answers structured questions.

2. Can locate and state significance of information found on the copyright page (date of publication).

T. explains the copyright date found on the copyright page and shows in book. ("Turn to the next page in your book. This page is called the copyright page. What is it called? It tells the copyright, the date when the book was published. Look for a year on the page. In what year was this book published? How many years ago was this book published? Was this book published recently or a long time ago? Why is it good to have a science book that was published recently?")

C. locates the copyright page.
C. locates the publication date.
C. answers structured questions.

3. Can locate and state purpose of the preface, introduction, and/or foreword.

T. explains the purpose for any introductory material and shows it to the children. Very few elementary content books include these materials.

C. locates introductory materials.
C. tells purpose of preface, introduction and/or foreword.
C. reads introductory material.

4. Can locate information in other aids in the book (e.g., appendix, lists of illustrations, maps and figures, footnotes, references at the end of chapters, and bibliography).

T. explains the purpose for these aids, how to read the aids and shows their locations.
*Note: These aids should only be introduced to the more advanced students when they occur in classroom textbooks.*

C. locates the aid.
C. tells the purpose of the aid.
C. reads and extracts information from the aid.

material with the written discourse. Though the teacher might follow all of these steps when introducing a new type of graphic aid, some steps (instruction on the organization pattern, use of symbols, and locating information) can gradually be faded and replaced with an emphasis on the higher level skills (interpretation of graphic aids and integration of graphic and discourse information). The steps are illustrated in Table 4.6.2 using a chart, map, table and graph.

## Locating Information in Reference Materials

Children in the intermediate grades should be taught to locate information in common reference materials such as the dictionary, encyclopedia, and atlas. The dictionary, the most frequently used of these reference materials, can help the learner determine the spelling, meaning, and pronunciation of a word as well as the part of speech, the spelling of derivatives, and origin of the word. Critical to all dictionary use is the ability to rapidly locate a word within the entries. Because of the complexity of this skill, it must be broken down into component skills, and the student must receive instruction on each component (e.g., saying the alphabet beginning with any letter; determining if a letter is in the front, middle or back of the dictionary; finding an appropriate starting point for the word search; and systematically using the guide words to turn to the front or back to quickly locate the word).

Another important reference material is the encyclopedia. Though primary children can be exposed to the wealth of information and illustrations presented in the encyclopedia, intermediate children need to be taught how to locate topics in the encyclopedia using designations on the volumes' spines, guide words in the volumes, and the encyclopedia index. Initially, they can look up information to supplement study in their content areas. Later, the encyclopedia can be used to research topics for short reports (verbal and written) and longer written reports.

Readability is the critical variable that must be considered when selecting a dictionary or encyclopedia for classroom use. Numerous dictionaries and encyclopedias have been written for children (see listings in table). Though more selective in their entries, these materials attempt to control for the difficulty of the words (both decoding and concept level) and to include more explanatory information (e.g., illustrations, diagrams) to assist the young learner.

Instruction on reference materials should not be limited to library references but should be extended to telephone books, newspapers, magazines, commercial catalogs, and schedules (radio, television, bus, train). These daily reference aids use many of the study skills discussed in regard to classroom textbooks: using the table of contents, using the index, locating information in alphabetized lists, determining possible entry words, and verifying the relevance of information to a specific problem. Motivation is often increased when these familiar reference aids are used for instructional purposes (e.g., teaching categorization using the yellow pages, teaching reading of tables using the TV guide). Not only are these materials interesting to children but also they are important to the children's daily functioning. For this reason, these reference materials deserve as much emphasis as the dictionary and encyclopedia.

To maximize understanding of the following formats, particularly location of a word in the dictionary, practice the procedures with the appropriate reference material.

## Locating Information in the Library

Locating materials in the library involves a number of complex skills: understanding the general arrangement of the library, use

(Continued on p. 416)

**TABLE 4.6.2** *Locating and Interpreting Information in Graphic Material*

| SKILLS | TEACHER RESPONSE | CHILD RESPONSE |
|---|---|---|
| A. *Can locate and interpret information presented in pictorial aids.* | (Additional examples and questions should be provided.) | |
| Component Skills: | | |
| 1. Can determine the topic of the pictorial aid and type of information presented. | T. introduces flow chart, how to locate the chart, and how to determine the chart's topic. ("Read pages 301 and 302. What did these pages talk about? How did you know when to look at the chart? Right, the author told us to look at the tuna's food chain and used a symbol to show you where to look. Often a chart or picture will have a title or caption to tell us what it is about. Does this chart have a title or caption? When no title is given, the author will either tell us what the chart is about or we can look carefully at the chart. Does the author tell us what the chart is about? Yes, it is the tuna's food chain.") | C. tells how author refers the reader to the chart. C. tells the topic of the chart. |
| *Types of pictorial aids:* | | |
| photographs | | |
| drawings | | |
| diagrams | | |
| schematic drawings | | |
| cartoons | | |
| time lines | | |
| flow charts | | |
| charts showing    organization | | |
|                   processes | | |
|                   comparisons | | |
|                   sequences | | |

**The Start of the Food Chain**

When you grew algae and protozoans, you were growing plankton, in a way. As you know, plankton is the name given to the drifting plants and animals in the waters. Algae and protozoans make up most of this drifting life.

Do you recall (from Unit 7) what young salmon in the rivers eat? They live mostly on plankton — on algae and protozoans. So, too, in the oceans. Even the huge fish depend on the plankton — as part of their food chain. Let's look at the huge tuna's food chain, for example. ◆ The huge tuna feeds on large fish. The large fish feed on smaller fish. The smaller fish feed on still smaller fish, or snails, or crayfish. These little animals feed on the tiniest animals, the animal plankton. And the animal plankton feed on the plant plankton.

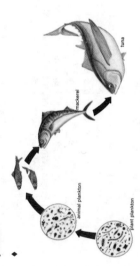

animal plankton
plant plankton
mackerel
tuna

From *Concepts in Science* (Orange) by Paul F. Brandwein et al. Copyright © 1975 by Harcourt Brace Jovanovich. Used with permission.

397

Table 4.6.2 cont'd.

| SKILLS | TEACHER RESPONSE | CHILD RESPONSE |
|---|---|---|
| 2. Can tell what the symbols used on the pictorial aid refer to and understands organization of information. | T. introduces symbols used in the chart and the organization of information. ("Look at the chart. Notice the black arrows. They tell us the direction to follow in the chart. Where should we start? Right, with the plant plankton. Where do we go next?") | C. tells meaning of symbols.<br>C. explains how chart is organized. |
| 3. Can locate information on chart. | T. tests children on locating information. ("Put your finger on the beginning of the food chain. Who feeds on the plant plankton? Who feeds on the animal plankton? Who feeds on the herring? Who feeds on the mackeral?") | C. locates information on the chart. |
| 4. Can make inferences based on the information presented in the chart. | T. tests children on conclusions reached from examining the chart. ("As you go up this food chain from the plant plankton to the tuna, what happens? Yes, the animals become bigger. Why is the plant plankton important to the tuna? Why is the plant plankton important to the herring? If there were no animal plankton, what would happen to the food chain? This food chain appears to end with the tuna. Is there any animal in the food chain after the tuna? Yes, larger fish might eat the tuna and certainly man eats tuna.") | C. reaches simple and more complex inferences based on the information in the chart. |
| B. Can locate and interpret information presented in a map.<br><br>Component Skills:<br>1. Can determine the topic of the map and the type of information presented.<br>Types of maps:<br>street, road, physical, relief, political, historical, vegetation, product, pictorial, population, weather | T. introduces map and how to determine the topic by reading the map's title. ("Look at the map on page 371. What is the title of this map? What is the map about? This type of map is called a *historical* map. What kind of map is this? An historical map tells about events in history. What events in history does this map tell about?") | C. reads title of map and determines what the map is about. |
| 2. Can tell what the symbols on map refer to. Special attention should be given to commonly used symbols for physical features, the map's scale and legend, and direction indicators. | T. introduces symbols used on the map, the scale (if given), and the legend. ("This is a world map. It shows all of the continents. The names of the continents are in dark black type. This continent is NORTH AMERICA. I will point to the other continents and you tell me their names. The names of the oceans are also written in dark print. This ocean is the Pacific Ocean. I will point to the other oceans and you tell me their names. Underneath the title of this map is its legend. The legend explains what the special symbols on the map represent. If land is blue on the map what nation | C. tells meaning of symbols on map.<br>C. reads legend and determines the meaning of each symbol. |

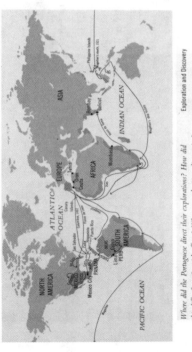

*Where did the Portuguese direct their explorations? How did this differ from Spanish efforts? What were the great discoveries?*

claimed that land? If the land is purple on the map what nation claimed that land?" The symbols introduced are very dependent on the map being used. Examine the map to determine the symbols that the children must understand to locate or interpret information on the map.)

Exploration and Discovery
Spanish claims
Portuguese claims

From Field Social Studies Program, *The Human Adventure: A Survey of Past Civilizations* by Frank J. Cappelluti and Ruth Grossman. Copyright © 1972 by Field Educational Publications, Inc.

| 3. Can locate information on the map. Practice in locating information on the map should be directed at those variables of particular importance to the specific map (e.g., physical features on a physical map; types of vegetation on a vegetation map; events on a historical map.) | T. tests for location of information on the map. ("Many of the early explorations began in Spain and Portugal. Look at the lines on your map. They show the routes of the explorers. This line is labeled Magellan. It shows the route Magellan took in his explorations. The arrow shows us which way Magellan went. Put your finger on Spain and Portugal. Find the line for Magellan's route. What continent did he go to first? After leaving South America, what islands did Magellan go to? What happened in the Philippine islands? Did Magellan's ship continue its journey? On what continent did the ship land next? Where did the ship go after leaving the southern tip of Africa? Did Magellan's ship go around the whole world?" Test children using additional location questions.) | C. locates information on the map. |
| 4. Can make inferences based on the information presented on the map (e.g., comparisons, contrasts, conclusions). | T. tests children on forming conclusions and comparisons based on the information presented in the map. ("Where did the Portuguese direct their explorations? How did this differ from the Spanish efforts? Which nation became involved in slave trade? How would you know this from the map? On what continents would you expect to find Spanish descendents? Why do you think the same language is spoken in Spain as in Mexico? Which nation claimed the most land? Can we determine that just by looking at this map?" Test using additional questions.) | C. makes simple comparisons and contrasts using the information in the map. C. reaches more complex conclusions, comparisons, and contrasts using the information found in the map. |

Table 4.6.2 cont'd.

| SKILLS | TEACHER RESPONSE | CHILD RESPONSE |
|---|---|---|
| C. *Can locate and interpret information presented in a graph.*<br>Component Skills:<br>1. Can determine the topic of the graph and the type of information presented.<br>Types of graphs:<br>*Line graphs* showing change in quantities.<br>*Bar graphs* using vertical or horizontal bars to show relationships and to compare quantities.<br>*Circle or pie graphs* showing how parts are related to wholes.<br>*Picto-graphs* showing quantities using pictures. | T. introduces graph and how to determine the topic of the graph by reading available titles and captions. ("On page 383 is a special kind of graph called a circle graph. We read the title of the graph to find out what the graph is about. What is the title of this graph? What will the information in the graph be about? What will we learn about Canada by studying this graph?")<br><br>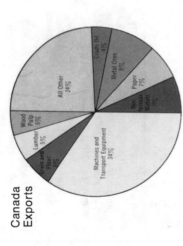 | C. reads available title and caption to determine the topic of the graph. |
| 2. Can tell how the graph is organized. | T. introduces the circle graph and how information is presented in the graph. ("The circle graph shows how parts are related to the whole. The whole circle represents 100% of Canada's exports. What does the whole circle represent? The circle is divided into parts. Each part shows one export. What does each part of the graph show? Look at the part labeled lumber. Five percent of Canada's exports are lumber. Each part of the circle graph tells us a percentage for one export out of the total exports. For example, lumber makes up 5% of Canada's total exports.") | C. tells what whole circle represents.<br>C. tells what parts of the circle represent. |
| 3. Can locate information in a graph. | T. models locating information in the graph and tests students on locating information. ("Let's look at the circle graph. I want to know what percentage of the total exports are grain and flour. I locate grain and flour on the circle graph and read the percentage. What percentage of exports are represented by grain and flour? Your turn, what percentage of Canada's exports are metal ores?" Test students on locating additional information in the circle graph.) | C. locates information in the circle graph. |

From Follett Social Studies, *Exploring Our World: The Americans*, by Herbert Gross et al. Copyright © 1977 by Follett Publishing Company. Used with permission.

4. Can make inferences based on the information presented in the graph (e.g., comparisons, contrasts, conclusions).

T. models making simple inferences (comparisons) using the graph and tests students on that skill. ("I want to know the major export from Canada. I look carefully at the graph and find the largest percentage. What is the major export from Canada? What are the three main exports from Canada? What total percentage do these three exports account for? Lumber and lumber products are important to Canada's economy. What evidence in the graph supports this statement? Canada relies greatly on its natural resources for exports. What evidence in the graph supports this statement? The United States imports many products from Canada. What do you think are some of the products shipped to the United States?")

C. makes simple comparisons and contrasts using the information.
C. reaches conclusions based on the data presented.
C. reaches more complex inferences based on data contained in the graph.

D. *Can locate and interpret information presented in a table.*
Component Skills:
 1. Can determine the topic of the table and the type of information presented.

T. introduces table, how to determine the topic by reading the title, and how to determine the type of information presented by reading the column headings. ("On top of page 174 is a table. A table presents number (statistical) information to go with what the book says. We read the title of the table to find out what the table is about. What is the title of this table? What is the table about? Yes, the table is about planets. We can read the headings at the top to find out what the table will tell us about planets. What is the first heading? Yes, the first heading is planets. Read the second heading. What is the second heading? What does this heading tell us about planets?" etc.)

C. reads title and determines what the table is about.
C. reads the column headings and determines what type of information will be provided in the table.

| INFORMATION ABOUT THE PLANETS | | | | |
|---|---|---|---|---|
| Planet | Distance from sun, in millions of miles | Diameter of planet, in miles | Length of year | Length of day | Weight of 100-pound human, in pounds |
| Mercury | 36 | 3,026 | 88 days | 59 days | 38 |
| Venus | 67 | 7,526 | 225 days | 244 days | 87 |
| Earth | 93 | 7,927 | 1 year | 1 day | 100 |
| Mars | 141 | 4,218 | 1.9 years | 24.6 hours | 39 |
| Jupiter | 483 | 88,700 | 11.9 years | 9.8 hours | 265 |
| Saturn | 887 | 75,100 | 29.5 years | 10.2 hours | 117 |
| Uranus | 1,780 | 29,200 | 84.0 years | 10.8 hours | 105 |
| Neptune | 2,800 | 27,700 | 164.8 years | 14 hours | 123 |
| Pluto | 3,670 | 3,500 | 247.7 years | 6.4 days | ? |

From The Silver Burdett Elementary Science Program, *Science: Understanding Your Environment* by George G. Mallinson et al. Copyright © 1975 by General Learning Corporation.

 2. Can tell how the table is organized and the units of measurement used.

T. introduces the concept of rows and columns and verifies if children understand the unit of measure used. ["The lines of information going DOWN the page are called columns (T. indicates on table.) What do we call the lists going *down* the page? The headings at the top of the columns tell us what type of information is in the columns. Put your finger on the heading for column two. What information is given in this column? Listen as I read down that column:

C. locates headings for columns.
C. reads information in columns.

Table 4.6.2 cont'd.

| SKILLS | TEACHER RESPONSE | CHILD RESPONSE |
|---|---|---|
| | 36 million miles, 67 million miles, 93 million miles, etc. What information is given in column three? Each of the numbers in this column refers to miles. Read the numbers in the column." Continue for remaining columns.] <br><br> [The lines of information going ACROSS the page are called rows (T. indicates on table.) What do we call the lists going across the page? Put your finger on the word *Mercury*. Mercury is a planet. The numbers in the same row as the word *Mercury* tell about that planet. Listen as I read across that row. 36—Mercury is 36 million miles from the sun; 3,026—Mercury is 3,026 miles in diameter; 88—Mercury's year is the same as 88 days on earth. (As you add explanatory statement, point to heading above column.) Find Pluto and read across the row. Be sure to read each of the numbers and tell what it means."] | C. locates headings for rows. <br> C. reads information in rows. |
| 3. Can locate information within a table (intersection of rows and columns). | T. models strategy for locating information within a table. ["I want to know the distance Pluto is from the sun. I put my finger (left-hand index finger) on the word *Pluto* and this finger (right-hand index finger) on the heading, distance from sun in million miles. Watch me. I run my right index finger down the column and my left index finger across the row. Where my fingers meet, I find the distance that Pluto is from the sun. How far is Pluto from the sun?" Model locating information with further examples. Provide ample practice locating information in the table.] | C. locates information at the intersection of rows and columns. |
| 4. Can make inferences based on the information presented in the table (e.g., comparisons, contrasts, conclusions). | T. models how to use the information in making comparisons and reaching conclusions. ["I want to know which of the planets is furthest from the sun. I find the column, distance from the sun, and read down the column to find the largest number. Which planet is furthest from the sun. Your turn. Find the planet that is closest to the sun. (Continue with additional comparisons.) I want to know which of the planets has the shortest year. Which column should I look in? Under the heading, length of year, which planet has the shortest year? Yes, Mercury has the shortest year. It takes Mercury the shortest time to get around the sun. Why do you think it takes Mercury less time to get around the sun? Yes, it takes less time for Mercury to get around the sun because it is closest to the sun. The closer the planet is to the sun, the shorter its year." T. should move from simple inferences (comparisons, conclusions and contrasts) to more complex inferences.] | C. makes simple comparisons and contrasts using the information. <br> C. reaches conclusions based on the data presented. <br> C. reaches more complex conclusions, comparisons, and contrasts using the data found in the table. |

**TABLE 4.6.3** *Locating Information in Reference Materials*

| SKILLS | TEACHER RESPONSE (Additional examples and questions should be provided.) | CHILD RESPONSE |
|---|---|---|
| A. *Can locate information using the dictionary.*<br><br>Component Skills:<br>Well-known dictionaries for children:<br>*The Holt Basic Dictionary of American English* (Holt, Rinehart and Winston)<br>*The Holt Intermediate Dictionary of American English* (Holt, Rinehart and Winston)<br>*Thorndike-Barnhart Beginning Dictionary,* Edward L. Thorndike & Clarence L. Barnhart, eds. (Scott, Foresman)<br>*Thorndike-Barnhart Junior Dictionary,* Edward L. Thorndike & Clarence L. Barnhart, eds. (Scott, Foresman)<br>*Webster's Dictionary for Boys and Girls* (American Book)<br>*Webster's Elementary Dictionary* (American Book)<br>*The Winston Dictionary for Schools,* Thomas K. Brown & William D. Lewis, eds. (Holt, Rinehart and Winston)<br>*The World Book Dictionary,* Clarence Barnhart, ed. (World Book—Childcraft International, Inc.) | | |
| 1. Can rapidly locate a word in the dictionary. Preskills: | | |
| a. Given a single letter, can tell if the letter is in the front (*a–h*), middle (*i–q*) or back (*r–z*) part of the dictionary. Example on board:<br>a b c d e f g h<br>i j k l m n o p q<br>r s t u v w x y z | T. introduces the alphabet divided into three groups. ["Here is the alphabet divided into three groups (T. points to alphabet on board.) These are the front letters, the middle letters and the back letters. What part? (T. points to the front, middle, or back letters.) Say the letters in the front part. Say the letters in the middle part. Say the letters in the back part. Is the letter *f* in the front, middle, or back? Is the letter *v* in the front, middle, or back?"] | C. tells if group of letters is in the front, middle, or back part of the alphabet.<br>C. says the letters in the front, middle, and back part of the alphabet.<br>C. says if letter is in front, middle, or back part. |
| b. Given any letter, can say alphabet beginning with that letter. (This skill enables children to decide whether to turn toward the front or back of the dictionary after opening to a certain page.) | T. models saying the alphabet beginning at any letter and tests on that skill. ("I can start at *f* and say the alphabet. Listen: *f g h i j k.* Your turn. Start at *f* and say the alphabet. Now say the alphabet starting with *i*." Continue with additional examples.) | C. says alphabet starting with various letters. |
| c. When given a single letter and a target letter, can determine whether to go to the front or back to get to the target letter. | T. leads students through strategy. ["Let's say we're at *f* and want to get to the letter *d*. When we say the alphabet we start at the letter *f* and go toward the *back*. Let's start at *f* and say the alphabet: *f g h i j k.* Did we get to *d*? No, so we can't go toward the back to | C. says alphabet beginning with a letter and continues until he comes to a target letter or completes the alphabet. |

403

Table 4.6.3 cont'd.

| SKILLS | TEACHER RESPONSE | CHILD RESPONSE |
|---|---|---|
| *Note: This strategy may seem awkward. However, it is not intended as the ultimate strategy students will use. With practice students will eventually be able to automatically turn toward the back or toward the front of the dictionary.* | get to *d*. We have to go toward the *front*. Now let's say we are at *g* and we want to get to *i*. Start saying the alphabet toward the back and see if we get to *i*: *g h i*. Do we get to *i* by going toward the back? Yes, so which way do we go to get from *g* to *i*? Now I am going to make it harder. We're at *e* and we want to get to *b*. Where do we start? Which way do we go to get to *b*? (Pause for students to say letters to themselves to decide if they go toward the back.) Right, we go toward the front.''] | C. says if you can get to the target letter by going to the back or by going to the front. |
| d. When given a guide word and a target word beginning with different letters, can determine whether to go to the front or back to get to the target word. *Note: The dictionary is not introduced until all preskills have been mastered.* | T. leads students through strategy. Pairs of words are written on the board. (''What is the guide word where we start? Right, *call*. What word do we want to get to? *Fast*. What's the first letter in *call*? What's the first letter in *fast*? We're at *c* and we want to get to *f*. Do we go toward the back or toward the front?'') | C. reads the guide word and target word.<br>C. tells first letter in words.<br>C. says if you get to the target letter by going to the back or by going to the front. |
| e. When given a guide word and a target word beginning with the same letter, can determine whether to go to the front or back to get to the target word. | T. leads students through strategy. Pairs of words are written on the board. (''What is the word where we start? Right, *cell*. What word do we want to get to? Right, *class*. What's the first letter in *cell*? What's the first letter in *class*? Are they the same? So we have to look at the second letter in each word. What's the second letter in *cell*? What's the second letter in *class*? Are they the same? So we look at those letters. We're at *e* and we want to get to *l*. Do we go toward the back or toward the front?'' Continue with many examples using different second letters. Extend practice to different third and fourth letters.) | C. reads the guide word and the target word.<br>C. tells first letter in words and if they are the same or different.<br>C. tells second letter in words and if they are the same or different.<br>C. says if you get to the target word by going to the back or by going to the front. |
| Subskills involving use of the dictionary. aa. Can locate guide words and tell how they are used in locating a page in the dictionary. *Note: This step introduces actual dictionary exercises.* | T. introduces guide words and which guide word to use when locating a word. [''Guide words appear at the top of every page in the dictionary (point to guide words on a number of pages in the dictionary.) The guide word on the left tells us the first word on the page. What does this guide word tell us? What is the first word on this page? The guide word on the right tells us the last word on the page. What will be the last word on this page? We always use the first guide word. The one on the left. Which of these guide words will we use? Here's how you use guide words. When you open the dictionary to a page, you look at the first guide word and ask yourselves, which way do I go to get to the word I'm looking for? If the answer is toward the back, you keep on going toward the back, still asking which way do I go. When the answer is toward the front, you've gone too far toward the back: the page just before you went too far has the word you want.''] | C. points to guide words at top of page.<br>C. tells purpose of left and right guide word.<br>C. tells which guide word is used in locating a word in the dictionary. |

| | | |
|---|---|---|
| bb. Can rapidly locate a *page* in the dictionary containing a specific word. | T. introduces a strategy for finding a page in the dictionary integrating prior steps. ["We're going to practice finding the right page in the dictionary. We're looking for the word *invention*. What is the first letter in *invention*? Is *i* in the front, middle, or back of the dictionary? Right, the middle. Watch, I open the dictionary to the middle. I opened the dictionary to a page with the guide word *pound* (point to left guide word.) Ask yourself, "Which way do I go to get from *pound* to *invention*? Which way do you go to get from pound to invention? Right, go toward the front. I quickly turn pages toward the front until I come to guide words that begin with the first two letters in the word I am looking for. What are the first two letters I'm looking for? Right, *in*. The first guide word with *in* is *involute*. Now what do you ask yourself? Right, 'Which way do I go to get from *involute* to *invention*?' Which way do we go to get from *involute* to *invention*? Right to the front. Watch me. (Turn page by page, looking at the left guide words.) I turn toward the front one page at a time and look at the left guide word. The guide word here is *intrigue*. Which way do we go to get from *intrigue* to *invention*? Right, to the back. We stop going toward the front so *invention* must be on this page." Model this process many times eliciting continuous responses from the children. When they understand the process, have them locate the correct page independently.] | C. tells whether dictionary should be opened to front, middle, or back.<br><br>C. reads guide word and tells whether to go toward the front or the back.<br><br>C. uses other letters to decide whether to go toward the back or front. |
| cc. Can rapidly locate a target word on a given page in the dictionary. | T. dictates page numbers and words and has students locate target words on specified pages. | C. locates page on which target word appears.<br><br>C. locates target word on a given page. |
| dd. Can rapidly locate words in the dictionary.<br>This step integrates all prior components for locating words in the dictionary. | T. tests children on locating words in the dictionary. ("Find the word *chemical* in your dictionary."<br>Provide much practice on the use of all previously taught components.) | C. locates words in dictionary. |
| ee. Can locate shorter words (*micro*) when longer words containing the same letters are also included. | T. presents the rule that shorter words with the same first letters come before longer words. T. tests children by presenting pairs of words (e.g., *orator* and *or; mono* and *monotype*) and having the children say which word comes first in the dictionary. | C. says which word comes first in the dictionary (shorter word with same initial letters as longer word.) |
| ff. Can locate base words in the dictionary when given a word with a prefix or suffix that is not listed. | T. presents the rule, if you cannot find a word that has an ending, cover up the ending and look up the base word. T. tests by presenting words with endings and having the child determine the base word. Extend similar instructions to prefixes. | C. states the rule.<br>C. covers up ending and says base word that should be looked up in the dictionary. |
| 2. Can locate, read, and use the dictionary definitions.<br>Subskills:<br>a. Can locate and read the meanings of target words in the dictionary. | See Section 4.3, "Vocabulary Instruction," for a discussion of teaching procedures. | C. locates word in the dictionary, reads the definitions, and refers to any supportive contextual sentences, diagrams, and/or drawings. |

Table 4.6.3 cont'd.

| SKILLS | TEACHER RESPONSE | CHILD RESPONSE |
|---|---|---|
| The child must be taught that words often have more than one meaning; that the meanings are numbered; that sentences using the word in context, drawings, or diagrams might be included to help explain a word's meaning. | | |
| b. When given a sentence with an unknown word, can locate the word in the dictionary and can select the best meaning for the context. | See Section 4.3, "Vocabulary Instruction," for suggested teaching procedures. | C. locates word in dictionary and selects best meaning for sentence context. |
| c. Can use dictionary definition to understand a statement in a book. | See discussion of glossary instruction in this section. | C. substitutes definition for word in sentence. |
| d. Can determine appropriate times to use dictionary to determine a word's meaning. | See Section 4.3, "Vocabulary Instruction." | C. states appropriate times to consult the dictionary to determine a word's meaning. |
| 3. Can determine the pronunciation of a word using the dictionary.<br><br>More able students can be introduced to additional information found in the dictionary entries (e.g., spelling of derivatives, synonyms for the entry word, and word origins) and supplementary information found in unabridged dictionaries (e.g., common abbreviations, given names, geographic locations, flags of different nations and English writing conventions). | The child should be taught the phonemes for common symbols, how to consult the pronunciation key at the bottom of the page and/or beginning of the dictionary, how to sound out words using those symbols, and how to use syllable divisions and accents to assist in decoding the world. | C. pronounces words. using the dictionary's pronunciation key. |
| B. *Can locate information in the encyclopedia.* | | |
| Well-known encyclopedias for children:<br>*Britannica Junior Encyclopedia*<br>(Encyclopaedia Britannica Educational Corp.)<br>*The Children's Hour* (Spencer International Press)<br>*Compton's Pictured Encyclopedia*<br>(F. E. Compton and Company)<br>*The Golden Book Encyclopedia*<br>(Golden Press) | T. introduces the encyclopedia and tells its purpose. ("This is an encyclopedia. An encyclopedia has many books called volumes. What do we call the books in an encyclopedia? Each volume has information on people, animals, places, and things. What kind of information is found in the encyclopedia? The topics are arranged in alphabetical order. How are the topics arranged?") | C. answers structured questions.<br>C. tells what kind of information is found in the encyclopedia.<br>C. tells how topics are ordered in the encyclopedia. |

*The New Book of Knowledge: The Children's Encyclopedia* (Grolier, Inc.)
*Our Wonderful World* (Grolier, Inc.)

Component Skills:

1. Can define encyclopedia and describe its purpose.

| | | |
|---|---|---|
| 2. Given a topic, can locate correct volume using the letters on the spines. | T. explains letter designations on volume spines and models locating a volume when given a topic. ["All of the volumes are numbered so we can put them away easily in the right order. How many volumes are in this set? Look at the letters on the spine of the volumes. These letters tell the first letter of the entries in the volume. Let's look at a volume. (Select a volume with a single letter designation.) What letter is on the spine? What should be the first letter of the entries in the volume? Let's check to see if all of the entries begin with this letter. (Write down some entries from the volume.) Some of the volumes have a letter followed by a dash and then another letter. This means that the volume includes words beginning with more than one letter. This volume is marked i-j. It has words that begin with *i* and *j*. What letters will the entry words begin with in volume 5, etc? In what volume would you find words beginning with *b*, etc? In what volume should I look for the topic, sheep?"] | C. determines number of volumes in set.<br><br>C. tells first letter of entries in volume.<br><br>C. tells correct volume when given a letter name.<br>C. tells correct volume when given a topic. |
| 3. Given a topic and the correct volume, can locate the entry using the guide words. (This assumes prior experience with guide words in the dictionary.) *Note: Guide words in encyclopedias are found on the top corners of the two facing pages. Many times the guide words are deleted because of illustrations at the top of the page. The child should be taught to use the first entry on the left-hand page or the last entry on the right-hand page when the guide words are deleted.* | T. explains how guide words are used in the encyclopedia. ["Encyclopedias use guide words similar to those in dictionaries to help us locate an entry. Look here. There are two pages facing you. This guide word (point to guide word on left-hand page) tells you the first entry on the left-hand page. This guide word (point to guide word on right-hand page) tells you the last entry on the right-hand page. We use the left guide words to help us locate words in the volume." Using the procedures introduced for the dictionary, test students on locating entries in the encyclopedia. "Find the entry *school* in this volume."] | C. locates entries in the volume. |

Encyclopaedia Britannica

Table 4.6.3 cont'd.

| SKILLS | TEACHER RESPONSE | CHILD RESPONSE |
|---|---|---|
| *Note: Remind children that names of people are listed last name first as in the index.* | | |
| 4. Given a topic, can locate the correct volume and corresponding entry. | This step incorporates component skills 2 and 3. T. should provide topics that children can locate in different volumes of the encyclopedia. Providing index cards with topics and a blank for the corresponding page numbers will allow children to use different volumes. | C. locates correct volume and correct entry using the guide words. |
| 5. Given a question or problem statement, with a single key word from the encyclopedia, can select key word, select correct volume, locate the entry in the volume, and read to find the answer to the question. | Use activities similar to those listed under component skill 7, "Locating Information in the Index." Many children's encyclopedias provide "detective" activities in which the children look up information to solve a particular problem. | C. selects key word from a question or problem statement, selects correct volume, locates entry in volume, and reads to locate the answer to the problem statement or question. |
| 6. Given a question or problem statement with more than one key word from the encyclopedia, can determine the best key word, locate the correct volume, locate the entry, examine the subheadings, and read the appropriate section to find the answer. Sample questions: How does the caste system work in *India*? What are the main crops in *Oregon*? How is *wine* made from grapes? | T. explains how to select the best key word and how to use the subheadings to locate the desired information. ["Read this question. What are the main crops in Oregon? What two key words might we look up in the encyclopedia? Which article is more likely to tell us about the crops in Oregon: the article on crops or the article on Oregon? Let's look up Oregon. (T. leads children through locating Oregon entry.) Under the major heading, Oregon, are subheadings. Listen as I read the subheadings: history, population, geography, industry, and agriculture. Under which of these headings will we find information concerning the crops in Oregon? Listen as I read that section. Did it tell us about the crops in Oregon?" T. leads children through additional examples and assigns independent practice activities.] | C. selects best key word from the problem statement. C. locates entry using key word. C. reads subheadings to locate section that might contain answer to the question. C. reads to find the answer. |
| C. *Can locate information in other library reference materials.* atlas almanac *Who's Who* specialized encyclopedias | Older intermediate children can be introduced to other library reference materials, the atlas being the most important. As with the dictionary and the encyclopedia, careful instruction on the contents of the reference material and how to locate information using their table of contents, index, and/or guide words is necessary. | |

D. *Can locate information in the telephone book.*

Preskills:
Can locate entries in an alphabetized list. Can locate entries using guide words.

Component Skills:
1. Can locate names of people, businesses, and governmental agencies in the white pages and corresponding addresses and phone numbers.

   Subskills:

| | | |
|---|---|---|
| a. Can tell what information is included in the white pages and how that information is organized. | T. introduces white pages and how information is organized. ("This section is called the white pages. The names of people, businesses, and agencies of the government in ＿＿＿ are listed in alphabetical order. The names of people are listed last name first.") | C. tells what information is listed in the white pages and how it is ordered.<br>C. tells how names of people are written in the white pages. |
| b. Can read entries in the white pages.<br>Various types of entries:<br>FINE G 305 N 14th .........687-9087<br>FINE I MD 13 Main St .......687-2245<br>FINE GROCERS INC<br>4560 18th Ave ..........688-2908 | T. introduces reading of white page entries. ("After the name of the person, business or government agency is their address and telephone number. Let's read these entries from the white pages." Give particular attention to common abbreviations—Dr., Rd., St.—symbols, initials, treatment of Mc and Mac in last names, and special typographic features used for businesses.) | C. reads entries in white pages including abbreviations and symbols. |
| c. Can locate entries in the white pages. | T. explains and models locating entries in white pages. ("To locate a person's name in the white pages we use the guide words at the top of each page." Model locating an entry in the white pages using the procedures suggested under dictionary. Provide ample practice under teacher supervision and independent assignments.) | C. locates names of persons, businesses and governmental agencies and corresponding addresses and telephone numbers in the white pages. |

2. Can locate information in the yellow pages of the telephone book.

   Subskills:

| | | |
|---|---|---|
| a. Can tell what information is included in the yellow pages. | T. introduces the yellow pages and the type of information in the yellow pages. ("The pages at the back of your telephone book are called the yellow pages. The yellow pages list the telephone numbers and address of businesses where you can buy *products* such as cars, boats, or furniture and where you can get *services* that you need such as your car fixed, your dog groomed, or your carpet cleaned. What information is found in the yellow pages? What are examples of *products* that businesses listed in the yellow pages might sell? What are examples of *services* that businesses listed in the yellow pages might provide?") | C. tells what information is given in the yellow pages.<br><br>C. gives examples of products and services. |
| b. When given an entry word in the yellow pages (product or service), can locate in yellow pages.<br>*Note: Special attention should be given to subheading delineations.* | T. introduces major headings and models how to locate heading in yellow pages. ["Products and services are listed in alphabetical order in the yellow pages and printed in dark black print. Look at the first page in the yellow pages and point to the major headings as I read them. How are the major headings ordered in the yellow | C. reads major headings.<br><br>C. tells how major headings are ordered. |

Table 4.6.3 cont'd.

| SKILLS | TEACHER RESPONSE | CHILD RESPONSE |
|---|---|---|
| Example:<br>Automobile—Body Repairing and Paint<br>Automobile—Dealers—New Cars<br>Automobile—Detailing<br>Automobile—Electric Service<br>Automobile—Glass<br>Automobile—Leasing | pages? What do the major headings refer to? Right, products and services." Model locating a major heading (product or service) using the suggested procedures under dictionary (subskills aa, bb, cc). Provide ample practice in locating major headings. This important skill is made somewhat more difficult by the unorganized nature of the yellow pages due to the inclusion of advertisements.] | C. tells what major headings refer to (products and services).<br><br>C. locates major headings in yellow pages. |
| c. When given a major heading in the yellow pages, can locate heading and businesses listed under the heading.<br>Note: Products are also listed under brand names under major headings. Example entries in yellow pages:<br>**PIANOS**<br>Baldwin Pianos<br> Thomas Music 2547 Main ...456-3429<br>Fred's Piano Shop<br> 4986 River Ave ..........456-8900<br>Kimbal Pianos<br> Jason Music Co. 1432 18th ..456-8765<br> (Please see advertisement Page 342)<br>MUSIC TODAY<br> Serving Redmond since 1949<br> A complete selection of fine consoles, uprights and grands.<br> Hours—9:00 to 6:00.<br> Open Monday and Saturday evenings.<br> 4593 Front St .............456-3290 | T. introduces listings found under major headings and accompanying advertisements. ["Under each of the major headings is a list of businesses that sell the product or do the service referred to by the heading. The names of the businesses are listed in alphabetical order. Look here. The heading is Pianos. Is this a product you can buy or a service? Right, a product. Under the heading Pianos are names of businesses that sell pianos. Their names are in dark black print that is smaller than the main heading. Listen as I read the names of the businesses listed under Pianos: Baldwin Pianos, Fred's Piano Shop, Kimbal Pianos. After the name of each business are its address and telephone number. What comes after the business's name? Read the addresses and telephone numbers for the piano stores. (Individual turns.) Some of the businesses pay for advertisements to go in the yellow pages. Their advertisements may be right with their listing in the yellow pages (show examples) or a page nearby. If it is not with the listing, it will say, Please see advertisement page _____. Look up gutters and downspouts. What businesses are listed? Which of the businesses paid for an advertisement in the yellow pages? Find the advertisement." Provide further practice in locating businesses under major headings and locating accompanying advertisements.] | C. tells how businesses are listed under the major headings.<br><br>C. tells what information is given after the business's name.<br><br>C. reads listings.<br><br>C. locates major heading, listings under heading, and accompanying advertisements. |
| d. Given a problem, can determine appropriate major headings and locate businesses providing the necessary service or product.<br>Note: Use problem situations that are familiar to the children so that they can make the necessary associations and determine appropriate headings. | T. poses problem situations and assists children in locating major headings and listings. ("I need to get a vet for my new puppy. What do I need? What major heading should I look under? I want to make reservations to fly to Spokane. Whom should I call to make the reservations? Right, an airline. What major heading should I look under? I want to build a dog house. What supplies will I need? What major headings should I look under?") | C. determines major headings.<br><br>C. locates major heading and listings under heading in response to problem statement. |

Note: Strategies for locating information in the 'yellow pages' can be extended to locating information in commercial catalogs (e.g., Sears Roebuck and Co., Montgomery Ward & Co., automotive supply catalogs, seed catalogs.)

3. Can locate additional information using aids in the telephone book including:
emergency numbers
information regarding making calls
billing and telephone service information
zip codes
governmental listings
time of day

T. introduces additional aids found in the telephone book and describes the use of each. Practice should be provided in locating each aid and information within the aid.

C. locates aid in phone book and specific information within the aid.

E. Can locate and understand information in the newspaper.

Note: The newspaper can be used for instruction on literal, inferential, and critical comprehension skills. The following is only a sample of the newspaper skills that can be introduced in the intermediate grades.
Component Skills:
1. Can tell the type of information found in each section of the newspaper:
national/international news
area/local news
editorials
columns
sports
classified ads
advertisements
schedules
entertainment
weather
information articles (cooking, home improvement, gardening)
financial

T. introduces separate sections of the newspaper and the type of information found in each. (example: "The front page of the newspaper has important news articles. These articles tell about things that have happened in the United States, in another country, or right in our own state or town. To be on the front page, it must be important news that many people will be interested in. What kind of news is on the front page? What will the important news articles be about? Read the first headline. What is this article about? Read the first paragraph. Is this article about something that happened in our country, another country, or in our city?" Introduce additional sections of the newspaper stressing the type of information provided. The introduction may be incorporated into lessons teaching comprehension and interpretation skills.)

C. labels each section and tells the type of information included in each section.

2. Can locate newspaper features using the newspaper's index.
Where to Look
Civic Calendar ............. 9A
Classified ............. 6–16C
Comics ............. 7B
Community Notes ............. 2C
Dear Abby ............. 7A

T. introduces the index and tests children on locating features when given the index entry or a question statement. ["Look at the bottom of the front page on your newspaper for the box labeled Where to Look. (Adapt to your local newspaper.) In this box is a special index that helps us find daily features in the newspaper. They are organized in alphabetical order. After each feature, it tells the section and page on which the feature is located. Look at the first entry. Civic calendar is found in section A, page 9. Where would

C. locates index on front page.

C. tells what information index includes (features, section, page)

C. locates feature when given index entry.

Table 4.6.3 cont'd.

| SKILLS | TEACHER RESPONSE | CHILD RESPONSE |
|---|---|---|
| Editorials ............ 10–11A<br>Financial ............ 4C<br>Horoscope ............ 7A<br>Newschool ............ 6B<br>Sports ............ Section B<br>Theaters/Entertainment ......... 8A<br>TV Schedule ............ 7A<br><br>From the *Eugene Registrar Guard*<br><br>*Note: The newspaper's index only includes regular features and doesn't usually include all features in the newspaper (e.g., local, national, and international news are not included in this index). Children must understand the type of information in each of these features before they can use the index.* | we find the sports page? the editorials? the comics? the TV schedule?<br>This is going to be harder. This time I want you to tell me what feature might have the information I want and the page and section of the newspaper. I would like to hire someone to clean my house. What feature would have that information? Right, the classified ads. What section, what page? I want to know what time the movie is playing tonight. What feature would have that information? What section, what page?"] | C. locates feature when given a problem statement. |
| 3. Can read the headline and lead paragraph in a news article (national, international, area, state, sports) and answer literal comprehension questions. | T. introduces the lead paragraph in news articles and the type of information contained in those articles. ["The first paragraph in a news article is called the *lead* paragraph. What is it called? The lead paragraph tells you the most important information. The lead paragraph usually answers these questions: *What* happened? *Where* did it happen? *Who* was involved? *When* did it happen? and sometimes *Why* did it happen? The lead paragraph tells us what, where, who, when, and why something happened. Read the first paragraph in this article. Let's answer the what, where, who, when, and why questions using this article. (Proceed with lead paragraphs from a variety of articles: national, international, area, state, or sports news.) What questions does the lead paragraph answer? Since the lead paragraph tells us the most important information, we often read these paragraphs to get a quick idea about the article. If it is interesting or is something we want to know more about, we can read the whole article. Why might we quickly read the lead paragraph of a news article?"] | C. tells the name for the first paragraph in a news article.<br><br>C. tells what questions are answered in the lead paragraph.<br><br>C. answers questions on specific article.<br><br>C. tells why they might read the lead paragraph before the whole article. |
| 4. Can read remainder of news article to find supportive details giving more information on what, who, where, when, and why. | T. explains the type of information found in the body of a news article and its relationship to the lead paragraph. ("What questions did the lead paragraph answer? The rest of the article is called the body. The body of the article gives more details about what happened, who was involved, where it happened, when it happened, and why it happened. Read the body of this article silently. The lead paragraph told us *what* happened. In the body of the article, what other details were given about what happened? The lead paragraph told us *who* was involved. In the body, what other details | C. tells the type of information found in remaining paragraphs (More details about who, what, when, where, and why.)<br><br>C. reads remaining paragraphs in article and answers questions on the supportive details included. |

were given about who was involved?" Continue, adding details from the body to information given in the lead paragraph. Extend to different types of news articles.)

---

5. Can read an editorial and determine: (1) what the issue is; (2) what side of the issue is represented; (3) what specific evidence is given to support that side; (4) what is the author's bias.

Editorials are the perfect means for teaching *critical* reading skills. See Section 4.4 for instructional formats for teaching critical reading.

C. determines issue addressed in editorial, the side of the issue represented in the editorial, the evidence given to support the author's conclusions or position, and the author's bias.

---

6. Can read advertisements including common abbreviations and locate information in the advertisement.

VACUUM BAGS

Assorted bags for most vacuums.

Stock up at this low price

2 pkgs. for $1.00    Reg. 89¢

T. introduces reading and locating information in advertisements. ("Many businesses pay to have advertisements in the newspaper. An advertisement is a printed announcement in the paper that usually tells us about something for sale. What do the advertisements usually tell us? Let's practice reading some of the advertisements. Turn to section B, page 1 in your newspaper. What business is advertising on this page? What are some of the things they are selling? Listen as I read this ad. Vacuum Bags. Assorted bags for most vacuums. Price, 2 packages for one dollar. Regular price 89¢. What abbreviation did they use for packages? What abbreviation was used for regular?" Give lots of practice reading advertisements stressing common abbreviations. Numerous math skills can be incorporated into the examination of ads, e.g., determining unit cost, the savings made, the total cost for a number of items. Have children locate specific information in the advertisement. "Look at the next advertisement. What is the product? What is its sale price? What is its regular price? How many can you buy?")

C. reads advertisement giving referent for abbreviations.

C. locates information in advertisements.

C. uses numerical information to answer questions (How much is saved? Would you save more by buying the large or small box?)

---

7. Can detect persuasive devices used in advertisements.
Types of persuasive devices that can be introduced:
*Glittering generalities*—Vague phrases (to influence reader) devoid of specifics.
*Plain folks appeal*—Relates product to common people to gain their support.
*Star appeal*—Uses highly popular or respected person to endorse product.
*Bandwagon effect*—Gives the impression that everyone is using the product.
*Winner appeal*—Gives the impression that you can be a "winner" by using this product.

T. presents persuasive devices, examples used in advertisements, and tests identification of persuasive devices. ("Businesses really want to buy their products. They do many things to convince us to buy their product. Sometimes they use 'glittering' words to describe their products. For example, they might use these words: *wonderful, fantastic, great, marvelous, beautiful, makes you happy, terrific.* We have to watch carefully when advertisements use these words. Look at this advertisement. What are they selling? Do they use any 'glittering' words to convince us to buy their sports car? Right, they say that the sports car is the 'sportiest car around,' 'small but luxurious,' and 'greatest car on the road.' Do they tell us why it is the sportiest car around? Why it's luxurious? Why it is greatest? No, they want you to believe them but they don't provide any details to support these statements. Look at this advertisement. Are any 'glittering words' used? Why were they included in the advertisement? Should you believe all of these statements?" Introduce each type of persuasive device coupled

C. identifies examples of persuasive devices in advertisements.

C. tells why device is used in advertisement.

C. identifies type of persuasive device used in specific advertisement.

Table 4.6.3 cont'd.

| SKILLS | TEACHER RESPONSE | CHILD RESPONSE |
|---|---|---|
| 8. Can read and interpret tables included in the newspaper. Examples: Radio & TV schedules, Game scores, Weather, Financial tables | with examples. When children have learned to identify a number of persuasive devices, test them on determining the device used. Magazine advertisements may also be used in these exercises.)<br><br>Much statistical and numerical information is presented in newspapers in tabular form. This is an excellent resource when teaching children to read and interpret tables. See suggested teaching procedures listed under "Locating . . . Graphic Material"—Tables. | |
| 9. Can read and locate information in the classified ads. Subskills: a. Can read the classified advertisements. | T. introduces classified advertisements, the type of information presented, and tests on reading advertisements. ("These are called the classified ads. They are short advertisements that individuals as well as businesses pay to have in the newspaper. The classifieds advertise *jobs* that are open such as, dishwashing, house painting, nursing, or accounting jobs. They also have advertisements for *products* that are for sale such as, houses, cars, TVs, and appliances. They also include advertisements on *services* that are available such as, cleaning your house, mowing lawns, and trimming hair. People also put in advertisements when they want a job, a service or a product to buy. For example, this ad says 'Wanted a part-time job babysitting.' This ad says 'Wanted—a 1976 Ventura.' Each word in an advertisement costs money. As a result, the advertisements are usually short with many abbreviations. Let's practice reading some classified ads." Provide practice reading ads stressing the use of abbreviations to shorten the ad. Ask questions that demand location of information within ads.) | C. tells where classifieds are located in the newspaper.<br><br>C. tells the type of advertisements found in the classifieds.<br><br>C. reads advertisements.<br><br>C. locates information in classified ads in response to a question. |
| b. Given a major entry in the classified index, can locate entry and corresponding location in classified ads. *Note: Classified indexes vary in different newspapers. They may be arranged topically or alphabetically.* Example—Topical organization: BUSINESS OPPORTUNITIES<br>250 Business for Sale<br>　　　Partnerships<br>255 Business Locations for Lease<br>260 Agents, Distributors<br>265 Franchise Available<br>Example—Alphabetical organization: | T. introduces use of classified index, numbering system used, and how to locate ads in classified section. The following procedures are written for a topical index. ("We find advertisements on the classified pages by using the classified index. Classifieds that advertise the same type of product, service, or job are grouped together. In the index, we find *major headings* that tell us the type of job, product, or service. Listen as I read the first main headings: merchandise, employment, business opportunities, and financial. Read the rest of the headings. Look at the main heading, merchandise. Subheadings listed under the main heading tell us different types of merchandise that people want to buy or sell. Read the subheadings with me." Continue reading other headings and subheadings. To use the classified index, the children must understand the categorization system used.) | C. locates index for the classified advertisements.<br><br>C. locates and reads main headings in the index.<br><br>C. locates and reads subheadings listed under each main heading.<br><br>C. locates number reference for each subheading in the index. |

From the Eugene Registrar Guard

CLASSIFIED
INDEX

All Classifications are Numbered
and Appear in Numerical Order
Acreage ...............180–186
Air Conditioning .........505
Antiques .................539
Antiques & Collectors Cars ...686
Apartments, Courts, Rent ..219–234
Apartments, Courts for Sale ...114

From the
*Oregonian*

Teach using the format in your local newspaper.
Examples of headings and subheadings and numeration system used in classified pages:

| | |
|---|---|
| Duplexes, Multiplexes, Unfurnished | 608 |
| Apartments, Unfurnished | 615 |
| Apartments, Furnished | 610 |

c. Given a problem, can determine appropriate main heading and sub-heading in index and corresponding advertisements.

*Note: Classified advertisements can be used in math instruction (comparing prices, determining the yearly rent on an apartment) and as a stimulus for teaching many important living skills (e.g., career education —career opportunities, type of training needed, salaries; home management—cost of rent, buying a home, appliances; consumer skills—warranties, guarantees, loans, interest.)*

T. introduces the numbering system used in the classifieds and the numerical organization of the advertisements. ("Look under the main heading, merchandise. Before each of the subheadings is a number. What number comes before toys? tools? clothing? What is the same about all of these numbers? Yes, they all begin with 100 . . . 102, 105, 110. What do the numbers begin with under employment, schools, and training? Right, 200. We use these numbers to find the ads we are looking for. The advertisements are arranged by numbers, beginning with the 100's, then the 200's, then the 300's, etc. Watch me. I want to find the advertisements for furnished apartments. I look under the main heading, rentals. Then I look for the subheading, apartments—furnished. What number comes before that subheading? Right, 615. I look at the numbers at the top of the page until I find the 600's. Then I look down the columns until I find 615. Now I can read the advertisements to find an apartment in the area of town that I need. Your turn. Find the subheading, motorcycles, under the main heading, automotive, in the index. What number is listed? Right, 823. What number should you look for at the top of the classified ads? Yes, the 800's. Find the 800's and then 823 in the classifieds." Continue with further testing of location in the ads when given the main heading and subheading.)

T. poses problem situations and assists children in locating appropriate headings and corresponding advertisements.
See the use of yellow pages for suggested teaching procedures.

C. determines the similarity in numbers listed under the main heading.

C. locates heading and subheading and locates advertisements on classified pages.

of the classification system employed in the library (Dewey Decimal System or Library of Congress system), use of the card catalog, and specialized location aids (*Reader's Guide to Periodical Literature*). In order to develop efficient library users and topical researchers, classroom teachers or school librarians must carefully teach and review these skills.

The most basic library skills involve understanding the different types of books contained in the library (fiction, nonfiction, picture books, magazines, audio-visual materials, biographies) and their general location in the library. These skills can be introduced to young primary children to broaden their library "browsing." When children have learned the requisite alphabetizing and numeration skills, the use of call numbers to locate books can be introduced. Most small school libraries use the Dewey Decimal System of classification or an adaptation of that system. The Library of Congress System should only be introduced if used in the school library or to more able students, when a "practice" library is available. Critical to using the Dewey Decimal System is the ability to classify books as fiction and nonfiction since separate organizational procedures are used for each type of book. Organization of fiction books should be introduced first because of its reliance only on alphabetizing skills. When learning to locate fiction books, the children must be introduced to the alphabetical arrangement of the books and the use of the first letters in the author's name on the book spine.

The arrangement of nonfiction books is much more complex. The books are arranged topically and assigned a class number that refers to a broad class in the Dewey Decimal System. Books within that class are given specific call numbers and arranged numerically on the shelves. Children must determine the row in which the book will appear using guides at the end of the rows, locate the shelves containing similar call numbers, and finally locate the specific book.

The use of call numbers in locating nonfiction books is only helpful when the correlate skill, locating cards in the card catalog, has been taught. The card catalog, though similar to other indexes, is a complex tool due to the use of three separate cards for each book (subject, author, title) and application of location skills to a file of cards rather than to an alphabetized listing. Children must be taught how to quickly locate cards and to record the information needed in locating books.

Skills in locating books using the card catalog will only be maintained if these skills are frequently used and occasionally reviewed. The teacher must continuously assign projects, problems, and tasks that are best solved by using the card catalog.

## Recording Information for Later Retrieval

When studying in the content areas, students must be able to sift through the mass of information presented, extract the most salient main ideas and details, and record this information for later retrieval and review. Note-taking, summarizing, and outlining are three procedures used by students to record the high points of content information. These procedures can be used to record information from a single textbook or reference book, from a number of sources, and from verbal input, such as lectures, movies, discussions or auditory tapes. Though recording of information for use in writing reports, preparing discussions, or studying for examinations is less critical in the elementary classroom, these skills must be introduced in the intermediate grades, and students must gain some facility with these skills prior to entering secondary schools where daily recording of information is required.

When recording information from a textbook, the critical main ideas and details may either be noted in the text or exter-

(continued on p. 423)

**TABLE 4.6.4** *Locating Information in the Library*

| SKILLS | TEACHER RESPONSE (Additional examples and questions should be provided.) | CHILD RESPONSE |
|---|---|---|
| A. *Can locate general sections within the school library:*<br><br>fiction<br>picture books<br>nonfiction<br>reference books<br>trade books on specific topics<br>biographies<br>magazines<br>audio-visual<br>hardware<br>software | T. or librarian introduces the general organization of the library. This should be done in the primary grades long before the card catalog or call numbers are introduced. | C. locates general section of library with desired type of book. |
| B. *When given a call number for a specific book, can locate book on shelves.*<br>Preskill:<br>Can locate an entry within an alphabetized list using the first, second, or third letter and within a numerical listing.<br>Component Skills:<br>1. Can determine if a book is fiction or nonfiction. | T. defines fiction and nonfiction and tests using titles from library books. ["Library books can be separated into two categories: fiction and nonfiction. Stories made up by an author from his own imagination are called fiction. What is fiction? These books are fiction. (Show examples of well-known fiction books.) Books that give *factual* or real information are called nonfiction. What is nonfiction? These books are nonfiction. (Show examples of nonfiction books including biographies.) I will read a title of a book. You tell me if it is fiction or nonfiction."] | C. defines fiction and nonfiction.<br><br>C. tells if book is fiction or nonfiction. |
| 2. Can locate a fiction book on the library shelves. | T. explains organization of fiction books within library, models locating a fiction book, and tests children on locating fiction books. ("Fiction books have their own location in the library. Fiction books in our library are located in these bookshelves. What kind of books would I find here? On the spine of each fiction book are the first two or more letters of the author's last name. The author's last name for this book is Cleary. On the spine is written *Clea* in large print so we can easily see it." Test with questions of this format: "Who is the author of this book? What letters are written on the spine?") | C. locates fiction books in library.<br><br>C. locates first letters of author's last name on spine of book. |

Table 4.6.4 cont'd

| SKILLS | TEACHER RESPONSE | CHILD RESPONSE |
|---|---|---|
| *Note: Children must be taught that fiction books are arranged alphabetically:* (1) *according to the author's last name;* (2) *according to the first name of the author when there are several authors with the same last name;* (3) *by the title of the book when an author has several books in the collection.* *Children must also be taught that fiction books are arranged on the shelves in alphabetical order from left to right and top to bottom.* | ["Fiction books are arranged alphabetically by the *author's last name* on the shelves. Look here. The first author's last name begins with A. (Show remaining books with author's names beginning with A and beginning of B's. Stress organization from left to right on the shelves and from top to bottom.) I want to find *Paddington Takes to TV* by Michael Bond. Would I look in the beginning, middle or end shelves for Bond? Right, the beginning shelves. I look on the spines and find the names beginning with B. Then I look for names beginning with Bo. When I find the Bo's, I look for Bond. Here is the last name Bond. When there are a number of authors with the same last name, those books are arranged in alphabetical order by the *author's first name*. Would I find Michael Bond before or after Ralph Bond? Before or after John Bond? Here are the books by Michael Bond. When the author has several books on the shelf, the books are ordered alphabetically *by the title of the book*. Which of these titles would I find first, *A Bear called Paddington* or *Paddington Takes to TV*. Here is our book. Your turn. I will give you a card with an author's name and the title of a book. Find the book and bring it to me."] | C. tells how books are arranged on the shelves: alphabetically by author's last name; alphabetically by author's first name when more than one author with same last name; alphabetically by title when several books written by same author. C. locates books when given author's name and title. |
| 3. Given the call number, can locate a nonfiction book on the library shelves. *Note: Children should not memorize the ten classes or subclasses in the Dewey Decimal System. However, they should realize that the books are organized by topic with books on the same topic found together in the library.* Main classes in Dewey Decimal System: 000–009 General works 100–199 Philosophy and Psychology 200–299 Religions 300–399 Social Sciences (Government, Law, Sociology, Education, Political Science, etc.) 400–499 Languages (Philology, Dictionaries, Grammars) 500–599 Pure Science (Mathematics, Chemistry, Earth Science, etc.) | T. explains organization of nonfiction books within the library, models locating a nonfiction book, and tests children on locating nonfiction books. ["Nonfiction books have their own location in the library. They are on these bookshelves (show location in your library). Look at the spine of these nonfiction books. There is a number with a letter or letters beneath it. The number is the *class number*. The *class number* is determined by the topic of the book. Books on the same topic will have the same or almost the same *class number*. (You may wish to introduce the classification chart in the library. Note, many of the class categories will be difficult for elementary children to use because of past experiential background.) All books on the same topic will be found in the same place in the library. Look here. These books all have the class number _____. They are all about _____. The letters underneath the class number are the first letter or letters in the author's name. We call the class number and the letters from the author's last name the *call number*. What is included in the call number? Read the call number on the spine of this book."] ["Nonfiction books are arranged *numerically* by the call number | C. locates section of library with nonfiction books. C. locates call number on spine. C. determines class number and explains that books on the same topic have the same or similar class number. C. reads entire call number. C. explains arrangement of nonfiction books (numerical order by call number). C. locates nonfiction book when given call number. |

418

600–699  Applied Science (Medicine, Engineering, Agriculture, Manufacturing, etc.)
700–799  Fine Arts and Recreation (Music, Painting, Sports, Photography etc.)
800–899  Literature
900–999  History, Biography, Travel

from left to right and top to bottom on the shelves. (Show numerical organization of books.) The numbers at the end of each row (in smaller library, on each shelf) indicate the call numbers of all books on the shelves in that row. What is the call number of the first book in this row? The last book? I want to find the book with the call number 598 L2. Let's look at the numbers at the end of the rows. Which row should I look in? Right, 454-621. I look in that row for the 500's. When I find the 500's I look to the very end of the 500's for 598. When I find 598, I look for my exact call number. Here is the book. (Demonstrate with additional examples.) Now it's your turn. I will give you a card with a call number on it. Find the book and bring it to me."]

4. When given the name of a famous person, can locate biographies about that person.
Note: *Biographies are usually located in a separate section of the library. The books may be classified under B(iography) or the call number 921. The books are arranged on the shelf alphabetically by the last name of the person the book is about. If there are more than one book about a person, those books are arranged alphabetically by the author's last name. Books containing more than one biography (e.g., Women Themselves by Johanna Johnson) must be located using the 920 call number.*

T. introduces biographies, and location of biographies in the library and explains how they are arranged on the shelves. ['A biography is a book that tells about a *real* person's life. All of the books on these shelves are biographies (show appropriate shelves). What will these books be about? Listen carefully. Biographies are arranged in alphabetical order by the last name of the person the book is about. Are they arranged by the author's last name? No, by the last name of the person the book is about. Here is a book about President Abe Lincoln. What letter is it alphabetized under? L, that is the first letter in Lincoln. I want to find a book about Marie Curie. What last name should I look for? Yes, Curie. Would I look at the beginning, middle, or end of the biographies? Yes, at the beginning. I find the C's; then I look for Curie. What is the title of the book? (Illustrate with examples found in your library.) Now it's your turn. I will give you a card with a number of famous person's names. You locate a book about the person. Or here is a list of famous people. You find a book about the person and write down the title and author of the book.']

C. defines biography.

C. explains how biographies are arranged alphabetically by the last name of the person the book is about.

C. explains how books about the same person are arranged alphabetically by the last name of the author.

C. locates biographies given the name of the person.

C. When given an author's name, title of a book or a subject, can locate card in card catalog and corresponding book on the library shelves.
Component Skills:
1. Can locate the card catalog in the library and tell its general purpose.

T. introduces the card catalog, its contents and when a student would use the card catalog. ("These drawers are called the card catalog. In these drawers are cards that contain information on all of the books in the library. The card catalog is an index of all of the materials in the library. We use the card catalog to help us locate books in the library. What do we call this collection of drawers? When would you use the card catalog?")

C. locates card catalog in library.

C. tells what is contained in the card catalog drawers (cards with information about all of the books in the library).

C. tells when the card catalog is used.

2. Can describe the information found on an author card, a title card, and a subject card.

T. introduces examples of each type of card beginning with the title card and where we might look for each type in the card catalog. ["Before we can use the card catalog to help us find books, we first

C. labels card title card.

C. reads information on title card.

Table 4.6.4 cont'd.

| SKILLS | TEACHER RESPONSE | CHILD RESPONSE |
|---|---|---|

**TITLE CARD**

636.7 Cole, Joanna
C675  My puppy is born. With photos by Jerome Wexter.
    New York, Morrow, 1973.
    40 p. illus.
    SUMMARY: Black and white photographs trace the
  first eight weeks in the life of a miniature
  dachshund puppy from the minute he is born.
  SF426.5 C64    636.7

**TEACHER RESPONSE:** need to understand the cards in the catalog. The first type of card is called a title card. If we know the title of a book and want to find it in the library, we can find the title card in the card catalog and then use the call number to find the book. Look at this title card. At the top of the card is the title of the book. What is the title of this book? Under the title is the author's name, the title again, the publisher of the book and year in which it was published. (Show a number of examples.) A title card has the title of the book at the top. Is this a title card? (Show examples and nonexamples of title cards). In the top left-hand corner is the call number. What is the call number of this book? When would we look up a title card? What information on the card would help us locate the book?"]

**CHILD RESPONSE:**
C. locates call number on title card.

C. tells when you would look for a title card.

**AUTHOR CARD**

636.7 Cole, Joanna
C675  My puppy is born. With photos by Jerome Wexter.
    New York, Morrow, 1973.
    40 p. illus.
    SUMMARY: Black and white photographs trace the
  first eight weeks in the life of a miniature
  dachshund puppy from the minute he is born.
  SF426.5 C64    636.7

**TEACHER RESPONSE:** T. introduces author card. ("Sometimes we know the author's name when we are trying to locate a book. Sometimes we read a book we really like and want to read other books by the same author. In these situations, we can look up the author card. Look at this author card. What is written at the top of the card? How is the author's name written? What is written below the author's name? What is the call number for this book? When would we look for the author card in the card catalog?")

**CHILD RESPONSE:**
C. labels card author card.
C. reads information on author card.
C. locates call number on author card.
C. tells when author card would be used.

**SUBJECT CARD**

    Dogs.
636.7 Cole, Joanna
C675  My puppy is born. With photos by Jerome Wexter.
    New York, Morrow, 1973.
    40 p. illus.
    SUMMARY: Black and white photographs trace the
  first eight weeks in the life of a miniature
  dachshund puppy from the minute he is born.
  SF426.5 C64    636.7

**TEACHER RESPONSE:** T. introduces subject card. ("Many times we don't have a specific book in mind when we come to the library. Instead, we want a non-fiction book on a *certain topic*, such as snakes, motorbikes, or sewing, or we want a fiction book on a *certain topic*, such as horse stories or sports stories. We can look in the card catalog for a third type of card, a subject card. Look at this card. What is written at the top? Right, dogs. This is about dogs. What is the subject of this book? What information is written below the subject? What is the call number for this book? When would we look for the subject card in the card catalog?")

**CHILD RESPONSE:**
C. labels card subject card.
C. reads information on subject card.
C. locates call number on subject card.
C. tells when subject card would be used.

**SKILLS:** 3. When given a title, author, or subject can locate the correct drawer in the card catalog.

**TEACHER RESPONSE:** T. explains the organization of the drawers (top to bottom, left to right). ["The title, author, and subject cards are arranged alpha-betically in the drawers. The alphabet begins with this top drawer

**CHILD RESPONSE:**
C. tells how cards are arranged in the card catalog.
C. labels the outside guides.

and continues down the drawers and then starts over at the top (show using actual card catalog). Some of the drawers contain cards whose titles, authors, or subjects begin with the same letter. Other drawers contain more than one letter. For example, this drawer labeled C–E contains letters *c*, *d*, and *e*. What letters would be in this drawer? We call these letters on the outside of the drawers *outside guides*. I will tell you a *subject*, you tell me the drawer I should look in. Cats, horses, music, helicopters. I will tell you an *author*; you tell me the drawer to look in. Remember, authors are listed by their *last name*. Virginia Lee, Avon Neal. I will tell you the *title* of a book and you tell me the drawer to look in. Listen, when the title begins with *a*, *an*, or *the*, they alphabetize the card by the next word in the title. *Me Nobody Knows. The Peter Pan Bag.* Good, you used the word after *the*, *Peter*, and told me to look in the drawer with *p* on the *outside guide*."]

C. tells letters contained in drawers.
C. tells drawer that contains subject card when given subject.
C. tells drawer that contains specific author card using last name.
C. tells drawer that contains specific title card using second word in title if the first word is *a*, *an*, or *the*.

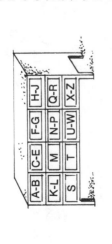
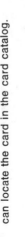

4. When given a title, author or subject, can locate the card in the card catalog.

T. introduces inside guides, models location of a card in the card catalog, and tests on that skill. ["Let's look inside the F–G drawer. In the drawer we find cards with tabs. These are called *inside guides*. They help us find a card quickly. The cards behind the first inside guide begin with the letters *FA* and continue alphabetically to *FO*. What will be the first two letters of the title, author, or subject on the card behind *FO? GA? GO?* Watch me find a card. I am looking for a subject card on flutes. The first two letters are *FL*. *FL* is to the back of *FA*. I go to the next tab. Is *FL* to the front or back of *FO?* (If the children have difficulty, use the same procedures suggested under dictionary for saying the alphabet to the back to determine if you go to the front or back.) Right, we go to the front. I turn the cards quickly looking for FL. When I find the FL words I look for flute.

Now, its your turn to find a title, author or subject card in the card catalog. I will give you a card with titles, authors, and subjects. You locate the card and write down the call number."]

C. tells how cards are organized alphabetically behind the inside guides.
C. locates title, author or subject cards in the card catalog.

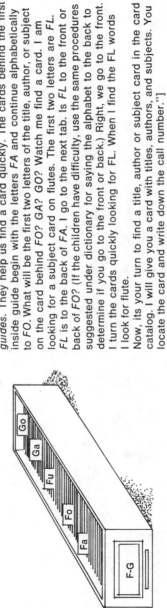

Table 4.6.4 cont'd.

| SKILLS | TEACHER RESPONSE | CHILD RESPONSE |
|---|---|---|
| 5. When given a title, author or subject, can locate the card, write down the necessary information, and locate the book in the library. | T. explains how to write down the necessary information from the title, author or subject card. ("Once we locate the card in the card catalog, we must write down the call number, the title of the book, and the author's name. What must we write down? If we don't write down all of this information, we may have difficulty finding the book. Watch me. I write down the call number first. It has to be right; so I check it. Then I write down the title and author on the same card. Now I can find the book. If I find more than one book listed in the card catalog that I am interested in, I make separate cards for each of those books. Your turn. Locate the author, title or subject on this card. Find the card in the card catalog, write down the necessary information and find the book.") | C. copies call number, author's full name, and the title of the book from the card in the card catalog.<br><br>C. locates book after writing down necessary information. |

```
629
D37h
    Delmar, Frank J.
    The new world of
    helicopters
```

| SKILLS | TEACHER RESPONSE | CHILD RESPONSE |
|---|---|---|
| As with other study skills, continual practice must be given on using the card catalog. The children must have real reasons to consult the card catalog (to locate subject area books for a report or for the classroom library, to locate other books by an author after reading one book in class). | | |
| C. Can locate articles in periodicals using the *Reader's Guide to Periodical Literature.* | The *Reader's Guide* can be introduced to older elementary children in conjunction with report writing on topics needing current information. The *Reader's Guide* to periodicals is arranged alphabetically by topic similar to an encyclopedia. After each topic, references are listed. To shorten the length of the guide, abbreviations are used extensively. Carefully introduce reading of the entries and using the table of abbreviations (names of journals) at the beginning of the guide. | |

nally. Indication of salient points within the text may be accomplished through underlining, color highlighting, marginal notes of key words or phrases, and marginal indicators of significant facts (e.g., vertical lines in margin parallel to important segments of discourse and stars next to key points). These procedures have a number of advantages. Not only do they require a minimum amount of writing, but also they allow the student to concentrate on the determination of significant main ideas and details rather than on the form of the recording system. When reviewing within-text notations, the student can refer to the overall structure of the material and can reread text discourse to clarify important information. Also, using within-text notations requires an active, overt response that should lead to more involvement in textbook reading. Despite its potential advantages, within-text recording systems are seldom feasible within the elementary school where students do not own their textbooks. However, these procedures can be introduced and practiced using newspaper articles, duplicated expository materials, weekly magazines commonly found in elementary classrooms, and expository articles found in supplementary workbooks.

Since few children in the public schools purchase their own textbooks, external recording systems such as outlining, note-taking, and summarizing should be introduced and used by students. The type of recording system used depends on the organization of the information, the type of input (verbal and written), the amount of information that must be recorded, and the intended use of the recorded information. When students are completing a general reading assignment or preparing for a general report on a topic, outlining can be used to record all of the salient points within the text material. Note-taking, on the other hand, is generally used to record specific information in response to a question, problem, or topic. Though outlining and note-taking involve the summarization of in-

formation, students may also write more formal sentence or paragraph summaries of information.

The most common types of outlining introduced to intermediate children are the topical outline and the sentence outline. In preparing a sentence outline, each of the main ideas and supporting details is written in complete sentences. Though this is less efficient than the recording of key words or phrases as in the topical outline, sentence outlines are useful when time will elapse between when the information is recorded and when the information is utilized for study or report writing. Both of these systems involve the recording of topics, main ideas or subtopics, and supporting details in a fashion that clearly indicates the subordination of ideas. The relationship of ideas in the sentence and topical outlines is shown through the use of indentation, numbers (Roman and Arabic), and letters (upper- and lower-case) (see Figures 4.6.2, 4.6.3, and 4.6.4).

A less formal type of outlining, indentation outlining, illustrates the subordination of ideas through systematic indentation of topics, main ideas, and supporting details. This system is far less complex than parallel systems using number and letter designations, allowing the child to focus on the relationship of ideas rather than the formality of the outlining system. This type of outlining is particularly adaptable to verbal input where the organization of ideas is less apparent and often less structured than written expository materials (see Figure 4.6.5).

Notes and written summaries are two additional ways to record information from text material. Notes simply involve the jotting down of information generally in response to a question or topic. The notes may take many forms: enumerated lists, sentences, or key words or phrases. If the notes are collected from a number of sources for later summary in a verbal or written report, they may be recorded on separate cards or pieces of paper for later

**FIGURE 4.6.2**  *Sentence Outline Following Paragraph Structure*

Title: Igneous Rock

I. The earth's crust is very thin.
   A. Under the continents the crust is about 20 miles thick.
   B. The earth's crust is thinner under the oceans.

II. Most of the earth is mantle rock.
   A. Mantle rock is under the earth's crust.
   B. Mantle rock is nearly 1800 miles deep.
   C. Mantle rock is very hot.

III. There are pockets of hot, liquid rock in the earth's crust and mantle.
   A. This hot, liquid rock is called magma.
   B. When magma cools and hardens it forms igneous rocks.
      1. Igneous means fiery.

IV. Magma can well up and spill out on the land and ocean floor.
   A. This magma is called lava.
   B. Volcanos are made from lava.
      1. Steam and hot lava may make the volcano blow its top.

V. There are two kinds of igneous rock.
   A. One kind of igneous rock cools and hardens on the surface.
   B. One kind of igneous rock cools and hardens underground.

VI. Igneous rock that cools and hardens on the surface has small grains.
   A. Obsidian and basalt are igneous rocks that are formed on the surface.
   B. Some of these rocks have grains that we cannot see.

VII. Igneous rock that cools and hardens underground has larger grains.
   A. Granite and granite pegmatite are formed underground.

reorganization by topic. Summaries, though demanding in organization and writing skills, are often effective ways to record information. When writing a summary, the student condenses the content of a number of paragraphs into a concise paragraph including a sentence that summarizes the topic of the discourse and additional sentences that summarize the main ideas presented in the paragraphs. Often summaries will be written after notes are collected or an outline prepared. At other times, the student may read in the textbook until the topic switches to a new topic, stop, and write a summary of the information to that point before proceeding.

One unique recording system that combines the structure of notes with the amount of information recorded using outlines is question-answer notes. Using this system, the child reads a paragraph or series of paragraphs, stops reading when the topic changes, considers the main points presented, writes questions that are answered in the material, and finally writes the answers to these questions using brief notations. This system has a number of advantages. The student must carefully consider the material in order to generate appropriate questions concerning the main idea or supporting details, thus avoiding the rote, copying responses that some students adopt when preparing notes, outlines, and summaries. This system also leads to efficient review and study. The questions are recorded on the left side of the paper with the answers in note form on the right side of the paper. Thus, the student can easily cover the answer, pose the written question, recite the answer, and check recall with the written answer (see Figure 4.6.6).

Whether the student is recording information using notes, summaries, or outlines, a common set of characteristics is desir-

**FIGURE 4.6.3**   *Sentence Outline Condensing Information from a Number of Paragraphs*

Note: Though paragraph-by-paragraph outlining is probably easiest to introduce to naive students, the result is often a long, detailed outline. When students have mastered simple outlining and understand the organization of information to show the relationship of ideas, they can be taught to combine ideas from a number of paragraphs, to delete less important details, and to write condensed information in outline form.

Types of Rock (title)

I. (Topic) Igneous Rock.
  A. (Main idea). Igneous rock is formed when hot, liquid rock cools.
      1. (Supporting detail) Hot, liquid rock is found in the earth's crust and mantle.
      2. (Supporting detail) This hot, liquid rock is called magma.
      3. (Supporting detail) Magma can well up and spill out on the land and ocean floor.
          a. (Supporting detail) This magma is called lava.
          b. (Supporting detail) Volcanos are made from lava.
  B. (Main idea) There are two kinds of igneous rock.
      1. (Supporting detail). One kind of igneous rock cools and hardens on the surface.
          a. (Supporting detail). These rocks have small grains.
          b. (Supporting detail). Some of the grains cannot be seen.
          c. (Supporting detail). Obsidian and basalt are igneous rocks that are formed on the surface.
      2. (Supporting detail). One kind of igneous rock cools and hardens underground.
          a. (Supporting detail). These rocks have larger grains.
          b. (Supporting detail). Granite and granite pegmatite are formed underground.
II. (Topic) Sedimentary Rock.

able across all recording systems. The student should use his own words whenever possible to avoid the habit of copying large segments of the discourse unless a direct quotation is needed. The information should be organized in a consistent fashion that clearly indicates the relationship of ideas. Generally, a block style of recording, in which ideas of the same level of subordination are aligned, is desirable for illustrating the relationship among topics, main ideas, and supporting details. With most notation systems, brevity and the use of key words and phrases should be stressed. However, it is critical that the notes or outline be complete enough to allow the student to accurately retell the content using the recording system.

Before introducing any system for recording information, the students must be introduced to three critical entry behaviors: determining the topic for a paragraph or series of paragraphs, determining the main idea for a paragraph, and determining which details support the main idea through explanation or examples. These entry behaviors must be carefully introduced primarily through presentation of examples and extensively practiced before a recording system is introduced.

**FIGURE 4.6.4**   *Topical Outline Following Paragraph Structure*

Title: Igneous Rock

I. Earth's crust—thin
   A. Under continents—average 20 miles thick
   B. Under oceans—thinner

II. Most of earth—mantle rock
   A. Under the crust
   B. 1800 miles deep
   B. Magma cools and hardens
   C. Very hot

III. Pockets of hot, liquid rock in crust and mantle
   A. Called magma
   B. Magma cools and hardens
     1. Kind of rock called igneous
     2. Igneous means fiery

IV. Magma spills out on the land and ocean floor
   A. Lava
   B. Volcanos—from lava
     1. Steam & lava make volcano blow its top

V. Two kinds of igneous rock
   A. Cooled & hardened ON SURFACE
   B. Cooled & hardened UNDERGROUND

VI. Cooled & hardened ON SURFACE—small grains
   A. Obsidian & basalt
   B. Cannot see some of the grains

VII. Cooled & hardened UNDERGROUND—larger grains
   A. Granite & granite pegmatite

**FIGURE 4.6.5**   *Indentation Outline (Partial)*

Igneous rock

Earth's crust—thin
   Under continents—average 20 miles thick
   Under oceans—thinner

Most of earth—mantle rock
   Under the crust
   1800 miles deep
   Very hot

Pockets of hot, liquid rock in crust and mantle
   Called magma
   Cools and hardens
     Forms igneous rocks
       Igneous means fiery

Magma spills out on the land and ocean floor
   Called lava
   Volcanos made from lava
     Steam and lava may make volcano blow its top

**FIGURE 4.6.6**   *Note-taking—Question and Answer Structure*

Subheading: Igneous Rock                                    pp. 179–184

| Question | Answer |
|---|---|
| What is the earth's crust like? | very thin<br>under continents—20 miles thick<br>under ocean—thinner |
| What is most of the earth made of? | mantle rock<br>under crust<br>very hot |
| What does the hot liquid rock do? | pushed around<br>goes up cracks |
| What is magma? | molten rock |
| What is igneous rock? | made of magma<br>cool and hard<br>igneous means fiery |
| What is lava? | magma that has spilled onto the surface<br>ocean or land |
| How is a volcano built? | from lava mixed with lots of steam<br>may blow off top |
| How many kinds of igneous rock are there? | two kinds<br>cooled and hardened on top of the surface<br>cooled and hardened under surface |
| What are igneous rocks formed on the surface like? | small grains<br>sometimes cannot see grain<br>obsidian, basalt |
| What are igneous rocks formed underground like? | larger grains<br>granite, granite pegmatite |
| Do all igneous rocks look the same? | no, different colors |

When children have mastered these entry behaviors, a system for recording information can be introduced. The teacher should carefully examine the classroom textbooks selecting the most highly organized textbook for use in this instruction. She should then select a recording procedure that is appropriate to the structure of the material. If the material has well-defined headings, subheadings, and main ideas, outlining, either topical, sentence, or indentation, can be introduced. If the material does not have well-defined headings and subheadings or a highly organized paragraph structure, question and answer notes or topical summaries may be introduced. Using the latter systems, the child reads until the topic changes and then makes notations on the content before resuming reading.

When introducing any of these recording procedures, the teacher should model the procedures stressing the organization of topics, main ideas, and supporting details as well as the structure of the recording system. Initial practice should be given at the paragraph level with part of the structure provided (e.g., a skeleton outline listing topics and main ideas). Gradually these prompts should be faded with more and more of the responsibility for independent recording placed on the child. It is important that the child read the discourse before making any notations either within the book or externally. Until the entire segment (paragraph or series of paragraphs on a single

(continued on p. 438)

**TABLE 4.6.5** *Note-taking, Outlining, and Summarizing*

| SKILLS | TEACHER RESPONSE<br>(Additional examples and questions should be provided.) | CHILD RESPONSE |
|---|---|---|
| A. *Can determine the topic for a series of paragraphs.*<br>Component Skills:<br>1. When given a number of choices, can select the topic for a paragraph.<br>Example item:<br>"The bones can be pulled closer together because there is a joint at your elbow. A joint is a place where two bones meet and can move against each other. As the biceps grows shorter and pulls at the bone in the lower arm, that bone turns at the joint. The lower arm moves upward, and the hand comes closer to the shoulder."<br>From *Intermediate Level A* of the GINN SCIENCE PROGRAM by J. Myron Atkin and others, Copyright © 1975, 1973, by Ginn and Co. (Xerox Corp.).<br>The topic of this paragraph is:<br>1. biceps<br>2. bones<br>3. joints<br>4. arms | T. defines topic, presents example paragraphs and topics. Present many examples before asking child to select topic. T. presents paragraph with four topic choices and assists children in selecting topic. ("Listen as I read this paragraph. This whole paragraph talks about _____. A *word* or *phrase* is used to state the topic. A topic tells about the whole paragraph. What does a topic tell about? What is the topic of this paragraph? Right, the topic of this paragraph is _____ because the whole paragraph talks about _____. Your turn. Read the next paragraph. Here are four topics. Which one is the topic for the paragraph?" Read each answer and assist students in eliminating topics that do not cover the content of the entire paragraph. Use questions of the following format. "Did the whole paragraph talk about _____?" Further corrections can be made by examining each sentence to see if the majority of sentences relate to the topic. Present many examples.) | C. defines topic.<br><br>C. selects topic from a number of choices. |
| 2. When given a paragraph, can read the paragraph and state the topic. | T. reviews definition for topic and demonstrates how to determine the topic of a paragraph when no choices are given. ["A topic is a word or phrase that tells about the whole paragraph. What does a topic tell about? Read this paragraph to yourself. The topic is _____. What does the whole paragraph talk about? Now it's your turn. Read the next paragraph and write down a word or phrase that tells what the whole paragraph is about. What is the topic of the paragraph? (individual turns.) If errors occur, use questions of the following type. "Did the whole paragraph talk about _____?" For a further correction, go through each sentence to determine if the majority of sentences talk about the given topic.] | C. defines topic.<br><br>C. states the topic of a paragraph.<br><br>C. writes down the topic of a paragraph. |
| 3. When given two or more paragraphs written on the same topic, can read the paragraphs and state the topic. | Use the same procedures as introduced with Component Skill 2. | C. states the topic of a series of related paragraphs. |

| Objective | T. (Teacher) | C. (Child) |
|---|---|---|
| 4. When given a longer piece of discourse, can determine when the topic changes.<br>*Note: Use discourse that does not contain explicit headings and subheadings for this exercise.*<br>*Note: Determining the topic of a paragraph or series of paragraphs is a necessary entry behavior for note-taking, outlining, and summarizing. When a student can determine the topic of a paragraph or series of paragraphs, it is much easier to determine the main ideas.* | T. introduces strategy for determining when the topic changes. ("Read the first paragraph. What is the topic of this paragraph? Read the next paragraph. Does it have the same topic? Ok, continue reading until the topic changes and then stop." Continue with additional examples.) | C. determines the topic of first paragraph.<br><br>C. determines when the topic changes. |
| B. *Can determine the main idea(s) for a paragraph or series of related paragraphs.*<br>Component Skills:<br>1. When given a number of choices, can select the main idea for a paragraph.<br>Example practice item:<br>"Indians used natural resources for all their needs. They hunted, fished, and grew crops. Their homes, clothes, and tools were made from animals and plants. They also used plants for medicines and dyes. Some tribes used shells, stone, copper, and silver for jewelry and art."<br><small>From Follett Social Studies, *Exploring Our World: The Americas* by Herbert H. Gross et al., Copyright © 1977 by Follett Publishing Co.</small><br>The topic of this paragraph is _____.<br>The main idea of this paragraph is:<br>a. Indians made their homes from animals and plants.<br>b. Indians hunted, fished, and grew crops for food.<br>c. Indians used natural resources for all their needs. | T. defines a main idea and its relationship to a topic. ("Listen as I read this paragraph. The topic is _____, because the whole paragraph talks about _____. Listen, the main idea is _____. A main idea is one sentence that summarizes or tells the most important information given about the topic. What is a main idea?" Present many example paragraphs and main idea statements. Include summary sentences as well as sentences containing the most important information given on the topic.)<br>T. leads children in selecting the main idea of a paragraph. ("Read this paragraph. What is the topic of the paragraph? Right, natural resources. We want to select the main idea for this paragraph. The main idea is one sentence that summarizes or tells the most important information about natural resources. Let's read the choices. Does the first choice summarize or tell the most important information given about the topic? No, it is one idea but the whole paragraph does not talk about how the Indians made their homes. Read the next choice. Does this sentence summarize or tell the most important information given about the topic? No, it is one idea but the whole paragraph does not talk about how Indians got their food. Read the last choice. Does this sentence summarize or tell the most important information given about natural resources? Indians used natural resources for all their needs. Let's reread the paragraph and see if the sentences tell how Indians used natural resources to meet their needs." Read each of the sentences given in the paragraph. Point out how each of the sentences explains the main idea or gives examples of the main idea. Continue with additional paragraphs. Point out that the author often includes a sentence with the main idea at the beginning or end of the paragraph.) | C. defines main idea.<br><br>C. determines the topic of the paragraph.<br><br>C. selects the main idea from a number of choices. |
| 2. When given a paragraph with an explicitly stated main idea, can read the paragraph and state the main idea. | T. leads children to select a main idea from the paragraph. ("We have seen how the author often includes a main idea sentence in the paragraph. Today we are going to find main idea sentences in paragraphs. Read this paragraph. What is the topic of the | C. reads paragraph and tells the topic. |

Table 4.6.5 cont'd.

| SKILLS | TEACHER RESPONSE | CHILD RESPONSE |
|---|---|---|
| | paragraph? Which sentence tells the main idea for the paragraph?" Use the following questions to correct errors and clarify correct responses. "Does this sentence summarize or tell the most important information about the topic? Does the whole paragraph talk about this idea?" A sentence by sentence correction can also be made. "Listen, you said the main idea was _____. The rest of the sentences should tell us more about this main idea. Let's read each sentence to see if it tells about the main idea." Continue with many examples.) | C. locates the sentence that summarizes the information presented about the topic (main idea sentence). |
| 3. When given a paragraph with no stated main idea, can read the paragraph and state the main idea of the paragraph. | T. models the process and leads students in stating a main idea when it is not explicitly presented in the paragraph. ["Listen as I read this paragraph. What is the general topic of this paragraph? Is there a sentence in the paragraph that summarizes the information presented about the topic?" Proceed sentence by sentence if students cannot determine if there is a main idea sentence. "No, this paragraph does not have a main idea sentence. We have to think of one sentence that summarizes the information presented about the topic. What did the whole paragraph tell us about _____ (topic)?" Have children suggest main idea statements. Use the following question to correct errors and clarify responses. "Does this sentence summarize or tell the most important information about the topic?" A sentence by sentence correction can also be used after children state possible main ideas (see corrections for Component Skill 2).] | C. reads paragraph and states the general topic. <br><br> C. reads paragraph to determine if a main idea is stated. <br><br> C. states a main idea for the paragraph. <br><br> C. rereads paragraph to determine if main idea statement summarizes the information presented about the topic. |
| C. Can determine the important details in a paragraph that explain or provide examples of the main idea. <br><br> Component Skills: <br> 1. When given a paragraph, can determine which details explain or provide examples of the main idea. <br> Note: The purpose of these lessons is to assist students in determining which of the details provided are important to understanding the main idea. | T. introduces details given in paragraphs that explain or expand on the main idea. ["Most paragraphs include details that explain or expand on the main idea. Listen as I read this paragraph. What is the topic of the paragraph? In one sentence, what is the main idea of the paragraph? Now let's look at each sentence. Read the second sentence (assume for this example that the first sentence includes the main idea). Does this sentence tell us more about the main idea or give us an example? Yes, it gives us an example of the main idea. Read the third sentence. Does it tell us more about the main idea or give us an example of the main idea? Yes, both the second and third sentences are important details. They tell us more about the main idea or give us examples of the main idea."] | C. states the topic of a paragraph. <br><br> C. states the main idea of the paragraph. <br><br> C. determines if the details explain the main idea or are examples of the main idea. <br><br> C. determines if the details are related to the main idea. |

T. assists children in determining if the details explain or expand the main idea. ("Read the next paragraph. What is the main idea? What is the topic? What is the main idea? Read the second sentence. Does it tell us more about the main idea or give an example of the main idea? Yes, it gives an example of the main idea. Read the next sentence. Does it tell us more about the main idea or give an example of the main idea? No, this sentence includes interesting information, but it does not tell us about the main idea. This detail is less important because it does not tell about the main idea." Continue with additional paragraphs that include details that are/are not related to the main idea.)

D. *When given a section of a content area textbook with explicit headings and subheadings, can outline the content.*

Component Skills:
1. When given a completed outline, can explain how topics, main ideas, and supporting details are indicated through indentation, numbers, and letters.

Example outline presented to students:
Title: United States Government (chapter heading)
I. Legislative Branch (chapter subheading)
  A. Congress makes laws for the country.
    1. Congress includes the House and the Senate.
    2. Both groups must agree on a bill.
    3. The president must sign a bill before it becomes law.
  B. Senate members are called senators.
    1. There are two senate members from each state.
    2. Senators are elected for 6-year terms.
  C. Members of the House of Representatives are called representatives.
    1. There are 430 representatives.
    2. States with larger populations have more representatives.
    3. Representatives are elected for two-year terms.
II. Executive Branch (chapter subheading)
(This is only a partial outline of chapter section.)

T. presents completed outline on section of content area textbook.

T. explains the use of indentation, numbers, and letters to show subordination of ideas (topics, main ideas, and supporting details). ["An outline lists the most important information presented in the chapter. Read the title of this outline. The entire outline will talk about the United States government. What will it talk about? Major topics are listed after Roman numerals. What major topic is listed after Roman numeral I? Roman numeral II? Roman numeral III? What is listed after Roman numeral I? Right, major topics. Look at the capital letters under Roman numeral I. After each letter is a main idea about how Congress makes laws for the country. What is given after each capital letter? Read the first main idea. What is the second main idea? What is the third main idea? What is given after each capital letter? Right, a main idea. Look, we indent the main ideas to show that they are talking about this major topic (Point to I on outline). Look under Roman numeral II. What are the main ideas about the executive branch? Why did we indent these main ideas? Look under Roman numeral I. What is the first main idea about the legislative branch? Under this main idea are three supporting details that tell us more about the main idea. Read the first supporting detail that follows number 1. Number 2. Number 3. Look we have indented numbers 1, 2 and 3 to show that these details tell us more about the main idea. Why did we indent numbers 1, 2 and 3?" Continue with additional examples.]

C. reads title of outline.

C. states the content of the entire outline.

C. reads the major topics in the outline.

C. states that major topics are indicated by Roman numerals.

C. reads the main ideas listed under a major topic.

C. states that main ideas are designated with capital letters.

C. explains the use of indentation to show the relationship of main ideas to major topics.

C. reads the supporting details listed under a main idea.

C. states that supporting details are designated with numbers.

Table 4.6.5 cont'd.

| SKILLS | TEACHER RESPONSE | CHILD RESPONSE |
|---|---|---|
| *Note: This format illustrates the use of a sentence outline. However, the same general steps may be used to introduce an indentation outline or a topical outline.* | | C. explains the use of indentation to show the relationship of supporting details to main ideas. |
| 2. When given a completed outline, can explain the relationship of the topics, main ideas, and supporting details to the section in the textbook. | T. presents example of outline based on section of content area textbook and shows children the relationship of the title, topics, main ideas and supporting details with the headings, subheadings and content found in the chapter. | |
| | ["Open your book to page _____. Find the major heading on this page. Good, the major heading is 'United States Government.' Find this on your outline. This is the title of the outline. The whole outline is about the United States Government. | C. locates major heading in textbook. |
| | | C. compares major heading with title of outline. |
| | Look for the first subheading under the heading 'United States Government.' What is the first subheading? Find this on your outline. How is it labeled? Right, with a Roman numeral I. I have used this subheading to tell the first major topic in the outline. Find the second subheading after 'United States Government.' What is the second subheading? Find it on your outline. How is it labeled on the outline?" Continue until all subheadings have been located and compared to the major topics on the outline. | C. locates subheadings in textbook. |
| | | C. compares subheadings to major topics listed in the outline. |
| | "Read the first paragraph after the subheading 'Legislative Branch.' What is the topic of this paragraph? Right, making laws. Tell me in one sentence the main idea of this paragraph. Right, that Congress makes laws for our country. Find this main idea on your outline. What is placed before this main idea? Why is the main idea indented? Read the next paragraph. What is the topic of this paragraph? Right, the Senate. On your outline find the second main idea under Roman numeral I. Read the main idea. What is placed before this main idea? Why is the main idea indented?" Continue examining remaining main ideas. Stress their relationship to paragraphs in the discourse and to the major topics (subheadings in the book). | C. reads paragraphs and states the topic and main idea of each paragraph. |
| | | C. compares the paragraph main ideas to the main ideas listed in the outline. |
| | "Let's go back to the beginning of the outline. What was the first major topic? What was the first main idea? This main idea came from the first paragraph following the subheading 'Legislative Branch.' Read the paragraph. What important supporting details are given in the paragraph about how Congress makes laws for the country? How are these details written in your outline? Why are the supporting details indented under the main idea?" Continue examining remaining supporting details. Stress their relationship to paragraphs in the discourse, the main idea of each paragraph, and the outline listings.] | C. reads paragraphs and states the supporting details for each main idea. |
| | | C. compares the paragraph's details to the supporting details listed in the outline. |

3. When given a partially completed outline containing the title, major topics, and main ideas, can complete the outline by adding necessary supportive details from the chapter.
   Title: United States Government
   I. Legislative Branch
   A. Congress makes laws for the country.
      1. _____
      2. _____
      3. _____
   B. Senate members are called senators.
      1. _____
      2. _____
      3. _____
   C. House of Representative members are called representatives.
      1. _____
      2. _____
      3. _____

T. assists students in locating supporting details to complete the partially completed outline.
("We have been looking at examples of outlines for a number of days. Today you are going to complete an outline of a section in your book. Open to page _____. Read the heading for this section. Find this heading on your outline. Good, this is the title of the outline. Read the first subheading under 'United States Government.' Find this subheading on your outline. What is placed before the major topic 'Legislative Branch'? Read the first paragraph. What main idea is listed in the outline for this paragraph? How many supporting details should we find in this paragraph? Read the paragraph again. Write down three important supporting details that explain or give examples of the main idea." Elicit responses from individuals. Correct responses with questions of the following types: Does this detail tell us more about the main idea? Does this detail provide an example of the main idea?" Continue through four or five more paragraphs, assisting children in determining the important supporting details for each main idea. Provide feedback on their choices. Have children complete the remainder of the outline independently. Continue work on this skill for a number of days.)

C. locates heading in textbook and compares to title of outline.

C. locates subheading in textbook and compares to major topic listed in the outline.

C. reads paragraph and determines the topic and main idea for the paragraph.

C. reads paragraph and determines the important supporting details that expand on the main idea.

C. writes down supporting details for each main idea.

---

4. When given a partially completed outline containing the title and major topics, can complete the outline by adding necessary main ideas and supportive details.
   Title: United States Government
   I. Legislative Branch
   A. _____
      1. _____
      2. _____
      3. _____
   B. _____
      1. _____
      2. _____
      3. _____
   C. _____
      1. _____
      2. _____
      3. _____

T. assists students in locating main ideas and supporting details to complete partial outline.
("Today, we are going to add main ideas as well as details to complete our outline. Read the title of our outline. Find that heading in your book. Now find the first subheading. Locate that subheading on your outline. How many main ideas should we find for this major heading? Good. Read the first paragraph. What is the main idea of this paragraph? Write this main idea after capital letter A in your outline. Now reread the paragraph to find three important supporting details that explain or expand on the main idea. Write these supporting details in your outline. Ok. Read the next paragraph. What is the main idea of this paragraph? Write the main idea after capital B in your outline. Now reread the paragraph to find two important supporting details that explain or expand on the main idea. Write these supporting details in your outline.") Continue through four or five more paragraphs, assisting children in determining the main idea and supporting details. Provide feedback on their choices. Have students complete the remainder of the outline independently. Continue work on this skill for a number of days.)

C. locates heading in textbook and compares to title of outline.

C. locates subheading in textbook and compares to major topic listed in the outline.

C. reads paragraph and determines the main idea for the paragraph.

C. records the main idea on the outline.

C. reads paragraph and determines the supporting details that explain or expand on the main idea.

Table 4.6.5 cont'd.

| SKILLS | TEACHER RESPONSE | CHILD RESPONSE |
|---|---|---|
| *Note: When students are skilled at determining the main ideas and supporting details when the number of main ideas and supporting details are designated, drop the capital letter and number designations and have children independently write down the main ideas and supporting details.* | | C. records the supporting details on the outline. |
| 5. When given a section of chapter with explicitly stated headings and subheadings, can outline the content. | This step involves a culmination of all previous steps. Independent outlining should not be expected until children are proficient at completing partial outlines. The teacher should model outlining stressing selection of outline title (major heading), outline major topics (subheadings), main ideas for each topic, and supporting details. Following modeling of outlining, have children copy the teacher's outline and complete remainder independently. When students are able to complete outlines following teacher modeling, assign them short segments of the chapter to outline and provide feedback on their outlining by showing them your outline of the same material. Do not look for exact replications of your outline. Instead, stress the subordination of ideas and the relationships of ideas shown by indentation, numbers, and letters. | C. copies first portion of outline prepared by the teacher and outlines remainder of section independently.<br><br>C. outlines section of text independently and compares to teacher's model. |
| E. *When given a section of a content area textbook or other expository material that does not contain explicit headings and subheadings that can be used in outlining, can outline the content.* | This skill is much more complex than similar outlining where headings and subheadings are given. This skill should not be introduced until students have mastered outlining discourse with headings and subheadings. The same steps presented for Skill D should be used in teaching this type of outlining: (1) providing supporting details to complete the outline, (2) providing supporting details and main ideas to complete the outline, (3) providing major topics, main ideas, and supporting details to complete skeleton outline and (4) independent outlining of section following teacher modeling of process. | |
| F. *Can take notes from a single source or number of sources to respond to a specific question or to a given topic.*<br><br>*Note: Outlining is used when the student wishes to record the majority of information presented in a chapter or article. However, many times the student may only wish to record information in response to a question or given topic. Notes can be taken in these cases. Generally, the* | | |

question or topic is recorded with the specific information listed under the question or topic. The notes may take many forms: sentences, listings, key words, or phrases. Just as in outlining, the notes must be adequate to communicate to the reader. As with outlining, indentation can be used to indicate the subordination of ideas.

Component Skills:
1. When given a series of questions or topics, the student can locate related information in a text and record the information in note form under or next to the topic or question.
Example notes:

What are the natural resources of the Southern states?
  clays
  coal
  hardwoods
  phosphates
  softwoods
  stone

Different ways to record text material.
Within-text
  Marginal Notes
  Underlining
  Symbols in margins
External
  Outlines
    Indentation
    Sentence Outline
    Topical Outline
  Notes
  Summaries

T. presents examples of notes using listings, phrases as well as sentences. Tells the purposes for taking notes and the use of indentation to show the relationship among ideas. ("We outline a chapter or article when we want to record all of the important information so that we can later study the information. Sometimes we only want to record or write a little information on a certain topic or to answer a specific question. Look at these notes. In the first example, I wanted to know the natural resources of the Southern states. What did I write down? Why did I put the answer in list form? Look at the next topic. The topic concerns different ways to record information. There are two major ways to record information: within the text and externally from the text. I wrote each of these down. What did I write under 'within-text'? What did I write under 'external'? Why did I indent the words under 'within-text'? Right, just like in outlining, I can indent to show that these words tell more about within-text recording of information." Continue with additional examples of notes. Point out brevity of notes, organization of notes using indentation, different style of recorded information depending on question or topic, and neatness of notes. "Your turn. Open to page 45. For each of the following topics write down brief notes.") If notes are to be compiled from a number of sources to summarize in a report, have the children write each note on a separate card or piece of paper. A brief citation can also be listed. However, early report writing should focus on writing notes in the child's own words with less focus on the source of the information.

C. tells when information is recorded in notes rather than outline form.
C. examines notes of various styles and explains desirable attributes of notes.
C. takes notes given a single source, topic, or question.
C. takes notes given more than one source.

G. *Can use a question/answer format for recording information.*

Component Skills:
1. When given the questions written on the left-hand side of a paper, can complete the question and answer notes.
Example Exercise

T. presents examples of question/answer notes based on a section of content area textbook. ["Our textbook answers many questions. Today we are going to learn a special type of note-taking called question and answer notes.

C. locates question column of notes.
C. locates answer column of notes.

Table 4.6.5 cont'd

| SKILLS | TEACHER RESPONSE | CHILD RESPONSE |
|---|---|---|
| *Question*     *Answer*<br><br>How does Congress make laws?    Senate and House agree on bill. President signs.<br><br>What are members of the Senate called?    Senators<br><br>How many years are they elected for?    6<br><br>How many Senators come from each state?    2<br><br>What are members of the House of Representatives called?    Representatives<br><br>How many years are they elected for?    2<br><br>What determines the number of representatives from each state?    population | Look at my notes (show example). On this side of the page (point to left column), I have written questions that I determined after reading the material. What did I write on the left-hand side of the paper? On this side of the page, I wrote the answers to my questions. What did I write on the right-hand side of the paper? Look at my answers. I wrote quick notes using key words and short sentences. What kind of notes did I write to answer the questions?"]<br><br>T. introduces exercise involving writing answers when the question is given. Stresses briefness in the answers.<br><br>("Today you are going to complete my question and answer notes. I have written the questions on the left-hand side of the paper. You only have to write the answers to the questions. Read the first paragraph. Now you are ready to answer the questions on this paragraph. There may be only one question or more than one question if the paragraph contained much important information. Answer all of the questions that were covered in the first paragraph. Look at my answers. Notice that I used brief notes including key words and short sentences.") Complete a number of paragraphs with children and then have them independently complete the notes. Continue practice for a number of days. | C. states the characteristics of notes (brief using key words and short sentences).<br><br>C. completes question and answer notes when the questions are given. |
| 2. When given a section of a content area textbook, can record notes using a question and answer format.<br><br>*Note: As with other recording systems, question/answer notes are developed at the paragraph level. However, larger segments could be read before questions are formulated.* | T. introduces a strategy for determining questions on the content and recording answers for questions.<br><br>("You have been completing question and answer notes on your textbook for a number of days. Today you are going to write the questions as well as the answers. Where do we put the questions? Where do we put the answers? Turn to page _____. Read the first paragraph. What is the most important information given in this paragraph? (Individual turns) Ok, now let's write questions that relate to information. Listen to me. One piece of important information is that Congress has two bodies, the Senate and the House. Now, listen to my question. What are the bodies of Congress? Where should I write this question? Where should I write the answer? What answer should I write down? Look at my answer. It is brief and includes key words.") Continue practice. Have children state the important information in a paragraph, translate these statements into questions, record the questions, and finally put the answer in note form. | C. locates question column of notes.<br><br>C. locates answer column of notes.<br><br>C. reads a paragraph and states the important information in the paragraph.<br><br>C. translates the important information into questions, writes the questions in the left-hand column.<br><br>C. writes answers to questions using brief notes. |

H. Can study notes, outlines, summaries, or teacher-prepared study guides using a read, cover, recite, check format.

*Note: This study strategy can be applied to notes, outlines, summaries as well as teacher-prepared study guides and end-of-unit questions. In all cases, the child reads the information, covers the information, recites the major points, and checks with the information. Children should be taught to repeat the four steps when any deletions are noted during the check step.*

T. models format and leads children in using the strategy. T. tests children on the steps in the strategy.

["Today we are going to learn how to study for a test using our outlines. What are we going to learn? Watch me and I will show you a special way to study for tests. First I read the topic following Roman numeral I. What is the topic? Next I read the main idea A and the details listed for main idea A. (T. orally reads the main idea and details.) What did I do? Watch, now I cover up the main idea and details with a piece of paper. What did I do after reading the information? Right, I covered up the information. Now, I am going to say the information out loud. We call this reciting. Listen. (T. says informaton out loud.) What did I do first? After reading, what did I do? After covering the information, what did I do? Now, I uncover the information and reread the main idea and details to check what I said. What do I do after reciting the information? Right, I check what I said by rereading the information. Let's write these steps on the board. What do we do first? Next? What do we do after covering the information? What do we do after reciting the information? (Write the four steps on the board: read, cover, recite, check.)] Lead children through additional sections of the outline, stressing use of the study strategy. Finally, give students a limited period of time to study their outline. During independent practice of the study procedure, rotate around the room reinforcing children for proper use of the strategy.

C. states the first step in the strategy—read.
C. states the second step in the strategy—cover.
C. states the third step in the strategy—recite.
C. states the fourth step in the strategy—check.
C. states all steps in the strategy.
C. uses the four steps in the study strategy to study his outline.

437

topic) has been read, the child will be unable to accurately determine the topic, main idea, and supporting details.

Students must be given practice using their notes, summaries, and outlines, including retelling the content verbally. This step in instruction is critical for a number of reasons: it provides feedback to the child on the adequacy of her notes and provides initial practice in studying recorded information. In addition, students should be taught a strategy for studying their notes, summaries, or outlines as well as teacher-prepared study guides. One strategy involves the following steps: read, cover, recite, and check. Using this strategy, the student first reads a small segment of the recorded information, covers the information, recites the information from recall, and finally checks recitation by uncovering the recorded information. Unless these final steps are taken, verbally retelling information using notes and studying from notes, recording skills may have little transfer to content area classes.

Because of the number of different retrieval systems, we have limited the following formats to representative skills including the necessary entry behaviors, sentence outlining, note-taking, question/answer notes, and a strategy for studying notes, outlines, or summaries.

## Scanning and Skimming

Students should be introduced to two specialized skills to assist them in reading expository materials: scanning and skimming. Scanning involves the rapid search for specific information. When looking for specific information or an answer to a question, there is no need to read every word in the discourse. Instead, the student can quickly scan the material for the specific answer. Initially, the child should practice scanning for a specific piece of information within the passage (e.g., a date, a person's name, a place, a number), moving to scanning for an answer that is worded like the question and finally to scanning for an answer that is not worded in the same way as the question (Thomas & Robinson, 1972). Scanning is also used for locating entries in the dictionary, table of contents, and index as well as specific information within graphic material, particularly tables and charts. In all cases, the student quickly runs her eyes over the material in an organized left to right fashion proceeding down the page in visual pursuit of the desired information. To maximize the scanning process, the child must (1) know what information is desired and the possible form in which it might be found, (2) swiftly look over the page while limiting attention to the desired information, and (3) read the surrounding discourse to verify the applicability of the information to the question (Spache & Spache, 1973). The student should be taught to use headings and subheadings to find approximate locations of the information before the scanning process is initiated.

While scanning involves the visual search for specific information, skimming focuses on determining the general gist of an expository article or textbook selection. The preview procedures discussed in the previous chapter are one form of skimming. Thomas and Robinson (1972) have termed this type of skimming, preview skimming: "rapid coverage to learn the general content before reading." As suggested earlier, the students would preview the introduction, concluding paragraphs, headings, subheadings, and illustrations to determine the general content of the chapter prior to a more thorough reading of the material. Another type of skimming is referred to as "overview skimming" (Thomas & Robinson, 1972) in which the child rapidly reads the expository material when no second reading is intended. Though the purposes differ (to decide whether or not to read an article in more depth vs. to skim with no intent to

(continued on p. 442)

**TABLE 4.6.6** *Scanning and Skimming*

| SKILLS | TEACHER RESPONSE<br>(Additional examples and questions should be provided.) | CHILD RESPONSE |
|---|---|---|
| A. *Can scan expository material to locate an answer.*<br><br>Component Skills:<br>1. When given a question demanding a specific piece of information for the answer, can scan to locate the information.<br><br>Types of questions that would lead to scanning for a specific piece of information:<br><br>Find the definition for *Olmec*.<br>(Scan for the word *Olmec*.)<br><br>Find the dates for the Olmec's classical period.<br>(Scan for dates. Watch carefully for stopper word, classical period.)<br><br>On what body of water is Greece?<br>(Scan for the name of a body of water. Look carefully for the word, *Greece*.)<br><br>In what year did Cyrus capture Babylon?<br>(Scan for date.) | T. introduces scanning for the specific piece of information. ("Listen to this question. Who was the first Spanish explorer? What information do you need to answer this question? Right, the name of an explorer. We don't need to read the whole section on explorers to find one name. Instead we can *scan* to find the name. When we scan, we move our eyes quickly down the page looking for names and ignoring everything else. When we come to the name, we stop and read carefully to see if that person was the first Spanish explorer. What are we looking for? How do you scan? When I hold up my hand begin scanning. Look up when you have the answer. Ready, scan.") Continue practice, scanning for different types of information: a number, a date, a given word or phrase. Timed activities can be used to increase speed as well as motivation.<br>*Note: Scanning is also used when looking for an entry in the dictionary, table of contents, index, encyclopedia, telephone book, or classified ads as well as specific information in graphic material.* | C. determines word, phrase, or specific type of information to scan for.<br><br>C. scans material, locates information, and reads carefully to determine if the information answers the stated question.<br><br>*Note: Prior to scanning for a specific piece of information, the students should use the headings and subheadings to locate probable locations of information.* |
| 2. When given a question for which the wording is similar to the answer in the material, can scan and locate the information. | T. introduces more difficult scanning skill. ("Now we are going to scan for an answer that is worded like the question. Listen to this question. How do roots hold a tree in the ground? Will one word answer this question? No, we need to find a longer answer. In this case, the answer is worded like the question. What words are the *key words* in this question? The most important words? Right, roots, tree and ground. These are your important words. You are going to concentrate on looking for these words. Scan by quickly looking down the page, stopping when you find one or more of these words. Then read the sentences around the word to see if the answer is there. Listen, the question is, How do roots hold a tree in the ground? Scan this section concentrating on the words *roots, tree*, and *ground*. Ready, scan.") | C. determines key words in the question.<br><br>C. scans to locate the key words, reads the surrounding sentences, determines if the answer is given. The child then stops reading or continues scanning. |

439

Table 4.6.6 cont'd.

| SKILLS | TEACHER RESPONSE | CHILD RESPONSE |
|---|---|---|
| 3. When given a question for which the wording is not the same as the answer in the material, can scan to locate the information. | T. introduces the most complex level of scanning—looking for an answer that is worded differently than the question. ["Sometimes the question does not use the same words as the answer in the material. First, we scan for the key words in the question, but if we can't find the answer, we need to think of other words that we can use. Listen to this question. What kind of climate does Alaska have? What are the key words that we could scan for? Right, *Alaska* and *climate*. We have looked for these words. The whole article is about Alaska so that key word is not too helpful. We looked for *climate* and could not find it. We have to think of other words that mean the same or almost the same as climate. What are some words? (rain, snow, temperature, sunshine, etc.) Ok, we are going to scan for any idea related to climate. This is harder. We can't scan as fast. We must look for words that are related to climate. When you come to a word related to climate, stop and see if it tells you about the climate in Alaska. You may have to stop more than once to learn all the information given about Alaska's climate. Ready, scan."] This is the most difficult aspect of scanning. Much practice must be given. In order to look for alternate words in the material, the concept must be fairly familiar so that the children can generate associations. This skill is best initially practiced with material that the children have already read. | C. determines key words (stopper words) and scans for the answer. If not located: C. scans for related words at a slower pace, stopping to read the information when a related word or idea is located. |
| B. *Can skim an expository article to gain the general gist or to determine if the article should be read more carefully.* Component Skills: 1. Can skim an article to gain a general idea of the content before more careful reading. Preview skimming is best introduced with highly organized expository materials that use introductory statements, explicit headings and subheadings, and supportive graphics. | T. introduces skimming for the purpose of previewing a chapter, unit or article. ("Before we carefully read a chapter, it is helpful to preview the chapter so we know the type of information that will be covered. When we skim a chapter before reading it more carefully, we just want to hit the most important aspects of the chapter that will quickly give us the general idea of the chapter. First, we can read the title of the chapter. This tells us the general topic of the chapter. This chapter's title is 'plants.' Now we have an idea what the chapter is about. Next we can read the headings and subheadings to learn more about the chapter's content. Let's read the headings and subheadings: Roots, Stems, Leaves, Plant Growth, Plant Reproduction. Now we know that this chapter will tell us about the parts of the plant, how plants grow and how plants reproduce. We can read the introduction to the chapter to get a further idea of the general content of the chapter. Read the introduction. What did it tell us about the general content? . . . We can also read the first sentences of paragraphs and the sentences around words printed in BOLDFACE print to get the general gist of the chapter. Let's review. To get the general gist of an article, chapter or unit before reading it more carefully, we can hit the high points in the material. What were some of the important 'high points'? . . . Right the introduction, the headings and subheadings, the | C. tells 'high points' of a chapter that would help convey the general gist of the chapter. |

| | | |
|---|---|---|
| | sentences around words written in BOLDFACE type, and the first sentences in paragraphs. It is also helpful to look at the pictures and graphs and the titles of these graphics. We want to do this fast . . . only hitting the important, high points in the chapter. Your turn to try this. I will give you 1 minute to skim this chapter for the general gist. Just hit the high points. Ready, skim.") | C. skims chapter or article when given a time limit and determines the general gist of the chapter. |
| 2. Can skim an article to gain the general idea of the content when a second reading is not planned. | T. introduces overview skimming and when it is appropriate to use this type of skimming. ("We can use skimming to gain the general gist when we don't intend to read the material again. For example, we might want to gain the general idea from a newspaper article, a magazine article, an interesting book in the library, a pamphlet that you find at the fair, or a chapter in a textbook that covers similar information as your textbook. Remember we can only get the general gist from skimming. If you need to know the details or need to thoroughly understand a material, you must read it more carefully.") T. leads children through skimming materials that may not be reread. The same procedures are used as in preview skimming: locating and reading important aspects of the material. The teacher may place a time limit on the skimming activity to encourage a quick overview of the material. Questions as a follow-up of skimming can also be provided. Children can also write short summaries of the information and verify the accuracy of their initial conclusions through more careful reading. | C. tells when skimming is appropriate. C. skims article or chapter to determine the general gist. |

reread), the process of skimming is very much the same.

Skimming and scanning should be introduced to students, stressing how to use the processes and when to use the strategies, with ample practice provided to develop the skills. After the introduction of these skills, the teacher should remind children when to use them and should guide children in their use.

## APPLICATION EXERCISES

The examples used in the following application exercises are taken from Follett Social Studies, *Exploring Our World: The Americas* by Herbert H. Gross et al., Copyright © 1977, by Follett Publishing Company.

1. Using the index involves a number of complex skills that students will need to practice. For each of the following skills, write two questions that will allow students to practice using the index. The questions should lead to one of the index entries provided.

   a. Locating main entries when a key word from the index is used in the question.

   b. Locating main entries when the question does not include vocabulary found in the index (e.g., students must generate alternate entries).

   c. Locating subtopics to answer a question.

COTTON

communications, *p.* 81
   colonial times, 79
   pony express, 316
   satellites, 349
   telegraph, 316, *p.* 81
communism, 348, 403
compass, 31, 93, *p.* 87
Conestoga wagon, *p.* 212
Confederate States of America, 270, 271, 272, *m.* 271
Congress, U.S., 194, 195, 214
Connecticut, 124, 125, 135, 165
   state summary, 141
   *See* also New England States
Connecticut River, 124
Connecticut River Valley, 136
conservation, 77
   animals, 78, 339, 350
   erosion control, 102, 292, *p.* 102, 103
   flood control, 236–237, 258–259, *d.* 236, *m.* 259
   forests, 76, 77, 259, 323, 339
   natural resources, 128–129
   soil conservation, 102, 103
   *See* also environment, erosion, and pollution
Constitution, U.S., 194
   amendments, 194, 274, 338, 339
Constitutional Convention, 193–194

2. One of the important glossary skills is the ability to substitute a definition for a word in context to assist the reader in understanding the content. For each of these glossary words, write a sentence that would allow practice in substituting definitions for words in context.

scurvy (skər′vē) A disease caused by lack of Vitamin C.

secede (si · sēd′) To leave an organized group; to give up membership in a group.

3. Examine this map carefully. What symbols need to be introduced before the student could locate or interpret information on this map?

4. Write three questions that could be used to test location of information on this map.

Important
Natural
Resources

5. Examine this graph. Write a format similar to that presented for a circle graph to explain the organization of information in this graph.

6. Using the same graph, write a format that involves modeling location of information in the bar graph, leading students in the location of information, and testing students on their ability to locate information within the bar graph.

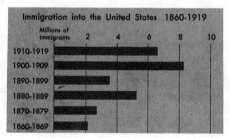

7. You are teaching students the preskills necessary for locating words in the dictionary. Write five pairs of words that could be used when determining whether to go to the front or back to get to the target word when the first letters are different and when the first letters are the same.

8. Develop four problem statements that will lead to location of services or products in the yellow pages. In writing the problem statements be sure that intermediate children could generate the necessary entry words.

9. You are going to introduce the lead paragraph and body of newspaper articles. From a local newspaper, select three articles that would clearly illustrate the parts of a newspaper article. Select a variety of articles (e.g., local news, international news, sports).

10. Your class has just completed a unit in social studies on the Civil War. You would like students to locate fiction and nonfiction books concerning the Civil War. Prepare a list of titles, subjects, and authors that can be located in the card catalog that would lead to location of Civil War books on the shelves.

For the remaining questions, use pages 445–46 from *Exploring Our World: The Americas.*

11. Skimming, like previewing, involves a quick survey of a material to determine the general gist. In skimming a material, the student attends to the highpoints that are heavily laden with information. In directing students to skim this selection, what features would you have them attend to?

12. You have given your students 1 minute to skim this selection. What questions might you pose to test their ability to determine the general gist of the selection using selective skimming?

13. Scanning is often done when a key word is given in the question. The student determines a key word in the question, reads until the key word is located, and then reads the surrounding discourse to determine the answer. Design three questions that would allow practice in this type of scanning.

14. The headings and subheadings of this chapter could easily be used in outlining this chapter. Prepare a skeleton outline that could be completed by students learning how to write topical outlines. Describe how you would fade prompts over lessons until the students were independently outlining a section of a chapter.

**126** In the center of most New England villages was a village green, or common. The church, school, and inn were often built around it. Nearby were the carpenter's shop and the blacksmith's. The mills were located near the river. Do you know why? The houses were made of boards and heated by fireplaces. Almost every family owned a cow and chickens.

# Life in Colonial New England

In the years after settlements were started and the Indians were driven off their land, life in New England became easier for the colonists. Their homes and villages became pleasant places.

| | | |
|---|---|---|
| *democratic* | *export* | *clipper ship* |
| *environment* | *import* | *profit* |

What was it like to live in homes and villages of colonial New England?

**The church.** Sunday was the most important day of the week. People began to prepare for this day on Saturday afternoon at three o'clock. At that time all work stopped.

On Sunday, a drummer called the people to worship. They listened to sermons that might take as long as three hours. Boys and girls enjoyed the singing of hymns, but they often found it difficult to sit still on the hard, wooden benches during the long sermon.

**The school.** Puritan leaders believed that all the people should be taught to read the Bible. They soon started schools where pupils were taught reading, writing, and some arithmetic. Books were scarce, but after 1690 the *New England Primer* was used. It contained prayers, spelling lessons, wise sayings, and questions about the Bible.

**The town meeting.** The villagers met from time to time to discuss problems and make laws needed in the colony. At the town meetings, any voter of the community had the right to make suggestions and take part in discussions. Problems were solved by majority vote.

In this way the colonists decided what taxes were needed and how to use tax money for building schools, roads, and bridges. They elected officials who saw to it that the decisions made at the town meetings were carried out. The town meetings gave the colonists a great deal of experience in governing themselves in a democratic way.

**Everyone worked.** Every member of a colonial family had work to do. The men and the boys plowed the fields, planted the seed, and gathered the crops. They cut trees. They used stones from the fields to build fences. They hunted and fished.

The women and girls worked in the fields, cooked the meals, and did the housework. They took care of the children and the garden. They made butter, cheese, soap, and candles. Clothes were washed in a big iron kettle that hung over a fire in the yard. They used a spinning wheel to make thread from the wool that the men cut from the sheep. They wove cloth and sewed it for clothes.

After a day's work, the family gathered about the fire. All enjoyed singing a song or two. Before going to bed, the father read a chapter from the Bible and said a prayer.

## Settlers Use New England's Resources

When the first colonists landed in New England, they began to use the natural resources of the region to feed, clothe, shelter, and protect themselves. It will be easy to remember these natural resources if you call them the four "F's"—fields, furs, forest, and fish.

**Fields.** Much of the land in New England is rocky and hilly. Despite this, the early colonists grew most of the food they needed for themselves and their farm animals. In addition to vegetables, the farmers grew corn, barley, rye, and wheat. They raised cows and pigs. From the woods surrounding the farm fields, colonists got berries, honey, maple syrup, and game.

**127**

**Furs and fur trading.** In the winter, when snow covered the fields, farmers often went into the woods to trap beaver, fox, mink, and other animals with valuable furs. They also gave the Indians cloth, knives, and axes in exchange for furs. The settlers sold these furs to traders, who shipped them to Europe.

**Forests and forest products.** When the Pilgrims came to New England, they found a land covered with forests. In order to have land for crops, they cut down the trees and used the wood to build their houses and barns and to heat their homes. They also made furniture, dishes, and farm tools out of this wood.

The forests also provided wood for shipbuilding. Nearly every group of settlers that came to New England included a

Hornbook

Spinning wheel

Cooking pot

Churn

Loom

Ax and adz

Bellows

Firearms

# Selecting and Using a Program

In this section, we will outline the components of an intermediate grade classroom reading program; summarize our suggestions for selecting materials; suggest testing, grouping, and placing procedures for the intermediate grades; and discuss starting points in the various program components. We also include discussion on meeting the needs of the remedial reader.

## Components of an Intermediate Grade Program

The components of an intermediate grade reading program are new word introduction, literature reading, reading comprehension, study skills, and content area instruction. Each of these areas was discussed in detail in earlier sections and will just be briefly reviewed here.

### New Word Introduction

Three types of words receive special attention: words which are fairly common (most students know their meaning) but difficult to decode, words which are not difficult to decode but are fairly uncommon (most students do not know their mean-

ing), and words which are both uncommon and difficult to decode. The words in these three groups would appear in decoding and/or vocabulary exercises. Words to be introduced would be drawn from the upcoming selections in literature and content area materials.

The formats for introducing new words incorporate use of the phonic, structural, and contextual cues taught during the primary stage. If necessary, remediation in these skills would be provided early in the school year.

### Literature Reading

One purpose of a literature component is to demonstrate to students that reading is an enjoyable activity. A secondary, but still important, purpose is to familiarize students with various types of literature. Care must be taken not to emphasize one objective at the expense of the other; i.e., students should not read too much literature that is of little interest to them.

The two main sources of material for literature reading are basal textbooks and soft- and hard-cover books. When using basal textbooks, teachers should be selective, not choosing selections with a readability level significantly above the students' reading level. Teachers should also attempt to generate interest and enthusiasm over a selection before students read it. Most selections should be read silently by students at their desks rather than orally in a reading group. Exceptions are made for students needing rate, comprehension, or expression training. A daily period which included oral reading would be planned to provide practice on those skills.

Teachers should try to see that students engage in at least a 1/2 hour a day of recreational reading. If the probability is high that students are not reading outside of school, the teacher should provide time during the school day.

## Reading Comprehension

A reading comprehension program during the intermediate grades should center on more complex skills such as, inference, summarization, and critical reading, rather than literal comprehension. The main sources of material are commercially prepared supplementary programs (oriented toward general or specific skills) and the workbook components of basal reading series. (It is not necessary to use the workbook from a basal series just because the textbook is being used. Usually, at the intermediate level, workbook activities are not based on stories in the textbook.)

## Study Skills

Study skill instruction encompasses a wide variety of skills: locating specific information in textbooks, interpreting visual and representational material (e.g., graphs, maps, diagrams, charts), using various reference aids (e.g., dictionary, encyclopedia, atlas), acquiring library skills, organizing information (e.g., note-taking, outlining), and learning methods for studying various types of material. Priority should be given to developing proficiency in study skills since success in content area in-

struction is dependent on proper application of study skills.

## Content Area Instruction

Content area instruction (e.g., science, social studies, health, etc.) should be integrated into the total reading plan. Words and strategies critical to understanding the material and doing written exercises should be pretaught. If time restraints dictate that content area subjects be taught to relatively large groups, differentiated assignments should be prepared. All students should receive assignments that are challenging and on which they are able to succeed.

## Remedial Instruction

Students not performing acceptably at their respective grade level will fall into one of the following four categories: nonreaders, confused decoders, moderately deficient decoders, and adequate decoders. Correctly classifying students in one of these categories is extremely important because the different deficits call for entirely different types of remediation.

### Nonreaders

Nonreaders are students who are virtually unable to decode. They may be able to identify about 100 words by sight; however, they will have no generalizable strategy for decoding words. These students will need a program that begins with the most basic skills: letter-sound correspondences, auditory preskills, and sounding out (see Section 2.8 for an overview of these skills). Our experience has shown that relatively few intermediate grade students will fall into the category of nonreader.

### Confused Decoders

Confused decoders are students who know most single letter-sound correspondences but demonstrate a confusion regarding how groups of letters represent sounds in words. Confused decoders will often demonstrate an overreliance on context usage. They'll make errors in which they look at a letter or two and say a word that makes sense in the context. They will not attend to endings of words, calling *hopping* "hopped" or *played* "plays." They will omit or add words in sentences. They will seem to vacillate in their approach, sometimes relying on phonic or structural cues and other times relying mainly on contextual cues.

A program for confused decoders should *not* include sounding out or auditory skills training but would concentrate on teaching phonic and structural units such as letter combinations, common affixes, the VCe rule, and minor sounds. It also should include exercises to teach students how to use a balanced combination of phonic, structural, and contextual cues (see Section 3.6).

### Moderately Deficient Decoders

Moderately deficient decoders will have mastered most of the phonic, structural, and contextual analysis skills taught in the primary stage. However, they will not have developed adequate proficiency in decoding multi-syllabic words. The deficiency in decoding multi-syllabic words will result in their having a halting, choppy rate of reading on intermediate grade level material. A program for these students should begin with a review of phonic and structural analysis skills taught during the primary stage and then emphasize strategies for decoding multi-syllabic words. A significant amount of oral and silent practice on passage reading should be provided to enable students to develop fluency (see Section 4.2).

Comprehension skills should also be taught to students who have decoding deficits. For nonreaders and confused readers, written comprehension exercises

will initially be limited to rather simple items because of the limited number of words that the students can decode. We recommend instituting an oral comprehension program for teaching more advanced comprehension skills to students with serious decoding deficits (see Sections 2.6, 3.5, and 4.3 for information on teaching comprehension skills). Moderately deficient decoders will be able to do more complex written problems. For these students, we recommend a supplementary comprehension program (see Sections 3.5 and 4.3).

### Adequate Decoders

The fourth type of remedial student, the adequate decoder, has no decoding deficits. She can decode material at her appropriate grade level with acceptable accuracy and speed. There are three possible causes of this student's problem: (1) vocabulary deficits (the student does not know the meaning of many words), (2) strategy deficits (the student does not have problem-solving strategies), or (3) a motivational deficit. Quite often the student's poor performance will be caused by a combination of these three deficits. A program for this type of student need not include intensive decoding instruction but should deal more with vocabulary and comprehension strategies and motivation.

## Classroom Plans

The type of programs instituted in an intermediate grade classroom depends on the students' skill levels. A student-centered activity, in which the teacher makes available various materials and students choose and complete assignments independently, is appropriate for students performing significantly above grade level. On the other hand, a highly structured teacher-directed program would be provided for students performing significantly below grade level. A program for students functioning around grade level might include a combination of structured and unstructured activities.

In schools that have few students performing below grade level, an entire class may be placed in a student-centered program. On the other hand, in schools that have a more heterogeneous mix of students, a classroom might include three programs: one for students above, one for students at, and one for students below grade level. The program for students performing above grade level will include minimal small group direct instruction. Student contact with the teacher will be mostly in the form of individual conferences. Group work will be in the form of discussions and reports on projects.

The program for students performing at about grade level will be more teacher directed. New terms and strategies to deal with difficult exercises will be pretaught in small group settings. The extent of teaching guidance depends on students' skills. If a group includes some students performing a little below grade level, the teacher might provide more extensive preparatory activities.

The final type of program is for students unable to function in materials written at their grade level. The content of the programs will be dependent on the students' deficits. Students functioning just about a year below grade level might be placed in a program similar to that of students functioning at grade level. The only difference will be that the materials used in the program will be easier, and the teacher will devote more time in remedying specific skill deficits. Students functioning several years below grade level require a specially planned program concentrating on skills usually taught during the primary stage.

Figure 4.7.1 shows what a daily schedule might look like in a classroom containing three groups functioning at different levels.

When looking at the schedule, note the following:

1. Lower-performing students receive more time in adult-supervised instruction. Students whose reading level is years below where it should be need to progress at an accelerated rate if they are to function at the level of their peers in later grades. The amount of practice the students receive must be geared to enable students to make this progress. As a general guideline, teachers might provide an extra 1/2 hour of adult-supervised instruction for each year a student is performing below grade level. Much of the supervised instruction will consist of oral reading. Volunteers or paraprofessionals can be used in providing this extra practice.

2. Included in a teacher-directed reading period are vocabulary and decoding, comprehension, and study skill instruction. Even though each of these areas was discussed in separate sections in this book, they can all be presented during one lesson.

3. We recommend a daily period devoted to language arts instruction. This would include spelling and other writing related skills. A major goal of language arts instruction is to teach students expressive written communication skills. A great deal of emphasis should be placed on these basic skills during the intermediate grades. Written expression becomes an increasingly important factor as reading comprehension and content area assignments switch from multiple choice type questions to questions requiring sentence or paragraph replies.

4. The higher and mid-groups are combined for language arts and content area instruction. This larger group instruction will be most effective if teachers cooperate to form homogeneous grouping.

**FIGURE 4.7.1** *Classroom Schedule for Three Groups at Different Levels*

| | Low Group Decoding at 2nd Grade Level | Mid-group Students Functioning at Grade Level | High Group Students Functioning above Grade Level |
|---|---|---|---|
| 8:30– 8:45 | correction of assignments from previous day | | teacher-directed discussion of activities for the morning |
| 8:45– 9:15 | rate-building exercise using an aide, volunteer, or older student | teacher-directed group instruction decoding & vocabulary discussion of story in basal text strategy teaching for reading comprehension exercises study skills | seatwork: students do reading comprehension and study skills |
| 9:15– 9:45 | teacher-directed reading group decoding & vocabulary passage reading strategy teaching for comprehension | seatwork: students do reading comprehension and study skill exercises | independent projects |
| 9:45–10:15 | seatwork activities: students complete reading and comprehension exercises | recreational reading | individual conferences between teacher and student |
| 10:15–10:30 | recess | recess | recess |
| 10:30–11:00 | language arts: writing, spelling, and related skills—15 min | seatwork: students complete reading comprehension and study skill exercises | seatwork |
| 11:00–11:30 | recreational reading | language arts instruction: spelling, writing, and related skills | |
| 11:30–12:00 | rate and expression training decoding and vocabulary training | seatwork: language arts related exercises | seatwork: language arts related exercises |
| 12:00–12:30 | lunch | lunch | lunch |
| 12:30– 1:15 | content area instruction—3 days a week on science and 2 days a week on social studies interclass grouping | | |
| 1:15– 2:00 | math | math | math |
| 2:00– 2:30 | music, gym, art | music, gym, art | music, gym, art |

## Selecting Materials

An intermediate grade teacher with a heterogeneous class will be using a wide variety of materials. One set of materials may be used for higher-performing students while mid-level students use a different set and still another set of materials is used for lower-performing students.

### Literature

When selecting material for the intermediate grades, the basal reading program should be looked at as just a part of a broad program in which many types of materials are used. In selecting textbooks, teachers should note the potential appeal of the stories and their readability level.[1] We recommended that during the beginning and primary stages, teachers use a program that employs a code-emphasis approach. This recommendation does not continue during the intermediate grades since both code-emphasis and meaning-emphasis programs take virtually the same approach to decoding and comprehension instruction. An intermediate grade textbook should be selected mainly on the suitability of stories and readability consistency.

### Comprehension

For teaching reading comprehension and study skills, we recommend using supplementary commercial programs that focus on comprehension rather than the basal workbooks, which suffer from a construction deficit which we call "too little of too much." The basal workbooks contain such a wide variety of activities that many students do not have the opportunity to master the skills and knowledge imbedded in the exercises. Moreover, basal workbooks are usually totally independent of

the textbook, with no coordination of words, introduction, or story content. Since workbooks and textbooks can be judged independently, teachers can use one but not the other.

When selecting a program to teach comprehension skills, the teacher should look for programs which do the following:

1. Include more complex skills (e.g., inference, summarization, critical reading)
2. Systematically introduce simple and then more complex skills
3. Provide adequate practice on each skill
4. Have reasonable control of readability. Passages do not contain an excessive number of words students are not likely to understand or be able to decode
5. Have clear written directions to the students
6. Have content which is interesting

### Content Area Material

Content area book selection should be based on the consistency of the readability level, the clarity of the text, and the appropriateness of the assignments. Readability is the most important factor. Many content area texts are written at a level several years above that designated by the publishers. Teachers should select texts written at readability levels appropriate to the grade for which the book is designed. The text should be written clearly, so that students become facile at using reading to learn rather than depending on teacher explanations to learn new material. Finally, the quantity and quality of written assignments should be considered. Written assignments should appear after each three-to-six page interval. Furthermore, the written assignments should be primarily text dependent, which means that information needed to answer questions is found in the text. This does not mean that complex inferential and deductive questions should not be included. Indeed, they should. However, the information needed

---

[1] A problem with many textbooks is that they often contain selections that are not interesting to intermediate students or that are written significantly above the grade level designated by the publisher.

to make the inference or deduction should be in the text. This last factor is especially important for teachers working with students who have a limited experiential background.

## Remedial Materials

If possible, teachers should obtain a comprehensive program integrating decoding and comprehension skills. One such remedial reading program is the *SRA Corrective Reading Series* by Siegfried Engelmann et al. © 1978. The series includes separate but coordinated components for decoding and comprehension skills. The programs are coordinated in that words do not appear in written comprehension exercises until students have been taught a strategy for decoding them. The decoding component includes three levels. The lowest level is designed for the nonreader. Instruction during this level concentrates on teaching students to decode regular words.

During the second level, students are taught the most common sounds of letter combinations and a strategy for decoding VCe words and VCe derivatives. They are also taught to decode two and three syllable words containing prefixes and/or suffixes. A unique feature of this level is the construction of the stories. Initially, stories are constructed with unpredictable syntax in order to discourage students from overrelying on context usage. Stories in the mid and later part of the program are written using conventional syntax. The themes are designed to interest older students.

The third level of the decoding program provides more emphasis on structural analysis skills as more and longer multisyllabic words are introduced. Stories in this level are also quite carefully controlled. Longer and more complex sentences, including passive voice construction and multiple clauses, are introduced. Nonfiction selections similar to those that students will encounter in content area books are interspersed among fiction stories.

The comprehension component of the *SRA Corrective Reading Series* also includes three levels. The first level of the program involves few written items. Nearly all tasks are presented orally. The type of tasks presented includes a mixture of basic facts: months, holidays, seasons, etc., and thinking operations such as, analogies, classification, deductions, true-false, synonyms-opposites, and inference. Although the program begins as an oral program, the proportion of written exercises increases as the students' decoding ability increases. Eventually all tasks involve written exercises.

An integral part of any remedial program should be establishing an independent reading program in which the student reads material which is easy for him to decode.

Recreational reading materials are available in the form of "high-interest–low-vocabulary books." These are books written at relatively low reading levels but which have themes geared to be of interest to the older student. Two popular series are the Scholastic Action Series and the Pal paperbacks.

If teachers cannot obtain a comprehensive program that coordinates decoding and comprehension instruction, they can construct a program by using various types of commercial material. For decoding instruction, we recommend a primary level code-emphasis program. Guidelines for selecting and using a code-emphasis program are discussed in Section 2.8, "Selecting and Using a Program" during the beginning stage and Section 3.6, "Selecting and Using a Program" during the primary stage. Teachers can use the word lists in Appendix A to supplement instruction in phonic and structural skills. An added variable to consider in selecting a program would be the format of the materials. Teachers should try to avoid formats with a "babyish" appearance. For remedial comprehension instruction, the teacher can use commercially prepared supplementary comprehension skills programs (see Section 3.5).

## Tests for Grouping and Placing Students

Testing, grouping, and placement procedures for intermediate grade students are more complex than for primary grade students because of the greater range of subject areas that must be considered and the wider range of student skill levels. The initial testing includes use of a reading comprehension test and a diagnostic test of word attack skills. After the initial testing, tentative groups can be established and instruction begun. During the first weeks of instruction, more thorough testing would be done on decoding skills, reading rate, and specific comprehension skills and study skills. Regrouping would be done based on the students' performance over the next week. Keep in mind that the procedure we outline is designed for a classroom teacher. Reading specialists and resource room teachers with low teacher-pupil ratios will be able to initially do more thorough testing.

## Reading Comprehension Skills Test

Nearly all commercial comprehension programs include series of written tests to place and/or evaluate student performance. We recommend using these tests as the initial instrument for testing students.

Before school begins, the teacher would inspect the testing component designed for the grade level he is teaching. A fifth grade teacher would look at the tests that correspond to the program designed for early fifth grade. He should inspect the test quite carefully, eliminating items which test relatively unimportant skills, which contain directions that are very confusing, or which do not provide clear diagnostic in-

formation. Copies of the test should be prepared for each student. If the program being used does not contain a testing component, the teacher can prepare a test by selecting and duplicating several worksheet pages. A teacher might reproduce five pages. The pages would include the following:

1. Summarization exercises (main idea or best title)
2. Inference exercises
3. Sequence exercises
4. Literal exercises (students find details in story)

## Diagnostic Test of Word Attack Skills

The intermediate grade test includes a list of 25 multi-syllable words. The words were selected from *Basic Elementary Reading Vocabularies* (Harris & Jacobson, 1971). Words 1 through 8 were extracted from the fourth grade list; words 9 through 18, from the fifth grade list; and words 19 through 25, from the sixth grade list.

| | |
|---|---|
| 1. announce | 13. professional |
| 2. championship | 14. definition |
| 3. collection | 15. convenient |
| 4. discovery | 16. satisfaction |
| 5. experience | 17. permanent |
| 6. original | 18. decision |
| 7. responsibility | 19. combination |
| 8. government | 20. accomplishment |
| 9. affectionate | 21. automatically |
| 10. contribution | 22. considerably |
| 11. disappointment | 23. examination |
| 12. appreciate | 24. opportunity |
| | 25. marvelous |

## Administering the Tests

It is possible to administer both the written comprehension test and the intermediate level word attack test on the first day of school.

### Written Comprehension Test

The teacher tells students prior to presenting the comprehension test that they may raise their hands if they need help reading any words. During the testing, the teacher helps students as needed. The purpose of offering the aid is to spot students who cannot decode well enough to function at this level. If a student is obviously unable to decode the words on the test, he is not required to complete the test. The teacher should have a supplementary exercise available for students who finish early or who do not have the decoding skills needed to read the test. These students will be given a test from a lower level of the program at a later time.

### Diagnostic Test of Word Attack Skills

A teacher needs to schedule about a 1 1/2 hour block of time for testing. During this period, students should be assigned independent seatwork assignments so that the teacher can test students individually. Included in the seatwork assignment should be a story writing exercise. Teachers will be able to determine much about a student's written language skills by examining a student's story. This information will be useful also in grouping.

While the students work independently at their seats, the teacher calls students individually to her desk. When administering the word attack test, the teacher needs a copy of the word list, a class record form (see Figure 4.7.2), and a stop watch. The teacher points to the list and asks the student to identify the words. The teacher starts the stop watch as soon as the student reads the first word.

1. If a student identifies the word correctly within 5 seconds, the teacher writes a plus on the record form across from the word.
2. If a student is not able to identify a word within 5 seconds and does not seem on the verge of identifying it, the teacher tells the student the word and says, "Let's try the next word." The skipped word would be counted as an error. The teacher makes a circle across from the word on the record form.
3. If a student mispronounces a word, the teacher says, "Look at that word again." If the student is able to identify the word within a second or two, the word would be counted as correct. The teacher marks a plus on the record form. If the student is unable to identify the word within another second or two, the teacher tells the student the word and says, "Let's try the next word." The missed word is counted as an error. The teacher makes a circle on the record form.
4. The teacher stops the watch as soon as the student identifies the last word.
5. The teacher records the number of words identified correctly and the time it took the student to read the list on the bottom of the form.
6. The teacher stops testing after the student misses five words in a row.

Students unable to read 13 or more words correctly on the intermediate diagnostic test of word attack skills should be given the primary level diagnostic test of word attack skills (see pages 280–83).

## Oral Reading Rate Test

We recommend that an oral passage reading rate test be administered to all students during the first two weeks of school. The purpose of the reading rate test is to determine which students would benefit from reading rate improvement exercises and to serve as a check to ensure that students can decode the selections from the material in which they are placed.

The selections the students read should be drawn from the reading comprehension

**FIGURE 4.7.2**  *Class Record Form—Diagnostic Test of Word Attack Skills*

Intermediate Level

| Students' Names<br>words | | | | | | | | | | | | | | |
|---|---|---|---|---|---|---|---|---|---|---|---|---|---|---|
| 1. announce | | | | | | | | | | | | | | |
| 2. championship | | | | | | | | | | | | | | |
| 3. collection | | | | | | | | | | | | | | |
| 4. discovery | | | | | | | | | | | | | | |
| 5. experience | | | | | | | | | | | | | | |
| 6. original | | | | | | | | | | | | | | |
| 7. responsibility | | | | | | | | | | | | | | |
| 8. government | | | | | | | | | | | | | | |
| 9. affectionate | | | | | | | | | | | | | | |
| 10. contribution | | | | | | | | | | | | | | |
| 11. disappointment | | | | | | | | | | | | | | |
| 12. appreciate | | | | | | | | | | | | | | |
| 13. professional | | | | | | | | | | | | | | |
| 14. definition | | | | | | | | | | | | | | |
| 15. convenient | | | | | | | | | | | | | | |
| 16. satisfaction | | | | | | | | | | | | | | |
| 17. permanent | | | | | | | | | | | | | | |
| 18. decision | | | | | | | | | | | | | | |
| 19. combination | | | | | | | | | | | | | | |
| 20. accomplishment | | | | | | | | | | | | | | |
| 21. automatically | | | | | | | | | | | | | | |
| 22. considerably | | | | | | | | | | | | | | |
| 23. examination | | | | | | | | | | | | | | |
| 24. opportunity | | | | | | | | | | | | | | |
| 25. marvelous | | | | | | | | | | | | | | |
| Total words correct | | | | | | | | | | | | | | |
| Time | | | | | | | | | | | | | | |

and content area materials being used. The students should read several 100-word selections from each book. An aide, parent, or an older student can test the students. The directions for the tester would be to tell the student any word which she is unable to identify within 5 seconds and to record the time it takes students to read the passage. The tester need not record errors. However, the tester should be in-structed to inform the teacher if any student misses more than three or four words in a passage. The teacher would retest any student whose reading rate is below 100 words per minute or who makes more than three or four errors per 100 words to determine if the student has been placed above her instructional level.

Rate training practice should be scheduled for students unable to read at a rate

**FIGURE 4.7.3**  *Sample Summary Sheet*

| Students' Initials | Read Comp. Test | Int. Word Attack #Correct/Time | | Primary Word Attack | Writing Skills |
|---|---|---|---|---|---|
| 1. B.F. | 95 | 25 | :34 | | above |
| 2. L.M. | 92 | 25 | :29 | | above |
| 3. J.S. | 92 | 24 | :38 | | above |
| 4. D.G. | 88 | 24 | :41 | | average |
| 5. T.J. | 88 | 23 | :40 | | above |
| 6. V.C. | 88 | 25 | :28 | | average |
| 7. M.F. | 87 | 23 | :43 | | above |
| 8. T.A. | 85 | 24 | :46 | | average |
| 9. S.C. | 81 | 23 | :31 | | above |
| 10. S.S. | 81 | 21 | 1:38 | | below |
| 11. B.G. | 78 | 25 | :43 | | above |
| 12. B.A. | 78 | 20 | 1:20 | | average |
| 13. T.M. | 78 | 19 | 1:30 | | average |
| 14. B.G. | 78 | 24 | 1:28 | | average |
| 15. F.T. | 75 | 23 | 1:18 | | average |
| 16. M.R. | 75 | 25 | 1:34 | | average |
| 17. C.A. | 75 | 18 | 2:23 | | below |
| 18. B.L. | 72 | 20 | 1:23 | | average |
| 19. F.G. | 72 | 20 | 1:28 | | average |
| 20. T.B. | 72 | 19 | 2:04 | | below |
| 21. R.F. | 72 | 18 | 1:40 | | below |
| 22. M.N. | 68 | 21 | 1:23 | | below |
| 23. B.T. | 61 | 17 | 2:01 | | below |
| 24. L.T. | 58 | 15 | 2:04 | | below |
| 25. R.B. | 58 | 6 | N.F. | 32 | below |
| 26. R.F. | 43 | 7 | N.F. | 35 | below |
| 27. A.T. | N.F. | 0 | N.F. | 6 | below |

N.F. = did not finish.

of about 150 words a minute. Suggestions for providing this practice appear on pages 237–40 of Section 3.4.

## Grouping and Placing

The teacher uses the results of the written comprehension test and the diagnostic test of word attack skills in setting up *tentative* groups. He lists students on a summary sheet according to the percent of items correct on the comprehension test. The teacher also lists the number of words correctly identified on the word attack tests and the time it took each student to read the words on the intermediate test. A final column on the summary sheet might indicate the student's story writing ability. When examining the student's written stories, the teacher notes the student's spelling, punctuation, grammar, and general phrasing. He marks them as above average, average, or below average. Figure 4.7.3 includes a list of the performance of the students in a sample classroom. Note that students with higher scores on the comprehension test are listed first.

When making initial groupings, the major factor is the students' performance on the reading comprehension test. Their performance on the diagnostic test of word attack skills and the quality of their written expression help place students who are on the borderline of two possible groups. With a borderline student, the teacher compares the number of words correct and the time it took the student to read the words with the performance of students in the higher group. If the student read the list significantly slower or with more errors than students in the higher group, the student would be placed in the lower group. Likewise, if a student's written answers indicate that she is substantially below the students in the higher group, a lower placement should be considered. For example, note that student 10 took about twice as long to read the word list as students scoring at a comparable level and scored below in writing ability. The teacher might consider placing this student in a lower group. Likewise, even though student 11 scored lower on the comprehension test, the teacher might consider placing her in a higher group since her decoding and writing performance are above average.

When forming groups for reading instruction (decoding, vocabulary, comprehension, and study skills), we recommend that teachers divide the class into three or four groups. When grouping students, the teacher may find that there is a significant range between higher- and lower-performing students in a group. For example, the highest group in a sixth grade room may contain some students able to function at an eighth or ninth grade level. Likewise, the lowest group may contain some students who are nonreaders and some reading at a late second grade level. The problem of a large ability spread can be dealt with more easily with higher-performing students than with lower-performing students. Teachers can generate independent assignments for higher-performing students. On the other hand, students functioning below grade level require very carefully structured instruction if they are to make significant progress in catching up with their peers. If a low-performing group

contains some students functioning at a second grade level and other students functioning at a third grade level, teachers will not be able to provide efficient instruction. This is not acceptable. Students performing below grade level must receive instruction appropriate to their needs.

There are several ways this can be accomplished. The first and most efficient alternative is interclass grouping. Several teachers across a grade level or in adjoining grade levels cooperate to form homogeneous groups for lower-performing students. Thus, one teacher may take all the students performing a little below grade level in one reading group. Another teacher might take all the nonreaders in another reading group. A second alternative is to set up more reading groups. Obviously, the problem with setting up more groups revolves around time limitations. Teachers have an enormous amount of material to cover (reading, writing, science, social studies, etc.). There simply isn't time for teaching more than three or four reading groups on a daily basis. A third alternative involves the use of supplementary personnel. Teachers can use peer tutoring, volunteers, and aides if available. One note of caution: Extremely deficient readers require very careful instruction. These students often are quite difficult to motivate and need very carefully controlled teaching demonstrations. Teachers should not relegate total responsibility for these students to peers, aides, or volunteers.

Let's refer to Figure 4.7.3. Note that three students were unable to read 13 or more words correctly on the intermediate level test of word attack skills and were thus given the primary level test. Their performance on the primary level test seems to indicate all are decoding below a fourth grade level. There is, however, a significant difference between student 27 and students 25 and 26. Student 27 appears to be essentially a nonreader (he read only 6 words correctly on the primary level test) while the other two students are not so deficient in decoding, having read 32 and 35 words correctly on the primary level test. Student 27 should not be placed in the same instructional group with the other two students since he requires a different type of instruction. Students 25 and 26 belong in the same group. Obviously, if the teacher has to form instructional groups for one student (27) and two students (25 and 26), his overall effectiveness will be hampered. Cooperative grouping between teachers is needed here. Perhaps the teacher might take some students similar to 25 and 26 from other classrooms while student 27 would be taught by another teacher who takes all the nonreaders. Assuming that students 25, 26, and 27 are grouped, we have 24 students left. These students may be divided into two or three groups. If the teacher divides them into three groups, the top group might include 10 students (1–9 and 11). Student 11 read the list more quickly and had better writing ability than student 10. The second group might include 8 students (10, 12, 13, 14, 15, 16, 18, and 19); and the third group, 6 students (17, 20, 21, 22, 23, and 24). Note that student 17 was placed lower because of a slower reading rate and poor writing skills.

Unfortunately, there is no easy formula that can be applied to all cases. In many instances, teachers will have to make trade offs, sacrificing what might be ideal for an individual on a short-term basis to what is better for the group of students over a longer-term basis. Likewise, beginning-of-the-year testing is often not highly reliable. Students' performance often improves significantly after a week or two of school. Therefore, regrouping is quite critical.

Regrouping should occur after the first week or two of instruction. Student performance on written comprehension exercises should be the prime factor considered when forming new groups. Students whose performance is significantly above or below the other students in the group should be moved to a higher- or lower-

performing group. Regrouping after about a week is very important since initial grouping based on a relatively small sample of a student's work is bound to be somewhat inaccurate. The student's performance during the first week gives the teacher more information. Regrouping should not be delayed unnecessarily. The earlier students are placed in an appropriate group, the more productive instruction will be for them.

Grouping for content area instruction will be different than for reading skills instruction since most classroom teachers will not be able to conduct content area instruction in small groups because of time limitations. There simply isn't time in the school day for small group instruction of all subjects. A teacher might create two groups. One group would include all middle- and higher-performing students. The other group would include lower-performing students.

Regardless of the procedure used, teachers must ensure that students receive appropriate instruction. If for one reason or another, students are placed in material somewhat more difficult than their instructional level, they should be provided with extra decoding and vocabulary practice and, if necessary, easier written assignments.

## Determining Starting Points in Programs

After administering the grade level written comprehension test and the diagnostic test of word attack skills, the teacher will be able to set up tentative groups. Further testing will be necessary, though, to determine specific starting points in the various reading program components.

### Reading Comprehension

As a general rule of thumb, students should be placed at a level at which they can perform with between 70–85% accuracy without preteaching of critical vocabulary or strategies. The assumption of this strategy is that preteaching exercises will enable students to perform at higher accuracy levels.

If some students in a group perform higher than an 85% level, they might be administered the written test from the next higher levels of the program to see if they can be placed at a level that would be more challenging.

If a student performs below a 70% level on the written comprehension test, the teacher should first try to determine if the student's poor performance on the comprehension test was caused by lack of motivation. This can be done by retesting the student on materials from his grade level. The teacher would construct the retest by assigning several workbook pages similar to those that were on the original test. To determine if motivation was a key factor, the teacher might incorporate a pay-off for accurate work. The teacher might say, "I want you to work as hard as you can. If you do a good job, you'll get some extra recess" (or other desired pay-off). The purpose of the retest is to determine whether lack of motivation was a factor in the student's initial poor performance. If the student performs above 70% on the test, the teacher should consider placing the student at the grade level from which the original test was drawn and should work on developing student motivation.

If a student scores below 70% even after a reward is offered, he probably has decoding, vocabulary, and/or strategy deficits. The teacher should place the student in lower level material. A suitable level can be determined by administering written tests from the lower levels until coming to a level at which the student performs above 70%.

At this point, we should emphasize that our recommendation for placing students at a level at which they perform at a 70–85% level is not based on any empirical data. Teachers may find an 80% rather than a 70% minimal pretest level more appropriate.

## Literature

A literature component has two aspects: recreational reading and teacher-directed reading. Most teacher-directed literature reading will be done in basal textbooks since using basal texts allows the teacher to prepare a group of students to read the same selection. Selections from basal textbooks should be at the student's decoding instructional level (95% decoding accuracy). The assumption is that the teacher will present difficult words in decoding and vocabulary exercises before the students read the selection. Since basal textbooks do not contain a progression within a book from easy to more difficult, the teacher will have to select stories from different places within the book. The teacher can determine the difficulty level of the stories by having one of the lower-performing students in the group read excerpts from the story or by computing the readability level.

## Content Area

The question in content area material is what grade level book to use with a group. The answer is determined in part by the composition of the group and in part by the difficulty level of the textbooks in a series.

The book from the selected series in which students are placed should be one in which the lower-performing students in the group can function successfully with the amount of teacher preparation that will be given. Higher-performing students in the group can be given supplemental assignments to make the workload appropriate. To determine if a book is appropriate for a group, the teacher can present some sample lessons from the book. For each lesson, the teacher would preteach difficult-to-decode words. The teacher should then have several of the lower-performing students in a group read 100-word passages from the pages. If the students struggle with more than 1 or 2 words per 100, the readability level of the book is probably too high. We set 1 or 2 words as a limit since the teacher will have already taught difficult key words. If the text is so difficult that even with preteaching of words students still have difficulty, a lower level text should be used.

## Study Skills

Study skills instruction includes a large number of rather discrete skills. These skills are described in Section 4.6.

At the beginning of the school year, the teacher should test students on their relative knowledge of the various skills. The test would include dictionary skills; index and table of contents usage; graph, chart, table and map reading; and encyclopedia and other resource book usage. The test can be prepared by using worksheet pages from the program being used to teach study skills. Individual testing would be done only when the student's performance indicates a deficit. Once specific deficits are determined, instruction can be integrated within reading and content area instruction.

## Remedial Instruction

Students unable to read 13 or more words on the intermediate level of the diagnostic test of word attack skills probably have not mastered the basic decoding skills taught during the primary stage and may need to be placed in a primary level decoding program.

Earlier in this section, we discussed remedial programs. We recommended obtaining a comprehensive remedial program. If obtaining such a program was not possible we recommended using a code-emphasis program for decoding instruction. In order to place students in a primary level program, we advise administering an informal reading inventory (IRI), which is an oral passage-reading test designed to place students at their instructional level. Procedures for constructing and administering the informal reading inventory are discussed in Section 3.6.

A final note on remedial instruction concerns moving students at an optimal rate. Once the teacher clears up some specific skill deficits and establishes an effective motivational system, the performance of students often will improve dramatically. After several weeks, the teacher should readminister various placement tests to see if a move to a higher level is possible. Other procedures for moving at an optimal rate include skipping lessons and teaching more than one lesson in a period (see Sections 2.7 and 3.6 for a more detailed discussion of these procedures).

---

### APPLICATION EXERCISES

1. Figure 4.7.4 is a summary of all testing done by Ms. Henderson (a fifth grade teacher) during the first 2 weeks of school. In the first column is each student's score on the highest level reading comprehension test at which a student scored acceptably. In the second and third columns is the student's score on the diagnostic test of word attack skills. In the fourth column the student's writing ability has been summarized. In the fifth column the student's oral reading rate is listed.

Your assignment is:
a. Make three instructional groups for reading comprehension instruction.
b. Set up a daily schedule for instruction. Include (1) ½ hour block for each group during which new words will be included in vocabulary, decoding, study, and comprehension exercises, (2) 1 hour's time for seatwork, (3) ½ hour recreational reading, and (4) extra ½ hour instruction for students performing below grade level.

**FIGURE 4.7.4**

| Student | Read Comp. Percent | | Word Attack Test Words | | Story Writing | Oral Reading Rate |
|---|---|---|---|---|---|---|
| | Level | % | Correct | Time | | |
| 1 | 6th | 85 | 25 | :32 | above | 190 |
| 2 | 6th | 82 | 25 | :34 | above | 152 |
| 3 | 6th | 80 | 25 | :31 | above | 146 |
| 4 | 6th | 80 | 25 | :40 | average | 149 |
| 5 | 6th | 76 | 24 | :43 | average | 163 |
| 6 | 6th | 76 | 25 | :28 | above | 148 |
| 7 | 6th | 76 | 24 | :42 | above | 153 |
| 8 | 6th | 74 | 24 | :37 | average | 160 |
| 9 | 6th | 70 | 18 | :30 | average | 145 |
| 10 | 5th | 90 | 23 | :28 | above | 153 |
| 11 | 5th | 88 | 22 | :58 | average | 115 |
| 12 | 5th | 78 | 20 | 1:25 | average | 121 |
| 13 | 5th | 78 | 21 | 1:10 | average | 138 |
| 14 | 5th | 78 | 20 | 1:26 | below | 100 |
| 15 | 5th | 76 | 19 | 1:20 | average | 103 |
| 16 | 5th | 76 | 21 | 1:58 | average | 93 |
| 17 | 5th | 76 | 20 | 1:08 | average | 137 |
| 18 | 5th | 76 | 21 | 1:14 | average | 135 |
| 19 | 5th | 70 | 14 | 2:01 | below | 81 |
| 20 | 4th | 80 | 16 | 2:14 | below | 78 |
| 21 | 4th | 78 | 18 | 2:10 | below | 90 |
| 22 | 4th | 76 | 15 | 2:30 | below | 86 |
| 23 | 4th | 72 | 16 | 2:15 | below | 82 |

2. Assume you are an intermediate grade teacher (fourth, fifth, or sixth) and are preparing for the school year.
    a. Examine several comprehension programs (both supplemental and basal) and select one. Explain your choice. Discuss how you might modify it.
    b. Examine several content area books and select one. Explain your choice. Discuss how you might modify it.
    c. Examine several remedial reading programs and select one. Explain your choice. Discuss how you might modify it.
    d. Obtain the testing component from a basal program or from a supplemental reading comprehension program. Examine the test from a specific grade level either fourth, fifth, or sixth grade. Tell which pages from the test you would include as a beginning-of-the-year reading comprehension skills test. Explain why you have included each page in the testing packet and why you excluded any pages, if you did.

# PART 5

# Motivation

# SECTION 5.1

## *Developing Student Motivation*

Regardless of how well a program is designed and how efficiently instruction is organized, some students may not do well in reading instruction unless the teacher has the skill to motivate them. Ideally, all students will want to learn to read, and the teacher will need only to design and present reading lessons so that learning is as easy as possible. Unfortunately, this is not the case. Many students come to school unprepared to learn to read. They are said to be unmotivated because they often ignore a teacher's presentation, participate only irregularly in group instruction, disregard corrective feedback, and do not complete written exercises. Obviously, the potential benefits from well-designed and appropriately presented lessons will not be realized under these circumstances.

Several factors determine how difficult it is to motivate a student, among which are student competence, student interest in reading material being presented, and student responsiveness to adult attention.

Student competence refers to the skills the students bring to a task. A student's skill level determines how difficult instruction will be for him. For example, a child who enters school with knowledge of letter-sound relationships, rhyming, and other reading-related skills will find it much easier to learn to read than the student who has not previously learned these skills. While the former child may need only 5 to 10 repetitions to master sounding out a new word type, the latter child may need 20 to 30 repetitions.

Student interest is obviously a factor since teaching is always easier when the students are interested in the materials being presented. Although providing interesting reading material is an important teacher responsibility, students will sometimes have to read materials that are not of a high interest level. When this is the case, teachers must have the skills to motivate students to complete their assignments.

The third factor, student responsiveness to teacher attention, is determined to a great extent by the students' home backgrounds and by their past experience in school. Some students are quite anxious to please teachers, while others do not consider teachers to be very important figures. Some students will persist at a task with which they are having difficulty if the teacher encourages them, while other students, at the first sign of difficulty, will attempt to escape from the situation.

Regardless of the cause of motivation problems, teachers, as professional educators, must be prepared to develop student motivation where none seems to exist. They cannot wait for students to become motivated or excuse students' failure by blaming them for being "unmotivated." Teachers must take the responsibility for developing the occurrence of appropriate behavior (participation in instruction and academic proficiency) and decreasing the occurrence of inappropriate behavior (disruptive social behaviors and frequent academic errors).

This section is designed to help teachers develop student motivation. First two major objectives are discussed: increasing appropriate behavior and decreasing inappropriate behavior. Next four general guidelines are briefly described. Teachers should provide (1) positive yet (2) minimal consequences only for (3) significant accomplishments and (4) collect data to ensure that appropriate behaviors are occurring more often. Six specific procedures for establishing a motivation system are then discussed in some detail: selecting reinforcers, designing a delivery system, identifying performance units, establishing rules, presenting units, and dealing with inappropriate behavior. To help teachers avoid the more common errors that are made in carrying out these procedures, we describe seven of the more common ones. With an awareness of these pitfalls, teachers are less likely to accidentally undermine the effectiveness of a system they might implement. The final area includes suggestions for classroom organization. The way in which a classroom is organized can have a strong influence on student motivation.

## Major Objectives

## Increasing Appropriate Behavior

Motivating students who have relatively few skills, are uninterested in most reading material, and are somewhat indifferent to teacher attention requires a great deal of skill. The teacher's main tool in developing student motivation is the use of *reinforcers.* For our purpose, a reinforcer is a teacher action occurring after a student behavior that results in the student behavior occurring more often. The example below illustrates a teacher action which functioned as a reinforcer.

Billy, a second grader in Ms. Garcia's class, usually spent about 10 of the 20 minutes allocated for seatwork actually working on his reading assignment. Ms. Garcia wanted to increase the proportion of time Billy spent actually working. She decided to try using praise. Each day she watched Billy carefully during the seatwork period. Twice during a period, after Billy had been working for several minutes, Ms. Garcia went over to Billy and praised him for working hard. After a week Billy spent approximately 17 minutes out of the 20-minute period actually working. The appropriate student behavior (working on the assignment) was followed by a teacher action (Ms. Garcia's praise) and the appropriate behavior increased. Ms. Garcia's teacher action (praise) acted as a reinforcer.

The critical aspect of a reinforcer is that it makes the behavior it follows occur more frequently. Praise in itself is not necessarily a reinforcer, as the following example illustrates.

Robert, another student in Ms. Garcia's class, was similar to Billy in that he spent only about 10 of the 20 allocated minutes actually working on his seatwork assignment. Ms. Garcia tried the same procedure she did with Billy. Twice during each seatwork period, after Robert had been working for a while, Ms. Garcia would praise him. After a week Robert still spent only about 10 of the 20 minutes working.

In this example, Robert did not attend more as a result of the teacher's praise. Praise functioned as a reinforcer for Billy but not for Robert.

Remember: *for a teacher action to be a reinforcer, it must strengthen the behavior it follows.* If a teacher action does not result in a student behavior happening more often, the action is *not* a reinforcer, even though the teacher might have intended it to be one. The importance of looking at what actually happens rather than what the teacher wants to have happen cannot be overemphasized. Wanting students to attend during reading instruction is not enough; teachers must make sure that the students do, in fact, attend. The teacher in the second example is not absolved from the responsibility of motivating Robert just because the praise did not work. Teachers must try different actions until they find ones that function as a reinforcer. Various types of possible reinforcers will be discussed later.

## Decreasing Inappropriate Behavior

Teachers not only work to increase appropriate behaviors, they also attempt to decrease inappropriate behaviors. One method for decreasing undesired behavior is punishment. Teacher actions that result in behaviors occurring less often are called *punishers.* There are many types of teacher actions that may function as punishers: scolding, withdrawal of privileges, and isolation. Just as teachers must examine the effect of intended reinforcers, they also must examine the effect of intended punishers. Let's look at the case of Kyle, a sixth grader. He frequently disrupted reading instruction at the beginning of the year by yelling to Casey. The teacher decided to punish the disruptive talking. She required Kyle to leave the group and sit in a "quiet seat," a chair facing the wall, for 5 minutes after each time he yelled to Casey. The first day the teacher used the procedure, she sent Kyle to the quiet chair three times; the next day once; and the third day not at all. The inappropriate student behavior (yelling to Casey) was followed by a teacher action (a command to leave the group), and the inappropriate behavior decreased. The teacher's action acted as a punisher.

. On the other hand, having Kyle leave the group could function as a reinforcer. For example, if after several days of having Kyle leave the group, the number of times Kyle yelled to Casey began to increase, the teacher action of having Kyle leave the group would be functioning as a reinforcer, not a punisher. Why do we say that this teacher action was a reinforcer? Because the more the teacher told Kyle to leave the group, the more he yelled to Casey. Note that the teacher's intention when having him leave the group was to decrease the inappropriate behavior. As quite often happens though, when teachers rely on negative actions, the intended result was not obtained. Kyle learned that yelling to Casey resulted in attention from the teacher and, thus, yelled more to Casey.

Teachers must be aware of the actual effects of negative consequences. In addition to not functioning as punishers, negative actions can involve undesirable side effects of damaging a student's self-image and developing an avoidance attitude toward school. Consequently, negative actions must be used very carefully.

A more desirable method for reducing inappropriate behavior is to ignore it and reinforce a student who is displaying an appropriate, incompatible behavior. Below is an example of a teacher who ignores an inappropriate behavior and reinforces another student for an appropriate behavior which is incompatible with the inappropriate behavior.

> During a reading group, John, a first grader, often fidgets in his chair. Each time the teacher sees John fidgeting, the teacher gives a handshake to *another* student who is sitting still. The teacher says, "I like the way Bill is sitting up and listening." John's fidgeting stops when the teacher says this. After John sits still for several minutes, the teacher praises John. After a week of praise and ignore, John's fidgeting behavior decreases dramatically.

The undesired behavior (fidgeting) was ignored, and the incompatible, desired behavior (sitting still) was rewarded with praise and a handshake. At first, the teacher rewarded other students displaying the appropriate behavior and ignored the inappropriate behavior. Next the teacher rewarded the target student for the desired behavior. When John sees Bill being praised for sitting still, John is more likely to sit still, at which time the teacher can praise John for sitting still. The ignored behavior (fidgeting) occurs less often, while the rewarded behavior (sitting appropriately) occurs more often. The notion of incompatible behavior is quite important since it switches the focus from keying on undesirable behaviors to keying on desirable behaviors. For example, instead of harping about sloppy writing, the teacher rewards writing neatly, which is incompatible with writing sloppily.

## General Guidelines for Developing Student Motivation

The teacher's primary goal in the area of motivation is to develop intrinsic motivation. Often intrinsic motivation is thought to mean an internal desire to act in a certain way. In the area of reading instruction, we believe that intrinsic motivation develops when the natural consequences of learning to read are positive and reinforce reading behavior. Positive natural consequences of learning to read include the enjoyment of the content of interesting material, pride in learning to read, and the recognition of parents, teachers, and peers for learning to read.

As pointed out earlier, many students are not intrinsically motivated to learn to read, often because they have not received instruction that would allow them to succeed or because their achievements have been ignored. With these students, teachers must rely on extrinsic motivation, which involves procedures for increasing appropriate behaviors and decreasing inappropriate behaviors. As teachers develop

plans for extrinsic motivation, they will use various procedures, depending on the instructional setting and on the students. Regardless of the particular procedure being used, teachers should always follow these three guidelines:

1. Positive consequences should be used more often than negative consequences.
2. Minimal reinforcers needed to do the job should be used.
3. The focus of reinforcement should be on significant rather than trivial student achievement.

## Positive Consequences

The first guideline is to use positive rather than negative consequences. Positive consequences are preferable because they contribute to positive student attitudes while negative consequences contribute to negative student attitudes. An extensive use of negative consequences may result in students' avoiding teachers and school and in their thinking that as students they are inadequate or defective. Strong negative consequences should be reserved for special situations in which a student's misbehavior is so extreme or frequent that appropriate behaviors are not occurring.

## Minimal Reinforcers

The second guideline is to use minimal reinforcers. Using minimal reinforcers is desirable because they make developing intrinsic motivation easier. The transition from a minimal reinforcer, such as membership in the good readers club or praise, to natural reinforcers, such as parental recognition or grades on assignments, is fairly easy. The danger of using stronger reinforcers than are necessary is that students may learn to attend and perform only when offered a sizable reward. Once students learn to expect strong rewards, replacing them with weaker consequences (such as teacher attention or grades) may be very difficult. In fact, some students learn that if they misbehave, they can force the teacher to offer an even stronger reinforcer. Whenever possible, teachers should use minimal reinforcers to motivate students and save stronger reinforcers for difficult-to-handle situations.

Although the reinforcers teachers use should be minimal, they must still be effective. At the beginning of the school year, teachers should select reinforcers that are very likely to work. Teachers working with older students who have experienced failure and have demonstrated behavior problems might begin the year with a variety of stronger reinforcers (e.g., a student's good work earns extra recess, gym, or a letter home to parents). Starting the year with more powerful rewards that are likely to function as reinforcers is better than starting with less powerful rewards that may not be effective. This point is very important. Using effective rewards enables the teacher to begin the year with positive student-teacher interactions. Once the positive interactions begin, reinforcers can be delivered less often and/or reduced. On the other hand, if a teacher starts with ineffective reinforcers, a negative interaction pattern can begin: appropriate behavior does not increase; misbehavior becomes more frequent; and the teacher ends up relying on negative actions.

## Significant Achievement

The third guideline is to focus on significant rather than trivial student achievements. The significance of an accomplishment varies from student to student according to each student's skill level. For example, reading a list of 10 new words without any errors is a significant achievement for a young student. In contrast, for the same student to read the familiar word *man* correctly is not significant. The teacher should treat reading the entire list without error as a significant accomplishment, praising the student; e.g., "That was really hard and you did it. I bet you're really proud." On the other hand, the teacher might simply say, "Good" when the student reads *man* correctly.

Similarly, attending, sitting quietly, watching the teacher may be a significant achievement for a young, unmotivated student and should be rewarded. However, for older, more sophisticated students such behaviors are trivial. With these older students, teachers should focus on reading performance, rather than attending, sitting quietly, etc. In all cases, teachers should shift their focus to academic behaviors as quickly as possible. If teachers praise students for performing well academically, listening and attending will take care of themselves. Also, it will be clearer to students that the teacher's goal is for students to learn new skills and that attending behaviors are just a means to that end.

## Collecting Data

In many situations, teachers will need to keep records of student behavior, e.g., how many times they disrupt a lesson or how many errors they make on their seatwork assignments. Because judgments of how well a motivation procedure is working are so likely to be clouded by what the teacher wants to have happen, objective measures of student performance are very important, as indicated in the following example:

Tim never finished his seatwork. During the first week of school, he finished 10, 11, 10, 9 and 11 items out of 20 on his worksheet. The next week, the teacher decided to use a reward system. Every time Tim finished 5 items, the teacher gave him a star. During the 2 weeks that Tim received stars, he completed 9, 10, 8, 7, 10, 11, 10, 7, 10 and 9 items out of 20.

Did the teacher reinforce Tim's item-completing behavior? No. The stars did not strengthen the behavior of completing more items. Tim actually completed fewer items when he was getting stars. If the teacher had not kept records of how many seatwork items Tim completed each day, she might have thought that the stars were working and that he completed more items when stars were used as rewards. Since the teacher had a record of the number of items completed each day, she knew that completing an average of nine items a day was *not* better than the first week's performance. Knowing this, the teacher would stop using stars as rewards and try something else.

## Establishing a Motivation System

There are six basic steps in setting up a motivation system:

1. Selecting reinforcers
2. Designing a delivery system for reinforcers
3. Dividing the day into performance units
4. Establishing rules
5. Presenting units
6. Deciding on techniques to use in reducing inappropriate behavior

## Selecting Reinforcers

Teachers have a wide variety of reinforcers from which to choose. The major types of reinforcers include praise, physical contact and gestures, activities, tangibles, and recognition.

### Praise

The most common (and easiest to use) reinforcers are *praise* statements, in which the teacher shows approval by what is said and/or how it is said. Here are examples of various praise comments intended to

strengthen or reinforce the behavior described in the comment:

1. "That sentence was hard, and you read all the words right."
2. "Very good. You said that sound just right."
3. "Terrific. Lisa wrote every letter so it touched the bottom of the line."
4. "You keep your place in the story just like the big kids do."
5. "You said those words so clearly. I bet you practiced at home last night."
6. "Look at Wendy. She doesn't give up. She looks for the answer to the question until she finds it."

Note that all the comments *describe the specific behavior that earned the praise.* Using descriptive or behavior-specific praise is important because it makes clear to the student what behaviors the teacher is reinforcing. Teachers cannot take for granted that students will know why they are being rewarded but must make the reason very clear.

In addition to being specific, praise should be delivered with appropriate emotion. This means that when a student does something that is significant, the teacher's reaction should be different from when the student's performance is just average. For example, the way a teacher says "Good" will be more emphatic for a student who reads 20 words correctly for the first time than for a student who usually reads 20 words correctly. Also, when delivering all praise, the teacher should smile or in other ways indicate that the student's behavior is pleasing.

Teachers working with preadolescent students must be quite careful in the way they use praise. The last thing that many older students want is to receive lavish praise from a teacher in front of their peers. As a general rule, teachers should keep their praise low key and descriptive with older students. More emotional types of praise should be saved for more private meetings between the teacher and student.

### Physical Contact

Physical contact is an extremely powerful reinforcer. Primary (K–3) students usually enjoy knee rides, tickles, pats on the back, and various types of handshakes. Teachers can make handshakes more fun by making up different kinds. For example, in a spaghetti handshake, the teacher might take a student's hand, let his arm go limp, and give a wiggly handshake. In a slapping handshake, the teacher can slap the student's palm with her palm. In a group handshake, the teacher takes the hands of all the students (up to eight or nine) and gives them a handshake all at once. With intermediate grade students, physical contact can involve pats on the shoulder or handshakes.

When initiating physical contact, the teacher's words and tone of voice should suggest that the contact is very desirable. If a teacher treats an activity as desirable, most students will too. Below is an example of how a teacher might do this with younger students. (Note the inclusion of behavior-specific praise.) "Here comes a handshake looking for a good reader who got all the words right. It starts up in the air and it comes down slowly. Then it sees the good reader and goes right to that person!" (The teacher would be smiling and talking in an excited fashion.)

### Activities

Making available certain activities can also be used to reinforce appropriate behavior. Activities popular with many different students include these:

1. Extra recess or gym periods
2. Being allowed to play teacher
3. Access to various classroom responsibilities: lunch count taker, attendance monitor, board cleaner, seatwork distributor, etc.
4. Access to free time corner which includes puzzles, games, records, tape recorders, audiovisual machines
5. Being tutors (older students can tutor younger students)

Teachers can determine what activities to use as reinforcers for particular students by observing what students do during free time or by keeping track of activities that students ask to do during the day. This observation technique is especially effective in working with hard-to-motivate students. With students who are able to read, teachers can pass out a checklist form on which students check off favorite activities. Remember, an activity must be effective with a particular student; otherwise, it is not a reinforcer. Do not offer extra gym to a student who does not like gym. Another procedure, especially powerful with older students, involves awarding an extra activity to the entire group because of the performance of one student. Peer approval is very effective with older students.

A note of caution: Sometimes a student may deliberately try to have a group lose gym or some other activity. If a student is trying to control the group through his misbehavior, change the situation so that this is not possible; i.e., do not make group reinforcement dependent on that student's behavior.

### Tangibles

Tangible rewards range from pieces of paper to toys, food, and other objects desired by students. The easiest and most practical types of tangibles are those that can be mass-produced at little cost. These include thermofax copied pictures of animals, popular sports, TV and movie personalities, or comic book characters, various puzzles, and word games.

A tangible reward that is effective with younger students but should only be used with difficult-to-motivate kindergarteners or first graders is food. Food will often function as a reinforcer with students for whom verbal praise, physical contact, and classroom activities are not effective. The most practical type of food to use as a reward is a piece of cereal, since it is relatively inexpensive and is eaten quickly. But keep in mind that the use of food is needed only with extremely unmotivated students.

### Recognition

Recognition rewards include a variety of rewards that acknowledge a student has mastered a certain skill. Included among recognition rewards are letters to parents, certificates, and marks on charts. Weekly letters sent home to parents can be very powerful reinforcers. Figure 5.1.1 shows a sample letter.

**FIGURE 5.1.1**

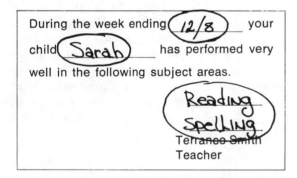

During the week ending ⟨*12/8*⟩ your child ⟨*Sarah*⟩ has performed very well in the following subject areas.

*Reading*
*Spelling*

~~Terrance Smith~~
Teacher

## Designing a Delivery System

A delivery system is the way in which teachers award reinforcers: when and how they reinforce students. In an efficient delivery system, teachers reinforce students quickly without disrupting instruction. The complexity of a delivery system is dependent on the skills and attitudes of the students. Teachers working with highly motivated and skilled students will not need a complex delivery system, since the teacher can rely primarily on praise as a reinforcer. The delivery system for reinforcers for these students might involve self-recording of performance on seatwork assignments. The only stronger reinforcer might be weekly reports taken home to parents.

Teachers working with less motivated and/or less skilled students will need more elaborate delivery systems since they will have to initially rely on stronger activities than praise to serve as reinforcers.

### Token Economy

Often, teachers select sizeable reinforcers that students cannot use during group instruction without interfering with the lesson (e.g., extra recess, game activities) or that occur periodically (e.g., a party or field trip). In both instances, some type of intermediary is needed so that students can see that they are working toward a sizeable reinforcer. Tokens in the form of stars, chips, or marks on a chart can serve as this intermediary.

In a token system, the teacher in effect sets up a wage-price economy. The students earn specified wages through their behavior and trade their wages for privileges or tangibles. Elaborate token systems need not be set up for most students in normal classroom situations. The systems in most classrooms can be quite simple. As a general rule, no more than 5% of instructional time should be used the first several days to administer the system.

In setting up a token system, the teacher must specify the behaviors desired of the students, and establish a wage-price scale that specifies how many tokens or points can be earned for certain behaviors and how many tokens or points will be charged for the reinforcers. For example, a teacher awards up to 10 points for behaving appropriately during teacher-directed reading group and during independent work. The teacher might make the system so that 10 points earn 5 minutes extra recess,

**FIGURE 5.1.2**  *Point Chart*

|         | M | T | W | Th | F | M | T | W | Th | F |
|---------|---|---|---|----|---|---|---|---|----|---|
| Ann     |   |   |   |    |   |   |   |   |    |   |
| Barbara |   |   |   |    |   |   |   |   |    |   |
| Calley  |   |   |   |    |   |   |   |   |    |   |
| Elton   |   |   |   |    |   |   |   |   |    |   |
| Galen   |   |   |   |    |   |   |   |   |    |   |
| Henry   |   |   |   |    |   |   |   |   |    |   |
| Iona    |   |   |   |    |   |   |   |   |    |   |
| Louise  |   |   |   |    |   |   |   |   |    |   |

9 points earn 3 extra minutes recess, 8 points earn regular recess, and below 8 points results in no recess. In a normal classroom situation (one teacher for 20–30 students), teachers often can rely on recording points on a group point chart like the one in Figure 5.1.2.

When awarding points, the teacher would go through the list quickly specifying what behaviors earned the maximal points and what students who did not earn 10 points must do next time to earn points.

1. "Ann got 10 points. She followed the rules all the time."
2. "So did Barbara. She also gets 10 points."
3. "Calley, you did a good job, but you have to look at the board all the time. You get 8 points."
4. "Elton worked hard during the whole group. He gets 10 points."
5. "Galen, next time remember to bring a pencil to group so I can give you 10 points. You only get 9 today."

## Identifying Performance Units

After teachers select a set of reinforcers and construct a delivery system, the reinforcement system can be implemented. One of the most difficult aspects of reinforcement is knowing how often to reinforce. Delivering reinforcers too often may interrupt a lesson or reduce the effectiveness of the reinforcers. Reinforcing too infrequently may result in lackadaisical student attitudes toward learning. To help teachers decide how often to reinforce, we recommend that teachers divide activities into performance units. A performance unit refers to a series of tasks on which students can be expected to work with no or minimal reinforcement.

The length of a performance unit depends on student interest in the material and its difficulty. Students cannot be expected to work as long on material that is not interesting to them or that involves lots of difficult tasks. When working with older students who enjoy school, a unit might include a series of tasks that require 30 to 40 minutes to complete, since these students will probably encounter little frustration and working for an extended period of time is something they have done many times before. In contrast, when working with kindergarten or first grade students, a performance unit should be short. During a reading lesson for beginning readers, the teacher might identify just two or three letters as a unit and reinforce the students with praise after they correctly say the sounds for those letters. A lesson might include five units each 2–4 minutes long. Before too long, however, the teacher would increase the size of the unit until it included all the letters in an isolated sounds task. Performance units should increase throughout the school year, so that students learn to work for longer and longer periods of time. Moreover, the teacher should inform the students when increasing the size of a performance unit. The teacher might say, "Yesterday we did four words in a row before we had our handshake. Let's see if we can do six words today."

## Establishing Rules

The rules should describe what students should do, rather than what they should not do. The rule, "Walk in school" is better than "Do not run." Rules should specify behaviors that are incompatible with undesirable behaviors. Watching the teacher is incompatible with staring off into space. Answering only when the teacher asks a question is incompatible with talking out. Sitting like good learners is incompatible with fidgeting.

The number of rules should be kept low. Possible rules during a small group lesson might be these:

1. Look and listen to the teacher
2. Talk only when the teacher calls on you
3. Keep your hands to yourself

At the beginning of the school year, teachers should remind students about the rules quite often. Teachers can post the rules for students to read. Rules might be expanded as new situations arise. For example, if a student continually rocks in his chair, the teacher might establish a new rule that all four chair legs must be on the floor.

## Presenting a Unit

There are three basic steps in presenting any performance unit:

1. Beginning the unit in a manner to increase the likelihood of student attentiveness

2. Structuring performance units to keep attentiveness high
3. Awarding major reinforcers at the end of the unit

### Beginning a Unit in a Motivating Manner

At the beginning of each unit, the teacher should take some type of action to get the unit off to a good start. At the beginning of a lesson, the teacher would remind students of the rules, make a quick motivating statement, and then immediately begin the first task. The purpose of a motivating statement is to increase the likelihood that the students will be attentive during a unit. The type of motivating statement used depends on the students and the relative difficulty of the task. For older students doing relatively well in reading, motivating statements can be minimal. Here is one example of a minimal motivating statement that arouses the students' curiosity. "Let's read this story and see what happened to Achilles after his mother bathed him in the magic waters." A challenge which involves the teacher's stating a certain criterion of performance and challenging the students to reach that criterion is a more powerful motivating statement. For example, a teacher might say, "Yesterday it took seven minutes to look up ten words in the dictionary. Let's see if we can look up ten words today in less than seven minutes." A special type of challenge that can be used occasionally with intermediate grade students involves the teacher's beginning a lesson with a quick explanation of a new concept and then immediately asking difficult questions about what was explained. The purpose of asking difficult questions is to point out to the students that they do not know the material being presented and must pay attention if they are to do well on the lesson. This technique is best reserved for students who usually succeed on difficult tasks.

Different motivating statements can also be used to encourage primary grade students to do well on a performance unit. One type of statement is a reminder of the consequences that will come at the end of the unit. The teacher might say, "I hope you kids work super well. I really want to play a hangman game with you when we finish reading the story. Remember, we're done when you read it with less than four mistakes." When making the statement, the teacher should communicate to the students that he really wants them to play the game.

Challenges can also be used with younger students. In one type of challenge, the teacher might tell the students that an upcoming task is very hard, and even though the students are smart, the task is just too hard for students their age. "Oh-oh. The next page is hard. You guys are good readers, but these words would even give fifth graders a hard time." At the end of the page, the teacher acts surprised that the students were able to do the task. Teachers should use challenges only if the students are likely to succeed.

Another type of challenge which students usually enjoy is the race. The teacher draws a score box on the board (see Figure 5.1.3.). After drawing the box, the teacher says, "We're going to have a race. The *T* is for teacher. The *S* is for students. Every time I win, I get a point. Every time you win, you get a point. For you guys to get a point, everyone must answer when I signal. If you don't get the answer on time, I get a point." Begin the race with easy questions, so that the students can get ahead. Pretend that you really want to win the race and are upset at being behind. If students make errors or respond late, give yourself a point. Do not give students a point unless they earn it. The students

must respond correctly as a group; otherwise, you get the point. If they are losing, use easier items. With younger students, the race should almost always end up with the students winning.

The teacher can begin a unit even if some students are inattentive. Instead of scolding the inattentive students, the teacher begins the unit and makes it clear that the students who are attending and responding will be the ones who will be reinforced. The teacher can make comments like, "Tony's working hard. I'll be able to give him that extra recess." (With young students, the teacher may give a quick handshake or tickle to students who are performing well.) The teacher should not attend to any inattentive student unless that student is interfering with the learning of other students or has been inattentive for a relatively long period of time. Suggestions for handling disruptive students will be presented later.

An activity that is particularly effective in beginning units with younger students is the stand up-sit down game. In this activity, the teacher starts with a challenge. "Listen carefully. I'm going to see if I can trick you. I'll say something. See if you can do what I say. Ready? (pause) Stand up. Sit down. Stand up. Sit down. Sit down. (Some students will probably stand up because of the alternating pattern the teacher established.) Tricked you. Let's play again. Stand up. Sit down. Stand up. Sit down. Sit down. Good. I didn't trick you. Stand up. Sit down. (point to a letter from the isolated sounds task and ask) What's this sound?" The purpose of the stand up-sit down game is to get the students into the general behavior of listening carefully and responding to what the teacher says. Once the students get into this general set of attentiveness, the teacher can quickly re-

**FIGURE 5.1.3**

| 😊 | T | |
|---|---|---|
| 😊 | S | |

place the movement instructions with an academic task. The game can also be played with instructions such as, "Touch your nose. Close your eyes. Smile."

### Structuring Tasks for High Attentiveness

Teachers should present units in a manner that minimizes the occurrence of inappropriate student behavior. The main tool in doing this is to structure lessons so that the tasks are at the student's instructional level, neither too easy, which causes boredom nor too difficult, which causes frustration.

Teachers should generally begin lessons with relatively easy material so that all students can succeed and be reinforced for answering correctly. Reinforcing students during the first unit is important, since it shows them that positive consequences result from appropriate behavior.

The pace and style with which a teacher presents a lesson are big factors in determining student attentiveness. Lessons should be presented at a lively pace and in an interesting manner. Teachers should treat the tasks as interesting and challenging.

While presenting a performance unit, a teacher should anticipate problems. If students are having difficulty with an exercise or are becoming restless, the teacher should move quickly to prevent misbehavior. Reacting to trivial behaviors that precede more serious misbehaviors can prevent the more serious misbehaviors from ever occurring. For example, if a teacher notices that a student who has been having a lot of difficulty with a task is becoming upset, the teacher can use a "change up." In a change up, the teacher makes a dramatic change in the way the lesson is being presented. A change up might involve a switch from a difficult to an easier task so that a frustrated student will succeed. Or it may involve simply taking a short break (15 to 30 seconds) during

which the teacher can acknowledge that the task is difficult but express confidence that the students will be able to succeed; e.g., "This list is really hard, but I know you kids don't give up. You're not quitters." After making a statement to express her confidence in the students, the teacher must be sure to provide the practice necessary for the student to master the material in the exercise. Sometimes problems arise with higher-performing students who get bored. One way to handle this problem is to acknowledge to those students that they have mastered the skills but you'd like them to keep responding so they can help the other students.

### Awarding Major Reinforcers at the End of a Unit

During a unit, the teacher may use brief praise comments like, "Good reading." However, the teacher should delay awarding stronger reinforcers until all the students have successfully completed the unit. Students must learn that reinforcement follows mastery of a substantial unit of academic work, not just a question or two. For example, if a performance unit is an isolated sounds task, which includes six letters, the teacher confirms correct responses during the unit ("Right," "Mmm") but delays more substantial reinforcers until all students identify all six letters correctly.

When awarding reinforcers at the end of a unit, the teacher should make it clear that students who worked hard throughout the entire unit receive special treatment. If students who did not obey group rules during the entire unit ask why they are not receiving special treatment, say that they worked only part of the time. Next, indicate confidence that the students will earn the pay-off in the next lesson. "I know you'll do better the next time we read." Do not be negative but at the same time, do not be too supportive. Quickly make your statements and then move on to the next performance unit. Do not argue with the student or allow him to engage in an extended verbal interaction. This procedure will let students know that you expect them to work hard all the time.

Occasionally, call attention to students who worked the hardest during a lesson. Tell the rest of the students that they worked well, but some of the students worked "super hard." The teacher might surprise students who worked super hard by saying, "Dina, stand up. Everybody, do you know that Dina worked so well that I'm going to give you all two extra minutes of recess? Let's clap for Dina." (Giving the whole group a reward because of the performance of one student will avoid jealousy and foster positive attitudes among students.)

## Dealing with Inappropriate Behaviors

As stated earlier, teachers should use positive rather than negative consequences since negative consequences can have undesirable side effects; students may develop negative feelings toward school and/or feelings of inadequacy about themselves. Another problem with negative consequences is that they often increase rather than decrease inappropriate behavior. For example, if a student enjoys spending time with adults, the intended punisher of staying in during recess may increase the inappropriate behavior that led to losing recess rather than decrease it. Therefore, since negative consequences can have undesirable side effects or unintentionally function as reinforcers, they must be used very carefully. A prime rule governing the use of a negative consequence is that when using it, teachers *must* be in control of themselves. Teachers must not become angry or frustrated (although they may act and appear so) over a student's behavior. They may choose to appear angry, but they must be in complete control of their emotions. This point is critical. A

teacher must always be able to objectively evaluate the effects of intended punishers to see if they are working as intended. A second rule governing the use of punishment is that just as teachers should use minimal reinforcers, so too should they use the most minimal type of negative consequences needed when dealing with a situation.

### Praise-Ignore

Praise-ignore is the initial method we recommend for dealing with most inappropriate behavior because it involves positive rather than negative consequences. (Note: Praise-ignore is *not* used when one student's actions are physically or emotionally abusing another student.) The general rule for using praise-ignore is to make one student's inappropriate behavior the cue for praising a student who is behaving appropriately. For example, if Alicia is answering in a low mumbly voice, the teacher might say to another student "Good answering, Roberta. You answered with a big voice." Quite often, the student displaying the inappropriate behavior will copy the behavior of the student being praised. The teacher would then praise that student for the appropriate behavior. "Good answering, Alicia."

### Reward-Ignore

If praise-ignore does not immediately stop a student's inappropriate behavior, the teacher must decide what to do next. The teacher's reaction depends on the type of inappropriate behavior being displayed. There are basically two sets of inappropriate student behaviors: those that interfere with the learning of other students and those that do not. The reaction to inappropriate behaviors that are not affecting the learning of other students is reward-ignore. Reward-ignore is essentially the same as praise-ignore except that a stronger reinforcer is given to students behaving appropriately. For younger students, the stronger reinforcer might be a tickle or handshake. For older students, the awarding of extra access to a desired activity is effective.

Remember: Reward-ignore is used to deal with behaviors that do not affect the learning of other students. For example, some kindergarten or first grade students who have just begun school are often reluctant to answer. When working with this group of beginning readers, the teacher would use very enjoyable reinforcers such as, knee rides, tickles, and handshakes, to reward students who are responding appropriately and would ignore nonresponding.

Older students often act uninvolved to impress their peers. If a student's performance on individual turns indicates that he is mastering the skills being taught, the teacher need not worry about apparent inattentiveness, unless of course his behavior is disturbing other students.

### Warnings

A different procedure is used when a student's inappropriate behavior is interfering with the learning of other students. For example, a student is distracting other students by tapping or talking out. The first step in dealing with this type of behavior is to issue a warning. To be effective, warnings should be issued quite early in a chain of misbehaviors and should make it clear that continuation of the behavior will lead to the loss of an activity. For example, if one student is whispering to another, the teacher might praise students attending to the teacher. If the student who is whispering does not stop, the teacher might say, "Ann, look up here and listen carefully so I can let you go to recess." Note that the wording is done so that the teacher lets the student know that the teacher wants the student to have something enjoyable but will have no choice in taking the activity away if the student does not behave properly. Issuing more

than one warning to a student during a lesson should generally lead to a loss of part of or an entire activity. At the end of the lesson, the teacher might tell Ann that she lost part or all of recess time because she was not following the group rules.

Backing up warnings with consequences is especially important at the beginning of the school year. Teachers must make it clear to the students that inappropriate behavior does not lead to a pay-off but rather leads to the loss of a desirable activity.

Warnings should be worded quite carefully. They should not imply there is something wrong with a student. They should focus on the student's action, not the student as a person. The theme of the warning should always be: you're ok, but that action was not. When issuing warnings, the teacher should not raise his voice. The warning can be issued in a matter of fact tone. This is important. It avoids a situation in which the only time students attend to the teacher is when the teacher raises his voice. Raising one's voice should be saved for occasions in which one student is physically or emotionally abusing another student. If, for example, a student has made fun of another student, a teacher might use a very harsh tone of voice, saying, "Don't ever make fun of anybody in this class again," glaring at the student in a foreboding way. After making the statement, the teacher should quickly return to the instructional task. A long lecture about the misbehavior is usually less effective than a short command. When returning to task, the teacher's tone of voice should be normal.

With younger students a negative command issued in a stern voice might be used in lieu of a warning. Younger students respond to more immediate types of consequences. A sternly said "Don't bother William" will sometimes be effective. Remember though that the negative command is used only if praise and ignore do not work, and one student is interfering with another student's learning.

### Expulsion from a Group

Sometimes a student will not stop misbehaving even after a teacher takes away an activity after issuing a warning. If the student's misbehavior is disrupting other students' learning and the student does not respond to the loss of an activity, the teacher must consider expulsion from the group. The advantage of expulsion is that it allows the teacher to continue instruction with the remaining students. The disadvantages of expulsion are the attention the student may receive, either from the teacher or from peers, and the loss of instructional time while out of the group.

Expulsion from a group is usually more effective with younger students. The teacher might say to the young student, "You're not acting like a big kid so you can't do this big kid work with us. When you can work like a big kid, you can join us." When removing the student, the teacher should avoid emotional reaction. He should act calmly. In no case should he argue with the student. The teacher puts the student's chair several feet outside the group and turns the chair in a direction so that the student is facing away from the group, but not toward any other students. The student should be in easy view of the teacher so that the teacher can make sure that the student is not receiving attention from other students. The teacher should not attend to the student unless, of course, the student continues to disrupt the group. During the ensuing time, the teacher should make the lesson extremely enjoyable for the other students, playing games, giving handshakes, etc. After the expelled student has sat quietly for several minutes, the teacher asks if she is ready to join the group. If the student says yes, she is returned to the group. If the student says no, she remains outside the group for the rest of the period. Instructional time missed by the student due to expulsion from the group should be made up during a period when other students are doing enjoyable activities. At that time, the teacher tells the student it is time to make up work that was missed when she was out of the group.

With older students the teacher should make it quite clear that any time the student spends out of the group must be made up at a later time, preferably during an activity that the student enjoys. To further decrease the probability that students will remain away from the group for a long period, the amount of time in the make-up activity could be several times longer than the amount spent out of the group. Each minute out of the group might mean 2 to 3 minutes of make-up work. When excluding a student from the group, the teacher should let the student know she can come back if she will cooperate. The teacher might say, "Go back to your seat. If you sit quietly for 5 minutes, you can come back. I hope that's soon, so you don't have to lose too much gym time making up your work." The 5-minute minimal period is to ensure that there will be some significant later loss of a privilege.

In summary, when dealing with inappropriate behaviors the teacher must distinguish between behaviors that disturb and do not disturb the learning of other students. Behaviors that do not disturb other students are dealt with by using more powerful reinforcers. Behaviors that disturb other students are dealt with through warnings or negative commands, depending on the nature of the behavior. One last note concerning inappropriate behavior involves a reminder on setting up a system to discourage the occurrence of inappropriate behavior. Reinforcers that are effective should be used from the beginning. Also, instruction should be at an appropriate level.

## Common Errors to Avoid in a Reinforcement System

Making a motivation system work is an unending task. We know of no simple formulas that will work in every situation with every student. A teacher must continually watch for behaviors that need to be strengthened or weakened and figure out effective procedures and consequences for changing those particular behaviors. If a teacher is having difficulty with student misbehavior or lack of motivation, he should examine his actions to determine how they are not functioning as intended. The following discusses some common teacher errors.

### The Criticism Trap

In the "criticism trap" the teacher relies on negative commands to the students ("sit down, don't talk out, don't be so sloppy"), rather than positive reinforcement. The criticism trap is easy to fall into since the negative command usually leads to a temporary cessation of the inappropriate behavior. The problem is that, in the long run, the negative commands do not decrease the frequency of the inappropriate behaviors.

### Inconsistency

Inconsistency is a second major error made by teachers. Inconsistency occurs when teachers vary their standards from day to day. If talking in group is permitted one day and not the next, students will become confused about how to behave during group instruction.

Just as a teacher's standards for acceptable behavior must be consistent, so too must a teacher's reaction to students who behave and misbehave. Behaviors must earn their promised consequence. When teachers forget or deny consequences to students who have earned them or feel guilty and reward students who did not behave well but cried, sulked, or whined, a reinforcement system will not work effectively. Teachers must make it clear to stu-

dents that behaving appropriately throughout an entire unit is the only way to earn reinforcement.

Teachers must watch out not to fall into a pattern of providing a reward for students who consistently misbehave during the early part of a lesson but then behave toward the end of the lesson. The reaction to such a pattern should be denial of the reward with a reassuring statement expressing confidence that the student will be able to earn the reward the next day or activity (e.g., "You really worked hard during the last part of the lesson. I bet tomorrow you'll work hard during the whole lesson. Then I'll be able to let you have recess").

### Not Reacting Early Enough

Misbehaviors usually occur as a chain of events. Teachers should consistently react to behaviors early in the chain rather than letting more serious misbehaviors develop and then trying to punish them. Delaying actions until misbehaviors have escalated is an error since the teacher demonstrates that a certain degree of misbehavior is tolerated.

### Bribery

Bribery occurs when a student does not do the work necessary to earn a promised reinforcer, and the teacher offers the student an even bigger reward for doing the work. For example, a student dallies when doing her seatwork assignment. The teacher says, "I'll give you five extra minutes of recess if you finish your seatwork."

Teachers, especially those working with older students, should carefully guard against falling into a bribery syndrome. Problems relating to bribery can be avoided by initially using reinforcers that are potent enough to motivate students and by making sure assignments are reasonable.

### Terminating a Motivation Procedure at the Wrong Time

Teachers can stop using a procedure too soon or too late. Sometimes teachers give up on a reinforcement procedure before it has had time to take effect. They use a reinforcement system quite diligently for the first few weeks of school and then drop it completely. Teachers can expect only minimal carry-over effects after abruptly dropping a reinforcement system. It should be gradually phased out.

A second error having to do with terminating a reinforcement procedure is acting too late. Teachers must carefully monitor the effects of procedures they use. If a procedure does not have any effect after about a week or 10 days, its use should be evaluated, and possibly the procedure should be changed. To avoid using a dysfunctional reinforcement procedure too long, teachers need to compile data on targeted student behaviors. Data allow teachers to decide whether a procedure is working.

### Using Withdrawal of Privileges Inappropriately

When withdrawal of privileges is used as a punishment, the student should be told what he must do to earn back the privilege. If a teacher takes away many privileges and does not allow the student to earn them back, the student is likely to become uncooperative since he has nothing to lose. For example, a student misbehaves on Monday. The teacher says, "You have lost your gym and recess for the rest of the week." An alternative might be telling the student that when she shows that she can behave appropriately for several days in a row, she will be allowed to go to the desired activities. Note that behaving ap-

propriately for only one day does not earn back the activity.

### Assumed Willfulness

Teachers sometimes misdiagnose student errors as resulting from a lack of attentiveness or a lack of effort, when in fact the cause of the error is a lack of knowledge. Increasing the motivation will not be effective in helping students solve a problem they do not know how to work. Teachers must not blame all errors on motivation. Many errors call for remediation in specific reading skills.

## Classroom Organization

Teachers usually do not teach all students in a room at once. During any one period, some of the students will be working independently, without direct teacher supervision. Planning what will be done during these times and transitions from activity to activity is very important.

## Transitions

Transitions include student movement between the reading instruction area and their desks and going to and returning from recess, gym, lunch or other activities outside classrooms. Transition periods are typically a time when behavior problems occur. The most important way to prevent problems during transitions is to establish rules and procedures about making transitions. These rules include the following:

1. Specifying the materials students are to bring with them: pencils, papers, notebooks, chairs, etc. If chairs are to be carried, teachers should show students how to carry them, so they do not bump into other students or desks and do not fall

2. Setting up traffic rules. Where are students to walk? Traffic rules avoid bumping into each other and engaging in talking and roughhousing
3. Specifying seat arrangements (separate students who talk to each other)

Teaching specific rules can be done through a combination of explanations and teacher models. For example, in explaining how to carry a chair, the teacher states the rule, "When you walk with a chair, carry it in front of you. Watch me." The teacher then models how to carry a chair. "Your turn. Show me how you carry a chair."

Performance units are as important in teaching transition rules as in teaching decoding or comprehension skills. The teacher prefaces the unit with a motivating statement, "Let's practice going back and forth to groups. When we do it perfectly, we'll go out to recess." During the first school days, the teacher should have students practice going to and from group areas until they do so quietly and follow the correct path. Successful completion of a unit should earn a reinforcer. "I liked the way you walked quietly to the group. Let's go to recess early."

Teachers of younger students should plan on spending 10 to 15 minutes each day during the first week of school teaching students how to make transitions from activity to activity. Setting up and practicing specific transition procedures at the beginning of the school year not only saves instructional time later in the year but also fosters a positive attitude, since a great deal of teacher nagging is avoided.

The teacher should set up a schedule so that students know where they are supposed to be at certain times. With older students, this can be done by posting the schedule on the board. With younger students, teachers would initially remind students of where they are to move to during a transition.

In order to facilitate transitions, teachers should give a signal (ringing a bell, etc.) a few moments before the transition is to take place. The signal notifies students to prepare to make the move to the next activity.

## Independent Work Periods

During independent seatwork, students may work on a number of activities either individually or in a small group. Activities that students work on individually might include comprehension worksheets, individual silent reading, handwriting practice, and story writing. Activities in which students might work in pairs include spelling practice, oral reading, and reading games. Students are more likely to make efficient use of seatwork time if teachers provide carefully structured assignments and institute a motivation system.

When assigning worksheet activities, the teacher should assign work that all students, both lower and higher performers, have an equal chance of successfully completing. Ideally, each student should be assigned work on which, with reasonable effort, 100% accuracy is possible. If this is to happen, exercises must be appropriate. An assignment is appropriate when students have been taught the skills necessary to successfully complete the assignment. Appropriate exercises are particularly important for younger students and older remedial students, since these students will be less likely to persist on materials that they do not know how to work.

Teachers should set up the classroom to encourage on-task independent work. A first step in teaching students to work independently is to arrange the classroom to minimize distractions. Desks should be spaced so that students are not too close to each other. Friends who talk a lot should be separated from each other. Desks should not be faced toward windows or other areas that might be distracting. The teacher should be located so that while he is teaching a group, he can observe the students as they work at their desks.

A second step involves setting up procedures for minimizing out-of-seat traffic. Problems associated with students' getting out of their seats can be avoided by making sure at the beginning of the day that students have enough materials at their desks. If each student has two pencils at her desk, the teacher will be spared numerous requests for pencils throughout the day. One of the before-school activities can be sharpening pencils. Problems revolving around students going to the restroom and to the drinking fountain can be minimized by restricting breaks to recess periods or by charging recess time for unscheduled breaks; e.g., a drink equals 5 minutes of recess. A procedure for seeking assistance while students remain at their desks involves a *need help* sign. When students come to exercises they cannot work, they circle the exercise, flip over their need help sign, and then proceed to the next exercise. (A need help sign can be a piece of paper attached to each student's desk with *need help* written on one side or simply a piece of colored paper which the student puts on his desk when he needs help.)

A third step in setting up a system to encourage independent work involves procedures for what a student is to do after he completes his work. After students complete their assignment, they might be allowed to select an activity. These after-work activities should be somewhat neutral. They should not be so enjoyable that students rush through their assignment to do them. On the other hand, they should be interesting enough to keep students quietly involved for the remainder of the seatwork period so they don't distract other students. Good choice activities for older students include reading a book or doing a crossword puzzle. For younger students who cannot yet decode, coloring exercises are possible activities. Whenever possible, activities should involve reading. Finished work should be left on the student's desk. At the end of the period, it may be passed up to the front of the room or collected by a monitor.

Teachers should establish a data-based motivation system for independent seatwork. In a data system, performance on assignments is recorded daily. The system for recording scores depends on the type of seatwork given. Recording student errors in terms of items missed or answered correctly is useful only when the number of items remains fairly constant from day to day. If 20 items appear on a worksheet one day and 5 the next, using a system that records the number of daily errors or items correct will not accurately reflect student performance. An alternate to recording the number of errors is to use percentages or letter grades: A, B, C, D. With letter grades, daily quotas are set according to how many items are in an assignment. The criteria for an A on one day might be three errors or less when there are 30 items and zero errors the next day when there are only 5 items. The advantage for the teacher of using letter grades over percentages is that less computation is necessary.

Keeping track of student performance will tell the teacher which students need extra help. If a student is performing poorly on independent seatwork, the teacher should go through a series of steps to diagnose the cause of the problem. The first step is to determine if the problem is caused by lack of motivation. To find out if consistent poor performance results from a lack of motivation, the teacher increases the reinforcement for good performance. For example, if the reinforcer for acceptable performance is extra recess at the end of the week, the teacher might increase the reinforcement by offering extra recess at the end of each day. If student performance does improve, the poor performance on worksheets likely resulted from a lack of motivation.

If the student's performance does not improve when the reinforcers are increased, the teacher should carefully examine the student's worksheets to identify error patterns. Procedures for diagnosing skill deficits and providing remediation are discussed throughout the book.

Below are examples of how several teachers used motivation systems in their classroom. The first description was written by Jane Cote with the assistance of Billie Overholser, both first-grade teachers in a school located in a lower socio-economic area. They describe procedures used at the beginning of the school year to teach Ms. Cote's students appropriate classroom behavior. Note the distinction made between more important behaviors and less critical behaviors. Also note that in her token system, she hands out tickets which can be turned in for activities. Keep in mind that the system she describes is designed for students with little or no prior school experience. The second description discusses a beginning-of-the-year system for intermediate grade students.

### Example One: First Grade

During the first days of school, I do not begin teaching reading lessons but concentrate instead on teaching appropriate independent seatwork behavior. The way I do this is by scheduling several 15-minute whole-class seatwork activities involving simple skills like coloring. During these periods, I walk around the room handing out tickets and praising students who are working appropriately. I'll hand out a ticket about every 30 seconds. Immediately after each session I have a fun activity. Students must trade in their tickets to participate in the fun activity. "Everybody who has a ticket, come up here; we're going to play a game." I pay special attention to students who earned the most tickets. After a day

or two of this, students begin to value the tickets. At this point, I start teaching groups.

During the first few days of teaching groups, I spend half my time actually teaching the group and the other half supervising students who are working at their desks. Throughout the group instruction, I teach for several minutes; then I leave the group and hand out tickets and praise several students who have been working appropriately at their seats during the time I was working with the group. Initially, I'll teach for about 3 minutes, then I hand out tickets for about 30 seconds, then teach another 2–3 minutes, then hand out tickets for another 30 seconds, etc. I repeat this pattern throughout the 25-minute group session. To control the behavior of students in the group during the time when I give tickets to seatworkers, I give tickets to students who waited quietly for me to return.

After each group lesson, I have a whole class fun activity. I'll start the activity by calling up students who have the most tickets. "Everybody with 5 tickets, come up here. You get to go outside first to play." In order to make it clear why these students go out first, I ask each child to tell how he earned the ticket. To make earning the tickets even more reinforcing, I'll have the children clap for the students who earned more than a certain amount of tickets. "Everybody, let's clap for the children who earned more than 3 tickets. They sure worked hard." If a student didn't earn any tickets, the student does not get to participate in the fun activity. I am not negative to those students. I might say in a friendly tone, "Sue, do you know how Alex earned all those tickets?" If the student says no, I'll tell her in a friendly way and then tell her that I have confidence that next time she'll act like Alex did, and she'll be able to go out. I then send the child back to her seat saying she can color or look at a book.

After several days of teaching groups, I make two changes. First, I *set up a vari-*

*able-interval reinforcement system.* Rather than leaving the small teaching group every 2 to 3 minutes, I become more unpredictable, sometimes waiting up to 5 minutes before getting up to give out tickets, and sometimes waiting only a minute or two. I switch to this variable system to teach children to work for longer periods of time. How quickly I increase the intervals between giving out tickets depends on the behavior of the students. With students who have had prior experience in school, I find that I can often progress to 10- to 15-minute intervals within the first few weeks of school. With students who have little independent seatwork behavior on entering school, the interval might remain at about 5 to 10 minutes for the first 2 months of school.

Secondly, I *set up free time tables.* I set up a special table for each reading group. On the tables are reading games at that group's appropriate reading level. I change games frequently to keep interest high. Each game has a price tag. When a student finishes his seatwork, he goes to the table, deposits the correct number of tickets in a can and takes the game to his desk. The purpose of the free time table is to eliminate the need for special whole class activities after each group, thus enabling the teacher to teach one small group after another.

The procedure I've described for teaching seatwork behavior requires a great deal of time and effort on my part, but it's worth it. In the long run, it saves me time. After the first month or so of school, most students will be able to work independently at their desks for extended periods of time. I can devote my energy to teaching. Equally if not more important is the positive classroom atmosphere. It is not only beneficial to the students but also is quite rewarding to me.

I have instituted these procedures myself in some years. At other times, I have used an aide or parent volunteer. It is absolutely vital that the assistant be well trained and monitored to maintain the positive level of interaction with the children. During the first several days of school, I have the person simply observe me. I explain why I praise certain behaviors and ignore others. I then have the person start giving out tickets. For the next day or two I observe the person quite carefully. I insist that the person be positive with the students. (For some adults, this is very difficult.)

### Example 2: Fifth Grade

I divide the day into four periods of about 1 1/2 hours each. A student can earn up to 10 points each period.

Students earn points by following classroom rules: attending during group, going to and from group quickly and quietly, and working industriously at seatwork. On the first day of school I explain the system and award points fairly loosely so that many students will receive the rewards. On the second day, I become much stricter. Each time I see a student misbehaving, I praise a student who is behaving appropriately. I keep track of students whose behavior warranted me to praise another student for an incompatible behavior. When awarding points I would say, "Tom, you worked hard, next time I hope you keep busy the whole period so I can give you all 10 points." I would then award less than 10 points to the student.

At the end of each school day, I have a grab bag in which students who earned 38 points or more may participate in selecting papers with various rewards on them from a can. Below are some of the rewards:

1. 2 minutes extra recess
2. Three pieces of red paper
3. First in line for lunch
4. Attendance book monitor
5. Extra gym period
6. An eraser
7. Being board cleaner
8. Lunch ticket monitor

9. 5 minutes extra recess
10. Use of ball during recess
11. Movie projector monitor
12. Good work letter

To back up the importance of the points, I set up a system in which all students receiving more than 38 points get a special bonus if more than 90% of the students earn 38 or more points. This creates some peer pressure but does not give one student the opportunity to keep the entire class from earning the bonus. I also make access to recess contingent on earning a minimum of 36 points, thus adding the possibility of a loss of activity for the student not cooperating fully. I keep track of points by writing them on a chart like the one in Figure 5.1.3.

I spend only about 10 minutes a day in awarding points. When awarding points, I write the points on the chart for each student making quick remarks as I go. "Bill got 10 points: he worked perfectly. Sarah got 9: next time carry your chair right so I can give you 10 points. Anne got 10," etc. After about a week, I award points only twice a day, then several weeks later, only once a day. Another major change I make is to incorporate a point system based on the students' performance on seatwork exercises. I find this to be very important since some students whose behavior is acceptable in a group setting will not initially concentrate on seatwork exercises without some type of pay-off system. The system I use involves the students' plotting their daily performance on a graph. I return the papers to the students and have them record their performances. At first, I

**FIGURE 5.1.3**

| Bill | 10 | 10 |
| --- | --- | --- |
| Sarah | 10 | 10 |
| Anne | 10 | 10 |
| Frances | 10 | 9 |
| Tyrone | 9 | 10 |

give daily pay-offs, such as extra recess; later I award pay-offs once a week.

## Professionalism and Reinforcement

Although the deliberate use of consequences can facilitate both the teaching and learning of reading, some teachers object to planned reinforcement as being too mechanistic. Others say that students should want to learn for the sake of learning; they should be intrinsically motivated to learn to read. We, too, wish that all students were intrinsically motivated to learn to read. The fact is, however, many students are not. If teachers do not use carefully planned reinforcement techniques to motivate students, many students' progress in learning to read will be hampered.

Some teachers feel that planned reinforcement is good but is not suited to their teaching style. This attitude is fine as long as all of the teacher's students are learning and feeling positive about themselves. However, if some students are failing or being negative, the teacher *must* use techniques that work. *The question is not primarily what the teacher feels comfortable doing but more what works with the teacher's students.*

## Building Self-images

A major goal of each reading lesson must be to build students' self-images. As students learn to read, they also learn about themselves; whether they can succeed, whether persistence pays off, whether they are as competent as their peers. Every time a teacher presents a reading exercise, the teacher is not only teaching reading skills but is also demonstrating to the student and the student's peers whether the student is capable. If a student succeeds often, the student learns that she is capable. On the other hand, a student who often fails learns that she is not capable.

By persistence, we refer to the ability to keep trying when one encounters difficulty. Persistence is a critical prerequisite to future academic success. Teachers can facilitate the development of persistence in several ways. First and foremost is assigning students appropriate work. If students are misplaced in instructional material, they will have little chance of obtaining the success which facilitates the development of persistence. Second is the way teachers handle situations in which a student has difficulty. Especially with younger students or students functioning below grade level, the teacher must show that if you persist you will succeed. To do this a teacher must be able to diagnose and remediate problems effectively. When students have diffi-

culty, teachers should acknowledge that the student is having difficulty and should express confidence that the student will eventually succeed ("Billy's working hard. These words are tough, but I know he's going to be able to get them."). When the child masters the difficult task, the teacher must treat this mastery as a significant accomplishment. The teacher should act excited. "I told you he would get it. He's smart. He knows if you work hard you'll be able to get it." Mutual support among students can be encouraged by rewarding all the students for the accomplishment of one student. "Everybody gets to go out to recess early because Andrea worked so hard. Let's all clap for Andrea."

---

## RESEARCH

The research on the systematic use of consequences is so extensive that we will not attempt to document it here. Instead, we refer the reader to two other books which discuss the research:

Becker, Engelmann, & Thomas. *Teaching I: Classroom management.* Chicago: Science Research Associates, 1976.

Walker, Hill, & Buckley, Nancy. *Token reinforcement techniques.* Eugene, Oreg.: E. B. Press, 1975.

These books provide excellent summaries of the research.

## APPLICATION EXERCISES

1. In each blank, write the teacher-delivered consequences and the student behavior. At the end of each series of teacher-student interaction, circle whether the teacher consequences were punishing, reinforcing, or had no effect.
   a. John sat reading at his desk for 3 minutes. Then he threw a ball of paper at Jane. The teacher glared at John.
   Student behavior that preceded the consequence _____.

   Teacher consequence _____.
   John started reading again. After 2 minutes, he threw a ball of paper at Lisa. The teacher said, "Stop it."
   Student behavior that preceded the consequence _____.

   Teacher consequence _____.
   John read for a minute. Then he threw a ball of paper at Mike. The teacher said, "John, put your head down."
   Student behavior that preceded the consequence _____.

   Teacher consequence _____.

The teacher consequences (reinforced, punished, had no effect on) throwing balls of paper.

b. John sat reading at his desk for 3 minutes. Then he threw a ball of paper at Jane. The teacher smiled at John.
Student behavior that preceded the consequence _____.

Teacher consequence _____.
John started reading again. After 2 minutes he threw a ball of paper at Lisa. The teacher said, "I like the way you're working."
Student behavior that preceded the consequence _____.

Teacher consequence _____.
John read for a minute. Then he threw a ball of paper at Mike. The teacher said, "You can go to recess now."
Student behavior that preceded the consequence _____.

Teacher consequence _____.
The teacher consequences (reinforced, punished, had no effect on) throwing balls of paper.

c. John sat reading at his desk for 3 minutes. He threw a ball of paper at Jane. Then he began reading. After reading 2 minutes, the teacher said, "You're really doing a nice job reading that story."
Student behavior that preceded the consequence _____.

Teacher consequence _____.
John read for 4 minutes and then looked up at the teacher. The teacher smiled.
Student behavior that preceded the consequence _____.

Teacher consequence _____.
John read for 6 more minutes. The teacher said, "John, I like the way you are quietly reading."
Student behavior that preceded the consequence _____.

Teacher consequence _____.
The teacher consequences (reinforced, punished, had no effect on) reading.

2. A group of students (Tom, Dick, and Harry) have been introduced to *s, m, e, i, t,* and *d.* The newest letter is *i,* with which students are still having difficulty. The students are well behaved and can quickly and accurately identify the other letters. Answer the question for each of the following student behaviors during isolated sounds instruction.
   a. Dick is sitting quietly. Is that a significant behavior?
   b. The group correctly identifies *m.* Is this a significant academic behavior?
   c. The group correctly identifies all the letters the first time they are presented in a lesson. Is this a significant academic behavior?
   d. In which instances, *a, b,* or *c,* would the teacher reinforcement be the greatest?

3. Mark the three statements which illustrate behavior-specific praise.
   a. Everybody has been so good today.
   b. John and Alice did a terrific job.
   c. John and Alice did a terrific job on their independent work. They only made one mistake.
   d. Good, Maxwell, the sound is /a/.
   e. I think you are a good student, Sam.

    f. Sam, you did a nice job summarizing the chapter on the industrial revolution.

4. Which three of the following units are appropriate performance units?
   a. Third graders identifying one letter.
   b. Fifth graders reading a sentence.
   c. Fifth graders completing a set of 15 study questions on a science chapter.
   d. Kindergarteners identifying three letters.
   e. First graders accurately decoding five sentences.
5. What are two major objectives of a motivation system?
6. How are punishers different from reinforcers?
7. A teacher's intentions have nothing to do with whether a teacher's action functions as a reinforcer or punisher. True or False? Explain why.
8. Tell two reasons why negative consequences must be used with extreme care.
9. What is meant by reinforcing incompatible behaviors as a means of weakening undesired behavior? Give three examples (not the ones discussed in book).
10. Why is the use of positive consequences preferable to the use of negative consequences?
11. What is meant by using minimal reinforcers? Explain why minimal reinforcers should be used.
12. What is meant by focusing on significant rather than trivial student achievement? Why is it important?
13. What are six basic steps in setting up a motivation system?
14. How can teachers determine what activities are likely to function as reinforcers for a student?
15. What is a delivery system; when is a token economy delivery system needed?
16. What is a performance unit?
17. What two factors does the length of a performance unit depend on?
18. Is this an appropriate rule: Do not doodle, daydream, talk to your neighbor, or make noise when you work at your desk. Write a shorter rule that states what students should do.
19. Describe several types of motivation statements.
20. Describe a procedure for beginning a lesson even though some students are not attentive.
21. Why is it important to begin a lesson with a relatively easy unit?
22. What is a change up? When should it be used?
23. Describe two types of inappropriate behavior and the type of reaction to each if praise-ignore does not result in the immediate cessation of an inappropriate behavior.
24. a. Under what circumstances might a student be expelled from the group?
    b. Describe the procedure discussed to make expelling younger students from the group effective.
25. What is the criticism trap? Why is this trap easy to fall into?
26. What is meant by reacting to misbehavior early in a chain? Why is it important?
27. What is bribery?
28. List three steps teachers can take to encourage on-task independent work behavior.
29. How can a teacher find out if a student's continual poor performance on seatwork is caused by lack of motivation?
30. Tell how teachers can develop student persistence.

# References

A secret report flunks schools. *Chicago Sun Times,* January 7, 1975, p. 1.

Aaron, I. A. What teachers and prospective teachers know about phonics generalizations. *Journal of Educational Research,* 1960, *53,* 323–330.

Abramson, T., & Kagan, E. Familiarization of content and differential response modes in programmed instruction. *Journal of Educational Psychology,* 1975, *67,* 83–88.

Abt Associates. *Education as experimentation: A planned variation model* (Vol. IV). Boston: Author, 1977.

Action Books. N.Y.: Scholastic Book Services, 1971.

Anastasiow, N. J., Sibley, S. A., Leonhardt, T. M., & Borich, G. D. A comparison of guided discovery, discovery, and didactic teaching of math to kindergarten poverty children. *American Educational Research Journal,* 1971, *7,* 493–510.

Anderson, R. C. The notion of schemata and the educational enterprise. In R. C. Anderson, R. J. Spiro, & W. E. Montague (Eds.), *Schooling and the acquisition of knowledge.* Hillsdale, N.J.: Lawrence Erlbaum Associates, 1977.

Arlin, M., & Arlin, P. K. *Operational level and children's recall for relevant and irrelevant information from stories.* Paper presented at the annual meeting of the American Educational Research Association, Toronto, March 1978.

Arter, J. A., & Jenkins, J. R. *Differential diagnosis—prescriptive teaching: A critical appraisal* (Tech. Rep. No. 80). Champaign: University of Illinois at Urbana-Champaign, Center for the Study of Reading, January 1978.

Asher, R. R., & Markell, R. A. Sex differences in comprehension of high and low interest material. *Journal of Educational Psychology,* 1974, *66,* 680–687.

Athey, I. Reading research in the affective domain. In H. Singer & R. B. Ruddell (Eds.), *Theoretical models and processes of reading.* Newark, Del.: International Reading Association, 1976.

Athey, I. Syntax, semantics, and reading. In J. T. Guthrie (Ed.), *Cognition, curriculum, and comprehension.* Newark, Del.: International Reading Association, 1977.

Ausubel, D. P. A cognitive-structure theory of school learning. In L. Siegel (Ed.), *Instruction.* San Francisco: Chandler, 1967.

Baily, M. H. The utility of phonic generalizations in grades one through six. *Reading Teacher,* 1967, *20,* 413–418.

Balow, B. The long-term effect of remedial reading instruction. *The Reading Teacher,* 1965, *18,* 581–586.

Baron, J., & Strawson, C. Use of orthographic and word-specific knowledge in reading words aloud. *Journal of Experimental Psychology: Human Perception and Performance,* 1976, *2,* 386–393.

*Basic reading.* Philadelphia, Penn.: J. B. Lippincott Co., 1975.

Bateman, B. D. *The essentials of teaching.* San Rafael, Calif.: Dimensions Publishing Co., 1971.

Beaton, A. E., Hilton, T. L., & Schrader, W. B. *Changes in the verbal abilities of high school seniors, college entrants, and SAT candidates between 1960 and 1972.* Princeton, N. J.: Education Testing Service, 1977.

Beck, I. L. Comprehension during the acquisition of decoding skills. In J. T. Guthrie (Ed.), *Cognition, curriculum and comprehension.* Newark, Del.: International Reading Association, 1977.

Becker, W. C. Applications of behavior principles in typical classrooms. In *Behavior Modification in Education,* The Seventy-Second Year Book of the National Society for the Study of Education, Chicago, Ill.: NSSE, 1973.

Becker, W. C. Teaching reading and language to the disadvantaged—What we have learned from field research. *Harvard Educational Review,* 1977, *47,* 518–543.

Becker, W. C. *The Follow Through data show that some programs work better than others.* Paper presented at AERA, Toronto, March 1978.

Becker, W. C., & Carnine, D. W. *Direct instruction—A behavior theory model for comprehensive educational intervention with the disadvantaged.* Paper presented at the VIII Symposium on Behavior Modification, Caracas, Venezuela, February 1978.

Becker, W. C., & Engelmann, S. *Analysis of achievement data on six cohorts of low income children from 20 school districts in the University of Oregon Direct Instruction Follow Through Model.* Technical Report 76-1, Eugene, Oreg. University of Oregon, 1976. (a)

Becker, W. C., & Engelmann, S. *Teaching 3: Evaluation of instruction.* Chicago: Science Research Associates, 1976. (b)

Becker, W. C., Engelmann, S., & Carnine, D. W. The direct instruction model. In R. Rhine (Ed.), *Encouraging change in America's schools: A decade of experimentation.* New York: Academic Press, in press.

Becker, W. C., Engelmann, S., & Thomas, D. R. *Teaching 1:* Classroom management. Chicago: Science Research Associates, 1976.

Berger, N. *An investigation of linguistic competence and organizational processes in good and poor readers.* Unpublished doctoral dissertation, University of Pittsburgh, 1975.

Biderdorf, J. R., & Pear, J. J. Two-to-one versus one to one student-teacher ratios in the operant verbal training of retarded children. *Journal of Applied Behavioral Analysis,* 1977, *10,* 506.

Biemiller, A. J. The development of the use of graphic and contextual information as children learn to read. *Reading Research Quarterly,* 1970, *6,* 75–96.

Bishop, C. H. Transfer effects of word and letter training in reading. *Journal of Verbal Learning and Verbal Behavior,* 1964, *3,* 214–221.

Blank, M., & Frank, S. M. Story recall in kindergarten children: Effect of method of presentation on psycholinguistic performance. *Child Development,* 1971, *42,* 299–312.

Bleismer, E. P., & Yarborough, B. H. A comparison of ten different beginning reading programs in first grade. *Phi Delta Kappan,* June 1965, pp. 500–504.

Bloom B. S. *Human characteristics and school learning.* New York: McGraw-Hill, 1976.

Bohannon, R. *Direct and daily measurement procedures in the identification and treatment of reading.* Unpublished doctoral dissertation, University of Washington, 1975.

Bond, G. L., & Dykstra, R. The cooperative research program in first grade reading instruction. *Reading Research Quarterly,* 1967, *2,* 5–142.

Borus, J. F., Greenfield, S., Spiegel, B., & Daniels, G. Establishing imitative speech-employing operant techniques in a group setting. *Journal of Speech and Hearing Disorders,* 1973, *38* (4), 533–554.

Bourne, L. E., Jr., & Pendleton, R. B. Concept identification as a function of completeness and probability of information feedback. *Journal of Experimental Psychology,* 1958, *56,* 413–420.

Bransford, J. D., & Johnson, M. K. Contextual prerequisites for understanding: Some investigations of comprehension and recall. *Journal of Verbal Learning and Verbal Behavior,* 1972, *11,* 717–726.

Bridge, J. T. Rank ordering of letters and letter combinations according to ease of learning their sound associations. In E. B. Coleman, Collecting a data base for a reading technology. *Journal of Educational Psychology Monograph,* 1970, *61* (4, Pt. 2).

Britton, Gwyneth, & Lumpkin, Margaret. *Readability—A consumer's guide computerized analysis of the Houghton Mifflin reading series.* Corvallis, Oreg.: Britton and Associates, 1977.

Britton, B. K., Westbrook, R. D., & Holdredge, T. *Reading and cognitive capacity usage: Effects of test difficulty.* Paper presented at the annual meeting of the American Education Research Association, Toronto, March 1978.

Brophy, J. E. *Teacher behaviors related to learning by low vs. high socioeconomic status early elementary students.* Paper presented at the annual meeting of the American Educational Research Association, Washington, D. C., April 1975.

Brophy, J. E., & Evertson, C. M. *Learning from teaching: A developmental perspective.* Boston: Allyn & Bacon, 1976.

Brown, A. L. Semantic integration in children's reconstruction of narrative sequences. *Cognitive Psychology,* 1976, *8,* 247–262.

Brown, A. L. Knowing when, where, and how to remember: A problem of metacognition. In R. Glasser (Ed.), *Advances in instructional psychology.* Hillsdale, N. J.: Lawrence Eralbaum Associates, 1978.

Brown, R. M. An examination of visual and verbal coding processes in preschool children. *Child Development,* 1977, *48,* 38–45.

Burmeister, L. E. Usefulness of phonic generalizations. *Reading Teacher,* 1968, *21,* 349–356.

Burmeister, L. E. Phonics in a reading program—Place and content. May 1970. (ERIC Document Ed 046–611) (a)

Burmeister, L. E. Selected word analysis generalizations for a group approach to correc-tive reading in the secondary school. *Reading Research Quarterly,* Fall 1970. (b)

Burmeister, L. E. Content of a phonics program based on particularly useful generalizations. In N. B. Smith (Ed.), *Reading Methods and Teacher Improvement.* Newark, Del.: International Reading Association, 1971, 27–39. (a)

Burmeister, L. E. Final vowel-consonant -e. *The Reading Teacher,* 1971, *24,* 439–442. (b)

Burmeister, L. E. Final vowel-consonant-e. *The ing.* Reading, Mass.: Addison-Wesley, 1975.

Calfee, R. C., Venezky, R. L., & Chapman, R. S. *Pronunciation of synthetic words with predictable and unpredictable letter-sound correspondences.* (Tech. Rep. No. 71). Madison, Wis.: University of Wisconsin, Wisconsin Research and Development Center for Cognitive Learning, February 1969.

Camp, B. W., & Dahlem, N. Paired-associate and serial learning in retarded readers. *Journal of Educational Psychology,* 1975, *67,* 385–390.

Canney, G. F. A study of the relationship between pupils' aural vocabulary and their ability to apply syllabication rules or to recognize phonogram patterns to decode multiple syllable words. *Journal of Reading Behavior,* 1976, *8,* (3), 273–288.

Carlson, J. G., & Minke, K. A. Fixed and ascending criteria for unit mastery learning. *Journal of Educational Psychology,* 1975, *67,* 96–101.

Carnine, D. W. *Conditions under which children learn the relevant attribute of negative instances rather than the essential characteristic of positive instances.* Unpublished manuscript, Follow Through Project, University of Oregon, 1976. (a)

Carnine, D. W. *Correction effects on academic performance during small group instruction.* In W. C. Becker & S. Engelmann (Eds.), *Technical Report 1976-1 Appendix B: Formative Research Studies.* Eugene, Oreg.: University of Oregon, Follow Through Project, April 1976. (b)

Carnine, D. W. Effects of two teacher presentation rates on off-task behavior, answering correctly, and participation. *Journal of Applied Behavioral Analysis,* 1976, *9,* 199–206. (c)

Carnine, D. W. Establishing a discriminative stimulus by distributing attributes of compound stimuli between instances and not-instances. In W. C. Becker & S. E. Engelmann, (Eds.) *Technical Report 1976-1 Appendix B.* Eugene, Oreg.: University of Oregon, Follow Through Project, 1976. (d)

Carnine, D. W. Similar sound separation and cumulative introduction in learning letter-sound correspondence. *Journal of Educational Research,* 1976, *69,* 368–372. (e)

Carnine, D. W. Phonics versus look-say: Transfer to new words. *Reading Teacher,* 1977, *30* (6), 636–640.

Carnine, D., & Fink, W. T. A comparative study of the effects of individual versus unison responding on the word reading performance of preschool children. In *Technical Report 1978-2, Formative Research on Direct Instruction,* Eugene, Oreg.: Follow Through Project, University of Oregon, 1978. (a)

Carnine, D. The effect of separating similar stimuli and similar responses from each other when integrating a new concept into a set of related concepts. In *Technical Report 1978-2: Formative Research on Direct Instruction.* Eugene, Oreg.: Follow Through Project, University of Oregon, 1978. (b)

Carnine, D. W. The effects of progressive increases in the number and/or magnitude of differences between positive and negative concept instances. In *Technical Report 1978-2, Formative Research on Direct Instruction.* Eugene, Oreg.: Follow Through Project, University of Oregon, 1978. (c)

Carnine, D. W. The effects of two correction procedures on word acquisition by preschool children. In *Technical Report 1978-2, Formative Research on Direct Instruction.* Eugene, Oreg.: Follow Through Project, University of Oregon, 1978. (d)

Carnine, D. W. Four procedures for introducing similar discriminations. In *Technical Report 1978-2, Formative Research on Direct Instruction.* Eugene, Oreg.: Follow Through Project, University of Oregon, 1978. (e)

Carnine, D. W. High and low implementation of direct instruction teaching techniques. In *Technical Report 1978-2, Formative Research on Direct Instruction.* Eugene, Oreg.:

Follow Through Project, University of Oregon, 1978. (f)

Carnine, D. W. The relative difficulty of selected vowel and consonant letter-sound correspondences. In *Technical Report 1978-2,* Formative Research on Direct Instruction. Eugene, Oreg.: Follow Through Project, University of Oregon, 1978. (g)

Carnine, D. W. Three procedures for presenting minimally different positive and negative instances. In *Technical Report 1978-2, Formative Research on Direct Instruction.* Eugene, Oreg.: Follow Through Project, University of Oregon, 1978. (h)

Carnine, D. W. Two letter discrimination sequences: High confusion alternatives first versus low confusion alternatives first. In *Technical Report 1978-2, Formative Research on Direct Instruction.* Eugene, Oreg.: Follow Through Project, University of Oregon, 1978. (i)

Carnine, D. W. Two procedures for sequencing instances in discrimination learning tasks: Simultaneously presenting minimally different instance pairs and changing a single stimulus to generate successive instance. In *Technical Report 1978-2, Formative Research on Direct Instruction,* Eugene, Oreg.: Follow Through Project, University of Oregon, 1978. (j)

Carnine, D. W. Undergeneralization as a function of examples used in training. In *Technical Report 1978-2, Formative Research on Direct Instruction.* Eugene, Oreg.: Follow Through Project, University of Oregon, 1978. (k)

Carnine, L., & Carnine, D. W. Determining the relative decoding difficulty of three types of simple regular words. *Journal of Reading Behavior,* in press.

Carnine, D. W., & Fink, W. T. *Effects of eye-contact on attending and correct responding during small group instruction.* Unpublished manuscript, University of Oregon, 1974.

Carnine, D. W., & Kameenui, E. *Teaching students to comprehend complex syntactic structure.* Unpublished manuscript, Eugene, Oreg.: University of Oregon, 1978.

Carnine, D. W., & Kameenui, E. *Use of discrimination word lists in teaching students* to decode VCe pattern words. Unpublished manuscript, Follow Through Project, University of Oregon, 1979.

Carnine, D. W., Kameenui, E. J., & Ludlow, R. Rule saying, concept application and rule application training in relation to rule application transfer performance. Unpublished manuscript, Eugene, Oreg.: Follow Through Project, University of Oregon, 1978.

Carnine, D., Prill, N., & Armstrong, J. Teaching slower performing students general case strategies for solving comprehensive items. In Technical Report 1978-2, Formative Research on Direct Instruction. Eugene, Oreg.: Follow Through Project, University of Oregon, 1978.

Carnine, D. W., & Stein, M. Two methods for teaching words with an unfamiliar letter combination. Unpublished manuscript, Follow Through Project, University of Oregon, 1979. (a)

Carnine, D. W., & Stein, M. Use of a deductive rule in teaching students to decode VCe pattern words. Unpublished manuscript, Follow Through Project, University of Oregon, 1979. (b)

Carroll, J. B. Learning from verbal discourse in educational media: A review of the literature. Princeton, N.J.: Educational Testing Service, 1971. (ETS RM 71-61)

Carroll, J. B. Developmental parameters of reading comprehension. In J. T. Guthrie (Ed.), Cognition, curriculum and comprehension. Newark, Del.: International Reading Association, 1977.

Carroll, J. B., Davies, P., & Richmond, B. The American Heritage Word Frequency Book. Boston: Houghton Mifflin, 1971.

Chall, J. Readability: An appraisal of research and application. Ohio State Bureau of Educational Research Monographs, 1958, 34.

Chall, J. Learning to read, the great debate. New York: McGraw-Hill, 1967.

Chall, J. Clues from research on programs for poor readers. In J. S. Samuels (Ed.), What research has to say about reading instruction. Newark, Del.: International Reading Association, 1978. (a)

Chall, J. The great debate: Ten years later, with a modest proposal for reading stages.

In L. B. Resnick & P. A. Weaver (Eds.), Theory and practice of early reading. Hillsdale, N.J.: Earlbaum, 1978. (b)

Chall, J. S., Roswell, F. G., & Blumenthal, S. H. Auditory blending ability: A factor in success in beginning reading. The Reading Teacher, 1963, 17, 113–118.

Chapman, C. A test of hierarchical theory of reading comprehension. Reading Research Quarterly, 1973, 9, 232–34. (Abstract)

Chapman, R. S., & Kamm, M. R. An evaluation of methods for teaching initial sound isolation, 1974. (ERIC Document ED 066-231)

Cheyne, W. M. Vanishing cues in paired-associate learning. British Journal of Psychology, 1966, 57, 351–359.

Chomsky, C. Reading, writing and phology. Harvard Educational Review, 1970, 40, 287–309.

Chomsky, C. After decoding: What? Language Arts, 1976, 53, 288–296.

Clay, M. M., & Imlach, R. H. Juncture, pitch, and stress as reading behavior variables. Journal of Verbal Learning and Verbal Behavior, 1971, 10, 133–139.

Clymer, T. The utility of phonic generalizations in the primary grades. Reading Teacher, 1963, 16, 252–258.

Coleman, E. B. Collecting a data base for a reading technology. Journal of Educational Psychology Monograph, 1970, 61 (4, Part 2).

Collins, R., Brown, A. L., Morgan, J. L., & Brewer, W. F. The analysis of reading tasks and texts, Technical report 43. Champaign, Ill.: Center for the Study of Reading, University of Illinois, 1977.

Cook, V. J., & White, M. A. Reinforcement potency of children's reading materials. Journal of Educational Psychology, 1977, 69, 231–236.

Corder, R. The information base for reading: A critical review of the information base for current assumptions regarding the status of instruction and achievement in reading in the United States. Washington, D.C.; USOE, Project No. 0-9031, 1971. (ERIC Document ED 054-922)

Cossairt, A., Hall, V., & Hopkins, B. L. The effects of experimenter's instructions, feedback, and praise on teacher praise and student attending behavior. *Journal of Applied Behavior Analysis,* 1973, *6,* 89–100.

Cowart, J., Carnine, D. W., & Becker, W. C. The effects of signals on attending, responding, and following in direct instruction. In W. C. Becker & S. E. Engelmann (Eds.), *Technical Report 1976-1 Appendix B.* Eugene, Oreg.: University of Oregon, 1976.

Cronbach, L. J., & Snow, R. E. *Aptitudes and instructional methods: A handbook for research on interactions.* New York: Irvington Publishers, 1977.

Cronnell, B. *Spelling-to-sound correspondences for reading vs. sound-to-spelling correspondences for writing.* Inglewood, Calif.: Southwest Regional Education Lab., U.S. Department of HEW, OEO, June 1971. (ERIC Document ED 057-024)

Cunningham, P. M. Investigating a synthesized theory of mediated word identification. *Reading Research Quarterly,* 1975–76, *11* (2), 128.

Dahl, P. An experimental program for teaching high speed word recognition and comprehension skills. In T. Lovitt (Ed.), *Communications research in learning disabilities and mental retardation.* Baltimore, Md.: University Park Press, 1979.

Dale, Edgar, & Chall, Jeanne S. A formula for predicting readability. *Education Research Bulletin,* January 21 and February 17, 1948, pp. 11–20; 37–54.

Davis, F. B. Research in comprehension in reading. *Reading Research Quarterly,* 1968, *3,* 499–545.

Davis, F. B. Psychometric research on comprehension in reading. *Reading Research Quarterly,* 1972, *7,* 628–678.

Denburg, S. D. The interaction of picture and print in reading instruction. *Reading Research Quarterly,* 1976, *12* (2), 176–189.

Diederich, P. B., II. *Research 1960–70 on methods and materials in reading.* Princeton, N.J.: Educational Testing Service, January 1973. (TM Report 22), ERIC Clearinghouse on Tests, Measurement and Evaluation.

*DISTAR Language I.* Chicago, Ill.: Science Research Associates, 1976.

Dooling, D. J., & Mullet, R. L. Locus of thematic effects in retention of prose. *Journal of Experimental Psychology,* 1973, *97,* 404–406.

Downing, J. *Learning to read with understanding.* Paper presented at the Annual Convention of the International Reading Association, Miami Beach, Florida, May 1977.

Duncan, C. P. Transfer after training with single versus multiple tasks. *Journal of Experimental Psychology,* 1959, *55,* 63–72.

Durling, R., & Schick, C. Concept attainment by pairs and individuals as a function of vocalization. *Journal of Educational Psychology,* 1976, *68,* 83–91.

Dykstra, R. Summary of the second-grade phase of the cooperative research program in primary reading instruction. *Reading Research Quarterly,* Fall 1968, *4,* 49–70.

Dykstra, R. Phonics and beginning reading instruction. In C. C. Walcutt, J. Lamport, & G. McCracken (Eds.), *Teaching reading: A phonic/linguistic approach to developmental reading.* New York: Macmillan, 1974.

Edelman, G. *The use of cues in word recognition in a basic research program on reading.* Ithaca, N.Y.: Final Report, Project No. 639, Cornell University and the U.S. Office of Education, 1963.

Egan, D. E., & Greeno, J. G. Acquiring cognitive structure by discovery and rule learning. *Journal of Educational Psychology,* 1973, *64,* 85–97.

Ehri, L. C. *Effects of word recognition training in a picture-word interference task: Automaticity vs. speed.* Paper presented at the annual meeting of the American Educational Research Association, Toronto, March 1978.

Eicholz, G., & Barbe, R. An experiment in vocabulary development. *Educational Research Bulletin,* 1961, *40,* 1–7.

Elkonin, D. B. In J. Downing (Ed.), *Comparative reading.* New York: Macmillan, 1973.

Ellis, N. R. The stimulus trace and behavioral inadequacy. In N. R. Ellis (Ed.), *Handbook on mental deficiency.* New York: McGraw-Hill, 1963.

Emans, R. The usefulness of phonic generalizations above the primary grades. *Reading Teacher,* 1967, *20,* 419–425.

Engelmann, S. *SRA Corrective Reading Program.* Chicago, Ill.: Science Research Associates, 1978.

Engelmann, S., & Bruner, E. *DISTAR reading level 1.* Chicago, Ill.: Science Research Associates, 1974.

Engelmann, S., & Bruner, E. *DISTAR reading level II.* Chicago, Ill.: Science Research Associates, 1975.

Engelmann, S., & Carnine, D. A structural program's effect on the attitudes and achievement of average and above-average second graders. In W. C. Becker, & S. Engelmann (Eds.), *Technical Report 76-1, Appendix B: Formative Research Studies.* Eugene, Ore.: University of Oregon, Follow Through Project, April 1976.

Engelmann, S., & Osborn, J. *DISTAR language level I.* Chicago, Ill.: Science Research Associates, 1976, 1977.

Engelmann, S., & Osborn, J. *DISTAR language level II.* Chicago, Ill.: Science Research Associates, 1977.

Engelmann, S., & Stearns, S. *DISTAR reading III.* Chicago, Ill.: Science Research Associates, 1973.

Fader, Daniel et al. The new hooked on books. New York: Berkeley Publishing Corp., 1976.

Farmer, A. R., Nixon, M., & White, R. T. Sound blending and learning to read: An experimental investigation. *British Journal of Educational Psychology,* 1976, *46,* 155–163.

Farr, R. *Reading: What can be measured?* Newark, Del.: International Reading Association, 1969.

Feldman, K. V., & Klausmeier, H. J. Effects of two kinds of definitions on the concept attainment of fourth and eighth graders. *Journal of Educational Research,* 1974, *67*(5), 219–223.

Feldman, S. M., & Underwood, B. J. Stimulus recall following paired-associate verbal learning. *Journal of Experimental Psychology,* 1957, *53,* 11–15.

Fink, W. T. *Effects of a pre-correction procedure on the decoding errors of two low-performing first-grade girls.* In W. C. Becker, & S. E. Engelmann (Eds.), *Technical Report 1976-1 Appendix B.* Eugene, Oreg.: University of Oregon, 1976.

Fink, W. T., & Carnine, D. W. Control of arithmetic errors using informational feedback and graphing. *Journal of Applied Behavioral Analysis,* 1975, *8,* 461.

Fink, W. T., & Sandall, S. R. *A comparison of one-to-one and small group instructional strategies on a word identification task by developmentally disabled preschoolers.* Unpublished manuscript, Center on Human Development, University of Oregon, 1977.

Flanders, D. *Teaching receptive and expressive usage of plurals to a language delayed mentally retarded child.* Unpublished Master's Thesis, University of Oregon, 1978.

Foss, D. J., & Swinney, D. A. On the psychological reality of the phoneme: Perception, identification and consciousness. *Journal of Verbal Learning and Verbal Behavior,* 1973, *12,* 246–257.

Fox, B., & Routh, D. K. Phonemic analysis and synthesis as work-attack skills. *Journal of Educational Psychology,* 1976, *68,* 70–74.

Francis, E. W. Grade level and task difficulty in learning by discovery and verbal reception methods. *Journal of Educational Psychology,* 1975, *67,* 146–150.

Frase, L. T. Learning from prose material: Length of passage, knowledge of results and position of question. *Journal of Educational Psychology,* 1967, *58,* 266–272.

Frase, L. T. Questions as aids to reading: Some research and theory. *American Educational Research Journal,* 1968, *5,* 319–332.

Frase, L. T. Maintenance and control in the acquisition of knowledge from written materials. In J. B. Carroll and R. O. Freedle (Eds.) *Language Comprehension and the Acquisition of Knowledge.* Washington, D.C.: V. H. Winston, 1972.

Frase, L. T. Comments on an applied behavior analysis approach to reading comprehension. In J. T. Guthrie (Ed.), *Cognition, curriculum, and comprehension.* Newark, Del.: International Reading Association, 1977.

Frase, L. T., Patrick, E., & Schumer, H. Effect of question position and frequency upon learning from text under different levels of incentive. *Journal of Educational Psychology,* 1970, *71,* 52–56.

Frase, L. T., & Schwartz, B. J. Effect of question production and answering on prose recall. *Journal of Educational Psychology,* 1975, *67,* 628–635.

Frederick, W. C., & Klausmeier, H. J. Instructions and labels in a concept attainment task. *Psychological Reports,* 1968, *23,* 1339, 1342.

Fries, C. C. *Linguistics and Reading.* New York: Holt, Rinehart and Winston, 1962.

Fry, Edward. *Elementary reading instruction.* New York: McGraw-Hill, 1977.

Fry, Edward. *Fry's readability scale.* Providence, R.I.: Jamestown Publishers, 1977.

Gagné, R., & Brown, T. Some factors in the programming of conceptual learning. *Journal of Experimental Psychology,* 1961, *62,* 55–63.

Gagné, R. M., & Wiegand, V. Effects of a superordinate context on learning and retention of facts. *Journal of Educational Psychology,* 1970, *61,* 406–409.

Gagné, R., Mayor, J. R., Garstens, H. L., & Paradise, N. E. Factors in acquiring knowledge of a mathematical task. *Psychological Monographs: General and Applied,* 1962, *76,* (7).

Gengler, C. R. A study of selected problem solving skills comparing teacher instructed students with librarian-teacher instructed students. Unpublished doctoral dissertation, University of Oregon, 1965, 310 pp.

Gibson, E. J. Learning to read. *Science,* 1965, *148,* 1066–1072.

Gibson, E. J. Trends in perceptual development: Implications for the reading process. In H. Singer & R. B. Ruddell (Eds.), *Theoretical models and processes of reading.* Newark, Del.: International Reading Association, 1976.

Gibson, E. D., & Levin, H. *The psychology of reading.* Cambridge: MIT Press, 1975.

*Ginn 720.* Lexington, Mass.: Ginn and Company, 1976.

Gipe, J. P. *Investigating techniques for teaching word meanings.* Paper presented at the annual meeting of the American Educational Research Association, Toronto, 1978.

Glaser, R. Foreword. In J. T. Guthrie (Ed.), *Cognition, curriculum, and comprehension.* Newark, Del.: International Reading Association, 1977.

Glass, G. G., & Burton, E. H. How do they decode? Verbalizations and observed behavior of successful decoders. *Education,* 1973, *94*(1), 58–64.

Golinkoff, R. A. Comparison of reading comprehension processes in good and poor comprehenders. *Reading Research Quarterly,* 1975–76, *4,* 623–659.

Gollin, E., Moody, M., & Schadler, M. Relational learning of a size concept. *Developmental Psychology,* 1974, *10,* 101–107.

Goodman, K. S. A linguistic study of cues and miscues in reading. *Elementary English,* 1965, *42,* 639–643.

Goodman, K. S. Behind the eye: What happens in reading. In H. Singer & R. B. Ruddell (Eds.), *Theoretical models and processes of reading.* Newark, Del.: International Reading Association, 1976.

Gordon, C., Hansen, J., & Pearson, P. D. *Effect of background knowledge on silent reading comprehension.* Paper presented at AERA, Toronto, 1978.

Gough, P. B. One second of reading. In H. Singer & R. B. Ruddell (Eds.), *Theoretical models and processes of reading.* Newark, Del.: International Reading Association, 1976.

Granzin, A. C., & Carnine, D. W. Child performance on discrimination tasks: Effects of amount of stimulus variation. *Journal of Experimental Child Psychology,* 1977, *24,* 332–342.

Grimes, L. *Effects of two error correction procedures on type of oral reading error.* Unpublished manuscript, Department of Special Education, University of Illinois, 1977.

Groff, P. Sequences for teaching consonant clusters. *Journal of Reading Behavior,* 1971–72, *4,* 59–65.

Groff, P. Limitations of context cues for beginning readers. *Reading World,* 1976, *16*(2), 97–103.

Gruenenfelder, T. M., & Borkowski, J. G. Transfer of cumulative-rehearsal strategies in children's short-term memory. *Child Development,* 1975, *46,* 1019–1024.

Gurren, L., & Hughes, A. Intensive phonics vs. gradual phonics in beginning reading: A review. *Journal of Educational Research,* 1965, *58,* 339–346.

Guthrie, J. T. Follow Through: A compensatory education experiment. *The Reading Teacher,* November 1977, 240–244.

Guthrie, J. T., & Seifert, M. Education for children with reading disabilities. In H. R. Myklebust (Ed.), *Progress in learning disabilities* (Vol. IV), in press.

Guthrie, J., & Tyler, S. Psycholinguistic processing in reading and listening among good and poor readers. *Journal of Reading Behavior,* 1976, *8,* 415–426.

Haddock, M. Effects of an auditory and an auditory-visual method of blending instruction on the ability of prereaders to decode synthetic words. *Journal of Educational Psychology,* 1976, *68,* 825–831.

Haddock, M. Teaching blending in beginning reading instruction *is* important. *The Reading Teacher,* 1978, *31,* 654–658.

Hall, V., Lund, D., & Jackson, D. Effects of teacher attention on study behavior. *Journal of Applied Behavior Analysis,* 1968, *1,* 1–12.

Hammill, D. D., & Larsen, S. C. The effectiveness of psycholinguistic training. *Exceptional children,* 1974, *41,* 5–14.

Hanna, G. S. Effects of total and partial feedback in multiple-choice testing upon learning. *The Journal of Educational Research,* 1976, *69,* 202–205.

Hanna, P. R., Hanna, J. S., Hodges, R. E., & Rudolf, E. H., Jr. *Phoneme-grapheme correspondences as cues to spelling improvement.* Washington, D.C.: U.S. Government Printing Office, 1966.

Hansen, C. *The generalization of skills and drills versus corrective feedback instruction to the independent reading performance of intermediate aged learning disabled boys.* Unpublished doctoral dissertation, University of Washington, 1976.

Haring, N. G., & Bateman, B. *Teaching the learning disabled chi'd.* Englewood Cliffs, N.J.: Prentice-Hall, 1977.

Harris, A. J., & Clark, M. K. *The Macmillan reading program,* teacher's annotated edition and guide to accompany *Opening books, A magic box, Things to see.* New York: Macmillan, 1965.

Harris, A. J., & Jacobson, M. *Basic Elementary Reading Vocabularies.* New York: Macmillan, 1972.

Harris, A. J., & Sipay, E. R. *How to increase reading ability* (6th ed.). New York: David McKay, 1975.

Hartley, R. M. A method of increasing the ability of first grade pupils to use phonetic generalizations. *California Journal of Educational Research,* 1971, *22,* 9–16.

Harzem, P., Lee, I., & Miles, T. R. The effect of pictures on learning to read. *The British Journal of Educational Psychology,* 1976, *46,* 318–322.

Helfgott, J. A. Phonemic segmentation and blending skills of kindergarten children: Implications for beginning reading acquisition. *Contemporary Educational Psychology,* 1976, *1,* 157–169.

Hershberger, W. A., & Terry, D. F. Typographical cuing in conventional and programmed texts. *Journal of Applied Psychology,* 1965, *49,* 55–60.

Higa, M. Interference effects of intralist word relatedness in verbal learning. *Journal of Verbal Learning and Verbal Behavior,* 1963, *2,* 170–175.

Hochberg, J. Components of literacy: Speculations and exploratory research. In H. Levin & J. P. Williams (Eds.), *Basic studies on reading.* New York: Basic Books, 1970.

*Houghton Mifflin Reading Series.* Boston, Mass.: Houghton Mifflin, 1976.

Houser, L. L., & Trublood, C. R. Transfer of learning on similar metric conversion tasks. *Journal of Educational Research,* 1975, *68,* 235–237.

Howard, D. P. The needs and problems of socially disadvantaged children as perceived by students and teachers. *Exceptional Children,* 1968, *34,* 327–335.

Huey, E. B. *The psychology and pedagogy of reading.* Cambridge: M.I.T. Press, 1908.

Humes, A. *A design for a vocabulary development program.* Southwest Regional Laboratory, Technical Note 3-76-09, December 1976.

Isakson, R. L., & Miller, J. W. Sensitivity to syntactic and semantic cues in good and poor comprehenders. *Journal of Educational Psychology,* 1976, *68,* 787–792.

Jarvella, R. J. Syntactic processing of connected speech. *Journal of Verbal Learning and Verbal Behavior,* 1971, *10,* 409–416.

Jeffrey, W. E., & Samuels, S. J. Effect of method of reading training on initial learning and transfer. *Journal of Verbal Learning and Verbal Behavior,* 1976, *6,* 354–358.

Jenkins, J. R. Oral Reading: Instructor and Measurement. In T. Lovitt (Ed.), *Communication Research in Learning Disabilities and Mental Retardation.* Baltimore, Md.: University Park Press, 1979.

Jenkins, J., Bausell, R. B., & Jenkins, L. M. Comparisons of letter name and letter sound training as transfer variables. *American Educational Research Journal,* 1972, *9,* 75–86.

Jenkins, J. R., & Fleisher, L. *The validity of multiple vs. single measure informal reading inventories.* Unpublished manuscript. Department of Special Education, University of Illinois, 1977.

Jenkins, J. R., & Larson, K. *Differential effects of error correction procedures for oral reading* (Technical Report No. 55). Champaign, Ill.: Center for the Study of Reading, University of Illinois at Urbana-Champaign, 1977.

Jenkins, J. R., & Larson, K. *Evaluating error correction procedures for oral reading* (Technical Report No. 55). Champaign, Ill.: Center for the Study of Reading, University of Illinois at Urbana-Champaign, July 1978.

Jenkins, J. R., Mayhall, W. F., Peschka, C. M., & Jenkins, L. M. Comparing small group and tutorial instruction in resource rooms. *Exceptional Children,* January 1974, 245–250.

Jenkins, J. R., Mayhall, W. F., Peschka, C. M., & Townsend, V. Using direct and daily measures to influence learning. *Journal of Learning Disabilities,* 1974, *7,* 14–17.

Jenkins, J. R., & Pany, D. *Curriculum biases in reading achievement tests* (Technical Report No. 16). Champaign, Ill.: Center for the

Study of Reading, University of Illinois at Urbana-Champaign, 1976.

Jenkins, J. R., & Pany, D. *Reading comprehension in the middle grades: Instruction and research.* NIE Deliverable. Champaign, Ill.: Center for the Study of Reading, University of Illinois at Urbana-Champaign, January 1977.

Johnson, D. D. *Suggested sequences for presenting four categories of letter-sound correspondences. Elementary English,* 1973, *50*(6), 888–896.

Johnson, D. D., & Pearson, P. D. *Teaching Reading Vocabulary.* New York: Holt, Rinehart and Winston, 1978.

Johnson, R. E. Recall of prose as a function of the structural importance of the linguistic units. *Journal of Verbal Learning and Verbal Behavior,* 1970, *9,* 12–20.

Johnson, R. J. *The effect of training in letter names on success in beginning reading for children of different abilities.* Paper presented at American Educational Research Association, Minneapolis, Minnesota, 1970.

Jorm, A. F. Children's reading processes revealed by pronunciation latencies and errors. *Journal of Educational Psychology,* 1977, *69,* 166–171.

Kameenui, E. & Carnine, D. W. Methods for teaching vocabulary and their effects on inference items. Unpublished manuscript, Follow Through Project, University of Oregon, 1979. (a)

Kameenui, E., & Carnine, D. W. Types of contextual meaning cues and their effects on vocabulary acquisition. Unpublished manuscript, Follow Through Project, University of Oregon, 1979. (b)

Keeney, T. J., Canizzo, S. R., & Flavell, J. H. Spontaneous and induced verbal rehearsal in a recall task. *Child Development,* 1967, *38,* 953–966.

Keisler, E. R., & McNeil, J. D. Oral and non-oral methods of teaching reading. *Educational Leadership,* 1968, *25,* 761–764.

Keith, C., & Carnine, D. W. *Recognition of syntax violation in oral and written sentences by good and poor readers.* Unpublished manuscript, Follow Through Project, University of Oregon, 1978.

King, E. M. Prereading programs: Direct versus incidental teaching. *The Reading Teacher,* 1978, *31,* 504–510.

Klausmeier, H. J., & Feldman, K. J. Effects of a definition and varying numbers of examples and non-examples on concept attainment. *Journal of Educational Psychology,* 1975, *67,* 174–178.

Klausmeier, H. J., Ghatala, E. S., & Frayer, D. A. *Conceptual Learning and Development.* New York: Academic Press, 1974.

Klausmeier, H. J., & Meinke, D. L. Concept attainment as a function of instruction concerning stimulus material, a strategy, and a principle for securing information. *Journal of Educational Psychology,* 1968, *59,* 215–222.

Kleinfeld, J. Effective teachers of Eskimo and Indian students. *School Review,* 1975, 301–344.

Kodroff, J. K., & Roberge, J. J. Developmental analysis of the conditional reasoning abilities of primary-grade children. *Developmental Psychology,* 1975, *11,* 21–28.

Koehler, John. *Interdependencies between words, context and comprehension.* Paper presented at the AERA, Toronto, 1978.

Krumboltz, John D., & Krumboltz, Helen Brandhorst. *Changing children's behavior.* Englewood Cliffs, N.J.: Prentice-Hall, 1972.

Kryzanowski, J. A. Praise effects on on-task behavior during small group instruction. In W. C. Becker & S. Engelmann (Eds.), *Technical Report 76-1, Appendix B: Formative Research Studies.* Eugene, Oreg.: Follow Through Project, University of Oregon, April 1976.

Kryzanowski, J. A., & Carnine, D. W. The effects of massed versus distributed practice schedules in teaching sound-symbol correspondences to young children. In *Technical Report 1978-2, Formative Research on Direct Instruction.* Eugene, Oreg.: University of Oregon, 1978.

Kucera, H., & Francis, W. N. *Computational analysis of present-day American English.* Providence, R.I.: Brown University Press, 1967.

Kurth, R. J., & Moseley, P. A. *The effect of copying or paraphrasing structurally-cued topic sentences on passage comprehension.* Paper presented at the annual meeting of The American Educational Research Association, Toronto, March 1978.

LaBerge, D., & Samuels, S. J. Toward a theory of automatic information processing in reading. *Cognitive Psychology,* 1974, *6,* 293–323.

Larson, K. L., & Jenkins, J. R. *Effects of word recognition corrections on reading comprehension.* Paper given at Council for Exceptional Children Annual Convention, Kansas City, May 1978.

Laumbach, J. D. Rank ordering two-sound words as to phonic blendability. In E. B. Coleman, Collecting a data base for a reading technology, *Journal of Educational Psychology Monograph,* 1970, *61*(4, Part 2).

Lerner, J. W. *Children with learning disabilities.* Boston: Houghton Mifflin, 1976.

Levin, J. R. Comprehending what we read: An outsider looks in. *Journal of Reading Behavior,* 1971–72, *4,* 18–29.

Liberman, I. Y. Segmentation of the spoken word and reading acquisition. *Bulletin of the Onton Society,* 1973, *23,* 65–77.

Lieberman, J. *The effect of direct instruction in vocabulary concepts on reading achievement.* Bloomington, Ind.: ERIC Clearinghouse on Reading, 1967. ERIC Document ED 010985.

*Lion's,* level 3B (teacher's edition). Boston: Houghton Mifflin, 1971.

Lovitt, T. C., & Hansen, C. The use of contingent skipping and drilling to improve oral reading and comprehension. *Journal of Learning Disabilities,* 1976, *9,* 481–487.

Madsen, C., Becker, W. C., & Thomas, D. R. Rules, praise and ignoring: Elements of elementary classroom control. *Journal of Applied Behavior Analysis,* 1968, *1,* 139–150.

*Manual level 1.* Glenview, Ill.: Scott, Foresman, 1971.

March, G., & Desberg, P. Stimulus and response variables in children's learning of grapheme-phoneme correspondences. *Journal of Educational Psychology,* 1974, *66,* 112–116.

Marchbanks, G., & Levin, H. Cues by which children recognize words. *Journal of Educational Psychology,* 1965, *56,* 57–61.

Martin, C. J. Mediational processes in the retarded: Implications for teaching reading. In N. Ellis (Ed.), *International Review of Research in Mental Retardation* (Vol. 9). New York: Academic Press, 1978.

Mason, J. M. Questioning the notion of independent processing stages in reading. *Journal of Educational Psychology,* 1977, *69,* 288–297. (a)

Mason, J. M. Refining phonics for teaching beginning reading. *The Reading Teacher,* November 1977, 179–184. (b)

Mason, J. M., & Kendall, J. R. *Facilitating reading comprehension through text structure manipulation.* Paper presented at the meeting of the American Educational Research Association, Toronto, March 1978.

Mason, J., Osborn, J., & Rosenshine, B. *A consideration of skill hierarchy approaches to the teaching of reading,* Champaign, Ill.: Center for Study of Reading, University of Illinois at Urbana-Champaign, April 1977.

Massad, V. I., & Etzel, B. C. Acquisition of phonetic sounds by preschool children. In G. Semb (Ed.), *Behavior analysis and education.* Lawrence, Kans.: University of Kansas, 1972.

Mathews, J. Skills *Education Digest,* 1975, *41,* 65.

May, Frank, *To help children read.* Columbus, Ohio: Charles E. Merrill Publishing Co., 1973.

Mayer, R. E., Stiehl, C. C., & Greeno, J. G. Acquisition of understanding and skill in relation to subjects' preparation and meaningfulness of instruction. *Journal of Educational Psychology,* 1975, *67,* 331–350.

Mazurkiewicz, A. J. Didactic vs. discovery phonics instruction effects on speech articulation. *Reading World,* 1977, *16,* 196–205.

McClelland, J. Letter configuration information in word identification. *Journal of Verbal Learning and Verbal Behavior,* 1977, *16,* 137–150.

McCullough, C. What does research in reading reveal about practices in teaching reading? *English Journal,* 1969, *58,* 688–706.

McCutcheon, B. A., & McDowell, E. E. Intralist similarity and acquisition and generalization

of word recognition. *The Reading Teacher,* 1969, *23,* 103–107.

McDermott, R. P. Achieving school failure: An anthropological approach to illiteracy and social stratification. In H. Singer & R. B. Ruddell (Eds.), *Theoretical models and processes of reading.* Newark, Del.: International Reading Association, 1976.

McDonald, F. J. *Beginning teacher evaluation study, phase II: Executive summary.* Princeton, N.J.: Educational Testing Service, 1976.

McFeely, D. C. Syllabication usefulness in a basal and social studies vocabulary. *The Reading Teacher,* 1974, *27,* 809–814.

Mead, M. Adolescence in primitive and modern society. In E. E. Maccoby, T. M. Newcomb, & E. D. Hartley (Eds.), *Readings in social psychology* (3rd ed.). New York: Holt, 1958.

Michalos, Alex C. *Improving your reasoning.* Englewood Cliffs, N.J.: Prentice-Hall, 1970.

Millman, J. Instructional planning and management. In J. Blaney (Ed.), *Program development in education.* Vancouver, B.C.: Education-Extension, University of British Columbia, 1974.

Milner, E. A study of the relationship between reading readiness in grade one school children and patterns of parent-child interaction. *The 62nd Yearbook of the National Society for Study of Education.* Chicago: University of Chicago Press, 1963.

Montgomery, J., & Bruning, R. *A field test of a rereading method of reading instruction.* Paper presented at the Annual Meeting of the American Educational Research Association, Toronto, March 1978.

Morrisett, L., & Hovland, C. I. A comparison of three varieties of training in human problem solving. *Journal of Experimental Psychology,* 1959, *58,* 52–55.

Muller, D. Phonic blending and transfer of letter training to word reading in children. *Journal of Reading Behavior,* 1973, *5* (3), 13–15.

Neef, N. A., Iwata, B. A., & Page, T. J. The effects of known-item interspersal on acquisition and retention of spelling and sight reading words. *Journal of Applied Behavior Analysis,* 1977, *10,* 738.

Neimark, E. D., & Slotnick, M. S. Development of the understanding of logical connectives. *Journal of Educational Psychology,* 1970, *61,* 451–460.

Neville, M. Effects of oral and echoic responses in beginning reading programs. *Journal of Educational Psychology,* 1968, *59,* 362–369.

Neville, D., Pfost, P., & Dobbs, V. The relationship between test anxiety and silent reading gain. *American Educational Research Journal,* 1967, *4,* 45–50.

*The New Open Highways.* Glenview, Ill.: Scott, Foresman, 1974.

New starts for America's third century. *Time,* April 12, 1976, p. 29.

Newman, A. P. Later achievement study of pupils underachieving in reading in first grade. *Reading Research Quarterly,* 1972, *7,* 477–508.

Oaken, R., Weiner, M., & Cromer, W. Identification, organization and reading comprehension for good and poor readers. *Journal of Educational Psychology,* 1971, *62,* 71–78.

Ohnmacht, D. D. *The effects of letter-knowledge on achievement in reading in the first grade.* Paper presented at the American Educational Research Association meeting, Los Angeles, 1969.

Olson, L. A. Concept attainment of high school sophomores. *Journal of Educational Psychology,* 1963, *54,* 213–216.

O'Malley, J. M. Stimulus dimension pretraining and set size in learning multiple discrimination with letters of the alphabet. *Journal of Educational Psychology,* 1973, *67,* 41–45.

Otterman, L. M. The value of teaching prefixes and word-roots. *Journal of Educational Research,* 1955, *48,* 611–616.

Otto, W. Design for developing comprehension skills. In J. T. Guthrie (Ed.), *Cognition, curriculum, and comprehension.* Newark, Del.: International Reading Association, 1977.

Otto, W., & Pizillo, C. Effect of intralist similarity on kindergarten pupils' rate of word acquisition and transfer. *Journal of Reading Behavior,* 1970–1971, *3,* 14–19.

Pace, A. J. *The influence of world knowledge on children's comprehension of short narrative passages.* Paper presented at the annual meeting of the American Educational Research Association, Toronto, March 1978.

Pace, A. J., & Golinkoff, R. M. Relationship between word difficulty and access of single word meaning by skilled and less skilled readers. *Journal of Educational Psychology,* 1976, *68,* 760–767.

Pal Paperback Kits. Middleton, Conn.: Xerox, 1974, 1975, 1976.

*The Palo Alto reading program: Sequential steps in reading.* New York: Harcourt Brace Jovanovich, 1973.

Pany, D., & Jenkins, J. R. *Learning word meanings: A comparison of instructional procedures and effects on measures of reading comprehension with learning disabled students.* March 1977. (ERIC No. ED 136237)

Pearson, P. D. The effects of grammatical complexity on children's comprehension, recall, and conception of certain semantic relations. In H. Singer & R. B. Ruddell (Eds.), *Theoretical models and processes of reading.* Newark, Del.: International Reading Association, 1976.

Pearson, P. D., & Studt, A. Effects of word frequency and contextual richness of children's word identification abilities. *Journal of Educational Psychology,* 1975, *67,* 89–95.

Pehrsson, R. S. V. The effects of teacher interference during the process of reading or how much of a helper is Mr. Gelper? *Journal of Reading,* 1974, *17,* 617–621.

Perfetti, C. A. Language comprehension and fast decoding: Some psycholinguistic prerequisites for skilled reading comprehension. In J. T. Guthrie (Ed.), *Cognition, curriculum, and comprehension.* Newark, Del.: International Reading Association, 1977.

Perfetti, C., & Hogalboom, T. Relationship between single word decoding and reading comprehension skill. *Journal of Educational Psychology,* 1975, 67, 641–649.

Petty, W., Herold, C., & Stoll, E. *The state of knowledge about the teaching of vocabulary.* Champaign, Ill.: National Council of Teachers of English, 1968.

Ramsey, W. Z. *Evaluation of assumptions related to the testing of phonics skills* (Final Report). St. Louis: National Center for Educational Research and Development, 1972. (ERIC Document ED 068-893)

Rayner, K., & Posnansky, C. Learning to read: Visual cues to word recognition. In A. M. Lesgold, J. W. Pellegrino, S. D. Fokkena, & R. Glaser (Eds.), *Cognitive psychology and instruction.* New York: Plenum Publishing, 1978.

Reynolds, G. S. Attention in the pigeon. *Journal of Experimental Analysis of Behavior,* 1961, *4,* 203–208.

Rhine, R. (Ed.). *Encouraging change in America's schools: A decade of experimentation.* New York: Academic Press, in press.

Richards, J. P. Processing effects of advance organizers interspersed in text. *Reading Research Quarterly,* 1975–76, *11,* 599–622.

Richardson, Ellis, & Collier, Lucy. Programmed tutoring of decoding skills with third and fifth grade non-readers. *Journal of Experimental Education,* 1971, *39* (3), 57–64.

Risley, T., & Reynolds, N. J. Emphasis as a prompt for verbal imitation. *Journal of Applied Behavior Analysis,* 1970, *3,* 185–190.

Rist, R. Student social class and teacher expectations: The self-fulfilling prophecy in ghetto education. *Harvard Educational Review,* 1970, *40,* 411–451.

Roberge, J. J. Recent research on the development of children's comprehension of deductive reasoning schemes. *School Science and Mathematics,* 1972, *72,* 197–200.

Roberts, T. Skills of analysis and synthesis in the early stages of reading. *British Journal of Educational Psychology,* 1975, *45,* (11), 3–9.

Rosenfield, S. *Cognitive style and the reading process.* Paper presented at the International Reading Association conference, New York City, 1975.

Rosenshine, B. The third cycle of research on teacher effects: Content covered, academic engaged time, and quality of instruction. In *Seventy-eighth Yearbook of the National Society for the Study of Education.* Chicago: University of Chicago Press, in press.

Rosenshine, B. V., & Berliner, D. C. Academic engaged time. *British Journal of Teacher Education,* 1978, *4,* 3–16.

Rosenthal, T. L., & Carroll, W. R. Factors in vicarious modifications of complex grammatical parameters. *Journal of Educational Psychology,* 1972, *63,* 174–178.

Rothkopf, E. Z. Two scientific approaches to the management of instruction. In R. M. Gagné & W. J. Gephart (Eds.), *Learning research and school subjects.* Itasco, Ill.: Peacock, 1968.

Royer, J. M., & Cabel, G. W. Facilitated learning in connected discourse. *Journal of Educational Psychology,* 1975, *67,* 116–123.

Rozin, P., & Gleitman, L. The reading process and the acquisition of the alphabetic principle. In A. S. Reber & D. Scarborough (Eds.), *Reading: The CUNY Conference.* New York: Laurence Earlbaum, in press.

Ruddell, R. B. Language acquisition and the reading process. In H. Singer & R. B. Ruddell (Eds.), *Theoretical models and processes of reading.* Newark, Del.: International Reading Association, 1976. (a)

Ruddell, R. B. Psycholinguistic implications for a systems of communication model. In H. Singer & R. B. Ruddell (Eds.), *Theoretical models and processes of reading.* Newark, Del.: International Reading Association, 1976. (b)

Ryan, W. *Blaming the victim.* New York: Vintage, 1971.

Rystrom, R. Linguistics and the teaching of reading. *Journal of Reading Behavior,* 1971–72, *4,* 34–39.

Samuels, S. J. Effects of pictures on learning to read, comprehension, and attitudes. *Review of Educational Research,* 1970, *40,* 397–408.

Samuels, S. J. Letter-name versus letter-sound knowledge in learning to read. *Reading Teacher,* 1971, *24,* 604–608.

Samuels, S. J. The effect of letter-name knowledge on learning to read. *American Educational Research Journal,* 1972, (1), 65–74.

Samuels, S. J. Effect of distinctive feature training on paired-associate learning. *Journal of Educational Psychology,* 1973, *64,* 164–170.

Samuels, S. J. Automatic decoding and reading comprehension. *Language Arts,* 1976, *53,* 323–325. (a)

Samuels, S. J. Modes of word recognition. In H. Singer & R. B. Ruddell (Eds.), *Theoretical models and processes of reading.* Newark, Del.: International Reading Association, 1976. (b)

Samuels, S. J., Biesbock, E., & Terry, P. R. The effect of pictures on children's attitudes toward presented stories. *The Journal of Educational Research,* 1974, *67,* 243–246.

Samuels, S. J., Dahl, P., & Archwamety, T. Effect of hypothesis/test training on reading skill. *Journal of Educational Psychology,* 1974, *66,* 835–844.

Samuels, S. J., & Jeffrey, W. E. Discriminability of words and letter cues in learning to read. *Journal of Educational Psychology,* 1966, *57,* 337–340.

Santa, C. M. Spelling patterns and the development of flexible word recognition strategies. *Reading Research Quarterly,* 1976–77, *12* (2), 125–144.

Savin, H. B. What the child knows about speech when he starts to learn to read. In J. F. Kavanagh & I. G. Mattingly (Eds.), *Language by ear and by eye.* Cambridge, Mass.: MIT Press, 1972.

Savin, H. B., & Bever, T. G. The nonperceptual reality of the phoneme. *Journal of Verbal Learning and Verbal Behavior,* 1970, *9,* 295–302.

Scribner, S., & Cole, M. Effects of constrained recall training on children's performance in a verbal memory task. *Child Development,* 1972, *43,* 845–857.

Shankweiler, D., & Liberman, I. Y. Misreading: A search for causes. In J. F. Kavanagh & I. G. Mattingly (Eds.), *Language by ear and by eye. The relationships between speech and reading.* Cambridge, Mass.: MIT Press, 1972.

Siegel, M. A. *An experimental investigation of teacher behavior and student achievement in the DISTAR instructional system.* Unpublished doctoral dissertation, University of Illinois, 1973.

Siegel, M. A. Teacher behavior and curriculum packages: Implications for research and teacher education. In L. J. Rubin (Ed.), *Handbook of Curriculum.* New York: Allyn & Bacon, 1977.

Siegel, M. A., & Rosenshine, B. *Teacher behavior and achievement in the Engelmann-Becker Follow Through Program.* Paper presented at the meeting of the American Educational Research Association, New Orleans, February 1973. (ERIC Document Reproduction Service No. ED 076-564).

Siegler, R. S., & Liebert, R. M. Effects of presenting relevant rules and complete feedback on the conservation of liquid quantity task. *Developmental Psychology,* 1973, *7,* 133–138.

Silberman, H. F. *Exploratory research on a beginning reading program.* Santa Monica, Calif.: System Development Corporation, 1964.

Siler, E. R. The effects of syntactic and semantic constraints on the oral reading performance of second and fourth graders. *Reading Research Quarterly,* 1973–74, *9*(4), 583–602.

Simons, H. D. Reading comprehension: The need for a new perspective. *Reading Research Quarterly,* 1971, *6*(3), 338–355.

Singer, Samuels, & Spiroff. The effect of pictures and contextual conditions on learning responses to printed words. *Reading Research Quarterly,* 1973, *9*(4), 555–567.

Skailand, D. B. *A comparison of four language units in teaching beginning reading.* Paper presented to the American Educational Rereach Association, New York 1971.

Smith, F. Familiarity of configuration vs. discriminability of features in the visual identification of words. *Psychonomic Science,* 1969, *14,* 261–262.

Smith, F. *Understanding reading.* New York: Holt, Rinehart and Winston, 1971.

Smith, H. D. The responses of good and poor readers when asked to read for different purposes. *Reading Research Quarterly,* 1967, *3,* 53–83.

Smith, Robert W. L. *Dictionary of English word-roots.* Totowa, N.J.: Littlefield, Adams & Co., 1966.

Smith-Burke, M., Reid, D. K., & Nicholich, M. J. *The relationship between class-inclusion and reading comprehension of the main idea.* Paper presented at the annual meeting of the American Educational Research Association, Toronto, March 1978.

Spache, G. D. A phonics manual for primary and remedial teachers. *Elementary English Review,* 1939, *16,* 147–150 and 191–198.

Spache, G .D. *Good reading for poor readers* (9th ed.). Champaign, Ill.: Garrad, 1974.

Spache, G. D., & Baggett. What do teachers know about phonics and syllabication? *The Reading Teacher,* 1965, *19,* 96–99.

Spache, G. D., & Spache, E. B. *Reading in the elementary school* (3rd ed.). Boston: Allyn & Bacon, 1973.

Spache, G. D., & Spache, E. B. *Reading in the elementary school* (4th ed.). Boston: Allyn & Bacon, 1977.

Speer, O. B., & Lamb, G. S. First grade reading ability and fluency in naming verbal symbols. *Reading Teacher,* 1976, *29,* 572–576.

Spoeky, K. T., & Smith, E. E. The role of syllables in perceptual processing. *Cognitive Psychology,* 1973, *5,* 71–89.

Stallings, J. A. Implementation and child effects of teaching practices in Follow Through classrooms. *Monographs of the Society for Research in Child Development,* 1975, *40* (7-8, Serial No. 163).

Stanford Program on Teaching Effectiveness. *A factorially designed experiment on teacher structuring, soliciting, and reacting.* Stanford, Calif.: Stanford Center for Research and Development in Teaching, 1975.

Starch, D. *Advertising.* Glenview, Ill.: Scott, Foresman, 1914.

Stein, M., & Carnine, D. W. Constant and variable introduction of letter-sound correspondences. In *Technical Report 1978-2, Formative Research on Direct Instruction.* Eugene, Oreg.: Follow Through Project, University of Oregon, 1978.

Steiner, R., Wiener, M., & Cromer, W. Comprehension training and identification for poor and good readers. *Journal of Educational Psychology,* 1975, *67,* 641–649.

Stolurow, K. A. C. Objective rules of sequencing applied to instructional material. *Journal of Educational Psychology,* 1975, *67,* 909–912.

Stoodt, B. D. The relationship between understanding grammatical conjunctions and reading comprehension. *Elementary English,* 1972, *49*(4), 502–504.

Stott, D. *Behavioral aspects of learning disorders: Assessment and remediation,* 1971. (ERIC Document ED 049-582)

Stromer, R. Modifying letter and number reversals in elementary school children. *Journal of Applied Behavioral Analysis,* 1975, *8,* 211.

Suchman, R., & Trabasso, T. Stimulus preference and cue function in young children's concept attainment. *Journal of Experimental Child Psychology,* 1966, *3,* 188–198.

Suppes, P., & Ginsberg, R. Application of a stimulus sampling model to children's concept formation with and without an overt correction response. *Journal of Experimental Psychology,* 1962, *63,* 330–336.

Taylor, A. M., & Whitely, S. E. *Overt verbalization and the continued production of effective elaborations by EMR children.* Research Report No. 38, Project No. 332189, Grant No. OE-09-332189-4533(032), University of Minnesota, Minneapolis, 1972.

Taylor, S. E., Frackenpohl, H., & Pattee, J. L. *Grade level norms for the components of the fundamental reading skill.* Bulletin #3, New York: Huntington Educational Development Laboratories, 1960.

Tennyson, R. D. Effect of negative instances in concept acquisition using a verbal learning task. *Journal of Educational Psychology,* 1973, *64,* 247–260.

Tennyson, R. D., Steve, M. W., & Boutwell, R. C. Instance sequence and analysis of instance attribute representation in concept attainment, *Journal of Educational Psychology,* 1975, *67,* 821–827.

Tennyson, R. D., & Tennyson, C. L. Rule acquisition design strategy variables: Degree of instance. *Journal of Educational Psychology.* 1975, *67,* 852–859.

Terry, P., Samuels, S. J., & LaBerge, D. The effects of letter degradation and letter spacing on word recognition. *Journal of Verbal Learning and Verbal Behavior,* 1976, *15,* 577–586.

Thomas, D. R., Becker, W. C., & Armstrong, M. Production and elimination of disruptive classroom behavior by systematically varying teacher's behavior. *Journal of Applied Behavior Analysis,* 1968, *1,* 35–45.

Thomas, E. L., & Robinson, H. A. *Improving reading in every class.* Boston: Allyn & Bacon, 1972.

Thorndike, E., & Lodge, I. *The Teacher's Word Book of 30,000 Words.* New York; Bureau of Publications, Teachers College, 1944.

Tikunoff, W., Berliner, D. C., & Rist, R. C. *An ethnographic study of the forty classrooms of the beginning teacher evaluation study known sample.* (Technical Report No. 75-10-5). San Francisco: Far West Laboratory for Educational Research and Development, October 1975.

Tinker, M. A. Prolonged reading tasks in visual research. *Journal of Applied Psychology,* 1955, *39,* 444–446.

Tobias, S., & Ingber, T. Achievement-treatment interactions in programmed instructions. *Journal of Educational Psychology,* 1976, *68,* 43–47.

Torgensen, J. K. Memorization processes in reading-disabled children. *Journal of Educational Psychology,* 1977, *69,* 571–578.

Trabasso, T. R. Stimulus emphasis and all or none learning in concept identification. *Journal of Experimental Psychology,* 1963, *65,* 398–406.

Twardosz, S., & Baer, D. M. Training two severely retarded adolescents to ask questions. *Journal of Applied Behavior Analysis,* 1973, *6,* 655–661.

Underwood, B. J., Runquist, W. N., & Schultz, R. W. Response learning in paired-associate lists as a function of intralist similarity. *Journal of Experimental Psychology,* 1959, *58,* 70–78.

The Valedictorian. *Newsweek,* September 6, 1976, p. 52.

Vandever, T. R., & Neville, D. D. Transfer as a result of synthetic and analytic reading instruction. *American Journal of Mental Deficiency,* 1976, *30,* 498–503.

Venezky, R. L. English orthography: Its graphical structure and its relation to sound. *Reading Research Quarterly,* 1967, *2,* 75–106.

Venezky, R. L. *The structure of English orthography.* The Hague: Mouton, 1970.

Venezky, R. L. *Language and cognition in reading* (Technical Report No. 188). Madison, Wis.: Wisconsin Research and Development Center for Cognitive Learning, University of Wisconsin, 1972.

Venezky, R. L. *Prereading skills: Theoretical foundations and practical applications* (Theoretical Paper No. 54). Madison, Wis.: Wisconsin Research and Development Center for Cognitive Learning, University of Wisconsin, May 1975.

Venezky, R. L., & Calfee, R. C. The reading competency model. In H. Singer & R. B. Ruddell (Eds.), *Theoretical models and processes of reading.* Newark, Del.: International Reading Association, 1970.

Venezky, R. L., & Shiloah, Y. *The learning of picture-sound associations by Israeli kindergartners* (Technical Report No. 227). Madison, Wis.: Wisconsin Research and Development Center for Cognitive Learning, University of Wisconsin, June 1972.

Venezky, R. L., Shiloah, Y., & Calfee, R. *Studies of prereading skills in Israel* (Technical Report No. 227). Madison, Wis.: Wisconsin Research and Development Center for Cognitive Learning, University of Wisconsin, 1972.

Waechter, M. *A methodology for a functional analysis of the relationship between oral reading and comprehension in beginning readers.* Unpublished doctoral dissertation, University of Oregon, 1972.

Walker, Hill, & Buckley, Nancy. *Token reinforcement techniques.* Eugene, Oreg.: E. B. Press, 1975.

Waugh, R. P., & Howell, K. W. Teaching modern syllabication. *The Reading Teacher,* October 1975, 20–25.

Weber, R. M. First graders' use of grammatical context in reading. In H. Levin & J. P. Williams (Eds.), *Basic studies on reading.* New York: Basic Books, 1970, 147–163.

Weiner, M., & Cromer, W. Reading and reading difficulty: A conceptual analysis. *Harvard Educational Review,* 1967, *37,* 620–643.

Weir, R. H., & Venezky, R. L. *Rules to aid in the teaching of reading.* (U.S. Office of Education Research Project No. 2584) Stanford: Stanford University, 1966.

Williams, J. P. Successive versus concurrent presentation of multiple grapheme-phoneme correspondences. *Journal of Educational Psychology,* 1968, *59,* 309–314.

Williams, J. P., & Ackerman, M. D. Simultaneous and successive discrimination of similar letters. *Journal of Educational Psychology,* 1971, *62,* 132–137.

Williams, P., & Carnine, D. W. *Introducing words in lists and in isolation.* Unpublished manuscript, Follow Through Project, University of Oregon, 1978.

Williams, M. S., & Knafle, J. D. Comparative difficulty of vowel and consonant sounds for beginning readers. *Reading Improvement,* 1977, *14,* 2–10.

Winschel, J. F., & Lawrence, E. A. *Short-term memory curricular implications for the mentally retarded,* 1975, *4,* 396–407.

Wittrock, M. C. Verbal stimuli in concept formation: Learning by discovery. *Journal of Experimental Psychology,* 1963, *54,* 183–190.

Wittrock, M., Marks, C., & Doctorow, M. Reading as a generative process. *Journal of Educational Psychology,* 1975, *67,* 484–89.

Wolf, C. G., & Robinson, D. O. Use of spelling-to-sound rules in reading. *Perceptual and Motor Skills,* 1976, *43,* 1135–1146.

Worthen, B. R. A study of discovery and expository presentation: Implications for teaching. *Journal of Teacher Education,* 1968, *19,* 223–242.

Zimmer, J. W. *A processing activities approach to memory for prose.* Paper presented at the annual meeting of The American Educational Research Association, Toronto, March 1978.

Zoref, L., & Carnine, D. A comparison of visual discrimination and letter-sound correspondence training with letter-sound correspondence training only. In *Technical Report 1978-2 Formative Research on Direct Instruction.* Eugene, Oreg.: Follow Through Project, University of Oregon, 1978.

# Appendix A

## Word Lists*

### Contents

### CVC Words Beginning with a Continuous Sound   (Section 2.4)

| a | i | o | u | e |
|---|---|---|---|---|
| | | | | fed |
| fad | | | | |
| fan | fin | | fun | |
| fat | fit | | | |
| lad | lid | | | led |
| lag | | log | | leg |
| lap | lip | | | |
| | lit | lot | | let |
| mad | mid | | mud | |
| | | mom | mum | |
| man | | | | men |
| map | | mop | | |
| mat | mit | | | met |

---

* Parentheses in Appendix A indicate a minimally different word that can be used in discrimination exercises.

| a | i | o | u | e |
|---|---|---|---|---|
|  |  | nod |  | Ned |
| Nat | nit | not | nut | net |
| nap | nip |  |  |  |
|  | rid | rod |  | red |
| rag | rig |  | rug |  |
| ram | rim |  | rum |  |
| ran |  | Ron | run |  |
| rap | rip |  |  |  |
| rat |  | rot | rut |  |
| sad | Sid | sod |  |  |
| Sam |  |  | sum |  |
|  | sin |  | sun |  |
| sat | sit |  |  | set |
| sap | sip |  |  |  |

## CVC Words Beginning with a Stop Sound    (Section 2.4)

| a | i | o | u | e |
|---|---|---|---|---|
| bag | big |  | bug | beg |
| bad | bid |  | bud | bed |
| bam |  |  | bum |  |
| bat | bit |  | but | bet |
| cap |  | cop | cup |  |
| cab |  |  | cub |  |
| can |  | con |  |  |
| cat |  |  | cut |  |
| dad | did |  | dud |  |
| Dan |  | Don |  | den |
|  | dig | dog | dug |  |
|  | dip |  |  |  |
| gas |  |  | Gus |  |
| gag |  |  |  |  |
|  |  |  | gun |  |
| had | hid |  |  |  |
| ham | him |  | hum |  |
| has | his |  |  |  |
| hat | hit | hot | hut |  |
|  | hip | hop |  |  |
|  |  | hog | hug |  |
|  |  |  |  | hen |
| jab |  | job |  |  |
| jam | Jim |  |  |  |
|  |  |  |  | jet |
|  | jig | jog | jug |  |
|  | kin |  |  | Ken |
|  | kid |  |  |  |

| a | i | o | u | e |
|---|---|---|---|---|
| pan | pin |  |  | pen |
| pat | pit | pot |  | pet |
|  | pig |  |  | peg |
|  |  | pop | pup | pep |
| tab |  |  | tub |  |
| tag |  |  | tug |  |
| tan | tin |  |  | ten |
| tap | tip | top |  |  |
|  | Tim | Tom |  |  |

## CVCC Words Ending with a Consonant Blend or Double Consonants (Section 2.4)

| a | | i | | u | | e | | o |
|---|---|---|---|---|---|---|---|---|
| act | (at) | fill |  | bump | (bum) | bend | (Ben) | golf |
| and | (add) | film |  | bunt | (bun) | bent | (Ben) | honk |
| ant | (an) | fist | (fit) | bust | (but) | best | (Bess) | lock |
| band | (bad) | hint | (hit) | dump |  | belt | (bell) | pond |
| bank |  | ink |  | dust |  | bent | (Ben) | pomp |
| camp | (cap) | lick |  | gulp |  | dent | (den) | rock |
| can't | (can) | lift |  | gust | (gut) | end | (Ed) | romp |
| cast | (cat) | limp | (lip) | hunt | (hut) | felt | (fell) | sock |
| damp | (dam) | milk |  | hung | (hug) | held | (help) | soft |
| fact | (fat) | mint | (mit) | jump |  | left | (let) |  |
| fast | (fat) | mist | (miss) | junk |  | kept |  |  |
| gasp | (gas) | sick |  | luck |  | melt | (mell) |  |
| hand | (had) | tilt | (till) | lump |  | mend | (men) |  |
| lamp | (lap) |  |  | must |  | neck |  |  |
| land | (lad) |  |  | punk |  | nest | (net) |  |
| last |  |  |  | runt | (run) | pest | (pet) |  |
| mask |  |  |  | rust | (Russ) | self | (sell) |  |
| mast | (mass) |  |  | suck |  | send |  |  |
| pant | (pan) |  |  | sung |  | sent |  |  |
| past | (pass) |  |  |  |  | test |  |  |
| raft | (rat) |  |  |  |  | tent | (ten) |  |
| sack |  |  |  |  |  | weld | (well) |  |
| sand | (sad) |  |  |  |  | went | (wet) |  |
| sank |  |  |  |  |  |  |  |  |

wind   (win)

## CCVC Words Beginning with a Consonant Blend   (Section 2.4)

bl—bled (bed), blot
br—brag (bag), brat (bat), bred (bed), brig (big), brim
cl—clad, clam, clan (can), clap, clip, clot, club (cub)
cr—crab (cab), cram, crib, crop (cop)
dr—drag, drip (dip), drop, drug (dug), drum
fl—flag, flap, flat (fat), fled (fed), flip, flop

fr—frog (fog), from
gl—glad, glum (gum)
gr—grab, gram, grim, grin, grip
pl—plan (pan), plop (pop), plot (pot), plug, plum, plus
pr—prop (pop)
sc—scan, scat (sat), scab
sk—skid, skim, skin, skip, skit
sl—slam (Sam), slap (sap), slat, sled, slim, slip (sip), slob (sob),
    slot, slug, slum (sum)
sm—smog, smug
sn—snag, snap (sap), snip, snub, snug
sp—span, spat (sat), sped, spin, spit (sit), spot, spun (sun)
st—stab, stem, step, stop, stun (sun)
sw—swam (Sam), swim
tr—trap (tap), trim (Tim), trip (tip), trot (tot)
tw—twig, twin (tin)

### CCVCC, CCCVC, and CCCVCC Words    (Section 2.4)

bl—blast, blimp, blunt (bunt), blond, blend (bend), blink, bliss,
    black (back), block, bluff
br—bring, brunt, brand (band), brass (bass)
cl—clamp (camp), clasp, cling, clump, clung, clink, class, cliff
cr—cramp, crust, craft, crisp
dr—drink, drank, drift, draft, dress, drill
fl—fling, flung, flunk
fr—frost, frank, frisk, frill (fill)
gl—gland, glint, glass (gas)
gr—gramp, grand, grump, grant, grasp, grunt, grass (gas), grill
pl—plant (pant), plump (pump), plank
pr—print, prank, press
sc—scalp
sk—skunk, skill
sl—slang, slant, slump, slept, sling
sm—smack (sack), smell (sell)
sn—snack (sack), sniff
sp—spend (send), spent (sent), spank (sank), spunk (sunk), spell (sell), spill
st—stand (sand), stamp, stump, sting (sing), stink (sink), stomp,
    still, stiff, stack (sack), stuck (suck)
sw—swift, swang (sang), swung (sung), swing (sing), swell (sell)
tr—tramp, trunk, trust, trend, trick (tick)
tw—twang, twist
spl—split (spit), splint, splat
str—strip, strap, strung, strand, struck
scr—scrap, scram, script

## *VCe Pattern Words in Which the Vowel Is Long*   *(Section 3.2)*

### 1. Words Beginning with a Single Consonant (CVCe)

| a | | i | | o | | u | | e | |
|---|---|---|---|---|---|---|---|---|---|
| vane | (van) | time | (Tim) | hope | (hop) | cute | (cut) | Pete | (pet) |
| fade | (fad) | like | (lick) | note | (not) | use | (us) | eve | |
| made | (mad) | site | (sit) | robe | (rob) | mule | | | |
| bake | (back) | Mike | (Mick) | home | | cure | | | |
| cane | (can) | mile | (mill) | joke | | pure | (purr) | | |
| tape | (tap) | ripe | (rip) | hole | | fume | | | |
| mate | (mat) | file | (fill) | nose | | mute | | | |
| hate | (hat) | tile | (till) | rope | | | | | |
| sake | (sack) | pile | (pill) | mope | (mop) | | | | |
| Jane | (Jan) | ride | (rid) | pope | (pop) | | | | |
| pane | (pan) | mite | (mit) | bone | | | | | |
| same | (Sam) | fine | (fin) | cone | (con) | | | | |
| cape | (cap) | wine | (win) | dope | | | | | |
| wave | | pike | (pick) | hose | | | | | |
| tame | (tam) | bite | (bit) | note | | | | | |
| take | (tack) | kite | (kit) | yoke | | | | | |
| save | | dime | (dim) | poke | | | | | |
| make | (Mack) | hide | (hid) | pole | | | | | |
| gaze | | pine | (pin) | rose | | | | | |
| | | tide | | rode | (rod) | | | | |
| | | side | (Sid) | | | | | | |
| | | hire | | | | | | | |
| | | fire | | | | | | | |
| | | wire | | | | | | | |
| | | dine | | | | | | | |
| | | dire | | | | | | | |
| | | line | | | | | | | |
| | | like | | | | | | | |
| | | dive | | | | | | | |
| | | five | | | | | | | |
| | | lime | | | | | | | |
| | | bike | | | | | | | |
| | | nine | | | | | | | |
| | | size | | | | | | | |

### 2. Words Beginning with a Consonant Blend CCVCe

| a | | i | | o | u |
|---|---|---|---|---|---|
| skate | | slide | (slid) | spoke | brute |
| state | | snipe | (snip) | broke | |
| trade | | gripe | (grip) | close | |
| stale | (stall) | prime | (prim) | drove | |
| scale | | spine | (spin) | globe | |
| snake | (snack) | spite | (spit) | froze | |
| slave | | bride | | scope | |
| slate | (slat) | crime | | smoke | |
| scare | | pride | | stone | |

|   a   |      |   i    |        |   o   |     | u |
|-------|------|--------|--------|-------|-----|---|
| plate |      | prize  |        | stove |     |   |
| plane | (plan) | smile |       | slope | (slop) |   |
| grape |      | stripe | (strip) |      |     |   |
| grade |      |        |        |       |     |   |
| frame |      |        |        |       |     |   |

### 3. Multi-syllabic Words with a VCe Syllable

|    a     |    i     |    o     |    u    |    e     |
|----------|----------|----------|---------|----------|
| careless | perspire | hopeless | excuse  | complete |
| escape   | dislike  | explode  | confuse | stampede |
| inhale   | likely   | backbone | reuse   |          |
| take-off | umpire   | pinhole  | costume |          |
| handmade | entire   |          |         |          |
| grateful | lifetime |          |         |          |
| pancake  | ninety   |          |         |          |
|          | timeless |          |         |          |

## Letter Combinations    *(Section 3.2)*

ai   aid, aim, bail, bait, claim, fail, fair, laid, maid, mail, main, pail, paid, pain, paint, plain, rain, tail, plain, stair, trait, afraid, complain, remain, explain, tailor, daily, ailment, maintain, obtain, aimed, failing, mailing, painter, raining, aid (add), aim (am), bait (bat), fair (far), maid (mad)

al   fall, call, tall, ball, small, wall, mall, salt, false, bald, waltz, also, always, almost, salty, all right, walnut, hallway, walrus, alter

ar   arm, bark, barn, card, cart, farm, far, star, hard, harm, mark, park, part, art, car, dark, mars, smart, start, yard, starve, shark, artist, darling, barber, target, party, carpet, partner, harvest, barking, starring, parked, smarter, started, bark (back), hard (hand), art (at), car (care), star (stare), bar (bare)

au   fault, vault, sauce, cause, taught, haunt, laundry, author, autumn, August, daughter, applaud, because, auto

aw   bawl, brawn, claw, dawn, hawk, jaw, law, lawn, paw, pawn, raw, saw, straw, crawl, shawl, yawn, awful, drawing, lawful, sawmill, lawyer, seesaw, outlaw, strawberry, awkward, awning

ay   day, gay, may, ray, say, clay, gray, play, pray, spray, tray, payment, today, played, saying, player, playing, prayed, praying, away, Sunday

ch   chap, chat, chip, chop, cheek, chug, charm, chimp, chain, cheap, chest, chill, chair, champ, catch, match, patch, pitch, switch, ditch, much, march, starch, crunch, arch, pinch, teach, touch, rich, hunch, chip (ship), chop (shop), chap (clap), ditch (dish), catch (cash), catcher, pitcher, pitching, chopped, teacher, touched, rancher, chuckle, chilly, marching

ea   bead, bean, beat, beast, dean, deal, fear, hear, heal, heat, Jean, lead, meal, least, mean, meat, neat, read, sea, seal, seat, speak, steam, east, eat, freak, leave, please, sneak, wheat, treat, bean (ben), beat (bet), beast (best), meat (met), speak (speck), reason, season, peanut, teacher, eastern, dealing, speaker, sneaker, treated, eating, leaving, hearing, healed, heated, steaming

ee   bee, bleed, creep, see, weed, deer, flee, free, green, keep, wheel, three, jeep, creep, beet, peep, creek, fleet, bleed (bled), beet (bet), peep (pep), weed (wed), beetle, between, canteen, fifteen, sixteen, indeed, needle, freedom, coffee, bleeding, creeped, wheeled, peeping

__eu__ cue, due, sue, rescue, argue, tissue, value, statue

__ew__ new, few, flew, chew, slew, stew, drew, grew, curfew, nephew

__ey__ hockey, money, donkey, turkey, whiskey, valley, alley, monkey, honey

__igh__ fight, light, right, tight, might, high, sigh

__ir__ bird, birth, dirt, first, shirt, sir, skirt, stir, third, whirl, bird (bid), first (fist), shirt (short), stir (star), dirty, birthday, stirring, whirled, thirsty, thirty

__kn__ knock, know, knee, knife, knight, knit, knob, knot, known

__oa__ boat, boast, coal, coat, cloak, float, load, road, roast, oak, oar, soap, throat, toast, boat (boot), coal (cool), load (loud), oar (our), oatmeal, toaster, unload, approach, railroad, seacoast, soapy, charcoal, coaster

__oi__ boil, coin, coil, foil, join, noise, point, spoil, soil, moist, oil, voice, coil (cool), foil (fool), coin (con), boiler, appoint, adjoin, disappoint, poison, avoid, joined, noisy, boiling

__ol__ bold, bolt, cold, colt, roll, fold, gold, hold, hole, scold, sold, told, toll, volt, control, enroll, folder, golden, holder, holster, roller, swollen, unfold, roller, folding, holding

__oo__ boot, cool, food, fool, hoop, mood, moon, moose, room, soon, tool, pool, stoop, shoot, smooth, tooth, too, spoon, shoot (shot), stoop (stop), soon (son), hoop (hop), cartoon, bedroom, noodle, poodle, shampoo, igloo, bamboo, fooling, moody, shooting, raccoon, teaspoon, harpoon

__or__ born, corn, for, lord, pork, port, porch, torn, short, stork, shore, fort, sport, torch, storm, north, corn (con), for (far), pork (park), port (part), short (shot), normal, order, organ, ordeal, border, conform, escort, forty, hornet, perform, inform, popcorn, story, morning

__ou__ bout, cloud, clout, loud, mouse, noun, pout, pouch, scout, mouth, blouse, count, ground, found, out, our, round, sound, about, aloud, amount, around, counter, thousand, trousers, outside, cloudy, counting, grounder, bout (boot), mouse (moose), noun (noon), mouth (moth), our (or)

__ow__ blow, crow, glow, grow, know, low, owe, row, slow, show, throw, shown, thrown, grown, elbow, fellow, below, follow, hollow, pillow, shadow, yellow, window

__oy__ boy, toy, joy, Troy, annoy, employ, enjoy, cowboy, oyster, royal

__ph__ phone, graph, photo, phrase, photograph, physics, typhoon, alphabet, elephant, dolphin, orphan, pamphlet, trophy, nephew, paragraph

__sh__ ship, shot, shop, shed, shin, shut, shack, shell, shun, cash, dish, fish, wish, rush, lash, flash, fresh, crash, brush, trash, shine, chime, shame, shape, share, ship (slip), shot (slot), shop (stop), shell (sell), shack (sack), cash (cast), fish (fist)

__th__ that, them, this, than, with, tenth, eleventh, twelfth, thirteenth, fourteenth, fifteenth, sixteenth, seventeenth, eighteenth, then (ten), than (tan)

__ur__ burn, church, curb, curl, cur, hurt, purr, spurt, surf, turn, burst, curse, curve, purse, nurse, purple, turkey, Thursday, disturb, further, return, turtle, injure, burn (born), fur (far), curl (Carl)

__wh__ when, whip, which, what, white, while

__wr__ wrap, wreck, wrench, wring, wrist, write, wrong, wrapper, wreckage, wrestle, wrinkle, writer, wrongful

### *Suffixes   (Section 3.3)*

<u>a</u> panda, comma, Anna, soda, drama, china, zebra, mamma, papa

<u>able</u> likeable, teachable, touchable, expendable, drinkable, enable, unable, portable, reasonable, returnable

<u>age</u> luggage, package, village, image, voyage, storage, passage, hostage, cottage, manage, language, wreckage, usage

<u>al</u> sandal, formal, postal, local, vocal, final, journal, metal, total, legal, criminal

<u>ance</u> clearance, entrance, performance, distance, instance, annoyance

<u>ed</u> hugged, killed, missed, ripped, tipped, bumped, helped, jumped, picked, rocked, clapped, dripped, dropped, flipped, grabbed, grinned, gripped, pressed, smelled, spelled, tricked, flipped, dotted, patted, petted, dusted, handed, landed, tested, lasted, hunted, ended, blasted, planted, slanted, trusted, twisted

<u>ence</u> absence, sentence, audience, patience, silence, influence, evidence, confidence

<u>er</u> batter, bigger, butter, fatter, hotter, letter, madder, sadder, bumper, faster, helper, hunter, blacker, dresser, slipper, speller, sticker, swinger, swimmer

<u>es</u> glasses, misses, passes, messes, foxes, mixes, taxes, boxes, wishes, dishes, fishes, mashes

<u>est</u> biggest, fattest, hottest, maddest, saddest, dampest, fastest, blackest, flattest, stiffest

<u>ful</u> handful, careful, useful, helpful, cheerful, mouthful, watchful, faithful, fearful

<u>ible</u> horrible, sensible, possible, flexible, admissible, responsible, permissible, convertible, terrible, invisible

<u>ic</u> traffic, picnic, arctic, antic, frantic, plastic, magic, tragic, comic, panic, basic, music, critic

<u>ing</u> batting, betting, cutting, digging, filling, getting, killing, letting, petting, bending, dusting, ending, helping, jumping, picking, testing, clapping, dripping, grabbing, grinning, planning, smelling, spending, swimming

<u>ion</u> fashion, champion, region, union, companion, opinion, religion, million, billion

<u>ish</u> snobbish, selfish, sluggish, publish, foolish, furnish, establish, accomplish, astonish, punish, finish, radish

<u>ive</u> active, captive, attentive, expensive, impressive, attractive, constructive, corrective, defective, destructive, positive

<u>le</u> battle, cattle, juggle, middle, paddle, riddle, saddle, wiggle, apple, bottle, giggle, little, puddle, handle, ankle, bundle, candle, jungle, uncle, grumble, twinkle, trample

<u>ment</u> agreement, argument, basement, attachment, development, employment, movement, payment, appointment, shipment

<u>less</u> endless, groundless, matchless, toothless, speechless, sleepless, helpless, careless, restless, lifeless, nameless, useless

<u>ness</u> madness, badness, freshness, dullness, witness, dryness, likeness

tion  action, mention, fraction, question, invention, inspection, section, suction, portion, construction, celebration, circulation, congratulation, combination, decoration, education, formation

ture  feature, creature, fracture, lecture, picture, puncture, structure, culture, venture, capture, torture, mixture, adventure, furniture, nature, future

ward  northward, inward, forward, backward, coward, skyward, onward, awkward

y  funny, muddy, penny, bunny, happy, jelly, silly, rocky, jumpy, handy, lucky, rusty, sandy, windy, candy, empty, fifty, sixty, smelly, snappy, sticky, clumsy, drafty, grumpy, plenty, sloppy, twenty

## Prefixes   (Section 3.3)

a  about, alive, alarm, around, along, amount, among, apart, asleep, atop

ab  absent, absentee, absorb, absurd

ad  address, adjust, admire, admit, adverb, advertise

ap  appear, appeal, appendix, applaud, appoint, approach,

at  attack, attempt, attend, attic, attach

be  because, become, before, begin, behave, behind, behold, belong, beneath, besides, between, beware

com  combine, command, commit, compete, complain, complex, compute

con  concrete, conduct, confess, confine, confirm, conflict, conform, confuse, connect, conserve, consist, control, consult, convict, conserve, contract

de  decay, declare, decoy, defeat, define, defrost, delay, delight, demand, depart, depend, describe, design, desire, destruct, detail, devote

dis  disappear, disappoint, discount, disconnect, discuss, dismiss, dismount, display, displease, disagree, disbelieve, discharge, dishonest, discolor, distance

ex  explain, expect, expense, expert, explode, expand, expire, export, explosive, extoll, exclaim, excuse, exact, exam, except, exit, examine, example

for

fore  forbid, forearm, forecast, forgive, forehead, forest, forget, forty, foremost, foreman, foreclose, forefront

im  imperfect, impact, impeach, impress

in  inclose, income, index, infect, inflate, inform, inspect, intend

mis  miscount, misdeal, misfit, misjudge, mislead, misplace, mistake, mistreat, misspell, misprint, mistrust, mismatch

non  nonsense, nonstop, nonprofit, nonconform, nonsupport

over  overall, overboard, overcast, overcome, overdue, overhead, overload, overlook, overrun, oversight, overtake, overtime, overturn, overstep, overshoes, overshadow

per  percent, perfect, perfume, perhaps, permanent, persist, person, perplex, perspire, perturb

post  postage, postcard, postman, postpone, postmark, postal

pre  predict, pretend, preheat, prepay, prepare, precook, preside, precede

pro  profile, protest, propose, produce, protest, provoke

re return, rebake, recall, recount, refill, reflex, reform, refresh, refuse, regain, regard, relay, release, remark, repair, repay, report, replay, reprint, respect, retreat, reverse

sub subdue, subject, submerge, submit, subnormal, subside, subsist, subtract, suburb, subway

super superman, supervise, supertanker, supersonic, supermarket, supersede, supernatural

trans transfer, transform, transit, translate, transmit, transparent, transplant, transport

un unable, unarm, uncage, unchain, unclean, unhappy, uneven, unlock, unreal, untie, unfair, unseen, unsafe, unlucky, unsure

under undercharge, underdog, undergo, underline, understand, underground, undertake, understood, underworld, underwear

up uphill, upkeep, uplift, upright, upsidedown, uptown, upward, uphold, upon, uproar, upstream

## CVCe Derivative Words   (Section 3.3)

(The words in parentheses are not minimally different. They are words derived from CVC words and would be used in a format to discriminate CVCe derivatives from CVC derivatives.)

### 1. Words with *s* Ending

| a | | i | | o | | e–u | |
|---|---|---|---|---|---|---|---|
| canes | (cans) | bites | (bits) | cones | (cons) | Petes | (pets) |
| cares | (cars) | files | (fills) | globes | (globs) | cubes | (cubs) |
| hates | (mats) | fines | (fins) | hopes | (hops) | uses | |
| mates | (hats) | miles | (mills) | mopes | (mops) | | |
| planes | (plans) | shines | (shins) | robes | (robs) | | |
| shakes | (shacks) | times | | | | | |
| stares | (stars) | wines | (wins) | | | | |

### 2. Words with *er* Endings

| a | | i | | o | | e–u | |
|---|---|---|---|---|---|---|---|
| later | (latter) | filer | (filler) | closer | (hotter) | cuter | (cutter) |
| shaver | (slammer) | diner | (dinner) | smoker | (robber) | ruder | (rudder) |
| crater | (batter) | finer | (winner) | homer | (logger) | user | |
| braver | (hammer) | riper | (hitter) | | | | |
| saver | (madder) | timer | (ripper) | | | | |
| | | biter | (bigger) | | | | |

### 3. Words with *ed* Endings

| a | | i | | o | | e–u | |
|---|---|---|---|---|---|---|---|
| hated | (tapped) | filed | (filled) | hoped | (hopped) | used | |
| named | (jammed) | smiled | (ripped) | closed | (robbed) | | |
| waved | (fanned) | timed | (kidded) | smoked | (nodded) | | |
| skated | (rammed) | piled | (fitted) | stoned | (rotted) | | |
| blamed | (batted) | glided | (fibbed) | roped | (logged) | | |
| faded | (matted) | | | | | | |

4. Words with *ing* Endings

| | a | | i | | o | | e–u |
|---|---|---|---|---|---|---|---|
| naming | (batting) | filing | (filling) | hoping | (hopping) | using |
| skating | (tapping) | riding | (hitting) | roping | (robbing) | |
| waving | (slamming) | timing | (ripping) | closing | (logging) | |
| hating | (napping) | piling | (kidding) | smoking | (stopping) | |
| shading | (snapping) | biting | (winning) | roving | (mopping) | |

5. Words with *y* Endings

| | a | | i | | o | | e–u | |
|---|---|---|---|---|---|---|---|---|
| gravy | (Tammy) | spicy | (Timmy) | bony | (Tommy) | cuty | (nutty) |
| shady | (batty) | shiny | | smoky | (Dotty) | | tummy |
| wavy | (fanny) | tiny | | stony | (foggy) | | |
| shaky | (Sammy) | wiry | | | | | |

6. Words with *est* Ending

| a | i | u |
|---|---|---|
| bravest | ripest | cutest |
| latest | wisest | rudest |
| safest | widest | surest |
| tamest | | |

## Y Derivative Words   (Section 3.3)

| | ier | iest | ied | ies |
|---|---|---|---|---|
| army | | | | armies |
| buddy | | | | buddies |
| bumpy | bumpier | bumpiest | | |
| clumsy | clumsier | clumsiest | | |
| foggy | foggier | foggiest | | |
| funny | funnier | funniest | | |
| greedy | greedier | greediest | | |
| greasy | greasier | greasiest | | |
| grumpy | grumpier | grumpiest | | |
| handy | handier | handiest | | |
| happy | happier | happiest | | |
| holy | holier | holiest | | |
| hungry | hungrier | hungriest | | |
| kitty | | | | kitties |
| lucky | luckier | luckiest | | |
| muddy | muddier | muddiest | | |
| party | | | | parties |
| penny | | | | pennies |
| rusty | rustier | rustiest | | |
| silly | sillier | silliest | | |
| skinny | skinnier | skinniest | | |
| smelly | smellier | smelliest | | |
| ugly | uglier | ugliest | | |
| windy | windier | windiest | | |
| baby | | | babied | babies |
| berry | | | | berries |
| body | | | | bodies |

| | *ier* | *iest* | *ied* | *ies* |
|---|---|---|---|---|
| bury | | | buried | buries |
| busy | busier | busiest | busied | |
| carry | carrier | | carried | carries |
| copy | copier | | copied | copies |
| country | | | | countries |
| hurry | | | hurried | hurries |
| lady | | | | ladies |
| marry | | | married | marries |
| sorry | sorrier | sorriest | | |
| study | | | studied | studies |
| worry | | | worried | worries |

## *Two-syllable Words with a Single Consonant in the Middle* (Section 3.4)

| *a* | *e* | *i* | *o* | *u* |
|---|---|---|---|---|
| paper | legal | Bible | frozen | music |
| satin | fever | visit | holy | bugle |
| travel | pedal | china | local | punish |
| cable | meter | prison | profit | human |
| label | clever | final | moment | super |
| planet | zebra | limit | copy | pupil |
| table | seven | finish | motor | humid |
| chapel | metal | minus | topic | study |
| rapid | defend | silent | robin | rumor |
| magic | second | tiger | poker | |
| crazy | seven | pilot | soda | |
| favor | devil | spinach | total | |
| vacant | petal | spider | solid | |
| taxi | evil | river | robot | |
| crater | | tiny | modern | |
| panic | | | proper | |
| maple | | | pony | |
| | | | comic | |
| | | | motel | |
| | | | motor | |
| | | | promise | |
| | | | model | |
| | | | robin | |
| | | | total | |

# Appendix B

## List of 400 Common Words

| | | | | | |
|---|---|---|---|---|---|
| a | bed | called | dress | friend | head |
| about | be | came | drink | from | hear |
| after | bee | can | drop | full | heard |
| again | been | can't | duck | fun | hello |
| airplane | before | car | each | funny | help |
| all | began | carry | eat | game | hen |
| almost | behind | cat | eight | gave | her |
| along | below | catch | end | get | here |
| also | best | children | enough | girl | hill |
| always | better | city | even | give | him |
| am | between | clean | ever | go | his |
| an | big | coat | every | goat | hold |
| and | bike | cold | fall | goes | home |
| animals | bird | colds | family | going | hop |
| another | birthday | come | far | gone | horse |
| any | black | could | farm | good | hot |
| anything | blue | cow | fast | good-by | house |
| are | boat | cry | fat | got | how |
| around | book | cut | father | grass | hurry |
| as | both | daddy | feet | great | hurt |
| ask | box | dark | few | green | I |
| at | boy | day | fight | grow | ice |
| ate | bring | did | find | guess | if |
| away | brought | didn't | fire | had | I'll |
| baby | brown | different | first | hair | I'm |
| back | build | do | fish | half | in |
| bag | bus | does | five | hand | into |
| ball | but | dog | fly | happy | is |
| balloon | buy | done | food | hard | it |
| bark | by | don't | for | has | its |
| barn | cage | door | found | hat | it's |
| bear | cake | down | four | have | jump |
| because | call | draw | fox | he | just |

520

| | | | | | |
|---|---|---|---|---|---|
| keep | much | pick | she | them | walk |
| kind | must | pig | shoe | then | want |
| kitten | my | picnic | should | there | warm |
| knew | myself | picture | show | these | was |
| know | name | place | side | they | wash |
| land | need | play | sing | thing | water |
| large | never | please | sister | things | way |
| last | new | pocket | sit | think | we |
| laugh | next | pony | six | this | well |
| left | night | pretty | sleep | those | went |
| leg | no | prize | so | thought | were |
| let | not | pull | soon | three | what |
| letter | nothing | put | some | through | when |
| life | now | rabbit | something | time | where |
| light | number | race | sound | to | which |
| like | of | rain | small | today | while |
| line | off | ran | start | together | white |
| little | often | read | stay | told | who |
| live | oh | ready | step | tomorrow | why |
| long | old | red | still | too | will |
| look | on | ride | stop | took | window |
| looked | once | right | stopped | town | wish |
| lost | one | road | store | toy | with |
| made | only | rocket | story | train | won't |
| make | open | room | street | tree | word |
| man | or | round | such | truck | words |
| many | other | run | sun | try | work |
| may | our | said | sure | turtle | world |
| maybe | out | same | surprise | TV | would |
| me | over | sang | table | two | write |
| men | own | sat | take | under | year |
| met | paint | saw | talk | until | yellow |
| might | pan | say | tell | up | you |
| miss | part | school | ten | upon | your |
| money | party | see | than | us | yes |
| more | peanut | seen | thank | use | zoo |
| morning | penny | set | that | used | |
| most | people | seven | the | very | |
| mother | pet | shall | their | wagon | |

# Appendix C

# *Books Popular with Intermediate Grade Students*

### Realistic Fiction

| Author | Title |
|--------|-------|
| Blume, Judy | *Are You There, God? It's Me, Margaret* |
| | *Blubber* |
| | *Deenie* |
| | *It's Not the End of the World* |
| | *Tales of a Fourth Grade Nothing* |
| | *Then Again, Maybe I Won't* |
| Burnett, Frances Hodgson | *The Secret Garden* |
| Cleary, Beverly | *Henry Huggins* |
| | *Ramona the Brave* |
| | *Ramona the Pest* |
| Farley, Walter | *The Black Stallion* |
| Fitzgerald, John D. | *The Great Brain* |
| | *The Great Brain Reforms* |
| | *More Adventures of the Great Brain* |
| Fitzhugh, Louise | *Harriet the Spy* |
| George, Jean | *Julie of the Wolves* |
| Hamilton, Virginia | *The House of Dies Drear* |
| Kerr, M. E. | *Dinky Hocker Shoots Smack* |
| Klein, Norma | *Mom, the Wolf Man and Me* |
| Konigsburg, E. L. | *From the Mixed-Up Files of Mrs. Basil E. Frankweiler* |
| Mann, Peggy | *My Dad Lives in a Downtown Hotel* |
| Rawls, Wilson | *Where the Red Fern Grows* |
| Smith, Doris B. | *A Taste of Blackberries* |
| Snyder, Zilpha | *The Egypt Game* |

### Fantasy

| | |
|--------|-------|
| Alexander, Lloyd | *The Marvelous Misadventures of Sebastian* |
| Atwater, Richard (Florence) | *Mr. Popper's Penguins* |
| Babbitt, Natalie | *Goody Hall* |
| | *Kneeknock Rise* |
| | *Tuck Everlasting* |
| Cleary, Beverly | *The Mouse and the Motorcycle* |
| Juster, Norton | *The Phantom Tollbooth* |

List prepared by Kathryn Vogel Duchin, librarian, Springfield, Oregon.

| Author | Title |
|---|---|
| LeGuin, Ursula | *A Wizard of Earthsea* |
| Merrill, Jean | *The Pushcart War* |
| Norton, Mary | *The Borrowers* |
| Pinkwater, Manus | *Lizard Music* |
| Sharp, Margery | *Miss Bianca* |
| | *The Rescuers* |
| Tolkien, J. R. R. | *The Hobbitt* |
| White, E. B. | *Charlotte's Web* |
| | *Stuart Little* |
| | *The Trumpet of the Swan* |

## Historical Fiction

| | |
|---|---|
| Eckert, Allan | *Incident at Hawk's Hill* |
| Haugaard, Erik C. | *A Slave's Tale* |
| | *The Untold Tale* |
| Hunt, Irene | *Across Five Aprils* |
| Pope, Elizabeth | *The Perilous Guard* |

## Books in Series

| | |
|---|---|
| Alexander, Lloyd (fantasy) | *The Book of Three* |
| | *The Black Cauldron* |
| | *The Castle of Llyr* |
| | *Taran Wanderer* |
| | *The High King* |
| Bellairs, John (fantasy-mystery) | *The House with the Clock in Its Walls* |
| | *The Figure in the Shadows* |
| | *The Letter, the Witch, and the Ring* |
| Cooper, Susan (high fantasy) | *The Dark is Rising* |
| | *The Greenwitch* |
| | *The Grey King* |
| | *Silver on the Tree* |
| L'Engle, Madeline (fantasy) | *A Wrinkle in Time* |
| | *A Wind in the Door* |
| Lewis, C. S. (fantasy) | *The Lion, The Witch and the Wardrobe* |
| | *Prince Caspian* |
| | *The Voyage of the Dawn Treader* |
| | *The Silver Chair* |
| | *The Horse and His Boy* |
| | *The Magician's Nephew* |
| | *The Last Battle* |
| McCaffrey, Anne (fantasy) | *Dragonsong* |
| | *Dragonsinger* (this series will probably be continued) |
| Wilder, Laura I. (historical fiction) | *By the Shores of Silver Lake* |
| | *Little House in the Big Woods* |
| | *Farmer Boy* |
| | *Little House on the Prairie* |
| | *Little Town on the Prairie* |
| | *The Long Winter* |
| | *On the Banks of Plum Creek* |
| | *These Happy Golden Years* |

# Appendix D

## *Outline of Lessons for Beginning Phonics Program*

Formats listed in this outline can be found on the following pages:

letter intro.—77
letter disc.—78
telescoping—67
segmenting—68

sounding out—97
sight reading—103
irregular word—120
passage reading—128

*Lesson One*
letter intro.—a
telescoping—sad, if, at
letter intro.—a

*Lesson Two*
letter intro.—m
letter disc.—m, a
telescoping—it, mad, am
letter intro.—a
letter disc.—m, a

*Lesson Three*
letter disc.—m, a
segmenting—am, it
letter disc.—m, a
segmenting—Sam, at

*Lesson Four*
letter intro.—t
letter disc.—t, a, m
segmenting—at, it, Sam
letter intro.—t
letter disc.—t, a, m
segmenting—am, sit

*Lesson Five*
letter intro.—t
letter disc.—m, a, t
segmenting—am, sad, sit

letter disc.—m, a, t
segmenting—mad, if

*Lesson Six*
letter intro.—s
letter disc.—m, a, s, t
segmenting—am, sit, Sid
letter intro.—s
letter disc.—m, a, t, s
segmenting—Sam, it

*Lesson Seven*
letter intro.—s
letter disc.—m, a, s, t
sounding out—am
letter disc.—m, a, s, t
segmenting—at, sit, if
sounding out—am

*Lesson Eight*
letter intro.—i
letter disc.—m, a, s, t, i
sounding out—am, at
segmenting—sat, it, am
letter intro.—i
letter disc.—m, a, s, t, i
sounding out—am, at

*Lesson Nine*
letter intro.—i

letter disc.—m, a, s, t, i
sounding out—sat, am
segmenting—if, fat, miss, fig
letter disc.—m, a, s, t, i
sounding out—mat, Sam

*Lesson Ten*
letter intro.—f
letter disc.—m, a, s, t, f, i
sounding out—am, sat
segmenting—mad, Sid, fit, rat
letter intro.—f
letter disc.—m, a, s, t, f, i
sounding out—at, sat

*Lesson Eleven*
letter intro.—f
letter disc.—m, a, s, t, f, i
sounding out—Sam, sit
segmenting—rag, fit, sad, add
letter disc.—m, a, s, t, f, i
sounding out—am, it, sat

*Lesson Twelve*
letter intro.—d
letter disc.—m, a, s, d, f, i
sounding out—mat, sit, sat
letter intro.—d
letter disc.—a, d, i
segmenting—lot, rag, luck

*Lesson Thirteen*
letter intro.—d
letter disc.—m, a, s, d, f, i
segmenting—not, nut, in, on
letter disc.—a, d, i
sounding out—if, fit, am, fat, Sam
passage reading—am
(sounding out)

*Lesson Fourteen*
letter disc.—a, m, s, t, i, f, d
segmenting—lot, rat, sick, rip
letter disc.—t, d, i
irregular—is
sounding out—Sid, mad, fat, sad, sit, if
passage reading—Sam
(sounding out)

*Lesson Fifteen*
letter intro.—r
letter disc.—m, a, s, i, t, r, d
irregular—is

sounding out—mad, sat, it, if, at, sad
letter disc.—r, a, i
segmenting—on, in, ran, rag
passage reading—am, Sam
(sounding out)

*Lesson Sixteen*
letter intro.—r
letter disc.—m, a, i, t, f, d, s, r
irregular word—is
sounding out—sad, sat, am, fit, mit, mad
letter disc.—r, i, s
segmenting—sick, sock, lot, on, in
passage reading—Sam is sad
(sounding out)

*Lesson Seventeen*
letter intro.—o
letter disc.—o, a, i, r, d, f, s, t
segmenting—lock, fig, cat, rag
sounding out—at, it, am, fit, mad, Sam
sight reading—at, it, am
passage reading—it, is, Sam
(sounding out)

*Lesson Eighteen*
letter intro.—o
letter disc.—o, a, i, r, d, f, s, t
segmenting—top, got, dad, Tag
sounding out—ram, rid, fit, am, rat, Sam, sit
sight reading—it, at, Sam, sit
passage reading—Sam is sad. Sid is mad.
(sounding out)

*Lesson Nineteen*
letter intro.—g
letter disc.—o, a, i, r, d, f, t, g
segmenting—rug, cut, cat, did, hot
sounding out—Sam, it, am, sat, rim, fit, mad
sight reading—Sam, it, am, sat
passage reading—Sid is mad at Sam.
(sounding out)

*Lesson Twenty*
letter intro.—g
letter disc.—o, a, i, r, d, f, t, g
segmenting—dad, got, can, dig, him
sounding out—mom, rod, rat, sit, at, Sid, fit,
   ram
sight reading—sit, am, at, sad
passage reading—Sam is fat. Mom is fit.
(sounding out)

# Publishers of Basal and/or Supplementary Reading Programs

Addison-Wesley Publishing Company
2725 Sand Hill Road
Menlo Park, Calif. 94025

Allyn & Bacon, Inc.
Rockleigh Industrial Park
Rockleigh, N.J. 07647

Barnell Loft, Ltd.
958 Church Street
Baldwin, N.Y. 11510

Bell & Howell Company
7100 McCormick Blvd.
Chicago, Ill. 60645

Benefic Press
10300 West Roosevelt Road
Westchester, Ill. 60153

BFA Educational Media
2211 Michigan Avenue
P.O. Box 1795
Santa Monica, Calif. 90406

The Continental Press, Inc.
520 E. Bainbridge Street
Elizabethtown, Pa. 17022

E-B Press
Division of Engelmann-Becker Corp.
P.O. Box 10459
Eugene, Oreg. 97401

The Economy Company
P.O. Box 25308
Oklahoma City, Okla. 73125

EDL/McGraw-Hill
1221 Avenue of Americas
New York, N.Y. 10020

EMC Corp.
180 E. Sixth Street
St. Paul, Minn. 55101

Fearon Publishers, Inc.
6 Davis Drive
Belmont, Calif. 94002

Follett Publishing Company
1010 W. Washington Blvd.
Chicago, Ill. 60607

Ginn and Co.
191 Spring St.
Lexington, Mass. 02173

Harcourt Brace Jovanovich, Inc.
757 Third Avenue
New York, N.Y. 10017

Harper & Row
10 E. 53rd Street
New York, N.Y. 10022

D. C. Heath
125 Spring Street
Lexington, Mass. 02173

Holt, Rinehart & Winston, Inc.
383 Madison Avenue
New York, N.Y. 10017

Houghton Mifflin Company
Pennington-Hopewall Road
Hopewell, N.J. 08525

Laidlaw Brothers
30 Chatham Road
Summit, N.J. 09701

J. B. Lippincott Co.
East Washington Square
Philadelphia, Pa. 19105

Lyons and Carnahan
407 East 25 St.
Chicago, Ill. 60616

MacMillan Publishing Company
866 Third Avenue
New York, N.Y. 10022

McGraw-Hill Book Company
1221 Avenue of the Americas
New York, N.Y. 10020

Charles E. Merrill Publishing Company
1300 Alum Creek Drive
Columbus, Ohio 43216

Open Court Publishing Company
P.O. Box 599
LaSalle, Ill. 61301

Random House
201 E. 50th Street
New York, N.Y. 10022

Reader's Digest Educational Division
Pleasantville, N.Y. 10570

Scholastic Magazine and Book Services
50 West 44th Street
New York, N.Y. 10036

Science Research Associates, Inc. (SRA)
155 North Wacker Drive
Chicago, Ill. 60606

Scott, Foresman and Company
1900 East Lake Avenue
Glenview, Ill. 60025

Webster/McGraw-Hill
St. Louis, Mo.

# Basic Vocabulary for Beginning Readers and Suggestions for Assessing Student Knowledge

1. *Colors* blue, red, black, orange, green, yellow, pink, brown, white, gray, gold, purple, olive

   *Testing Suggestion* Use crayons to make marks of each color. Point to each mark and ask, "What color?"

2. *Prepositions* (Synonyms are in parentheses.) in, on, under (below), over (above), next to (beside), between (in the middle of), in front of (ahead), in back of (behind)

   *Testing Suggestion* Use a pencil and two cups. Place the pencil in various positions and ask, "Where is the pencil?"

3. *Common Objects and Locations*
   classroom: board, window, reading corner, teacher's desk, bookcase, bulletin board, light switch, doorway, chalk, clothing area, globe, map, stapler, clip, folder, calendar, lunch card holder
   foods:
   > *fruits:* apricot, apple, cherry, pear, plum, grape, orange, grapefruit, pineapple, blueberry, strawberry
   > *vegetables:* beet, broccoli, cabbage, carrot, celery, onion, pepper, radish, squash
   > *meats:* chicken, ham, liver, steak, turkey
   > *dairy products:* cottage cheese, yogurt, Swiss cheese, American cheese
   > *miscellaneous:* mustard, catsup, salt, pepper, sugar, honey, puddings, bread, cereal
   locations: park, zoo, restaurant, grocery store, drug store, shoe shore, department store, school, garage, church, library, post office, hotel, hospital, forest

   *Testing Suggestion* Obtain pictures or real objects. Ask, "What is this?"

4. *Pronouns*
   subject—he, she, they, it, you, we
   object—him, her, them, you
   possessive—his, her, their, your, its

   *Testing Suggestion* Get several pictures that are identical except for gender of people, e.g., a picture of girl running and a picture of boy running. Point to appropriate picture and ask questions such as: "Touch *her* hair. Touch *his* hair. Touch the picture that shows *he* is running. Touch *them*."

5. *Parts of Objects*
    match—stick, head
    pencil—eraser, point, shaft
    hammer—handle, head, claw
    purse—bag, clasp, handle
    wagon—wheels, handle, body
    shoe—sole, heel, laces, top, tongue
    egg—yolk, white, shell
    jacket—hood, zipper, front, back, sleeve
    clock—case, hands, face
    cabinet—handle, doors, shelves
    refrigerator—door, handle, body, freezer door, shelves
    tree—roots, branches, trunk, leaves
    chair—seat, back, legs, rungs
    door—doorknob, key hole, hinges, lock, rod
    cup—bowl, handle
    pot—body, lid, handle
    table—top, legs
    umbrella—frame, handle, covering
    fish—body, tail, fins
    nail—head, shaft, point
    flower—roots, stem, leaves, petal
    glasses—frame, earpieces, lenses
    shirt—collar, pocket, sleeves, cuffs, buttons
    window—frame, lock, handle, panes
    coat—sleeves, collar, buttons, button holes, front, back
    pants—zipper, legs, cuffs, pockets
    broom—handle, bristles
    toothbrush—handle, bristles
    glove—thumb, fingers, cuff, palm
    car—wheels, fenders, windows, doors, bumpers, hood, windshield, head-
        lights, seats, seat belts, steering wheel
    rake—handle, prongs
    fork—handle, prongs
    knife—blade, point, handle
    dashboard—speedometer, glove compartment, radio, clock, gas gauge
    shovel—handle, scoop
    jar—lid, mouth, neck, body, label
    belt—strap, buckle, prong, loop, holes
    lamp—shade, stand, cord, switch, bulb
    garbage can—handles, lid, body
    spoon—handle, bowl
    staircase—railing, post, stairs
    person
        *face:* hair, eyebrow, eyelash, forehead, nostrils, chin
        *upper body:* waist, shoulder, upper arm, lower arm, index finger, ribs, back-
        bone, hips, wrist, elbow, palm, knuckles
        *lower body:* ankle, knee, arch, hips, thigh

    *Testing Suggestion* Obtain pictures or actual objects. Ask, "What part is this?"

6. *Characteristics* (adjectives)

| | | |
|---|---|---|
| long–short | few–many | dark–light |
| big–little | same–different | deep–shallow |
| hot–cold | old–new | raw–cooked |

| | | |
|---|---|---|
| full–empty | skinny–fat | stale–fresh |
| wet–dry | clean–dirty | ripe–spoiled |
| straight–crooked | fast–slow | early–late |
| rough–smooth | young–old | happy–sad |
| wide–narrow | tiny–huge | sick–well |
| quiet–noisy | mild–stormy | easy–difficult |
| safe–dangerous | ugly–beautiful | careful–careless |
| sharp–dull | open–closed | tight–loose |
| whole–part | shiny–dull | |
| wild–tame | cool–warm | |

*Testing Suggestion* Obtain pictures of objects or actual objects that contain a characteristic. Ask either, "Is this _____?" or "Which one is _____?"

7. *Occupations*

| | | |
|---|---|---|
| baker | jeweler | secretary |
| barber | librarian | shoe repairperson |
| brick layer | lifeguard | stewardess or steward |
| bus driver | logger | taxi driver |
| carpenter | maid or butler | teacher |
| cashier | mail carrier | telephone repair person |
| clerk | mechanic | truck driver |
| cook | milkman | TV repair person |
| custodian | minister | veterinarian |
| dentist | nurse | waiter or waitress |
| dishwasher | painter | |
| doctor | paper carrier | |
| dressmaker | photographer | |
| druggist | pilot | |
| electrician | plasterer | |
| elevator operator | playground supervisor | |
| farmer | plumber | |
| firefighter | police officer | |
| fisherman | priest | |
| forest ranger | printer | |
| garbage collector | rabbi | |
| grocer | roofer | |
| hair dresser | | |

*Testing Suggestion* Obtain pictures. Ask, "What do we call this person?"

8. *Quantity Words* all, some, none, most, a few, a lot

*Testing Suggestion* Put five pencils on a table. Ask, "Give me _____ (all, some, none, most, a few, a lot) of the pencils."

9. *Materials* cardboard, cloth, fur, glass, leather, metal, plastic, rubber, wood, brick

*Testing Suggestion* Obtain a piece of material or a picture. Ask, "What is this made of?"

10. *Figures* circle, square, rectangle, oval, triangle

*Testing Suggestion* Draw each figure. Ask, "What is this?"

11. *Patterns* plaid, striped, plain, spotted, flowered, checkered

*Testing Suggestion* Fill in squares with different patterns. Ask, "What pattern is this?"

# Index

**DATE DUE**

| | | | |
|---|---|---|---|
| | | | |
| | | | |
| | | | |
| | | | |
| | | | |
| | | | |
| | | | |
| | | | |
| | | | |
| | | | |
| | | | |
| | | | |
| | | | |
| | | | |
| | | | |
| | | | |
| | | | |
| | | | |

DEMCO 38-297